Canadian Securities Regulation

Canadian Securities Regulation

David L. Johnston

BUTTERWORTHS
Toronto

CANADA:	BUTTERWORTH & CO. (CANADA) LTD. TORONTO: 2265 MIDLAND AVENUE, SCARBOROUGH, M1P 4S1
UNITED KINGDOM:	BUTTERWORTH & CO. (PUBLISHERS) LTD. LONDON: 88 KINGSWAY, WC2 B 6AB
AUSTRALIA:	BUTTERWORTH PTY. LTD. SYDNEY: 586 PACIFIC HIGHWAY, CHATSWOOD, NSW 2067 MELBOURNE: 343 LITTLE COLLINS STREET, 3000 BRISBANE: 240 QUEEN STREET, 4000
NEW ZEALAND:	BUTTERWORTHS OF NEW ZEALAND LTD. WELLINGTON: 26/28 WARING TAYLOR STREET, 1
SOUTH AFRICA:	BUTTERWORTH & CO. (SOUTH AFRICA) (PTY.) LTD. DURBAN: 152/154 GALE STREET

Johnston, David L
  Canadian securities regulation

(Canadian legal text series)

Bibliography: p.
Includes indexes.
ISBN 0-409-84120-X

1. Securities — Canada. I. Title. II. Series.

KE1065.J63   346'.71'092   C77-001266-3

To my wife Sharon and to John Willis
and my colleagues on the Ontario
Securities Commission.

Canadian Legal Textbook Series

CARROTHERS:	*Collective Bargaining Law in Canada*
WILLISTON AND ROLLS:	*The Law of Civil Procedure*
REID:	*Administrative Law and Practice*
LINDEN:	*Canadian Negligence Law*
SACK AND LEVINSON:	*Ontario Labour Relations Board Practice*
SOPINKA AND LEDERMAN:	*The Law of Evidence in Civil Cases*
FEENEY:	*The Canadian Law of Rules — Probate*
CASTEL:	*Canadian Conflict of Laws*
RUBY:	*Sentencing*
WILLIAMS:	*The Law of Defamation*

Preface

This book is intended to provide a broad description and analysis of the principal features of securities regulation in Canada. It concentrates primarily on the provincial securities acts and the administrative agencies responsible for those acts and, within that group, on the Ontario Securities Act and the Ontario Securities Commission.

The book is not intended to be an exhaustive analysis of each provincial securities act although major differences are usually noted. The major reason for the paramount focus on Ontario is simply that I am more familiar with this jurisdiction than the legislation and its administration elsewhere. Moreover since the major reforms in securities regulation over the last two decades have frequently been initiated in Ontario and the most current reform bill, The Securities Act, 1977 (Bill 20), is presently before the Ontario Legislature, this jurisdiction is a useful starting point. I must be quick to add, however, that the other major jurisdictions have usually contributed significantly to the other Ontario reforms and followed with uniform legislation.

In an area of law which has experienced as much change as securities regulations recently it is impossible to fix a precise date from which point of time the book speaks. In general I have tried to analyze the legislation in effect and jurisprudence as at the commencement of 1976 although some of the major cases decided in early 1976 have been considered as well. A substantial portion of the book is given over to Ontario Bill 20, The Securities Act, 1977 which received first reading on April 5, 1977 and thus the analysis of reform initiative dates from this point in time. The index to all the reported decisions of the Ontario, Quebec and British Columbia Securities Commissions are complete from the beginning of publication of the reports to mid 1975.

I am indebted to a remarkable group of friends — students, colleagues at the University of Western Ontario and University of Toronto law faculties and the Ontario Securities Commission and working associates — who have made this book possible. Since I can never truly repay this debt with an appropriate description of their assistance I do not more than mention them here: Marion Morris and Kathryn O'Rourke laboured like saints with the typing of many drafts. Valerie McGarry, Fred Baxter, David Jackson, John Layton, Ronald McCloskey, Peter Mercer, Leslie Rose and Brent Swanick toiled with uncommon zeal on the background research, the preparation of numbers of manuscripts and indexing the cases. Shirley Hinterauer edited the final manuscripts with industry and intelligence in cheerful combination.

I owe a special debt to two of my colleagues on the Ontario Securities Commission — Harry Bray and Stanley Beck — with whom I also shared duties as a member of the drafting committee for the new Ontario securities legislation. They have been generous as they have been patient and stimulating in sharing their enormous fund of knowledge and experience. And in the best traditions of friendship they were always willing to return to first principles in educating their colleague. Persons interested in securities regulation in Canada will recognize the special acknowledgement to Professor John Willis whose contribution to administrative law in Canada is the stuff of which legend is made and whose insights into securities legislation — which he shared so enthusiastically with me before I had the honour to succeed him on his retirement from the Ontario Commission — always reflected his profound and pervasive wisdom and his sparkling candour. May I finally record in these tributes my gratitude to the Canada Council, the Ontario Law Foundation and the law faculties of the universities of Toronto and Western Ontario for welcome financial assistance with the research.

And having made full true and plain disclosure of my intellectual debts in the traditions of securities regulation, I leave two formal caveats to the end. First, the responsibility for errors is, of course, mine. Secondly, although I am a member of the Ontario Securities Commission the views expressed herein are mine alone and should not be taken to reflect views of the Commission.

D. L. JOHNSTON
London, Ontario
April, 1977

Table of Contents

ix

Chapter 1
Philosophy and
Scope of
Regulation

A. Philosophy of Regulation

1.01 Purpose

The traditional goal of securities regulation has been the protection of the investor. That statement has an appeal which is misleading in its simplicity. It focuses on only one of a number of parties to a securities transaction. Moreover, it fails to reflect the fact that the goal of protection must be achieved while taking into account a diverse range of other objectives, some of which compete with one another.

We may begin by observing that the political system which erects laws for the protection of the investor operates on the basis of a number of implicit assumptions. These may not receive the same public emphasis as investor protection but nonetheless must be taken as a "given" by any regulatory framework. Two current examples in Canada are: first, investor protection is to be achieved without an excessively heavy burden of cost or rigidity; secondly, an element of risk for private capital, with an attendant chance of loss or failure, is an inherent feature of our national economy to which both investors and business enterprises must consider themselves subject.

Besides the goal of protection, with its somewhat negative tendency to repress and restrict, the regulatory thrust is expressed positively in the attempt to ensure that Canadian capital markets operate efficiently and fairly and command a full measure of public confidence.[1]

---

[1]For some recent studies of Canadian capital markets with particular emphasis on the securities industry see (complete citations in Appendix I): Atlantic Acceptance Report (Hughes Report); J.C. Baillie, "The Protection of the Investor in Ontario"; Bouchard Report, Interim 1971, Final 1972; G.R. Conway, *The Supply of, and Demand for, Canadian Equities*; D.H. Fullerton, *The Bond Market in Canada*; Gordon Report; OSC Industry Ownership Report; Kelly Report; Kimber Report; Law Society of Upper Canada Special Lectures, 1972; OSC Merger Report; Moore Report; Mutual Funds Report; E.P. Neufeld, *The Financial System of Canada*; Parizeau Report; J.R. Peters, *Economics of the Canadian Corporate Bond Market*; Porter Report; D.C. Shaw and R.T. Archibald, *The Management of Change in the Canadian Securities Industry*, especially study one, "Canada's Capital Market"; J.P. Williamson, *Securities Regulation in Canada*, 1960, and 1966 Supplement; *Studies in Canadian Company Law*, J.S. Ziegel ed., Vol. 1 (1967), Vol. 2 (1973).

An analysis of the conditions necessary to achieve this goal of capital market efficiency discloses three requirements which have particular relevance to securities regulation.[2] First, the system of regulation should encourage the most rational and sensible allocation of financial resources. Throughout Canadian history economic development has held a high priority. Domestic financial resources have been comparatively meagre. The resulting tension between supply of and demand for capital has underlined the need to ensure that financial resources are distributed prudently among different growth sectors of the economy which compete for priority.[3]

The second of the three requirements is the mobility and transferability of capital. It is important that an investor with financial resources at his disposal should be able to convert them from one form into another with a minimum of obstruction and expense. Thus, as our system presently operates, an investor with cash in hand today may purchase a share in a corporation tomorrow, knowing that in a week's time he may sell that share and apply the proceeds to the purchase of a government bond, all with minimal transfer costs and delays.

Thirdly, the goal of efficiency requires a permanent framework for the realistic pricing or evaluation of investments. Traditionally this is provided in a market economy by bringing the forces of supply and demand together in as concentrated a manner as possible and with the fullest possible current information available to the participants.

So much for the goal of efficiency. The objective of increasing and maintaining public confidence in the persons and institutions operating in the capital markets is less directly linked to the goal of efficiency than the protection of the investor. The methods employed to this end in recent years have included an attempt to ensure the honesty and competence of traders, the promulgation of rules and norms which achieve fairness and accord with the public interest and the enforced disclosure of information about issuers on terms which make it equally accessible to all investors. A concurrent objective has been to encourage more individuals to own investment securities; the assumption is that the participation by a wider group of Canadians in the ownership of the economy (a kind of "people's capitalism", as it were) will have a broadly beneficial effect from both a social and a political standpoint.

Finally, there is the objective of directing the speculative interest of Canadians into an arena that produces a significant return to the economy as a whole. It is assumed that certain individuals are willing to risk their money freely in the hopes of substantial gain, though fully cognizant of the chance of loss. It has been considered sensible to channel the funds so made available into speculative stock. This use

---

[2]Kimber Report, para. 1.06.

[3]See, for example, the OSC Industry Ownership Report, which dealt with the twin issues of foreign ownership and public ownership of the Canadian securities industry. In assessing Canada's future capital needs in terms of supply to demand, it noted (para. 3.03) the conclusion of the Economic Council of Canada that annual expenditures on new plant and equipment should increase by 5.8 per cent annually during the 1970's in order to sustain satisfactory economic growth.

of the money involves at least the possibility of generating a productive business enterprise, in contrast to encouraging lotteries or other forms of gambling; the latter activities have not (traditionally at any rate) had the popularity in Canada which they enjoy in some other countries. Much of the effort by regulators in this speculative area has been to ensure that the game is played with a minimum degree of honesty.

These varied objectives outlined above are better understood by looking at the techniques of securities regulation.

1.02 Techniques of Securities Regulation

There are three basic regulatory techniques traditionally used in Canadian securities law. These are anti-fraud measures, registration of persons and of institutions, and registration of securities.[4]

Anti-fraud measures define fraudulent or otherwise wrongful conduct, provide civil or criminal penalities for engaging in such conduct, and create investigatory and enforcement tools to identify and suppress it. They are essentially prophylactic or preventative and usually not directly remedial. Their very presence is expected to deter, presumably in direct proportion to their effectiveness in application. An attempt is made by such measures to combat illicit activity before it has had time to achieve its objective or become well established; or at any rate to minimize damaging consequences. But what is not always realized is that anti-fraud measures only apply to wrongful conduct after it has clearly manifested itself and usually only after some loss or damage has occurred.

The registration or licensing of persons and of firms or institutions[5] participating in the securities industry is designed to ensure that active participants in the business have achieved a minimum standard of honesty, good reputation and competence, and maintain that

---

[4]This conceptual framework is fully described in the seminal U.S. treatise, Loss, *Securities Regulation*, 6 vols., 3rd ed. (1960) and supplement (1969) (hereinafter cited: Loss), vol. 1, p. 33 and following.

[5]This rather awkward designation "persons and firms or institutions" is necessary because the definition of person does not include a corporation, in the Ontario Securities Act, R.S.O. 1970, c. 426 (hereinafter in the text itself and footnotes referred to as "the Act"). It includes (s. 1(1)12; s. 1(1)27 in Bill 20) "an individual, partnership, unincorporated association, unincorporated organization, unincorporated syndicate, trustee, executor, administrator or other legal personal representative". "Company" on the other hand is defined (s. 1(1)4) as "any incorporated corporation, incorporated association, incorporated syndicate or other incorporated organization." These terms will be used throughout and will have the meanings given to them by the Act when precision so requires, but normally "registration of persons" should be taken to mean the licensing of persons, firms and institutions. In *Re Skynner Lake Gold Mines Ltd.*, [1947] O.W.N. 945, [1948] 1 D.L.R. 540 (C.A.), the court permitted a corporation to appeal an OSC decision even though the Act gave the right only to a "person"; it reasoned somewhat generously that the legislature intended to give the word "person" a broader meaning when used in relation to appeals than that contemplated in the definition section.

competence together with observing minimum standards of fair dealing.[6]

More recently, the factor of competence—measured by standards which have been set progressively higher—has received growing emphasis, as the industry has achieved a professional identity. Under the ordinary registration procedure, an individual must apply for and receive a licence from the appropriate regulatory authority before engaging in some segment of the securities business. He must give evidence of competence and integrity, which must be maintained at a satisfactory level as he is expected to renew the licence on a periodic basis. In some instances the applicant must submit to an examination of his past record. The licence may be revoked temporarily or permanently if he falls below the standards as declared and amended from time to time.

The registration of firms or institutions is slightly more complex. The basic structure of regulation is the same, but the requirements embrace not only the competence and integrity of the human participants (which include in this area the capacity of senior persons to supervise employees), but also attempt to import a uniform set of standards with respect to operational strength and stability of the firm. Furthermore the ultimate sanction of the removal of recognition of the institution is weightier in the case of a firm because the consequences may impinge upon a great number of people—employees, customers and perhaps even the industry in general.

The third regulatory technique involves the registration of securities. In Canada this approach relies heavily on disclosure of information, but it encompasses a broad spectrum of administrative discretion which is not confined to requiring the release of pertinent data. A useful overview of this technique is provided by a survey of the various ways it can be used (by no means exclusive of one another) at the time of an initial issue of securities. At one end of the spectrum is mere notification. Here the obligation on an issuer is simply to notify a regulatory agency on or before the time of issue. The degree of disclosure may be minimal or somewhat more substantial, depending upon the amount of detail about the issue which must be contained in the notification statement. The effectiveness of such disclosure is in turn dependent on how the content of the statement is made available to the potential investor. There is a considerable difference between keeping the information in private files of the regulatory agency and making it available on a public file so that any interested person may have access to it; most effective of all is the requirement that data be disseminated in a document circulated to offerees.

Moving away from this purely passive form of registration one soon encounters the concept of "qualification". This essentially means that

----

[6]The classic and oft-quoted statement of the first two items in this list of objectives belongs to Lord Atkin in *Lymburn v. Mayland*, [1932] A.C. 318 at p. 324, [1932] All E.R. Rep. 291, [1932] 2 D.L.R. 6 (P.C.): "There is no reason to doubt that the main object sought to be secured in this part of the Act [registration of persons] is to secure that persons who carry on the business of dealing in securities shall be honest and of good repute, and in this way to protect the public from being defrauded."

the issuer, before it may distribute its securities, must satisfy the regulator that it meets legislative standards in its disclosure of information, whether the disclosure is solely to the regulatory agency itself, or in the case of a scheme involving the widespread dissemination of a selling document, to purchasers and prospective purchasers. If this approach is taken a step further the administrator may be given discretion to require additional disclosure beyond that expressly stipulated in the legislation, or to impose certain terms and conditions on the modalities of distribution or on the application of the proceeds raised therefrom. Finally, at the farthest extreme from mere notification, some jurisdictions require that the administrator be satisfied regarding the over-all fairness or financial viability of the proposed venture before the distribution may commence.

The examination this far has covered the registration of securities at the time of original issue. The same regulatory approach has been applied with important consequences to the period subsequent to the initial issuing of the securities while they are traded in secondary markets. The past ten years have witnessed in Canada the imposition of a variety of substantial obligations regarding the reporting and dissemination of information in what is referred to as secondary trading. Such provisions are comprised under the general rubric "continuous and timely disclosure". Generally they involve the placement of a report on public file with a regulatory agency and the dissemination of information directly to securities holders. The addition of these post-issuance disclosure requirements involves a kind of metamorphosis in which what began as a technique of registration of securities emerges as a technique of registration of the issuer, with obligations cast upon the latter long past the initial marketing of its securities. When Bill 20, the proposed Securities Act, 1977, comes into force this transformation of the registration of securities technique to registration of the issuer will be largely complete.

Canadian securities law has for some time involved a mixture of these three techniques. However, the emphasis placed on one or the other of them has varied right from the beginning, both from an over-all national standpoint, and within the separate provincial jurisdictions. In recent years it is the third technique which has received the greatest emphasis, and within that third technique, issuer registration with continuing obligations has eclipsed the registration of securities.

1.03 Current Framework of Securities Regulation

The current framework of securities regulation in Canada consists of a network of provincial and federal statutes and their administering agencies, together with a variety of national and local self-regulatory organizations possessing the power to admit and discipline members and issuers.

(1) LEGISLATION

Each of the ten Canadian provinces as well as the two territories has a securities statute or ordinance.[7] Five of these—the statutes of

---

[7]Securities Act, R.S.A. 1970, c. 333, as am. 1971, c. 102; 1972, c. 85; 1974, c. 14 and c. 65; 1975 (2nd Sess.), c. 9; Securities Act, 1967 (B.C.), c. 45, as am. 1968,

British Columbia, Alberta, Saskatchewan, Manitoba and Ontario—
comprise one similar or uniform group, originating with the 1966
Ontario Act as amended.[8] These five jurisdictions are called the
uniform act provinces. The statutes of the four Atlantic Provinces
(New Brunswick, Nova Scotia, Prince Edward Island and Newfoundland) form another separate uniform group, based on what prior to
1966 was a national model. These provinces did not incorporate the
1966 uniform act changes into their legislation, and have not, in fact,
effected any substantial amendments within the past eight years. The
Ordinances of the Yukon and Northwest Territories are simpler but
not dissimilar to those of the Atlantic group. Quebec's statute is a
hybrid; it is based on what was an earlier national model on to which
has been grafted[9] most of the principal features of the 1966 uniform
act.

   More recently Ontario introduced an "exposure draft" bill, Bill 154
in 1972.[10] This was followed by a substantially amended exposure
draft, Bill 75.[11] It was intended to consolidate in a systematic fashion
various amendments which the uniform act had accumulated since
1966. In addition the new Bill was to give effect to three major law
reform reports: a 1969 national report on mutual funds and investment contracts, those parts of a 1970 OSC report on disclosure which
had not already been recognized by legislative amendment, and a 1973
Ontario Select Committee on Company Law report. Bill 75 had been
discussed in detail with the other nine provinces in earlier forms. The
Ontario Minister in his statement introducing it anticipated that it
would find acceptance as a uniform provincial securities act.[12] A
revised version of the Bill, "Bill 75 Revised", appeared early in 1975;[13]
it contained numerous changes which attempted to refine the legislation in the light of criticisms and suggestions provoked by the
appearance of the unrevised version. Another revision, Bill 98, was

---

c. 50; 1970, c. 43; 1971, c. 58; 1973, c. 78; 1974, c. 82; 1975, c. 17, s. 194, c. 37, s.
6(1), c. 65, s. 4(a) and c. 70; Securities Act, R.S.M. 1970, c. S50, as am. 1970,
c. 23; 1971, c. 31; 1972, c. 58; 1976, c. 30; Security Frauds Prevention Act,
R.S.N.B. 1973, c. S-6; Securities Act, R.S.N. 1970, c. 349, as am. 1971, No. 65;
1974, No. 118; Securities Act, R.S.N.S. 1967, c. 280, as am. 1968, c. 53; 1969, c.
72; Securities Act, R.S.O. 1970, c. 426, as am. 1971, Vol. 2, c. 31; 1972, c. 1, s.
55; 1973, c. 11; Securities Act, R.S.P.E.I. 1974, c. S-4; Securities Act, R.S.Q.
1964, c. 274, as am. 1966-7, c. 17, ss. 14 to 16 and c. 82, s. 2; 1971, c. 77; 1973,
c. 67; Securities Act, 1967 (Sask.), c. 81, as am. 1968, c. 70; 1969, c. 59; 1970, c.
65; Securities Ordinance, R.O.N.W.T. 1974, c. S-5; Securities Ordinance,
R.O.Y.T. 1971, c. S-5.
[8]1966 (Ont.), c. 142. The latter statute was fathered by the 1965 Kimber
Report.
[9]"An Act to amend the Securities Act", 1973 (Que.), c. 67.
[10]Bill 154, "The Securities Act, 1972" (2nd Sess.), 29th Legislature, Ontario.
[11]Bill 75, "The Securities Act, 1974" (4th Sess.), 29th Legislature, Ontario;
CCH Canadian Securities Law Reports, Special Report No. 100, Extra
Edition, June 24, 1974.
[12]"A Statement to the Ontario Legislature by the Honourable John T.
Clement", June 1974 OSCB 105-108.
[13]Bill 75 Revised, CCH Canadian Securities Law Reports, Special Report No.
107, Extra Edition, Feb. 18, 1975.

introduced into the Legislature on May 30, 1975;[14] however, the Legislature rose before this Bill could be given detailed consideration by the Legal Bills Committee and subsequent third reading. On April 5, 1977, Bill 20, The Securities Act, 1977,[15] which contains a number of revisions from Bill 98, was given first reading in the Ontario Legislature with the expectation that it will come into effect in 1978.

In addition to regulations under the statute, each of the ten provincial jurisdictions has issued policy statements. These set out in detail procedures to be followed in complying with the legislation, and provide guidance as to how the discretion vested in administrators or tribunals under the acts will be exercised. The statements are divided into three groups: national, uniform and local.[16] National statements are issued jointly by all ten provincial jurisdictions; uniform statements are issued jointly by the five uniform act provinces; and local statements are issued by one provincial jurisdiction for application within that province only.

All ten provinces as well as the Federal Government have enacted legislation for the incorporation of companies. Not surprisingly this legislation overlaps in places with securities legislation. This is particularly so in the case of federal companies legislation, since the Federal Government has never enacted a securities act as such. Recently the Federal Department of Consumer and Corporate Affairs released a working paper which contained proposed legislation to regulate mutual funds on a national basis and under Federal Government authority.[17]

(2) ADMINISTRATION

Each of the securities statutes cited above works with the aid of a government administrative agency. These agencies show a great variation in size and sophistication, ranging from a securities commission in Ontario with a staff of 100 to a registrar in each of the Territories who has as one minor part of his duties responsibility for the securities legislation of that jurisdiction.[18] There is a considerable

---

[14]Bill 98, "The Securities Act, 1975" (5th Sess.), 29th Legislature, Ontario; CCH Canadian Securities Law Reports, Part 1, No. 112, June 19, 1975.

[15]Bill 20, "The Securities Act, 1977" (4th Sess.), 30th Legislature, Ontario.

[16]See CCH Canadian Securities Law Reports (hereinafter "CCH"), which reproduces all of these statements on an up-to-date basis. See also Appendix II which lists these statements and contains a reference to where they are cited in the text.

[17]See J.C. Baillie and W.M.H. Grover, *Proposals for a Mutual Funds Law for Canada*, vol. 1 especially the Appendix, "The Constitutionality of Federal Regulation of Mutual Funds", by P.W. Hogg. For guidance on Canadian corporations statutes see: W. K. Fraser and J. L. Stewart, *Handbook on Canadian Company Law*; W. K. Fraser and J. L. Stewart, *Company Law of Canada; Studies in Canadian Company Law*, J. S. Ziegel ed.; F. W. Wegenast, *The Law of Canadian Companies;* E. E. Palmer and D. D. Prentice, *Cases and Materials on Company Law;* S. Lavine, *The Business Corporations Act;* Law Society of Upper Canada Special Lectures, 1972, 1968, 1950. See also Ontario Corporation Manual; Canada Corporation Manual; J. A. Mullin and R. A. Davies, *Canadian Corporation Precedents;* CCH Company Law Reporter.

[18]For a detailed discussion of the machinery of regulation see chapter 2.

sharing of services and responsibilities between the different regions to avoid duplication, but the actual pooling of administrative staff has never gone beyond the discussion stage.

(3) SELF-REGULATION

Looking within the industry itself there are various self-regulating institutions. Occupying a premier place are five operating stock exchanges in Canada, the Vancouver, Alberta, Winnipeg, Toronto, and the Montreal stock exchanges, the last being the result of a recent merger of the separate Montreal Stock Exchange for seasoned securities and the Canadian Stock Exchange on which more junior issues were listed.[19] A sixth, in Halifax, exists as a legal entity but has never operated. All five are creatures of provincial legislation. All impose a pattern of rules and standards on their members and listed issuers.

Particular trade segments of the securities industry have established self-regulatory associations. The Investment Dealers' Association includes in its national membership most of the larger investment dealers and is divided for organizational purposes into a second tier of regional divisions. On a more local basis the Ontario Broker-Dealers' Association (and until its recent demise the British Columbia Broker-Dealers' Association) comprises smaller dealers whose business is more concentrated in the junior industrial or resource company area. Again at the local level, the Toronto Bond Traders' Association and the Vancouver Bond Traders' Association have established codes of conduct and procedures for their members. The Canadian Mutual Funds Association is a national organization composed of mutual fund dealers, advisers, and management firms, but excluding trust companies which issue mutual funds. On the periphery of securities regulation are such organizations as the Canadian Life Assurance Association, the Canadian Life Underwriters, the Society of Financial Analysts, the Canadian Sales Finance Company Association, the Canadian Bankers Association and the Trust Companies Association of Canada.

(4) OTHER RELATED REGULATION

Securities regulation cannot be considered in isolation. The laws, agencies and organizations described above should be seen as one piece (or pieces, if we think in terms of diversity rather than unity) in a whole mosaic of economic regulation. To obtain an accurate picture of the general field within which the securities laws operate one must include federal and provincial taxing statutes, the federal Bank Act, federal and provincial legislation regulating and supervising loan, trust and insurance corporations, and the broad though ill-defined sphere of regulation and administration within and subordinate to each of those statutes. Securities law must also be perceived in relation to monetary and fiscal policy dictates of government authorities, though the impact of these dictates on the industry is much more subtle and difficult to define. As an example we may take the short-term money market in which vast sums of money are raised by issuing notes ranging in terms from a day to three years. The key to its

---

[19]The Canadian Stock Exchange is still legally in existence, though dormant. See CCH, vol. 3, para. 83-014.

functioning is the recognition given by the Bank of Canada to fifteen investment dealers as official money market dealers who enjoy "lender of last resort" privileges with the Bank of Canada to carry on their operations. A restrictive or liberal monetary policy may be determined in part by the Bank of Canada's transactions with these dealers.

1.04 History of Securities Regulation

Securities regulation as we know it today in Canada has evolved through various statutes. A list of these would include laws relating to the incorporation of companies, the reporting of information by companies, the sale of shares, securities fraud prevention, and the licensing of brokers, with the final product of this evolution being comprehensive securities acts. In tracing this development one may adopt as a framework the three techniques of regulation discussed earlier: registration of persons, registration of securities and anti-fraud measures. All three have their roots in English antecedents. More recently they have been influenced significantly by federal and state legislation in the United States.[20]

(1) REGISTRATION OF PERSONS

The beginning of securities regulation can be traced to 1285 England. The Court of Aldermen issued licences to brokers in the City of London under the authority of a statute of Edward I. Prosecutions of unlicensed brokers have been recorded before 1300.[21] Four centuries later in 1696 a special commission reported to the House of Commons that:[22]

> "The pernicious art of Stock-jobbing hath, of late, so wholly perverted the End and Design of Companies and Corporations, erected for the introducing, or carrying on, of Manufacturers, to the Private Profit of the first Projectors, that the Privileges granted to them have commonly, been made no other use of, by the First Procurers and Subscribers, but to sell again, with Advantage, to ignorant Men, drawn in by the Reputation, falsely raised and artfully spread, concerning the thriving State of their Stock."

A statute was passed one year later designed to frustrate concerted plans by jobbers to manipulate prices. It introduced penalties for unlicensed trading, limited commissions to one-half of one per cent and established a requirement that stock transactions be recorded.[23] In 1707 the statute was not renewed and fell into oblivion. Twenty-three years later, however, the South Sea Bubble burst and in the ensuing panic, legislation was passed which sought to stifle the trade

---

[20]The best detailed account of the history of Canadian securities legislation is by J.P. Williamson, *Securities Regulation in Canada*, 1960, chapter 1, on which much of this following section relies. See also Loss, vol. 1, pp. 440-9, and for the earlier history, Mulvey, *Company Capitalization Control*, 1913 (a report prepared by the Canadian Under Secretary of State).

[21]Killik, *The Work of the Stock Exchange*, 2nd ed. (1934), p. 12, as quoted in Loss, vol. 1, p. 3, footnote 1.

[22]11 H.C. Jour. 595 (1696).

[23]1697, 8 & 9 Wm. 3, c. 32, as quoted in Loss, vol. 1, p. 3; see also Lane, "The Years Before The Stock Exchange" (1957), 7 History Today 760, at p. 761 and Frankfurter, "The Federal Securities Act", 8 Fortune 53, Aug. 1933.

in company charters; the same law insisted in addition, upon the forfeiture of licences by brokers trading in the shares of companies with "secondhand" charters. From this time on it was the registration of securities that claimed greater legislative attention in England, particularly with the growth of the corporate form of business from 1844 onward.

In 1911 the State of Kansas enacted the first "blue-sky" legislation,[24] so named because it was designed to prevent slick Eastern salesmen from selling Kansas farmers a fee simple in the blue sky. It provided for registration of issuers, their salesmen and the securities to be sold. The Kansas statute served as a model for similar legislation in various North American states and provinces. First to the mark among Canadian jurisdictions was Manitoba, which passed a Sale of Shares Act in 1912. This Act required issuers and other sellers of securities to obtain a licence from the Manitoba Public Utility Commission. Saskatchewan and Alberta in 1914 and 1916, and New Brunswick in 1923 followed with rather similar statutes. Quebec first enacted a statute requiring registration of securities in 1924; then a 1928 amendment to the Quebec Licence Act prohibited brokers from selling securities which had not been qualified under the previous Act. The licensing power was made more comprehensive in Manitoba in 1926 when its Sale of Shares Act was absorbed by the Municipal and Public Utility Board Act.

The next major step was the Ontario Security Frauds Prevention Act of 1928. It required brokers and salesmen to be registered, and contained a prohibition against trading without registration combined with an extremely comprehensive definition of trade. The legislation was made workable by numerous exemptions. Prince Edward Island, Alberta and Saskatchewan enacted statutes on the Ontario model in 1929. Under the impetus provided by the 1929 financial crash, Alberta, British Columbia, Manitoba, Ontario, Quebec and Saskatchewan produced a "uniform" Security Frauds Prevention Act, which was enacted in all seven jurisdictions in 1930. This was followed by a similar statute in Newfoundland in 1931; New Brunswick acceded to the rest in 1935. A major feature of all these statutes dating from the year 1930 and after was the increasing supervision of registrants. The period also displays a zealous urge towards uniformity in provincial legislation, a tendency which had yet to run its course when it was struck by an ill wind from across the ocean.

In *A.-G. Man. v. A.-G. Can.*[25] the Privy Council nullified that portion of the Manitoba Sale of Shares Act which required a federally incorporated company to obtain leave of the provincial administrator before offering its securities in Manitoba. It concluded that the licensing provision trespassed upon the Federal Government's power to incorporate companies. The provincial statutes affected were largely concerned with anti-fraud provisions and the licensing of persons. In the next fifteen years however a number of jurisdictions added a requirement that certain information (usually a satisfactory

---

[24]Kan. L. 1911, c. 133.
[25][1929] A.C. 260, [1929] 1 D.L.R. 369, [1929] 1 W.W.R. 369 (P.C.).

prospectus) be filed with the registrar before any registrant could use his licence to sell those securities. Thus by building on the provincial right to impose licensing requirements on persons selling securities and only indirectly regulating the federally incorporated issuer the provinces leapt over the constitutional hurdle. In that period also the English Prevention of Fraud (Investments) Act, 1939[26] was passed, requiring dealers or salesmen to be licensed by the Board of Trade.

The year 1945 saw the first comprehensive Canadian securities legislation in the Ontario Securities Act. Its appearance at this time owed something to the revelation of frauds in mining shares, the first maxim of securities regulation being that fraud spawns legislative activity. In fairness, however, it should be said that a desire to encourage more legitimate resource promotion in the province was a major motivating factor as well. Among other provisions the Commission was empowered to terminate trading on the Toronto Stock Exchange (TSE) and stiffer audit requirements were imposed on licensed persons. Two years later the Legislature passed the Broker-Dealers' Act, forcing self-regulation on a reluctant group of mining promoters. The 1945 Ontario Act was followed in Saskatchewan in 1954 and in Alberta in 1955; the same year saw a largely parallel statute passed in Quebec. British Columbia followed in 1962. The next major change was the 1966 Ontario Securities Act. That Act brought only minor changes in the area of registration of persons, since the basic patterns had already been established.

(2) REGISTRATION OF SECURITIES

The passage of the English Joint Stock Companies Act in 1844 marked the beginning of the era when the use of the corporate legal personality as a framework for business first became widespread and popular. The addition of limited liability some twelve years later provided a swift boost to that popularity. The requirements of the 1844 statute combined in summary fashion registration of the issuer and registration of the securities. Promoters were required to provide a concise statement of information about themselves and the company, along with a prospectus and any advertisements to be used. In the years before 1867 the solid foundation thus laid was weakened rather than strengthened by the alterations that were made. The Companies Act of 1867, however, restored the situation somewhat. In particular, invitations to purchase the company's shares required details of the company's contracts to be disclosed and the threat of civil liability was added to encourage compliance.

It was the next stage, however, that marked the coupling of civil liability to all the disclosure requirements on the initial distribution of the shares. The precipitating event was the House of Lords decision in *Derry v. Peek*,[27] which effectively put an end to the common law attempt to encourage complete truth in securities distribution. In that celebrated case the court insisted on proof of intent to defraud as a requirement for recovery of damages resulting from a false statement in a prospectus. The response of Parliament came as early as the

---

[26]1939 (U.K.), c. 16.
[27](1889), 14 App. Cas. 337, [1886-90] All E.R. Rep. 1 (H.L.).

following year in the form of the Directors Liability Act, 1890, which attached liability for misstatement to those authorizing a defective prospectus. Additional detailed specifications for the contents of the prospectus were prescribed in the U.K. Companies Act ten years later. The Act also recognized some of the practical realities of company promotions by requiring the same disclosure in a prospectus used by promoters selling their own shares as that prescribed for shares being sold by the company itself. At this stage the decision whether or not to issue a prospectus was entirely optional. The next step came in 1907, when a statement in lieu of a prospectus was required of companies that had chosen not to issue a prospectus. The latter document was defined as a written solicitation of subscriptions. Having thus broadened the coverage of the registration requirement, the British Legislature then introduced a compensating relaxation of the same requirement in the form of an exemption for private companies.

Companies legislation in Canada imitated with little or no deviation these developments in England. In 1869 the Canada Joint Stock Company Letters Patent Act was passed by the Dominion Parliament. A successor Act in 1877 followed the English example in requiring disclosure of the company's contracts. Several of the provinces and territories employed prospectus requirements in company statutes. In 1891 Ontario acted with despatch in copying the U.K. Directors Liability Act. English precedent evoked a tardier response in the Ontario Companies Act of 1907, which provided more precisely detailed requirements regarding the content and scope of the prospectus. All companies with more than ten securities holders were now compelled to file a prospectus, and it was further enacted that the purchaser could avoid the contract to purchase if he had not been supplied with the prospectus. In 1912 Ontario adopted the English exemption respecting the private company and the requirement of a statement in lieu of a prospectus.

By way of contrast, 1912 was also the year in which Manitoba imitated the Kansas "blue-sky" precedent in its Sale of Shares Act which required registration of securities and issuers; these requirements were extended to secondary trading as well as primary distributions. As mentioned earlier several other provinces followed the Manitoba initiative.

With the Dominion Companies Act of 1917 one finds a renewed manifestation of the English influence. The prospectus and statement in lieu of prospectus requirements were adopted, as well as the provisions for directors' liability. It was additionally stipulated that shareholders be furnished with an annual balance sheet and that a statement of income and expense be placed before the annual meeting. This stipulation served as a talisman for the outpouring of continuous and timely disclosure requirements which were to follow and foreshadowed the gradual shift which has led to greater emphasis on continuous post-distribution disclosure as opposed to the traditional prospectus at the time of initial distribution; in this regard at least, Canadian legislation led the English. The 1917 Act included the private company exemption. The companies legislation of a number of provinces developed along similar lines.

The next English innovation to lend fresh impetus to change in Canada was the Companies Act of 1928, which required prospectuses of underwriters who had purchased a company's securities with the intent to distribute them to the public. The Dominion Companies Act enacted a similar requirement in 1935. In 1934 the same Act had been changed to require that a subscriber receive a copy of the prospectus at least one full day prior to the acceptance of his application. The amendments of 1935 were notable also for the first steps, admittedly not overly bold, to curb insider trading. Directors were required to provide a report of their transactions in the company's securities, which was to be available on request to shareholders at the annual meeting. They were also prohibited from "speculating" in the company's securities.

We have seen how the Ontario Security Frauds Prevention Act of 1928 was followed by the 1930 statute adopted uniformly by a number of provincial jurisdictions. This statute required issuers to register but avoided comprehensive disclosure requirements in view of the fact that various companies information acts already imposed such obligations. Numerous extensions to that uniform act in different provinces over the next fifteen years gradually added registration of securities requirements.

Ontario again took the initiative with its Securities Act of 1945. It was, among other things, a registration of securities statute. The speech which accompanied the introduction of the enacting bill in the Legislature stated that the primary objective was to provide full, true and plain disclosure about the securities offered, and to ensure that this information found its way to the purchaser. It was not, said the Attorney-General, intended to give an administrator a "blue-sky" discretion to prohibit a promotion on grounds of insufficient financial viability. In fact on a literal interpretation the statute gave him just that discretion, though it took him some years to discover and exercise it. Various provinces (Saskatchewan in 1954, Alberta in 1955, Quebec in 1955 and New Brunswick in 1955—the latter province enacted only the prospectus requirements) followed the Ontario pattern. Nova Scotia in 1945 and Newfoundland in 1952 enacted further registration of securities provisions. And in 1963, at a time when the urge toward uniformity was shortly to show renewed vigour, the Ontario style act was adopted in British Columbia.

(3) ANTI-FRAUD MEASURES

The combatting of fraud as a distinct element in Canadian securities law has included amendments to the Criminal Code as well as substantive anti-fraud provisions in various pieces of provincial securities legislation. Minor measures such as inspection powers in federal and provincial companies legislation round out the picture. Perhaps the most significant innovation has been the acquisition by the provincial securities commissions of investigatory personnel armed with the power to carry out their function appropriately.

The earliest anticipation of present day laws in this area may be found in companies legislation. With the introduction of limited liability in England in 1856, the Board of Trade was empowered to investigate a company at the request of 20 per cent or more (in number and value) of its shareholders. In 1902 the Dominion Companies Act introduced similar provisions, followed by Quebec in 1907 and New Brunswick in 1916. Manitoba showed a characteristic willingness to innovate in adopting the Dominion Act inspection provisions in 1905 and extending their applicability in 1912 to situations where "the interests of justice" so required. British Columbia and Ontario in 1897 and the Yukon Companies Ordinance in 1914 introduced inspection rights into their respective companies legislation. In 1914 Ontario recognized the potential dangers presented by the corporate pyramid. Where a single shareholder had been unfairly dealt with by the majority and the unfairness resulted from interrelated companies being controlled by the same group he was permitted to apply to a judge for an investigation. The remedies included compensation for any loss sustained or appraisal rights which enabled him to be bought out at a fair price. In 1931 ten shareholders were empowered to apply for an audit of the company's accounts.

The Manitoba Sale of Shares Act of 1912 introduced anti-fraud measures directly into the field of securities law as such. Its significant innovation was the establishment of a bureaucracy whose attention was primarily directed to initial distribution of securities but it was also directed to uncovering frauds at an early stage and this provided a focus for a continuing review of the issuer. Periodic reports were required, as well as the maintenance of records which would be subject to inspection by the administrator. These measures were coupled with a power to supervise "investment companies" and to investigate "out of province" issuers. The Manitoba tribunal was also empowered to approve (or refuse to approve) stock exchanges. These provisions were made more effective by the enactment two years later of a power to examine persons and documents. The popularity of the Manitoba model in other provinces has already been referred to.

The years before and after 1930 saw some further developments in the company law area. The English Companies Act of 1928 introduced a prohibition on door-to-door sales of securities. This was followed in the Dominion Companies Act of 1934. In 1932 Manitoba introduced inspection provisions in its companies legislation and in 1933—presumably as a response to the harshness of those times—the Attorney-General was empowered to search and to seize documents without a warrant.

However, it was the Ontario Security Frauds Prevention Act of 1928, followed by the uniform act in 1930, which laid the essential foundation for current anti-fraud measures. These statutes introduced an extensive set of definitions branding certain conduct as fraudulent. The Attorney-General was given wide investigatory powers to ferret out the guilty. The privilege of remaining silent was denied and failure to provide information constituted an offence. Powers to seize and hold assets were introduced and a privative clause denied a victim of the bureaucracy the opportunity to employ judicial remedies. Manitoba however had anticipated Ontario if only by a little with its own Security Frauds Prevention Act, incorporating extensive definitions of fraud coupled with wide investigation powers. That Act left the registration of brokers and securities to be administered under the Municipal and Public Utility Board Act.

With the adoption by eight provinces of the uniform Security Frauds Prevention Act in 1930 followed by the accession of a ninth, New Brunswick in 1935 (Newfoundland had adopted the Act in 1931 but did not become part of Confederation until 1949), uniformity was (temporarily) achieved. Symbolic of this desirable state of affairs was a provision facilitating the "backing" by a magistrate in one province of a warrant for a violation of a securities act in another. Unfortunately the uniformity was short-lived, and within a few years it had disappeared.

The next important legislative milestone was the Ontario Securities Act of 1945. The previous Act (of 1928), despite its extensive definitions of fraud, had been notably unsuccessful in exorcising the demon, and the provisions of the new law reflected a recognition of this fact. While the Securities Commission found its discretionary powers with respect to the registration of persons and securities expanded, its investigating powers were split up and reduced, with part of them being transferred to the Attorney-General. As indicated above, that Ontario Act was followed with some variations by a number of provinces.

1.05 Modern Reforms

The watershed of the modern era is the work of the Kimber Committee. In 1963 the Attorney-General of Ontario formed a committee headed by the chairman of the Ontario Securities Commission to recommend up-to-date legislation. The committee's terms of reference are a catalogue of some of the deficiencies of the legislation existing at that time:[28]

"To review and report upon, in the light of modern business conditions and practices, the provisions and working of securities legislation in Ontario and in particular to consider the problems of takeover bids and of 'insider' trading, the degree of disclosure of information to shareholders, the requirements as to proxy solicitation, procedures as to primary distribution of securities to the public and like matters, and generally to recommend what, if any, changes in the law are desirable."

The stimulus which led to the appointment of the committee was twofold. At a general level it was widely felt that the rapid maturation of the Canadian economy during and after World War II made it necessary to subject Canadian securities laws to a thorough overhaul; the presence of comprehensive legislation in this field in the neighbouring U.S. could only make this feeling more acute. More particularly, widespread allegations of the use of inside information in a take-over bid involving two major oil companies had aroused considerable concern and given an immediacy to the felt need for reform which might otherwise have been lacking.

---

[28]Kimber Report, para. 1.01.

The recommendations of the Kimber Report in 1965 received rapid legislative enactment with the Ontario Securities Act of 1966, which came into effect in May, 1967. This owed something to the appearance of certain other reports at about the same time, whose voices added strength to the swelling chorus demanding change in securities laws. First came the Porter Report on Banking and Finance in 1964, which contained unsparing criticisms of the securities industry. Even less deferential was the Kelly Report in 1966, which dealt with a scandal involving market manipulation and wash trading in junior mining stocks on the TSE. The report was particularly scathing with regard to the institution involved, Canada's leading securities exchange, but it also drew attention to more general inadequacies in the regulatory scheme as a whole. There was also the collapse of the Atlantic Acceptance Company Ltd. in 1965, with indicated losses of over 100 million dollars. This catastrophe led to the creation of the Hughes Royal Commission, whose hearings continued through 1965 and 1966 and helped ensure that the problems of the securities industry were the subject of unremitting public attention. The final event in the series was the uncovering of a substantial degree of fraud in the affairs of the Prudential Finance Co., resulting in considerable losses for many small investors. Their plight led to direct pressure being brought to bear on the Ontario Cabinet and provided an additional impetus toward reform if any was still needed at this stage.

Two of the most noteworthy aspects of the 1966 Act are its emphasis on continuous disclosure and concern for secondary trading in securities; but the improvements it effected in the system for the initial distribution of securities through a prospectus should not be overlooked. Particular requirements introduced by the Act include annual and semi-annual financial disclosure by issuers, regulatory standards to govern take-over bids, proxy solicitation and the information circulars accompanying the solicitation, and the reporting by corporate insiders of their trading, together with civil liability provisions for improper use by them of inside information. These requirements in the Act applied to companies incorporated outside Ontario which thereafter effected a prospectus distribution or which had shares listed on the TSE. Parallel changes in the Ontario Corporations Act imposed the same requirements on Ontario incorporated companies. Another, though minor, innovation introduced at that time was a requirement that the prospectus be in narrative form for easier reading. The Kimber Report had recommended increased administrative support for securities regulation, and this also was provided for in the legislation. The Act, which was followed by the four Western Provinces in as many years, was also a model for amendments to the Canada Corporations Act, and influenced the changes made to the Quebec Securities Act in 1971.

A report by a Committee of the Ontario Securities Commission into matters involving the disclosure of information[29] and the report of the Canadian Committee on Mutual Funds and Investment Contracts[30]

---

[29]Merger Report, 1970.
[30]Mutual Funds Report, 1969.

resulted in amendments to the Ontario Act in July of 1971. This was followed less than a year later by the introduction in the Ontario Legislature in June 1972 of Bill 154.[31] Though produced after consultation with the other provinces, that Bill was a draft intended to provoke comment and discussion, and it died on the order paper. The new provisions of its successors, Bill 75, Bill 98 and Bill 20[32] which introduce considerable modifications, will be the subject of more particular discussion throughout this book.

1.06 Co-ordination of Jurisdictions

Securities regulation in the U.S. involves both federal and state administrative agencies, although the federal Securities and Exchange Commission (SEC) is the dominant force. In Canada, to date, federal authorities have not attempted to exercise any jurisdiction in securities regulation proper. However, some of the requirements imposed on federally incorporated companies through the Canada Corporations Act overlap with provisions of the provincial securities acts. From time to time there have been proposals to merge the provincial securities administrations into some type of national agency with or without Federal Government presence. In 1967 Ontario proposed the creation of the Canadian Securities and Exchange Commission (CANSEC), which would have effected the delegation of administrative responsibility for the provincial acts, in connection with interprovincial issues of securities, to a national organization assembled from the existing provincial agencies.[33] Several years later the Federal Government proposed a federal securities act for interprovincial issues with a Federal Government administrative agency. Neither of these proposals went beyond the discussion stage.

Notwithstanding this lack of progress towards any degree of formal integration, for a number of years the provincial agencies have met semi-annually to co-ordinate administrative efforts. One innovation that has resulted attempts to eliminate, by means of a national policy, the most obvious case of duplicated effort: the need to clear a prospectus independently through two or more provincial jurisdictions. In National Policy No. 1,[34] all ten provinces have agreed to a

---

[31]"The Securities Act, 1972" (2nd Sess.), 29th Legislature, Ontario.

[32]Bill 75, "The Securities Act, 1974" (4th Sess.), 29th Legislature, Ontario; CCH Canadian Securities Law Reports, Special Report No. 100, Extra Edition, June 24, 1974. Bill 75 Revised, CCH Canadian Securities Law Reports, Special Report No. 107, Extra Edition, Feb. 18, 1975. Bill 98, "The Securities Act, 1975" (5th Sess.), 29th Legislature, Ontario; CCH Canadian Securities Law Reports, Part 1, No. 112, June 19, 1975; Bill 20, "The Securities Act, 1977" (4th Sess.), 30th Legislature, Ontario. For a good review of Bill 98 see P.J. Dey, "Securities Reform in Ontario: The Securities Act, 1975" (1975), Canadian Business Law Journal, vol. 1, No. 1; and for more generalized reviews see J.C. Baillie, "Securities Regulation in the Seventies"; H.G. Emerson, "An Integrated Disclosure System for Ontario Securities Legislation" in *Studies in Canadian Company Law*, Ziegel ed., vol. 2, pp. 343 and 400 respectively.

[33]See J. A. Langford and D. L. Johnston, "The Case for a National Securities Commission".

[34]"Clearance of National Issues", CCH vol. 2, para. 54-838.

procedure by which one jurisdiction chosen by the issuer serves as "principal jurisdiction" to co-ordinate the deficiency comments of all the jurisdictions with which the issuer has filed. In similar co-operative spirit all ten jurisdictions have agreed on 27 different national policy statements,[35] most of which apply to prospectuses, as a result, uniform administration in broad terms is possible. In addition the five uniform act jurisdictions have agreed on twelve different uniform act policy statements,[36] several of which are also concerned with prospectuses. The same five jurisdictions together with Quebec publish individual policy statements as well.

In the absence of a clear determination of the issue of federal *versus* provincial jurisdiction in securities regulation, the outlook is for continuing co-operation among the provincial agencies, both through national and uniform policy statements and through a widespread acceptance of Bill 20.

1.07 Fundamental Issues of Current Regulation

It is useful to identify at an early stage some of the fundamental issues or continuing tensions of securities law and its administration. Some of these issues will simply be stated here in order to provide a preliminary overview of the crucial problem areas, leaving to a later stage the necessary elaboration. However, like Wagnerian themes, at one time subdued and scarcely apparent, at another time rising to a crescendo of conflicting energies, these issues keep reappearing and are never fully resolved.

The first tension was implicit in our previous discussion. What proportion of limited public resources should go into securities regulation and its administration? One may disguise this issue somewhat by requiring a securities commission to finance itself from the fees collected from registrants and issuers. This allows the cost of regulation to escape the scrutiny of a treasury board intent on paring department budgets and avoids the unwelcome publicity of a Legislature debate on projected expenditures. However, the same question must still be asked with a self-financing scheme—how heavy a burden can the regulated participants in the scheme endure for a given level of investor protection. In some jurisdictions securities laws have been a very welcome revenue collector,[37] though it is clear that this is a rather unhealthy way of filling the public purse.

Another broad issue is that of self-regulation *versus* government regulation. Where a combination of the two is used—the case in all Canadian jurisdictions—the question becomes what compromises or relationships may be worked out between the agencies in each regulatory sphere. There are several facets to this problem. Success depends substantially on the extent to which the securities industry or various segments in it evince a desire to self-regulate prudently and in the public interest. And assuming the existence of this desire, it is not at all easy to determine whether and to what extent the threat of

---

[35]CCH vol. 2, paras. 54-838 to 54-865 and CCH vol. 3, para. 66-025.
[36]Nos. 2-01 to 2-12, CCH vol. 2, paras. 54-871 to 54-882.
[37]See Loss, vol. 1, p. 106.

government intervention held in reserve should be used to maintain it. Certainly those persons or institutions whom it is proposed to leave to self-regulation will almost invariably find it more palatable to be governed by their peers rather than by some anonymous bureaucrat removed and perhaps insulated from the economic setting. The advantages gained in terms of more amicable relationships between government and the industry will be somewhat derisory, however, unless self-regulation can be made to work fully and effectively in the public interest. Can the self-regulatory institution establish effective techniques and sanctions to achieve this goal?

Of a somewhat more technical nature, but nevertheless fundamental, is the question of whether to regulate by means of notification or by qualification requirements. Notification is by far the easier of the methods to administer. It simply requires that the law specify clearly and in detail what is adequate disclosure in particular circumstances and that it provide a remedy after the fact for the investor who suffers because such standards have not been met. It does not require a large bureaucracy with expertise. Nor does it require the difficult exercise of judgment on the part of the administrator to determine whether the standards have been met. At the other extreme, qualification, according to some, "fair, just and equitable standard" demands that an assessment be made of such matters as the viability of a particular venture. This can be extremely difficult when the issuing concern has no previous earnings history, or the project involves launching a new product or entering a new field. It may be proposed, for example, to employ business practices or techniques which depart radically from those used in the past. If a regulatory agency assumes the responsibility of evaluating such schemes or proposals, what should be the legal consequences, if any, of a failure to discharge this responsibility adequately? This is surely a question of considerable significance. It is at least possible to argue that the agency should be required to compensate investors for their losses on the grounds that it had encouraged them to suspend their own judgment regarding the viability of a venture in the belief that the task had been undertaken for them at an earlier stage by the government regulatory body.

Another fertile breeding ground of conflict and tension lies on the ill-defined border between political and administrative needs and functions. On the one hand there is the responsible Minister in the area of securities law; as a political representative he must answer to the public through the Legislature. Facing him are civil servants who have no such direct public exposure. This poses questions regarding the extent of the Minister's existing responsibility and whether it might ideally be desirable for him to be responsible for all features of securities administration. Also, should he interfere in that administration whether or not he is responsible? And if he is not to take an active role, how is the public will to be reflected in the shaping of current regulatory norms?

Within the securities administration itself there are tensions between the functions of policy formulation, administration and enforcement. This prompts an examination of the effectiveness of combining all these functions in a single agency, and of the gains or losses to be had by the establishment of a number of separate agencies. A particular example of potential conflict between different functions concerns the administrative agency in its anti-fraud role; in exercising its powers it acts in due course as investigator, prosecutor and judge. The dubious propriety of such an arrangement leads naturally to a different though related problem, the extent to which the administrative tribunal as judge should be circumscribed by the courts.

A continuing difficulty concerns the rules to be devised by the administrative agency: should they be extended to have universal application requiring all participants to conform in an equal manner, or should they have a more corrective bent, aiming at those errant individuals whose activities are the most dangerous and reprehensible, or at any rate unacceptable? This problem arises both in the creation of the rules and in their administration and enforcement. To use a specific example, what proportion of their time should administrators spend in reviewing notification disclosure documents as opposed to following up specific complaints against traders or issuers?

A frequently debated issue concerns the amount of discretion that should be vested in or exercised by regulatory authorities. On the one hand the duties of the regulator and the manner in which they are to be discharged may be fully articulated in all particulars through very clear detailed legislation which provides for a minimum of delegation and autonomy in both the making of policy and its execution. At the other extreme one may find an agency with a substantial discretion untramelled by specific rules and detailed criteria, and important questions regarding the mode of its exercise immediately arise. In fundamental terms the question is whether there can be rule entirely by law or rule largely by men appointed under the law. To the extent that the latter obtains, rules must be laid down regarding the tenure, answerability to the public and removal from office of those appointed.

A characteristically Canadian problem, already adverted to, is that of competing jurisdictions and jurisdictional confusion between and among different governments. And even within a particular regional division, overlapping jurisdiction between agencies of the same government is an important source of difficulty. For example, in Ontario the Superintendent of Insurance and the Securities Commission are both responsible for life insurance companies issuing variable annuity policies. The latter because of their nature are sometimes considered to be mutal funds. Another Ontario example, a single problem involving several layers of government as well as a number of governmental bodies, is the matter of police investigation. The diverse roles of the R.C.M.P., the various provincial and city police forces, investigators of the Attorney-General's Ministry and the Securities Commission must be examined, categorized, and ideally, harmoniously coordinated.

Before attempting at a later stage to fathom fully the deep and difficult problems raised by the various tensions, one must first survey the boundaries of securities law and endeavour to plot the scope of regulation.

B. Scope of Regulation

1.08 Boundaries
The boundaries for securities law in Canada are difficult to establish precisely. To emphasize in fact how indistinct these boundaries are, it is perhaps appropriate to state the two fundamental legal concepts involved in the form of questions: what is a security and when is there a trade? Our earlier discussion of the three main techniques of securities regulation made it clear that "trading in securities" has two stages, a primary and a secondary. The issuer, persons and institutions professionally involved in the trading of securities, and the individual members of the investing public are all affected by regulation both at the time of the initial issuance of the security (primary distribution) and as long as subsequent trading in the securities continues to take place (secondary trading).

1.09 Summary Statement of the Regulatory Framework
Before examining in detail the concepts of trade and security it is necessary to state concisely the existing regulatory framework. The five propositions that follow do this for Ontario:

(1) Whenever a person (broadly defined to include company and unincorporated association) trades in a security, he must first obtain registration unless legislative exemption is available or an exempting order is secured.

(2) Whenever an issuer first distributes securities, it must produce a prospectus acceptable to the Commission which makes full, true and plain disclosure about the issue and the issuer absent an exemption or exempting order.

(3) After registration, regular traders must satisfy certain minimum standards of conduct to maintain registration.

(4) After distribution, issuers must make regular, continuous and timely disclosure about their affairs and persons closely connected with them must follow certain standards of conduct and satisfy reporting obligations relating to trades in their securities.

(5) There exists a wide variety of institutions, mechanisms and sanctions to discourage and penalize fraud in securities transactions, and to ensure that the registration of traders as well as that of securities operates effectively in the public interest.

1.10 Security
(1) IN GENERAL
The Act contains fourteen separate branches to the definition of the word "security". As if even that degree of articulation were insufficient, the introductory sentence of the definition states that it *includes* each of the fourteen separate instances, with the suggestion that the fourteen items should not be viewed as exhaustive but more as particular examples of the one general idea. The intention of the Legislature in framing the concept is clear. The definition is cast as wide as possible to ensure that the regulatory scheme effectively

covers contingencies. That having been done, certain exemptions from the definition are provided in specific instances when a literal adherence to the definition produces an undesired or inconvenient result. In addition the administration is granted discretion to modify the exemptions so as to prevent the definition from resulting in the application of the Act to certain instruments.[38]

The definition of security[39] is much the same in the securities acts of

---

[38]The exemptions and discretionary relief orders are considered in chapters 3 and 4 in connection with the requirements for the registration of persons and securities.

[39]Section 1(1)22 of the Ontario Securities Act defines "security" as follows:
   "22. 'security' includes,
   i.   any document, instrument or writing commonly known as a security,
   ii.   any document constituting evidence of title to or interest in the capital, assets, property, profits, earnings or royalties of any person or company,
   iii. any document constituting evidence of an interest in an association of legatees or heirs,
   iv.   any document constituting evidence of an option, subscription or other interest in or to a security,
   v.   any bond, debenture, share, stock, note, unit, unit certificate, participation certificate, certificate of share or interest, preorganization certificate or subscription,
   vi.   any agreement providing that money received will be repaid or treated as a subscription to shares, stock, units or interests at the option of the recipient or of any person or company,
   vii. any certificate of share or interest in a trust, estate or association,
   viii. any profit-sharing agreement or certificate,
   ix.   any certificate of interest in an oil, natural gas or mining lease, claim or royalty voting trust certificate,
   x.   any oil or natural gas royalties or leases or fractional or other interest therein,
   xi.   any collateral trust certificate,
   xii. any income or annuity contract not issued by an insurance company or an issuer within the meaning of *The Investment Contracts Act*,
   xiii. any investment contract, other than an investment contract within the meaning of *The Investment Contracts Act*, and
   xiv. any document constituting evidence of an interest in a scholarship or educational plan or trust,
   whether any of the foregoing relate to a person, proposed company or company, as the case may be;"
Bill 20, s. 1(1) 38(xv), (xvi) and (xvii) adds three more, namely, agreements for periodic use or occupancy of vacation properties and commodity futures options and contracts other than those governed by The Commodity Futures Act, 1977 (*infra*, footnote 62).
   The definition of security in the TSE by-laws (s. 1.01) is basically similar to that in the Ontario legislation, although it varies in a few particulars. It does not include the most recent addition to the Act's definition, "any document constituting evidence of an interest in a scholarship or educational plan or trust" (s. 1(1) 22 xiv; Bill 20, s. 1(1) 38(xiv). It does, however, contain several

the ten provinces and the securities ordinances of the two territories, although this approximation to uniformity has been achieved by somewhat different paths, for example through amendment to the Regulation rather than to the Act. And since there are some differences in the definition among the jurisdictions careful attention should be given to the legislation in question in any specific case. Only a few general features of the definition receive comment here.

First, the uniform act definition does not require that a security always be a written document. An oral agreement will suffice for some branches of the definition.[40] Secondly, the aspect of security subjected to definition varies (resulting at times in confusion) from the tangible *res* or physical instrument itself to the intangible legal relationship.[41]

Most of the acts terminate their section defining security by a statement that the various clauses relate both to persons, broadly defined in the legislation to include certain legal entities as well as human beings,[42] and companies.

Careful attention must be paid to the exact phraseology employed in a particular act because the uniform model has been articulated

<hr>

paragraphs listing items not separately expressed to be securities in the Act, *viz.* "any bankers' share, any trustee's share, and any investment participating bond or investment trust debenture". The by-laws of the Montreal and Vancouver Stock Exchanges do not contain definitions of security, although rule 100.6 of the Vancouver Stock Exchange defines "listed security" to mean "a stock that is posted for trading on the floor".

The American Law Institute Federal Securities Code (Tentative Draft No. 1, April 25, 1972) generally follows the simple and relatively standardized definition in the U.S. federal legislation and the Uniform Securities Act, reading:

"Sec. 297 (a) [*General*] 'Security' means a bond, debenture, note, evidence of indebtedness, share in a company (whether or not transferable or denominated 'stock'), preorganization certificate or subscription, certificate of interest or participation in a profit-sharing agreement, investment contract, collateral-trust certificate, equipment-trust certificate, voting-trust certificate, certificate of deposit for a security, fractional undivided interest in oil, gas, or other mineral rights, or, in general, an interest or instrument commonly known as a 'security,' or a certificate of interest or participation in, temporary or interim certificate for, receipt for, guaranty of, or warrant or right to subscribe to or purchase or sell, any of the foregoing.

"(b) [*Exclusions*] 'Security' does not include currency, an annuity or optional annuity contract under which an insurance company promises to pay a fixed sum of money either in a lump sum or periodically for life or some other specified period, or an insurance policy issued by an insurance company."

[40]For example s. 1(1), para. 22(vi), (viii) and (x).

[41]For examples of the latter see subparas. vi and x. Subparagraphs v, vi, viii, xii, and xiii may be open to either interpretation. A similar confusing mixture of tangible and intangible concepts exists in the Business Corporations Act, R.S.O. 1970, c. 53 (hereinafter referred to as BCA), in particular those sections—ss. 1(1) 24, 63(1) (i) and 67—where security is on one hand treated as the document such as a share certificate and on the other hand as a legal relationship such as a debt obligation.

[42]*E.g.*, s.1(1)12 of the Act. Bill 20, s.1(1)19 deftly telescopes the two broad concepts by including persons and companies in the definition of "issuer".

differently in several instances. Whether this is the result of inadvertence or conscious intent is difficult to determine.[43]

Finally, it is noteworthy that the Atlantic Provinces have achieved substantial conformity with the definitions of the uniform act by means of regulations made under their securities acts. Their method of enlarging the meaning of the term "security" to meet new situations provides a speed and flexibility which cannot be matched by a resort to formal statutory amendment. The inclusive character of the definition, as determined by its introductory words, probably protects such a procedure from being assailed as *ultra vires*.

Relatively few Canadian court cases have directly faced the question "is 'this' a security?" Hence the prevailing judicial attitude to the interpretation of this part of the statute is not easy to determine with any precision. However, a few general conclusions may be drawn.

In the first place the Act, at least insofar as the definition of security is concerned, is to be interpreted as remedial rather than punitive legislation. Accordingly the definition of security is to be given a broad and liberal construction. This absence of punitive intent is manifested in the fact that the legislation does not absolutely prohibit transactions which come within its regulatory framework but rather simply requires that the issue be qualified and the participating traders be registered as a protection for the public. The appropriate interpretation therefore is one which expands the statute's scope.[44]

Secondly, Canadian courts have shown in recent years a welcome determination to look to substance rather than to form. In the *Great Way*[45] decision the Alberta Appellate Division referred to the leading U.S. authority, *Securities & Exchange Comm. v. W.J. Howey Co. et al.*[46] There the U.S. Supreme Court stated:

"The term 'investment contract' is undefined by the Securities Act or by the relevant legislative reports. But the term was common in many state 'blue sky' laws in existence prior to the adoption of the federal statute and, although the term was also undefined by the state laws, it had been broadly construed by state courts so as to afford the investing public a full measure of protection. Form was disregarded for substance and emphasis was placed upon economic reality. An investment contract thus came to mean a contract or scheme for 'the placing of capital or laying out of money in a way intended to secure income or profit from its employment.'...This definition was uniformly applied by state courts to a variety of

---

[43]*E.g.*, subpara. vii in the Ontario, British Columbia, Alberta and Saskatchewan, and Northwest and Yukon Territories legislation distinguishes between the terms "trust" and "estate" by separating those two words with a comma. In the Manitoba, New Brunswick, Nova Scotia, Newfoundland and Prince Edward Island legislation, and that of Quebec by a slightly different route, "trust" and "estate" are telescoped into the much narrower concept "trust estate" by the omission of the comma.

[44]*A.-G. Alta. v. Great Way Merchandising Ltd.*, [1971] 3 W.W.R. 133, 20 D.L.R. (3d) 67, 3 C.C.C. (2d) 463, *sub nom. R. v. Great Way Merchandising Ltd.* (Alta. C.A.).

[45]*Ibid.*, at p. 146 W.W.R.

[46](1946), 328 U.S. 293 at p. 298, 66 S. Ct. 1100 at p. 1102.

situations where individuals were led to invest money in a common enterprise with the expectation that they would earn a profit solely through the efforts of the promoter or of some one other than themselves."

Another leading U.S. case on the form *versus* substance issue is *Tcherepnin v. Knight*.[47] Both *Howey* and *Tcherepnin* looked at the whole of the transaction to determine if it had in substance the character of an investment. In *Great Way*,[48] the Alberta Court went still further, however, and embraced *Securities & Exchange Commission v. United Benefit Life Insurance Company*,[49] which adopted the reverse reasoning, that a contract need not in some instances be characterized in its entirety. A court may detach one part of a contract from the rest and declare that part to be an investment contract.[50]

The use of U.S. judicial precedents by Canadian courts is still a matter of debate and the scene remains confused. The *Great Way* case analyzed the concept of security in a broad fashion and made very sensible and thorough use of U.S. authorities.[51] On the other hand, in *Green v. Charterhouse Group Canada Ltd.et al.*[52] the court explicity eschewed the use of U.S. precedent, relying on the fact that the Canadian insider-trading liability legislation (under interpretation in that case) was couched in slightly different language. This approach was taken notwithstanding the fact that the Canadian provision had direct roots in the U.S. federal legislation and there was a great wealth of American jurisprudence on which to draw. This tendency in some Canadian courts to ignore and exclude U.S. jurisprudence in the field of securities regulation is unfortunate; many regulatory techniques and often the statutory language itself have been borrowed from U.S. models, and American legal literature is rich with instances where that language has been tested and interpreted.[53]

---

[47](1967), 389 U.S. 332, 88 S. Ct. 548; referred to in the British Columbia case of *Re Bestline Products of Canada Ltd. et al. and The Securities Commission* (1972), 29 D.L.R. (3d) 505, [1972] 2 W.W.R. 245 *sub nom. Securities Commission v. Bestline Products of Canada Ltd. et al.* (B.C.C.A.).

[48]*A.-G. Alta. v. Great Way Merchandising Ltd.*, [1971] 3 W.W.R. 133, 20 D.L.R. (3d) 67, 3 C.C.C. (2d) 463, *sub nom. R. v. Great Way Merchandising Ltd.* (Alta. C.A.).

[49](1967), 387 U.S. 202, 87 S. Ct. 1557.

[50]See *Re Western Ontario Credit Corp. Ltd. and Ontario Securities Commission* (1975), 9 O.R. (2d) 93, 59 D.L.R. (3d) 501 (Div. Ct.), and *Re Ontario Securities Commission and Brigadoon Scotch Distributors (Canada) Ltd.*, [1970] 3 O.R. 714, 14 D.L.R. (3d) 38 (H.C.) for an approach which similarly looks broadly to substance rather than form. In *Western Ontario Credit* the court upheld the Commission's finding that a "mix" of documents could constitute a security and preferred an expansive flexible interpretation of security, quoting with favour from Frankfurter J. in *Howey* (at p. 102): "'Investment contract' is not a term of art; it is a conception dependent upon the circumstances of a particular situation."

[51]See also *Western Ontario Credit Corp. Ltd.*, *supra*, footnote 50, especially at pp. 101-2.

[52](1975), 12 O.R. (2d) 280 (C.A.); affirming [1973] 2 O.R. 677, 35 D.L.R. (3d) 161 (H.C.).

[53]It is ironic that U.S. courts are now inclined to use Canadian authorities in

High authority at a relatively early date for a generous use of U.S. authority may be found in *Clarke v. Baillee*,[54] where the rights of a broker to deal with a customer's securities purchased on margin was in issue. The court based its view on common commercial practice. Anglin J. stated:

"It is common knowledge that the business of stockbrokers in this country is conducted in a manner more closely resembling that which prevails in the United States, and particularly in the State of New York, than that which obtains in England. Many customs and usages of English brokers are unknown in Canada; and many practices prevalent in our markets, which have come to us from the United States, would not be recognized on the London Stock Exchange. For this reason, and also because of a dearth of English authority...I have drawn for authorities, perhaps more freely than is usual in our courts, upon American sources."

We may close this section by noting that Canadian courts have displayed a welcome tendency to consider the purpose and spirit of the legislation in determining whether a particular instrument falls within the regulatory definition. For example, in *Re Ontario Securities Commission and Brigadoon Scotch Distributors (Canada) Ltd.*[55] it was necessary to construe subpara. (ii) of the broad definition of security in the Act (security includes "any document constituting evidence of title to or interest in the capital, assets, property, profits, earnings or royalties of any person or company"). Hartt J. declared that this definition should not be taken to include documents of title to goods bought for purposes other than investment, *e.g.* bills of lading and receipts for goods purchased for inventory or consumption. In giving his reasons he stated: "Such an interpretation...can be inferred from the basic...purpose of the *Securities Act, 1966*, [to protect] the investing public through full, true and plain disclosure....A statute should be construed to harmonize with the intention of the Legislature and the aim and object of the statute:...".[56]

(2) IN PARTICULAR

Of the fourteen individual subparagraphs making up the definition, only the more important receive separate treatment here.

"i. any document, instrument or writing commonly known as a security".

The first question posed by this definition is the type of evidence to

---

appropriate instances. The leading U.S. treatise in the field comments extensively on Canadian jurisprudence and has a passage which dilates on the value of Canadian and other Commonwealth authority: Loss, vol. 1, at p. 427.
[54](1911), 45 S.C.R. 50 at p. 76.
[55][1970] 3 O.R. 714, 14 D.L.R. (3d) 38 (H.C.).
[56]See also *A.-G. Alta. v. Great Way Merchandising Ltd.*, [1971] 3 W.W.R. 133, 20 D.L.R. (3d) 67, 3 C.C.C. (2d) 463, *sub nom. R. v. Great Way Merchandising Ltd.* (Alta. C.A.); *Re Skynner Lake Gold Mines Ltd.*, [1947] O.W.N. 945, [1948] 1 D.L.R. 540 (C.A.) and also *Re Western Ontario Credit Corp. Ltd. and Ontario Securities Commission* (1975), 9 O.R. (2d) 93 at p. 100, 59 D.L.R. (3d) 501, where the Ontario Divisional Court acknowledged a drafting flaw in the legislation, implying that an additional exemption could be judicially inferred. The same Court also approved the statement of Hartt J. referred to above.

be adduced in determining "common knowledge". The Quebec Securities Commission answered this question in the context of a commodity futures case by drawing on trade usage. It heard evidence and relied on information "sought from persons engaged in the trade of securities and commodities."[57] The only documentation of the transaction was "a confirmation slip or invoice issued as a result of such trading". Although it could perceive similarities with stock broking, in particular a resemblance to trading in puts and calls, the Commission cited a U.S. test:[58]

> "The test...(of the definition of a security)...is what character the instrument is given in commerce by the terms of the offer, the plan of distribution and the economic inducements held out to the prospect..."

and concluded that:[59]

> "Proof of common knowledge must be based on an overwhelming set of facts and conclusive evidences. On that basis and notwithstanding the fact that they are viewed by the securities industry as speculative opportunities, we are unable to conclude that commodity futures contracts are commonly known as securities in the trade, at the present time."[60]

"ii. any document constituting evidence of title to or interest in the capital, assets, property, profits, earnings or royalties of any person or company".

This subparagraph has the widest scope, and cases involving it usually turn on whether an appropriate document can be found. In the *Gelderman* case,[61] however, the QSC found that the documentation accompanying a commodity futures contract was not a security because "at the time trading is made, the 'company...or person' is not known and is impossible of determination."[62] The Ontario Supreme

---

[57]*Re John T. Gelderman & Co. Inc.*, July 1972, 3 QSCWS No. 65. It held that no security within the meaning of the Act was being traded. Trading in commodity futures was summarily described as consisting of "an undertaking to deliver or take delivery of a specified amount of the commodity at a specified time and place for a specified price. The hope of profit arises from the speculative expectation that the market price of the...commodity would change in favour of the investor, permitting purchases or sales at a profit."

[58]*Securities & Exchange Commission v. C.M. Joiner Leasing Co. et al.* (1943), 320 U.S. 344, 64 S. Ct. 120.

[59]*Supra*, footnote 57.

[60]The concluding words suggest a certain precariousness to the decision. See *R. v. Bird and International Claim Brokers Ltd.* (1963), 43 W.W.R. 241 (B.C.S.C.), where the court held that a telephone and literature campaign to sell individual mineral claims constituted trading in securities either under this definition, or the one describing evidence of title to capital assets, or the one dealing with a certificate of interest in a mineral lease or mineral claim, without identifying which one and without any reasons.

[61]*Supra*, footnote 57.

[62]For a somewhat different conclusion on the role of commodity futures, and their similarity to puts and calls, see the Canadian Mutual Funds Report, paras. 12.12, 12.13 and 12.24. For a brief and lucid description of how commodity futures markets operate, see N.C. Miller, *The Great Salad Oil Swindle*, New York, Coward McCann, 1965, chapter 4. The matter is an

Court was not faced by this obstacle of the anonymity of one of the participants to the transaction when it held that Scotch whisky warehouse receipts were securities.[63] In *Brigadoon Scotch Distributors*, Hartt J. issued a restraining order in a cryptic judgment which held that such receipts fell within this paragraph. He referred to *R. ex rel. Swain v. Boughner*,[64] where the Ontario High Court held that the documents of title to a one-half interest in a pair of breeding chinchillas, the animals being kept in the vendor's possession, were a security in the purchaser's hands. Both cases suggest that an investment or speculative purpose to the purchase of the title documents will attract the jurisdiction of the paragraph.[65] The court in *Boughner* applied the traditional rule of statutory interpretation that the statute

---

important one in Canada because of the country's very substantial production and export of commodities. In certain items, for example, nickel, newsprint, grain, copper, iron ore, it is among the world leaders, a fact which could lead to the development of an international commodity and futures market here. In a move which shows an awareness of this possibility, the Ontario Government recently struck an inter-ministerial committee headed by the Vice-Chairman of the OSC to study a number of aspects of trading in commodity futures. Its report, released in mid-1975, calls for regulation of commodity futures trades by a special branch of the OSC. See Report of the Interministerial Committee on Commodity Futures Trading (Bray Report), introduced in the Ontario Legislature on April 25, 1975. See May 1975, OSCB 147. On April 5, 1977, Bill 19, "The Commodity Futures Act, 1977" (4th Sess.), 30th Legislature, Ontario, was given first reading in the Ontario Legislature. It adopts the recommendations of the Bray Report for commodity futures traded on a recognized commodities exchange or clearing house. Bill 20 (s. 1(1) xvi and xvii), introduced the same day, adds two new definitions of security, which will regulate under the Act commodity futures options and commodity futures contracts not traded through a recognized exchange. Both Bills 19 and 20 exempt from regulation professional hedge training done by firms which use commodities in their business concerns.

[63] *Re Ontario Securities Commission and Brigadoon Scotch Distributors (Canada) Ltd.*, [1970] 3 O.R. 714, 14 D.L.R. (3d) 38 (H.C.).

[64] [1948] O.W.N. 141 (H.C.).

[65] One might still argue, however, that the paragraph should be narrowly interpreted so far as purely speculative investments are concerned. Protection of the public should be confined to situations where the investor has a rational hope of making a profit through sound management of the concern to which he has allocated his money. The commodity futures market, where a multitude of sellers and buyers dealing in a homogeneous product prevents any one person from influencing future prices, can be said to resemble gambling more than investing; the *Gelderman* case may yet turn out to be sound in principle, even if the principle was not clearly expressed in the reasons given. It is possible of course that rational predictions may be made in the commodity futures market (even if it remains a gamble), but the factual basis for such predictions does not arise from what the individual seller can disclose about his product, but on general market conditions. By contrast the proprietor of a potential mine is in a position to provide the information which will be of decisive importance in deciding on its profitability prospects—quantity and quality of ore. In the case of a bushel of wheat nothing turns on how good that particular bushel of wheat is, once it is assigned to one of a number of standard grades.

should be construed to harmonize with the intention of the Legislature and the aim of the statute.[66]

"v. any bond, debenture, share, stock, note, unit, unit certificate, participation certificate, certificate of share or interest, pre-organization certificate or subscription".

This subparagraph is the most straightforward one; its terms denote the most common type of specific security interests and taken together they encompass the overwhelming majority of instruments currently regulated by the Act. Bill 20[67] enlarges this definition in two ways. First the phrase "or other evidence of indebtedness" is inserted after "note" to ensure that all debt obligations are included. The second and more controversial change involves the addition, at the end of the subparagraph, of terminology designed specifically to cover variable annuity contracts:

"any agreement under which the interest of the purchaser is valued for purposes of conversion or surrender by reference to the value of a proportionate interest in a specified portfolio of assets."

It is important to note, however, that any consideration of variable annuity contracts must also take into account the exemption which follows.

"xii. any income or annuity contract not issued by an insurance company or an issuer within the meaning of *The Investment Contracts Act*".

The Ontario Investment Contracts Act[68] does not define an income or annuity contract as such, but it does define an investment contract.[69] The same Act also defines issuer for its own purposes in a rather circuitous fashion.[70] The result of these definitions is that an

---

[66]See the conclusion of Hartt J. in *Brigadoon Scotch Distributors, supra,* footnote 63, that an intention to regulate trading in this sort of document could be inferred from the basic purpose of the Act to protect the investing public through full, true and plain disclosure. See text, *supra,* footnote 55.

In *A.-G. Alta. v. Great Way Merchandising Ltd.,* [1971] 3 W.W.R. 133, 20 D.L.R. (3d) 67, 3 C.C.C. (2d) 463, *sub nom. R. v. Great Way Merchandising Ltd.* (Alta. C.A.) another opportunity to consider the scope of this paragraph was lost. In that case the Alberta Appellate Division found it unnecessary to consider whether a pyramid selling scheme was caught by sub-para. ii because it concluded the documents were investment contracts within the meaning of sub-para. xiii. See also *R. v. Bird and International Claim Brokers Ltd.* (1963), 43 W.W.R. 241 (B.C.S.C.) and *R. ex rel. Irwin v. Dalley* (1957), 8 D.L.R. (2d) 179, 118 C.C.C. 116, 25 C.R. 269, [1957] O.W.N. 123 *sub nom. R. v. Dalley* (C.A.).

[67]Section 1(1)37.

[68]R.S.O. 1970, c. 226.

[69]Section 1(b) (paraphrase): an agreement by an issuer to pay a determinable maturity value on a determinable date and containing optional settlement values the consideration for which consists of installment or single sum payments excluding contracts within the meaning of the Insurance Act. See *R. ex rel. Irwin v. Dalley, supra,* footnote 66, where the Ontario Court of Appeal held that fractional interests in non-assignable government permits to prospect for oil and gas were documents within the meaning of this paragraph.

[70]Section 1(c) reads: "'issuer' means a corporation that offers for sale, sells,

"income or annuity contract" issued by other than an insurance company or "issuer" will fall within this subparagraph of the Act's definition of security. Furthermore the definition of "income or annuity contract" quoted here does not exhaust the meaning of this term for the purposes of the Act. It is thus conceivable that an agreement could fall within a broader meaning of "income or annuity contract", in which case it could be held to be a security notwithstanding that it was issued by an insurance company or issuer as defined by the Investment Contracts Act.

"xiii. any investment contract, other than an investment contract within the meaning of *The Investment Contracts Act*".

The Ontario Investment Contracts Act definition of "investment contract" has been set out earlier.[71] The cases interpreting this subparagraph have in a number of instances involved "pyramid selling" schemes—a form of speculation which has enjoyed recent popularity. In *A.-G. Alta. v. Great Way Merchandising Ltd.*[72] the Alberta Appellate Division dismissed a private company's appeal from its conviction on a charge of trading in securities without registering. The case turned on the nature of the agreements which the company had entered into with its "authorized representatives". In holding that the agreements were investment contracts, the Court defined investment as "in essence the putting out of money", adopting the formulation of a New Zealand case.[73] Decisive in its view was the fact that each authorized Great Way representative contributed money to the company and received in return a commission on certain sales made by others in the chain of distributors. This was sufficient to make the transaction as a whole, one of investment, notwithstanding the fact that other parts of the contract tended to give it a contrary character so that extra commissions received could with some plausibility be seen as a reward for services rather than the fruits of invested capital.

In looking at the nature of the contract, the court used the language of causation: the investment element was the *sine qua non* of the whole project. Were it not that a part of the distributor's money contribution was not related to the cost of goods purchased, the scheme would not go forward. Conversely the distributor would only be interested in the venture because of the commission he would earn, resulting in part from his investment of moneys. The upshot was that the Court was able effectively to disregard the "non-investment" parts of the contract. It stated that once an agreement contained provisions for investment, the fact that these provisions were mixed and intermingled with non-investment matters did not remove the resulting contract from the reach of securities legislation.

---

makes or enters into investment contracts of its own issue, but does not include an insurer within the meaning of *The Insurance Act* or a corporation within the meaning of *The Loan and Trust Corporations Act*".
[71]*Supra*, footnote 69.
[72][1971] 3 W.W.R. 133, 20 D.L.R. (3d) 67, 3 C.C.C. (2d) 463, *sub nom. R. v. Great Way Merchandising Ltd.* (Alta. C.A.).
[73]*Commissioner of Taxes v. Australian Mutual Provident Society* (1903), 22 N.Z.L.R. 445 (C.A.).

The British Columbia Court of Appeal was confronted by a pyramid scheme in *Re Bestline Products of Canada Ltd. et al. and The Securities Commission.*[74] The Court found that the purchase of distributorships was not the purchase of an investment contract because the distributors made money through their own sales efforts. In its citation of authority the B.C. Court referred to *Great Way* and a number of U.S. decisions. It concurred in the view that the emphasis should be on economic reality, form being disregarded for substance, and gave its approval to what is perhaps the most important principle to emerge from *Great Way*, that elements both of an investment and a non-investment nature can combine to form an investment contract. On the question of when there is an investment in securities, however, it applied the U.S. *Hawaii Market Center*[75] "risk-capital" test that "the salient feature of securities sales is the public solicitation of venture capital to be used in a business enterprise, subjecting the investor's money to the risk of an enterprise over which he exercises no managerial control."[76] So far as the Bestline Company was concerned, the Court concluded that at all three levels of the pyramid the purchaser of a distributorship paid only the price of the products to be distributed together with other legitimate merchandising charges and therefore the "risk-capital" test was not met.

More recently the Ontario Court of Appeal has applied both the "risk-capital" test and the "common enterprise" test from *Howey* in *Pacific Coast Coin Exchange.*[77] There the OSC had issued a cease trading order on concluding that a commodity account agreement entitling the purchaser to a bag of silver coins was an investment contract and *ipso facto* a security. In applying the "common enterprise" test, the Court of Appeal concluded that the agreements were investment contracts—money was being invested in a common enterprise with the expectation of profit solely or largely from the effort of others.[78] The investor's expectation of profit was governed not only by

---

[74](1972), 29 D.L.R. (3d) 505, [1972] 2 W.W.R. 245 *sub nom. Securities Commission v. Bestline Products of Canada Ltd. et al.*

[75]*State of Hawaii, Commissioner of Securities v. Hawaii Market Center, Inc.* (1971), 485 P. 2d 105 at p. 197.

[76]That test requires a combination of the following four elements (see *Bestline, supra*, footnote 74, at p. 510):

"(1) An offeree furnishes initial value to an offeror, and

"(2) a portion of this initial value is subjected to the risks of the enterprise, and

"(3) the furnishing of the initial value is induced by the offeror's promises or representations which give rise to a reasonable understanding that a valuable benefit of some kind, over and above the initial value, will accrue to the offeree as a result of the operation of the enterprise, and

"(4) the offeree does not receive the right to exercise practical and actual control over the managerial decisions of the enterprise."

[77]*Re Pacific Coast Coin Exchange of Canada Ltd. et al. and Ontario Securities Commission*, November 1974 OSCB 209, upheld on appeal (1975), 7 O.R. (2d) 395 (Div. Ct.); 8 O.R. (2d) 257 (C.A.).

[78]The Divisional Court had referred to the case of *S.E.C. v. Koscot Interplanetary, Inc.* (1974), 497 F. 2d 473 (5th Circ. C.A.) and reliance was placed on

the general state of the silver market but by the appellant's internal market. In hedging against future commitments and soliciting orders for the purchase and sale of silver, the appellant was in part determining a price by its own operations. The amount of the investor's profit depended for practical purposes on the efforts of the appellant.[79]

1.11 Instruments Related to Securities—Franchises

Recently franchises have come within the ambit of securities regulation in Canada. In 1971, the Franchises Act[80] was passed in Alberta, the first such legislation in Canada. It is presently administered by the Alberta Securities Commission. In the same year a committee on franchises appointed by the Ontario Minister of Financial and Consumer Affairs produced a final report recommending somewhat similar legislation,[81] and a draft bill to be administered by the OSC is currently in preparation.

The Ontario Bill will probably adopt the definition found in the

---

the statement, at p. 479 of that decision, that the mere fact that an investor's return is independent of that of other investors in the scheme is not decisive of the absence of a common enterprise. The operation was dependent for its success upon the skill and efforts of the management of Pacific in hedging properly to cover the futures contracts and this supplied the necessary commonality.

[79]See also *Re Western Ontario Credit Corp. Ltd. and Ontario Securities Commission* (1975), 9 O.R. (2d) 93, 59 D.L.R. (3d) 501 (Div. Ct.) where the Ontario Divisional Court applied *Pacific Coast Coin Exchange* and both the "common enterprise" and "risk-capital" tests in finding the sale of interests in mortgages to constitute investment by the purchasers.

See also *Re Sanderson and Ontario Securities Commission*, [1972] 3 O.R. 329, 28 D.L.R. (3d) 171 (C.A.) where the Court of Appeal held there was an investment contract with scarcely a word in the way of reasons, reversing the verdict of the trial judge that no security existed. The case was notable in that it showed the regulatory authorities applying the Act to a scheme the proceeds of which were applied to gambling on horse-races. The procedure adopted was an application by the OSC for a compliance order requiring the issuer to register for trading in securities. Newspaper advertisements had been used to solicit deposits which the firm's entrepreneur, described as an "old pro", was to use in betting on horse-races in the U.S.A. Many persons had accepted this offer of a 180 per cent return on investment in less than four months.

An interesting postscript to this decision was reported in "The Financial Post", October 21, 1972, p. 1: "$200 Will Get You $34 A Week—So He Said". The article alleged that the *Sanderson* promotion was a gigantic "chain letter" type of scheme which came to its natural conclusion with the disappearance of its promoter, leaving only $350,000 available to repay a total investment of $2,800,000. According to the same story Sanderson then repeated the scheme in California. Accused of violating the state securities laws in collecting "betting investments" at horse-racing tracks, he entered a guilty plea but subsequently disappeared, resulting in the issuance of a bench warrant for his arrest anywhere in the U.S.A. At the preliminary hearing on fraud charges in Ontario, the judge refused to commit for trial on grounds of insufficient evidence.

[80]1971 (Alta.), c. 38 as amended.
[81]The Grange Report, 1971.

Alberta Franchises Act,[82] which is remarkable for its breadth.[83] The Ontario legislation, although largely modelled on the Western Canadian example (which in turn derived from the equivalent California statute and other U.S. state legislation), will require franchisors both to obtain registration and qualify a prospectus before negotiating a franchise agreement. By contrast the Alberta Act imposes only the prospectus requirement. In addition the OSC will have a discretion to refuse registration if the franchisor is not honest and of good repute and integrity. The discretion regarding the approval of a prospectus is of the "fair, just and equitable" or "blue-sky" variety, and a failure in the franchise agreement to contain terms reflecting a reasonably equal bargaining relationship will constitute grounds for prospectus refusal, as will unacceptable advertising literature produced by the franchisor or a lack of appropriate provision for the arbitration of disputes between the parties.[84]

1.12 Trade
(1) TRADING FUNCTIONS
The Ontario Act has set the interpretation of the concept "trade" into

---

[82]1971 (Alta.), c. 38 as amended.

[83]Section 1(1) cl. 6:

"6. 'franchise' means a contract, agreement or arrangement, either expressed or implied, whether oral or written, between two or more persons by which a franchisee is required to pay directly or indirectly a franchise fee in consideration for any of the following:

(i) the right to engage in the business of offering, selling or distributing the goods manufactured, processed or distributed or the services organized and directed by the franchisor, or

(ii) the right to engage in the business of offering, selling or distributing any goods or services under a marketing plan or system prescribed or controlled by the franchisor, or

(iii) the right to engage in a business which is associated with the franchisor's trademark, service mark, trade name, logotype, advertising or any business symbol designating the franchisor or its associate, or

(iv) the right to engage in a business in which the franchisee is reliant on the franchisor for the continued supply of goods or services, or

(v) the right to recruit additional franchisees or subfranchisors;

but excluding contracts, agreements or arrangements between manufacturers or where the franchisor is the Crown, a Crown agency or a municipal corporation;"

By contrast, the Grange Report (p. 36) summarized the chief features of a franchise as:

"essentially the grant of a right to operate a business, which business involves the use of the grantor's trademark or trade name, and some substantial control of the grantee's operation of the business by the grantor."

[84]The Ontario Government is currently considering the recommendation of the Bray Report that a special branch of the OSC regulate commodity futures trades. See, *supra*, footnote 62.

four separate subparagraphs.[85] Like the extended definition of security,[86] they are introduced by the word "includes" and should therefore not be viewed as exhaustive. A common limiting element is the requirement of consideration. Before a trade can take place there must be, at least in contemplation, a consideration flowing from each party. The qualification "in contemplation" means that a trade may occur before consideration has moved from one party to the other, and indeed before there has been a joinder of offer and acceptance.

The Securities Act is a "selling" Act rather than a "dealing" Act. This means that it is designed to require registration (and in the case of an original issuer or control-block holder a prospectus) when one person attempts to sell another a security. It is not designed to require registration when one person attempts to buy another's securities. This interpretation requires that the phrase "or other dealing in" (subpara. i of the definition) be read according to the *eiusdem generis* rule to mean an activity closely analogous to the meaning of "solicit, sell"; the contrary approach would view "dealing" as a separate independent test which could be used to constitute "buying" activities as "trading".[87]

It follows that if a course of conduct can be classified as "purchasing" rather than "selling", it will avoid the operation of the Act. An example is *Prudential Trust Co. Ltd. et al. v. Forseth and Forseth*,[88] a Supreme Court of Canada case interpreting the Saskatchewan Act. There a farmer granted an oil lease to a company; he later assigned an undivided one-half interest in all oil rights in the land, subject to the prior lease, to the defendant, in return for a cash payment. In holding that no "trade" had taken place and that accordingly no rescissionary remedy, express or implied, was available, Martland J. construed the defendant's activities to be the purchase of an interest in mineral rights in land and the acquisition of an option to lease mineral rights. By contrast the extended meaning of trade in the Securities Act seemed "to contemplate the soliciting of subscriptions for or the making of sales of security by the person trading and do not contemplate the soliciting for or making of purchases of securities by such a person."[89] Thus even the person who makes a business of paying cash for securities "issued" in an isolated fashion by others is not trading in securities. The *Prudential* case does suggest, however, that subse-

---

[85]Section 1(1)24. Bill 20, s. 1(1)40 adds a fifth (actually (iv) in the enumeration) covering the transfer, etc. of securities of an issuer as collateral for a *bona fide* debt.

[86]The definitions of trade in the ten provincial securities acts, two territorial securities ordinances and the federal companies' legislation vary somewhat. The TSE by-laws define trade in a limited fashion to mean "a contract for the purchase and sale of a security". The Vancouver and Montreal Stock Exchanges' by-laws do not define the term.

[87]Bill 20, s. 1(1)40 clarifies the matter by deleting the phrase "other dealing in" from the definition and adding the words "does not include a purchase of a security". The same approach should be used in interpreting the words "conduct or negotiation" in subpara. v.

[88][1960] S.C.R. 210, 21 D.L.R. (2d) 587, 30 W.W.R. 241.

[89]*Ibid.*, at p. 225, S.C.R.

quent transfers of the collected securities or documents by the buyer (whether a person or a company) might constitute trading within the Act.[90]

A converse result was reached in *Meyers et al. v. Freeholders Oil Co. Ltd. et al.*,[91] another case involving the Saskatchewan Act in which the plaintiff based his claim for rescission on breaches of the licensing requirement and the prohibition on soliciting at a purchaser's residence. The court found that the issuing by the defendant company of shares rather than cash as consideration for the assignment of mineral rights constituted a trade. It rejected the defence's argument that the transaction was in essence an agreement for the acquisition of mineral rights to which the issuance of shares was incidental; such an argument could not succeed where the agreement itself contained the provision for the issuance of shares as consideration.[92]

The ambit of the trading definition is not however so wide as to cover all activities that fall into the "selling" category. Some limits exist even in the case of those whose business is directly related to the selling of securities and who are thus a part of the securities industry. In *Re Ontario Securities Commission and C.A.P. Ltd.*,[93] the Ontario High Court held that registration was not required of a firm which provided bookkeeping and administrative facilities to mutual fund dealers. A trust company handled the funds and paid a commission to the defendant firm whose task it was to consolidate into larger amounts suitable for investment the accumulated periodic payments from contractual plan mutual fund subscribers as well as dividends and interest from the fund's portfolio designated for reinvestment. The Court held that the defendant firm was not a dealer, even though a dealer would ordinarily perform these services for itself, because they were merely administrative. Furthermore, the trade which was the subject of registration had already been completed and there was no "furtherance of trade", because the work was only that which a registrant's "back office" would do.

(2) GEOGRAPHICAL BOUNDARIES

The geographical boundaries of trade in its statutory definition are of special significance in Canadian securities regulation, since the law

---

[90]In *Prudential Trust Co. Ltd. et al. v. Olson*, [1960] S.C.R. 227, 21 D.L.R. (2d) 603, involving similar facts with a different plaintiff, Martland J. applied the same reasoning with a similar result.

[91][1960] S.C.R. 761, 25 D.L.R. (2d) 81, 33 W.W.R. 193.

[92]In *Re Sanderson and Ontario Securities Commission*, [1972] 3 O.R. 329, 28 D.L.R. (3d) 171, the Ontario Court of Appeal held that the activities there described were sufficient to bring the transactions within the term "other dealing" to constitute trading under the Act.

[93][1972] 1 O.R. 205, 22 D.L.R. (3d) 529 (H.C.). Although the sense of the decision is justifiable, the cryptic reasoning in the case is less satisfactory. The distinctions applied are question-begging. When do aspects of a trade become merely "administration"? The issue is this: when does the performance of administrative services become sufficiently vital to the safeguarding of funds, and the consequence of failure sufficiently serious, that the protection of the investor requires regulation through licensing together with appropriate protective standards and supervision?

properly speaking lacks a federal component and is in consequence the product of ten provincial jurisdictions. In general the reach of a province's laws extends only so far as its borders. For example, in *Hretchka et al. v. A.-G. B.C., B.C. Securities Commission and Superintendent of Brokers*,[94] it was contended that an order of the BCSC purported to prohibit trading by named persons in a specific company's shares anywhere; in response to this Martland J. in an *obiter* statement (because the order was not before the court) stated "like any other order of the Commission, it would have application only in the Province of British Columbia."[95]

The more difficult question is what activity must take place within the geographical boundaries of a province before an order may issue. Two cases, which are roughly mirror images of each other, show a tendency of the courts to be liberal in recognizing the existence of a province's jurisdiction. They also establish that two provinces could in some circumstances each have jurisdiction over one transaction. In *Gregory and Co. Inc. v. The Quebec Securities Commission*[96] Gregory, a registrant with a Montreal head office, promoted four mining companies operating within the province by publishing weekly bulletins relating to the shares of these and other companies. The persons to whom the bulletins were mailed and with whom the firm dealt were *all* resident *outside* of the province. The Commission not only cancelled Gregory's licence, but also seized its books and put a freeze on its funds and securities. In all these actions it was upheld. Fauteaux J. (as he then was) said that the paramount object of the Act was to ensure that persons who carry on the securities business in the province should be honest and of good repute; it was hoped in this way to protect the public, in the province or elsewhere, from being defrauded as a result of certain activities initiated in the province by persons who carry on business there.[97]

While *Gregory* held that the initiation of trading activities within a province's boundaries gave it jurisdiction, the decision in *R. v. W. McKenzie Securities Ltd. et al.*[98] reached the same result where the target or victim of the activities, but not the initiator, was within its boundaries. The Manitoba Court of Appeal held that when a broker located in Ontario contacted Manitoba residents over an interprovincial telephone link this constituted trading in Manitoba requiring registration under the Manitoba Act.

---

[94][1972] S.C.R. 119, 19 D.L.R. (3d) 1, [1972] 1 W.W.R. 561.
[95]*Ibid.*, at p. 126, S.C.R. See also, *post*, part 7.03, footnote 20.
[96][1961] S.C.R. 584, 28 D.L.R. (2d) 721.
[97]See also *Re Chapman*, [1970] 3 O.R. 344, 11 C.R.N.S. 1 *sub nom. R. v. Chapman* (C.A.); leave to appeal to Supreme Court of Canada refused [1970] 3 O.R. 353*n*, which rejected the view that the fraud provisions of the Criminal Code are designed to protect only the *Canadian* public against fraud.
[98](1966), 55 W.W.R. 157, 56 D.L.R. (2d) 56 (Man. C.A.).

Chapter 2
The Machinery of
Regulation

2.01 Introduction

This chapter concerns itself with the manner in which securities legislation is administered, and within that general topic the focus will be on government institutions and procedures. The machinery of self-regulation is considered in Chapter ten. The administration of business corporation legislation or statutes specifically concerned with loan, trust, mortgage or insurance companies, or other related financial institutions, will receive only marginal attention. There is one exception to this restriction, however: in the absence of any federal securities administration, the CCA and CBCA contain certain requirements similar to the uniform provincial securities acts; accordingly some discussion of the regulatory apparatus under those acts is included.

The primary emphasis in this chapter will be on the role of the Ontario Securities Commission.[1] It is two-tiered in structure. The first level consists of eight commissioners, two of them, the chairman and vice-chairman, serving full-time, with the other six part-time. A staff of approximately 100 forms the second tier.[2] To a large extent, the structure by which the other uniform acts are administered is substantially similar to the Ontario model although on a smaller scale.[3]

The uniform act provinces borrow from the common pattern of U.S. administrative structures in that the securities commissions are not branches within a department of government but rather stand somewhat apart and independent from the departmental chain of command, although reporting to the Minister. The degree of independence of the Commission and the extent to which it is "accountable" to the

---

[1]The "OSC". Where there is a significant difference in another provincial jurisdiction, it will usually be footnoted.

[2]It is the third largest securities administration in North America after the U.S. SEC and that of the State of California. From a technical standpoint, a reference to the "official Commission" should be interpreted to mean the body of eight commissioners; that is, the upper tier excluding the supporting staff. In practice, persons dealing with the regulatory authority often use the term "commission" in a variety of senses; reference may be intended to the entire administrative structure, to members of the administrative staff, to the upper tier or merely to a quorum of commissioners, depending on which organ is being dealt with at the time. Throughout this book it is the first of these four conventional usages which is employed, unless the context suggests otherwise. The strict or technical sense is well illustrated by the immunity provision of Bill 20 (s. 140), which states: "No action or other proceeding for damages shall be instituted against the Commission or any member thereof, or any officer, servant or agent of the Commission...".

[3]All of the uniform act jurisdictions, as well as Quebec and New Brunswick have two-tiered administrations.

Minister are exceedingly complex issues which are best dealt with in the context in which they arise.

In the four Atlantic Provinces, by contrast, securities legislation is administered within a government department in a fashion closer to British civil service traditions. In each of these provinces, the responsible person is an official of the Attorney-General's department with other, often more demanding, tasks to perform. There have been recent discussions in the Maritime Premiers' Council (which brings together officials of the New Brunswick, Nova Scotia, and Prince Edward Island Governments—but not Newfoundland) concerning a Maritime Provinces Securities Commission which would serve as an administrative tribunal for all three provincial acts. In the Yukon and Northwest Territories the securities ordinance is administered on a part-time basis by an official with numerous other commitments and responsibilities. The CCA and the CBCA are administered by the corporations division of the federal Department of Consumer and Corporate Affairs. The division is headed by a registrar who answers to one of two assistant deputy ministers in the department.[4]

In April 1972, the Ontario Statutory Powers Procedure Act, 1971[5] and the Judicial Review Procedure Act, 1971[6] began to apply to the OSC. Those two Acts provide the procedural framework for hearings before most administrative tribunals in Ontario and appeals from such hearings to the courts. This book does not deal directly with those two Acts; but it should be noted that they have paramountcy in the case of any conflict with a procedural provision of the Act.[7]

---

[4]The present structure for administering the Act stems largely from the 1966 Kimber Committee reforms and from the implementation of a consulting report's recommendations on internal organization which that committee requested. Kimber Report, ch. 8. The administrative framework of the various jurisdictions may be summarized in tabular form as follows:

Province	Section of Securities Act	Chairman	Vice-Chairman	Members	Quorum	Appmt
Ont.	s. 2	1 full-time	1 full-time	6 part-time	2	L-G in Council
Alta.	s. 3	1 full-time	1 part-time	1 part-time	2	L-G in Council
B.C.	s. 14	1 part-time	1 part-time	3 part-time	3	L-G in Council
Man.	s. 2	1 full-time	1 part-time	3 part-time	2	L-G in Council
Sask.	s. 3	1 full-time	1 part-time	1 part-time	2	L-G in Council
Que.	s. 2	1 full-time	2 full-time	2 part-time	2	L-G in Council
N.B.	s. 3	Administrator	1 Deputy-Administrator			L-G in Council
N.S.	s. 2	1 Registrar	1 Deputy Registrar			L-G in Council
P.E.I.	ss. 1(f), 3	1 Registrar				L-G in Council
Nfld.	s. 3	1 Registrar	1 Deputy Registrar			L-G in Council

[5]1971 (Ont.), Vol. 2, c. 47.

[6]1971 (Ont.), Vol. 2, c. 48.

[7]For detailed background to these two general Acts see the Report of the Royal Commission Inquiry Into Civil Rights (called "the McRuer Report" after its single Commissioner, a distinguished former Chief Justice of Ontario),

2.02 Creation and Nature of the Commission

The OSC takes its origin from the legislation in a curious manner. First created in 1937, the "official Commission" is given responsibility for the administration of the Act and then throughout the Act is clothed with certain powers.[8] But at the same time it is not established as a distinct corporate entity. Rather it is defined in terms of its composition—eight persons who have been appointed commissioners by the Lieutenant-Governor in Council.[9] The structure of the new body was altered somewhat in 1945 when a chairman was placed at its head, assisted by not more than two other part-time members.[10] In 1947, provision was made to designate one of the two other members as a vice-chairman.[11] The number of commissioners in addition to the chairman was increased to four in 1966 at the time of the introduction of the new Ontario Act, to five in 1969, and to seven in 1971. The purpose of this increase in personnel from 1966 was to broaden the range of expertise at the disposal of the Commission, as well as to help it cope with an increasing work load. Perhaps the next major structural change in Ontario will be to increase the number of full-time commissioners, while decreasing or maintaining at the present level the number of part-time members. Quebec recently opted for this "mix" by promoting its two full-time commissioners to vice-chairmen and appointing two new part-time commissioners.

The Act stipulates that the chairman shall devote himself on a full-time basis to the Commission's work, whereas the others are required to give such "time as may be necessary for the due perform-

---

Queen's Printer, Ontario, Report No. 1, 1968, Report No. 2, 1969, Report No. 3, 1971; J. Willis, "The McRuer Report: Lawyers' Values and Civil Servants' Values", 18 U. of T. L.J. 351 (1968); R.F. Reid, *Administrative Law and Practice* (Toronto, Butterworths, 1971); S.A. de Smith, *Judicial Review of Administrative Action*, 3rd ed. (London, Stevens, 1973); D.W. Mundell, *Manual of Practice on Administrative Law and Procedure in Ontario*, Department of Justice, 1972; and R.G. Atkey, "The Statutory Powers Procedure Act, 1971", 10 Osgoode Hall L.J. 155 (1972). The Reid and Mundell books are particularly useful to the practitioner.

[8]Section 2(1). Bill 20, s. 2(1) is neater, it explicitly "continues" the Commission.

[9]The evolution of the eight-man "official Commission" reflects the growth in size and complexity of Canadian securities markets, which has entailed corresponding changes in the regulatory structure. A registrar supervised the administration of Ontario's first Security Frauds Prevention Act in 1928, and the Attorney-General enforced the Act. In 1931, the Attorney-General's enforcement powers (to grant, deny or suspend registrations, make investigations and generally to ensure compliance with the Act) were turned over to a newly created board. In 1937, this board was renamed the Ontario Securities Commission, to be composed of one or more persons appointed by the Lieutenant-Governor in Council to hold office during pleasure.

The OSC will add a ninth commissioner—someone with expertise in commodities trading—when Bill 19, "The Commodity Futures Act, 1977" (4th Sess.), 30th Legislature Ontario, becomes law (see Bill 20, s. 2(2)).

[10]1945 (Ont.), c. 22, s. 2.

[11]1947 (Ont.), c. 98, s. 2(1).

ance of their duties".[12] Since 1967, the chairman and vice-chairman have been full-time public servants; the other six commissioners attend the regular weekly Commission hearings and various special hearings, and are present at other meetings as required.

Actions of the "official Commission" or its staff without or in excess of its jurisdiction were, until the advent of the Judicial Review Procedure Act, 1971, subject to review by way of *certiorari* or prohibition; a failure to act could be reviewed by way of *mandamus*.[13] Now a simple action to review under that legislation replaces the former prerogative writs. The Commission is not capable, however, of being sued in damages. The leading case is *Westlake et al. v. The Queen*,[14] where a motion to dismiss an action brought against the OSC was upheld. The plaintiffs, holders of securities issued by Prudential Finance Company Limited, alleged that the OSC had failed to perform its duties properly in regard to prospectuses and other disclosure documents filed by Prudential with the Commission prior to the company's failure.[15] They sought damages for breach of trust, breach of contract, deceit, common law negligence and negligence in performing statutory duties. The court held that the OSC was a non-corporate body which was not by the terms of the statute creating it or by necessary implication liable to be sued for damages; it was, however, a legal entity whose actions could be reviewed through *certiorari, mandamus* and prohibition.[16]

---

[12]Section 3(1).

[13]*Bishop v. Ontario Securities Commission*, [1964] 1 O.R. 17, 41 D.L.R. (2d) 24 (C.A.), appeal to S.C.C. dismissed 46 D.L.R. (2d) 601, [1964] S.C.R. v.

[14][1971] 3 O.R. 533, 21 D.L.R. (3d) 129 (H.C.); affd [1972] 2 O.R. 605, 26 D.L.R. (3d) 273 (C.A.); affd 33 D.L.R. (3d) 256n, [1973] S.C.R. vii.

[15]The Prudential story is, with the Windfall and Atlantic sagas, one of a trinity of financial tragedies which have profoundly influenced recent securities reform in Canada. Each of these unfortunate events is separately described in Appendices VI, VII, and VIII.

[16]In coming to this conclusion the High Court expressed the view that the Securities Act and the Ontario Labour Relations Act were "remarkably similar", and accordingly applied a principle from an analogous action against the Labour Board (*Hollinger Bus Lines Ltd. v. Ontario Labour Relations Board*, [1952] O.R. 366, [1952] 3 D.L.R. 162 (C.A.)) where the Ontario Court of Appeal rather emphatically stated at pp. 377-8:

"The whole scheme and purpose of the [Labour Relations] Act is to deal with certain phases of the employer-employee relationship. The Board does not carry on any business. Its function is primarily administrative and it has been given power to exercise certain functions of a judicial nature. There is nothing in the Act remotely suggesting that it was intended by the Legislature that the Board should have the capacity either to sue or be sued."

Weintraub v. The Queen, [1972] F.C. 611, 27 D.L.R. (3d) 513; appeal to Federal Court of Appeal dismissed [1972] F.C. 619, 29 D.L.R. (3d) 497, a proceeding against the Minister of National Revenue dealt with the same problem.

On top of all the other difficulties facing a plaintiff there is the privative clause in the Act requiring the Minister's consent for proceedings against any person acting in the administration of the Act (s. 145). Section 140 of Bill 20 removes the requirement for the Minister's consent but provides complete

The distinction between the two levels of responsibility within the Commission is set out in the Act with a brevity which is almost cryptic: the chairman is to be the chief *executive* officer; the director is to be the chief *administrative* officer, subject to the direction of the "official Commission".[17]

2.03 Appointment

The Ontario legislation is silent as to the tenure and removal of commissioners. They are appointed by order of the Lieutenant-Governor in Council[18] usually for a three-year term.[19] A commissioner may be removed without stated reasons during his term by order-in-council since he holds office at the pleasure of the Lieutenant-Governor in Council.[20]

The Quebec Act is the only one with specific provisions in this area. Commissioners are to hold office for a fixed period not to exceed three years, whereas for the chairman and two vice-chairmen the period is not to exceed ten years.[21] The Quebec Act also empowers the Lieutenant-Governor in Council to dismiss a commissioner during his term after inquiry, upon a motion by the Minister and a report by the Court of Appeal. Given the unusual sensitivity of these positions, Quebec's express provision as to removal is to be preferred.

---

immunity for actions performed in good faith in the course of duty. See also *Executors of the Woodward Estate v. Minister of Finance*, [1973] S.C.R. 120, 27 D.L.R. (3d) 608; *Robertson v. Deputy Superintendent of Brokers and A.-G. B.C.*, [1973] 3 W.W.R. 643, 35 D.L.R. (3d) 451 *sub nom. Re Robertson and Scott* (B.C.S.C.); appeal allowed [1974] 2 W.W.R. 165, 42 D.L.R. (3d) 135 (C.A.) and *Ontario Securities Commission v. Dobson et al.*, [1957] O.W.N. 183, 8 D.L.R. (2d) 604 (H.C.).

[17]Sections 3 and 4. See also, *infra*, part 2.05.

[18]Section 2(2).

[19]The last few appointments of chairmen have been for five-year terms and the vice-chairman's appointment has been for an unlimited term.

[20]The federal U.S. practice is more satisfactory as a matter of law in ensuring the independence of commissioners, once appointed, from political pressures. Professor Loss, commenting on the SEC, says (vol. 3, pp. 1881-2):

"In the nature of the American political system, the Commission is perhaps more independent of both branches (Executive and Legislative) when the Administration party does not control Congress. In any event, the Canons of Ethics adopted by the SEC for its members in 1958 provide that, 'under the law, this is an independent Agency, and in performing their duties, members should exhibit a spirit of firm independence and reject any effort by representatives of the executive or legislative branches of the government to affect their independent determination of any matter being considered by this Commission.' Moreover, it now seems quite clear that the legislative silence does not empower the President to remove members of an 'adjudicatory body' like the SEC, except presumably for 'inefficiency, neglect of duty or malfeasance in office.'"

This passage should be read, however, in the light of the events leading up to the resignation of the SEC's Chairman in 1973. The salutary lesson to be learned from that event, perhaps, is that a legalistic regime is at best a partial answer to the problem of ensuring the independence of persons in these positions.

[21]Section 2.

In practice the appointment of the chairman of the Ontario Commission may be carried out in various ways. Either the Premier or the Minister may take the initiative, although the Premier and Cabinet make the final decision.[22]

When it comes to the appointment of part-time commissioners, the initiative usually comes from the chairman and vice-chairman of the Commission who discuss the matter with the other commissioners and then with the Deputy Minister and the Minister; in the normal course of events this is followed by Cabinet approval.

2.04 Balance in the Commission

One objective in selecting members of the Ontario Commission has been to bring together persons with a diversity of experience in the many areas of securities regulation which involve knowledge and skill of a specialized kind.[23] The other provincial commissions have not altogether followed Ontario in this respect. For example, until 1973 Quebec retained a smaller complement of three full-time commissioners only, thereby eschewing a wide range of expertise. This policy was reversed with the appointment of two additional part-time commissioners in 1975. British Columbia and Alberta have named judges as part-time commissioners, underscoring in this manner the judicial side of the commission's responsibilities.[24]

---

[22]The professional and other qualifications of the chairman have also been a topic of some discussion. In particular, a requirement that he be a lawyer has been considered, but it has never been expressly enacted. The OSC chairman has traditionally been a lawyer, but the predecessor of the current chairman was a banker. The Kimber Committee said (para. 8.04): "Since the Commission performs important functions which are judicial in nature, the appointment of a chairman with a legal background has been desirable and should be continued." Generally this is the practice in other provincial jurisdictions. The Canadian Bar Association has suggested that legal qualification be a prerequisite to office. (Canadian Bar Association, Ontario Commercial Law Section Special Committee, Brief on Bill 154, 1972.)

[23]The Kimber Report (paras. 8.04 and 8.06) was quite explicit on the importance of substantial expertise, though was perhaps less concerned about the range of experience which the individuals chosen should possess. It said:

"It has been traditional that the members of the Commission, other than the Chairman, serve on a part-time basis. One of the Commissioners has frequently been a Master of the Supreme Court of Ontario and another a representative of the Department of Mines.

"....[W]ith the increasing complexity of the securities industry and in view of the amendments to securities legislation recommended by the Committee, the Commission would be greatly strengthened by the inclusion of persons who have special skill or experience in matters relating to the securities industry....

"...whether drawn from investment dealers, brokerage houses or the legal and accounting professions."

[24]The breadth and variety of experience within the OSC is apparent from a consideration of its composition in mid-1974. The chairman left a senior executive position with one of the chartered banks to join the Commission. The vice-chairman was a lawyer whose entire practising lifetime had been in the public service with particular emphasis on securities regulation. The most senior of the part-time commissioners, a former vice-chairman, was also the

2.05 Powers of the Commission

Section 2(1) vests in the Commission the general responsibility for the administration of the Act. Scattered throughout the Act are other references to its powers and duties, but the only other provisions articulating its responsibilities in Parts I and II are those which grant it the power to delegate and to appoint experts. Any commissioner may exercise the powers of the Commission and perform its duties, with two exceptions: hearings on appeal from a disposition of the director and decisions to issue investigation orders.[25] A quorum for such hearings or orders is two, although customarily for hearings a panel of three commissioners is struck by the chairman, and for matters of unusual complexity or ones which raise questions of fundamental importance a greater number may sit.[26]

Superintendent of Insurance for Ontario. Although professionally qualified as a chartered accountant, he had been a business executive and chief executive officer of a major manufacturing concern for many years. Another part-time commissioner had retired from a senior position with a large investment dealer and had served as chairman of the Board of Governors of the TSE. Traditionally the Commissioner of Mines or a senior geologist in the government service has served as a part-time commissioner, and the practice of choosing a mining representative was being continued at the date this survey was made. Another part-time commissioner had retired from a position as the senior partner of a major accounting firm; he had also been a member both of the Kimber Committee and the Financial Disclosure Advisory Board. The remaining two part-time members of the Commission were law professors with a specific interest in securities and corporate law. Customarily at least one of the three legally trained commissioners sits on each panel and drafts the Commission's decision where reasons are required.

[25]Section 3(2). Bill 20, s. 3(2) removes these limitations on the delegation of powers to a single commissioner.

[26]Ontario recently has increased the scope of the director's responsibility to make decisions in the initial instance which are then subject to appeal to the Commission (usually represented by a panel of three commissioners). For many years however a different practice was followed in the province. A single commissioner would make an initial decision which could then be appealed to two or more different commissioners. The former Ontario practice is still followed in some of the other two-tiered provincial administrations where there are fewer commissioners. Under the former Ontario practice, it was not always clear that the commissioner of first instance must absent himself from the appeal. A former Ontario chairman said (O.E. Lennox, "Securities Legislation and Administration", p. 87):

"The three-man Commission with a full-time Chairman, replacing the former single Commissioner, was first established under the provisions of the 1945 Act. The advantages of this establishment are, I think, generally conceded, despite the fact it undoubtedly invites the criticism that the Chairman sits on appeals from his own rulings. Whatever may be the merits of this, the establishment of a three-man Commission is one redeeming feature from my point of view, as the lot of a Commissioner is not an easy one and the knowledge that the most difficult decisions I am called on to make involving suspension or cancellation of registration, are subject to review by the full Commission, is most comforting."

But it is now settled that a commissioner who hears and decides at first instance must absent himself from the appeal (s. 3(3)). And see *Re Alberta Securities Commission and Albrecht* (1962), 38 W.W.R. 430, 36 D.L.R. (2d)

More difficult problems arise, however, where the Commission hears evidence from its staff and decides to launch an investigation which subsequently reveals that there is sufficient evidence in a particular case to question continued fitness for registration. It then instructs an investigation counsel to draw up a notice of hearing containing the allegation and the case to be met, and proceeds to hear and decide the case. The Commission is here acting in the roles of investigator, prosecutor and judge. Can it be free from bias? Conceivably a further structural separation of the two tiers could insulate the commissioners from the investigation of a case, but to a large extent the conflict is implicit in the present legislation which gives the chairman chief executive responsibility.[27] This issue was squarely faced in *Re W.D. Latimer Co. Ltd. and A.-G. Ont*[28] where an attempt was made to stay an OSC disciplinary hearing by alleging bias due to the mixing of the three roles of investigator, prosecutor and judge in one of the commissioners. It was held that the whole structure of the Commission as set up by statute involved the intermingling of these three functions, and something more was required to show bias.[29]

The Commission's power to appoint experts [30] has been exercised on a more permanent basis by the appointment of a part-time geological consultant who reports to the deputy director-filings and who analyzes engineering reports filed in connection with resource company prospectuses. From time to time expert witnesses or special counsel are retained on a temporary basis for hearings or research projects. The ability to retain unusually skilled individuals in this manner frees the Commission from confining civil service salary categories.

Three additional organs should be mentioned before concluding a technical description of the Commission. They are the Financial Disclosure Advisory Board (FDAB), the Commission secretary and the chief counsel.

2.06 Financial Disclosure Advisory Board
The FDAB is expressly created by the statute,[31] with members (including a chairman) appointed by the Lieutenant-Governor in Council to hold office at pleasure. It meets at the call of the Commission to consult with and advise the Commission concerning financial disclosure requirements contained in the Act and the regulations. The five members of the board are drawn from the fields of accounting and financial analysis and are paid a modest *per diem*

---

199 *sub nom. R. v. Alberta Securities Commission, Ex. p. Albrecht* (Alta. S.C.). See also *Law Society of Upper Canada v. French* (1974), 49 D.L.R. (3d) 1, [1975] S.C.R. ix; application for rehearing dismissed.
[27] On the tension produced by joining investigatory, prosecutory and judicial roles in one body, see the incisive comments of C. R. Thomson, "Concepts and Procedures in Hearings Before the Ontario Securities Commission", pp. 107-108.
[28] (1973), 2 O.R. (2d) 391, 43 D.L.R. (3d) 58 (Div. Ct.).
[29] See also *Law Society of Upper Canada v. French, supra,* footnote 26 and *Metropolitan Properties Co. (F.G.C.) Ltd. v. Lannon et al.,* [1969] 1 Q.B. 577, [1968] 3 All E.R. 304 (C.A.).
[30] Section 13(1). Bill 20, s. 5(1).
[31] Section 146. Bill 20, s.4; Bill 20 assigns a separate part (II) to the FDAB.

allowance for their work at the meetings and in connection with the other business of the board. Nothing is specified as to term of service of the members, but a custom has developed of staggered five-year terms for the five members with one member retiring each year. This system is obviously designed to balance continuity and experience with new ideas.

Advisory boards have been experimented with in other areas of government regulation with varying results. The OSC's FDAB was a direct result of the new emphasis on financial disclosure in the Kimber Report.[32] The statutory provision for creation of the board first appeared in the new Act of 1966. It has developed a practice of meeting regularly twice a year with the Commission; on other occasions it meets *ad hoc* in response to OSC requests for advice. A sampling of its recent activities would include consultation in the preparation of a policy statement (subsequently issued by the OSC) which attempted a definition of the term "generally accepted accounting principles", the initiation of a study on financial forecasting, and the production of a report dealing with the question of whether source and application of funds statements were meaningful for all types of companies. It also studied and gave advice on proposed amendments to the Act, and at the Commission's request provided a critique of the unusual method employed by issuers of a particular industry to show deferred tax liabilities in their financial statements.

If experience establishes that advisory committees of this kind have value in securities regulation, one may expect that they will be used in connection with a broader range of issues. Besides assisting in the development of financial disclosure requirements, the FDAB can provide a positive information input regarding business condition changes and help the OSC to anticipate regulatory problems. One caveat is necessary, however, to avoid conflicts of interest and to ensure that the board functions on a policy-making plane it would seem important that it not be drawn into direct consideration of specific cases.

Besides playing a wider role, it may be that the FDAB will in the future draw upon more diverse groups for its members. Already the range of expertise furnished by the board has expanded beyond that suggested by the Kimber Committee to include financial analysts as well as chartered accountants. One professional organization[33] has suggested that issuers be represented as well. For some years the American Bar Association has provided a committee of distinguished members of the securities bar to consult with the SEC on evolving legal problems.[34]

---

[32]In its chapter on "Disclosure in Financial Statements" (para. 4.32), the Kimber Report recommended "the formation of an Advisory Committee to the Ontario Securities Commission drawn from members of The Institute of Chartered Accountants of Ontario which could assist and advise the Commission on financial disclosure requirements to be embodied in the Regulations from time to time."

[33]Canadian Bar Association, Ontario Commercial Law Section, Special Committee, Brief on Ontario Bill 154, 1972.

[34]See for example the "Summary of the Meeting between Members of the Securities and Exchange Commission and Representatives of the Federal

The FDAB model will probably be imitated in other jurisdictions in Canada. The Quebec Minister of Financial Institutions has announced plans to establish a consultative committee on financial affairs[35] composed of representatives from "financial institutions and the public". It will review legislation and regulations on "insurance company law, insider trading, takeover bids and commercial matters".

2.07 Secretary
The office of secretary to the Commission has existed as a civil service position for some time, but without recognition by express legislative provision. In making amends for this neglect, Bill 20 ascribes various powers to the position; among other things these enable the holder to accept service on behalf of the Commission and to certify directives and other dispositions of the Commission.[36]

2.08 Chief Counsel
One of several structural recommendations of the Kimber Committee, yet to be carried out, called for the appointment of a chief counsel:
> "whose function would be to render legal opinions to the Commission, to represent the Commission in major court proceedings and generally to act as legal adviser to the Commission. His duties would not entail day-to-day or routine functions in the registration, investigation or prospectus review procedures."[37]

This officer would also take the lead in promulgating regulations and publishing statements to clarify the principles and policies which guide the Commission in those substantial areas where it has discretion.[38]

Regulation of Securities Committee" (1975), 30 The Business Lawyer 1341, where one of these interchanges is reported. Recently the chairman and a former member of the Bar Association Committee were appointed commissioner and chairman respectively of the SEC. The author suggested in an address to the Commercial Law subsection of the Ontario branch of the Canadian Bar Association in June, 1973 that a similar committee might be established for liaison with the OSC.

[35]Financial Times, Jan. 22, 1973, p. 12.

[36]Section 10.

[37]Para. 8.06, item 3.

[38]The Kimber Committee (*ibid.*, item 4) anticipated that:
> "The Chairman and the other members of the Commission, with the assistance and advice of the Chief Counsel, should, if the Commission were otherwise adequately staffed, be free to devote more attention to formulation of policies to be recommended to the Lieutenant Governor in Council for embodiment in regulations to be passed under The Securities Act. Section 72 of the Act has provided reasonably adequate scope for the promulgation of policy regulations, but has not, in the past, been sufficiently resorted to, with the result that Commission policy at the present time is largely a matter of so-called "departmental policy" prevailing from time to time. In our opinion, the policy-making functions of the Commission, especially in the significant areas of primary distribution and jurisdiction over stock exchanges, should be embodied in published regulations. Section 72 and other pertinent sections should be carefully analysed to determine whether the scope of such provisions are adequate to permit the formulation of necessary policies by regulations passed under section 72".

Under the present Act, the matters in respect to which regulations may be made are listed in s. 147. Bill 20, s. 141 increases the scope of this power to

Even though a chief counsel has not been appointed, the OSC has become much more active in publishing policy statements.[39] The Commission's standard practice now is to publish these in draft form, inviting comments from the industry and the professions concerned before making them final. With the growing complexity of regulation, however, the need for a chief counsel and for the members of the Commission to devote more attention to policy matters and to the formulation of new regulations has become acute. It would be difficult to over-emphasize how enormous is the discretion given to the Commission, often with no more in the way of detailed instructions than a general injunction to act in the public interest.[40] The policy statements therefore have the vital function of giving some indication of how this power will normally be exercised.

2.09 Staff

Just as the executive responsibilities of the Commission may be said to devolve upon the chairman, so the director is the locus of administrative responsibility and is in charge of the staff. The following chart represents the administrative structure in schematic form. The director, as chief officer, reports directly to the chairman. The four divisions of the Commission are shown, three under deputy directors and the fourth under the chief legal investigation officer, all of whom report to the director.

This structure, with a director and operating divisions, is outlined, though imprecisely, by various sections of the Act.[41] The director is subject to the direction of the Commission, and if the latter body chooses to delegate, either he or any deputy director may exercise powers and perform duties vested in the Commission by the Act or the

---

permit regulations which impose financial standards and conditions on issuers. Paragraphs 9 and 10 are new and provide for regulations governing the fees and sales charges of management companies, distribution companies, and contractual plan service companies in connection with the management of mutual funds and the sale of units in such funds. Paragraph 13 includes the word "release" to allow regulations pertaining to the use of press releases under the new timely disclosure provisions of the bill. Paragraph 23 gives effect to the Mutual Funds Report, which recommended that "knowledge necessary to enable potential purchasers to compare mutual funds should be communicated to them through regulations concerning the content of material distributed by salesmen...". Paragraph 26 gives the Lieutenant-Governor in Council power to pass regulations concerning the form and content of a takeover bid circular and a director's circular. Paragraph 27 provides for a penalty for early redemption of shares of mutual funds.

[39]Since the coming into effect of the Securities Act, 1966, in May, 1967, the number of OSC policy statements on record has increased from only a few in 1966 to 27 national, 12 uniform act and 32 local statements in mid-1975: see Appendix II.

[40]See, for example, ss.7, 19(5), 59, 61, 144.

[41]See in particular ss. 1(1)6 and 4. Section 4 provides that the director, or any deputy director, may exercise the powers and shall perform the duties vested in the director by the Act; any one of the three deputy directors may thus act in the place of their chief. In Bill 20 the relevant sections are 1(1)10 and 6. Section 6 deletes the words "or any Deputy Director", but the definition of director includes deputy director.

CHART "A"
THE ONTARIO SECURITIES COMMISSION*

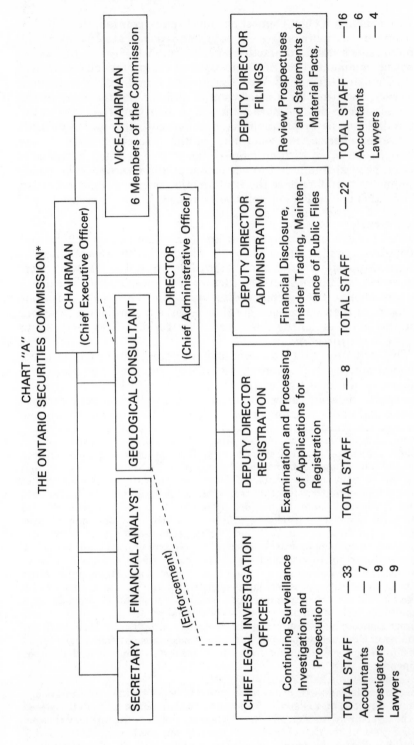

CHAIRMAN
(Chief Executive Officer)

VICE-CHAIRMAN
6 Members of the Commission

SECRETARY

FINANCIAL ANALYST

GEOLOGICAL CONSULTANT

(Enforcement)

DIRECTOR
(Chief Administrative Officer)

CHIEF LEGAL INVESTIGATION OFFICER

Continuing Surveillance Investigation and Prosecution

TOTAL STAFF	—33
Accountants	— 7
Investigators	— 9
Lawyers	— 9

DEPUTY DIRECTOR REGISTRATION

Examination and Processing of Applications for Registration

TOTAL STAFF — 8

DEPUTY DIRECTOR ADMINISTRATION

Financial Disclosure, Insider Trading, Maintenance of Public Files

TOTAL STAFF —22

DEPUTY DIRECTOR FILINGS

Review Prospectuses and Statements of Material Facts,

TOTAL STAFF	—16
Accountants	— 6
Lawyers	— 4

*According to 1972 complement structure.

regulations. Exempted from the range of items that may be delegated are reviews by the Commission of dispositions by the director and orders for investigation.[42]

The director also has important original as opposed to delegated functions. These are specified in various provisions of the Act. For example, he grants registration and renewal of the same, to persons requiring a licence to trade in securities (although the deputy director-registration will make the actual decisions).[43] The Act also vests in the director substantial discretion in accepting prospectuses for filing in connection with a public distribution. Once again it is the deputy director-filings who exercises this responsibility in practice. Generally the director performs a supervisory and managerial function, intervening personally only in certain extraordinary matters (*e.g.* formal hearings). The day-to-day administration of the Act is performed under the direct supervision of the three deputy directors and the chief legal investigation officer in the four functional divisions.

The largest of these divisions in terms of professionally qualified persons is the investigation section, headed by the chief legal investigation officer. He is assisted by a number of accountants, investigators and lawyers. This division is responsible for continuing surveillance of the securities markets, investigation and prosecution. It also prepares for consideration by the "official Commission" most applications for rulings and exemptions under the Act (and, where relevant, the BCA). The smallest division is headed by the deputy director-registration; its responsibility is the examination and processing of applications for registration. Hearings in connection with such applications take place before the director. The third division is headed by the deputy director-administration. This section, which has a large clerical staff, is responsible for financial disclosure, insider-trading reports and maintenance of the public files. The fourth division is presided over by the deputy director-filings; it is responsible for reviewing prospectuses and statements of material facts. This task is performed by a group of accountants and lawyers who usually operate in teams made up of one accountant and one lawyer. The deputy director of this division holds his own hearings, and appeals from his decisions go to the Commission.

2.10 Administrative Proceedings and Appeals
The uniform act sets out basic procedural rules for hearings before the director or Commission in one detailed section[44] and for appeals to the

---

[42]Sections 3 and 4. In February, 1968 (Feb. 9, 1968 OSCWS 3A) the OSC assigned to the director its power to grant exemptions from the proxy and proxy solicitation, insider trading and financial disclosure requirements of the Act, subject to the right of appeal by way of hearing and review to the Commission (ss. 104(2), 116(1) and 132(1); Bill 20, ss. 89(2), 120(2) and 81(c)). The BCA vests certain of these exempting powers in the Commission in the case of Ontario incorporated business corporations, but without expressing a power to delegate. Thus we have the anomaly of the Commission sitting as an appellate body on exemption decisions for non-Ontario incorporated companies but as judge of first instance for Ontario corporations.

[43]Section 7. A panel of commissioners suspends or cancels registration (s. 8).

[44]Section 5.

Commission or to the courts in two other sections.[45] In Ontario more
particular and paramount guidance is given by the Statutory Powers
Procedure Act, 1971 and the Judicial Review Procedure Act, 1971.[46]

Bill 20 joins the statement of rules for administrative proceedings
and appeals in a new Part V. Sections 8 and 9 of the same Bill deal with
the mechanics of appeal from the director to the Commission and from
the Commission to the Court of Appeal, containing minor amendments to the delineation of those rights in ss. 28 and 29 of the Act.
Both the right to a hearing within the structure of the Commission and
the right to a further appeal once such internal avenues of redress have
been exhausted are set out in a straightforward fashion. The Act[47]
stipulates that any person or company primarily affected by a
disposition of the director may appeal to the Commission for a hearing
and review.[48] Bill 20[49] substitutes "directly" for "primarily" apparently
in the belief that the right of appeal will be narrowed and be available
only to those who, at common law, are entitled to be parties to the
proceedings. In fact, the substitution may have the opposite effect.
Two different persons might be directly affected, but only one of them
would bear the primary force or brunt of the decision. In practice the
phrase "primarily affected" is given a generous interpretation. If, for
example, the director has issued a cease-trading order against an
incorporated issuer, a shareholder who is not part of management will
ordinarily be heard on appeal along with the corporation's management.[50] The disposition of the director which may be appealed is

---

[45]Sections 28 and 29.

[46]1971 (Ont.), Vol. 2, c. 47 and c. 48 respectively. As a result of the passing of
the Statutory Powers Procedure Act, 1971, the procedural rules section has
been deleted from the new Bill 20.

[47]Section 28.

[48]"Person" is defined in the Act (s. 1(1)12) to mean "an individual, partnership, unincorporated association, unincorporated organization, unincorporated syndicate, trustee, executor, administrator, or other legal personal
representative". In Bill 20 the definition (s. 1(1)27) adds a reference to "trust".
Its wide scope would appear to be satisfactory, but, as we have already seen,
ante, chapter 1, footnote 5, "person" for the purposes of the Act does not
include a company; company must be separately included throughout the Act.

It should be noted that notwithstanding the request for a hearing and
review the direction etc. under review takes effect immediately, but the
Commission may grant a stay until the disposition of the hearing and review
(s. 28(3)).

[49]Section 8(2).

[50]There is no Canadian jurisprudence in the field of securities regulation that
deals directly with this question. Certainly the parties to whom the order is
directed are primarily (or directly) affected. The question is whether third
parties have standing. In *Re Day & Ross Ltd. v. Jumbo Express Ltd.* (1972),
4 N.B.R. (2d) 658, 27 D.L.R. (3d) 115 (C.A.), s. 17A (enacted 1965, c. 28, s. 3)
of the Motor Carrier Act, 1957 (N.B.), c. 12 was in issue. It provided that "An
appeal lies to the Court of Appeal from any order...of the Board involving any
question as to its jurisdiction or any question of law." A third party objector
appealed a decision of the Board which retroactively amended the licence of
the respondent. The Court at p. 119 (D.L.R.) held s. 17A gave a right of appeal
"not only to a person who has made an application to the Board but also to any
person who, having a legitimate interest in any order or decision which might

described by the Act as "a direction, decision, order or ruling".[51] To take one example this language is broad enough to render subject to appeal a probationary condition attached to a positive decision of the director. The time within which an appeal must be lodged is limited to 30 days after the mailing of the notice of the director's disposition. There is, however, no stipulated time-limit within which the Commission must grant the hearing. As a practical matter the ability of the eight-member Commission to sit in panels of three, or on occasion two (a quorum), should ensure that most appeals will be heard within 30 days of their being requested.

A difficult question involves the nature and scope of the "hearing and review" of the director's disposition. One extreme of interpretation, emphasizing the first and not the last of these words, would require the hearing and review to be in the nature of a trial *de novo*, in which all evidence and witnesses are once again heard from beginning to end. The other extreme, giving paramountcy to the word review, would limit the appeal to a simple perusal of the record of the initial disposition, with the Commission's power extending only to reverse findings which it believed to be unreasonable or unsupported by the evidence. If one attempts to take an intermediate position, there are a number of issues to be faced, none of them susceptible of easy resolution. The chief questions, broadly speaking, are what material, evidence, and argument the Commission may consider, and what is the scope of its decision-making power; is it permitted, for example, to substitute a new decision completely contrary to that of the director, or must the matter be sent back to him with additional guidance for his own deliberation? The words "hearing and review" are not defined elsewhere in the Act. The fact that they are linked conjunctively might suggest a limitation on the form and nature of the appeal, *viz.*, that there is to be a hearing, but only for the purpose of reviewing the director's disposition. Alternatively one might by analogy assimilate this reviewing power to the jurisdiction of the Court of Appeal at the next stage, the appeal from the Commission, where the Act provides more explicit guidance.

The OSC has set out in a policy statement some simple guidelines for hearing and review appeals.[52] The party appealing is required to

---

be made on such an application, has opposed the application before the Board." For the Commonwealth jurisprudence see S.M. Thio, *Locus Standi and Judicial Review*, Singapore University Press (1971), pp. 216-31. A not dissimilar phrase which has been the subject of judicial comment and analysis is "aggrieved person" or "person aggrieved". See *Ex parte Sidebotham* (1880), 14 Ch. D. 458; *Maurice v. London County Council*, [1964] 2 W.L.R. 715, [1964] 1 All E.R. 779 (C.A.), and *A.-G. of the Gambia v. N'Jie*, [1961] 2 W.L.R. 845, [1961] 2 All E.R. 504 (P.C.).

[51]Bill 20 neatly avoids this prolixity by speaking throughout of decision and defining it to mean "a direction, decision, order, ruling or other requirement made under a power or right conferred by this Act or the regulations" (s. 1(1)9).

[52]Ontario Policy 3-20, CCH vol. 2, para. 54-914. The Quebec Securities Commission has also done so in Quebec Policy 2, CCH vol. 3, para. 66-013. In addition, see the Practice Statement of the British Columbia Corporate and Financial Services Commission in CCH vol. 2, para. 29-990.

order and deliver to the Commission transcripts of the proceedings to be reviewed and file a notice (which need not be a formal document) indicating "with sufficient certainty the decision appealed from and the interest of" the appealing party. The statement continues:

> "While the review of the evidence in no way prevents the introduction of new or additional relevant evidence by any party to the hearing and review before the Commission, where possible a statement of the points to be argued or of fact and law should be filed with the Commission at least 48 hours before the date fixed for the hearing and review."

On the face of it, therefore, the hearing is not limited to a narrow review of the record. Apart from what is contained in the form of written policies, customary practices of the OSC in regard to appeals may be summarized as follows. It will not allow documentary material which simply repeats evidence on the record before the director, preferring to use the record. New evidence is normally allowed to be filed only where it has come to light since the director's decision or where for some explainable reason it was not put before him.[53] However, the same witnesses who testified before the director may give evidence before the Commission. Moreover, evidence to support a novel legal argument may be adduced. Insofar as its power to dispose of the matter before it is concerned, the Commission sees the scope of its jurisdiction as complete, entitling it to substitute its discretion for the director's.[54]

---

[53]See *Re Whitelaw and Bd. of Police Commissioners of City of Vancouver* (1973), 35 D.L.R. (3d) 466 (B.C.C.A.).

[54]This latter practice is now justified by *Hretchka et al. v. A.-G. B.C.,* [1972] S.C.R. 119, 19 D.L.R. (3d) 1; appealing [1971] 1 W.W.R. 163 *sub nom. Re Hretchka et al. and Chromex Investments Ltd.,* 16 D.L.R. (3d) 273 *sub nom. Re Chromex Nickel Mines Ltd.* (B.C.C.A.). See also *Robertson v. Deputy Superintendent of Brokers and A.-G. B.C.,* [1974] 2 W.W.R. 165, 42 D.L.R. (3d) 135 (B.C.C.A.); reversing [1973] 3 W.W.R. 643, 35 D.L.R. (3d) 451 *sub nom. Re Robertson and Scott* (B.C.S.C.). In *Hretchka,* the Supreme Court of Canada held that a provision of the Supreme Court Act, R.S.C. 1952, c. 259 (now R.S.C. 1970, c. S-19, s. 44(1)), precluded an appeal where an earlier court decision was made in the exercise of judicial discretion. The British Columbia Commission had held a full hearing with *viva voce* evidence in reviewing a decision of the deputy superintendent to issue a cease-trading order. It confirmed his order, although varying it in certain particulars. On appeal to the Court of Appeal the order was sustained in substance, although this time the Commission was directed to effect certain changes in detail. The decision of the appellate court involved a holding that the Commission was not limited to a determination of whether or not the deputy superintendent's order was valid but was empowered to make its own order; it was on this point that the decision was upheld by the Supreme Court of Canada. But the highest court also suggested that the admission of evidence by the Commission along the lines of a trial *de novo* had the advantage of nullifying any errors which might have been made at the first hearing; implicity, therefore, the decision encourages the holding of an extensive hearing at the Commission level.

The Supreme Court quoted the reasoning of Bull J.A. in the lower court with approval at pp. 128-9, S.C.R.:

One question that remains open is this: does the Commission

"'It is apparent from the record that the record that the whole matter and the surrounding circumstances were canvassed in detail before the Commission. Extensive *viva voca* evidence was led, the appellants were represented, sworn testimony was given on their behalf and exhibits filed. Oral submissions were made that the public interest was not served by the prohibitions ordered by the Deputy Superintendent. In my view, the hearing was full and complete and in compliance with the principles of natural justice. In short, whether or not the Deputy Superintendent's order was valid or invalid, the appellants were present or represented at the hearing held before the Commission at their requests to convince it, not only that the earlier order was bad, but that it should not, in the public interest, make or affirm an order prohibiting [trading]...

...

"'Here the power to make an order to prohibit trading lay in the Commission itself under s. 77A, and the power purported to be exercised by the Deputy Superintendent was merely a delegated power under s. 5(1), and from which s. 30 *provides not only a "review" but a "hearing"*. The extent of that hearing is indicated by the specific power given in the section, not only of confirming the order or ruling of the Superintendent but of making such "other direction, decision, order or ruling as the Commission deems proper". That goes far beyond appellate jurisdiction in the strict sense of deciding merely whether a lower decision be right or wrong.'"
(Emphasis added.)

See also *Posluns v. Toronto Stock Exchange and Gardiner*, [1966] 1 O.R. 285, 53 D.L.R. (2d) 193 (C.A.); appeal dismissed [1968] S.C.R. 330, 67 D.L.R. (2d) 165 and *Re Clark and Ontario Securities Commission*, [1966] 2 O.R. 277, 56 D.L.R. (2d) 585 (C.A.). These two cases show an approach, and arrive at a result, similar to that of *Hretchka*. A somewhat different approach, however, can be seen in *Libman v. General Medical Council*, [1972] A.C. 217, [1972] 1 All E.R. 798, where the relevant legislation on appeal from the medical disciplinary committee to the Privy Council gave a broad invitation to the latter to "include power to vary or revoke the Order by a subsequent Order made in the like manner...subject to annulment in pursuance of a resolution of either House of Parliament". The Privy Council declined this invitation, stating at p. 800, All E.R.:

"...although the jurisdiction conferred by the statute is unlimited, the circumstances in which it is exercised in accordance with the rules approved by Parliament are such as to make it difficult for an appellant to displace a finding or order of the committee unless it can be shown that something was clearly wrong either (i) in the conduct of the trial or (ii) in the legal principles applied or (iii) unless it can be shown that the findings of the committee were sufficiently out of tune with the evidence to indicate with reasonable certainty that the evidence had been misread. Or, of course, an appellant can rely cumulatively or in the alternative on any combination of the three."

And for similar guidance on this matter closer to home see *Caswell v. Alexandra Petroleums Ltd.*, [1972] 3 W.W.R. 706, 26 D.L.R. (3d) 289, 2 L.C.R. 229 (Alta. C.A.), which suggests that if a trial *de novo* is intended much more emphatic encouragement from the legislation is required.

Contrast the dispositive position of the Commission on appeals from the TSE under s. 140(3) (Bill 20, s. 22(3)), where the Commission is somewhat more circumspect. See, *post*, part 10.03(4), and in particular *In The Matter of E.A.P. Williams*, May 1972 OSCB 87 and *Lafferty, Harwood & Partners Ltd.*, Feb. 1973 OSCB 26.

exercise an original jurisdiction or a limited appellate jurisdiction where the lower official is exercising a deliberative power specifically granted to him by the Act and not, as was the case with the cease trading order in *Hretchka*, delegated to him by the Commission? Although the judgment in *Hretchka* is *obiter* with respect to this question, the interpretation it gave to "hearing and review" extends logically to the Commission's consideration of both kinds of decisions by a lower official—those delegated to him by the Commission and those specifically entrusted to his charge by the Act. Furthermore, an analysis of Bull J.A.'s judgment,[55] which was approved by the Supreme Court of Canada, suggests that he concluded in favour of original jurisdiction in the Commission because it and no one else was the body which had the power under the terms of the statute to make whatever "other" order it deemed proper "where the final body to hear the appeal of the person aggrieved had the sole power to decide the point in issue."[56]

Until 1973, when it was deleted[57] as superfluous in view of the Judicial Review Procedure Act, 1971, the right of appeal from the Commission set out in the Act was couched in language similar to that employed in the case of appeals from the director to the Commission.[58] The only difference was that the jurisdictional phrase "hearing and review" was displaced by a broader statement as follows:[59]

"...the practice and procedure upon and in relation to the appeal shall be the same as upon an appeal from a judgment of the judge of the Supreme Court in an action, provided that the Rules Committee may vary or amend such practice and procedure...that shall be applicable to appeals taken under this Act."

This pre-1973 Ontario language continues to be used in the other uniform act jurisdictions.

The Act still contains detailed guidance with respect to the materials to be placed before the Court of Appeal[60] as well as the kinds of disposition which the Court of Appeal may cause to be made. The Court has the discretion to "direct the Commission to make such direction, decision, order or ruling or to do such other act as the Commission is authorized and empowered to do under this Act or the regulations and as the Court deems proper, having regard to the material and submissions before it" and the legislation.[61] Although the

---

[55][1971] 1 W.W.R. 163 at pp. 172-174, 16 D.L.R.(3d) 273 *sub nom. Re Chromex Nickel Mines Ltd.* (B.C.C.A.); appeal denied *sub nom. Hretchka et al. v. A.-G. B.C.*, [1972] S.C.R. 119, [1972] 1 W.W.R. 561, 19 D.L.R. (3d) 1.

[56]*Ibid.*, at p. 173. This interpretation enabled him to distinguish *Leary v. National Union of Vehicle Builders*, [1970] 3 W.L.R. 434, [1970] 2 All E.R. 713 (Ch. D.), where the plaintiff was held to be entitled to both a hearing *and* an appeal. In so doing he applied *King v. University of Saskatchewan*, [1969] S.C.R. 678, 6 D.L.R. (3d) 120, 68 W.W.R. 745.

[57]"An Act to amend The Securities Act", 1973 (Ont.), c. 11, s. 2.

[58]Note that there is no appeal from rulings under s. 59.

[59]Section 29(2).

[60]Section 29(3) and (5). Bill 20, s. 9(3) and (5).

[61]Section 29(5) (Bill 20, s. 9(5)).

injunction might seem superfluous, an explicit duty is imposed on the Commission to comply with the Court's directive. This is not the end of the matter, however. Notwithstanding an order of the Court of Appeal the Commission is empowered "to make any further direction, decision, order or ruling upon new material or where there is a material change in the circumstances", subject of course to a further right of appeal.[62]

For guidance on the nature and scope of the Court of Appeal's power on appeal from the Commission *Hretchka et al. v. A.-G. B.C.* is a ready guide.[63] The Supreme Court of Canada there held that the decision under appeal of the provincial Court of Appeal was one involving the exercise of judicial discretion and was thus not itself appealable. It said:

> "On the merits, the majority of the Court of Appeal held that, under all the circumstances, a prohibition against trading...which the Commission sought...to impose, was merited. The Court exercised its powers...to direct the Commission as to the nature of such order and varied, in certain respects, the Commission's order. In my opinion the Court, under the provisions of that subsection [s. 31(5)], had the power to make the order which it did. The appeal to it had been taken under s. 31 of the Act, and subs. (5) provides that, where such an appeal is taken, the Court of Appeal may direct the Commission to make such order, as the Commission is empowered to make under the Act, as the Court deems proper.
>
> ...
>
> "The Commission is an administrative tribunal which has authority, in specified instances, to conduct hearings, make decisions and issue orders....It can make a determination, not on the basis of fixed legal rules, but on the basis of its own opinion as to what is in the public interest. In my opinion this is a discretionary power.
> "...the Court, on appeal, has the same discretionary powers as has the Commission. The test which the Court had to apply in its determination of the appeal was not a legal test, but a test as to what was considered to be in the public interest."

However, the Court of Appeal may feel obliged to use restraint in exercising this discretion. The majority judgment of Bull J.A. in the Court of Appeal in the same case suggests as much. He said:[64]

---

[62]Section 29(6) (Bill 20, s. 9(6)). This jurisdictional give and take was subjected to a series of tests in *Re Niagara Wire Weaving Co. Ltd.*, [1971] 3 O.R. 633, 21 D.L.R. (3d) 305 (C.A.) and *Re Niagara Wire Weaving Co. Ltd. (No. 2)*, [1972] 3 O.R. 129, 27 D.L.R. (3d) 548 (C.A.) discussed, *post*, part 5.07(3).
[63][1972] S.C.R. 119 at pp. 129-30, [1972] 1 W.W.R. 561, 19 D.L.R. (3d) 1.
[64]*Re Hretchka et al. and Chromex Investments Ltd.*, [1971] 1 W.W.R. at p. 176, 16 D.L.R. (3d) 273 *sub nom. Re Chromex Nickel Mines Ltd.* See also *Re The Securities Act and Morton*, [1946] O.R. 492, [1946] 3 D.L.R. 724 (C.A.). A similar solicitude for the autonomy of the Commission within its proper sphere is found in other more recent cases. In *Re Western Ontario Credit Corp. Ltd. and Ontario Securities Commission* (1975), 9 O.R. (2d) 93 at pp. 98-9, 59 D.L.R. (3d) 501 (Div. Ct.). Hughes J. said: "[Section 29 providing for an appeal from the Commission's decision]...confers wide powers on the Court

"The full power given this Court to have the Commission make a proper order satisfies me that it is our function to consider on the merits whether or not the Commission erred in finding that the public interest required the stop-trading order. The members of the Commission are appointed, unquestionably, because of their knowledge and experience in matters involving corporate securities and the trading thereof, and it cannot be said that we have that advantage to any degree. With that in mind, I think the proper position that we should adopt is that stated by Laidlaw J.A. in *Re Securities Commission and Mitchell*, [1959] O.W.N. 595 at 599:

"'The opinion of the Commission should not be set aside or altered upon an appeal unless the Commission has erred in some principle of law or unless it appears clearly that the Commission has not proceeded to form its opinion in a judicial manner or unless it appears that the opinion of the Commission is so clearly wrong as to amount to an injustice requiring a remedy on appeal.'"

(1) ORDERS WITHOUT A HEARING

The Commission and the director are empowered in a number of instances to make orders which affect the rights of persons or companies without first affording them the opportunity for a hearing.[65] The directives which may be issued in this fashion include the denial of exemptions from the registration or prospectus qualification provisions, commencement of an investigation, freezing of funds and cessation of trading in specified securities.[66] This last type of order is the one most frequently used by far, and the need to interpret its scope has given rise to a not inconsiderable amount of litigation. When denials of exemptions or cease-trading orders are issued in this peremptory fashion, a hearing must be granted within fifteen days. By

---

and is consistent with the practice followed in recent years by the Legislature of Ontario and, indeed, by the Parliament of Canada in several statutes, of inviting it to consider appeals from regulatory tribunals on their merits and in excess of the inherent power of superintendence which the Court has historically assumed by way of prerogative writs and which has received statutory recognition by the *Judicial Review Procedure Act...*" He applied the statement of Aylesworth J.A. in *Re Maher Shoes Ltd. and Ontario Securities Commission*, [1971] 2 O.R. 267 at p. 268, 17 D.L.R. (3d) 519 (C.A.): "It is common ground that, apart from some question of failure of natural justice before such a Commission with the powers that the Commission has, the only ground for interference by an appellate Court would be demonstration to the Court of a plain and vital mistake as to what the evidence was which the Commission had to consider." Hughes J. concluded at p. 103: "...where a regulatory tribunal, acting within its jurisdiction, makes an order in the public interest with the experience and understanding of what that interest consists of in a specialized field accumulated over many years, the Court will be especially loath to interfere."

For guidance on what is a Commission order and appealable, as distinct from a condition which is not, see *Re Glass*, [1951] O.R. 629, [1951] 4 D.L.R. 117 (C.A.).

[65]See *Re Fournier; Re Securities Act*, [1942] O.W.N. 647, [1943] 1 D.L.R. 231 (Ont. Bd. of Review).

[66]Section 19(5) (Bill 20, s. 127); s. 21 (Bill 20, s. 11); s. 26 (Bill 20, s. 16); ss. 62 and 144 (Bill 20, ss. 71 and 126) respectively.

contrast no hearing is required to initiate an investigation or to freeze funds.

Some check is placed on the uninhibited use of denials of exemption and cease-trading orders by the legislative requirement that the power not be exercised "unless in the opinion of the Commission the length of time required for a hearing could be prejudicial to the public interest." In the case of the general power to order a cessation of trading the temporary order which is to expire within fifteen days if no hearing is ordered "may be extended for such period as the Commission considers necessary where satisfactory information is not provided to the Commission".[67]

In *Rodney Gold Mines Ltd. and Claybar Consultants Ltd. v. Ontario Securities Commission*[68] it was held that the Commission had jurisdiction to extend a temporary order after a hearing, pending further information. In that case the OSC had issued a temporary cease-trading order and had forwarded a notice of hearing to show cause why the order should not be made permanent. The hearing was held within the required fifteen days and adjourned to the following day with provision for the order to stay in effect; it was then again adjourned for a full week, without any lifting of the ban on trading. On the resumption of the hearing the OSC concluded that there was a need for further intensive investigation, and the hearing was adjourned until this was done and the information made available; at no time was any provision made for interrupting the cease-trading order. An application to quash what had now become a prohibition of indefinite duration was denied. The words of the Act permitting a temporary order to remain in effect, "where satisfactory information is not provided to the Commission" within fifteen days, were interpreted by the Court rather generously in the Commission's favour as placing a burden of providing information on the person or company against whom the order was made. And where the information did not satisfy the Commission it was allowed to extend the temporary order. An onus of this sort could operate harshly in cases where trading in a company's securities has been halted due to activities of third persons and the Commission's investigation has not reached the stage of providing satisfactory information regarding these activities.

Cease-trading orders and denials of exemptions are both severe sanctions, and careful consideration is required before they are used. The courts have been conscious of this fact in cases where the propriety of such orders has been an issue. In *Re Clark and Ontario Securities Commission*[69] the chairman of the OSC found that Clark, unknown to the shareholders, had "resigned" as auditor of a company to become a signing officer; he then participated in raising money from shareholders, less than a third of which found its way into the company treasury. Without waiting for a hearing the chairman denied trading exemptions to Clark and "any company of which he was an officer or director while he was such". On a hearing and review the

---

[67]Section 144(2).
[68]July 1972 OSCB 159, unofficial record of an Ontario Supreme Court oral judgment by Donnelly J.
[69][1966] 2 O.R. 277, 56 D.L.R. (2d) 585 (C.A.).

Commission affirmed the order. In the Court of Appeal it was held that although the failure by the chairman to give a hearing was a denial of natural justice which would entitle the Court to nullify any directive made by him, the full hearing before the Commission[70] had laid a sufficient basis for a valid order. In the written reasons of the Commission there appeared this passage, to which the appellate court gave its approval:

"'The hearing before us is a full hearing and review. The applicant is present and can call any evidence he wishes. It is on the basis of the material before us that our order is made and any defect in the first proceeding does not deprive us of our jurisdiction to deal with the matter on its merits.'"[71]

On the other hand the Court found that the Commission had erred in extending its ban beyond the one individual, since he was the only "person or company" stated in the initial order to have been guilty of misconduct. A power to constrain trading in other companies, which he served as an officer or director, purely because it was anticipated that he would engage in improper activity in the exercise of his functions, would require an amendment to the legislation.

The Court of Appeal decision in the *Hretchka* case[72] laid down more detailed guidelines, for the use of the same power. The first (and most specific) finding was that the British Columbia Commission had erred when it ordered that shares held by an individual whose securities were already subject to a cease-trading order should in addition be placed in escrow. Apparently the Commission was not content to let the force of the order deter trading, or it wished to prevent the securities being traded out of the jurisdiction. At all events its attempt to freeze the securities in the hands of a third party by an escrow was held to be abortive. The second point to be gathered from this decision is that a court looks with disfavour on open-ended cease-trading orders. The Commission had ordered that trading cease "until the Commission otherwise orders". In the Court of Appeal, the majority judgment did not expressly decide whether such an indefinite prolongation of the order was "for a period" as the statute required, because Bull J.A. decided that the imposition of such a "period" was unfair to the persons affected in the particular case; he directed that the order should last for one year or until such earlier time as the Commission determined. He added that:

"At the end of the year the Commission could, if it saw fit so to do, hold a new hearing, and thereat the interests of both the public and of the appellants would undoubtedly be considered and served."[73]

---

[70]On the authority of *Posluns v. Toronto Stock Exchange and Gardiner*, [1966] 1 O.R. 285, 53 D.L.R. (2d) 193 (C.A.); affirmed [1968] S.C.R. 330, 67 D.L.R. (2d) 165.

[71][1966] 2 O.R. at p. 278. See also *Re Cardinal and Board of Commissioners of Police of City of Cornwall* (1973), 2 O.R. (2d) 183, 42 D.L.R. (3d) 323 (Div. Ct.) and *Hretchka et al. v. A.-G. B.C.*, [1972] S.C.R. 119, [1972] 1 W.W.R. 561, 19 D.L.R. (3d) 1.

[72][1971] 1 W.W.R. 163, 16 D.L.R. (3d) 273 *sub nom. Re Chromex Nickel Mines Ltd.* (B.C.C.A.).

[73]*Ibid.*, at p. 177, W.W.R. The dissenting (on another point) judgment in the

A third lesson to emerge from *Hretchka* is that the official who holds the hearing must also make the resultant order. It was thus an error for the deputy superintendent to issue a cease-trading order for reasons given at a hearing before the superintendent of brokers alone.

(2) INVESTIGATIONS

Part III of the Act determines the scope of investigations by the Commission and the methods to be employed in pursuing them.[74] The seven sections of this part contain the basic tools which enable the regulatory authority to fulfil its role in the prevention and combatting of fraud. The powers involved are rather sweeping, and the investigation, since it is an administrative rather than a judicial proceeding, is not subject to the rules of natural justice or to the Statutory Powers Procedure Act, 1971.[75]

Investigations (formal and informal) constitute an important part of the Commission's work.[76] They are usually conducted with a minimum

---

case went further, holding that orders of no definite term were in principle invalid. Robertson J.A. stated at p. 186:

"Apart from practical results, I think that the requirement that the order mention a period is not met by words such as were used here. I think that words which do not specify a finite length of time, but prohibit one from doing something until the tribunal or another makes an order, do not mention a period within the intention of the section. The section gives a drastic power to the Commission and one which may have serious financial effects on those affected by its exercise, and I am of the opinion that the Legislature, in using the words it did, intended that the person prohibited from trading should know precisely how long his prohibition is to last."

See also *Posluns v. Toronto Stock Exchange and Gardiner*, [1966] 1 O.R. 285, 53 D.L.R. (2d) 193 (C.A.); affirmed [1968] S.C.R. 330, 67 D.L.R. (2d) 165.
[74]Bill 20, Part VI contains few changes in this area.
[75]See *St. John v. Fraser*, [1935] S.C.R. 441, [1935] 3 D.L.R. 135, 64 C.C.C. 90 and see, *infra*, footnote 100. For an acute criticism of this state of affairs, see J.C. Baillie, "Discovery Type Procedures in Security Fraud Prosecutions". This article is an excellent short review of the procedures used by securities commissions (primarily that of Ontario) in uncovering and obtaining information in the investigation which precedes a securities fraud prosecution. Mr. Baillie suggests that a greater effort must be made to carve out procedural safeguards for persons under investigation but not accused of securities fraud. He argues that this can be done without endangering the flexibility needed at the early detection stage of such prosecutions. The same author concludes that courts have been too complaisant in their treatment of wide-ranging investigation orders issued by securities commissions although granting that the permissive language of the statute encourages this approach. Mr. Baillie makes a remark which gives rise to some disquieting reflections in a wider context, at p. 500:

"So wide is this authority [of provincial securities commissions, particularly over registrant firms] and so important is it to a firm to retain the goodwill of the commission that requests made by commission staff members are often complied with even if not directly supported by the statutory powers of the commission".

See also C.R. Thomson, "Concepts and Procedures in Hearings Before the Ontario Securities Commission".
[76]In mid-1972 the OSC Chairman stated that there were about one hundred investigations proceeding at any one time (Address by Mr. E.A. Royce to the Junior Investment Dealers Association, Toronto, Ontario, April 10, 1972).

of publicity since the investigation takes place prior to any determination whether an offence has been committed; many of the matters considered are resolved or dropped at this pre-prosecution stage.

There are three ways in which a formal investigation may commence. The first requires a statement under oath—usually made by a member of the OSC staff after preliminary inquiries—that it appears probable that there has been a contravention of the Act or the Criminal Code in connection with a securities trade.[77] The Commission then has a discretion to appoint one or several persons to make such investigation as it deems expedient. The persons appointed are usually, though not always, members of the OSC staff.[78] Ordinarily a three-man team of a lawyer, accountant and investigator is named to carry out the investigation. The Commission must outline the scope of the enquiry in the appointing order, although if the line is initially drawn too narrowly, amendment is permitted.

The second method of commencing an investigation requires less in the way of preliminary evidence. No statement under oath concerning a probable offence is necessary. Rather the Commission is simply empowered to begin an investigation "for the due administration of this Act or into any matter relating to trading in securities".[79] This

---

Figures from earlier years reveal the following:

INVESTIGATIONS

Period Jan. 1-Dec. 31	Outstanding	FORMAL Opened	Closed	Outstanding
1967	17	15	13	19
1968	19	10	6	23
1969	23	15	16	22
1970	22	23	N/A	N/A
1971	N/A	4	N/A	N/A
				Opened & Closed
1972				21
1973				20
		INFORMAL		
1967	14	253	159	249
1968	157	241	170	228
1969	228	200	257	171
1970	171	311	N/A	N/A
1971	N/A	195	N/A	N/A

Source: Department of Financial and Commercial Affairs Annual Reports—not published for more recent years. The Statistical Review 1972-73, Ministry of Consumer and Commercial Relations, provides much more limited information.

[77]Section 21(1).
[78]Section 21(1) states that "any person" may be appointed. In the Prudential Finance proceedings, Appendix VI, a leading firm of chartered accountants was appointed to perform the accounting part of the investigation. This was done under the specific power conferred by s. 21(8) but it could have been done under s. 21(1) as well. On occasion staff of the TSE or of another provincial securities commission have been added to the investigation team by naming them in the order.
[79]Section 21(2) (Bill 20, s. 11(2)).

method was introduced by the 1968 amendments[80] in the belief that the investigative powers, which among other things permit the seizure of documents and the inspection of bank accounts, should on occasion be invoked before it can be shown that a probable offence has occurred. As things currently stand this procedure is the one more frequently employed.

Finally the Minister has a separate power to initiate an investigation which he considers expedient for the due administration of the Act; the person appointed in such a case enjoys a status similar to that enjoyed by an appointee of the Commission.[81] This ministerial discretion was introduced with the Act of 1966; it is however rarely used.[82] Moreover its presence evokes curiosity. The transfer of responsibility for securities matters from the Attorney-General to the new Minister of Financial and Commercial Affairs, a step which coincided with the passing of the Act, was thought to reflect the removal of the day-to-day administration of the Act from the sphere of the Minister's immediate authority. The granting of an initiating power to the Minister seems out of keeping with the trend toward administrative autonomy.[83]

Wide scope is given to an investigation. The person entrusted with the responsibility for carrying it out is empowered to investigate, inquire into and examine the affairs of a person or company: the list of items and relationships which might be comprehended by such affairs[84] is an exceedingly broad one. If such tools were placed in the hands of the uniformed police, one could expect strenuous objections from civil liberty organizations and members of the Legislatures.[85] The justification for these wide-ranging powers is that securities frauds are often exceedingly complex, requiring formidable weaponry to combat. The disagreeable features of such provisions are mitigated somewhat by the fact that their full force is felt by only a narrow group of individuals and institutions.[86]

---

[80]1968 (Ont.), c. 123, s.8.

[81]Section 23 (Bill 20, s. 13).

[82]1966 (Ont.), c. 142, s. 23; "a trade" was amended to "trading" in 1968 (Ont.), c. 123, s. 9.

[83]For a discussion of the Minister's role and the Commission's accountability, see, *infra*, part 2.13.

[84]Section 21(3) (Bill 20, s. 11(3)).

[85]Note, for example, the pressure which caused the then Attorney-General of Ontario to resign following the introduction of the "Police Powers" Bill, Bill 99 in the Legislature of Ontario Debates, 27th Legislature (1st-2nd Sess.), 1964, p. 1797.

[86]See *Torny Financial Corp. Ltd. v. Marcus et al.*, [1951] O.W.N. 733, [1951] 4 D.L.R. 762 (H.C.). What is perhaps most startling about these powers is that in exercising them the Commission must play a role of investigator and judge combined. As examples we may take the seizure of documents, and the freezing of assets. According to traditional procedural rules the investigating agency must go before a separate court to secure an order before doing either. And in a third case—the power to compel evidence—according to traditional procedural rules not only must the investigator go before a court, but in the most crucial instance (questions in which the accused might incriminate himself) the investigator is precluded from inquiring. Not so under the Act.

The investigator's power relating to witnesses and documents is similar to that of the Supreme Court in the trial of civil actions.[87] The failure or refusal of a person to attend or answer questions, or to produce documents or other things that are in his possession, renders him liable to committal for contempt by a Supreme Court Judge to the same extent as if he were in breach of an order or judgment of the Court. Persons giving evidence at an investigation are entitled to be represented by counsel.

Frequently in the investigation of a suspected securities fraud the trail leads to banking records, for example cancelled cheques. A special provision precludes a bank or any of its officers or employees from pleading the Evidence Act[88] to resist production of documents.[89]

An additional prerogative of the investigator which arouses considerable controversy because of its disruptive effect on business is his authority to seize any documents, securities or property.[90] The person or company whose property is seized must be actually named in the investigation order, and not simply connected with the matter in question. In fact, however, the protection afforded by this limitation is somewhat illusory, because investigation orders tend to be comprehensive in naming parties. And if time permits, an order may easily be amended to name the omitted person. The party from whom the property has been seized is entitled to have it available for inspection and copying at a mutually convenient time and place.[91]

The Commission also has a specific discretion, once an investigation has commenced, to appoint accounting and other experts to examine property of those under investigation.[92] An investigation or examination normally ends with the making of the required report of the results to the Commission, together with recommendations.[93]

It is only after the presentation of this report that the way lies open for the formal involvement of the Minister, although in matters of serious concern he will often be informally advised at an earlier stage. If it appears to the Commission from the investigation report that someone may have contravened securities legislation or committed a criminal offence in connection with a securities transaction, the sending of a complete report of the investigation to the Minister is

---

[87]Section 21(4) (Bill 20, s. 11(4)).

[88]Section 34(4) of the Ontario Evidence Act, R.S.O. 1970, c. 151, provides that banks need only produce books when required by court order.

[89]Another question which may arise is the right of those investigated to secure disclosure of information assembled by the Commission. This is part of the subject of Crown privilege: see *Gagnon v. Commission des Valeurs Mobilières du Québec et al.*, [1965] S.C.R. 73, 50 D.L.R. (2d) 329 *sub nom. Gagnon v. Quebec Securities Commission.*

[90]Section 21(6) (Bill 20, s. 11(6)).

[91]Section 21(7) (Bill 20, s. 11(7)).

[92]Section 21(8) (Bill 20, s. 11(8)). This power was exercised shortly after the commencement of the Prudential Finance investigation and a separate accountant's report was produced (see Appendix VI). Section 21(8) is technically superfluous given that the Commission is elsewhere empowered to appoint experts to assist in "such manner as it may deem expedient" (s. 13(1)).

[93]Section 21(9) (Bill 20, s. 11(9)).

mandatory.[94] The documents and other information placed before him must include the reports received by the Commission itself, any transcript of evidence, and any related material in the Commission's possession.[95] The fact that the Minister receives such full reports in anti-fraud matters is an accurate reflection of his very substantial involvement in this area. By contrast his participation in matters of registration, whether of persons or securities, is slight.

This part of the Act also contains a rather curious provision designed to suppress early publicity in connection with investigations. Section 24[96] prohibits any person from disclosing without the consent of the Commission (except to his counsel) any information or evidence obtained in the investigation. The intent of this provision is twofold: first, it aims to prevent persons who have evidence they may wish to suppress from being "tipped off" before the investigator has reached them or their records.[97] The second purpose is to ensure that innocent persons are not injured unfairly by publicity arising from an investigation. It is this goal which causes investigations to be conducted in practice with as much anonymity as possible.[98] For the same reason both the Minister and the Commission are under no compulsion to release reports; at all stages the question of publication remains a matter for ministerial discretion. The provisions of the Act which circumscribe this discretion are not skillfully drafted,[99] but they

---

[94]Section 22. The use of the word "may" at this stage in respect to the commission of the offence is curious. In the first type of investigation it was necessary that the offence be "probable" before an investigation was commenced in the first instance.

[95]Literally interpreted this could make up a rather bulky package in view of the large quantity of material that is normally stored both in the public and the private files of the Commission.

[96]Bill 20, s. 14.

[97]It is unlikely, however, that prohibition has much practical impact in instances of serious wrong-doing. If a person under investigation has some advantage to be gained by informing an associate, he undoubtedly will do so, any rules to the contrary notwithstanding. A careful investigator therefore will lay a proper foundation before approaching anyone so that all relevant persons can be contacted at the same time; only thus can intercommunication and the possible destruction of documents be prevented. See Ontario Policy 3-28, "Applications for Commission Consent to Obtain Transcripts of Evidence Taken During Investigations or Hearings", CCH Vol. 2, para. 54-953.

[98]In *R. v. Ben Smith*, [1963] 1 O.R. 249, 36 D.L.R. (2d) 613 (C.A.), the Court of Appeal indicated that the trial judge correctly used his discretion in not ordering Crown counsel to make available to the accused statements made under oath by persons who became witnesses at the trial, on the ground that the consent of the Commission to the release of these transcripts had been specifically denied under s. 24.

[99]See especially s. 25 (Bill 20, s. 15). Section 25 states that the Commission *may* report the result of an investigation to the Minister when the Commission has ordered it. Section 22 as we saw *requires* the Commission to report to the Minister where it appears that a person or company may have contravened the Act, the regulations or the Criminal Code. Thus the Commission's discretion in s. 25 relates by negative inference to a situation where there has not been such a contravention but where the Commission believes the Minister should be informed. The same section requires an investigator appointed indepen-

appear to cover any instance where a report has been produced by an investigation, whether at the instigation of the Commission or of the Minister himself.

A person being examined in the course of an investigation is not entitled to have an associate present, other than his counsel. Nor is he entitled to cross-examine other witnesses.[100]

As part of its anti-fraud function the Commission is given extensive powers to freeze funds and apply for a receivership. These powers, which are discretionary, may be exercised in three different fact situations as broadly defined by the Act.[101] An order may be issued before, during or after an investigation, in connection with the suspension or cancellation of a registration, or where criminal or *quasi*-criminal proceedings relating to securities have been or are about to be instituted under provincial legislation or the Criminal Code.[102]

The provision which authorizes intervention in the third of these three situations is curious in that it gives the Commission a power to freeze assets in contexts outside the normal scope of securities

---

dently by the Minister (under s. 23) to report to him the results of the investigation, including the evidence, findings, comments and recommendations. This brings us to the discretion of the Minister (as opposed to that of the Commission), which is the operative part of the section. He may cause "the report" to be published in whole or in part in such manner as he deems proper. The report so referred to here clearly includes that of the Minister's own investigator, and a reasonable interpretation would be that it includes also the discretionary report of the Commission to the Minister under s. 25 (where it does not "appear" that an offence has occurred). Not covered, it would seem, is the report which must be made by the Commission where an investigation shows a probable offence, although in all likelihood the Minister will exercise his discretion here as well and in precisely the same way. The lack of explicit provision for this latter situation is surprising. There is greater reason, one would suppose, for the Minister to publicize at least the pertinent parts of a report disclosing that an offence has probably taken place: once the information is laid, the allegations of wrongdoing against the person concerned will be made public, and whatever damage that is done to his reputation will arise from prosecution rather than publication of the report. However, to ensure a fair trial, parts of the report which deal with evidence to be laid before the court should be withheld until the trial is over.

[100]Both these privileges were denied in *St. John v. Fraser*, [1935] S.C.R. 441, [1935] 3 D.L.R. 465, 64 C.C.C. 90, on the ground that investigation under the Act was an administrative and not a judicial procedure. The principle of this case applies to investigations generally, not just the specific issue of cross-examination or the right to have persons present. This principle was approved in *Guay v. Lafleur*, [1965] S.C.R. 12, 47 D.L.R. (2d) 226, [1964] C.T.C. 350, 64 D.T.C. 5218, which held that another interested person was not entitled to attend the examination of witnesses in an investigation under the Federal Income Tax Act. The same administrative-judicial distinction resulted in a ruling that s. 2(e) of the Canadian Bill of Rights, 1960 (Can.), c. 44 (now R.S.C. 1970, App. III) which guarantees "the right to a fair hearing in accordance with the principles of fundamental justice", does not apply.

[101]Section 26 (Bill 20, s. 16).

[102]For an example of the second situation see *Ord, Wallington & Co. Ltd.*, Apr. 1968 OSCB 113. Bill 20, s.16 adds a fourth situation—where the Commission is about to make or has made a cease-trading order.

regulation. The section reads as follows: "where criminal proceedings...are about to be instituted against any person...that in the opinion of the Commission...arise...out of any business conducted by such person...". On a literal interpretation activities far removed from those normally associated with the securities industry (*e.g.* trafficking in stolen goods) would fall within the purview of the section.[103]

Once such an order affecting funds or securities is given to their custodian the Commission may direct him to hold funds or securities for any interim receiver, custodian, trustee, receiver or liquidator, or until written notice is received from the Commission revoking the direction or consenting to release. The Commission is thus given a power of life or death over any business so affected. And the responsibility involved in the exercise of such a power can be uncomfortable where the investigation is exceedingly complex and drawn out.[104] If someone receiving a direction which freezes funds or securities is in doubt concerning its applicability to certain assets, he may apply to a judge of the Supreme Court, who has the discretion to direct the disposition of the funds or security.[105]

The same three circumstances which permit the issuance of a freeze order also give the Commission a discretion to apply to a Supreme Court Judge for the appointment of a receiver or a receiver-manager or trustee of the property of a person or company.[106] When an application for a receiver is made, the judge must first be satisfied that the appointment is in the best interests of creditors or anyone else

---

[103]See *Centennial Mortgage Corp. et al. v. B.C. Securities Commission* (1969), 72 W.W.R. 100, 9 D.L.R. (3d) 357 (B.C.C.A.), which makes it clear that this power extends to private companies whose shares are not being sold to the public and who are thus exempted from the registration and prospectus provisions of the Act. The case concerned the issuing of a receiving order against a company under s. 29 of the British Columbia Act.

[104]There are several incidental immunities from the freeze order. Funds or securities in a stock exchange clearing-house or in process of transfer by a transfer agent are not to be restrained unless the freeze order expressly states. Furthermore, with respect to banks or loan or trust companies, the direction applies only to the offices, branches or agencies specifically named in the order (s. 26(1)).

The Commission's power to freeze funds also permits it to give notice to a registrar of deeds, master of titles or mining recorder that proceedings are being or are about to be taken which may affect land or mining claims belonging to the person or company referred to in the notice. The latter document must in such a case be registered or recorded against the lands or claims referred to therein. The effect is the same as registration of a certificate of *lis pendens*, with the additional proviso that the Commission may revoke or modify the notice (s. 26(3); Bill 20, s. 16(4)).

[105]Section 26(2). This power is removed from the Court in Bill 20, s. 16(2) because it was thought that the Commission was a more appropriate body, as the source of the original order, to resolve any doubts or ambiguities regarding its application to particular funds or securities.

[106]Section 27. Bill 20, s. 17(1)(b) and (e) add a fourth and fifth case where such an appointment may be made: where the Commission is about to make or has made a cease-trade order and where a firm fails to comply with minimum net asset or capital requirements or restrictions with regard to investment or ownership.

whose property is controlled by the person or company against whom the appointment is sought.[107] Where the application is *ex parte* by the Commission, the appointment is not to exceed eight days.[108] The powers of the receiver, once appointed, relate to all of the property belonging to or controlled by the firm under appointment. Furthermore, he has authority to wind up or manage the business with all powers necessary or incidental thereto, if so directed by the judge.[109] The enforcement of a receiving order is similar to that of any order or judgment of the Supreme Court, with a power vested in the Court of varying or discharging the order upon application made by notice; in addition the rules of practice of the Supreme Court govern the procedure when application is made for a receivership.[110]

The OSC is reluctant to use this power. It takes the position that generally the responsibility for making an application of this sort should lie with creditors. Consequently, instances where the regulatory authority has intervened are few.[111] It is most apt to do so in instances where the creditors and shareholders are extremely scattered and their individual holdings so small that it is unlikely any creditor group will come forward with the necessary funds for an initial application. However, the guiding principle overall remains that if an individual is capable of exercising his civil remedies unaided, the Ontario Commission will not intervene. Other provincial commissions, for example those of British Columbia and Quebec, have not shown the same reluctance.

(3) AUDITS

The Commission has another anti-fraud device which is largely preventive and prophylactic, designed more to deter than to apprehend. This is the power to impose and carry out audits.[112] The legislative provisions in this area are somewhat misleading, however, since they describe the Commission's powers with respect to audits where the Commission has not delegated its power to one of the self-regulatory organizations.[113] Most firms carrying on business in the securities industry are members of one of these organizations and are audited according to the internal rules of the body in question. It is clear however that the Commission has an overriding auditing power existing independently and in spite of any delegation that may have

---

[107]Section 27(2). Bill 20, s. 17(2) adds others whose "best interests" must be considered: in a proper case the shareholders or security holders of or subscribers of an issuer against whom the appointment order is sought.

[108]Section 27(3), extended to fifteen days in Bill 20, s. 17(3).

[109]Section 27(4). Bill 20, s. 17(4) adds flexibility by replacing "all of the property" by "all or any part of the property".

[110]Section 27(5) and (6) (Bill 20, s. 17(5) and (6)).

[111]*In the Matter of Waite Reid & Co.,* June 1966 OSCB 4 and July-Aug. 1966 OSCB 1, is one of these. There a brokerage firm was suspended from the TSE and when creditors' claims on the industry contingency fund were imminent the firm was placed in bankruptcy.

[112]Sections 30-33. See also the conditions of registration, CCH vol. 2, para. 54-981, which contain a more detailed statement of OSC auditing requirements for registrants.

[113]As described, *post,* chapter 10, text at footnote 46.

been made to a self-regulatory organization.[114] It may in its discretion at any time, by written direction, appoint any person to examine the financial affairs of a registrant or any issuer whose securities have been qualified with the Commission.[115] The authcrity of the auditor so appointed is extended to the preparation of such financial or other statements or reports as the Commission may require.[116] And finally, to aid him in his task, the auditor is given extensive powers of access to the relevant records.[117]

2.11 Three Major Investigations

There have been three stunning financial collapses centred in Ontario in the decade of the 60's which have had a significant impact on securities regulation. Each of these three illustrates vividly both the need for regulation in the securities area and, conversely, the important limits to the application of regulatory techniques which are inherent in the legislation and the machinery by which it is administered.[118]

The first episode, in the summer of 1964, involved large fluctuations in the price of shares of Windfall Oils and Mines Ltd. trading on the TSE. It resulted in the appointment of a Royal Commission of Inquiry, whose recommendations influenced reforms that have taken place subsequently on the TSE and in the regulation of junior mining financing in Ontario.[119]

The second case history is that of Prudential Finance Corporation Ltd. This company made initial distributions of its securities which were accompanied by material misrepresentations in the required disclosure documents. Substantial sums of money were raised from small investors under these conditions. These sums were totally lost in the corporation's collapse.[120]

Finally, we briefly consider here the investigation of Atlantic Acceptance Ltd. The centre of an empire of finance companies, Atlantic borrowed most if its money by using exemptions in the Act to issue short-term debt obligations in the money market; the principal purchasers of its notes were large highly sophisticated institutional investors throughout North America. The money thus raised was lent out in a diversified credit financing business which subsequently proved to be riddled with fraud and mismanagement.

There are several reasons for discussing Atlantic Acceptance in this chapter at some length. First of all the report of the inquiry into its collapse, the most detailed and expensive investigation in Canadian financial history, is an exemplary specimen of its kind, and as such is instructive from a technical standpoint. Secondly, the Atlantic disas-

---

[114]Section 33(1) (Bill 20, s. 18(1)).

[115]*Ibid.* Bill 20 also permits the books and records of a custodian of assets of a mutual fund (or of shares or units of a mutual fund) to be examined.

[116]*Ibid.*

[117]Section 33(2) (Bill 20, s. 18(2)).

[118]A detailed analysis of these three case histories is contained in Appendices VI, VII, and VIII.

[119]Windfall is discussed in chapter 10 and summarized in Appendix VIII.

[120]Prudential is examined in chapter 4 and summarized in Appendix VI.

ter contains some important lessons regarding the machinery of regulation and its inadequacies. It also demonstrates that the theory of the sophisticated investor being able to find out the facts for himself (the "need to know" test), upon which many of the exemptions from securities regulation are based, can be found wanting, when severely tested. Finally, the case illustrates how, in a complex financial world capital markets are greatly dependent on the restraints and checks provided by other institutions and regulations, public and private alike, and rely on high standards of conduct on the part of professional persons. The balance of forces thus established is a fragile one when challenged by ingenious and unscrupulous entrepreneurs.

All three of these *causes célèbres* in the field of securities regulation will be the subject of continual reference both here and throughout this book. In Windfall and again in Atlantic, though not in Prudential, a Royal Commission composed of a single judge was appointed to conduct the investigations and inquiries under the Public Inquiries Act.[121] In the case of the Atlantic Royal Commission, which was appointed two months after Atlantic's collapse, the commissioner's task was broad and general. He was first of all to inquire into the failure of Atlantic itself, the activities of related companies and persons, and the effect on the money market; further terms of reference embraced a consideration of the adequacy of current corporations legislation and of the laws regulating loan, trust and finance corporations and their activities in the money market generally, the findings on all these matters to be the subject of a report with appropriate recommendations.[122] The investigation took four years, including a year and a half of public hearings, and resulted in a report of four volumes, the text alone of which exceeded 1,700 pages. By the time the report was published nine of the persons who gave evidence had been charged with criminal offences. Two lawyers were disciplined by the Law Society of Upper Canada, one being disbarred and the other, a life bencher of the Law Society, resigning from that position with a reprimand. Four accountants were disciplined by the Ontario Institute of Chartered Accountants. An extensive series of recommendations for legislative change and administrative action resulted, some of which have been adopted; in fact significant alterations in the existing law were made even before the enquiry itself had been completed.

In Prudential, the investigation was conducted by the Commission although an outside accounting report was commissioned as well. In retrospect it would seem preferable to have employed a Royal Commission in this case also. In Atlantic most of the securities traded were exempt under the Act and were thus not qualified by a prospectus. In Prudential there were immediate accusations of bureaucratic negligence, culminating in a lawsuit against the Commission for damages;[123]

---

[121]R.S.O. 1960, c. 323 (now R.S.O. 1970, c. 379).
[122]Atlantic Report, pp. iii-iv, summarized in Appendix VII.
[123]*Westlake v. The Queen*, [1971] 3 O.R. 533, 21 D.L.R. (3d) 129 (H.C.); affirmed [1972] 2 O.R. 605, 26 D.L.R. (3d) 273 (C.A.); affirmed 33 D.L.R. (3d) 256n, [1973] S.C.R. vii; see also part 2.02, *supra*, and, *infra*, part 2.13.

it was alleged that the OSC had been at fault in not examining the issuer more thoroughly when it qualified its securities for public distribution. The fact that the Commission itself made the investigation left the way open for insinuations that the report lacked objectivity and was an exercise in self-justification. This might conceivably have been averted if the entire course of events relating to Prudential's affairs, including the Commission's role, had been subjected to the scrutiny of an outside tribunal. In Windfall, conflict of interest on the part of the OSC's director was alleged.[124] This by itself was perhaps reason enough for appointing a Royal Commission. In the Atlantic case, however, where there was an absence of suggestions that the OSC had not fulfilled its responsibilities properly prior to the collapse, the major reason for employing an external investigating authority was insufficient resources in the OSC itself.[125] There was an additional practical reason for appointing an outside commission, not seen on the face of the record but implied in it. The downfall of Atlantic had shocked the financial community; a government which assumed responsibility for investor protection and a stable economic environ-

---

[124]This allegation resulted in a charge of breach of trust in public office being laid from which the accused was subsequently acquitted: *R. v. Campbell*, [1967] 2 O.R. 1, [1967] 3 C.C.C. 250, 50 C.R. 270 (C.A.); affirmed 2 C.R.N.S. 403 (S.C.C.).

[125]See the Atlantic Report (pp. 23-4 and p. 1691):

"Steps had been taken by the Attorney-General of Ontario immediately after the Atlantic default to institute an investigation by the Ontario Securities Commission. By the end of July it had become apparent that an inquiry limited by the jurisdiction of the Securities Act, and by the paramount preoccupations of the Securities Commission over the whole field of securities regulation in Ontario, did not do justice to a situation which had produced the heaviest loss of any financial disaster in Canadian history, and the appointment of a Royal Commission was decided upon.

...

"As soon as the failure of Atlantic Acceptance Corporation Limited became known, the Attorney General...instructed the Ontario Securities Commission to examine its affairs. Its Chairman...took the lead in urging the appointment of a Commission of Inquiry upon the Government because he had early experience of the size and complexity of the task and thereafter put the services of the Securities Commission and its staff at my disposal to assist the Royal Commission in the commencement of its investigations. The help and cooperation then extended continued throughout the period of his chairmanship and that of his successor."

In Quebec, where securities investigations are performed by the Department of Financial Institutions on behalf of the Commission, even those which fall entirely within the jurisdiction of the Securities Act of that province, the limiting factor of insufficient resources is less significant.

ment concluded that dramatic measures were necessary to ameliorate that shock.[126]

2.12 Funding

The funding of the Commission forms part of the annual budget for the Ministry of Consumer and Commercial Relations.[127] The fees collected by the OSC are not applied directly to its own expenses. But even if they were, the present level of operations would require a substantial increase in subsidy. The problem of adequate funding was an important concern of the Kimber Committee, which recommended substantial overall increases to the Commission's budget and a pay scale within the Commission greater than established civil service

---

[126]It is interesting to contrast the rather optimistic tone of Ontario's Premier in appointing the Royal Commission with Mr. Justice Hughes' less sanguine concluding remarks after close to four years of study of the Atlantic debacle, report at pp. 1677-8:

"The protracted investigation of the affairs of Atlantic Acceptance Corporation, British Mortgage & Trust Company and of the many companies and individuals which were intertwined with them, must provoke general reflections at the conclusion of this report. It will be recalled that the Prime Minister of Ontario, at the conclusion of his statement announcing the constitution of this Commission...said:

'It will be our intent to ask the Royal Commission to also make recommendations as to what steps might be taken to ensure that the events which have been revealed in connection with Atlantic Acceptance Corporation Limited are not repeated in the future.'

"I have endeavoured, in the specific recommendations made in this concluding chapter, to suggest changes and safeguards in legislation, and by way of regulation, which will, if adopted, I hope make a repetition of the Atlantic disaster more difficult, coming as it did like a sudden and violent storm out of a cloudless sky in a season of sunny prosperity. After the storm many prospects were found to have darkened, and the wreckage left in its wake may still be discerned. There can be no guarantee that such a convulsion will not occur again, whatever legislation may be enacted or regulatory policy devised, because it had its origins in fraud and concealment, and it is yet to be demonstrated that laws of general application can be wholly successful in providing against the resolve of any human agency to twist and break them. In the case of fraud and theft, as in that of other forms of rapine, a great advantage lies with the aggressor whose determination to transgress, and to profit from his transgressions, may for long be successfully concealed. Thus, in a free society, the deterrent effects of vigilance by authority and condign punishment of offenders must inevitably be the main safeguards which law-abiding citizens can aspire to erect."

[127]Figures from the Ministry's annual reports showing OSC levels of revenue and expenditure for certain years are set out on the following page. The dollar value of prospectuses filed are set out separately because the fee levied as a percentage of the dollar value of the securities to be offered in a prospectus constitutes the largest revenue source. Consequently a poor year for public offerings results in a substantial fall-off in revenue directly generated by the OSC.

levels. To date the first of these two goals has been realized only to a very limited extent and the second not at all.[128]

Yr. End	Expenditure	Directly Generated Revenue
1968	$ 837,409.	445,495.
1969	890,573.	759,310.
1970	939,178.	829,556.
1971	1,078,152.	834,769.

Yr. End	Dollar Value of Prospectuses Filed ($000)	Value of Statements of Material Facts ($000)	Value of Private Placements ($000)	Total Financing in Ontario ($000)
1963*	673,317			
1964*	659,946			
1965*	592,977			
1966*	764,086			
1967*	786,495			
1968**	649,289			
1969**	1,005,179			
1970**	1,802,185			
1971**	1,810,761			
1972	1,903,715	1,519	571,539	2,476,773
1973	1,570,699	1,790	775,725	2,348,214

*Shares, unit offerings (preference and common shares), bonds and debentures.
**Based on preliminary filings of mining and oil and industrial companies.
Source: Department of Financial and Commercial Affairs Annual Reports 1967 to 1971. These have not been published in recent years. The Statistical Review, 1972-73, Ministry of Consumer and Commercial Relations provides much more limited information.

[128]In 1965 the Kimber Committee reported that (para. 8.02):
"There have been occasions in the past when the Commission has been criticized for an apparent lack of organization and efficiency, particularly with respect to the review and filing of prospectuses. For the purpose of the comments which follow it will be assumed that at least some of this criticism has been justified. Even a cursory examination of the structure of the Commission, for example, discloses that the Commission is and has been seriously understaffed. In addition, the Commission has apparently been expected to operate on a self-sustaining financial basis. Consequently, the Chairman and the Commissioners have been handicapped in effecting necessary reorganizations and additions to personnel to make the Commission a more efficient and effective administrative agency."
It recommended that (para. 8.06):
"The Commission should be established as an independent administrative agency and not as a branch of the Department of the Attorney General. The Commission would thereby acquire authority to procure and administer its own budget and would report to the Legislature, through a member of the Executive Council, on an annual basis as to its activities in the preceding year 'and submit its budget requirements for the ensuing year. This suggestion would have the beneficial effect, among others, of permitting the Commission to establish its own job classifications, personnel qualifications and salary ranges for its staff. Without such freedom, it seems doubtful whether the Commission will be able to attract and retain the competent legal, accounting and other personnel it will urgently need."

The personnel of the OSC increased from 85 to 97 in the seven years immediately following the Kimber Report, whereas the growth in the volume of its business has been proportionately far greater.[129] One solution to the funding problem would be to increase fees, particularly the levy imposed when qualifying a prospectus,[130] to a level which would permit the Commission to carry on as a self-financing agency. This would seem to be a feasible alternative even in the smaller Canadian jurisdictions, since national coverage for a prospectus is a desirable objective, at least on large issues. However, there are dangers in this approach. First of all, in a year in which new issues of securities were few, the fees generated might not be sufficient to meet the budget. And it would be precisely in such a difficult season, when the temptation for the black sheep of the industry to engage in questionable practices is greatest, that the regulatory agency might be forced to reduce staff. Secondly, any increase in the fees levied on registrants and issuers would be passed on directly to investors. To accept such a consequence would suggest that those broader goals of securities regulation which go beyond investor protection, such as more efficient capital markets and sustained economic growth, are of minimal significance. If one accepts that success in achieving these latter objectives would benefit society as a whole, it follows that the expenses incurred in pursuing them should be defrayed from the general funds of the state.

2.13 Accountability

The question of the accountability of the Commission is particularly complex.[131] The basic issue is the extent to which the Commission

---

However, Commissioner Hughes in the Atlantic Report took a rather different view on one aspect of the staffing and funding issue (p. 1676):

> "I have had some experience, in another field of activity [as chairman of the Federal Public Service Commission] of the departmental argument that staff should be multiplied and salaries raised to cope with the costs of increasing business, and to provide comparison with the large earnings of leaders in private practice; this is usually coupled with the argument that eminent counsel may be attracted to the public service by these means. The answer surely is to let the private practitioner do the laborious work and enjoy the emoluments of a successful professional career, but to establish the opportunity and, by custom, the requirement for his services from time to time to be placed at the disposal of the Crown."

[129]To take just one index of growth in the volume of business, the OSC processed prospectuses with an aggregate dollar value of under $600 million in 1965, the year in which the Kimber Committee reported. The comparable figure six years later was three times greater. See, *supra*, footnote 127. Financing of similar agencies has long been a problem in other jurisdictions (see the extensive comments of Professor Loss on U.S. federal and state administrations in, vol. 1, pp. 105-6, vol. 3, pp. 1884-9, vol. 4, pp. 2267-8 and vol. 6, pp. 4013-7).

[130]It stands presently at 1/100 of one per cent of the maximum aggregate price at which the securities are offered (R.R.O. 1970, Reg. 794, s. 8(1)(h)). Since the qualification fee is such an incidental portion of the total amount to be raised by the issue, the impact of an increase is minimal.

[131]See the Kimber Report, para. 8.06, quoted, *supra*, footnote 128.

should be responsible to the Minister and through him to the Legislature. The recommendations of the Kimber Report resulted in an approach being taken to this problem (in the Act of 1966) which gave a greater measure of independence to the administrative agency but did not divorce it altogether from direct ministerial supervision. The OSC was transferred from the Department of the Attorney-General to the newly created Department of Financial and Commercial Affairs.[132]

The traditional view of the accountability of administrative agencies which has prevailed in Canada stems from British practice, and is to be clearly distinguished from the theory prevalent in the U.S., where an entirely different legislature-executive relationship exists. In the Anglo-Canadian tradition the agency is accountable to the electorate through a responsible Minister who introduces its budget and answers for it in the Legislature. And in Britain at least, if the agency commits a serious error, the Minister is held responsible. In the U.S., the constitutional separation of powers, accompanied by a series of checks and balances, fragments accountability. The administrative agency is part of the executive branch of government and its head is appointed, subject to the Senate's consent, by the elected head of that branch, the President. While the agency is dependent on the will of the Legislature in respect to its funding and must respond to congressional committee inquiries, it has no direct and overall responsibility to the legislature, nor for that matter to the Presidency itself.

The provisions of the Ontario statute do not expressly lay down any general rules regarding the accountability of the Commission to the Minister. It is apparent, however, from our earlier discussion of the basic techniques of securities regulation, that only in the area of anti-fraud measures is the Minister given a direct role. The Commission as we saw may commence an investigation, but must forward a full report to the Minister as soon as it concludes that someone may have committed a criminal offence or contravened the legislation. It is the Minister's responsibility to proceed when full particulars have been placed before him.

The Minister's special position in the anti-fraud area is also underlined by his separate power to order independently of the Commission an investigation "for the due administration of the Act owing to any matter relating to trading in securities".[133] Furthermore,

---

[132]As the Report had recommended (para. 8.03):
"The Commission has traditionally been a branch of the Department of the Attorney General, which relationship was clarified by statute in the amendments to The Securities Act in 1962-63. This relationship may have been appropriate when securities regulation was first introduced in Ontario, since the legislation was primarily directed to the prevention of fraud in the sale of securities. However, such relationship is of limited importance today and will continue to be of less importance in the future. The administration of securities legislation should not be directed primarily to criminal and quasi-criminal law enforcement but rather to the enhancement of the position of the securities industry in the economic life of the province."

[133]Section 23 (Bill 20, s. 13).

no enforcement proceedings under the offence sections may be instituted except with the consent or under the direction of the Minister.[134]
Prosecutions for Criminal Code offences become the responsibility of
the Attorney-General, and counsel in his ministry have the carriage of
them, although they work closely with Commission personnel where
the alleged offence involves securities. Finally no action or proceedings
may be taken against any person administering the Act without the
consent of the Minister.[135]

The organizational structure outlined above is a curious one—some
responsibility devolves upon the Minister, but by no means all, even
in the anti-fraud area. In the area of registration of persons and
securities he has no directly imposed statutory duties whatsoever. The
explanation for this may simply be that in earlier years, when
securities regulation was administered by a branch of the Attorney-
General's Department rather than by a separate commission, the
anti-fraud responsibilities of this branch were of principal importance.
In the period since the Commission was created, and particularly since
the Ministry of Consumer and Commercial Relations (the successor to
the 1967 Department of Financial and Commercial Affairs) assumed
responsibility for the Commission, the registration of persons and
securities techniques of regulation have assumed a much more substantial role.

Notwithstanding the absence of involvement of the Minister in
supervising the registration of persons and securities, the question of
his responsibility to the electorate for the work done by the OSC in
these areas became a central issue in connection with the collapse of
Prudential Finance. The creditors of the corporation, it will be
recalled, alleged negligence on the part of the Commission in permitting a Prudential prospectus to be filed and its securities to be sold to
the public at a time when there was reason to suspect, certainly from
the information available to the Commission, that the financial
viability of Prudential was extremely tenuous. At the time when the
Minister delivered a statement on the matter in the House, several of
the individuals connected with Prudential had been convicted under
the Criminal Code or the Act. Charges against several others had been
discontinued owing to a successful technical defence which established
that the Minister (the Attorney-General) responsible for the predecessor Act, and not the Minister (of Financial and Commercial
Affairs) responsible for the current Act, should have signed the
prosecuting documents.[136] In concluding his statement the Minister
gave the following explanation of the Commission's accountability
through him:

> "There has been a series of prosecutions, all of which were
> conducted in open court, the results of which have been available to
> the news media. The steps taken by the trustee in bankruptcy in

---

[134]Section 138 (Bill 20, s. 122).

[135]Section 145.

[136]For a reported case determining *which* Minister's consent to prosecute must
be obtained when the responsibility for the Act was transferred from the
Attorney-General to the Minister of Financial and Commercial Affairs, see *R.
v. Coles*, [1970] 1 O.R. 570, 9 D.L.R. (3d) 65, [1970] 2 C.C.C. 340 (C.A.).

fulfilling his role under The Bankruptcy Act have resulted in a series of public actions.

"The philosophy underlying the securities legislation aimed at freeing the Ontario Securities Commission from political interference or from intervention of political persons is well known. It must be a free and independent body with respect to its day-to-day operations. The commission and its staff collectively represent many years' experience in every branch of the securities field. I submit that the Minister is entitled to rely on the legal opinions presented to him with the endorsement of the Chairman of the Commission involved, not only the recommendations as to the charges which ought to be laid, but also as to the procedures to be followed as conditions precedent to the laying of those charges.

"I refer you to the actual facts. I refer you to the results of the prosecutions and their conclusions. I personally regret that all the charges were not successful, but the fact remains they were, in the main, successful.

"It seems strange to me that those who most strenuously urge that the Commission should operate without political interference, as the facts I have presented so clearly demonstrated it did in the present case, should now attack the Minister involved."[137]

It is hard to disagree with this submission when the accepted wisdom of recent times has been that the only political pressures to which regulatory agencies in the business sphere should be subject are changes in the legislation which they administer.

Another aspect of accountability is the degree to which the government which has established agencies for investor protection should provide compensation for loss when protection fails. The Atlantic Report gave extensive consideration to the question of compensation from the public purse for losses of the kind experienced in the Atlantic and Prudential Finance collapses. The latter case received particular attention because it involved a decision of the OSC which in hindsight at least was questionable. Mr. Justice Hughes came to this conclusion:

"The holders of Prudential obligations, which yielded an unusually high rate of interest sufficient to proclaim the risk attendant upon purchasing them, have sought full compensation from the Province of Ontario for the unusual reason that their losses were due to the fraudulent conduct of the company's president and its auditor, and that they were entitled to rely on the Securities Commission for protection which was not forthcoming. Since the securities concerned were sold under 'high pressure' and their yield was in excess of what a prudent investor might expect to receive at the time, it is permissible to doubt the advisability of employing public funds for such a purpose. Although the operations of Prudential were on a much smaller scale than those of Atlantic, their failures have one feature in common; the presidents of both of them used their unchallenged authority dishonestly and in their own interests,

---

[137]Ontario Debates, 28th Legislature (2nd Sess.), 1969, p. 6405.

which were in conflict with those of their companies and those investors and lenders who had confidence in them."[138]

In the Commissioner's opinion the question of compensation could only arise, even in cases where there has been fraud, if a wrongful act or failure to perform a duty on the part of a Crown servant is the proximate cause of the loss suffered.[139] Liability would appear to be imposed on the Crown in such situations by s. 5(3) of the Proceedings Against the Crown Act,[140] although the right of recovery conferred by that section is always subject to specific enactments negativing the liability of Crown servants in particular situations.[141] Mr. Justice Hughes concluded that the issue of compensation was essentially one of political judgment,[142] and he was of the opinion that this judgment should not in general be exercised in favour of claimants. But the events surrounding the fall of Atlantic prove that the role of government is not necessarily entirely passive in such circumstances. The provincial government had of necessity to intervene quickly if other financial institutions were not to be carried away in the crisis of confidence catalyzed by the collapse. Accepting the challenge posed by the situation, the government served as guarantor of public deposits in a trust company caught in the Atlantic vortex and sponsored the merger of that trust company with another.[143]

---

[138]Atlantic Report, p. 1608.

[139]*Ibid.*, pp. 1608-9.

[140]1962-63 (Ont.), c. 109 (now R.S.O. 1970, c. 365).

[141]*Ibid.*, s. 5(4).

[142]Mr. Justice Hughes referred to the immunity clause in the Act (s. 145) and concluded at p. 1609:

"Whether or not this section is 'an enactment that negatives or limits the liability of the servant of the Crown' may be a matter for judicial interpretation, but it would appear to be so. If it is, then the question as to whether holders of securities can look to public funds for compensation where loss has been suffered by reason of a fraud, successful only because of the tortious act or neglect of a servant of the Crown whose duty it was to prevent it, is within the discretion of a minister of the Crown to decide. In other words the decision is political, and a claim for compensation could not apparently be entertained by the courts unless permission to sue were first granted by the executive. Since without this type of protection it would be difficult for public authorities to function, even if they could recruit the necessary personnel, it would not appear to be practicable to seek compensation from the public treasury under existing legislation as a matter of right. I have not found it necessary or desirable to recommend legislative change which would result in the automatic compensation of the imprudent investor at the expense of the general taxpayer."

Commissioner Hughes' factual conclusion was this (p. 1679): "Nowhere in the long and complicated history of Atlantic Acceptance and British Mortgage and Trust Company have I discovered an example of dereliction of duty by any public servant in Ontario."

[143]British Mortgage and Trust Company, through its president's position on the Atlantic board, had a substantial investment in Atlantic's securities. It also held securities in some of the worthless enterprises that Atlantic had shored up in a disastrous squandering of its resources. This unfortunate involvement was made possible by the close personal association of the presidents of British Mortgage and of Atlantic. Had it not been for the

publicly announced intervention of the Government of Ontario in guarantee-ing the public's deposits with British Mortgage, that company too would almost certainly have collapsed. Government funds did not have to be used owing to the fact that the existence of the guarantee limited the run on deposits. As it was, the Atlantic Report estimated that the loss to British Mortgage on its approximately $12,000,000 investment in securities and loans to individuals and corporations in the Atlantic group was approximately $7,000,000 (p. 1583). Immediately prior to the Atlantic collapse British Mortgage's shares were priced at $32. On amalgamation with another loan and trust company their value was $2.50.

Chapter 3
The Licence—
Registration of Persons

3.01 History and Development

The licensing or registration of persons as a technique of securities regulation has an ancient and honourable history. As early as 1285, English legislation[1] required stock brokers in the City of London to obtain a licence to carry on their business. The development of the licensing power in Canada essentially begins with the Manitoba legislation in 1914 and is extended in the Ontario Security Frauds Prevention Act of 1928 and the uniform legislation that followed. The basic thrust of this development was to ensure that persons engaged in the securities business were "honest and of good repute".[2] This aim remains primary, but since 1945 and in particular during the decade of the 1960's, more ambitious goals have been sought through the registration requirement—in particular minimum standards of education and ethical dealing. Ontario and the self-regulatory organizations have shown the way in this movement.[3]

3.02 Industry Defined

The securities industry has been the subject of several recent studies which examine its inner workings and outline the significant role it plays in the economy generally.[4] The OSC's Industry Ownership Report defined the industry to include "those financial intermediaries required to obtain registration in some principal capacity under The Securities Act".[5] It declared their primary function to be influencing, directing and managing the investment of the savings of Canadians. One might add to this the influence exercised by the securities industry in Canada on the direction taken by the substantial amounts of foreign capital which flow into the country.

The limiting boundary of the securities industry as set by the requirement of registration in the Act. This severs from the securities industry a number of other financial intermediaries who also make it their business to attract investment savings. Many members of this

---

[1] Cited in Loss, vol. 1, p. 1, and Killik, *The Work of the Stock Exchange*, 2nd ed. (1934), p. 12.

[2] *Lymburn v. Mayland*, [1932] A.C. 318 at p. 324, [1932] All E.R. Rep. 291, [1932] 2 D.L.R. 6 (P.C.).

[3] See, *ante*, part 1.04, for a capsule history of this and other techniques of securities regulation.

[4] OSC Industry Ownership Report; Porter Report; D. C. Shaw and R. T. Archibald, *Canadian Capital Markets Study*.

[5] *Ibid.*, para. 4.01, p. 35. By itself this definition begs the question. Instead of saying those in the securities industry as defined should be registered it says those who are required to be registered are in the industry.

broader group are regulated by their own specific legislation, although occasionally the Act refers to them.[6]

3.03 Who Must Register

The persons or companies who must be registered under the Act may be categorized in terms of three principal functions, namely, acting as dealer, adviser or underwriter.[7] Registration as a concept under the Act emerges from a consideration of these three activities, and anyone engaging in one of them must register in the appropriate class of dealer or adviser or as an underwriter. The requirements are worded in very general terms, necessitating a series of statutory exceptions and exemptions to limit their range of application.[8] Salesmen, whose task is to assist the dealer in the performance of its function, receive separate treatment.

A dealer is "a person or company who trades in securities in the capacity of principal or agent".[9] A principal buys or sells a security for or from his own account. An agent buys or sells securities for the account of his principal, usually earning his reward by charging a commission for the service provided. One who acts in the capacity of agent is normally regarded in the industry as a broker. It is unfortunate—and a source of confusion—that the statutory definition of dealer covers both brokerage and trading on one's own account, since the custom of the industry reserves the designation "dealer" for the principal who trades for his own account as a business.[10]

The second activity requiring registration is advising. The definition of adviser exemplifies legal "bootstrapping".[11] Perhaps the best com-

---

[6]Some of the major Ontario and federal statutes regulating this larger group are: Credit Unions Act, R.S.O. 1970, c. 96, especially s. 38; Insurance Act, R.S.O. 1970, c. 224, especially Part XVII; Investment Contracts Act, R.S.O. 1970, c. 226; Loan and Trust Corporations Act, R.S.O. 1970, c. 254, especially s.150 ff, and R.R.O. 1970, Reg. 570, s.11; Pension Benefits Act, R.S.O. 1970, c. 342, and R.R.O. 1970, Reg. 654, s. 14; Trustee Act, R.S.O. 1970, c. 470, especially s. 26 ff; Bank Act, R.S.C. 1970, c. B-1; Cooperative Credit Associations Act, R.S.C. 1970, c. C-29; Canadian and British Insurance Companies Act, R.S.C. 1970, c. I-15; Foreign Insurance Companies Act, R.S.C. 1970, c. I-16; Investment Companies Act, 1970-71-72 (Can.), c. 33; Loan Companies Act, R.S.C. 1970, c. L-12; Pension Benefits Standards Act, R.S.C. 1970, c. P-8.
[7]The statutory treatment across the Canadian provinces is not uniform: see, *infra,* footnote 46.
[8]All of the reported decisions of the OSC, QSC and BCSC (the only commissions which publish regular reports) are indexed in Appendix III. The great majority of these decisions involve matters of registration.
[9]Section 1(1)5 (Bill 20, s. 1(1)8). The key concepts of "securities" and "trade" have been discussed earlier, *ante,* parts 1.10 and 1.12.
[10]Until 1969 the Ontario Act followed trade usage with separate definitions of broker and dealer in the Act. The regulations do subdivide the dealer category according to trade usage. Other Canadian jurisdictions did not follow the 1969 Ontario change.
[11]The editor of Underhill's *Principles of the Law of Partnership,* 9th ed. (London, Butterworths, 1971), p. 3, irreverently chides the draftsman of the Partnership Act for this sin—there defining "partnership" as "carrying on a business in common with a view of profit", which he compares to the definition of archdeacon as "a person who performs archdiaconal functions".

ment is simply to cite the words of the Act: "a person or company engaging in or holding itself out as engaging in the business of advising others as to the advisability of investing in or buying or selling securities".[12] The murky picture created by this definition is clarified somewhat by the exemptions from registration as an adviser, but the result is still unsatisfactory.

The third activity requiring registration is that of underwriting. An underwriter is:

"a person or company who, as principal, purchases securities from a person or company with a view to, or who as agent for a person or company offers for sale or sells securities in connection with, a distribution to the public of such securities, and includes a person or company who has a direct or indirect participation in any such distribution, but does not include a person or company whose interest in the transaction is limited to receiving the usual and customary distributors' or sellers' commission payable by an underwriter."[13]

We are concerned with activities in connection with a "distribution to the public of securities",[14] for present purposes, meaning simply the initial sale by an issuer[15] of its securities or a sale by a holder of securities whose holdings materially affect control of an issuer. An underwriter can function either as agent or principal. The phrase "direct or indirect participation" gives the definition a wide sweep. It should, for example, discourage a group of unregistered persons who lack an intent to hold for investment from causing one of their number to purchase a large block of securities from an issuer (using an exemption for large-size purchases) and then quickly reselling the securities through the group to members of the public. In this instance each person within the group, if not registered as an underwriter, commits an offence under the Act whether participating directly or indirectly.

An underwriter is not permitted to deal with the public by virtue of its registration as underwriter alone.[16] To do so it must either avail

---

[12]Section 1(1)1. Bill 20, s. 1(1)1 reads "holding *himself or* itself out" and strikes from "advising others as to the advisability of investing in" the phrase "advisability of".

[13]Section 1(1)25. Bill 20, s. 1(1)40, eliminates "to the public" after distribution, and expands the exceptions from one to four, the three additional ones being mutual funds accepting their units for surrender followed by resale, companies purchasing and reselling their own shares, and chartered banks trading in government guaranteed debt instruments or similar securities of banks, loan, trust or insurance companies.

[14]This complex concept is discussed in detail in part 4.02(1), *post.*

[15]"Issuer" receives a definition for the first time in Bill 20 (s. 1(1)19): "a person or company that has outstanding, issues or proposes to issue, a security".

[16]But the statutory basis for this proposition is not entirely firm. A broad reading of the definition of underwriter and in particular the two phrases "in connection with a distribution to the public" and "includes [one] who has a direct or indirect participation" suggests that the definition includes one who deals with the public as part of the underwriting. Moreover, the need to sever off from the definition one "whose interest in the transaction is limited to receiving the usual and customary distributor's or seller's commission payable

itself of an exemption or, more usually, trade through someone who possesses the appropriate registration; not infrequently the underwriter itself is registered as a dealer. Those dealers whose particular class of registration permits them to sell securities as principal are deemed to be registered as underwriters as an incident of dealer registration.[17]

Unlike underwriters, dealers and advisers are broken down in the Regulations into classes; these are distinguished chiefly on the basis of the type of functions performed within the securities industry but also according to whether the registrant is or is not a member in one of the recognized self-regulatory organizations.

---

by an underwriter or issuer" might suggest that the distinguishing mark of the underwriter is simply that it receives as profit the full difference between the negotiated price paid to the issuer and the price for which the issue is sold to the public, whereas the ordinary selling agent, being less deeply involved in guaranteeing the distribution, receives as his "cut" a lesser percentage. In other words the underwriter deals with the public *qua* underwriter. Finally, the fact that Bill 20 (s. 1(1)41) exempts from the definition mutual funds reselling surrendered units, companies purchasing and reselling their own shares, and banks selling their own or government debt securities, situations all of which normally involve sales to the public, suggests the broad interpretation.

On the other hand certain provisions of the Act and Regulation suggest a narrow interpretation of underwriter—one not envisaging direct trades with the public. Section 2(3) of R.R.O. 1970, Reg. 794 as amended states that one who is registered as a broker-dealer, investment dealer, or securities dealer is deemed to have been granted registration as an underwriter. This is confirmed by Form 1 of the Regulations which says that these three classes of dealer need not obtain registration in an underwriting capacity. The converse proposition—that one who obtains registration in the underwriter category need not obtain registration in the three classes of the dealer category listed above—is nowhere stated. Rather From 1 states as a "Note" in the body of its instructions that "an underwriter may not trade with the public". Form 1 itself has the force of a Regulation. Section 3(1) of the Regulation states that an applicant for any category of registration *shall* complete and execute the form. But does a "note" to the form have the force of law, especially in the face of such an ambiguous definition of underwriter? In *R. v. Revenue Properties Co. Ltd.*, 1971, CCH vol. 3, para. 70-028 the defendant company and some of its directors were convicted under the Act of preparing a misleading prospectus. The court treated an instructional note to a required form as appropriate guidance as to whether misrepresentation had occurred.

This more restricted view of the powers and capacities incident to underwriter status is supported by a learned comment as to the historical purpose of this category of registration. OSC Vice-Chairman Bray (in *Studies in Canadian Company Law*, Ziegel ed., vol. 1, p. 422) states that in the Securities Act, 1966 "To the previous categories requiring registration [dealer and adviser] has been added that of underwriter" and explains that: "In the field of mining and oil company financing the non-dealer underwriter has played an important role. At the same time his financial strength may be such as to dominate the dealer he engages to distribute the securities underwritten. His market activities were not previously subjected to the same restraints as those of dealers. Accordingly, if not already registered, the underwriter must now obtain registration."

[17]*Ibid.*

(1) ADVISERS—TREATMENT BY THE REGULATIONS

Turning first to advisers, they are subdivided into the classes of "investment counsel" and "securities adviser".[18] An investment counsel advises as to investment in specific securities or "is primarily engaged in giving continuous advice as to the investment of funds on the basis of the individual needs of each client". The securities adviser advises "either directly or through publications or writings, as to the advisability of investing in or purchasing or selling specific securities".[19] The two classes may be distinguished partly on the basis of clientele. The investment counsel generally deals with the needs of specific investors. Typically he will guide Mr. X or corporation Y or fund Z in the acquisition and maintenance of a portfolio of investments, advising the client of when it suits his or its needs to make a change in the portfolio. The securities adviser will normally deal with a much wider clientele, typically through a newsletter to subscribers in which he may comment on peculiar features of the securities markets, as well as trends in particular industries or individual securities. The basic difference is that the investment counsel tends to act on behalf of the investor himself whereas a securities adviser evaluates securities in general terms apart from the unique needs of the individual and may often be acting on behalf of an issuer or promoter. But with respect to the advice which is tendered at a particular time regarding specific securities, there may be no distinction between the two. They may unite in recommending the shares of company ABC or in counselling a switch from shares to bonds.[20]

(2) DEALERS—TREATMENT BY THE REGULATIONS

The Regulation[21] divides the dealer category of registrant into seven distinct classes. Membership in one of the self-regulatory organizations and differentiation of function are relevant to these distinctions. Frequently a single dealer will have several classes of registration; one

---

[18]See R.R.O. 1970, Reg. 794, as amended by O. Regs. 168/71, 182/71, 316/71, 524/71, 160/72, 491/73, 541/73, 645/73, 95/74, 495/74, 600/74, 14/75, 155/75. Hereafter the Regulation under the Act will be designated simply as "Reg. 794" followed by a section number.

[19]*Ibid.*, s. 2(2). And for conditions which must be satisfied see Reg. 794, ss. 3(1), 6(9) to (11) and (17). Bill 20, s. 1(1)28, defines "portfolio manager" as "an adviser registered for the purpose of managing the investment portfolio of clients through discretionary authority granted by the clients", borrowing the definition from the current Regulation, and regulates self dealing by portfolio managers in s. 117.

[20]The number of securities advisers registered in Ontario is a handful contrasted with 40 or 50 investment counsel. Recently the OSC gave special attention to a number of counsel who held full investment discretion over clients' securities in addition to providing advice. Consequently the Regulations have been amended to create a new category of adviser, namely, the "portfolio manager", so that specialized safeguards could be applied (Reg. 794, ss. 2(2)1a, 6(20a) and (20b) explained in "Proposed Regulation, Portfolio Managers", May 29 1975 OSCWS 1).

[21]Section 2(1), items 1 through 7. And for conditions they must satisfy see Reg. 794, ss. 3 to 6.

example combines broker and investment dealer status with permission to underwrite as well.[22]

(a) Broker

A broker is:

"...registered exclusively to trade in securities in the capacity of an agent, which person or company is a member of a stock exchange in Ontario recognized by the Commission."[23]

The only stock exchange physically located in Ontario, and recognized by the Commission, is the Toronto Stock Exchange (TSE).[24]

(b) Broker-dealer

A broker-dealer is one who carries on a securities trading business either as agent or principal and holds membership in the Broker-Dealers' Association of Ontario (BDA), a self-regulatory organization which came into being in 1947.[25] This class of registration is best understood in contrast to the investment dealer category.[26]

(c) Investment Dealer

An investment dealer carries on a securities trading business either as agent or principal and "is a member, branch office member or associate member of the Ontario District of the Investment Dealers' Association of Canada" (IDA).[27] Thus the only formal distinction between broker-dealer and investment dealer is the membership of the former in the BDA and of the latter in the Ontario district of the IDA. The practical differences between these two organizations are substantial, turning largely on the investment quality of the securities in which their respective memberships normally deal. The IDA is the older organization of the two, emphasizing high-grade investment securities, whereas the BDA deals generally with more speculative and junior stocks, usually unlisted shares. Typically much of BDA members' business consists of trading in as yet unproven natural resource ventures. A firm cannot hold membership in both organizations.

---

[22]The OSC Industry Ownership Report, ch. 4, discusses the categories and classes of registration more completely, see esp. pp. 36-39.

[23]Reg. 794, s. 2(1).

[24]See Ontario Policy 3-17 "Recognition of Toronto Stock Exchange", CCH vol. 2, para. 54-911. In 1973 the OSC "recognized" the Calgary (now Alberta) Stock Exchange (ASE) for purposes of accepting a statement of material facts in lieu of a prospectus qualifying a distribution of securities through that Exchange. See June 1973 OSCB 78, which announces the reciprocal gesture of the Alberta Securities Commission recognizing the TSE for the same purpose. This recognition of the ASE was not extended to enable members of that Exchange to act as "brokers". If they wished to function in Ontario as agents for trading in various kinds of securities, they would have to obtain Ontario registration as securities dealers, otherwise called non-member brokers.

[25]Reg. 794, s. 2(1)2. See, *post,* part 10.05 for a discussion of the BDA.

[26]*Re Larrimore Securities Ltd.,* [1956] O.W.N. 501, 4 D.L.R. (2d) 727 (C.A.), was a case involving a refusal by the BDA to admit the appellant as a member, and the appellant's subsequent application to the OSC for registration. See also *Re Clark and Ontario Securities Commission,* [1966] 2 O.R. 277, 56 D.L.R. (2d) 585 (C.A.).

[27]Reg. 794, s. 2(1)3. See, *post,* part 10.04 for a discussion of the IDA.

(d) Mutual Fund Dealer

A mutual fund dealer is registered exclusively for trading in mutual fund securities.[28] Mutual fund is not defined in the Act but is defined in Bill 20 to include:

"an issuer of securities that entitle the holder to receive on demand, or within a specified period after demand, an amount computed by reference to the value of a proportionate interest in the whole or in a part of the net assets, including a separate fund or trust account, of the issuer of such securities."[29]

One can anticipate a further splitting up of this mutual fund dealer class depending on whether or not the mutual fund dealer is a member of the Canadian Mutual Funds Association (CMFA), the major self-regulatory organization in the mutual fund industry.[30]

(e) Scholarship Plan Dealer

A scholarship plan dealer trades exclusively in securities of a scholarship or educational plan or trust, terms which are not defined in the Act.[31] There are only a few such dealers now registered in Ontario; their function is to sell an investment which at some future time provides funds to finance the education of the beneficiary of the plan, usually at a post-secondary level, provided the beneficiary in fact advances to that level of scholastic attainment. The security issued under the plan is sold to a subscriber, usually the parent of a young child, with terms which customarily provide for regular instalment payments spread over the intervening years until the beneficiary reaches the normal age for entrance into an advanced institution of learning. A variable payment is then made to the beneficiary who enters the institution. The amount of the pay-out varies directly with the growth of his benefactor's contribution to the plan over the years and the number of other subscribers whose beneficiaries did not for whatever reason enter an institution of the type in question.

(f) Securities Dealer

A securities dealer is defined as one registered for trading in securities and engaged either full or part time in the business of trading in securities as agent or principal.[32] This category is really a catch-all designed to provide for those dealers that are not members of one of the recognized self-regulatory agencies and do not deal exclusively in one of the two types of specialized securities, mutual funds or scholarship plans. The very existence of this classification suggests that the movement toward comprehensive self-regulation in Ontario—which at one time made it official policy to force dealers of any

---

[28]Reg. 794, s. 2(1)4.

[29]Section 1(1)25. Bill 20 implements most of the recommendations of the Mutual Funds Report. See, *infra*, part 3.19, for a detailed consideration of this report.

[30]See the CMFA brief to the OSC on Bill 154. Sections 19 and 20 of Bill 98 added the CMFA to the list of recognized self-regulatory organizations, but when the CMFA decided to relinquish its self-regulatory audit roles effective April 1, 1976, these provisions were deleted from Bill 20. See, *infra*, footnote 122.

[31]Reg. 794, s. 2(1)5.

[32]Reg. 794, s. 2(1)6.

description into one or other of the self-regulatory organizations—has spent much of its force. The BDA was created in 1947 as a product of this policy.[33]

(g) Security Issuer

A security issuer, the final class, engages in the distribution to the public of securities exclusively of its own issue.[34] This last grouping is intended for those who "self-underwrite", that is, who effect a distribution of their securities without finding it necessary to use some other registrant.[35]

Dealers often hold several classes of registration. For example many firms, especially larger ones, hold membership in both the TSE (and exchanges elsewhere) and the IDA.[36]

3.04 Business Activities of Dealers

In order to understand fully the technical requirements for registration, the conditions of maintaining it and the limits beyond which it does not apply, one must first understand the several types of business carried on by dealers. Unfortunately from the standpoint of achieving

---

[33] A watershed was reached in the history of this development in *Re Clark and Ontario Securities Commission*, [1966] 2 O.R. 277, 56 D.L.R. (2d) 585 where the Ontario Court of Appeal held that the OSC could not deny registration on the bare ground that the applicant had been refused membership in the BDA. See also *Re Larrimore Securities Ltd.*, [1956] O.W.N. 501, 4 D.L.R. (2d) 727 (C.A.).

[34] Reg. 794, s. 2(1)7.

[35] When this happens exemptions for trades to an underwriter or through a registered agent (s. 19(1)6 and 7; Bill 20, s. 35(1)9 and 10(a)) are not available and registration is required.

[36] The OSC Industry Ownership Report (p. 53) shows the numbers in various classes within the dealer and adviser categories in Ontario, as of September 30, 1971, to be as follows:

*Investment Dealers, Investment and Securities Dealers, Investment Dealers and Brokers	90
**Brokers (TSE)	12
***Brokers and Broker-Dealers, Broker-Dealers	31
Securities Dealers	19
Mutual Fund Dealers	33
Scholarship Dealers	2
Investment Counsels	34
Securities Advisers	4
	TOTAL 225

*This entry lumps together firms which were either exclusively registered in one of the three classes there described or through separate branches or divisions within the firm were represented in several of the classes of registration.

**This entry includes firms which held registration only in the brokers class, *i.e.*, membership in the TSE and in no other class. Since the membership of the TSE then totalled close to 100, it is apparent that the vast majority of its members were represented in other classes of registration as well.

***This entry lumps together firms which are members both of the TSE and BDA, and firms which are BDA members only.

symmetry, as well as conceptual clarity, these different business activities in the securities industry do not neatly coincide with the distinctions between classes of registration.

(1) INITIAL DISTRIBUTION

We may begin our analysis of the role of the dealer with the point at which the securities are traded for the first time. Five different kinds of initial distribution have been identified:[37]

(1) A negotiated public offering, either through a firm which agrees to underwrite the issue or on a best efforts basis, where the issuer and the dealer negotiate the terms on which the security is to be offered. This is the usual way in which provincial and municipal government debt is financed and the public distribution of the securities of a corporation follows the same pattern.

(2) A stock offering to shareholders usually through a right to purchase shares which is based on the number of shares already owned. The success of such a rights offering will often be assured through arrangements with a dealer which guarantee that a minimum amount will be raised for the issuer. Either the dealer will underwrite the whole (or a part) of the issue or he will agree to distribute whatever shares are not taken up by the shareholders.

(3) A private placement where the dealer acts as the agent of the issuer in negotiating a sale to one or more buyers who are usually institutional investors such as insurance or trust companies, mutual funds or pension funds.

(4) A dealer's purchase of all or part of an issue arranged either by inviting a number of dealers to bid or sending out a call for public tenders. In earlier years certain provinces and municipalities employed this technique with some frequency. It is now unusual except in the case of smaller municipalities.

(5) A distribution through the stock exchanges. This traditionally was permitted for mining issues only; more recently the TSE has permitted some industrial issues to be distributed in this manner. In Ontario this method requires the filing of a statement of material facts acceptable to the OSC and the TSE. Different rules prevail on other Canadian stock exchanges. This method is anomalous because stock exchanges are normally associated with secondary trading on an auction process.

(2) TYPES OF SECONDARY TRADING MARKETS

Once an initial distribution of securities has taken place they may be sold and bought in what are known as secondary trades. In this area industry custom provides a convenient demarcation into four identifiable markets.[38]

The first market is a recognized stock exchange where the securities of a given issuer are listed and posted for trading.[39] To obtain listing

---

[37]These are set out in the Moore Report (p. 23) and also discussed in the Industry Ownership Report (p. 41), from which sources this description is taken.

[38]See the Industry Ownership Report, pp. 42-43, which forms the basis of the discussion here.

[39]Generally shares only and not debt securities are listed. The TSE does, however, list certain hybrid securities such as warrants and real estate investment trust (REIT) units. See, *post*, part 10.03(2), footnote 20.

privileges an issuer must first satisfy and then maintain certain minimum standards relating variously to amount of net assets, earnings history and breadth of share distribution. Broker-members of the exchange execute trades in listed securities acting either as agent or principal.

The second market is popularly called the "over-the-counter" market. The "counter" in the phrase refers to the desk or table in the dealer's office on which the trade takes place; there is no other physical setting such as the floor of a stock exchange for the negotiations leading up to the trade, with the result that there is no central forum on which the activities of traders converge. This second market is also called the "between-dealers market", because much of the trading takes place through the telephone contact of one dealer to another in the absence of one meeting place facilitating contact.

At an earlier stage of its history the second market was called the "curb" market, a name drawn from the fact that dealers who traded between and among themselves frequently did so not in their offices or inside the stock exchange, but out on the street at the edge of the curb. A fourth appellation "the unlisted market" derives not from the manner of trading, but rather from the dealer's stock-in-trade, securities not listed on a stock exchange. Hence the market includes trading of shares which are not listed on a recognized stock exchange and also trading in some debt securities—those of medium and long term issued by government authorities or corporations. With respect to the debt securities part of the market (usually known separately as the "bond market") the dealer frequently acts as principal, but it is common for him to carry on an extensive agency trade on behalf of clients as well. This over-the-counter market is much smaller in Canada than in the U.S., partly because lower listing standards in Canada permit less well-established securities to be listed on a stock exchange, and also because public ownership in the U.S. is more widely diffused, giving rise to more extensive trading networks with heavier volumes.[40]

The third market involves the trading of *listed* securities between investors and dealers who are not members of the stock exchange on which the securities are listed.[41] The result is a by-passing of the established stock exchanges, a development which as yet has been almost wholly confined to the United States. Exchange members are nervous about the spread of third market activity; not only does it deprive them of commissions but it also removes liquidity and market breadth from the exchange. Behind this simple statement of conse-

---

[40]An elaborate computer assisted trading system, codenamed NASDAQ for the National Association of Securities Dealers Automated Quote System, is used for trading some unlisted stocks in the U.S. Supervised by the NASD, it provides a visual display, similar to that obtainable by closed-circuit television, of quotes and trades in each member dealer's office across the U.S. Bids or asks may be followed up by telephone contact to the quoting dealer and the transaction consummated over the telephone.

[41]Stock exchange rules generally require members to execute all trades through the exchange with rare exceptions.

quences lies a fundamental problem which will confront securities markets in the future. If one eliminates the third market one also eliminates competition and the possibility of lowering the cost of securities transactions.[42] On the other hand a strong stock exchange has traditionally been seen as an important contributor to an economy's stability and growth because it furnishes a permanent identifiable market for trading in securities. Trades must be disclosed on an exchange and can thus be monitored. Also it is more readily subject to regulation in the public interest, whether by its own rules or by outside agencies.

The term fourth market denotes a facility which merely matches orders in listed securities. It involves no intervention by a broker in the true sense of the word attempting to "marry up" buyers or sellers; rather the buyer and seller "find" each other using the facility. This fourth market is used by some institutional investors in the United States but not with any frequency in Canada.[43]

Related to the second market, but nevertheless to be seen as a discrete entity, is the "money-market". It receives both a broad and a narrow definition in terms of the number and character of its participants. The narrow money market comprises fifteen "officially recognized" money-market dealers, whereas the broader money market includes those fifteen and many more. This market derives its name from the short-term debt securities in which its participants trade; the short-term aspect makes it an appropriate outlet for

---

[42]Third market commissions are negotiable and may be cheaper than exchange commissions. Also, when a large block is sold in a single transaction to a third market dealer buying as principal, the total price may be lower than the cumulative price (commission plus average purchase price) for which the same block could be absorbed on the exchange.

[43]One of the major facilities for the fourth market in the U.S. is "Instinet" Institutional Networks Incorporated. A limited number of large institutional investors have subscribed to this organization. These subscribers are linked by terminals to a central computer which provides quotations of securities the members wish to buy or sell; they then use this information to effect large "block" trades with one another without the intervention of a dealer. Instinet extended its activities across the border into Canada by enlisting as a member a large Canadian mutual fund. The OSC ordered the fund to sever its connection with the U.S. firm on the grounds that Instinet was not registered for trading in Ontario. In the event that it applied for registration at least three issues would arise. First, does it seek registration as a dealer (broker classification) or official recognition as a stock exchange. (Note in this connection *Re Ontario Securities Commission and C.A.P. Ltd.*, [1972] 1 O.R. 205, 22 D.L.R. (3d) 529 (H.C.)) where certain administrative activities in support of mutual fund dealers were held not to be trades requiring registration as a dealer.) Secondly, how will it be affected by the non-resident ownership restrictions (Reg. 794, s. 6a; *infra*, part 3.12)? Thirdly, as a matter of policy, will the regulatory authorities permit a trading mechanism which, while allowing its member institutions to achieve efficiencies, impairs the functioning of the established exchanges by reducing their liquidity and market breadth, lessening members' incomes and detracting from the open nature of trades on the exchange? For more detailed discussion of Instinet and some of these issues see I.F.G. Baxter and D.L. Johnston, "New Mechanics for Securities Transactions".

investors who have a temporary cash surplus which they wish to put to use. The terms of maturity run up to three years, but substantially shorter periods such as thirty or sixty days are more usual. The securities traded include those of various government agencies— federal, provincial and municipal—and business corporations. They may be either newly placed (and thus part of an initial distribution) or already outstanding (and thus purchased in a secondary trade). Frequently the term "commercial paper" is used to describe such short-term notes or debentures. The dealers in the money market may trade either as agent or principal.

The fifteen "official" money-market dealers have all received official approval or designation from the Bank of Canada. This designation provides them with a line of credit which enables them to use the Bank of Canada as a lender of last resort and which also entitles them to special borrowing privileges with the chartered banks. The fifteen include among their number the larger and more established members of the securities industry; moreover they are subject to supervision by the Bank of Canada, which scrutinizes their financial affairs in an effort to satisfy itself as to their stability. These dealers use their borrowing privileges at the chartered banks by pledging as collateral government treasury bills, short-term bonds and certain bankers' acceptances. Considered to be particularly susceptible to moral suasion by the Bank of Canada, the "official" dealers are one of the instruments employed by the central monetary authority in the implementation of its policies.

(3) OTHER DEALER ACTIVITIES

Certain ancillary dealer services deserve mention. One of the most important is the provision of advice by dealers to their clients. This investment advice often takes the form of market commentaries and recommendations, accompanied perhaps by a detailed analysis of several securities. A related service is portfolio management, which may also be performed on an exclusive basis by investment counsel. Some specialized dealers provide a management service for one or more pooled accounts which are known as "in house" mutual funds; these are qualified for sale through a prospectus.[44]

Other services, sometimes paid for directly and sometimes provided as a convenience, include the carrying of accounts on margin (permitting a customer to purchase securities by paying less than their market value and authorizing the broker to pledge the securities with a bank furnishing the firm with the funds to carry the credit), providing custody for securities of clients and collecting interest and dividends. Some securities firms are active as fiscal agents in the private placement of securities. The latter role is sometimes closely related to yet another activity pursued by many securities firms—advising corporate clients on a fee basis regarding a wide range of business problems, including mergers, acquisitions, and corporate re-organizations; even economic forecasting and the planning of future expansion

---

[44]This specialized service recently received special attention, "tailored" regulation, as it were, in anticipation of the enactment of new legislation: see Ontario Policy 3-32, "'Dealer Managed' Mutual Funds", July 1975 OSCB 183; CCH vol. 2, para. 54-957.

may come at times within their province.

The activities of two other categories of registrant, advisers and underwriters, as well as those of the specialized classes of dealers, securities issuers, mutual fund dealers and scholarship plan dealers, may be adequately comprehended from their definitions as set forth earlier. They are not normally involved in the same wide range of activities as the types of dealers we have been discussing, and if they wish to participate in such activities, they must seek registration in the appropriate class.

3.05 Scope of Licensing Requirement

The licensing requirement is a comprehensive one. In s. 6 of the Act[45] this takes the form of a rather sweeping prohibition, decreeing that no person or company shall trade in a security (or act in connection with a trade) or function as an underwriter or adviser unless registered in the appropriate category.[46] The all-encompassing nature of this provi-

---

[45]Section 24 in Bill 20.

[46]It is useful to compare the basic licensing requirement across the Canadian jurisdictions. Section 6(1) of the Ontario Act reads:

"6(1) No person or company shall,

(a)   trade in a security unless such person or company is registered as a dealer, or as a salesman of a registered dealer;

(b)   act as a partner or officer of or on behalf of a person or company in connection with a trade in a security by such person or company unless such person or company is registered...;

(c)   act as a salesman of or on behalf of a person or company in connection with a trade in a security by such person or company unless he is registered as a salesman...;

(d)   act as an underwriter unless such person or company is registered as an underwriter, or is a bank...;

(e)   act as an adviser unless such person or company is registered as an adviser..."

Section 7(1) of the British Columbia Act is similar to the Ontario Act, with the following significant differences; s. 7(1)(b) reads "act as partner or *director*", and cl. (f) reads "advise others by means of a publication or writing as to the advisability of investing in or purchasing or selling a security specified therein unless the person or company [is exempted]". Alberta (s. 6(1)); Manitoba (s. 6) and Saskatchewan (s. 6) have provisions similar to the Ontario provisions, except that all add a clause like s. 7(1)(f) in the British Columbia Act; however they do not speak of "directors" as the British Columbia Act does.

The Quebec Act, s. 16 reads:

"16 No *one* shall:

(a)   trade in any security unless he is registered as a broker or security issuer or as salesman for a broker or security issuer registered as such;

(b)   act as an employee, officer or agent of a person or company in connection with trading in any security...unless he...or such person or company is registered as a broker or as a security issuer;

sion, when taken in conjunction with the broadly framed definition of trade,[47] makes necessary a rather extensive series of intricately drafted exemptions whose purpose is to remove certain types of securities as well as certain trades from the reach of the section where it is apparent that registration would be inappropriate in the circumstances.

(1) HISTORICAL PREAMBLE—FEDERAL COMPANIES AND THE CONSTITUTIONAL QUESTION

The two-pronged prohibition attaching to both persons and companies is necessary because the truncated definition of person does not include companies.[48] The prohibition against distribution to the public without a prospectus similarly wears a double aspect.[49] Beneath this dual terminology, apparently so straightforward, lies a fascinating but still potentially treacherous reef of constitutional history.

In *A.-G. Man. v. A.-G. Can.*[50] the Privy Council struck down that portion of the Manitoba Sale of Shares Act which gave the administrative board under the Act a discretion to refuse a licence to a federally

---

(c) act as investment counsel without being registered...;

(d) act as salesman for a person or company, in connection with trading in any security by such person or company, unless he is registered as a salesman for a duly registered broker or security issuer."

The Nova Scotia Act, s. 3 reads:

"3(1) No person shall,

(a) trade in any security unless he is registered as a broker or as a salesman of a registered broker; or

(b) act as an official of or on behalf of any partnership or company in connection with any trade in any security by the partnership or company, unless he and the partnership or company are registered under this Act; or

(c) act as a salesman of or on behalf of any partnership or company in connection with any trade...by the partnership or company unless he is registered as a salesman of a partnership or company which is registered as a broker;

...

"3(2)...any partnership or company may be registered as a broker..."

New Brunswick (s. 5(1)(a)) includes "or sub-agent of a registered broker". Newfoundland (s. 4) and P.E.I. (s. 2) are similar to Nova Scotia.

[47]See, *ante*, part 1.12.

[48]Section 1(1)12. See, *ante*, chapter 1, footnote 5. "Person" is defined in s. 1(1)27 of Bill 20.

[49]Section 35 (Bill 20, s. 54). Section 35 at one time spoke only of companies. The distribution prohibition was extended by a later section (s. 66) to cover a "person, trust or other entity", but this is clumsy and inconvenient. Bill 20, s. 54 solves the problem neatly by using the comprehensive term "issuer".

[50][1929] A.C. 260, [1929] 1 D.L.R. 369, [1929] 1 W.W.R. 369 (P.C.). For a review of the constitutional issues, see *Laskin's Canadian Constitutional Law*, Rev. 4th ed., A. S. Abel, ed. (Toronto, Carswell, 1975), pp. 359-61; Williamson, *Securities Regulation in Canada*, 1960, chapter 7, and 1966 Supplement; *Studies in Canadian Company Law*, Ziegel ed., vol. 1, chapter 5; Banwell, "Proposals for a National Securities Commission"; Kimber Report, chapter 9; J.A. Langford and D. L. Johnston "The Case for a National Securities Commission".

incorporated company. That legislation required such a company to obtain a licence before selling its shares in the province. It was this licensing requirement, as it applied to a creature of federal jurisdiction, and not the substantive criteria established by the legislation for the granting or refusal of the licence (the major requirement was prospectus disclosure of the "qualification" as opposed to the "notification" type) to which the Privy Council took exception. In holding as it did the Judicial Committee followed *Lukey and A.-G. Sask. v. Ruthenian Farmers' Elevator Co.,*[51] in which the Supreme Court of Canada five years earlier had declared *ultra vires* a similar provision of the Saskatchewan Sale of Shares Act in its application to federally incorporated companies; two other important background cases were *John Deere Plow Co. Ltd. v. Wharton,*[52] and *Great West Saddlery Co. Ltd. v. The King,*[53] where the Privy Council rendered null and void attempts by a province to impose licensing requirements which neutralized or sterilized the capacities and powers of federally incorporated companies.

Notwithstanding this to say the least unreceptive attitude on the part of the courts, ingenious provincial draftsmen redefined "person" to exclude company and continued the prohibition on unlicensed vendors; this of course applied to officers or other employees selling shares of their employer, whether a federally incorporated company or not. The Privy Council gave its approval to this sleight of hand three years later in *Lymburn v. Mayland,*[54] where it upheld the Alberta Act. The court reasoned that so long as an exemption existed whereby a federally incorporated company could sell its shares through provincially licensed brokers acting as agents on its behalf, the power of such a company to raise funds in the province was not rendered sterile by the disputed enactment.[55]

Had the Privy Council in *Lymburn* chosen to follow in the wake of *Lukey* and *A.-G. Man.* and denied Alberta's careful drafting the

---

[51][1924] S.C.R. 56, [1924] 1 D.L.R. 706, [1924] 1 W.W.R. 577.
[52][1915] A.C. 330, 18 D.L.R. 353, 7 W.W.R. 706 (P.C.).
[53][1921] 2 A.C. 91, 58 D.L.R. 1, [1921] 1 W.W.R. 1034 (P.C.).
[54][1932] A.C. 318, [1932] All E.R. Rep. 291, [1932] 2 D.L.R. 6.
[55]One can imagine the supporters of provincial rights uttering a triumphant "Aye amen" on reading Lord Atkin's *exegesis* on this rather contrived qualification (at pp. 9-10, D.L.R.):

"There is no reason to doubt that the main object sought to be secured in this part of the Act is to secure that persons who carry on the business of dealing in securities shall be honest and of good repute, and in this way to protect the public from being defrauded. Incidentally the net has been drawn so wide as to cover the issue of shares by a public company, with the result that a company cannot issue its shares to the public unless for that purpose it employs a registered broker or salesman, or unless the company itself is registered. It is said that these provisions as far as they affect Dominion companies are *ultra vires* according to the principles adopted by this Board in *John Deere Plow Co. v. Wharton; Gt. West Saddlery Co. v. The King* and *A.-G. Man. v. A.-G. Can.* [citations omitted].

course of securities regulation in Canada might well have been different. A defeat for the provinces in *Lymburn* might have supplied the impulse which would have led to a substantial Dominion presence in this field. Such speculations gain added point in the light of social and economic conditions in 1932, the year of the decision. The effects of "the Great Depression" were at their most severe. In the U.S. an aroused public opinion was inclined to blame economic failure and the desperate plight of many on the unregulated activities of stock marketeers; despite the existence of considerable regulation under state laws, there was a demand for new and tougher regulation at the national level. Congress was intensely preoccupied at the time with a dramatic investigation of securities markets which led to the creation of the federal Securities and Exchange Commission (SEC) in the following year.[56] The year 1933 also saw the first federal "Truth in Securities Act", the Securities Act of 1933, come into effect, followed by the Securities Exchange Act of 1934; the former regulated initial distributions, the latter the subsequent trading of the securities on the exchanges (and the exchanges themselves), both these statutory schemes being furnished with elaborate machinery for their enforcement. Four additional statutes directed more at specific problems were enacted in the next six years; these also were to be administered by the SEC.

So far as Canadian developments were concerned, the *Lymburn* decision simply held that provincial legislation of general application did not preclude federal companies from causing their securities to be traded through a registered broker. In the absence of any supervening federal legislation, the case continued to stand. An opposite decision would have been tantamount to a clear invitation to the Federal Government to establish machinery for the qualification of at least the initial distribution by a federal company of its securities. Indeed, had Parliament legislated prior to or immediately after the *Lymburn* decision, the constitutional validity of its enactments would likely have been upheld, and to the extent that existing provincial legislation conflicted therewith, the latter might have been rendered inoperative through the application of the doctrine of paramountcy. As it was, the *Lymburn* decision must surely have weakened the case (and also

---

"In those cases there was a general prohibition to companies either to trade at all or to issue their capital unless the company was registered. The legislation was held *ultra vires* because the legislative powers of the Province are restricted so that 'the status and powers of the Dominion company as such cannot be destroyed' (*John Deere Plow Co.*) and legislation will be invalid if a Dominion company is 'sterilized in all its functions and activities' or 'its status and essential capacities are impaired in a substantial degree' (*Great West Saddlery Co.*). It appears to their Lordships impossible to bring this legislation within such a principle....As to the issue of capital there is no complete prohibition as in *A.-G. Man. v. A.-G. Can.* in 1929; and no reason to suppose that any honest company would have any difficulty in finding registered persons in the Province to whom it could lawfully issue its capital."

[56]See Loss, vol. 1, chapter 1.

perhaps lessened the ardour) of those advocating a major federal initiative in securities legislation.[57]

Today the debate continues. Provincial regulatory powers have been extended everywhere to encompass the dual techniques of licensing and prospectus filings under supervision of a provincially constituted authority, though the federal companies legislation recently has introduced take-over bid and insider-trading regulations similar to those enacted by the provinces.[58] And recently proposals similar to those of the 1935 Royal Commission on Price Spreads have been emerging from Ottawa with greater frequency and in a tone of increasing insistency; most significantly the contents of such proposals range far beyond the issue of federal jurisdiction over federally incorporated companies which was the nub of conflict in an earlier day.[59]

---

[57]It is apparent that the federal official most concerned with national securities regulation was acutely aware of the direction in which the wind was blowing in constitutional matters. In the Dominion Parliament in 1934 (Canada, House of Commons Debates, 17th Parl. (5th Sess.) 1934, vol. 4, p. 3508) a proposal was made to amend the federal Companies Act along the lines of the English model in the matter of prospectus distribution. This would have resulted in a prospectus being required under the Companies Act for the sale of a federal company's securities by an underwriter who had purchased as principal and was now proposing to re-sell what was technically his own property. The Secretary of State gave an opinion to the effect that Parliament had no constitutional authority to regulate the sale by their owner of the securities of a Dominion company. As a result of such inhibiting considerations, the prospectus requirements of the Companies Act were made applicable to public offerings of federal company securities by or on behalf of that company, that is, either by itself or through an agent. They did not apply when an intervening dealer bought and then resold as principal to the public, however short the interval involved.

Certainly federal legislators were not moved to any display of activity by the appearance of the Report of the Royal Commission on Price Spreads in 1935 (pp. 41-2), which called for substantial amendments to the Companies Act in order to provide the provinces with leadership in strengthening their companies legislation. The Commission had in mind constitutional change which would either permit the Federal Government to pre-empt the field occupied by the existing provincial regulation or provide a base for co-operative efforts on the part of the provincial and federal governments, with uniformity the desired end. In particular it recommended as a minimum step the establishment of a federal administrative body which would supervise the initial issuance of securities by a federal company.

[58]In its Proposals for a New Business Corporations Law for Canada the Federal Government suggested the establishment of its own prospectus screening agency, rather than accepting prospectuses for federal companies provided they were screened by a provincial securities authority. However in the revised version of the new Act, this proposal was dropped in favour of the *status quo*. See part 15.00 of the Draft Proposals as compared with s. 186 of the Act as passed.

[59]See the Green Paper on mutual funds legislation with a draft federal act (W. Grover and J. C. Baillie, *Proposals for a Canada Mutual Fund Law*) which proposes to effect at a national level the regulation of mutual funds, now done provincially through policy statement (and in future through legislation when Bill 20 is enacted) and see P. T. Banwell, "Proposals for a National Securities Commission".

3.06 Trading Prohibition

Section 6 contains the basic prohibition against trading without registration. With s. 35,[60] which governs trades in the course of distribution to the public, it is the sure foundation upon which most of the remainder of the Act is built. But the architecture of this foundation is not so simple.[61] There are five subsections, the first of which is split into five different parts with an unnecessary amount of overlapping and repetition. Three of the parts of s-s. (1) are concerned with the three main categories of registration: dealer, adviser and underwriter. One of those three parts also establishes the salesman of a registered dealer as a separate class prohibited from "trading" without registration. Of the two remaining parts, one deals with those human agents of a registered "trader" who belong to the high echelons of the firm and the other deals with the somewhat humbler class of salesmen. Essentially both groups are prohibited from carrying out their functions unless their employer is registered. This additional provision means that a salesman must not only refrain from trading himself without registration; he must also not act as a salesman on behalf of another unless that other is registered. The remaining four subsections of s. 6 contain various subsidiary provisions with respect to these various human agents of the three categories of registrant; these specify a grant of certain powers to the director over the people in question.

The prohibition in s-s. (1) applies to "persons and companies"[62] and may be summarized this way: No one (meaning person or company) may:

(1) trade unless registered as a dealer or a salesman of a registered dealer,

(2) act as an underwriter unless registered as such,

(3) act as an adviser unless registered as such,

(4) act as a partner or officer of a firm unless the firm is registered for trading,

(5) act as a salesman on behalf of a firm unless registered as a salesman and the firm is registered as a dealer.

Given the definition of trade it is likely that "underwriting" would require registration as a dealer under item 1. A broad reading of the trade definition suggests the same applies to advising. It is only the separate requirements in items 2 and 3 that establish underwriting and advising as separate registration categories. The requirement of registration as an underwriter is expressly stated not to apply to a chartered bank.[63]

Bill 20, besides implementing the recommendations of the Mutual Funds Report in the registration area, rearranges and consolidates

---

[60]Section 54 in Bill 20.

[61]A simpler approach might have legislated a single prohibition stating that no one shall trade without registration in one of the categories or classes within a category as provided by the Regulations.

[62]See, *supra*, part 3.05(1) for the reason for the dual formulation.

[63]This exception would be more logcially expressed if placed in company with the other exceptions and exemptions in ss. 18 and 19. See, *infra*, part 3.16.

somewhat the parts of s-s. (1) in the interests of greater simplification. Registrants, their partners or officers, and their salesmen are grouped together, followed separately by underwriters and advisers.[64] The rest of the subsection, which is new, extends the ban on acting without registration to mutual funds, management companies, and contractual plan service companies.[65]

Registration is effected by written notice of such from the director. Where he has attached terms and conditions, it is contingent on compliance with them.[66]

Ontario has provided some guidance on interrelated categories and classes of registration, and in particular dual registration, in a policy statement which contains a number of prohibitions and permissions.[67] These directives have as their essential aim the linking of an individual or firm in a permanent manner to his or its function or role in relation to trading in the securities business. "Special grounds" must be shown to exist for the director to depart from them. A salesman cannot directly hold another registration in another category, nor can he act as an officer of a corporate registrant. To do so he must receive "designation" by the director as a trading officer.[68] Registration in any combination of broker, broker-dealer and investment dealer is permitted and affiliated companies are treated as the same company.[69] Dealers or underwriters, other than investment dealers or brokers, may not directly or indirectly hold separate registration as securities advisers or investment counsel. Names other than an individual's or corporation's own name are not permitted without a "sound reason". Companies registered as investment dealer, broker-dealer, adviser or underwriter cannot have a second registration in the same class. Valid "business reasons" must be shown for seeking a registration where there is an interlocking relationship between the applicant and an existing registrant arising from their having common directors or the same principal shareholders. Separate registration as an underwriter is not available to broker-dealers, investment dealers or advisers. Where an individual applying for registration other than as a salesman is an "associate"[70] of another individual who is already registered or permitted to trade or who is a principal shareholder of a registrant, then the applicant must satisfy the director that he is a principal who will act independently of the individual with whom he is associated.

---

[64]Bill 20, s. 24 (1)(a) to (c).
[65]Bill 20, s. 24(1)(d) to (f). It gives effect to para. 7.20(2) of the Mutual Funds Report.
[66]Section 6(1) (Bill 20, s. 24(1)).
[67]Policy 3-10, "Dual Registration under the Securities Act", CCH vol. 2, para. 54-904.
[68]Section 6(2) and (3) (Bill 20 does not repeat these provisions). However the Regulations when they appear may contain detailed provisions regarding officers and partners. See, *infra*, footnote 75.
[69]For the definition of "affiliated companies" see s. 1(2) to (5) in the Act and in Bill 20.
[70]Section 1(1)2 in the Act and in Bill 20.

3.07 Agents of the Firm

In s-ss. (2) through (5) of s. 6[71] there is a series of requirements which permits the director to single out and subject to supervision some of the more important human agents who will act on behalf of the registered firm. The effect of these provisions may be summarized as follows:

(1) Partners or officers of any registrant must obtain "designation" as such before acting and, whenever a new partner or officer is appointed by a registered firm, the registrant must obtain written permission for him to trade.[72]

(2) A salesman's registration is withdrawn when he changes firms until the director is notified in writing of his employment by his new firm and approves it.

(3) The director has a discretion to designate as "non-trading" employees, persons other than registered salesmen employed by a registrant where these persons do not usually sell securities to the public.

In connection with item 2, the Ontario Commission has warned that frequent transfers by salesmen are not in the public interest because the individual can gain little knowledge of his employer's business or establish good client-dealer relations. The OSC's policy statement

---

[71]Modified in Bill 20, s. 24(2) and (3). The subsections dealing with the termination of salesmen and the designation of non-trading employees have been retained with virtually no changes.

[72]Section 6(2) and (3). The drafting of these subsections has left at least one important ambiguity. Section 6(3) empowers the director to designate certain partners or officers as "trading officers". One reading of that provision would suggest that punitive action cannot be taken against the officer himself for any shortcomings, but rather must be visited on the firm. The argument is that where the trading officer, who does not himself hold a registration, engages in practices which would ordinarily result in an action by the Commission to reprimand, suspend or cancel the licence of a registrant, there is no licence held by the individual trading officer which could be the subject of such action. One could thus infer that action must be taken against the firm which holds the licence, with the expectation that it will, in turn act in some manner against its trading officer. Section 8(1) empowers the Commission, as contrasted with the director, to suspend or cancel, after an opportunity for a hearing has been given, "any registration" where in its opinion such action is in the public interest. The officer permitted in s. 6(3) by the director to trade does not by that permission, narrowly read, obtain a registration, but rather simply a recognition. In fact, however, the Commission has used its power in s. 8 to affect the designation of a trading officer rather than the registration of the firm. The best example is provided by *In the Matter of A.E. Ames & Co. Ltd. et al.*, June 1972 OSCB 98, where the president of the *Ames* company was suspended for one week and a vice-president reprimanded. Both steps were taken with no accompanying action against the firm's registration. The power to act directly against trading officers rather than indirectly by affecting the registration of the firm is a necessary one and the Act should be amended accordingly. A firm and all the rest of its employees may be damaged severely if subjected to the direct impact of punitive action designed solely to correct the activities of one of its officers. If it is the officer who is solely responsible, then it is he who should be singled out for direct treatment. See also, *post*, chapter 9, footnote 5.

advises that the Commission will examine "the suitability for the securities business, of individuals who ask for approval of too frequent transfers" and the director "will consider the circumstances" before approving a third transfer in a twelve-month period.[73]

Section 6(5), which gives the director the necessary discretion for item 3, is a rather curious provision. The director may designate as "non-trading" individual employees or a class of employees of a registered firm where those employees do not "usually sell securities to the public". One would have thought it unnecessary to give the director an explicit power to cancel such a "non-trading" classification once granted, but the subsection goes on to state expressly that he may cancel the "non-trading" designation with respect to any employee or class of employees where he is satisfied that registration as a salesman should be required.[74]

3.08 Grant of Registration

The director is given wide discretion in granting or renewing registration.[75] The touchstone against which the exercise of this discretion

---

[73]Ontario Policy 3-09, "Transfers of Salesmen", CCH vol. 2, para. 54-903. A Quebec policy statement requires brokers or security issuers to advise the Commission as soon as a registered salesman leaves their employ and to give the reasons: Jan. 1973, 4 QSCWS No. 6.

[74]It is unclear whether the existence of this "non-trading" designation requires the director to keep a constant picture of the total number and identity of all employees of a registrant firm and to be informed of any changes. In practice he does not.

[75]There is considerable dissimilarity in the grant of registration provision of the various Canadian Acts. Section 7 of the Ontario Act reads:

"7(1) The Director shall grant registration or renewal of registration to an applicant where in the opinion of the Director the applicant is suitable for registration and the proposed registration is not objectionable.

"(2) The Director shall not refuse to grant or refuse to renew registration without giving the applicant an opportunity to be heard.

"(3) The Director may in his discretion restrict a registration by imposing terms and conditions thereon and, without limiting the generality of the foregoing, may restrict the duration of a registration and may restrict the registration to trades in certain securities or a certain class of securities."

Section 8 of British Columbia; s. 7 of Manitoba; s. 7 of Saskatchewan and s. 7 of Alberta are all provisions similar to the Ontario provision with the following significant differences: British Columbia, s. 8(3): "The Superintendent may...attach...such terms, conditions or restrictions as may be deemed necessary by him"; Manitoba, s. 7(3) is like Ontario, s. 7(3) except it adds the words "either at the time of registration or subsequently" after the word "discretion"; Alberta has s. 7(4), which requires delivery of a bond by an applicant where the director so orders.

Sections 24, 24a, 24b, of the Quebec Act (as enacted by 1973 (Que.), c. 67, s. 13) read:

"24. The granting or renewal of registration is at the discretion of the Director.

"24a. The Director must, whenever he refuses the granting or renewal of registration to a person or company, give him or it the opportunity to be heard.

is to be measured is expressed in the dictum of Lord Atkin in *Lymburn v. Mayland:*[76]

"...the main object [of registration] ...is to secure that persons who carry on the business of dealing in securities shall be honest and of good repute, and in this way to protect the public from being defrauded."

These words were spoken however in 1932, when prevention of fraud was the dominant purpose of securities regulation. Since then, there has been an increasing stress on professionalism as a necessary supplement to the basic need for trust and integrity. Just as the intent of modern securities regulation in general is to encourage the development of efficient capital markets in order to aid in attaining this overall goal so the particular technique of registration is aimed at stimulating the growth of professional competence and specialized excellence.[77]

The one procedural check on the director is that he must give the applicant the opportunity for a hearing before refusing registration or renewal.[78] The director is also empowered to attach conditions and

---

"24b. No registration may be granted to an applicant not qualified therefor under this act and the regulations."

Section 11(1) of the Nova Scotia Act reads:

"11(1) The Minister may order that:

(a) any application for registration, renewal...shall or shall not be granted for any reason which he may deem sufficient; or

(b) the application of any person...shall not be granted where it appears that such person proposes to use or is using a trading name other than his own, or that of his partner, where such trading name is apt to lead the public to believe it is that of a business firm of longer established standing in Nova Scotia, or is calculated to conceal from the public the identity of the applicant, or is for any reason objectionable; or

(c) any temporary entry in the Register shall be made, suspended or cancelled for any reason which he may deem sufficient; or

(d) any registration shall be reduced to a temporary registration or suspended or cancelled for any reason which he may deem sufficient; or

(e) the registration of any broker or salesman shall be suspended...by reason of default in filing a bond...; or

(f) the registration of any broker or salesman shall be suspended as provided in Section 23;

and no order of the Minister shall be subject to review in any way in any court."

Section 2(1) and (2) of Prince Edward Island; s. 8(1) and (2) of Newfoundland and s. 5(1) to (3) of New Brunswick are not substantially different from Nova Scotia. The Prince Edward Island and New Brunswick provisions are brief compared with those of the other two Atlantic Provinces. Section 5(1) (a) of New Brunswick adds "sub-agent of a registered broker" to the types of registration which may be held.

[76][1932] A.C. 318 at p. 324, [1932] All E.R. Rep. 291, [1932] 2 D.L.R. 6 at p. 9 (P.C.).

[77]One of the most emphatic statements of the theme of professionalism may be found in the brief of the IDA Ontario section to the OSC Industry Ownership Study.

[78]Section 7(2) (Bill 20, s. 25(3)). Bill 20 adds "or reinstate", thus covering the situation where a would-be registrant has been suspended or at any rate has ceased to hold a registration previously held.

terms to a registration which may be of a restrictive type.[79] In earlier years the most common example was the requirement that a specified education course provided by a self-regulatory organization be successfully completed within a stated period if cancellation of registration was to be avoided. This permitted a new registrant to pursue the course and earn a living at the same time. This arrangement is now not normally permitted in Ontario.[80] Another type of limiting condition is one which restricts a registrant to trades in certain types of securities.[81] Mutual fund salesmen, for example, are permitted by their registration to sell mutual fund securities but no others, with one important exception for life insurance which is discussed below. It is also possible for a conditional registration to be confined to certain named securities.

One area where Ontario made explicit the manner in which discretion will be exercised in granting registration is that of part-time salesmen. Less than full-time involvement was prohibited with certain exceptions.[82]

For many years it was the undeclared policy in Ontario to refuse

---

[79]Section 7(3) (Bill 20, s. 25(2)).

[80]Under Ontario Policy 3-06, "Educational Qualifications for Salesmen", CCH vol. 2, para. 54-900, which took effect May 1, 1973, applicants for mutual fund salesman registration were required to have completed and passed the Canadian Mutual Fund course; applicants for registration as general securities salesmen were to have completed and passed the Canadian Securities course. With the publication of O. Reg. 14/75 this policy statement was cancelled as of February 1, 1975 and these and other educational qualifications are now incorporated in Reg. 794, s. 6(9) to (17). See also British Columbia Policy 3-14 "Course Requirements for Salesman's Registration (Other Than Mutual Funds)", CCH vol. 2, para. 29-964; Manitoba Policy 3.03 "Mutual Fund Salesmen—Course Requirements", CCH vol. 2, para. 34-993; Quebec Policy 17 "Conditions of Registration for Securities Salesmen", CCH vol. 3, para. 66-028; British Columbia Policy 3-15 "Salesman Registration", CCH vol. 2, para. 29-965; British Columbia Policy 3-11 "Execution of Form 4 by Applicants for Registration as Salesmen", CCH vol. 2, para. 29-961.

[81]This condition is expressly provided for in s. 7(3) (Bill 20, s. 25(2)).

[82]Policy 3-07 "Registration of Part-Time Salesmen", CCH vol. 2, para. 54-901, cancelled February 1, 1975 and now incorporated in Reg. 794, s. 6(18) and (19). (The similar Alberta Policy 3-08, CCH vol. 1, para. 24-508, however, is still in force.) It reaffirms a "long standing policy" that full-time employment is required, on the ground that "a person selling securities should be willing to devote the time and effort required to place him in a position of being able to properly advise and handle the affairs of his client". Certain exceptions to this policy are considered:
(a) students pursuing a part-time business, commercial or financial course;
(b) post-graduate students pursuing business, commercial or financial courses preparatory to a career in the securities business;
(c) the other occupation, though productive of occasional income, is primarily a hobby or recreational or cultural activity and does not interfere;
(d) the other occupation is seasonal (six months or less) (see *Michael Blum*, Feb. 1971 OSCB 18);
(e) part-time mutual fund salesmen in remote and sparsely populated areas where full-time employment is not economically feasible.

dual licensing to mutual fund salesmen and life insurance agents. With the growth of variable annuity policies sold by the life insurance companies, together with a practice followed by some life insurance companies in recent years of deleting the life insurance provisions from such policies, the matter came to a head. It has been resolved (and the traditional position reversed) in a policy statement which permits dual licensing if the individual satisfies the educational requirements for selling the securities offered and the supervising employers meet certain conditions established by the Ontario Commission and the Ontario Superintendent of Insurance.[83]

3.09 Application for Registration

The procedures to be followed and the information required in an application for registration have rather sensibly been left largely to the Regulations. The Act simply requires a written application on the form prescribed by the Regulation and provided by the Commission, accompanied by a fee similarly prescribed.[84] An additional stipulation is that an address for service in Ontario be stated in the application; this has the result that notices which are delivered or sent by pre-paid mail to the latest address on the application are deemed to have been adequately served, always assuming that there is no more explicit provision elsewhere in the Act.[85] A second supplementary provision gives the director a further discretion, one which is probably unnecessary in view of his broad general powers. He may require any further information or material to be submitted by either an applicant or registrant within the time he specifies, and may insist upon verification by affidavit or otherwise of any information or material supplied then or previously. In addition the applicant or registrant may be required to submit to an examination under oath.[86] This latter discretionary power is occasionally used to test the knowledge of an applicant, and thus gauge his suitability for the securities business (or some part of it) at first hand rather than relying solely on the course and written examination administered by the self-regulatory organizations.

(1) APPLICATION FOR DEALER, ADVISER OR UNDERWRITER REGISTRATION

We may begin by considering dealers, advisers, and underwriters to the exclusion of salesmen. The appropriate application form required

---

[83]Ontario Policy 3-11 "Dual Licensing: Life Insurance Agents", CCH vol. 2, para. 54-905. A similar approach has been taken in other jurisdictions: Alberta Policy 3-09, CCH vol. 1, para. 24-509; British Columbia Policy 3-16, CCH vol. 2, para. 29-966; Manitoba Policy 3.02, CCH vol. 2, para 34-992; Quebec Policy 9, CCH vol. 3, para 66-020; Quebec Policy 10, CCH vol. 3, para. 66-021; Saskatchewan Policy 3, CCH vol. 3, para. 69-304.

[84]Section 10 (Bill 20, s. 28).

[85]Section 11 (Bill 20, s. 29).

[86]Or any partner, officer, director, or employee of the applicant or of the registrant (s. 12; Bill 20, s. 30). Bill 20 makes further additions to the list of those who may be examined on oath: governors and trustees as well as anyone performing a function akin to that of any of the persons in the preceding list apart from employees.

to be completed is Form 1,[87] which starts off by requiring that the class of registration desired be stipulated. These classes—ten in all—include investment counsellor, securities adviser, broker, broker-dealer, investment dealer, securities dealer, mutual fund dealer, scholarship dealer, security issuer, or underwriter. If an applicant's activities cover more than one class in the dealer category all his sub-groupings must be included as well. To choose a common example, if a firm trades securities both as principal and agent and is a member of the TSE and IDA then his listings under the dealer category of registration should include the classes of broker and investment dealer. Separate registration as an underwriter is not required for any registrant that has obtained registration as a broker-dealer, investment dealer or securities dealer.[88]

Twelve different items of fact must be sworn to on the application. Besides the address for service in Ontario, the bank and branch at which the applicant maintains accounts must be specified. The applicant must also indicate whether registration of any branch offices is desired. The names of any partners, officers, or directors of the would-be registrant must be set out in full,[89] and particulars must be supplied of any case where the applicant, or any partner, officer, director, associate or affiliate, has been registered or applied for registration in any capacity under the Act, or has ever been registered to deal with the public in another jurisdiction[90] or been disciplined by another securities jurisdiction. If the applicant, its agents or associates have held membership (or had membership refused or suspended) in one of the self-regulatory organizations in any jurisdiction, or if they have operated or carried on business under any other name, details must be disclosed.

A question to which civil libertarians have long voiced objections is that which seeks to elicit whether the applicant (or any partner, officer, director, associate or affiliate) has ever been "charged, indicted or convicted, under the law of any province, state or country, excepting minor traffic violations".[91] In a number of cases the failure to respond truthfully has resulted in a subsequent cancellation of the licence. The question poses a dilemma for the applicant with an embarrassing past, since he cannot but assume that an affirmative answer giving particulars of a criminal record will measurably diminish his chances of success. The Commission's position, reiterated in several cases, has been that a complete and truthful answering of the application form

---

[87]Reg. 794, s. 3(1). The Regulations to Bill 20 have not yet appeared.
[88]Reg. 794, s. 3(3).
[89]The applicant must also state the names and positions of the particular officers or partners for whom a trading designation is sought.
[90]The query relating to licensing in any capacity in which a licence is required for dealing with the public (item 6(b)) clearly extends beyond securities legislation. In the instructions to the question the following occupations are suggested: insurance agent, real estate agent, used car dealer, mortgage broker.
[91]To avoid any misunderstanding the instructions state that the question "refers to *all* laws, *e.g.* Criminal, Immigration, Customs, Liquor, etc., of any province, state or country in any part of the world."

is the first test of suitability to obtain a licence and carry on a securities business, and that if this test cannot be successfully met, the administrator can have little confidence in the applicant's ability to fulfil the obligations of trust which the business imposes. Accordingly, the applicant with an unfortunate past is expected to make full disclosure and hope that he can satisfy the director either that such conduct does not reflect upon his present ability to carry on business properly or that he has so reformed himself as to render the repetition of such conduct very unlikely.[92]

The same "infamous question nine" also requests an answer, with particulars in the case of an affirmative response, as to whether the applicant (or any partner, officer, director, associate or affiliate) has ever been a defendant or respondent in any civil proceedings in any jurisdiction anywhere in the world wherein fraud was alleged. No definition of the word "fraud" is suggested; undoubtedly its meaning will be from time to time the subject of some fine distinctions, in which a considerable range of synonyms of the term, not to mention euphemisms, will receive full play. Finally, question 9 requests information relating to past bankruptcies or refusals of fidelity bonds. There is one additional requirement for those seeking registration as an adviser: a letter must be furnished from each person who will act on behalf of the applicant in the giving of investment advice, outlining directly related experience; the director will then determine whether such person can be designated so to act.

The last major area of the application form concerns capitalization. The disclosure regarding the applicant's financial structure requested here should be seen as designed to assist in the implementation of the minimum net free capital requirements discussed below. There are two parts, one for companies and the other for partnerships and sole proprietorships. To begin with companies, information is sought with respect to both financial structure and control: the first requirement is a statement of authorized and issued capital broken down into preferred shares or common shares, both the number of shares and their dollar value being shown in terms of authorized and issued capital. In addition the application must state the total dollar value of the company's debt securities, including bonds, debentures, notes and any other loans, with the source of the loan and maturity dates being given in this "other loan" category. Following this the names and addresses of registered and beneficial owners of each class of security or obligation issued are to be given, accompanied by details of the nature and extent of the holdings attributable to each.

The director has permitted some modification of this requirement in the case of branch operations in Ontario of firms which have distributed their securities to the public in another jurisdiction. The latter must supply the name, addresses and extent of holdings of each registered holder but not of beneficial owners. Furthermore they need only supply information from the shareholders or debt holders registry

---

[92]For a rather bizarre application of this test of truthfulness see *In Re Michael Thomas*, June 1972 OSCB 118.

at one point in time and are not obliged to inform the director of changes in those registered holdings unless they are material.[93]

There are various other questions designed to establish an accurate picture of the ownership and control of the company. The names and addresses, with particulars, of every depository holding any of the assets of the company must be given. It must also be indicated whether any person or company has undertaken to act as guarantor in relation to the financial or other undertakings of the applicant, and whether anyone whose name is not disclosed has any interest in the applicant, "beneficially or otherwise".[94] Finally, there is a query as to whether a subrogation or subordination agreement has been executed with a creditor in relation to loans owing by the applicant.[95]

---

[93]If the recommendations of the OSC's Industry Ownership Report in Ontario and the Bouchard Report in Quebec are adopted to permit public ownership of the securities of registrants (not presently available in Canada), presumably the same sort of accommodation will be accorded Canadian-owned firms. (Public is used here in the sense of the general public rather than the government.)

[94]Again the director is permitted to qualify these requirements in the case of branch operations of firms publicly owned elsewhere. As of February, 1974, non-resident owned corporate registrants were required to incorporate their branches in Canada. See s. 6c(c) of Reg. 794 as added by O. Reg. 95/74.

[95]Subrogated or subordinated loans have been permitted by the OSC if an agreement satisfactory to the Commission has been entered into between the creditor and debtor. (A prescribed form for these agreements is set out in the Conditions of Registration, Schedule 1 to Appendix 2 of the Conditions of Registration, CCH vol. 2, para. 54-981.) The purpose of a subrogated loan is to permit debt as opposed to equity capital to be injected into a securities firm and improve its ability to meet net free capital requirements. The lender agrees to subordinate his claim to repayment of principal and interest so as to rank behind all of the creditors of the firm. Thus the loan can be used to increase the net free capital of the firm. However, the loan must be repaid before there can be any withdrawal of capital, and in any distribution of assets on winding-up it takes priority over the claims of partners or shareholders of the firm. Not infrequently the creditor who makes such a loan will be a shareholder of the firm who has pledged his shares in the firm with a bank or other lender for a sum of money; this sum he then lends to the firm and enters into a subordination agreement at the same time. The OSC Industry Ownership Report noted with some alarm the substantial growth in subordinated loans in recent years in Ontario and sounded a note of caution with respect to their use. It stated (p. 51) "there is now some evidence that lending institutions are in a position to exert influence on the policies of the firm, particularly when they agree to subordinate the loans so as not to impair free capital." The information gathered by the Report regarding the use of subordinated loans was broken down by class of registration. It showed (p. 54) that in the seven years to March 31, 1971, while share capital in 71 resident-owned investment dealers grew by 45 per cent, subordinated loans leapt by 267 per cent. In dealing with five firms registered solely as brokers and functioning only in that capacity the same Report referred to "the somewhat precarious balance on which this segment of the industry hangs" (p. 60). The 1971 balance sheets of these firms showed a debt-equity ratio of 3.3:1 when subordinated loans were considered as capital or equity rather than debt; but when such loans were regarded as debt rather than capital or equity, the ratio became 5.8:1. The share capitalization of this same group of five

The disclosure requirements for partnership and proprietorships are substantially similar, although tailored somewhat to reflect the different legal form. As in the case of companies, the aim is to provide a general picture of the resources of the enterprise and the degree of control held by each of the participants.

(2) APPLICATION FOR DESIGNATION AS PARTNERS, OFFI-CERS OR DIRECTORS OF A REGISTRANT

Any person applying for designation as a partner or officer of a registered firm is required to complete an information sheet accompanied by a sworn affidavit.[96] The questionnaire has thirteen parts, many of which ask the same questions as we saw were addressed to the applicant firm. The additional items of information requested relate to matters such as continuous residence in Canada and current residence in Ontario as well as the employment record and business activities of the applicant. Full disclosure is required of all these matters, including even periods of unemployment, for the entire fifteen-year period immediately preceding the date of the statement.[97] The applicant must indicate whether he has ever been discharged by any employer for "cause", with a request for particulars in the case of an affirmative response, and give three references. One of the latter must be the manager or some other officer of a bank or trust company to whom reference can be made for further information and to whom the business reputation and character of the applicant is well known. The final section of the statement requires details of size and physical appearance for purposes of identification and citizenship information.[98]

Reflecting the concern of regulatory authorities to know who manages registrants, reports must be made[99] of any change in the partners of a partnership or in the officers, directors, or shareholders of a company and these reports must specify *inter alia* the names of new partners or officers for whom designation is sought. Each of the newcomers must complete a new information statement.[100] In addition the firm must detail any changes which have occurred in its financial structure which would make previous information filed misleading and declare that there are no other material changes in relation to the information furnished.

---

declined in the seven years, whereas subordinated loans almost doubled in the period and were at one point twice the amount of share capitalization.
[96]Reg. 794, s. 6(2) and (3); Form 2.
[97]Ontario has built some flexibility into the current residence requirement. A policy statement indicates that "where special circumstances warrant" a non-Ontario resident officer of a dealer registered in Ontario may be considered for registration in Ontario. See: Ontario Policy 3-08 "Registration—Non-Residents", CCH vol. 2, para. 54-902, and, *infra*, footnote 106.
[98]Of the Canadian jurisdictions Quebec alone requires a recent photograph (which must be renewed periodically). Consideration has also been given to fingerprinting registrants, but no jurisdiction has made this a requirement.
[99]On Form 3, pursuant to s. 5 of the Regulation and s. 15 of the Act.
[100]Form 2.

(3) APPLICATION FOR SALESMAN REGISTRATION

The application form for salesmen[101] is almost exactly the same as the information statement required in the case of a sole proprietor, partner, officer or director, with the exception that the name of the registered dealer by whom the applicant is to be employed must be listed. The same dealer must provide a certificate to accompany the application stating that:

"On the basis of due and diligent inquiry made of the background of the applicant named above and other information available, the [certifying employer] believes this person to be of good character and reputation and has the qualifications to undertake and successfully complete one of the courses of study approved by the Commission and all reasonable assistance to that end will be furnished by us."[102]

3.10 Registration Renewals

Every registration[103] expires on the day next preceding the anniversary date of the initial registration or renewal. Anniversary date is defined to mean the day and month on which the registration was granted.[104] The application for renewal of registration must be made not later than 30 days before the date on which the registration expires, with the full particulars of any change in the facts set forth in the latest application for registration on record.[105]

3.11 Conditions of Registration

The requirements regarding conditions of registration present an interesting example of delegated legislation.[106] Although the Commis-

---

[101]Reg. 794, s. 3(4), Form 5.

[102]Reg. 794, s. 3(5), Form 6. *Cf., supra,* footnote 80.

[103]Reg. 794, s. 4(3).

[104]Reg. 794, s. 4(1). In *Commercial Life Assurance Co. of Canada v. Drever,* [1948] S.C.R. 306, [1948] 2 D.L.R. 241, the respondent's licence under the Alberta Real Estate Agents' Licensing Act expired in July and was renewed August 26. The court held the renewal was not retroactive so as to validate the respondent's claim for commission on a sale where the statute prohibited an unregistered person from selling and precluded such a seller from being entitled to compensation.

[105]Fees of varying size must be paid for all types of registration or the renewal thereof (Reg. 794, s. 8), and there are some differences in amounts from one jurisdiction to another. In addition the fee levied for a given registration requirement in metropolitan regions differs from that imposed in less heavily populated areas, both from the standpoint of particular provinces and throughout the country. This is designed to encourage the securities business in those parts of the country where population is less concentrated.

[106]This footnote merely draws attention to the more prominent features of the conditions of registration in each province.

In Ontario see Reg. 794, ss. 6 to 6f and in particular the OSC requirements made pursuant to s. 6 (CCH vol. 2, para. 54-981). The latter establish the following conditions of registration: minimum free capital, bonding or insurance, contingency fund participation, standards for the keeping of business records, a residence requirement and a "know your client rule" (Appendix, schedule 1). The conditions are very comprehensive.

sion may change these conditions at any time on its own initiative, it

In Quebec much of the same ground is covered by Policy Statement 21, "Conditions of Registration of Brokers", CCH vol. 3, para. 66-032, which is likewise very comprehensive. "Broker" is defined in s. 1(4) of the Quebec Securities Act as any person other than a salesman who, directly or through an agent, devotes all or part of his time to trading in securities.

In British Columbia, Policy 3-22, "Requirements for Registration", CCH vol. 2, para. 29-972, sets out the conditions of registration in skeleton form: minimum free capital, bonding, contingency fund participation, experience requirements and a residence requirement. Full amplification is provided in the British Columbia Conditions of Registration Statement, CCH vol. 2, para. 25-403, which resembles in content and structure its Ontario analogue. The section on instructions to auditors of registrants is fuller in the Ontario version, whereas the section on margin requirements is abbreviated in the British Columbia statement. Both contain the "Know Your Client" rule in almost identical terms.

In Manitoba the only condition of registration in the legislation is the residence requirement of s. 14.

Section 15 of the Saskatchewan Act imposes the following residence requirements: one year combined with an intention on the part of the applicant to make Saskatchewan his permanent home.

The Alberta Regulations (s. 6) set out conditions of registration regarding minimum free capital, bonding, and business records that are similar to the Ontario conditions (see CCH vol. 1, paras. 23-977 to 23-983). Section 14 sets out the residence requirement.

Section 11(1)(a) to (f) of the Nova Scotia Act sets out certain terms and conditions of registration. Section 12(1)(a) to (f) of the Newfoundland Act and s. 7(1)(a), (b), (c), (e) and (f) of the Prince Edward Island Act are similar to the Nova Scotia Act. Section 12(1)(a) and (b) of the New Brunswick Act is similar to those provisions of the Nova Scotia Act. However s. 12(1)(c) of the New Brunswick Act and s. 7(1)(d) of the Prince Edward Island Act provide that the Board (the Provincial Secretary in Prince Edward Island) may suspend or cancel registration when any of five events occur, one of which is the institution of criminal proceedings against a broker.

In Nova Scotia, s. 9 provides for bonding, and the Regulations made under the Securities Act, March 10, 1942, s. 18, contain a curious provision that requires a salesman who has not resided in Nova Scotia for three months prior to his application to send two photographs with the rest of his documentation (see CCH vol. 2, paras. 45-175 and 46-081). New Brunswick Regulations under the Security Frauds Prevention Act, Reg. 150 of the Consolidated Regulations of New Brunswick 1963, filed Nov. 1, 1963, as am. Reg. 67-80 (Reg. s. 23, and s. 10 of Act); Newfoundland (s. 10 of Act, s. 14 of Securities Regulations 1954); Prince Edward Island (s. 5 of Act, s. 20 of the Regulations under the Securities Act, P.E.I. Reg. No. EC 38/76, effective Jan. 15, 1976), all have similar requirements. Newfoundland is the only Atlantic Province with a meaningful residency requirement: s. 8(5) and (6) gives the Attorney-General discretion to refuse registration of a person or company or partnership not resident in Newfoundland for at least one year immediately prior to the date of application with the intention of making Newfoundland a permanent home.

The Policy Statements (in addition to those referred to above) relevant to registration and continued fitness for registration are the following:

National Policy Statements: applying to all provinces except Newfoundland and Nova Scotia (the two latter provinces are being consulted regarding possible participation: see CCH vol. 2, para. 54-838); No. 17 "Violations of Securities Laws of other Jurisdictions—Conduct Affecting Fitness for Continued Registration," CCH vol. 2, para. 54-854; No. 18 "Conflict of Interest—

must notify registrants of the proposed changes and provide an opportunity for a hearing before they become effective.[107] An extensive and detailed statement of conditions of registration has been published by the OSC. It may be examined under five main headings: Minimum Free Capital, Bonding or Insurance Requirements, Contingency Funds, Business Records and Procedures, and Financial Statement and Audit Requirements. A brief summary is presented here.

Registrants Acting as Corporate Directors", CCH vol. 2, para. 54-855; No. 22 "Use of Information and Opinion Re Mining and Oil Properties by Registrants and Others", CCH vol. 2, para. 54-859; No. 25 "Registrants: Advertising: Disclosure of Interest", CCH vol. 2, para. 54-862.

Uniform Policy Statements: applying to Ontario and the Western provinces: No. 2-06 "Use of Shareholders' Lists by Registrants", CCH vol. 2, para. 54-876.

Local Policy Statements: Ontario: No. 3-08 "Registration—Non-Residents", CCH vol. 2, para. 54-902; No. 3-10 "Dual Registration under the Securities Act", CCH vol. 2, para. 54-904; No. 3-11 "Dual Licensing: Life Insurance Agents", CCH vol. 2, para. 54-905; No. 3-30 "Suspension of Registration Pursuant to Section 8: Criminal Charges Pending", CCH vol. 2, para. 54-955.

British Columbia: No. 3-11 "Execution of Form 4 by Applicants for Registration as Salesmen", CCH vol. 2, para. 29-961; No. 3-13 "Sales Commission 'Charge Backs'", CCH vol. 2, para. 29-963; No. 3-14 "Course Requirements for Salesman's Registration", CCH vol. 2, para. 29-964; No. 3-15 "Salesman Registration—(Mutual Funds)", CCH vol. 2, para. 29-965; No. 3-16 "Dual Licensing—Life Insurance Agents and Investment Contract Salesmen as Mutual Fund Salesmen", CCH vol. 2, para. 29-966; No. 3-17 "Customers' Free Credit Balances Carried by Brokers and Broker Dealers", CCH vol. 2, para. 29-967.

Manitoba: No. 3.02 "General Policy Requirements in Respect of Dual Registration of Mutual Fund and Life Insurance Salesmen", CCH vol. 2, para. 34-992; No. 3.03 "Mutual Fund Salesmen—Course Requirements," CCH vol. 2, para. 34-993; No. 3.04 "Mutual Fund Distributors Supporting Staff and 'Know Your Purchaser'", CCH vol. 2, para. 34-994; No. 3.06 "Range of Trading Permitted Registrants Holding Restricted Registrations", CCH vol. 2, para. 34-996.

Saskatchewan: No. 2 "Refunds", CCH vol. 3, para. 69-303; No. 3 "Dual Licensing", CCH vol. 3, para. 69-304; No. 7 "Foreign Ownership of Canadian Securities Firms", CCH vol. 3, para. 69-308.

Alberta: No. 3-06 "Registration of Broker-Dealers, Investment Dealers", CCH vol. 1, para. 24-506; No. 3-07 "Examination Program for Salesmen", CCH vol. 1, para. 24-507; No. 3-08 "Registration of Part-Time Salesmen", CCH vol. 1, para. 24-508; No. 3-09 "Dual Registration—Life Insurance Agents", CCH vol. 1, para. 24-509.

Quebec: No. 9 "Dual Licensing of Mutual Fund Salesmen and of Life Insurance Agents", CCH vol. 3, para. 66-020; No. 11A "Conditions of Registration of University Scholarship Plans", CCH vol. 3, para. 66-022; No. 17 "Registration for Securities Salesmen", CCH vol. 3, para. 66-028; No. 18 "Conditions of Registration for Brokers", CCH vol. 3, para. 66-029.

None of the Atlantic Provinces has made any local policy statements. All the policy statements are reproduced in CCH vols. 1, 2 or 3. And see Bill 20, ss. 31 and 32.

[107]Reg. 794, s. 6(7).

(1) MINIMUM NET FREE CAPITAL

The minimum free capital requirements address the financial stability of registrants. Varying amounts have been established for the different categories. For dealers, except security issuers, it is the greater of $25,000 or an amount equal to ten per cent of the first 2,500,000 of adjusted liablities, plus seven per cent of the next $2,500,000, plus six per cent of the next $2,500,000, plus five per cent of adjusted liabilities in excess of $10,000,000. In the case of advisers it is a basic amount of $5,000 subject to an adjustment upwards (maximum $25,000) at the discretion of the director where control of a client's funds or securities is involved. For underwriters the sum is $10,000.[108] The definition of minimum free capital and of adjusted liablities, together with the methods of calculation, are set out in a complex manner in the conditions of registration.[109] The formula used for these calculations is somewhat different in Canada from that used in the U.S.

(2) BONDING OR INSURANCE

Bonding or insurance is required for each category of registrant. A minimum bond of $100,000 is required for dealers, except mutual fund dealers and security issuers. Mutual fund dealers must cover each employee in the amount of $25,000 with the director having the discretion to set a maximum coverage for each employer. Security issuers and advisers as well as underwriters must maintain a minimum amount of not less than $10,000, although this coverage may be reduced at the discretion of the director.[110]

(3) CONTINGENCY FUND

Each category of dealer other than securities issuers must participate in a contingency or compensation fund.[111] The fund must be approved by the Commission and either established by one of the self-regulatory organizations recognized by the Act or by a trustee in accordance with the terms and conditions contained in Form 8 of the Regulation.

As matters presently stand there is only one national contingency fund, the participants in which are the members of the Toronto, Montreal and Vancouver Stock Exchanges and the IDA.[112] The bankruptcy of a Toronto broker in 1971 completely depleted that fund and new levies were required to restore it.[113]

---

[108]Reg. 794, s. 6(1).

[109]For a case and statute which give a rather unusual definition of paid-up capital (upon which provincial corporation tax is assessed) see *Re City Parking Canada Ltd. and Minister of Revenue of Ontario*, [1972] 3 O.R. 340 (H.C.); appeal allowed 1 O.R. (2d) 425, 40 D.L.R. (3d) 513 (C.A.) and s. 70 of the Corporations Tax Act, R.S.O. 1970, c. 91.

[110]Reg. 794, s. 6(3).

[111]Reg. 794, s. 6(4).

[112]For details of the fund see the Canadian Securities Course, pp. 221-222.

[113]The OSC's Industry Ownership Study gave passing consideration to the contingency fund and the protection of clients generally, drawing parallels with experience in the United States (paras. 4.46 and 4.47):

"The public interest demands that a securities firm should be sufficiently well financed to avoid failure. It is true that increasingly comprehensive sets of safeguards have been devised and implemented by the Commission and the self-regulatory bodies under our jurisdiction to prevent such occurrences. Net free capital requirements have been reviewed. Audit and

(4) BUSINESS RECORDS AND PROCEDURES

Dealers, advisers and underwriters must maintain business records and procedures in accordance with the Commission's published requirements.[114] The conditions of registration statement[115] goes into considerable detail regarding the books and other records which registrants must maintain in order to keep track of their business transactions and financial affairs; as a result most of them have been forced into computerized record-keeping.

In the area of supervision and control of customers' accounts the statement introduces an important procedural guide called the "Know Your Client" rule. This directive requires the registrant to obtain from a new client certain information relating to the client's investment objectives and capabilities which will help to determine the advice he is given. The registrant is prohibited from accepting an order from an unknown individual until his credit and reputation are established. A

---

surveillance procedures have been tightened. This notwithstanding, a major brokerage bankruptcy occurred in Toronto during the summer of 1971. The circumstances of this bankruptcy are still under investigation. It is of some satisfaction to note that as a result of the establishment of the National Contingency Fund no public client will suffer a loss. It is also satisfying to recognize that such occurrences have been comparatively rare. However, dealers and other non-public clients who will claim as unprotected creditors will suffer from the bankruptcy mentioned above. Furthermore the investment dealer and broker community across Canada, which supports the National Contingency Fund, has in fact born its *pro rata* share of the loss, reducing, or [sic] requiring an infusion of new capital. The Committee has no solution. Net free capital requirements may have to be raised to provide a bigger cushion. Contributions to the contingency fund may have to be increased. Certainly each firm owes a duty to all others to be diligent to protect their joint interest by bringing unusual activities or patterns immediately to the attention of the appropriate authority so that the facts may be considered quickly and before failure occurs.
"By contrast the picture in the United States has been bleak.

. . .

"[I]n the past two years, four of the twenty largest U.S. firms in terms of net worth had failed, were required to be merged or suffered major difficulties leading to a complete change of control, and that during the same period the NYSE found it necessary to intervene directly in the affairs of 200 of its members, i.e. more than half of the NYSE members dealing with the public. The TSE brief suggests that these difficulties were due in part to the improvident use of capital, the failure of management to adequately control its business, and a method of financing through subordinated loans not permitted under the current Ontario regulations. The end result has been the passage of the Securities Investor Protection Act of 1971, which came into force in April 1971. The plan, which has the backing of the U.S. Treasury, received an initial $75,000,000 with the power to borrow an additional $1,000,000,000 from the U.S. Government. This is the apparent reason for the SEC's present concern with the effectiveness of U.S. self-regulatory bodies."

For a discussion of a broker's bankruptcy, reorganization and subsequent bankruptcy before the establishment of the contingency fund see *Trustee of Stobie, Forlong & Co. v. Colwell*, [1938] S.C.R. 193, [1938] 2 D.L.R. 209.
[114]Reg. 794, s. 6(5).
[115]*Supra*, footnote 106.

concrete step to aid in gathering adequate data has been the development of a "Know Your Client" information card which must be completed and maintained on file together with supporting documents. It is clear that a failure to follow the "Know Your Client" rules will bring the registration of an individual or firm into question.[116] However questionable whether such a failure will create a basis for a client to refuse a claim for payment by his broker.[117]

The same published statement of conditions establishes some new guidelines in the area of internal supervisory procedures. A registered firm must have a written summary of such procedures and "note each step in the supervisory process in sufficient detail to enable those with supervisory responsibilities to understand their obligations".[118]

An area singled out for detailed treatment is the segregation of funds and securities. Provided they are not subject to any lien or charge in favour of the registrant, fully paid-for securities of clients which are still in the possession of the registrant are to be segregated and placed in a separate container. However an exemption from this requirement is given to members of the IDA and the TSE because of the "adequate compensation funds maintained by both organizations".

The same guidelines provide for a statement of account to be sent to each client at the end of each month in which he has effected a transaction where there is a debit or credit balance or securities are being held by the registrant. Where either funds or securities are held on a continuing basis, a statement must be sent every three months. The guidelines also contain specific and detailed rules for the settle-

---

[116]See for example the trilogy of disciplinary cases before the OSC in 1972: *United Investment Services Ltd.*, Feb. 1972 OSCB 20; *W.R. Williamson*, Sept. 1971 OSCB 135; and *Davidson and Company*, Jan. 1972 OSCB 7. The latter two dramatically display the impact of the "Know Your Client" rule on a registrant.

[117]In *R.H. Deacon & Co. Ltd. v. Varga; DuDomaine Third Party*, [1973] 1 O.R. 233, 30 D.L.R. (3d) 653 (C.A.) where a broker's action to recover against his client was upheld, the client argued that there was a "legal duty on the broker to investigate the financial status of the customer and to protect him against improvident stock transactions." To this Evans J.A. replied: "I know of no authority for such a startling proposition—[counsel] did not cite any—and his arguments did not convince me." On appeal to the Supreme Court of Canada the Court affirmed the judgment of the Ontario Court of Appeal: 41 D.L.R. (3d) 767n. Abbott J. said: "...the finding of the jury that the appellant did not rely on the respondent or the third party to discover and make disclosure of facts necessary to enable him to give informed instructions, negatives...the existence of a fiduciary relationship between the appellant and the respondent." This case is an unfortunate blow to the extension of the "Know Your Client" principle to the area of civil consequences and imposes a greater regulatory load on the conditions of registration.

[118]The guidelines state: "The object of the procedures is to establish and enforce written supervisory procedures under the continuous scrutiny of firm management. This will enable management to supervise the opening and handling of customers' accounts, the supervision of the salesmen and clerical personnel, and to assure compliance with securities laws and regulations, Commission policies, the special requirements applying to members of a self-regulatory body and any other conditions attached to the registration."

ment of cash accounts. Finally, it should be noted that these Ontario provisions regarding financial records have been supplemented by a national policy statement,[119] which requires a registrant, other than an underwriter or salesman, whose head office is outside of the province, to keep in the province such records as are necessary to provide complete details of each transaction from or within that province.

(5) FINANCIAL STATEMENTS AND AUDITS

The fifth part of the conditions of registration does not apply so broadly as the preceding four, owing to the existence of an alternative auditing procedure imposed through the self-regulatory organizations.

One of the basic provisions of the Act which is relevant here is s. 12,[120] empowering the director to require any further information or material to be submitted by an applicant or a registrant. He may require verification by affidavit and examine under oath personnel associated with a firm which is registered or seeking registration. Part V of the Act[121] deals specifically with audits. The very considerable reliance placed on self-regulation in an area of strategic importance in securities regulation is manifest. A panel of senior auditors must be selected by the three self-regulatory organizations, the TSE, the IDA (Ontario) and the BDA. In addition, each organization must employ as its auditor a member of the profession whose appointment is subject to the Commission's approval.[122]

The TSE, IDA and BDA are required to ensure that each of their members (where the member is of a class for which the Commission designates an audit requirement) appoints an auditor from the panel to examine its financial affairs and report to the organization's auditor.[123] Furthermore the by-laws, rules and regulations of the organizations respecting the examination of members' financial affairs, along with the examinations made thereunder, must be satisfactory to the Commission.[124] As well as periodic inspections at regular intervals, the self-regulatory organization may conduct surprise audits of members.

Those registrants not governed by the audit requirements of the

---

[119]National Policy 16, "Maintenance of Provincial Trading Records", CCH vol. 2, para. 54-853.
[120]Section 30, Bill 20.
[121]Sections 30 to 33 (ss. 19 to 21 of Bill 20).
[122]Section 30 (Bill 20, s. 19). Recently in its statement of Conditions of Registration pursuant to Reg. 794, s. 6 (*supra*, footnote 106) the Commission gave formal recognition to the Canadian Mutual Funds Association (CCH vol. 2, at p. 10,297-51). See also Saskatchewan Policy 5, CCH vol. 3, para. 69-306. This recognition carried with it approval of the Association's procedure for audit surveillance and of its by-laws, rules and regulations regarding the examination of members' financial affairs, with the result that a number of mutual fund dealers would have been exempt from the requirements of the statement as regards the preparing of financial statements. But in an unfortunate reversal the CMFA decided to relinquish self-regulatory responsibility for auditing as of April, 1976. Consequently the provisions in Bill 98 (ss. 19 and 20) adding the CMFA to the other three self-regulatory organizations with audit responsibility were deleted in Bill 20 (ss. 19 and 20).
[123]Section 31(1) (Bill 20, s. 20(1)).
[124]Section 31(2) (Bill 20, s. 20(2)).

three self-regulatory organizations are required to keep appropriate books and records and file with the Commission annually, and at any other time the Commission requires, satisfactory financial statements and any other information the Commission may require.[125] The Commission has an overriding authority to make an audit of the financial affairs of a registrant or an issuer at any time.[126] This is a provision of formidable scope: it permits the Commission to examine the internal financial affairs of any issuer without a formal investigation order. Free access to all documents and records must be provided. There can be no withholding or refusal to give any information or anything reasonably required in the audit.[127] To crown it all the Commission is entitled to charge a fee prescribed by Regulation for this examination.[128]

The bulk of registrants have their financial affairs examined and audited by auditors from the self-regulatory organizations as described above. If not they are required to comply with the following rules. Financial statements must be reported upon by a person acceptable to the Commission and completely independent of the registrant. The statements must be prepared and submitted annually in a prescribed form and forwarded by the auditor to the director within 90 days of the end of the registrant's fiscal year. The registrant is required to issue a direction to its auditor instructing him to act. Likewise, if the Commission or the director so request an interim audit must be conducted, with the expense to be borne by the registrant.[129] Detailed guidelines and questionnaires to be completed are set out in the public statement of conditions of registration; there are separate divisions for advisers and mutual fund dealers and a third grouping for all others except security issuers.

3.12 Restrictions on Non-Resident Ownership of Registrants

One of the major policy questions in recent years with regard to conditions attached to registration is resident ownership or control of registrants. Several government and industry studies have identified the securities industry as a "key sector" in Canada requiring certain measures to be taken in order to ensure that control of the industry remains in Canada.[130] Ontario amended its Regulation in July of 1971 to bar any new registered dealers in cases where non-Canadian ownership in aggregate exceeded 25 per cent or where any single

---

[125]Section 32 (Bill 20, s. 21).

[126]Section 33. The equivalent provision in Bill 20 is s. 18(1)(a), which substitutes "reporting issuer" for "person or company". Section 18(1)(b) is a new provision which brings in mutual funds specifically. The Commission may examine the books and records of a custodian of the assets (or shares or units) of such a fund.

[127]Section 33(2) (Bill 20, s. 18(2)).

[128]Section 33(3) (Bill 20, s. 18(3)). Reg. 794, s. 8(1), para. (o) establishes a surprisingly low rate of $100 per day per auditor unless the Commission otherwise directs.

[129]Reg. 794, s. 6(6)5.

[130]Moore Report; OSC Industry Ownership Study; Foreign Direct Investment in Canada, Ottawa, Information Canada, 1972 (Gray Report); Report of the Joint Industry Committee on the Moore Report, Toronto Stock Exchange,

foreign owner held more than ten per cent.[131] Existing registrants, whose non-Canadian ownership exceeded those figures, called "grandfathers", had growth limitations imposed on them related to an "industry average" formula and were required to obtain Commission approval before any significant change in ownership occurred.[132]

A new element entered the discussion with the publication of the Final Report of the Study of the Securities Industry in Quebec. While adopting a position similar to that of the OSC Industry Ownership Study (which favoured some public ownership of securities firms), that Report came to a different conclusion regarding non-Canadian ownership and recommended acceptance of non-resident owned registrants if the QSC finds their business objectives to be in the interests of the Quebec public.[133]

1971; Report of the Task Force on the Structure of Canadian Industry, Queen's Printer, Ottawa, 1968 (Watkins Report).

[131]Reg. 794, ss. 6a to 6g. The spirit of the regulations seems to be directed at dealers only, but the text would seem to capture advisers and underwriters as well.

[132]*Ibid.* These severe restrictions on new non-resident owned registrants came in the form of a surprise announcement in July, 1971. The reasons of policy underlying the change were outlined briefly by Ontario's Premier in introducing the new amendment (July 1971 OSCB 83):

"In the view of the Government, one very large and critical area to the firm establishment of Canadian determination is the investment community. ...

"...In parallel areas of concern, in particular loan and trust companies, we enacted legislation restricting foreign ownership.

"The Canadian investment community, which has assumed the responsibility for the direction of vast sums of capital in the country, is no less important. The investment community must be responsible and responsive to the particular needs of Canada. Its owners must be amenable to these needs and aspirations.

"We believe it to be essential that ownership of investment companies remain substantially Canadian.

"...[These restrictions] would also apply where there is a material change in the control of an existing registrant."

Elsewhere, Manitoba has amended its Act to give the director a discretion to refuse registration to an applicant who does not have the "usual residence qualification" as defined (1972 (Man.), c. 58, s. 3) and Saskatchewan Policy 7 "Foreign Ownership of Canadian Securities Firms", CCH vol. 3, para. 69-308, imposes limits similar to Ontario.

[133]The Bouchard Report, issued by the Department of Financial Institutions, Companies and Co-operatives, June 1972, preceded by the Interim Report, August 24, 1971. It thus touched the sensitive nerve of development of national *versus* regional capital markets.

The Bouchard Report recommendations were founded on three substantive findings. First of all, it concluded that in terms of the number of underwritings, the range of institutions dealt with and over-all profitability, the Quebec industry was dominated by securities firms controlled in Ontario. Those firms whose controlling interest was held in provinces other than Quebec or Ontario or outside Canada were not considered to be substantial competitors. As a result, unlike the situation in Ontario, there was no significant concern in Quebec about the encroachments of non-Canadian ownership. Secondly, the Report concluded that a heavier capitalization of securities firms would allow greater diversity of function (desirable given the cyclical nature of the industry) and increase over-all efficiency. From this conclusion flowed the

3.13 Continued Fitness for Registration

All of the provincial securities administrations have outlined certain situations which will cause the registration of an individual or firm to be placed in jeopardy.[134] For example, one national policy statement issues a terse warning:

---

recommendation that additional capitalization be provided for Quebec securities firms through public ownership, or in lieu of this through public distribution of both their debt and equity securities. Thirdly, the Report concluded that economic development in Quebec would best be served by more large securities firms with significant operational control in Quebec. It specifically recommended that at least 25 per cent of the voting shares were to be held by officers and employees of the firm resident in Quebec.

Consequently the QSC was given a broad discretion to pass on the fitness for registration of all registrants, the guiding criterion to be the benefit to be obtained for Quebec from the initial or continued registration of the firm. This discretionary power was specifically designed to to allow decisions upon the question of firms owned outside Canada operating in the province. The Bouchard Report set out five factors to guide the QSC in its exercise. They were:
1. The ability to distribute Quebec securities on the various markets;
2. The firms' capacity to increase the volume of transactions on the Quebec financial market;
3. The firms' contribution in terms of know-how and special qualifications;
4. The need to establish and maintain an equilibrium at any given time in order to avoid undue outside influence;
5. The maintenance of sound competition in the industry.

Two major U.S. firms, First Boston and Morgan Stanley, were accepted for registration by Quebec in pursuance of this policy. First Boston had applied in Ontario for an exemption from the non-resident ownership guidelines. The firm relied on the fact of having held a previous limited registration for the purpose of underwriting a single issue and on the additional circumstance that its application for permanent registration was almost completed when the July 1971 restrictions came into effect. Nevertheless the application was refused (Sept. 1971 OSCB 140). See Quebec Policies 4 and 21, CCH vol. 3, paras. 66-015 and 66-032.

[134]The Commisson is empowered to "suspend or cancel any registration where in its opinion such action is in the public interest" (s. 8(1) (Bill 20, s. 26(1)). It is unfortunate that the current legislation does not expressly empower the Commission to take disciplinary action less harsh than suspension or cancellation. In *Re Registrar of Used Car Dealers and Salesmen and Robert Rowe Motors Ltd.*, [1973] 1 O.R. 308, 31 D.L.R. (3d) 35 (C.A.) the Ontario Court of Appeal construed rather similar disciplining language under the Used Car Dealers Act, R.S.O. 1970, c. 475, s. 17(1)(b):
"17(1)   The Tribunal may, after the hearing,
    (b)   where the hearing is an application for suspension or revocation of a registration, dismiss the application or order that the registration be suspended or revoked, and the Tribunal may attach such terms and conditions to its order or to the registration as it considers appropriate."
The Tribunal found that the dealer and salesmen had systematically turned back the odometers on used cars and revoked their licences. However, it "suspended" the revocation for a probationary period during which the

"Notice is hereby given to all securities registrants that violations of the securities laws of any jurisdiction is considered in principle to be prejudicial to the public interest and may affect their fitness for continued registration."[135]

A far more complicated situation, involving potential conflicts of interest, arises where a registrant serves as a corporate director. This topic also has been the subject of a national policy statement.[136] The difficulties inherent in this area are reflected in the circumspect language of the statement. It notes that the position of a registrant serving as a director "is fraught with the possibility of a conflict of interest", particularly with respect to insider information, trading and timely disclosure. It suggests that registrants must weigh the burden

---

registrants were not to contravene any relevant regulation and would be periodically checked with provision for the order to be rescinded at the end of the period. Instead of probation the Court of Appeal imposed a suspension of three months. It observed that the Tribunal's powers were limited to dismissing the application on the one hand or suspending or revoking the registration on the other. Because the Court concluded the Tribunal had given insufficient weight to the public interest in imposing a penalty of probation with terms "which for practical purposes have no meaning at all" it concluded that discretion had been exercised on a wrong principle; accordingly it was not "necessary to decide whether..." the Tribunal had the power to make the kind of order it did.

Bill 20, s. 26(1) resolves this problem by adding the words "restrict or impose terms and conditions upon" to the Commission's power to suspend or cancel registration.

In seeking to identify the public interest as used in the limited form of order imposed in *Rowe* the Court considered the interests of the dealer's employees and referred to *Re The Securities Act and Morton,* [1946] O.R. 492 at p. 494, [1946] 3 D.L.R. 724 (C.A.), where Robertson C.J.O. said:

"The Commission is to suspend or cancel a registration where, in its opinion, such action is in the public interest... A registered broker or salesman has no vested interest that is to be weighed in the balance against the public interest. I have no doubt the Commission will, on proper occasions, give consideration to the possible serious consequences of taking away a man's livelihood, and of making the business of a broker or salesman a precarious occupation. Such considerations may have their proper place in determining what is in the public interest. It is, however, the public interest that is to be served by the Commission, and not private interests or the interests of any profession or business, in the exercise of the Commission's powers of suspension or cancellation of the registration of any broker or salesman."

Two cases which emphasize the broad discretion of the Commission in cancelling registration are *Re Glass,* [1951] O.R. 629, [1951] 4 D.L.R. 117 (C.A.) and *Re Mitchell and Ontario Securities Commission* (1957), 12 D.L.R. (2d) 221, [1957] O.W.N. 595 (C.A.).

[135]National Policy 17, "Violations of Securities Laws of other Jurisdictions—Conduct Affecting Fitness for Continued Registration", CCH vol. 2, para. 54-854. The uniform act jurisdictions have declared that trafficking in shareholders' lists other than for purposes connected with the corporation (see, for example, the BCA, ss. 163 to 165) will affect fitness for continued registration (Uniform Policy 2-06, "Use of Shareholders' Lists by Registrants", CCH vol. 2, para. 54-876).

[136]National Policy 18, "Conflict of Interest-Registrants Acting as Corporate Directors", CCH vol. 2, para. 54-855.

of dealing in an ethical manner with the problem of conflict of interest against the advantages of holding corporate directorships where many of the shareholders will be clients.[137] The statement simply exposes the tip of the iceberg of conflicts of interest in the securities industry.[138]

3.14 Surrender of Registration

The uniform act jurisdictions have stated policy for the surrender of registration, other than for salesmen.[139] Once it receives notice of a desire to terminate registration, the Commission will suspend the registration; then as soon as evidence demonstrating that all obligations to clients have been discharged is received the suspension will be removed and the registration regarded as voluntarily terminated. Disciplinary action by the Commission under s. 8 of the Act would appear to be foreclosed by a registrant's surrender of his registration.[140]

3.15 Exemptions from Registration and Distribution Requirements

The broad scope of the definition of trade and of the registration requirement under the Act have already been noted. Thus the exemptions from those requirements are of particular importance. In this part we deal only with those exemptions expressed in ss. 18

---

[137]It defines acceptable conduct thus (quoting from a TSE statement of December 5, 1968):

"Every director has a fiduciary obligation not to reveal any privileged information to anyone not authorized to receive it. Not until there is full public disclosure of such data, particularly when the information might have a bearing on the market price of the securities, is a director released from the necessity of keeping information of this character to himself. Any director of a corporation who is a partner, officer or employee of a member organization, should recognize that his first responsibility in this area is to the corporation on whose board he serves. Thus, a [registrant] director must meticulously avoid any disclosure of inside information to his partners and employees of the firm, his customers or his research or trading departments.

"Where a representative of a [registrant] is not a director but is acting in an advisory capacity to a company and discussing confidential matters, the ground rules should be substantially the same as those that apply to a director. Should the matter require consultation with other personnel of the organization adequate measures should be taken to guard the confidential nature of the information to prevent its misuse within or outside of the [registrant firm]."

The statement warns that continued fitness for registration will be measured in terms of the standards set out in the above quotation.

[138]For a broad ranging discussion of this and related problems see M. Hershmann, "An Overview—Regulation of Securities and the Securities Markets: A Timely Report to the Bar" (1972-3), 28 The Business Lawyer, 375 at pp. 378-9.

[139]Uniform Policy 2-07, "Surrender of Registration—Other than Salesmen", CCH vol. 2, para. 54-877.

[140]*Wisener, MacKellar & Co., Ltd. & C.R. Wisener & the Application of Steen and Van Silfhout*, Nov. 1973 OSCB 181, applying the principle of *Re Cambrian Realty Corp. Ltd. et al. and Registrar, Real Estate and Business Brokers*, [1973] 3 O.R. 593, 37 D.L.R. (3d) 516 (Div. Ct.).

through 20 of the Act,[141] which are exemptions solely from the registration requirement; these are called "pure registration exemptions". There are other exemptions (called "double exemptions") in s. 19 which through the added effect of s. 58[142] also serve as exemptions from the distribution requirements. These "double exemptions", as well as certain provisions in s. 58 which are "pure distribution exemptions", will be discussed in detail in chapter 4. For a complete synopsis therefore of exemptions from registration, reference should be had not only to the discussion of pure registration exemptions in this chapter but also to the treatment of double exemptions in chapter 4.[143]

The pure registration exemptions in ss. 18 and 19 have been arranged in certain logical groupings. Section 18[144] contains certain exemptions from the requirement of registration as an adviser, the basis of qualification being, for the most part the professional occupation of the party involved. Section 19[145] contains two general types of exemptions from the requirement of being registered to trade. The first deals with *trades* which because of their peculiar nature or the parties involved do not require registration for one or both of the parties to the trade. In the second type of exempt situation, the focus is on the type of *securities* involved in the trade. The underlying rationale for the securities exemption embraces such factors as the sophistication of one or both of the parties, which may indicate that they have no need for the information in the prospectus ("need to know test"), the high investment quality of certain types of securities (in some instances the result of a government guarantee), considerations of business efficiency and ' finally the realization that some trading occurs on such a small scale that regulation would be unduly burdensome and not worth the protection obtained. Since these securities exemptions are all double exemptions, they are not discussed further in this chapter.

3.16 Exceptions for Chartered Banks from Underwriter Registration

Chartered banks are presently excepted from the requirement of registering as underwriters.[146] Bill 20 removes this exception. As a substitute it simply excludes a chartered bank from the definition of underwriter where it is involved in trades of certain government guaranteed debt securities or those issued by banks, loan, trust or insurance companies. The deletion of the blanket exemption may invite constitutional litigation. The banks will probably contend that underwriting may be included as a banking activity and thus is

---

[141]Bill 20, ss. 33 to 35.
[142]Bill 20, ss. 73 and 74.
[143]For a clear and precise discussion of exemptions under the Act, see P.J. Dey, "Exemptions under The Securities Act".
[144]Bill 20, s. 33.
[145]Bill 20, s. 35. Bill 20, s. 34, contains provisions for exempting investment clubs, trust companies etc. from having to register as mutual funds if they fulfil certain conditions.
[146]Section 6(1)(d).

exclusively regulated by the federal government under the Bank Act;[147] the provinces will respond that underwriting is part of the securities business and if the banks wish to continue carrying on this activity they must register as underwriters under the provincial act.[148]

Returning to the Act, it is not certain whether the exception from underwriter registration would permit a bank to deal with the public in the distribution of an issue it was helping to underwrite or whether it would be limited to non-public activities in connection with the underwriting. The question depends on whether a broad or narrow interpretation is given to the phrase "acting as an underwriter".[149] If it does not include trading with the public, it follows that the bank and those of its employees so dealing with the public require registration as dealer and salesmen respectively under the Act.[150]

3.17 Exemptions from Adviser Registration

Exemptions from adviser registration are grouped into four categories.[151] The first grants exemption to certain "otherwise regulated financial institutions". On the federal side are banks chartered under the Bank Act (Canada)[152] and the Industrial Development Bank incorporated under the Industrial Development Bank Act (Canada),[153] both of which are regulated by federal statute. Then there are loan and trust companies registered under the Loan and Trust Corporations Act[154] and insurance companies licensed under the Insurance Act,[155] all of which are governed by provincial statutes. The reason for exempting the chartered banks and the industrial development bank is in part to avoid sensitive constitutional issues.[156] In addition, from a pragmatic standpoint there is a recognition that their activities are already heavily regulated and thus do not need the overlapping regulation of the Act; it is this latter rationale which is solely applicable in the case of the loan corporations, trust companies and insurance companies.[157]

---

[147]R.S.C. 1970, c. B-1.

[148]The British North America Act 1867, 30 & 31 Victoria, c. 3, s. 91(15) reserves exclusively to the Federal Parliament the regulation of banking. The issue is what is comprehended by the term banking. Unhappily there is little jurisprudence to assist in determining which banking activities do not fall within provincial securities jurisdiction. *White v. Bank of Toronto*, [1953] O.R. 479, [1953] 3 D.L.R. 118 (C.A.) gave a generous interpretation to banking activity, holding that the Bank Act did not limit a bank from dealing in shares of its corporate debtor when those shares were not collateral. See generally, I.F.G. Baxter, *The Law of Banking*, 2nd ed. (Toronto, Carswell, 1968), pp.4-5, 196-198.

[149]See, *supra*, footnote 16.

[150]Unless the exemption for certain "bank" trades expressed in s. 19(1)3 obviates the need for such registration. See, *infra*, part 3.18(3).

[151]Bill 20, s. 33(e), adds a fifth category of "management company".

[152]R.S.C. 1970, c. B-1.

[153]R.S.C. 1970, c. I-9.

[154]R.S.O. 1970, c. 254.

[155]R.S.O. 1970, c. 224.

[156]See, *supra*, part 3.16 for the discussion of this issue in connection with banks as underwriters.

[157]Federally chartered loan corporations, or trust or insurance companies

The second category of exemption is based on professional occupation and relieves from the registration requirement "a lawyer, accountant, engineer or teacher, whose performance of such services is solely incidental to the practice of his profession". These occupations are not defined in the Act nor is the word "profession". To determine whether someone is within one or other of these groups, the primary test is whether that person is licensed by one of the professional organizations to which licensing and accreditation powers have been granted by the provincial government.

No interpretation has been given to the words "solely incidental". The clear situations can easily be identified. For example, an accountant auditing the financial statements of an industrial company which has invested surplus funds in shares or debt obligations may apply some recognized standards to the investment or speculative quality of those investments in establishing their value or setting up a reserve for loss in their value at some future time, particularly if there is not a ready market for them to which reference might be had for valuation purposes. Although the application of such standards may not amount to advising, a further suggestion by the accountant that "nonconforming" investments be traded off and replaced by conforming investments (particularly if he insists on his valuation criteria being followed before he will give a clean opinion of the client's financial statements) is probably advice. However admonitions that go no further than this may be reasonably regarded as solely incidental to the exercise of a professional function. On the other hand if the same accountant actively takes over the management of his client's investments and recommends a sale of all of the speculative securities followed by an investment in specific quality securities, the whole portfolio to be monitored by himself in return for financial remuneration, he is no longer advising in a manner which is "solely incidental" to his professional function.[158]

A third category exempts persons or companies already registered for trading in securities, either as dealer—including in this the classes in the Regulation—or as underwriter, and any partner, officer or employee of such registered firm. Again the performance of the services must be solely incidental to the conduct of the business for which registration has been obtained. In this category, however, the words "solely incidental" are rather more difficult to understand. One would expect a principal function of a broker (registered as a dealer), or any of its employees (registered as salesmen), to be that of advising with respect to the quality of securities in the light of the investment needs of particular clients.

---

which have been chartered in another jurisdiction outside Ontario, must be registered or licensed under the appropriate Act to carry on business in Ontario.

[158]It appears that there are certain anomalies in this area, however. For example, in the case of lawyers, it seems that the compensation fund maintained by the profession's governing body and the compulsory insurance program in which its members are enrolled will not compensate a client for moneys he has lost by following his lawyer's advice on securities investments, whether or not the advice was given as solely incidental to the practice.

The final category of exemption is extended to certain publishers. Here the description of publishers who qualify has been given rather elaborate drafting. The provision exempts only a publisher

"...of any *bona fide* newspaper, news magazine or business or financial publication of general and regular paid circulation distributed only to subscribers thereto for value or to purchasers thereof, who gives advice as an adviser only through such publication and has no interest either directly or indirectly in any of the securities upon which the advice is given and receives no commission or other consideration for giving the advice and who gives the advice as solely incidental to the conduct of his business as a publisher..."[159]

All of the individual points listed above must be satisfied by a publisher to obtain the benefit of the exemption. Examining some of these in order, there is first of all the stipulation that the publication must have a general and regular paid circulation, and that it must be sold for value rather than given away free of charge. The exempting criteria are thus more concerned with the manner in which the advice is given than with the substantive characteristics of the publication in question. The advice must be given only through the publication and not additionally in some other format. The publisher must have no interest in any of the securities with respect to which the advice is given, must receive no commission or other consideration for the advice, and once again must satisfy the solely incidental test. This last requirement presents the same interpretation difficulties discussed in the case of registered dealers: the opinions of the publisher of a financial newspaper specializing in investments and the financial markets can only with difficulty be construed as "incidental" to his work. The prohibition of any interest—directly or indirectly—in any of the securities for which the advice is given also creates difficulties. A rigorous interpretation of this prohibition would require that the publisher either ensure that he has no interest whatever—material or non-material—in the securities discussed, or that no such discussion takes place with respect to securities in which he has an interest.

The latter course would seem impossible, whereas the former course is not the practice at the present time of many well-remunerated publishers. Furthermore, there is a definitional problem with regard to the term "publisher". It could conceivably mean the individual

---

[159]Section 18(d). Bill 20, s. 33(d) adds the words "or any writer for" after "a publisher of". It has been suggested that the solely incidental exemption should be drafted to include radio and television broadcasters whose commentary on the market and specific securities may technically put them in breach of the Act (P. J. Dey, "Exemptions under The Securities Act", p. 171). Perhaps the exemption should also extend to spokesmen of government regulatory agencies or officials of the various self-regulatory bodies. At a time when there is a great deal of speculative trading with substantial use of margin provisions, an official of the exchange, for example, may issue a public statement suggesting that the public exercise caution in connection with the speculative securities of all high-risk exploration ventures with activities in a certain district considered to be a "hot prospect"; he may indeed go so far as to single out one or two companies. Clearly the official is giving advice, but without technically being registered to do so. For an example see, *post,* chapter 10, at footnote 27.

actually writing the column giving the advice, the publisher of the newspaper or journal, or the entity which owns and publishes the paper, whether corporation, partnership or sole proprietorship. It is this third interpretation which raises the greatest problems. A strict interpretation of the prohibition of direct or indirect interests might, for example, prevent the firm's pension fund from purchasing securities of any kind or even preclude a trust company or other administrator from managing it. The investment of any surplus cash would also seem to be precluded; apparently it would have to be kept as a bank deposit.

A final provision exempts from the adviser registration requirement, such other persons or companies as are designated by the Regulation.[160] None have been promulgated.[161]

3.18 Exemptions from Trading Registration Generally

In this section we consider what we have earlier termed "pure registration exemptions", those which by their nature are not also exemptions from the distribution requirements. These are defined in terms of situations which are types of or are in the nature of trades.

(1) ADMINISTRATIVE OFFICIALS

The first is an exemption for a trade at a judicial sale by an official in any one of a number of recognized administrative proceedings. The persons who qualify are "an executor, administrator, guardian or committee or...an authorized trustee or assignee, an interim or official receiver or a custodian...receiver...or liquidator" performing certain functions under various statutes.[162] The trades involved are not continuous and are limited only to the disposal of the estate or other corpus being handled by the administrator. Their nature is such that, given the public position of the party engaged in transacting them, an exemption from the registration requirement is warranted.

(2) ISOLATED TRADE

The next exemption concerns "an isolated trade in a specific security by or on behalf of the owner, for the owner's account...".[163] With the exception of the registrant's exemption,[164] it is the most frequently used and one of the least understood. There are two additional qualifications which narrow somewhat its scope: the trade must not be

---

[160]Section 18(e) (Bill 20, s. 33(f)).

[161]Bill 20 adds s. 34, which concerns exemptions of mutual funds from registration. The section provides that registration as a mutual fund is not required by an investment club if certain conditions are met (the shares are not held by more than 50 people, it does not pay fees under a management contract, all members contribute in proportion to the shares each holds), by a trust company registered under the Loan and Trust Corporations Act in the case of certain types of pooled or common trust funds, by insurance companies licensed under the Insurance Act, and by such other persons or companies as are designated by the Regulation.

[162]Section 19(1)1 refers to the Bankruptcy Act, R.S.C. 1970, c. B-3; the Judicature Act, R.S.O. 1970, c. 228; the Corporations Act, R.S.O. 1970, c. 89; the Business Corporations Act, R.S.O. 1970, c. 53 and the Winding-up Act, R.S.C. 1970, c. W-10. Bill 20, s. 35(1)1.

[163]Section 19(1)2 (Bill 20, s. 35(1)2).

[164]Section 19(1)7.

"made in the course of continued and successive transactions of a like nature", and it must not be made by one "whose usual business is trading in securities".

The term "isolated" with no other contextual factors would mean "one" or "single". It must be viewed, however, within a time dimension. One trade in one year would be isolated with respect to that year. However, if the time period under examination is reduced to one month or one business week or two consecutive trading days, the exemption becomes remarkably broader. The next question then is what is the appropriate time frame. The desire to avoid too short a period being chosen is probably the reason for the first qualifying phrase barring a trade made "in the course of continued and successive transactions of a like nature", although one is still left with the question of how a continued and successive pattern is shown.

R. v. McKillop[165] gives some guidance. There the defendant was convicted both of unlawful trading in securities without registration as a dealer or salesman and of unlawful trading in securities through engaging in primary distribution to the public without a prospectus. The accused offered three defences. The first, directed to the count of trading without registration, was that the sales fell within the exemption of an "isolated" trade as being occasional transactions only. There had in fact been at least ten trades over approximately twenty months in which the accused was "vitally interested financially and during the course of which he took an actual part". All were in the securities of one company. The Provincial Court Judge found as a fact that these trades were not isolated and elaborated:[166]

"In my opinion something that is isolated is kept alone. In other words, an isolated trade is a single transaction, the word 'isolated' connoting the singular as opposed to the plural.

"In my opinion as well the course of conduct of the accused as illustrated by the various sales indicated continued and successive transactions of a like nature. I would draw attention to the fact that in no case was a refusal to sell to any of the prospective purchasers received from the accused, but, rather, in every case he appeared to be a quite willing seller. After hearing the evidence of all the witnesses, and here I include the accused, I was left with the impression that while only certain sales were made, as proved in the evidence, the accused was open to all and any buyers who would be interested in purchasing shares from him."

Some assistance may also be sought in the fact that where rather similar but not precisely the same phraseology is used in another part of the Act, the term "isolated trade" is pluralized. In s. 58(2)(c), an exemption from the distribution requirement is created for securities listed on the TSE and distributed by "control persons" through the

---

[165][1972] 1 O.R. 164, 4 C.C.C. (2d) 390 (Prov. Ct.). See also *R. v. Malcolm and Olson* (1918), 13 A.L.R. 511, 42 D.L.R. 90, [1918] 2 W.W.R. 1081 (C.A.); *Canadian Bank of Commerce v. Johnson* (1926), 22 A.L.R. 346, [1926] 4 D.L.R. 248 (Alta. S.C.); affirmed 22 A.L.R. 346 at p. 356, [1926] 4 D.L.R. 1179 (C.A.) and *Re Western International Exploration Ltd.*, April 9 1974 QSCWS 8.

[166][1972] 1 O.R. 164 at p. 167.

Exchange "by way of isolated *trades* not made in the course of continued and successive transactions of a like nature". If that latter exception was deliberately expressed in terms of the plural so as to permit several trades, special significance may attach to the use of the singular form of the phrase in the exemption from registration.[167] At the least it would seem that the number of trades contemplated by the term "isolated trade" must be less than the several permitted by the term "isolated trades", whatever that latter number may be.

When can there be continued and successive transactions that are *not* of a like nature? Consider the following example. A person owning 100,000 shares of a company sells 80,000 of them today because he is approached by a buyer who is prepared to pay a substantial premium above the market price for such a large block. From the vendor's point of view this is an unsolicited sale induced by the prospect of a substantial premium. It may be, however, that now, having given up his position as a significant shareholder, he no longer wishes to retain an interest in the company. To effect the liquidation of his remaining holdings he enters the market and finds the bid at market price which will absorb the largest quantity of securities. Suppose that the market can handle only 15,000 of these shares. Must this sale take place in one transaction involving all 15,000 shares, or could they be put on the market to be sold off in pieces and still avoid falling back into the category of "successive transactions of a like nature"? There is a case for saying that this second trade is of a different nature from the first because it is one offered to the market at market price. Suppose further that the same vendor, fearing that a further trade on the market would be similar in nature to the second trade, then approaches another shareholder of the company and solicits a purchase by that shareholder at a price slightly below that prevailing in the market, thus disposing of his remaining 5,000 shares in the company. Arguably the third trade is again of a distinctly different nature. It is made to another shareholder who presumably has some knowledge about and confidence in the company, it is solicited by the vendor, the purchaser is induced to buy at a price below the market, and the transaction is off the market, therefore not appearing on the volume and price tape. Finally, the prime motive for the trade was that the buyer wanted out of his tag-end position, not for any reason that relates to the company's affairs, but rather because it was expedient in relation to the personal investment affairs to the vendor. However, despite the various grounds that exist for distinguishing between such transactions, the counsel of greatest prudence would suggest that only the first trade is exempt.

To qualify for this exemption the trade must be in a "specific" security. How narrowly the lines must be drawn in the definition of specific one can only conjecture. Clearly it would seem that it must be a security of one issuer, but could it combine debt obligations and shares, or preferred shares and common shares, or classes of preferred

---

[167]Note of course that this argument conflicts logically with that of the judge in *McKillop*, who felt that "isolated" in s. 19 means a single occurrence. If isolated in s. 58 means the same as in s. 19, this cannot be so.

shares, or indeed different series within a class of shares or debt obligations?

Finally, the trade must be by or on behalf of the owner of the security and for the owner's account. The use of the word "owner" gives rise to a rather thorny problem in this area. Is this exemption limited to sales of already outstanding shares or debt securities or is it wider so as to embrace in addition the issue by a corporation of previously unissued securities? It is submitted that the qualifying phrase "by or on behalf of the owner, for the owner's account" narrows the exemption to comprehend only transfers of already outstanding shares, on the premise that a corporation does not own its authorized but unissued capital. This view has been consistently adopted by courts and administrators in the U.S. when interpreting a similarly phrased exemption in a number of state statutes.[168]

---

[168]The Merger Study flatly states this narrower view (p. 77): "The isolated trade exemption in section 19(1)2 is of little assistance [to an issuer] when previously unissued securities are intended to be the consideration [for a business acquisition]...An issuer cannot own its authorized and unissued securities". The Quebec Securities Commission adopts a similar position in *Re Western International Explorations Ltd.*, Apr. 9, 1974 QSCWB 8. One respected Canadian writer, Professor W. H. Grover in his review of the Merger Report, (1971), 23 Administrative Law Review 309, labels this as an obvious error of law and prefers the wide interpretation. He suggests that the Merger Study must have been relying on the English case of *Re V.G.M. Holdings Ltd.*, [1942] Ch. 235, [1942] 1 All E.R. 224 (C.A.) in arriving at its conclusion, and that it has neglected the Ontario High Court case of *J.M.P.M. Enterprises Ltd. v. Danforth Fabrics (Humbertown) Ltd.*, [1969] 1 O.R.785, 4 D.L.R. (3d) 131 (H.C.). Professor Grover concludes that the *J.M.P.M.* case has overruled *Re V.G.M.* and stands as authority for the broader view.

It would seem, however, that neither case is authority for the interpretation of the exemption. Each construed the word "sales" or "purchases" in connection with an issue of shares, but did not deal directly with the question of whether a corporation owns its unissued shares. In *Re V.G.M.*, Lord Greene M.R. held that an issue of shares to a director was not a purchase by him so as to violate a prohibition in the U.K. Companies Act against the company providing financial assistance for "a purchase" of its shares. Since the U.K. Companies Act used the words "issue, subscription, allotment" when it wished to describe the issue by a company of previously unissued shares, it was open to his Lordship to suggest that the word purchase was not intended to cover such a situation. Using a more conceptual type of reasoning, he characterized the difference between an issue to a subscriber and a purchase from existing shareholders as the difference between the creation and the transfer of a chose in action. He concluded: "A chose in action implies the existence of some person entitled to the rights, which are rights in action as distinct from rights in possession, and until the share is issued, no such person exists."

In the *J.M.P.M.* decision the dispute centered around the construction of a lease, one provision of which gave the lessor the right to terminate the lease "if by sale or other disposition the control (of the lessee corporation) changes". Control did change through the issue by the corporation of additional previously unissued shares. Osler J. concluded that "sale or other disposition" did not refer exclusively to shares of the corporation but must also be applied to the word control, and, on the facts, control had changed by a transaction which involved a sale. He rejected the contention by the defence that the decision in *Re V.G.M.* gave authority to the position that the issue of treasury shares was not a sale, using as a basis the difference between British and Ontario corporations legislation. There were two instances where the Ontario statute (R.S.O. 1960, c. 71, s. 87(2)9 and s. 24(1)) used the word "purchase" in application to treasury shares. Moreover, the broad description of authorized capital in the Canadian Act carried with it the suggestion that there was no important difference between issued and unissued shares.

The two cases are at odds on the meaning of sale, and in view of the fact that it was the Ontario case which characterized an issue of previously unissued shares as a sale, it could be argued that the issuer therefore owns the shares so as to bring it within the exemption. In fact, however, the *J.M.P.M.* case did not really consider the question of whether the corporation owns its own treasury shares. (See also P.J. Dey, "Exemptions under the Securities Act of Ontario".)

The position of the OSC chairman in 1950 was that the narrow view of this exemption prevailed. He said (O.E. Lennox, "Securities Legislation and Administration", p. 83):

"These exemptions [from registration and prospectus requirements]...are of great practical importance. These exemptions are in keeping with democratic principles, otherwise for instance a person could not even sell his own securities without first ascertaining whether the issue was still qualified and without enlisting the services of a broker or dealer. A person is permitted to sell his own securities for two reasons. First, as the securities are already in the hands of the public, the sale is not made in the course of primary distribution and secondly, the transaction is an isolated transaction and accordingly exempted from the operation of the Act. On the other hand you may find a client suggesting that a company may meet a pressing obligation by issuing a block of stock to a creditor before the issue is qualified on the ground that it is an isolated transaction, but that is definitely primary distribution and the transaction is barred under the second main prohibition."

This is also the view adopted by Professor Williamson, with no consideration given to a possible contrary interpretation in *Securities Regulation in Canada*, p. 22:

"Isolated trades made by or on behalf of the owner of a security and not made in the 'course of continued and successive transactions' were also exempted. This left the security-holder free to dispose of his own securities so long as he did not make too much of a business of it...An issuer, of course, was required to register (as a broker)..., because the isolated trade exemption applied only to sales of a security-holder."

The same writer (*ibid.*, at p. 125) also states that "since Canadian companies are forbidden to purchase their issued securities, such a company could never be the 'owner' of securities of its own issue." In fact it has only been the purchase by a company of its common shares that has been precluded by the rule in *Trevor v. Whitworth* (1887), 12 App. Cas. 409, [1886-90] All E.R. Rep. 46 (H. of L.). Purchases of preferred shares and debt securities have been permissible. Moreover the BCA now permits an Ontario incorporated company to buy back its own common shares without necessarily cancelling the same. Probably that company owns the shares so purchased and comes within the exemption. Bill 20, s. 1(1), para. 12(ii) seems to recognize this by adding as a definition of distribution "a trade by or on behalf of an issuer in previously issued securities of that issuer which have been redeemed or purchased by or donated to that issuer".

A significant change effected by Bill 20, s. 73(1)(b) is to make the isolated trade exemption a double exemption, that is, an exemption from the distribution requirements also. This will provide relief for control persons. This change is in part intended to offset the reduction in exemptions from the

(3) REGULATED INDUSTRY

The next category in the series of registration exemptions depends on one of the parties to the trade being a member of an industry or involved in an activity already undergoing some degree of careful regulation. Those affected are chartered banks, the Industrial Development Bank, loan, trust and insurance companies, a government or a government agency, or officers thereof, or a company or person other than an individual who has obtained specific recognition by the Commission as an exempt purchaser.[169] When the designated person or company is the purchaser of the securities and has the requisite investment intent, that is to say is purchasing for investment rather than resale, this exemption is also an exemption from the distribution requirement. By way of contrast, the exemption from registration in respect of the trade requires only that the designated person be a party, whether as vendor or purchaser.[170]

(4) DEBT LIQUIDATION

The next category of trades which are exempted from registration embraces sales by a creditor of securities which have been deposited as security for a debt. Thus registration is not required for a trade

"... by or for the account of a pledgee, mortgagee or other encumbrancer for the purpose of liquidating a *bona fide* debt by selling or offering for sale a security pledged, mortgaged or otherwise encumbered in good faith as security for the debt."[171]

---

distribution requirements which will follow from the removal of the concept "public" from the definition of distribution.

[169]Section 19(1)3 (Bill 20, s. 35(1)3). Bill 20 changes this exemption somewhat to require that the persons or institutions listed be purchasing as a principal, and not just be a party to the trade. The exemption for parties recognized by the Commission as exempt purchasers is placed separately in s. 35(1)4. This is followed by s. 35(1)5, a registration exemption for a purchaser purchasing as principal, where the acquistion cost of the security is not less than $97,000. This is the equivalent of the old private placement exemption, s. 19(3) of the Act, except that the requirement of investment intent on the part of the purchaser has been deleted.

The requirement that the trade be one where the "regulated industry" purchases as principal and not simply as a party was aimed primarily at the banks, who interpret the existing exemption under the Act as permitting them to sell to the public free of registration in the distribution of a new issue or to act as agent for a customer in a secondary trade. The change in the Bill will require that the banks (and certain of their officers) obtain registration for such trades. The banks may resist this change on constitutional grounds. (See, *supra*, parts 3.16 and 3.17.) But some amelioration is allowed by s. 35(1)10, which exempts trades from the registration requirement where someone places an unsolicited order with a bank or trust company for execution by a registered dealer.

[170]Though the investment intent requirement in the distribution exemption precludes this exemption from being a true double exemption, it will be discussed in detail in chapter 4.

[171]Section 19(1)4. Bill 20, s. 35(1)7 substitutes the more precise words "as collateral for" for "as security for". Note that the initial pledge by a control person under Bill 20, s. 1(1), para. 40(iv) will be a trade. While a specific exemption for such a pledge (s. 35(1)6) or the isolated trade exemption (s. 35(1), (2)) will free it from registration, an insider trading report will ordinarily be required.

This exemption is based on commercial expediency. It is assumed that debt liquidations will not amount to a substantial part of securities trading and that in larger sized transactions the liquidator will usually be an institution such as a bank which is already regulated to some degree. The double *bona fide* requirement (covering both the debt and the encumbrance) is inserted to ensure that the securities were first placed as collateral for a valid debt and not to masquerade as a pledge with the real purpose of using the exemption. The aim is to prevent a clandestine sale being effected by means of a purported debtor-creditor transaction in which the "debtor" pledges securities with the "creditor" in return for payment, the intent being that the latter will resell the securities on the prearranged staging of an event of default.

(5) REGISTRANT'S EMPLOYEES

The next exemption is designed as a matter of accommodation for certain employees of a registered firm who are designated by the director as non-trading, whether the designation is given to individuals or to a class of employees.[172] The exemption only applies if the trade is one that "may occasionally be transacted" by such employees and "where they do not usually sell securities to the public" and have obtained the "non-trading" designation. These phrases present interpretive difficulties similar to those encountered with the isolated trade exemption.

(6) EXEMPTION BY REGULATION

Finally there is an exempting provision for a "trade in respect of which the regulations provide that registration is not required";[173] no trades have been so designated in Ontario to this date.[174] It should be noted that all fourteen categories of exemption from registration are subject to the Regulation and could be significantly affected by order-in-council.

3.19 Mutual Fund Industry

No survey of the licensing process would be complete without a separate consideration of the mutual fund industry. Until the introduction of Bill 20 and its predecessor bills there was little legislative recognition of the fact that mutual funds have particular problems of their own. Basically these funds issue their securities to the public and invest the amounts so raised in a portfolio of securities designed to spread risk. The purchaser is granted a right to be redeemed at his option at a price equal to his proportionate interest in the current value of the portfolio. At the present the distinct legislative recognition accorded to mutual funds has been limited to the establishment of a separate dealer classification—mutual fund dealer—as set out in the Regulation, with specialized capital requirements, a separate prospectus form, and six accompanying national policy statements,

---

[172]Section 19(1)5 (Bill 20, s. 35(1)8).
[173]Section 19(1)11 (Bill 20, s. 35(1)19).
[174]The situation is otherwise in a number of other jurisdictions which use their regulation power where Ontario uses the Act.

along with a number of local policy statements. The national policy statements deal with such matters as sales changes, management fees, the computation of net asset value per share, forward pricing for sales and redemptions, the conditions of redemption and change in management or investment policies and several specialized requirements for financial statements.[175] Bill 20 includes many changes, the majority of which are only adumbrated in the legislation; substantial work will be required in the detailed drafting of regulations and the careful articulation of appropriate policy statements to serve as a guide for the industry replacing the current national policy statements 6 through 11, which will be superseded with the passage of the Bill. These changes are almost entirely the result of recommendations in the report of the Canadian Committee on Mutual Funds and Investment Contracts, a provincial and federal study released in 1969. The report is unique, at least in the securities regulation field, in that it was sponsored jointly by the Federal Government and the ten provincial Governments.[176]

The purpose of this study was to consider the adequacy of regulation of the Canadian mutual fund industry and the related investment contract industry and make recommendations accordingly.[177] A number of factors influenced the decision to commence such a study. First

---

[175]Chapter 4, footnote 57, *post.*

[176]Hereinafter in this book the "Mutual Funds Report", and in the remainder of this chapter, "the Report". Since a not inconsiderable number of the recommendations in the Report affecting participants in the mutual fund industry are concerned with the conditions of registration, the present chapter would seem to be the appropriate point for a brief initial summary of its contents. Frequent reference will be had to relevant portions of the Report throughout this book where its discussion and recommendations bear on matters of securities regulation in general and more particularly on the mutual fund industry in aspects apart from licensing.

The Federal Government contributed one-half of the costs of the study. Each of the provinces paid the balance according to a formula based on the amount of personal disposable income in each province (Backgound Notes to the Report, p. 1). The proposals contained in the study have the status of recommendations only, submitted for the consideration of the governments of the sponsoring provinces, as well as of the industry and the public; they do not reflect government policy in any province. Nevertheless the fact that the document came from senior government officials charged with much of the responsibility for securities matters in six of the participating governments augured well for its acceptance.

[177]The initiative which led to its commissioning was taken by the Kimber Report in 1965 (Kimber Report, Appendix D, p. 92). The report referred to a number of briefs on mutual funds submitted to the Committee and also to some similarities between the mutual fund industry and other Canadian institutions offering savings programs to individuals such as life insurance and trust companies. It recommended a special study of mutual funds which should also review the relationship of their industry to those related institutions, observing that as a practical matter, it would be better for the new study to be conducted separately from the project on which the Kimber Committee was itself engaged. The recommendation was ratified at the October, 1965 conference of the Canadian Securities Administrators and the decision to proceed was taken in August 1966 at a meeting of the Prime Minister and provincial Premiers. The study committee was organized in November 1966,

was the remarkable growth of the mutual fund industry in Canada, the assets of which increased from $300,000,000 in 1957 to approximately $3.4 billion in 1968. By contrast the investment contract industry showed a much flatter growth rate, with contract liabilities creeping from about $320 million at the end of the 1962 to about $410 million at the end of 1967.[178] The Report estimated that as of its date of release (December 1969) more than one million Canadians held mutual fund shares or investment contracts.[179] A second factor was the lack of a uniform pattern of regulation in the mutual fund and directly related industries. Different government departments regulated various aspects of the industry, resulting in considerable overlapping, and in addition, some glaring gaps in the structure. A leading objective therefore of any movement for reform was to ensure that all aspects of the industry were subjected to a fair and appropriate form of regulation through an efficient co-ordination of regulatory activities between and within governments. A third factor undoubtedly was the fact that mutual funds have been largely covered by regulation in the U.S. since the passage of the Investment Contract Act of 1940, which is administered by the SEC. A number of studies analyzing the industry in the U.S., the most important of which was the Report to Congress on Investment Companies[180] published in 1966, revealed peculiar problems which required attention in the U.S. and, by inference, Canada as well.[181]

The proposals of the Report were many and varied. Some of the major ones are listed here. First of all it was suggested that the encouragement of competition in the industry rather than detailed government regulation should be the underlying philosophy of new legislation. In particular greater competiton should be encouraged by means of less uniformity in sales charges and management fees, less emphasis on luring salesmen from competing organizations, a decrease in the importance ascribed to short-term investment results, and a

---

at a meeting of the Federal-Provincial Conference of Officials on Financial Disclosure and Securities Regulation (Preface to the Report, p. iii).
[178]The Report, para. 17.13.
[179]Report Press Release, December 9, 1969.
[180]CCH Federal Securities Law Reporter, Special Studies 1963-1972, p. 65215.
[181]Although the study did not conduct public hearings, it was based on very substantial contact with the securities industry in general and the mutual fund industry in particlar. Besides having impressive financial support and a complete and well-organized staff, it profited from the frequent use of outside consultants and research surveys. The Committee took sufficient time (more than three years from its formation) to produce a careful and deliberate report with detailed reasoning to support its conclusions, which were accompanied by draft legislation. The result of all this effort will serve as a model for a subsequent study of major policy issues in Canada. Not the least of the achievements of the study was that it demonstrated the possibility of co-operation between the federal and provincial governments, and brought forward recommendations which show a high probability of achieving the goal of uniform or at least co-ordinated legislation and administration for the mutual fund industry throughout Canada. Bill 20 in Ontario reflects most of the legislative changes recommended by the Report.

prohibition on price fixing between distributors and sales agencies. The Report recommended that there be a simplified or short form prospectus, stating investment objectives and practices, costs of management and of purchase, and investment results for the previous five years, to be supplied to every offeree before any sales presentation was made. A full prospectus should be available if the purchaser so requests. Instalment plan purchases of mutual fund shares should have lower "front-end loading" of sales charges. Otherwise, if such charges absorb a high portion of the purchaser's payments in the early stages of his contractual plan, proportionately little will be available for investment resulting in a minimal return in the event of an early redemption.

The Report also contained suggestions for the development of greater public knowledge about mutual funds and investment contracts in order to render effective competition more feasible. It recommended specific regulatory requirements in the area of minimum capital, custodial arrangements, share-pricing procedures, insider trading and self-dealing transactions with persons associated with the fund. The Report placed heavy emphasis on administrative discretion as a tool to be employed by securities administrators and suggested incorporating greater flexibility into the regulatory system. In particular the licensing system should permit a salesman to sell more than one product (for example mutual funds and life insurance); it should allow unsolicited house calls by mutual fund salesmen and the wider use of part-time salesmen; and provision should be made for the operation of "funds on funds", *i.e.,* mutual funds that invest in the shares of other mutual funds. As a move to stimulate greater flexibility in investment practices, it was proposed that a division be created between conventional and non-conventional funds.[182]

As indicated the Report emphasized the need for administration at a national level in order to secure uniform regulation—whether by co-ordination between existing provincial administration, federal-provincial co-operation or complete federal regulation; understandably it gave little specific guidance as to how such uniformity might in fact be achieved. The federal-provincial nature of the Report, which meant in this case the involvement of all ten provinces, was in itself a considerable step towards the goal of a nation-wide co-ordination of effort. The Report also envisaged the technique of self-regulation playing a large role, but acknowledged that the self-regulatory agencies already existing in the field had not yet reached the level, even as established by minimum criteria, at which there could be delegation to them by government agencies of the full range of regulatory responsibilities enjoyed by similar bodies in other areas in the securities industry.[183]

We may turn now to examine the proposed implementation of the Report, as far as the licensing requirement is concerned, in Bill 20. The proposed definition of the term "mutual fund" recognizes two chief

---

[182]Even "non-coventional" funds, however, would be restrained from certain hazardous investment practices such as short selling, pending the anticipated development of a greater level of public sophistication.

[183]See chapter 10.

features: an interest in a variable portfolio of assets and the ability to obtain redemption on demand. It reads:[184]

"mutual fund includes an issuer of securities that entitle the holder to receive on demand, or within a specified period after demand, an amount computed by reference to the value of a proportionate interest in the whole or in a part of the net assets, including a separate fund or trust account, of the issuer of such securities."

The new legislation avoids focusing on only one aspect of the process by which mutual fund shares or units are created and delivered to the public. Instead Bill 20 recognizes four distinct elements in the industry and requires registration of all four. These are the mutual fund or mutual fund issuer, the management companies who through a contractual arrangement with the mutual fund issuer provide investment advice and administrative services, the distribution companies (termed mutual fund dealers in the current Regulation) who distribute mutual funds securities either on a lump sum or contractual plan basis, and finally contractual plan companies who receive the money from a purchaser of mutual funds on a contractual plan, forward it to the issuer and receive the securities on the purchaser's behalf.[185]

The Commission will be given a discretion to determine whether new kinds of instruments which are substantially similar to mutual funds should require registration as mutual funds. The regulations will include as conditions of registration a number of matters affecting the mutual fund such as bonding requirements, the right to inspect records, custody of fund assets, capital requirements, minimum subscriptions (including the consequences of reducing the capital below the minimum required and the power to apply for the appointment of a receiver). It is to be anticipated that some matters already dealt with in national policies affecting mutual funds will find their way into the regulations as conditions of registration. These may include provision for registration of redemptions, and a definition and method of calculation of "net asset value per share" to determine offering and redemption prices. Other conditions precedent to registration which one would expect in the regulations are a right of the security holder to vote on changes of management or distribution contracts, major changes in investment policy and a change of auditors.

Bill 20 also requires registration of mutual fund management companies, defined[186] to mean: "a person or company that provides investment advice, under a management contract." Perhaps unnecessarily, the Bill exempts management companies from the requirement of obtaining registation as an adviser.[187] It also defines management contract as:[188]

---

[184]Section 1(1)25.
[185]Sections 1(1)25, 20, 8 and 7 respectively. Section 24 of Bill 20 does not have a separate registration requirement for distribution companies but these must register as dealers (s. 24(1)(a)); they will fall into the category of "mutual fund dealer" in s. 2(1)4 of the current Regulation.
[186]Section 1(1)20.
[187]Section 33(e).
[188]Section 1(1)21.

"a contract under which a mutual fund is provided with investment advice, alone or together with administrative or management services, for valuable consideration."

One may anticipate that the substantive requirements affecting such companies will be found as conditions of registration. The latter will include bonding, the carrying of required insurance, a minimum investment in the mutual fund being managed, and biennial approval of the management company by securities holders of the funds for which it acts. Included in this approval will be the stipulation of maximum management fees.

The term "distribution company" is rather uninformatively defined as: "a person or company distributing securities under a distribution contract".[189]

The conditions of registration affecting the mutual fund dealer will probably have to be amended to encompass the distribution contract, which is defined in the Bill as:[190]

"a contract between a mutual fund or its trustees or other legal representative and a person or company under which that person or company is granted the right to purchase the shares or units of the mutual fund for distribution or to distribute the shares or units of the mutual fund on behalf of the mutual fund."

The conditions of registration for such companies will include bonding and insurance requirements, adequate provision for the inspection of records and restrictions with respect to when a plan may be entered into. Additional provisions are expected to deal with the appropriate procedures for handling securities, the commission load on plans and the making available of information to plan holders on a continuing basis.

Investment clubs meeting specified criteria, certain pooled or common trust funds of trust companies, and licensed insurance companies are exempted from the requirement of obtaining registration as mutual funds.[191] The three qualifying requirements for the investment club exemption are:

(1) its shares or units are held by not more than 50 persons;

(2) it does not pay or give any remuneration under a management contract or in respect of any trade in securities except normal brokerage fees; and

(3) all of its members are required to make contributions in proportion to the shares or units each holds for the purpose of investment.

All three criteria must be met.[192]

---

[189]Section 1(1)13.

[190]Section 1(1)14.

[191]Section 34.

[192]The 50 persons test is familiar from its use as the limiting number for the private company (see the definition of private company in Bill 20, s. 1(1)30). However, by using the word "persons" rather than "individual", it contains the same potential problems as the private company test. For example, 60 individuals might form themselves into a partnership or unincorporated association and cause that partnership or association to hold the share or unit, thus taking up only one of the total permitted number of 50 persons (see the definition of person in s. 1(1)12; s. 1(1)27 in Bill 20). This new exemption will

Finally, s. 34(d) exempts such other persons and companies as are designated by the Regulation.

---

provide welcome relief for the small *bona fide* investment club consisting of a group of friends, all of whom as the law stands are trading with one another (and violating the registration requirements of the Act) simply by the creation of participation units in the club for each member, particularly if those units are somehow documented. Reducing the arrangement to writing or a written certificate of some kind would clearly bring the document within the definition of security. The requirement that contributions should be in proportion to the units held, and thus not necessarily equal, is designed to accomodate a club in which some members are more affluent than others. The difficulties which investment clubs at present experience are illustrated by the case of *Hawkesbury Golf and Curling Ltd.*, July 1968 OSCB 161.

Chapter 4
Distribution

4.01 Types of Distribution—The Functional Framework

There is no typical example of distribution of a security to the public. One example is provided by the small family-owned company with a stable earnings history over the past few years, a proven product and capable management, which is anxious to expand and requires substantial increments of capital. It decides to raise this capital by selling some of its shares to the public through an underwriter. If the company's growth and need for capital continue, it may effect a number of subsequent distributions of the same sort so that eventually its securities become widely held, with many institutions and individuals looking to their investments in these securities for a profitable return. And if capital needs of the enterprise over that period have been both substantial and complex, it may have outstanding several categories of debt obligation—bonds, debentures and notes; these may be further subdivided into classes and series with different maturities and interest rates. The firm's equity capital structure may also be variegated, with several classes of preferred shares resting on a common share base.

The Act requires a prospectus to be qualified with the Commission before a "distribution to the public" may take place.[1] All provincial securities jurisdictions have this requirement; so does the CCA (though not the CBCA) for federally incorporated companies.[2] However, where the company must qualify a prospectus in another jurisdiction, it is sufficient for the purposes of the CCA if that prospectus is simply deposited with the federal department.[3] However, before examining the mechanics of prospectus obligations and exemptions, it may be helpful to examine briefly the characteristics of the different types of distribution which occur in practice.[4] There are three

---

[1]Section 35 (Bill 20, s. 54). Bill 20 speaks only of distribution; the concept of public has been dropped.
[2]Section 76.
[3]Section 78. The CBCA (s. 186) recognizes that the "deposit exemption" in s. 78 makes the s. 76 federal prospectus qualifying provision a dead letter and therefore drops it.
[4]For a more detailed treatment of this subject see for example, the OSC Industry Ownership Study, chapter 4; The Moore Report, chapter 2; J.P. Williamson, *Securities Regulation in Canada*, chapter 11; the Porter Report, chapters 16 and 17; C.C. Potter, *Finance and Business Administration in Canada*, 2nd ed. (Toronto, Prentice Hall, 1970), chapters 20, 21, and 23. For English and U.S. practice see L.C.B. Gower, *Modern Company Law*, 3rd ed. (London, Stevens, 1969), chapter 14, and Loss, *Securities Regulation*, chapter 2. Several U.S. court cases provide most illuminating detail on the underwriting process, including *U.S. v. Morgan* (1953), 118 F. Supp. 621 (U.S. Dist. Ct., S.D.N.Y.); *Escott v. BarChris Construction Corp.*(1968), 283 F. Supp. 643 (U.S. Dist. Ct., S.D.N.Y.) and in connection with the latter, "Proceedings,

main functional categories: the direct issue, the offer to sell, and the best efforts "underwriting".

(1) DIRECT ISSUE

The direct issue is the simplest distribution to understand. It is the most difficult to effect if the issue is large and the issuer relatively unknown. In a direct issue the company or person proposing to sell its securities, called the "issuer", does so by making direct contact with potential purchasers of its securities, without the services of an investment dealer or broker. This procedure will be most successful where a small group of purchasers who have intimate knowledge of the company's affairs can absorb the entire issue. A frequent example is a rights issue by a company to its shareholders. The company offers existing shareholders an opportunity to purchase newly issued shares, usually on a basis which enables each shareholder to maintain his proportionate holding in the company.

Another method of direct issue is the private placement of securities with one or more institutional purchasers. In order to arrange the transaction, the issuer negotiates with the investor either directly or through an investment dealer who participates on a purely agency basis. Under the Act such placements receive exemption from the registration and prospectus requirements if the purchaser agrees to take the securities for investment and not with a view to resale or distribution. Formerly this method was employed almost exclusively in the case of debt securities held by the purchaser to maturity, but more recently substantial blocks of shares have been issued in this manner.

(2) OFFER TO SELL

In the offer to sell, the issuer negotiates a firm underwriting agreement with an investment dealer. The latter agrees to purchase all of the securities of the issuer for resale to purchasers whom he locates through his own business resources. The dealer's profit results from his purchasing the securities from the issuer at a discount from the price at which he will offer them for sale to his purchasers; the difference is referred to as the underwriter's "spread". The phrase "firm underwriting" requires explanation. The transaction is firm in the sense that the investment dealer is committed to purchase the securities from the issuer, subject to any escape or "market out" clauses included in the underwriting agreement, and the issuer is thus assured of receiving the amount agreed to between it and the underwriter. By contrast underwriting in the literal or classic sense is based on an insurance principle whereby the underwriter only becomes obliged to purchase securities from the issuer if members of the public do not purchase the entire issue, and even then only that part of the issue not taken up by the public. Derived from this classical type of underwriting is the modern device of a stand-by underwriting. Here an investment dealer agrees to step in and purchase the unsold balance (or some fixed amount) if the selling efforts of the issuer, or the dealer, or other brokers do not result in the distribution of the entire issue. Stand-by

---

National Institute 'The BarChris Case: Prospectus Liability' " (1969), 24 The Business Lawyer 523.

underwriting is very often coupled with a rights issue of the sort discussed earlier as a form of direct issue.

The techniques used in firm underwritings have become very sophisticated and complex with a view to minimizing the risk of an unsuccessful issue. In the case of a very large offering the underwriter may join as his associates one or several other investment dealers who will contract directly with the issuer to buy the securities. The liability of this "purchase group" may be joint and several or, alternatively, several only with each member of the purchase group being obligated to take no more than a fixed percentage. Normally one underwriter (the "lead" or "managing" underwriter) will act on behalf of the purchase group in dealing with the issuer; he will do the negotiating, sign the underwriting agreement and prepare the necessary documentation.

Whether or not the lead underwriter chooses to form a purchase group, he will invariably, in an issue of any significant size, assemble a number of other investment dealers to join what is known as a banking group. Under this arrangement the underwriter (or the purchase group if the lead underwriter has formed such) will contract with other investment dealers, each of whom agree to take some fixed percentage of the issue from the lead or managing underwriter. Places in the banking group are taken according to a very competitive pecking order.

The purchasing underwriter, or the purchasing group if one is used, realizes its profit on the difference between the price it pays to the issuer for the securities and that for which it sells them. Thus it may pay the issuer $96 for a share which is sold to the public at $100. Where the share is sold to another member of the banking group, the lead underwriter will realize as profit the difference between what is paid for the share and what it receives for it from the banking group member. The remaining members of the banking group realize their profit on the basis of a slightly lower discount. They might, for example, purchase the same share from the lead underwriter or purchase group at $97 and sell to their public clients at $100. Since their risk is somewhat less than that of the purchase group, so their profit is less.

Finally the lead underwriter and the banking group may choose to form a "selling group", to ensure a wide-spread distribution of the issue to public clients. Such a group, when formed, could include all members of the Investment Dealers' Association (IDA). In the previous example the selling group members might buy a designated amount of the securities from the banking group at $98 and thus be liable as principals to pay for that amount. Selling group members would then resell them to the public at $100, thus realizing a $2 gross profit.

Occasionally the underwriting agreement results from competitive bidding for the issue by various dealers, or in response to public tender by the issuer. More commonly, however, the issuer simply negotiates directly with the dealer who has traditionally served as its fiscal agent. Some critics of practices in the Canadian industry have suggested more frequent competitive bidding or at least negotiations with several underwriters by a potential issuer would be desirable.

The "tombstone advertisement"[5] on the following page illustrates some of these points. It announces the distribution of $90,000,000 in securities of a trust and a related corporation. The two underwriters who constitute the purchase group, Dominion Securities Corporation Limited and A.E. Ames & Co. Limited, appear as the first names in the banking group, distinctly separated from the other members of the group. Dominion's name appears first, since it is the lead underwriter.

The names of those in the banking group are usually arranged in a distinct order. The higher the place in the list, the greater the amount of the issue which the particular member has agreed to "bank" or be liable for to the purchase group. The names of the selling group members do not appear here. In fact, on this issue every member of the IDA was included.

(3) BEST EFFORTS UNDERWRITING

In a best efforts underwriting a dealer contracts with the issuer to give his best efforts to sell the issue. The dealer expects to distribute the entire offering successfully, but does not agree to purchase the securities as principal; he therefore incurs no loss in the event of failure. His incentive is a commission from the issuer over and above the amount which he will receive from his purchasing clients for acting as broker on each sale. The best efforts type of underwriting has many variants. For example, an issue may be underwritten partially on a firm basis and partially on a best efforts basis. Or it may be an "all or nothing" arrangement under which the entire issue must be sold within a specified time before any commission is paid. On a rights issue by an issuer to its shareholders, a dealer may in the absence of a stand-by underwriting contract for an extra commission from the issuer for using his best efforts to encourage the sale of rights to shareholders or to other members of the public who are not shareholders.[6]

---

[5]This sombre sobriquet for a marketing technique draws its name from the fact that the securities laws impose severe restrictions on what preliminary advertisements may contain by way of a description of the issue, *viz.* only the barest essentials.

[6]A peculiar type of distribution technique has developed for the financing of junior natural resource issuers. It does not neatly fall into any one of the categories referred to above, but is almost invariably used in the more junior speculative type of exploration or resource development venture. The regulatory framework within which this financing takes place is described later in the chapter when dealing with prospectus qualifications. Resource financing was the base on which a much more sophisticated financial network was built up in Canada. It should be noted that some of the scandals in junior resource financing have had a profound influence on the shaping of Canadian securities law. For more detailed recent descriptions see the Windfall Report and the Beatty Report, and for an earlier account the Report of the Royal Commission on Mining, Toronto, 1944 ("Urquhart Report"). Finally, the stock exchanges in Canada are rather unique in permitting some types of distribution to take place through their facilities.

This advertisement is not to be construed as a public offering in any Province of Canada unless a prospectus relating thereto has been accepted for filing by a securities commission or similar authority in such province. The offering is made by the prospectus only and copies thereof may be obtained from such of the undersigned and other dealers as may lawfully offer these securities in such province.

New Issues

$90,000,000

consisting of

$40,000,000

BM-RT Realty Investments

(A trust created under the laws of the Province of Ontario)

4,000,000 Trust Units

Price: $10.00 per Trust Unit

Applications have been made to list the Trust Units on the Montreal, Toronto and Vancouver Stock Exchanges. Acceptance of the listings will be subject to the filing of required documents and evidence of satisfactory distribution, both within 90 days.

$50,000,000

BM-RT Ltd.

(Incorporated under the laws of the Province of Quebec)

6¼% Debentures

And Trust Unit Purchase Warrants

To be dated March 28, 1973   To mature April 1, 1978

Price: 100 and accrued interest, if any

Trust Unit Purchase Warrants in bearer form will be mailed to the holders of Debentures of record at the close of business on June 29, 1973, entitling the bearers to purchase Trust Units at the price of $12.50 per Trust Unit on or prior to April 1, 1978, on the basis of 20 Trust Units for each $1,000 principal amount of Debentures. Further particulars of the Warrants are set out in the prospectus.

A.E. Ames & Co. Limited

Dominion Securities Corporation Limited

Wood Gundy Limited
Greenshields Incorporated
Midland-Osler Securities Limited
Pitfield, Mackay, Ross & Company Limited
Burns Bros. and Denton Limited
Walwyn, Stodgell & Co. Limited
Mead & Co. Limited
Graham Armstrong Securities Ltd.
MacDougall, MacDougall & MacTier Ltd.

Richardson Securities of Canada
Fry Mills Spence Limited
Cochran Murray Limited
Lévesque, Beaubien Inc.
Harris & Partners Limited
R.A. Daly & Company Limited
Casgrain & Company Limited
C.J. Hodgson Securities Ltd.
Odlum Brown & T.B. Read Ltd.
Scotia Bond Company Limited   Tassé & Associés, Ltée

McLeod, Young, Weir & Company Limited
Nesbitt Thomson Securities Limited
Merrill Lynch, Royal Securities Limited
Bell, Gouinlock & Company Limited
Gairdner & Company Limited
Crang & Ostiguy Inc.
Cliche et Associés, Ltée
Houston, Willoughby and Company Limited
Pemberton Securities Limited

4.02 Regulation of Distribution

The starting point in the regulation of distribution is the prohibition contained in s. 35 of the Act. It bans trades which are in the course of distribution to the public unless both a preliminary prospectus and a prospectus are qualified with the Commission.[7] There are three key

---

[7]The distribution requirements of the other Canadian jurisdictions are substantially similar in that they insist upon a prospectus. However there are significant differences in form.

All of the uniform act provinces except British Columbia require a preliminary prospectus plus a prospectus for a distribution to the public. The Manitoba, Saskatchewan and British Columbia Acts use the older phraseology "primary distribution" whereas Alberta and Ontario have moved to the simpler concept "distribution": (British Columbia, s. 37; Manitoba, s. 35(1); Saskatchewan s. 42(1); Alberta, s. 35(1)).

In Quebec however the provisions are much different. Section 50 states "...no issue of securities shall...be the object of an initial sale...to the public before the Commission has permitted trading..." and s. 53 stipulates: "Every issue of securities which is subject to...section 50 must, unless the Commission otherwise determines, be accompanied by a...prospectus...".

The Atlantic Provinces have retained the old style of Act. In Nova Scotia (s. 12(1)) and Newfoundland (s. 13) trading in any security is not permitted until a registration statement has been filed. The registration statements require information similar to that found in prospectuses in the other provinces. In both provinces copies of prospectuses must be filed (s. 18(1) and s. 19).

In New Brunswick no person shall trade where such trade would be in the course of primary distribution, without first obtaining a certificate from the Board authorizing such trading (s. 13(1)). Section 13(3) requires filing of a prospectus where the securities are those of a mining company, industrial company or investment company.

In Prince Edward Island no person shall trade until he has the written consent of the Registrar (s. 8) and copies of prospectuses must be filed (s. 12).

In the Northwest (s. 23) and Yukon (s. 23) Territories no person shall trade in any security issued by a mining company, investment company or industrial company unless, among other things, a prospectus is filed. The companies legislation of some of the provinces also provides for the filing of prospectuses, though deferring to securities legislation for their qualification.

The CCA provides that securities shall not be offered to the public unless a prospectus has been filed (s. 76(1)). But a subsequent provision (s. 78(1)) permits the company to file a prospectus qualified in another jurisdiction when it offers its securities in "any province or foreign country" in satisfaction of the requirement, subject to an overriding discretion in the Minister (s. 78(4)) to insist on a CCA prospectus where he deems it in the public interest. The CBCA (s. 186) drops the prospectus qualification provision altogether, simply requiring that a prospectus qualified in another jurisdiction be deposited with the director. The result of the CBCA change is that no control is exercised through prospectus qualification when a federal company distributes offshore in a jurisdiction which lacks securities regulation laws. A few situations where unscrupulously managed enterprises obtain Canadian incorporation to exploit this lack of control and foreign investors are consequently victimized could tarnish the image of Canadian corporations generally in foreign eyes.

Ontario, British Columbia, Manitoba, New Brunswick, and Prince Edward Island companies legislation no longer requires prospectuses to be filed, leaving that responsibility entirely to securities law and raising the same problem for offshore distributions referred to in the case of the CBCA. But the

concepts in this comprehensive prohibition: "trade", "distribution" and "public". The first of these, "trade", was discussed earlier.[8] It will be remembered that "trade" is all-encompassing in its scope. It includes not only an offer, a solicitation and an invitation to treat, but also any acts in furtherance of the foregoing.

(1) DISTRIBUTION

One term of wide import·is succeeded by another: the prohibition extends to trades in the "course of distribution". This phrase both anticipates and extends beyond the central act of distribution, the actual sale of a newly-issued security to a member of the public, and when taken together with "trade", operates to subject a whole range of activities to the requirements of the section.[9] In particular the concluding portion of the definition of distribution, which expressly mentions trades to underwriters, makes it clear that it is the entire process which is meant to be enjoined. Just when that first step is taken which triggers the operation of s. 35 is a matter of some conjecture. A literal interpretation would suggest that the first informal discussion with a potential underwriter by a company wishing to sell its securities generally would be in the course of a distribution: a distribution is contemplated and the discussion would constitute an act in furtherance thereof. Since the Act expressly exempts trades between an issuer and an underwriter (and between underwriters),[10] however, neither registration nor a prospectus is required. But the first discussion with a potential purchaser "to sound out the potential market" for a direct issue could be fixed upon as the first step in the course of the distribution, and there is no exemption which would cover discussions with public purchasers.

A more realistic view would suggest that only when a reasonably firm decision to effect the distribution has been made is an act part of a chain of events which is governed by the section. This interpretation would suggest that the "course of distribution" does not begin at least until the issuer and underwriter in an offer-to-sell underwriting have had some opportunity to discuss and decide upon important points of principle.

Saskatchewan Companies Act (s. 36(1)), requires a public company to file a prospectus when issuing shares in conjunction with "its formation or organization for business"; the Alberta Companies Act (s. 93(1)) and the Northwest Territories companies legislation (s. 85(3)) require all prospectuses other than preliminary prospectuses to be filed; and the Newfoundland Companies Act (s. 260(4)), requires public companies to file prospectuses. Nova Scotia takes a slightly different tack. Its Companies Act requires a prospectus complying with the Act to accompany securities distributions and requires a copy of the prospectus to be filed (ss. 92(8) and 91(2)). In Quebec, the Companies Information Act (s. 2(1)) requires a prospectus to be filed when any one of four circumstances occur, one of which is merely the establishment by a company of an office in the province.

[8]See, *ante*, part 1.12.

[9]Bill 20, s. 54 alters the "no trade in the course of a distribution to the public without a prospectus" provision. "Public" is deleted. Moreover, s. 54 speaks of a distribution rather than "in the course of distribution". "A distribution" may have a narrower ambit than "in the course of distribution".

[10]Sections 19(1)6 and 58(1)(c) (Bill 20, ss. 35(1)9 and 73(1)(o)).

Continuing the focus on distribution, the Act contains a two-pronged definition of "distribution to the public": the first branch relates to trades by an issuer of newly issued securities ("primary distribution") and the second branch to trades by "control persons" of previously issued securities ("secondary primary distribution" or "control person distribution"). It reads:

"6a. 'distribution to the public', used in relation to trading in securities, means,

i. trades that are made for the purpose of distributing to the public securities issued by a company and not previously distributed to the public, or

ii. trades in previously issued securities for the purpose of distributing such securities to the public where the securities form all or a part of or are derived from the holdings of any person, company or any combination of persons or companies holding a sufficient number of any of the securities of a company to materially affect the control of such company, but any person, company or any combination of persons or companies holding more than 20 per cent of the outstanding equity shares in a company shall, in the absence of evidence to the contrary, be deemed to materially affect the control of such company,

whether such trades are made directly to the public or indirectly to the public through an underwriter or otherwise, and includes any transaction or series of transactions involving a purchase and sale or a repurchase and resale in the course of or incidental to such distribution."[11]

The definition deals only with securities issued by a company. On its face it excludes securities of a trust, syndicate or other non-incorporated form of business enterprise. This omission is rectified by the concluding section in the prospectus part of the Act, which reads:

"If any securities proposed to be distributed would, if distributed by a company, be in the course of primary distribution to the public, this Part and the regulations apply *mutatis mutandis* to the person, trust or other entity proposing to distribute the securities."[12]

---

[11]Section 1(1)6a as added by 1971 (Ont.), Vol. 2, c. 31, s. 1(2). (Bill 20, s. 1(1)12).

[12]Section 66. Bill 20, s. 54(1) refers to person or company and, in general, uses the comprehensive term "issuer". As a drafting matter it would seem far simpler just to add "or person" to the phrase "issued by a company" to the definition; this is the formula used in most other instances in the Act. See for example s. 6, the basic registration section. Indeed, in extending the application of the prospectus provisions, s. 66 perhaps displays an excess of drafting zeal, since it speaks, in addition to a "person", of "trust, or other entity". Do these last two concepts have a meaning exclusive of s. 1(1)12 of the Act which defines "person" to mean: "an individual, partnership, unincorporated association, unincorporated organization, unincorporated syndicate, trustee, executor, administrator or other legal personal representative"? Perhaps s. 1(1)12 does not include trust. But it would be more satisfactory to employ the term person, comprehensively defined (or "issuer", as does Bill 20), and avoid having to close the gap by means of a provision tacked on as a kind of addendum to the distribution requirements.

The first branch of the definition does not do much to interpret the words defined. Assuming for our purposes here that there is no difference between the words "distributed" and "issued",[13] branch one catches the movement of securities from the issuer to a purchaser who is a member of the public, whether directly, or indirectly through a purchaser who is not a member of the public.

Branch two of the definition deals with sales by "control persons".[14] There are a number of ways one might become a "control person". The original promoter who took securities in return for assets, a cash contribution or services would normally be such. The control position might also arise through purchases by private agreement or placement, or a take-over bid. Alternatively a major creditor of the company or one of its substantial debt obligation holders may find itself in a control position in the company through the debtor's default.

The need for special regulation of control through prospectus disclosure has been justified on the following premises:

"(a) Because of his special relationship the control person might well have access to information not available to the remaining shareholders and the public enabling him to buy and sell to his personal advantage.

"(b) He has a special interest in ensuring that the market price of his securities does not fall and is exposed to a temptation to manage the company's affairs so as to cast them in the best light during those periods when he wishes to sell, or perhaps equally important, when he wishes to use his securities as collateral for a loan or margin for his brokerage account...

"(c) The precipitate sale of a control block may have a disastrous effect on an orderly market to the detriment of all shareholders.

"(d) The control person may actively participate in or influence the quality of management—he is frequently the vital force in the

---

[13]There probably is a difference between "issued" and "distributed". Issuing is the act which releases the securities from the issuer usually by means of a resolution of the board of directors rendering authorized but hitherto unissued shares available as issued and outstanding shares. To distribute literally means to scatter or spread the shares around. One can thus envisage either a one or a two-step operation; shares can be released and spread around simultaneously or they can be released first and then spread around at a later stage. And if one does not confine the concept of distribution to an actual movement of paper, the two steps can be reversed, with the dissemination occurring first as opportunity offers and without any act of releasing having yet occurred—the shares to be issued on an "if, as and when" basis. See further, *McAskill v. Northwestern Trust Co.*, [1926] S.C.R. 412, [1926] 3 D.L.R. 612, 1 C.B.R. 440.

[14]The phrase "control person" is used here as a short form for the person or company caught by this branch of the definition. It is somewhat misleading because the operative condition is material effect on control rather than control itself. Furthermore the securities holder himself may not have any direct material effect on control but may be caught by this branch by virtue of his participation in a combination which does. See Appendix IV for a comparison with the definitions of the other Canadian jurisdictions and the U.S. federal legislation.

company—and his decision to withdraw from the company may be a piece of essential investor information."[15]

As already noted the critical requirement is not control *per se*[16] but *material effect* on control. Although not expressly so defined, in ordinary circumstances control means the ability to exercise a majority of the voting rights at shareholders' meetings, and more particularly the power to elect a majority of the board of directors.[17] Furthermore, it is *de facto* or practical control rather than *de jure* control. Thus the percentage holding of voting shares required to exercise control will vary with the size of the company, the number of outstanding shares, and the manner in which they are held. The determination of what size and type of shareholding constitutes control of a widely held corporation is a difficult task: this difficulty is greatly compounded when the concept of a "material effect on control" is introduced. The area is accordingly one which demands clarification. Suggestions for reform usually take the form of a call for more objective standards: the introduction of a specific percentage requirement, perhaps one which would vary inversely with the number of different shareholders; or the replacement of the material effect on control test with a *de jure* control test, including perhaps freedom for the person or group holding *de jure* control to sell without restriction those securities which are surplus to their absolute control needs.

One change towards objective guidelines has been implemented, but it is a negative one from the standpoint of providing greater freedom for the control person. The Merger Report recommended[18] that a holding of more than 20 per cent of the outstanding equity shares be deemed a position materially affecting control "in the absence of evidence to the contrary"; this suggestion became law with the 1971 amendments.[19] The 20 per cent test is adopted from the take-over bid definition in the Act; the figure is an arbitrary one chosen to give a certain definition of control adequate for the purposes of that part. It has yet to be determined, however, what contrary evidence is required and to whom it must be shown or proved. In doubtful cases a safe

---

[15]The Merger Report, para. 4.04. It concluded that the four factors listed could be neutralized, and control persons released from the distribution requirements, if a system of continuous disclosure was implemented, provided that the control person made no special selling efforts in disposing of his securities and immediately filed insider-trading reports. Its conclusion was motivated by a concern to remedy the "thinness" of the Canadian securities markets in stocks where large percentages were held by control persons, resulting in a "light float" which was susceptible to wide price fluctutation. See, *infra*, part 4.15.

[16]As it is in the 1933 U.S. Securities Act. For U.S. federal interpretation of the concept see Appendix IV and Loss, vol. 1, chapter 5, and in particular p. 772.

[17]See the discussion of the concept in the Merger Report, chapter IV, and in *Deer Horn Mines Ltd.*, Jan. 1968 OSCB 12. See also the definition of "control" for subsidiary companies (s. 1(4)) and the discussion of control in the Kimber Report, paras. 3.09 to 3.11, in connection with the definition of a take-over bid, and, *post,*, part 7.03.

[18]Para. 4.14(1).

[19]Section 1(1)6a. Of the other jurisdictions only Alberta has added this provision: s. 2(1)6.1, 1972 (Alta.), c. 85, s.2(d).

course of action would be a ruling by the Commission on a s. 59 application.[20]

Holdings of less than 20 per cent may still constitute control. In one case, *e.g.* the OSC held that fourteen per cent was sufficient to materially affect control.[21] But how far does the material effect test take us? Consider the situation where group A holds 49 per cent, group B, 49 per cent, and group C, two per cent. It seems clear that C has a material effect on control. So, of course, does either A or B.

The peculiar language *"derived* from the holdings of...[one] holding a sufficient number of *any* of the securities...to materially affect control"* makes it tolerably clear that non-voting securities are included in the prohibition, provided of course the person or group also has voting securities which materially affect control. The operative word is holdings. Inclusion of voting shares materially affecting control as part of the holdings colours the whole of them, with the result that any sale of securities from the holdings will fall into the category of a distribution. From the standpoint of policy this is a logical conclusion, since it is the possibility of a control person using inside information in the sale of any securities—debt or equity—that provides the major part of the rationale for the prospectus disclosure requirement. The history of the legislation buttresses this interpretation as well.[22]

---

[20]Section 75(1) in Bill 20. It is worth noting that the enthusiasm for certainty has not always existed. For some years prior to 1971 the Alberta Act used the even vaguer test "holding a *substantial* number of the securities of the company" for the second branch of the distribution definition, obviously inviting applications to the Commission for a determination.

[21]*Deer Horn Mines Ltd., supra,* footnote 17. That case did, however, present some additional features. The Commission said:

"In reviewing the filings which were made at the time Patricia [the applicant] acquired its interest in Deer Horn, Patricia described the arrangements as 'purchase of shares and acquisition of control of Silver Regent Mines Limited and Deer Horn Mines Limited'. The Boards of Directors of Deer Horn and Silver Regent are nominated by Patricia and the latter company is, in fact, at the present time in control of the operations of Deer Horn. The Commission is of the opinion that the question whether or not a block of shares materially affects control is not one capable of arithmetic measurement alone. There are undoubtedly many cases where a holding of 14.6 per cent would not constitute control. On the other hand, in the present instance and as already noted by the words of the applicant itself, the applicant does control the company with a holding of that size."

[22]In 1966, by 1966 (Ont.), c. 142, s. 1(1)16, the words "sufficient number of any of the securities of a company" (the present words) were substituted for "sufficient quantity of such securities" thus indicating—it is submitted—non-voting as well as voting securities. However, this interpretation has not always prevailed. At one point the OSC (*Inland Chemicals Canada Limited,* Oct. 1967 OSCB 56) decided that the definition governed only securities to which voting rights were attached. It did not regulate the total holdings of persons or companies (or groups of the same) even if the individuals or organizations in question were "control persons" by virtue of their voting securities. That conclusion was reversed, at least in part, by a later decision of the Commission (*Famous Players,* May 1969 OSCB 83). In that case Paramount International Films held in the form of long-term warrants rights to 49.5 per cent of the voting shares of Famous Players Co. although there were some 3,800 share-

The concept of derivation must however have its logical limits. For example once a stranger to the control group purchases securities from a control person, they are no longer subject to this branch of the definition.

Further perplexity is provided by the use, without any additional clarification, of the word "combination". We may begin with the clearest case, a group of persons or companies whose shareholdings are subject to a shareholders' agreement, which in its operation materially affects control; provided that the agreement deals with voting rights, a combination in the sense of the definition would seem to be present. But this is much less certain where the agreement deals only with other incidents of ownership, such as restriction on transfer, or where the agreement stipulates certain individuals shall hold certain offices, or where the agreement is based on an oral understanding rather than on an executed document.

What is the position of directors? It may be argued that a director is elected by the control group, and is thus sufficiently allied to that group to be considered a part of its combination. Yet one can think of examples where an individual has no connection with any group of shareholders but simply enjoys the confidence of a majority of shareholders because of peculiar expertise, impressive reputation in the business community, or, to take a more obvious instance, because he holds an internal management position. A cursory examination of insider-trading reports makes it clear that a great many directors do not hold the view that they are part of a control group and restricted in their sales. What is more plausible is that where the directors in aggregate hold enough shares to control, then their holdings may be combined, and in the absence of anyone else exercising *de facto* control, the directors may be looked to as a controlling combination.

---

holders. When Famous Players made a new distribution of warrants to all existing shareholders, Paramount received as its share 49.5 per cent of the new issue. The OSC made it clear that any disposition by Paramount of the warrants (and, one would presume, of the underlying securities after exercise of the warrants) would be caught by the second branch of the distribution definition, a category then called secondary primary distribution. The Commission said:

"the Commission considers that any disposition by Paramount...would be a secondary primary [distribution]. The order of the Commission [permitting the distribution] is conditional on the owner of the control block undertaking not to dispose of any of its warrants without qualifying the same through a prospectus or statement of material facts in the usual manner. In addition any interested party may apply to the Commission under the provision of Section 59(1a) in connection with any proposed or intended trade in these warrants.

"In considering this matter, the Commission had before it its decision in the matter of *Inland Chemicals Canada Limited*, made on October 19th, 1967. It is the opinion of the Commission that the earlier decision should be considered as overruled insofar as it indicated that trading in warrants which were convertible into voting stock was not to be considered as trading in securities which might affect control of the company."

Another and more general ambiguity concerns the type of combination that is meant. Is it merely potential, its presence or absence to be judged on the basis of objective criteria, or must the combination be manifested by some tangible form of co-operation related to the enterprise? In view of the preventive nature of these provisions, and in the interests of simplicity, the former interpretation seems preferable, but there is still room for argument in detail. For example, it seems clear that one cannot take the definitions of "associate" and "affiliate"[23] and equate them or either of them with the term "combination". It seems rather that a concept is intended which is both broader in its scope and at the same time more closely related to the facts of a particular situation, although in most cases an associate, for example, would doubtless be found to have combined.

The concluding part of the distribution definition precludes any "staging" of a distribution. Thus, for example, where directors take shares from the company, a distribution which is non-public and thus exempt, option them immediately to friends, and the friends exercise their options shortly thereafter and resell the shares on the public market, the directors would not be immune. This whole network of trading would be caught by the closing paragraph of s. 1(1)6a.

The final phrase of the definition also makes it clear that any market maintenance or stabilizing operations carried out by underwriters during a distribution renders the shares purchased by them on the market subject to the public distribution requirements on resale.[24] One may query how long this prohibition lasts. Presumably market support operations after primary distribution has technically ended would not be affected, but the answer is not certain.

Before leaving the subject of distribution, a look at the modifications introduced by Bill 20 is in order. A new definition of distribution with five branches replaces the two-branch definition, and the phrase "to the public" is eliminated.[25] Branch one simplifies its predecessor by describing the initial distribution curtly as "a trade in securities of an issuer which have not been previously issued".[26] The new branch two extends the concept of distribution to trades by or on behalf of an issuer in *previously* issued securities redeemed or purchased by or donated to it. Branch three repeats the control person restriction in branch two of the Act with some minor simplification. Branch four brands as a distribution resales of exempted trades which do not meet the new objective criteria for resale articulated in s. 73. Branch five adds to the definition of distribution the first trade in previously

---

[23]Section 1(1)2 and (2).
[24]See *Consolidated Montclerg*, June 1967 OSCB 12 and *J.D. Carrier Shoe* Sept. 1967 OSCB 32.
[25]Section 1(1)12. The disappearance of "to the public" has meant the elimination of the concluding paragraph discussed in the text above extending the definition to trades both direct and indirect and to trades in support of the market during distribution; the result is a gain in clarity and simplicity.
[26]The definition deals with securities traded by an issuer. "Issuer" is defined in s. 1(1)19 to mean "a person or company that has outstanding, issues or proposes to issue a security". There is thus no necessity for a section like s. 66 of the Act.

issued securities of a company that has ceased to be a private company.[27]

(2) THE PUBLIC

The third core element in s. 35 is that indicated by the phrase "to the public". No interpretive problem is so perplexing as this one. The Merger Report attempted to define public, and then having decided it was impossible, recommended deletion of the concept.[28] The first general point is that public is such a broad and amorphous concept that it must be interpreted in the context in which it is used—in this case corporations and securities legislation. Accordingly, meanings attributed to the concept under other legislation such as public hospitals or public schools acts, or in the case law defining offences against public morals or public nuisance, are of little help.

There are at least three views in the Canadian jurisprudence on the proper interpretation of the concept of "the public" in securities legislation.

(1) The first view is that the *whole community* is the public. Thus *every* member in a given community unit must be approached before there is a dealing with the public. This view derives from more generalized legislation than securities law. Although it is raised in several securities cases as a possibility, it is largely academic.

(2) The second view is that *anyone* is the public. Thus an approach to any single person, no matter what his relationship to the issuer may be, is a dealing with the public. This view has at least the virtue of certainty, but little more.

(3) The third view is that the public comprises those members of the community who need the protection of the Act, and particularly the information in the prospectus to make an informed investment decision. That need is determined by either of two tests:

(a) the need to know test which analyzes the state of knowledge about the issuer and the sophistication of an offeree to discover whether he needs prospectus information, or

(b) the close personal friend or close business associate test which analyzes the relationship between the issuer or its representative and the offeree to discover whether the offeree needs the objective pro-spectus information and the other protections of the Act.

Traditionally Canadian lawyers have agreed that the proper approach to the problem was based on view number three, provided it was clearly understood that public could be singular as well as plural. To state the proviso another way, there could be an offering to the public even when one person only had been approached if *he* needed

---

[27]This was added in Bill 20 to plug a glaring loophole observed by the practising bar commenting on Bill 98. Without it, it would be possible to incorporate a company with private company restrictions, issue securities through the private company exemptions free of registration and prospectus requirements and then remove the private company restrictions and trade freely in the securities.

[28]See chapter 3, paras. 3.10 to 3.15 of that Report, and Bill 20, ss. 1(1)12 and 54 which implement this recommendation. The discussion which follows borrows from the author's article "Public and Non-Public Offering Companies under the BCA...".

the protection of the Act. Equally there could be approaches to a number of people which would not be an offering to the public if *they* did not need the protection of the Act. Given this approach the difficult question remained of whether a specific person needed the protection of the Act. If he did, then any dealing with him would require that a prospectus be qualified first. This factual determination, however, was one which the practitioner could and did make on his own. The Merger Report disturbed this somewhat neat and tidy picture. It addressed the issue ambiguously:

"The word 'public' must be viewed in the light of the regulatory scheme in which it is found. In the context of a distribution to the public three alternative meanings for 'public' have been suggested: first that the distribution must be to *every* member of the community, next to *any* member of the community, and lastly, the distribution may be to all but *certain* members of the community. It may be concluded that our present legislation represents a combination of the second and third alternatives. Section 35, as we noted previously, appears to direct its attention to each and every one of us. The exemptions then go on to provide a specific list of exceptions to the general requirement."

But then it concludes emphatically (if the word "virtually" may be ignored):

"We have concluded that the Legislature intended that the protection of the Act should in fact be afforded to virtually everyone excepting those that it specifically exempted from its protective umbrella."[29]

The suggestion that emerges from this Report is that "virtually everyone" is the public and *only* those specifically exempted by statute either are not, or do not require the protection of the prospectus. It follows that if a specific statutory exemption cannot be found, or if a s. 59 ruling is not obtained, any other dealing with any other person in the course of distribution is a dealing with the public requiring a prospectus.[30]

---

[29]Paras. 3.11 and 3.14. See also para. 8.01 which sums up the discussion of "public" thus: "This conclusion is based on the premise that the legislation intends to protect everyone."

[30]Proponents of this view reject the "close personal friends" or "close business associates" test and distinguish the "need to know" test as one based on the U.S. Securities Act, 1933 and therefore inappropriate under our Act. Suggesting that the structure of the U.S. Act is significantly different, they note that s. 5 of that Act states broadly that it is unlawful for anyone, by any interstate commerce or use of the mails, to sell or deliver any security unless a registration statement (prospectus) is in effect. Section 4(1) then exempts from this prohibition transactions not involving a public offering. By contrast our Act prohibits a trade which would be a distribution to the public without prospectus disclosure and then sets out a great many categories of specific exemptions. These numerous and intricately designed express exemptions eliminate the need for the kind of interpretive flexibility which is required by the U.S. Act with its single broadly stated exempting concept "non-public". Furthermore, in case the specific exemptions are not sufficiently exhaustive, s. 59 of our Act gives a discretion to the Commission where any doubt remains. In particular, one of these specific statutory exemptions (ss. 19(1)10 and

Canadian jurisprudence which might resolve the controversy is unfortunately sparse and imprecise. But what there is clearly suggests that the "need to know" test enunciated by the U.S. Supreme Court in *SEC v. Ralston Purina Co.*[31] is applicable to the interpretation of public in Canadian securities legislation and the "close personal friends" or "close business associates" test may be used as well. The latter test has the added advantage of being employed elsewhere in our Act[32] in the regulation of trading generally to establish an exception to the general prohibition on calling at a residence to sell a security whether in distribution or not.[33]

58(1)(c)) permits trades by a company to its employees, precisely the trade which the U.S. Supreme Court in *SEC v. Ralston Purina Co.* (1953), 346 U.S. 119, 73 S. Ct. 981 specifically determined to be a trade with the public which required a prospectus. The exemptions in our Act are based in part on the "need to know" test, the difference being that the Legislature has applied this test and established those categories where it deemed the need to know did not exist.

By contrast proponents of the "need to know" view reply that if the "anyone" view were intended, our Act would never have used the concept "public" at all. In requiring a prospectus, s. 35 simply would have banned trading with anyone (as s. 6, the licensing requirement, does), without introducing the concept of public. It then would have provided specific exemptions. Furthermore the categorical distinction between public and non-public is implicit in some of the exemptions from both registration and prospectus, for example, trades in

(a) certain mortgages, or other encumbrances upon real or personal property,
(b) securities evidencing indebtedness due under any conditional sales contract or other title retention contract providing for the acquisition of personal property, or
(c) securities of a private company issued by the private company, if the securities are not offered for sale to the public, and
(d) securities of a prospecting syndicate agreement if they are not offered to the public and are sold to not more than 50 purchasers (s. 19(2), paras. 4, 5, 9 and 12 and s. 58(2)(a)). If the "public" meant every single person then the proviso which turns on the concept "public" would be meaningless in these exemptions.

[31]*Supra*, footnote 30.
[32]Section 68. See, *post*, part 8.07, text at footnote 65.
[33]The rough pattern woven by diverse threads in the case law is this. In *Ralston* the U.S. Supreme Court decided that sales by the defendant company of its own securities to its own employees totalling $2,000,000 over four years under a stock investment plan was a distribution to the public, because only some of the employees held positions in the company which would render the giving to them of prospectus type information superfluous. The others, more junior employees such as a foreman at the lowest level of supervision, had a "need to know". Mr. Justice Clark speaking for the court said (346 U.S. at pp. 124-5):

"The design of the statute is to protect investors by promoting full disclosure of information thought necessary to informed investment decisions. The natural way to interpret the private offering exemption is in light of the statutory purpose. Since exempt transactions are those as to which 'there is no practical need for [the bill's] application', the applicability of section 4(1) should turn on whether the particular class of persons affected needs the protection of the Act. An offering to those who are shown to be able to fend for themselves is a transaction 'not involving any public offering'.

"The Commission would have us go one step further and hold that 'an offering to a substantial number of the public' is not exempt under s. 4(1). We are advised that 'whatever the special circumstances, the Commission has consistently interpreted the exemption as being inapplicable when a large number of offerees is involved'. But the statute would seem to apply to a 'public offering' whether to few or many. It may well be that offerings to a substantial number of persons would rarely be exempt. Indeed nothing prevents the Commission, in enforcing the statute, from using some kind of numerical test in deciding when to investigate particular exemption claims. But there is no warrant for superimposing a quantity limit on private offerings as a matter of statutory interpretation."

In making the statement: "But the statute would seem to apply to a public offering whether to few or many", Justice Clark forged a link to the British jurisprudence and footnoted Viscount Sumner's frequently quoted dictum in *Nash v. Lynde*, [1929] A.C. 158, 98 L.J.K.B. 127 (H.L.), reproduced below. That case is from an external jurisdiction more frequently referred to by Canadian courts. There a jury finding had established an offer to the public on the facts and the House of Lords was directly concerned only with the issue of whether the documents concerned were a prospectus. However, there are several *dicta* relating to the question of who is the public, *per* Lord Hailsham at p. 164:

"[I]t is sufficient...that the prospectus...should be proved to have been shown to *any* person *as a member of the public* and as an invitation to that person to take some of the shares referred to in the prospectus..."

Per Viscount Sumner at pp. 168-9:

"I am anxious not to say anything that would make the way of the share canvasser less hard than s. 81 makes it already, but to me it is difficult to think of a prospectus being issued without some measure of publicity, however modest, and I think it is also impossible to do so, unless the steps taken are taken with the intention of inducing a subscription by the person invited to subscribe for the securities. I do not think that the term is satisfied by a single private communication between friends, even if they are business friends, or even though preparations have been made for other documents to be used in other communications if none such take place. In the present case all that constituted the "issue" was that one of the directors, in the course of a general endeavour to find money, was furnished with some copies of these typewritten documents and gave one of them to a friend, who as requested, passed it on to a friend of his own. I cannot believe that any one in business would call this the issue of a prospectus.

...

"Though literally it is true that the issue is not expressly said in the section to be an issue to the public, I think that it must be so in substance, otherwise any private letter, written by a person engaged in forming a company and advising his correspondent to take shares, would become an issued prospectus if other letters were written by him asking others to do the same. 'The public'...is of course a general word. No particular numbers are prescribed. Anything from two to infinity may serve: perhaps even one, if he is intended to be the first of a series of subscribers, but makes further proceedings needless by himself subscribing the whole. The point is that the offer *is such as to be open to any one* who brings his money and applies in due form, whether the prospectus was addressed to him on behalf of the company or not. A private communication is not thus open...."

Per Lord Buckmaster at p. 170:

"The question of what does or does not amount to an issue is a question of fact in each case and is not capable of a rigid and exact definition, but in my opinion it certainly does not necessarily involve a general application impartially made to all members of the public. A distribution of a prospectus *among a well defined class of the public* would be a issue within the meaning of s. 81..."

(Emphasis added.) Here the basis of the distinction is not the "need to know" but rather the degree of closeness and familiarity in the relationship between the parties; communications involving a limited group of friends or business associates are exempt.

R. v. Empire Dock Ltd. (1940), 55 B.C.R. 34 (Co. Ct.), one of the earliest Canadian reported decisions, is not particularly helpful; because of the facts the answer was obvious. There an appeal by a private company from its conviction for inviting the public to subscribe for its securities was dismissed where the invitation was made to 1,400 persons, of whom 600 were complete strangers. Those so canvassed included two-thirds of the lawyers in Vancouver. Judge Lennox stated at pp. 37-8:

"...not only reason but all the authorities stress the point that the meaning of the words 'the public' cannot be tied down to a specific quantity and that, when the term is used, it must be considered as relative to the question at issue and the circumstances of each particular case. Even the words 'friend' 'customer' and 'connection' must also not be narrowed to the particular from the general. A man may call another his friend and yet he may be a mere nodding acquaintance....

"...there must be some point (to be decided in each case) where 'private' ends and 'public' begins."

R. v. Piepgrass (1959), 29 W.W.R. 218, 23 D.L.R. (2d) 220, 125 C.C.C. 364, 31 C.R. 213 (Alta. C.A.) a more recent Canadian case, is more helpful because it reviews other authorities. It builds on the friends and business associates test from *Nash v. Lynde.* There the accused, a director and officer of a private company, sold shares in the company to five people, with four of whom he had previous business dealings. However, they were not "in any sense friends or associates of the accused, or persons having common bonds of interest or association". In addition to the five subscriptions accepted by the company "the accused turned in a 'lot of them that were refused' because the persons applying were not financially capable of putting in the required money." He was convicted of trading without registration as a broker and could not use the exemption for "securities of a private company...where the securities are not offered for sale to the public". Mr. Justice Macdonald stated at pp. 227-8, D.L.R.:

"If the word 'public'...is to be construed in its widest sense it would include all members of the community. In the Shorter Oxford Dictionary 'public' is defined in part as follows: 'That is open to, may be used by, or may or must be shared by, all members of the community.' If the word 'public' then is to be construed in its widest sense it is clear that unless there would be a general invitation to all members of a community by a person offering shares in a private company, such person would not be in breach of the statute.

"That view, in my opinion, is far too wide considering the objects of the statute and the rigorous manner by which the public generally are protected by its other provisions from offering of securities.

"It seems to me that the very essence of a private company envisages the idea that it is of private, domestic concern to the people interested in its formation or in later acquiring shares in it. It is one thing for an individual or group of individuals to disclose information to friends or associates, seeking support for a private company being formed or in existence, pointing out its attractions for investment or speculation as the case may be, but it is quite another thing for a private company to go out on the highways and byways seeking to sell securities of the company and particularly by high pressure methods, that is, by breaking down the sales resistance of potential purchasers and inducing them to purchase.

"It is clear from the cases cited and from the authorities cited that it is impossible to define with any degree of precision what is meant by the term 'offer for sale to the public'. It follows that in each instance the Court will be called upon to determine whether or not the sale of the securities of the private company transcended the ordinary sales of a private domestic concern to a person or persons having common bonds of interest or association. It is clear from the authorities that whether or not there was an offering to the public is a finding of fact."

In *R. v. Golden Shamrock Mines Ltd.*, [1965] 1 O.R. 692, [1965] 3 C.C.C. 72 (C.A.), the court found that an offer for sale to the public was made through a general newspaper advertisement. Unfortunately the reasoning is rather terse, and, like *Empire Dock*, the facts of public solicitation—through a newspaper—are so obvious as to admit of little doubt.

A more helpful inferior court case is *R. v. McKillop*, [1972] 1 O.R. 164, 4 C.C.C. (2d) 390 (Prov. Ct.) where a more limited group of persons was solicited and it was found to be an offering to the public either on the basis of a need to know or the absence of a friendship or business association nexus such as would remove the transaction from the public realm. The provincial court judge held that the transactions were with the public referring both to *Ralston Purina* and *Piepgrass*, and offered the following commentary of fact and law on the concept of "public" at p. 168:

"In my opinion the sales made by the accused to the various named individuals were not of a strictly private nature. In other words shares were not only available to those particular people to the exclusion of all others. While it is true that the individuals who purchased the shares constituted a small number in proportion to all residents of this community, nevertheless, they were not a favoured few, so far as possessing knowledge of the availability of the shares was concerned. They were not, so to speak, in on a secret. To the contrary, information concerning the company and concerning the availability of shares from the accused was apparently of common knowledge, fairly widespread in the community, as [one witness] discussed it with individuals over lunch in a public restaurant. While it is true that the number of those who availed themselves of the opportunity to purchase the shares is not shown to be large, nevertheless the availability of the shares was known to the public generally. In my opinion the number of people involved is not the important criterion. A public meeting may be called and advertised one way or another and then only be attended by a small group of five or ten people. Just because so few attend is of no real moment. The meeting is still a public meeting."

He also referred (at p. 169) to *Jennings v. Stephens*, [1936] Ch. 469 (C.A.), where Lord Wright stated at p. 476:

"'The public' is a term of uncertain importance; it must be limited in every case by the context in which it is used. It does not generally mean the inhabitants of the world or even inhabitants of this country. In any specific context it may mean for practical purposes only the inhabitants of a particular village or such members of the community as particular advertisements would reach, or who would be interested in any particular matter, professional, political, social, artistic, or local. In the case of a dramatic work the public may be regarded as including persons to whom the drama appeals,

However, interpretive releases of the U.S. SEC on the "need to know" test may provide useful criteria for practitioners advising their clients. One of these U.S. guides[34] states that "whether a transaction is one not involving any public offering is essentially a question of fact and necessitates a consideration of all surrounding circumstances, including such factors as the relationship between the offerees and the issuer, the nature, scope, size, type and manner of the offering". On the issue of number of offerees the release states "the number of persons to whom the offering is extended is relevant only to the question whether they have the requisite association with the knowledge of the issuer which makes the exemption available." On the identity of offerees it says "consideration must be given not only to the identity of the actual purchasers but also the offerees". On sale to promoters it states "the sale of stock to promoters who take the initiative in founding or organizing the business would come within the exemption. On the other hand, the transaction tends to become public when the promoters begin to bring in a diverse group of uninformed friends, neighbours and associates". The release then considers in some detail other factors such as size of offering, facilities used, acquisition for investment, period of retention, change of circumstance in investment intent, and integration and related series of offerings, all of which serve as additional distinguishing features in determining whether or not an offer is public.

To summarize, it seems the Canadian law distinguishes among three classes of people:
(1) those who are not members of the public either because
(a) they do not have a need to know the information contained in a prospectus, or
(b) they are close friends or business associates of an issuer,
(2) those who are members of the public, and

---

but that again must be limited by local and other conditions. Thus it is clear that by 'public' is meant in the words of Bowen L.J. 'a portion of the public'...It may be observed that in this country actions are in general tried in public...though the number of the public present at any hearing may not be more than half a dozen."
He also quoted from *Morrisons Holdings Ltd. v. Inland Revenue Commissioners*, [1966] 1 All E.R. 789 at p. 798 (Ch.D.):
"Looking at the subsection for a moment apart from authority, it seems to me that the word 'public' is appropriate to denote those outside the immediate circle of those who control the company."
See also *Crawford v. Bathurst Land and Development Co. Ltd.* (1918), 42 O.L.R. 256, 43 D.L.R. 98 (C.A.); reversed on other grounds 59 S.C.R. 314, 50 D.L.R. 457 *sub nom Fullerton v. Crawford*, [1919] 3 W.W.R. 843 and *R. v. Slegg*, [1974] 4 W.W.R. 402, 17 C.C.C. (2d) 149, 16 *Crim. L.Q.* 225, April 5, 1974 BCSCWS (Prov. Ct.). Finally see *Chandor Mines Ltd.*, June 4, 1974 QSCWB 1, CCH vol. 3, para. 70-066 where the QSC applied both the need to know and the close association tests evenhandedly without any attempt to assign a relative weight.
[34]*Securities Act*, 1933, S.E.C. Release No. 4552, Nov. 6, 1962, CCH Federal Securities Law Reporter, vol. 1, para. 2770. The release is a guide only, produced for a substantially different business and regulatory environment than that existing in Canada, and it must accordingly be used with caution.

(3) those who are members of the public but have been statutorily exempted from the forced disclosure provisions.
A trade to the third category of person is still a distribution to the public but without compulsory prospectus disclosure. Moreover there is an overlap between categories one and three because in a number of instances the common law tests from category one are used to create a statutory exemption in category three.

Bill 20 adopted the Merger Report recommendation and deleted the concept of "public".[35] However when the concept of public is dropped some flexibility is lost. Bill 20 seeks to restore this by the addition of several exemptions, *viz.* "the isolated issue" and "the limited offering" exemptions.[36]

4.03 The Prospectus

Assuming that a distribution is contemplated and no exemption is available, a prospectus must be qualified with the Commission. The Regulation[37] establishes seven different types of prospectus which are to be used, depending on the category of issuer. The information required to be contained in each is set out in accompanying forms. These categories are: finance, industrial, investment, mining, mining exploration, mutual fund, and insurance companies issuing variable policies with an equity base.[38] The director has a discretion to designate an issuer as falling into one or other of these categories.[39] Detailed formal definitions are given for the finance company and for the mining exploration company only. The special treatment accorded the former is a rather grim monument to the demise of Atlantic Acceptance and Prudential Finance and provides practical evidence for the "first law" of securities regulation—financial disaster and scandal breed legislation. Special treatment for mining exploration companies—ventures raising $100,000 or less from the public with at least 65 per cent being applied to actual exploration and development work on the property—is a legacy of the Beatty Report in 1968, which sought to expedite the raising of "shoe string" capital for early stage exploration.[40]

The qualification process begins with the filing of a preliminary or "red herring"[41] prospectus with the director. He simply issues a receipt

---

[35]Section 54. The Report at para. 3.20 reasoned:
"Since the proposed regulatory scheme is intended to be all inclusive, with the residual discretion vested in the Commission, the reference to 'public' should be removed. Section 35 would then prohibit a 'distribution' to anyone unless a prospectus had been accepted for filing...This plan has the merit of both simplicity and certainty."

[36]Section 73(1)(b) and (m), discussed, *infra,* part 4.12(3)(a) and (b).

[37]Sections 13 through 19.

[38]Forms 13 to 19.

[39]Reg. 794, s. 12(2).

[40]One incentive for mining development in its initial stages has been available for a long time—the exemption from full prospectus documentation in the case of the $50,000 prospecting syndicate. See s. 34 and, *infra,* part 4.12(1). Bill 20, s. 53, raises the limit on the capital of such syndicates to $100,000, reflecting the inflationary trends of recent years.

[41]The preliminary prospectus must bear a red ink statement on its face warning that it is not final and the securities may not be sold until the final

therefore without detailed scrutiny[42] unless the document fails to comply in a fundamental way as to form and content with the law.[43]

The preliminary prospectus will ordinarily contain everything except price, date of issue and perhaps the amount of securities to be offered, subject to any changes arising from deficiency requests. The deputy director-filings normally assigns it to a team of one accountant and one lawyer who analyze it according to the broad tests established in s. 41(1), this subsection requires a prospectus to provide full, true and plain disclosure of all material facts relating to the security proposed to be issued. Much of the substantive detail fleshing out the requirements of this test is now found in the Regulation.[44] This was not always the case. Prior to the Kimber Report recommendations incorporated in the 1966 Act, much of the detail was prescribed in the Act itself. The Kimber Committee was impressed by the clearer and far more detailed rules in SEC regulations and the narrative and more understandable form of prospectus which resulted from them. It recommended a similar scheme to replace the rather wooden "response to question" form used in Canada.[45]

The scrutiny by the Commission's prospectus team often results in a deficiency letter requiring changes to the draft prospectus before it

---

prospectus is accepted (s. 39). In fact it is the deputy director-filings who has director status for these purposes and who considers the prospectus. Pre-filing conferences with the director are encouraged where an issuer anticipates that substantial interpretive problems might develop midway through the qualification process, leaving insufficient time to resolve them before the issuer's target date for offering the issue. See Bray, "Recent Developments in Securities Administration in Ontario: The Securities Act 1966"; Alberta Policy 3-03, "Preliminary Prospectuses and Prospectuses", CCH vol. 1, para. 24-501; British Columbia Policy 3-02, "Prospectuses in Draft submitted to the Commission for Vetting", CCH vol. 2, para. 29-952 and British Columbia Policy 3-03, "Requirements re Filing of Prospectuses and Preliminary Prospectuses", CCH vol. 2, para. 29-953.

[42]Section 35(2) (Bill 20, s. 56).

[43]Section 40(1).

[44]On the authority of s. 41(2) and (3) (Bill 20, s. 57(1) and (2)).

[45]The Kimber Report, para. 5.15 said:

"There are several possible ways of providing for the use of forms: (a) by incorporating the forms in The Securities Act or as a schedule thereto; (b) by providing for the promulgation of forms by regulation; or (c) by the Commission requiring compliance with forms prescribed by it as a matter of administrative policy. Alternative (c) is unacceptable, even if it could be considered permissible under the present legislation: a radical change in the form and content of the prospectus should have legislative authorization. Alternative (a) suffers from the defect of inflexibility; amending a statute is too cumbersome a method of making changes in the forms which will be required from time to time. Therefore the Committee recommends that the forms should be prescribed by regulation."

In fact, with the growing use of policy statements to regulate prospectus content a combination of alternatives (b) and (c) is currently used with the emphasis on (c), notwithstanding the Kimber Committee's abhorrence of it. See, for example, Policy Statements 3-02, "Junior Mining Exploration and Development Companies", CCH vol. 2, para. 54-896, and 3-25, "Mortgage and Real Estate Investment Trusts and Partnerships", CCH vol. 2, para. 54-919.

will be accepted. These deficiencies may be met fully, a change more acceptable to the issuer negotiated, or again the deputy director may be satisfied on further explanation that there is no deficiency. If there is no change either in the issuer's position or that of the deputy director, the director must give the issuer a hearing; in the event of a decision rejecting the prospectus, it must be in writing.[46] The issuer may then appeal the director's decision to the Commission.[47] In fact the appeal to the Commission is often illusory, since the issuer cannot afford the delay involved in the exercise of his rights. Thus the director's requirements will frequently be complied with even where the issuer believes itself to have a reasonable chance of success on appeal.

There is a required "waiting period" of at least ten days between filing the preliminary prospectus and the receipt for the prospectus itself.[48]

4.04 Multi-Issuer Prospectus

May several related issuers combine to qualify their issues by a single filing or must there be a separate prospectus for the securities of each issuer in a distribution? Neither the Act nor the Regulation provides much specific guidance on this question. Section 35 does not, on its face, preclude two or more issuers from combining to make their offerings in a single prospectus. The Regulation, moreover, stipulates a separate fee "for each additional...unit offering...where the prospectus involves...more than one unit offering";[49] this suggests that for fee purposes at least two unit offerings by two different issuers in one prospectus might be permissible. However, probably the question falls ultimately to be determined by the director's residual discretion.

The problem emerges most clearly in the case of one parent mutual fund organization wishing to offer several different funds, *e.g.* a bond fund emphasizing income and an equity fund emphasizing capital gain, within the pages of one prospectus even though each fund is a separate issuer. At the most general level one would suppose that the test as to whether such a prospectus would be accepted is whether it provides "full true and plain disclosure of all material facts relating to the security proposed to be issued".[50] It may be argued, and with some force, that the effectiveness of disclosure is increased by combining in a single document several funds whose investment objectives vary but which share overriding common characteristics such as a common parent. The potential purchaser will have alternative possibilities clearly presented to him before making a commitment. The counter-argument is first that the average investor finds it sufficiently taxing to consider the information about a single issuer, and a combination

---

[46]Section 61(2). Bill 20, s. 62(3) omits the requirement that the decision be in writing but s. 62(5) requires the director to state the question and relevant facts in writing.
[47]Section 28.
[48]Section 36(1) (Bill 20, s. 66(1)). See, *infra*, part 4.09.
[49]Section 8(1)(h)(ii).
[50]Section 41(1).

document only imports additional confusion and second that comparisons can better be made when the alternative issue is contained in a separate and therefore obviously distinct booklet.

For almost two decades the OSC accepted multi-issuer mutual fund prospectuses which shared a single sponsoring entity. This was not however a frequent practice until changes in the tax laws in recent years resulted in the popularity of registered retirement savings plans. In early 1975 there were at least seven different mutual fund groups that made use of the multi-issuer prospectus in Ontario. The largest number of issuers to be qualified in the one prospectus was five.

This practice was terminated in 1975 with the issuance of a notice by the provincial securities administrators requiring a separate prospectus for each fund, notwithstanding a common sponsoring entity.[51] This decision is however phrased in cautious terms, admitting the possibility that a different view of s. 61 may come to prevail.

4.05 Director's Discretion

The director's receipt[52] for a prospectus is necessary for it to become effective. His discretion—to accept or reject a prospectus—is enormous, and the section granting it, subtly worded. Section 61 states "the Director *may*, in his discretion, issue a receipt for a prospectus filed under this Part, unless it appears to him that" it fails to comply with one of six specific conditions. Thus if one of the six conditions is not met he *must* refuse the prospectus. But even if all of the six specific conditions are met he *may* refuse the prospectus.

The language of s. 61 leaves no doubt that the Act is not limited to a full, true and plain disclosure regime of the SEC type. Rather it confers also, at least in part, a fair, just and equitable jurisdiction of the sort found in American state "blue-sky" legislation. The former is sometimes referred to as a "rotten egg" regime—one may sell rotten eggs so long as he makes it patently clear that they are rotten. Under the "blue-sky" regime the administrator has the responsibility to decide whether it is fair for the public to be allowed to buy a "rotten" security; disclosure is not enough. In fact the uniform act provinces in Canada administer their legislation in a manner somewhere in between these two polar extremes. It may be questioned, however, whether such a compromise position accurately reflects the precise wording of the statute. In fact, though not in form, the section consists of two distinct parts. In the first of these the permissive "may" (supplemented unnecessarily by the phrase "in his discretion") rather than "shall" suggests that the director is free to impose standards of his own choosing, limited only by the requirement that he apply standards appropriate for the purposes of the legislation.[53] In theory at least such

---

[51]See Sept. 1974 OSCB 158. See also *In the Matter of Royal Trust Managed Funds*, Apr. 1975 OSCB 132, where a multiple-issuer prospectus was rejected.
[52]In practice the phrases "final receipt for a prospectus", "receipt for a final prospectus" and "final receipt for a final prospectus" are used interchangeably. Properly there are two documents and two receipts therefore, *viz.* a receipt for a preliminary prospectus and a receipt for a prospectus (sections 35 and 36; Bill 20, ss. 54 and 66.)
[53]A recent case, *Voyager Explorations Ltd. v. Ontario Securities Commission et al.*, [1970] 1 O.R. 237, 8 D.L.R. (3d) 135, 60 C.P.R. 153 (H.C.), makes clear

language would seem to authorize the full blue-sky approach.

In the second part the section sets out the six situations alluded to above, the existence of which, either singly or in combination, makes it mandatory for the director to refuse to issue a receipt. The less than straightforward wording which lays all the stress on the six cases where there is no discretion and allows the word "may", establishing the residual discretion, to pass almost unnoticed, may have effectively masked from the proponents of a disclosure only regime the full extent to which a "blue-sky" provision of the paternalistic type has been implanted in the legislation. When the present wording was first introduced, it was suggested that the government's aim was to eschew the U.S. blue-sky approach and insist instead on full, true and plain disclosure. But this purpose would have been achieved if the provision read that the director *shall* issue a final receipt *if* the prospectus meets the stipulated disclosure requirements. Presumably the legislative draftsman sought what he conceived to be the best of both worlds: the director should not be made to appear as an implied guarantor of the success of a promotion but the statute should ensure that he retains the power to nip in the bud a venture which he had reason to believe would be wasteful and not financially viable.

Bill 20, s. 62 alters the formal statement of the director's discretion. The director *shall* issue a receipt for a prospectus unless it appears that it is not in the public interest to do so.[54] He *shall not* issue a receipt if any one of eight situations exists.[55] This two-pronged approach—one positive and one negative—results in greater formal clarity and a change of emphasis, but little more. The residual discretion for the director still exists in the phrase "unless it is not in the public interest to do so". The limitation that the decision be made according to the public interest is new, but it exists impliedly under the Act. The major

---

how unrestricted this discretion is. Ironically, the OSC chose in that case to exercise its discretion in a manner which limited the focus of attention to the question of adequate disclosure. Voyager Petroleums Ltd., an Alberta company, had filed a preliminary prospectus with the OSC. Voyager Explorations Ltd., a company incorporated in Ontario thirteen years earlier and trading over the counter, brought suit to enjoin the OSC from accepting the prospectus and the TSE for listing the shares on the ground of confusion of names. It had previously submitted its argument formally to the OSC where it was rejected by the chairman on the ground that the Commission had already disposed of the matter by requiring a face page note on the prospectus stating that the Alberta company was not the same as the Ontario company. Pennell J. dismissed the application, saying that a determination whether to accept a prospectus under s. 61 is an administrative not a judicial act and "seems to be in the unfettered discretion of the Director".

Furthermore, there seems to be no requirement that the discretion be exercised consistently. In *Japan Fund of Canada Ltd.*, Oct. 1970 OSCB 138 the same issue of similar names arose as in the *Voyager* case; the director's decision (upheld by the Commission) was to refuse to accept the prospectus. It applied this test: "Would the similarity of names   confuse the average investor of reasonable intelligence acting with ordinary caution or merely an unwary, uncautious or hurried securities buyer."

[54]Section 62(1).
[55]Section 62(2).

formal difference is that at present the issuing of the receipt is not expressed to be mandatory even when there is no bar from the standpoint of the public interest.

The above exposition has been concerned with the theoretical limits on the director's power in this area, and we have seen that it is wide indeed. The practical difficulty, of course, is that if the director were to attempt to pass judgment in detail on the viability of new enterprises, he would have to have at his disposal a staggering number of highly sophisticated experts from various disciplines. The result would be an economy heavily subject to public regulation, to a much greater extent than Canadians have been accustomed. Since this objective is both impossible to achieve and probably unworthy of attempt, the administrators have as described above attempted to steer a middle course, emphasizing disclosure but using with comparative freedom their wide discretion to refuse prospectuses or impose terms and conditions where such action appears appropriate.[56] There are thus a number of instances where the regulatory authorities have considered an insistence upon disclosure criteria inadequate and have applied the "blue-sky" approach to distributions. On some occasions these have been *ad hoc* decisions that the particular venture was not financially viable; they have also taken the form of regulations or policy statements issued on an *a priori* basis and applying to a whole class of ventures, such as junior mining companies or real estate companies. Unhappily several of these initiatives have occurred as belated responses after an abuse has manifested itself. Thus, for example, the imposition of a more onerous level of disclosure on finance companies, both by a special statutory provision and by regulation, occurred after the Atlantic and Prudential collapses.

---

[56]Indeed, 27 years ago the OSC chairman suggested that it was this middle position that was intended by the legislation. See O.E. Lennox, "Securities Legislation and Administration", at pp. 84-5.

Whatever the legislative intention, the Kelly Report has stressed the extent to which *de facto* the OSC at the present time has arrogated to itself wide discretion to intervene and regulate. The Report refers (p. 95) to a "self-conferred" extension of the power conferred by the relevant statutory provision to reject prospectuses.

In *Great Pine Mines Ltd.*, Feb. 1966 OSCB 7, the OSC commented on this passage in the Kelly Report, stressing that it had acted *de jure*:

"After reading what Mr. Justice Kelly says in the light of the context we do not think that by the word 'self-conferred' he meant that the Commission has as a matter of law no such power. All he meant, in our view, was that the Legislature, having failed to specify the grounds upon which the director could and the grounds upon which he could not, exercise what is on its face an unfettered discretion to refuse to accept a prospectus, the Commission had, lacking the guidance of the Legislature, been forced to work out those grounds for itself."

For examples of discretionary imposition of conditions see, National Policies 4, 5, 14, 19, CCH vol. 2, paras. 54-841, 54-842, 54-851, 54-856; Saskatchewan Policy 4, CCH vol. 3, para. 69-305; British Columbia Policies 3-07, 3-08, 3-21, CCH vol. 2, paras. 29-957, 29-958, 29-971; Quebec Policies 3, 7, 11A, 13, 16, 20, 25, CCH vol. 3, paras. 66-014, 66-018, 66-022, 66-024, 66-027, 66-031, 66-080; Manitoba Policies 3.01, 3.05, CCH vol. 2, paras. 34-991, 34-995.

A recent example of more extensive regulation based on this residual discretion is an OSC policy statement establishing detailed minimum criteria for qualification of real estate investment trusts (REIT).[57] As the name implies, the money invested in such trusts is in turn invested in real estate, whether in the form of direct ownership or mortgages; additional moneys are raised by the trust in the form of loans, to secure the advantages of leverage. One of the major reasons for choosing the trust rather than the corporate form was the tax advantage resulting from the fact that trust income is taxed only in the beneficiaries' hands, thus avoiding two levels of taxation. This new type of financing vehicle had just begun to be used in Canada when the policy statement was introduced. Although the REIT had achieved considerable popularity in the U.S. and U.K., several failures had caused it to be the target of adverse publicity in those jurisdictions,[58] due to the fact that as a trust it was not subject to the same constraints as a corporation in its operation; in particular there was an absence of the kind of rules governing the internal transaction of business which are to be found in corporations legislation.

There were a number of concerns which prompted this policy statement: the need for sophistication on the part of management to cope with the high-risk element in this type of venture; the need for substantial resources to provide a safe range of investments; the conflict between the adviser investing its own funds in a deal as opposed to those of the trust; the absence of the regulation of management conduct and protection for the unit holder found in corporations legislation owing to the organization of the venture as a

---

[57]Ontario Policy 3-25, "Mortgage and Real Estate Investment Trusts and Partnerships", CCH vol. 2, para. 54-919. On trusts generally, see Aug. 31, 1972 OSCWS 68-90 and the related Policy 3-26 on "'Closed-End' Income Investment Trusts and Partnerships", CCH vol. 2, para. 54-951. Other instances are National Policies 6 through 11 and 23, 24 and 26 dealing with mutual funds, CCH vol. 2, paras. 54-843 to 54-848, 54-860, 54-861 and 54-863, and National Policy 15, dealing with scholarship or educational plans, CCH vol. 2, para. 54-852. The former group is a particularly striking example since it establishes an entire registration regime based on the prospectus discretion, with very considerable restrictions. It foreshadows the legislation of a registration regime for mutual funds in Bill 20. For a particular case example in contrast to broader policy see *In the Matter of Shoppers Investments Ltd.*, Oct. 1972 OSCB 215, where a discretionary refusal to review a prospectus was used to attach conditions ensuring a greater spreading of investment risk and improved minimum secured assets ratios in the case of an investment company. The appellant public company, a residential mortgage financing firm, was heavily involved in lending money for second mortgages. The influence of the Prudential Finance and Atlantic Acceptance Reports was apparent in the conditions imposed. However, also apparent was the flexibility of the Commission displayed in its willingness to enter the realm of business judgment and make an *ad hoc* appraisal of soundness. In the background perhaps was a consciousness of the shortage of mortgage financing in Canada for residential housing, a pressing social need at that time.
[58]See K.C. Aldrich, "Real Estate Investment Trusts An Overview" (1972), 27 The Business Lawyer 1165; Financial Post, August 26, 1972.

trust; finally an element of doubt as to whether the unit holder was immune from liability incurred by the trust itself.

In attempting to meet these concerns the policy statement imposed a wide range of rather detailed requirements on unincorporated issuers of this type. The influence of the BCA manifests itself at many points, but at the same time many of the provisions are tailored to the peculiar needs and characteristics of real estate trusts.[59]

This and other examples of the exercise of s. 61 discretion raise fundamental questions. Is it proper, whether in view of the legislative intent or on general policy grounds, that the OSC (or its director) should make these kind of decisions; and if in some instances it does so, which ones? What, if any, should be the responsibility of government for those situations in which there has been an oversight by the Commission or its judgment has faltered?

Despite its importance in any discussion of the director's powers, the exercise of general or residual discretion as described above remains exceptional. In the ordinary course a prospectus is refused because of the existence of one of the six stated situations or bars in s. 61. In these situations as we have seen the director has no choice but to refuse, though clearly he has wide powers of interpretation.[60] These conditions are now briefly examined in turn.

(1) SUBSTANTIAL NON-CONFORMITY OR MISREPRESEN-TATION

The first of these is that,

"(a) the prospectus or any document required to be filed therewith,
(i) fails to comply in any substantial respect with any of the requirements of this Part or the regulations,
(ii) contains any statement, promise, estimate or forecast that is misleading, false or deceptive, or
(iii) conceals or omits to state any material facts necessary in order to make any statement contained therein not misleading in the light of the circumstances in which it was made".[61]

---

[59]The contents of the policy are grouped into no less than thirteen sections, of varying length. First the issuer must have a minimum equity capital of $5,000,000. In addition, appropriate records must be kept, and the head office must be in Ontario or a province with similar laws. There are also limits on the amount of borrowing in relation to equity. The number of trustees, their manner of election, and the duties imposed upon them are also subjected to regulation. Another important section concerns the adviser or management company of the trust, which is subject to certain restrictions in regard to conflicts of interest and the fees which it can charge the issuer. The adviser must also have a certain minimum capital, a percentage of which must be invested in the issuing trust or partnership. The statement also requires full disclosure of the investment policy of the trust. Furthermore there are restrictions aimed at preventing excessive concentration on investments of any one type; the percentage that can be invested outside Canada is also limited. There are also provisions for the continuous filing of information as well as guidelines regarding the nature of the information which must be disclosed in the prospectus.

[60]The words "unless it appears to the Director" are indicative of this wide leeway to interpret.

[61]Section 61(1)(a). In Bill 20, branch (iii) is simplified to "contains a mis-

This is essentially a disclosure provision. Branch (i) is straightforward enough and seems superfluous. However, it does have the effect of precluding the director from overlooking or waiving the legislative requirements in special circumstances unless he has been granted an express power to do so.[62] The director uses his residual discretion in refusing prospectuses which do not comply with any of the policy statements relating to prospectuses, since these statements are not expressed to be requirements to be met in this branch.

The importance of branch (ii) lies in the fact that it governs statements respecting future matters or events. It is in fact the general policy of the director to refuse a prospectus containing *any* promise, estimate or forecast whether or not it can be specifically shown to be "misleading, false or deceptive".[63] This policy is currently under review. An earnings estimate is one of the primary tools used by research analysts in commenting upon a new issue. Should they not have the protection of the statutory requirement of full, true and plain disclosure, backed by promoters' and underwriters' certificates, with respect to these statistical data? Moreover, several related jurisdictions (the U.K. and U.S., in particular the SEC) have a more relaxed attitude towards forecasts.[64] On the other hand forecasts by their very nature are imprecise. Permitting them might encourage investors to take them for more than what they are—predictions—and might give credence to exaggerated claims by issuers who are cavalier with the truth.

Branch (iii) is designed to eliminate "half truths", *i.e.*, statements which in isolation are literally true but when viewed in full context are misleading.[65]

---

representation" which in turn is defined actively and passively to mean an untrue statement of material fact or an omission to state a material fact (ss. 62(2)(a)(iii) and 1(1)24).

[62]One of the few examples of such an express power relates to disclosure of sales or gross revenue. Section 28(1)(a) of the Regulation specifically requires such disclosure in the prospectus. Section 28(3) authorizes the Commission, but not the director, to provide an exemption. See for example *Irwin Toy Ltd.*, Apr. 25, 1969 OSCWS 1A.

[63]Section 41 of the Regulation allows such forecasts to be included in a prospectus with the permission of the director.

[64]The U.S. SEC in a 1973 release reached the following conclusions regarding forecasts: CCH Fed. Sec. Law Rep., vol. 2, para. 23-508. Disclosure of forecasts should not be *required* except in two cases: first, where an issuer discloses forecasts apart from filings with the Commission, the issuer must file such forecasts with the Commission. Secondly, any issuer subject to the Exchange Act who discloses a forecast should be required to include in its annual report a statement of the forecast, the circumstances under which it was disclosed and a comparison of actual results with the forecast.

Though not required, forecasts *may* be included in filings with the SEC by reporting issuers who meet certain standards with respect to earnings histories and budgeting experience; these forecasts must however meet certain standards: the assumptions on which the forecast is based must be included, the forecast should relate to sales and earnings and be stated as a reasonably definite figure, and the forecast should be for a reasonable length of time.

[65]The language of the statute is the same as was used in *R. v. Lord Kylsant*, [1932] 1 K.B. 442, 101 L.J.K.B. 97 (C.C.A.). In that case the Court of Criminal

(2) UNCONSCIONABLE CONSIDERATION

The second stated condition is that,

"(b) an unconscionable consideration has been paid or given or is intended to be paid or given for promotional purposes or for the acquisition of property."[66]

What is "unconscionable" is for the director to decide. However, the OSC has articulated this discretion in the case of junior mining financing, where the amount of vendor's consideration for property sold to the enterprise is restricted and the underwriter's profit regulated through his "take-down" of options.[67]

(3) INSUFFICIENT PROCEEDS

(4) ESCROW

(5) LODGING PROCEEDS

The third, fourth and fifth conditions, in relation to insufficient proceeds, escrow and lodging in trust funds from the distribution[68] are best illustrated by detailed policy statements of the OSC relating to junior mining financing.[69] However, they are interpreted and applied in the director's discretion to industrial and other types of companies as well. They are:

Appeal upheld the conviction and jailing of a member of the House of Lords who in making the statement in a prospectus that average profits for the past ten years were a specified amount had neglected to point out that the figures presented had been inflated in early years by war and that in the last few years of the period continuous losses had been sustained.

[66]Section 61(1)(b) (Bill 20, s. 62(2)(b)).

[67]Ontario Policy 3-02, "Junior Mining Exploration and Development Companies", CCH vol. 2, para. 54-896.

[68]Section 61(1)(c), (d) and (e) (Bill 20, s. 62(2)(c), (f) and (g)).

[69]See National Policy 2 and Ontario Policies 3-02 (recently revised, effective April 1, 1976, Feb. 1976 OSCB 36), 3-03 and 3-27, CCH vol. 2, paras. 54-839, 54-896, 54-897 and 54-952. See also Alberta Policy 3-01, CCH vol. 1, para. 24-501; Quebec Policy 8, CCH vol. 3, para. 66-019; British Columbia Policies 3-07, 3-08, 3-10, 3-21, 3-25, CCH vol. 2, paras. 29-957, 29-958, 29-960, 29-971, 29-980. See also the Beatty Report.

The director has some discretion to depart from a strict adherence to these policy statements. In addition, while there are no policy statements governing the application of escrow and related provisions to types of companies other than mining and oil, these policy statements may serve as a rough guide. The conditions which permit release from escrow are different in some of the other provinces. Ontario seems willing to conform when another province with a less stringent escrow policy releases first: see *Kimberly Copper*, Sept. 1968 OSCB 224. A number of the provinces have stated policies on transfer within escrow: see Alberta Policy 3-02, "Mining Companies Including Oil and Gas Companies: Vendor Consideration, Escrow Agreements, Transfers and Releases from Escrow", CCH vol. 1, para. 24-502; British Columbia Policy 3-09, "Transfers Within Escrow", CCH vol. 2, para. 29-959; Ontario Policy 3-03, "Mining and Oil Companies: Vendor Consideration, Retained Interest, Escrow Agreements, Transfers and Releases from Escrow, Amalgamation and Escrowed Shares", CCH vol. 2, para. 54-897. See *Consolidated Manitoba Mines Ltd.*, Dec. 1966 OSCB 5, for a discussion of the Commission approval of transfer within escrow as the basis for revitalizing a company and making a public distribution. See also *Watson v. Canada Permanent Trust Co.*, [1972] 4 W.W.R. 406, 27 D.L.R. (3d) 735 (B.C.S.C.).

Insufficient Proceeds
"(c) the proceeds from the sale of the securities to which the prospectus relates that are to be paid into the treasury of the company, together with other resources of the company, are insufficient to accomplish the purpose of the issue stated in the prospectus;"

Escrow
"(d) such escrow or pooling arrangement as the Director considers necessary or advisable with respect to securities has not been entered into;"

Lodging Proceeds In Trust
"(e) such agreement as the Director considers necessary or advisable to accomplish the objects indicated in the prospectus for the holding in trust of the proceeds payable to the company from the sale of the securities pending the distribution of such securities has not been entered into."

(6) FINANCE COMPANIES

The final condition applies exclusively to a prospectus issued by a finance company; it relates to certain specifications in the Regulation regarding the provision of security and other financial arrangements in connection with this type of issuer.[70] This provision requires the director to refuse a receipt where he is not satisfied with the proposed plan of distribution of the securities being offered, if he is not satisfied with the manner, terms or means upon which they are secured, or if the offering company has failed to meet financial and other conditions contained in the Regulation.

Finance companies receive further special treatment in a provision which permits the director to require additional disclosure from a finance company while a distribution of its securities is continuing.[71] This information may include a statement of source and application of funds or of cash receipts and disbursements, or such other information as may be required to permit the director to satisfy himself as to the matters set out in the preceding paragraph. The director has a wide discretion to stipulate the form which this additional information must take and the period of time which it is to cover. The failure of an issuer to satisfy the director empowers the Commission to order a cessation of trading in its securities.[72]

Further authorization to regulate would seem unnecessary but the Act provides specifically in s. 61(3) for the making of regulations in regard to any of the matters which form the basis for a rejection of a prospectus in s. 61(1)(f). In more specific terms regulations may be made with respect to the paid-up capital and surplus requirements of a finance company, the liquidity of its assets, the ratio of debt to paid-up capital and surplus, audit procedures, the furnishing of interim financial statements, and the provisions of trust indentures including the role of the trustee.[73] This invitation has resulted in the

---

[70]Section 61(1)(f) and Reg. 794, ss. 12(1)(d) and 67 to 71.
[71]Section 63(1) (Bill 20 relegates this provision to the Regulations).
[72]Section 63(2).
[73]Section 61(3) (Bill 20, s. 141, para. 22).

passing of regulations which subject finance companies to particular prospectus provisions. They are also obliged to file detailed continuous reporting obligations (and may be required to give undertakings to do so) even though they might have escaped the continuous reporting obligations of the Act through not being a listed company or not making a prospectus distribution since the coming into force of the Act in May, 1967.[74]

The special regulatory regime for finance companies comes as a result of the failures of Atlantic Acceptance and Prudential Finance.[75]

(7) NEW CONDITIONS

Bill 20 contains three new conditions.[76] The first two were inserted to give the director discretion to refuse to issue a receipt where the financial position or past conduct of an issuer or officer, director, promoter or controlling security holder of the issuer affords reasonable grounds to suppose that the issuer cannot be expected to be financially responsible in the conduct of its business, or where the business of the issuer will not in all likelihood be conducted in accordance with law and with integrity. These subsections operate to extend the power of the Commission to inquire into the soundness of any company that proposes to issue securities. The third entitles the director to refuse a prospectus where one who has prepared or certified any part of a prospectus or has prepared or certified some other related prospectus document is not acceptable. This is not novel in one respect. It is simply a rearrangement of the current Act's provision regarding experts involved in the prospectus document.[77] However the fact that Bill 20 does not restrict it to experts will give it a novel and extended application.

4.06 Continuous Disclosure Undertakings

Each of the uniform act provinces will refuse a prospectus from a company not incorporated in the province until it has delivered undertakings to comply with the proxy, insider trading and financial disclosure provisions.[78] The only sanction for ensuring that these undertakings are subsequently fulfilled where an individual who fails to conform is out of the jurisdiction is an order against the issuer to cease trading or a refusal to accept subsequent prospectuses from it.

---

[74]Reg. 794, ss. 67 to 71. The term "finance company" is expressly defined according to certain traditional hallmarks associated with that type of financial institution (Reg. 794, s. 12(1)(d)). The director has an overriding discretion to designate a company as a finance company (Reg. 794, s. 12(1)(d)(ii)). There is a prescribed prospectus form for such companies (Reg. 794, s. 13 and Form 14) and an issuer whose primary business is something other than finance cannot qualify a prospectus if the word "acceptance", "credit", "finance", "loan" or "trust" is part of its name, unless it is registered under the Loan and Trust Corporations Act (Reg. 794, s. 67(1)).

[75]See Appendices VII and VI.

[76]Section 62(2)(d), (e) and (i).

[77]Section 50(6).

[78]Sections 107, 117, 133; Uniform Policy 2-01, "Undertakings—Extra-Provincial Companies", CCH vol. 2, para. 54-871 and for their rationale see the Kimber Report, chapter 9, and discussion, *post*, part 5.06 at footnotes 38 and 39.

This may not be unfair where the individual is a director or officer of the issuer and to that extent within its power. It may however be unfair when the recalcitrant individual is a ten per cent shareholder failing to file insider reports.

4.07 Mandatory Trust Indenture Provisions

A recent development in corporate-securities legislation in Canada is the introduction of mandatory trust indenture provisions. They are considered here because they are obligatory in a public issue of debt in Ontario.[79] Although the statutory code might perhaps best be categorized as an anti-fraud device it is convenient to consider it here within the broad rubric of distribution of securities. The provisions appear in the BCA alone, and apply to all corporations with outstanding debt obligations issued or guaranteed under a trust indenture if a prospectus or take-over bid circular therefor has been filed under Ontario legislation.[80]

---

[79]British Columbia recently introduced similar provisions into its Companies Act, 1973 (B.C.), c. 18, ss. 94 to 105. So has the CBCA, ss. 77 to 87. They were recommended by the Ontario Select Committee on Company Law, Interim Report, 1967, and are borrowed from the U.S. Trust Indenture Act of 1939, but with notable omissions both in substance and in the procedure for ensuring their application to particular trust indentures. The Select Committee's report did not refer specifically to the series of trust indentures under which Atlantic Acceptance issued its debt obligations. But it is probably fair to say that the loose way in which trustee responsibilities were defined in those documents constituted one factor in permitting that fraud to carry on for a longer period of time and to reach larger proportions than would have been possible under the stricter U.S. provisions. The Prudential Finance fiasco may also claim a share in the parenthood of these new provisions. In the aftermath of that unfortunate disaster the Ontario Government undertook to underwrite the cost of a legal opinion on possible rights which creditors might have for breach of duty by the trustee under the trust indenture. The resulting opinion was pessimistic regarding the chances of recovery; the reason, apart from the state of the general law, was the low standard of trustee obligations in the particular trust indenture provisions. It is fair to say that the trustee arrangements in the Atlantic Acceptance and Prudential Finance situations were largely representative of the norm in large-scale debt issues in Canada at that time.

Ironically, the Atlantic Report recommended that the mandatory trust indenture provisions of the BCA (which was still in Bill form at the time the Report was released) be aborted. It argued that these were an unjust interference with freedom of contract and would have damaging consequences for the development of the Canadian money-market. It concluded that the duties imposed on trustees by those provisions would require substantially higher payments to them. Furthermore it argued that the consequences in Canada would parallel those which the Report observed in the U.S., where the enactment of the U.S. Trust Indenture Act of 1939, the model for the Ontario provisions, resulted in finance companies ceasing to borrow on the security of trust deeds but rather relying simply on the strength of their covenant to repay and preparation of a prospectus or any other periodic information the creditors might insist upon (pp. 1606-7).

[80]Sections 57 to 62. This is one of the few instances where the BCA regulates corporations other than those incorporated in Ontario. For that reason these provisions should more logically be lodged in the Act. For a general consideration of these provisions see the Select Committee Report, *supra*, footnote 79,

The U.S. Act on which these provisions are based resulted from an extremely detailed study under the direction of Professor (later Mr. Justice) William Douglas.[81] The SEC concluded from his report that the public interest in the protection of investors required (1) that the trustees under these indentures be disqualified from acting or serving if they have or acquire conflicts of interest incompatible or inconsistent with their fiduciary obligation, and (2) that they be transformed into active trustees with the obligation to exercise that degree of care and diligence which the law attaches to such a high fiduciary position.[82]

Consequently Congress passed the Trust Indenture Act stating three primary purposes:

(1) To provide full and fair disclosure, not only at the time of original issue of bonds, notes, debentures and similar securities, but throughout the life of such securities.

(2) To provide machinery whereby such continuing disclosure may be made to securities holders, and whereby they may get together for the protection of their own interests.

(3) To assure that the securities holders will have the services of a disinterested indenture trustee, and that such trustee will conform to the high standards of conduct now observed by the more conscientious trust institutions.[83]

With this background we may turn to consider the new Ontario provisions. A minor preliminary point concerns their applicability to organizations other than corporations. *Prima facie* the debt obligations of institutions such as trusts are not affected. However the director may use his discretion to refuse the prospectus of an unincorporated organization which is distributing debt obligations to the public if it does not include similar contractual obligations and rights in its trust deed.[84]

---

at p. 99; the Atlantic Report, pp. 1266-1342 and 1573-74; J.G. Ware, "The Role of the Trustee Under Trust Indentures"; D.L. Johnston "Public and Non-Public Offering Companies under the Ontario Business Corporations Act, 1970"; F. Iacobucci, "The Business Corporations Act, 1970, 'Creation and Financing of a Corporation' and 'Management and Control of a Corporation'".

[81]SEC, Report on the Study and Investigation of the Work, Activities, Personnel and Functions of Protective and Reorganization Committees, Part VI, Trustees Under Indentures (1936) pp. 2-6. See also Loss, vol. 2, pp. 719-25. Subsequent to that study Mr. Justice Douglas became a commissioner and later chairman of the SEC from which vantage point he had the opportunity to shape the administration of his legislative recommendations. His report painted a rather unhappy picture of the way the system of trust indentures was operating at that time. His main criticism was that the wide powers granted to such trustees to protect the security of the investors were not coupled with any duty to exercise them properly. He viewed the security holders as the victims of a situation where freedom of contract had become illusory, and recommended that statutory minimum standards be imposed.

[82]SEC Protective Committee Report, *ibid.*, at p. 110.

[83]H.R. Rep. No. 1016 at 25 and S. Rep. No. 248 at 1-2, 76 Cong., 1st Sess. (1939) 25; see also Trust Indenture Act, s. 302, as quoted in Loss, vol. 1, at p. 725.

[84]The policy statement for real estate investment trusts is a good illustration of this point, *supra*, text at footnote 57. It requires as a condition of acceptance

In order that the statutory code may apply there are three necessary ingredients: a document, the issuance or guaranteeing of debt obligations in accordance with the terms of that document, and the naming of a trustee for the holders of the securities so issued.[85] The document is a "trust indenture", which is defined rather inelegantly but comprehensively to mean "any deed, indenture or document howsoever designated, including any supplement or amendment thereto, by the terms of which a body corporate issues or guarantees debt obligations".[86] The term "debt obligation" is elsewhere defined in the BCA in a broad fashion as "a bond, debenture, note or other similar obligation of a body corporate, whether secured or unsecured".[87] The term "trustee" is defined to mean "any person appointed as trustee under the terms of a trust indenture, whether or not the person is a trust company authorized to carry on business in Ontario".[88] At least one of the trustees must be resident or authorized to do business in Ontario.[89]

Three sets of mandatory provisions regarding the obligations and qualifications of the trustee are deemed to be part of every trust indenture, whether or not they are actually set out in the documents. First a duty of care, diligence and skill is imposed on the trustee. The wording of this duty derives ultimately from the common law; the immediate source is the language used for directors' and officers' duty in s. 144 of the BCA which introduced this test into a corporation statute for the first time. The trustee is required to "exercise that degree of care, diligence and skill that a reasonably prudent trustee would exercise in comparable circumstances." The scope of the duty is indicated by the introductory phrase "in the exercise of the rights and duties prescribed or conferred by the terms of a trust indenture".[90] The duty cannot be waived by agreement of the parties in the form of an exculpatory clause in the indenture.[91]

---

that the trust indenture provisions of the BCA be inserted in the declaration of trust establishing the investment trust, or in the indenture, if any, under which debt obligations are issued.

[85]The mandatory provisions have a retrospective application in that they apply to any trust indenture in existence at the time the BCA came into force (January 1, 1971), as well as those entered into thereafter (s. 62).

[86]Section 57(1)(a).

[87]Section 1(1)11. There is no definition at all in the Act. Caution is needed in dealing with these terms because of varying usages in the U.S., Britain, and Canada. Precision is impossible, but in common Canadian financial parlance a "bond" is a long-term debt secured by some charge on real property, fixed assets or collateral security. A "debenture" is also a long-term debt but either unsecured or secured by a floating charge only. Bonds may be long or short term. A note is similar to a debenture, but usually with a term of less than one year.

[88]Section 57(1)(b).

[89]Section 57(3).

[90]Section 58(1).

[91]The duty imposed on directors and officers in the original bill which became the BCA was also measured against the supposed conduct of "a reasonably prudent director"; however, a "directors' lobby", fearful that such a yardstick implied a professional class of directors with particular hallmarks of excel-

A second provision permits the trustee to rely on information from others in discharging his responsibilities, subject always to the overriding consideration that he is acting in good faith. The trustee must examine the material submitted to him on which he proposes to rely, and determine that it complies with the requirements of the legislation or the trust indenture.[92]

The third provision requires the trustee to give notice to the security holders of every event of default. This must be done within a reasonable time of the event, not to exceed 30 days after the occurrence of the event. The requirement applies only to an event of default that continues at the time the notice is given. However, there is a discretionary qualification to the obligation. The trustee may withhold notice where he in good faith determines that such restraint is in the securities holders' best interests provided he advises the corporation accordingly.[93]

In addition to imposing certain standards of performance upon a trustee, the statutory scheme expands his duty of good faith to prohibit material conflicts of interest. A person is not to be appointed as trustee under a trust indenture if a material conflict of interest exists in the trustee's role as a fiduciary thereunder. The determination of the existence of such a conflict is to be made at the time of such appointment. It is expressly provided that a violation of this prohibition does not affect the validity or enforceability of the trust indenture or the security created by it or issued under it. Rather the trustee is obliged within 90 days after ascertaining that a material conflict of interest exists to eliminate it or to resign.

Only one conflict of interest is expressly defined. A trustee and any person "related" may not be appointed as receiver, receiver and manager, or liquidator of the issuer or guarantor.[94] This prohibition has come under fire for very practical reasons.[95] It is often quickest and cheapest to permit the trustee, who will often be the person most knowledgeable regarding the debtor's or guarantor's affairs, to operate as receiver after an event of default occurs. Possibly a more satisfactory solution which furnishes an adequate safeguard is to provide for the barring of the trustee from the position of receiver by court order on application by a security holder who can show proof of actual conflict. The U.S. Act on which these provisions are modelled does contain several declarations of what constitutes a conflict of interest.[96]

---

lence, convinced the legislative drafting committee to insert the word "person" for "director". No similar change was made in the trustee provision suggesting perhaps that it is an easier task to identify the characteristics of the reasonably prudent trustee as a professional person.

[92]Section 60(6).

[93]Section 62.

[94]Section 61. The term "related person" (s. 1(1)23) is defined somewhat more narrowly than the term "associate" (s. 1(1)3) which is used to describe other types of related or connected persons or organizations in the BCA.

[95]Brief of the Ontario Commercial Law Subsection of the Canadian Bar Association Relating to the BCA, 1968 and Business Corporations Information Act, 1968, February, 1969; see also, the Atlantic Report, pp. 1573-4.

[96]It is uncertain whether or not an Ontario court interpreting the Ontario

The next mandatory provision relates to the evidence of compliance required to be furnished by the obligor to the trustee. The purpose of this requirement is to establish that the conditions precedent contained in the trust indenture have been complied with. The four matters to which this evidence must relate are: certification and delivery of debt obligations, release or substitution of property, satisfaction and discharge of the trust indenture itself, and the taking of any other action at the request of or on the application of the issuer or guarantor.[97] Unfortunately, the timing for furnishing evidence of compliance is not described in detail and leaves a good deal to the imagination. However the statutory scheme requires the obligor to furnish to the trustee annually, its certificate that the issuer or guarantor has complied with all requirements in the trust indenture, non-compliance with which would constitute an event of default.[98] The same provision imposes the same obligation "at any other reasonable time if the trustee so requires". Further, the issuer is required to furnish to the trustee on request evidence as to any action required or permitted to be taken by the issuer under the trust indenture, or as a

---

provisions would feel bound to adopt all of the U.S. express declarations of conflict of interest. For a discussion of the uses of U.S. jurisprudence to interpret Canadian legislation which has a U.S. counterpart, see, *ante*, chapter 1, text at footnote 50.

The language which provides the test for a prohibited conflict differs slightly from one statute to the other. Whereas the U.S. Act requires the indenture to disqualify any trustee who has "any conflicting interest" (s. 310(b)), the Ontario legislation deals only with a *material* conflict of interest, a term which is nowhere defined in the BCA. But see s. 1(1)22 of Bill 20 for a definition of "material" in a broader context. A useful survey of the kinds of conflict of interest caught by the U.S. Act is provided in Loss, vol. 2, pp. 730-1. He sets out six situations in which a trustee is deemed to have a conflicting interest. The first of these is where the trustee acts as trustee under more than one obligation of the same borrower (subject to certain fairly obvious exceptions). Secondly, there is such a conflict if a director or executive officer of the trustee is liable upon the indentures or is an underwriter of any of the obligations in question. The third conflict arises where the borrower or the underwriter directly or indirectly controls the trustee, or *vice versa* (or if both sides are directly or indirectly subject to common control). Fourthly, there is a conflict if the trustee on the one hand and the borrower or underwriter on the other have more than one director or executive officer in common. This restriction extends to the situation where such director or officer is a "partner, employee, appointee, or representative" of the borrower (or of any such underwriter). It is relaxed somewhat if the trustee's board of directors is large enough. The fifth situation is one where more than certain specified percentages of the trustee's voting securities are beneficially owned by the borrowers and underwriters and their respective officials. The last conflict is the converse situation where the trustee owns beneficially more than specified percentages of the securities of the borrower or underwriter or of a person who stands in a control relationship with the borrower (or owns substantial percentages of its securities).

[97]Section 60. The same section outlines the modes of compliance and gives further guidance on the nature of the examination which gives rise to the statements produced.

[98]Section 60(4).

result of an obligation imposed on it by the indenture.[99] Conceivably an extremely nervous trustee, in the absence of statutory guidelines as to the frequency with which such requests should be made, could insist on receiving detailed evidence of compliance daily. It is doubtful however that the obligor (who of course pays the trustee's fees) would suffer such demands indefinitely. Probably the number of such additional requisitions going beyond the statutory minimum of once a year will be in direct proportion to the indications of difficulty in the affairs of the obligor.

These mandatory provisions lay down a basic framework for the contents of first indentures. They do not prevent additional provisions being included so long as they are not in conflict with those required by statute. The setting of a minimum standard below which individual indentures must not fall is not intended to prevent a more demanding obligation being placed on the trustee.

We may note in conclusion a major point of difference between these provisions in Ontario corporations legislation and those in the U.S. Act. Any trust indenture to which the American statute applies must be scrutinized and qualified by the SEC in much the same way as a prospectus. This is not the case with the Ontario enactment, which does not interpose administrative vetting. This restraint is consistent with the Kimber Committee recommendations in several other areas such as take-over bids and proxies where the major thrust was to create statutory obligations but leave it to the parties to carry them out with the support of civil and criminal sanctions.[100]

4.08 Contents of the Prospectus

The Act contains a skeleton guide to the contents of the prospectus. More detailed information is supplied by the Regulation and policy statements.[101] Only the most basic provisions will be discussed here.

The typical prospectus today is a narrative document giving extensive background information about the issuer and its operations as well as a detailed description of the proposed use of the money being solicited from the public. It is probably true to say however that the heart of the prospectus lies in the accompanying financial statements—the balance sheet and statement of profit and loss. These statements provide the data which the most knowledgeable investors will use to make their decisions.[102] The prospectus must include the report of an auditor acceptable to the director on the financial statements signed with the usual opinion that they

---

[99]Section 60(5).

[100]For example, see Part IX of the Act.

[101]See ss. 42 to 53 of the Act; ss. 12 to 43 of the Regulation with Forms 13 to 19; National Policies 1, 12, 13; Uniform Policies 2-02, 2-03, 2-04, and Ontario Policies 3-01 and 3-04, CCH vol. 2, paras. 54-838, 54-849, 54-850, 54-872, 54-873, 54-874, 54-895 and 54-898; and Saskatchewan Policy 2, CCH vol. 3, para. 69-305; ss. 42 to 51 of the present Act will be in the regulations after the passage of Bill 20. For requirements applying to statements of material facts, see ss. 51 to 63 of the Regulation.

[102]Section 43 sets out the basic types of statement that must be included.

"...present fairly the financial position of the company, the subsidiary or the business acquired o₁ to be acquired, as the case may be, and the results of their respective operations for the years and periods under review in accordance with generally accepted accounting principles applied on a consistent basis."[103]
The report may not be qualified in any way where it is reasonably practicable for the presentation of the final financial statements to be revised.[104]

Important in this connection is a national policy statement,[105] which declares that securities administrators will regard pronouncements by the Accounting and Auditing Research Committee of the Canadian Institute of Chartered Accountants to the extent set out in the research recommendations of the "CICA Handbook" as "generally accepted accounting principles" wherever the term is used in securities or companies law.[106]

The auditor is given some statutory guidance as to the contents of his report. He is required to make examinations necessary to his report and to comment or qualify where:
(1) the required financial statements do not agree with the issuer's accounting records,
(2) he has not received all the information and explanations that he has required,
(3) proper accounting records have not been kept, or
(4) the financial statements have not been prepared as required by the legislation.[107]

Unaudited financial statements are permitted for the period subsequent to the last financial year of an issuer, provided they are made up to date not more than 90 days before the issuance of a receipt for the preliminary prospectus and do not cover more than one year after the last completed financial year, with a discretion in the director to permit a longer delay.[108] Financial statements are to receive the express approval of the issuer's board of directors, as evidenced by the signatures of two duly authorized directors, thus rendering potentially liable all members of the board.[109] The director has a discretion to require separate financial statements from a subsidiary, whether or not its financial statements have been consolidated.[110]

---

[103]Section 46(1).
[104]Section 46(4).
[105]No. 27, "Generally Accepted Accounting Principles", CCH vol. 2, para. 54-864. See also, Quebec Policy 7, "Financial Statements", CCH vol. 3, para. 66-018.
[106]CICA Committee on Accounting and Auditing Research, Bulletin Nos. 17 and 23. National Policy 27 applies to continuous disclosure filings as well as to prospectuses. See, *post*, chapter 5 at footnote 33.
[107]Section 46(3).
[108]Section 46(5).
[109]Section 47 (Bill 20, s. 59). Uniform Policy 2-03, "Prospectuses and Amendments—Certification (Section 52), Supporting Documentation", CCH vol. 2, para. 54-873 stipulates that the supporting documents should include the names of all directors present at the authorizing meeting.
[110]Section 49.

The Act also provides for the filing of various consents from experts involved in preparing or certifying the prospectus. This category includes solicitors, auditors, accountants, engineers, appraisers, or any other person whose profession gives authority to his statement.[111] The director has the discretion to waive this requirement if it would be impracticable or unduly harsh.[112] The consent of the auditor or accountant who has prepared the audited financial statements has given rise to considerable disquiet within the accounting profession. A statement is required that the auditor "has read the prospectus and that the information contained therein, which is derived from the financial statements contained in the prospectus *or which is within his knowledge*, is, in his opinion, presented fairly and is not misleading".[113] Some auditors argue that while they are quite prepared to take responsibility for the financial statements—that part of the document falling within their area of expertise[114] —they should not be expected to have any responsibility for the non-financial sections. They contend that they do not have the professional skills to test the narrative part of the documents against any information which might be within their knowledge, acquired in expert capacity or otherwise, and should not therefore have to pronounce on whether the information is "presented fairly and is not misleading". For example, the narrative portion of the prospectus may suggest that there is no litigation which might have material effect on the issuer's position. Yet the auditor may have learned during a casual conversation with the issuer's manager of research that one of its products might violate a patent. The auditor's position is that the information and the test of whether the statement in the circular is misleading lies within the lawyer's field of expertise and not the accountant's, and the accountant should be absolved from any responsibility with regard to it.[115]

By contrast with auditors, solicitors are treated much more gingerly. There is no statutory provision which makes the solicitor responsible on his filed consent for all items within his knowledge. Furthermore a uniform policy statement[116] further calms the fears of lawyers by

---

[111]Section 50(1).
[112]Section 50(2).
[113]Section 50(3), emphasis added.
[114]A leading case on the standard to be applied in judgment on accountant's performance in his area of strict competence is *Guardian Ins. Co. of Canada v. Sharp*, [1941] S.C.R. 164, [1941] 2 D.L.R. 417. See also *Re Hurley and Institute of Chartered Accountants of Manitoba*, [1949] 1 W.W.R. 481, [1949] 2 D.L.R. 801, 93 C.C.C. 345 (Man. K.B.) and such celebrated recent U.S. authorities as *Escott v. Barchris Const. Corp.* (1968), 283 F. Supp. 643 (S.D.N.Y.) and *SEC v. National Student Marketing Corp.* (1973), 360 F. Supp. 284 (D.C.D.C.).
[115]Some auditors avoid this particular kind of dilemma by inserting the conjunctive word *and* for the disjunctive word *or* when reproducing the statutory language in their consent letters. This purports to limit their representation regarding the narrative part of the prospectus to matters "derived from" the financial statements.
[116]Policy 2-04 "Consent of Solicitors—Disclosure of Interest (Section 50)", CCH vol. 2, para. 54-874.

limiting their responsibility. Merely because a law firm's name appears on the face page of the prospectus as the solicitor on whom the underwriter or issuer relies does not establish that he is named as having prepared or certified any part of the prospectus or a valuation report; a consent letter or disclosure of interest is not therefore required of him. On the other hand, where the prospectus makes a statement that summarizes or relies upon a legal opinion (for example, that the securities may be purchased by insurance companies under the relevant insurance company regulation), then the consent and disclosure of interest of that legal counsel as an expert is required.

The experts involved in the preparation of the documents are required to disclose any direct or indirect interest they might have in the securities or property of the issuer or affiliates; and if they anticipate election or appointment to office or employment with the issuer or an affiliate, this must also be divulged.[117] Notwithstanding such disclosure the director may refuse to issue a receipt for a prospectus if the expert is not acceptable to him.[118] The grounds for refusal are not expressly limited to matters of conflict of interest of the kind which could be resolved by disclosure; as a result this section probably permits the director to refuse a prospectus on the ground of lack of confidence in the professional competence of the expert. The same official has a further discretion to require a supplementary consent of the expert for any material change in the prospectus affecting the prior consent.[119] The power to "blacklist" certain experts has occasionally been used against particular professionals, but the customary practice where the director has reason to question the professional competence or integrity of an expert is to refer the circumstances to the appropriate professional disciplinary body. Recently the Ontario Commission exercised this power to "pass" on the qualifications of experts by stipulating that engineering or geological reports for junior mining issues would be acceptable only if emanating from professionals licensed by a Canadian professional body.[120]

This part of the Act has a special provision to assist the "control person" making a distribution under branch two ("secondary primary" distributions) of the definition. The director is given discretion to order the issuer to provide that person with information and to waive signature requirements.[121] This discretion might be necessary where, for example, an individual has had a falling out with other members of the family in a family-controlled company and his desire to sell his shares is opposed by the family.

Anyone intending to engage in a public distribution must notify the Commission before doing so, and also when, in his opinion, he has

---

[117]Section 50(4) and (5).
[118]Section 50(6). See British Columbia Policy 3-01 "Engineering Reports— Requirements for Submitting to Commission", CCH vol. 2, para. 29-951; Quebec Policy 23, "Guide for Mining Engineers, Geologists and Prospectors Submitting Reports to the Commission", CCH vol. 3, para. 66-078.
[119]Section 51.
[120]Feb. 1974 OSCB 18; CCH vol. 2, para. 54-952.
[121]Section 60 (Bill 20, s. 65).

ceased.[122] These notifications are published in the OSC weekly summary. Where a material change occurs during a distribution an amendment to the prospectus must be filed "as soon as practicable" and in any event within ten days of the change.[123] The Act provides little guidance regarding what is a material change. The test is stated broadly in terms of effect—whether the change "makes untrue or misleading any statement of material fact" contained in the prospectus. The prospectus is "fresh" for one year. If the distribution is still continuing, a new prospectus must be qualified, *i.e.*, a receipt obtained therefor, within 20 days of the end of the twelve-month period beginning on the date a receipt was obtained for the preliminary prospectus.[124]

Where a receipt for a prospectus has been issued and the Commission subsequently determines that any of the six conditions specified in s. 61(1) are present, it may order the distribution to the public of those securities to cease, thus bringing all trading to a halt.[125] Such an order may be made with or without a prior hearing, but in the later case it expires within fifteen days.[126] The order has the effect of revoking the director's receipt for the prospectus.[127] Moreover the Commission has a general cease trade power which may be exercised "in the public interest."[128]

4.09 Waiting Period

The Act regulates selling efforts during a distribution by imposing a delay, called the "waiting period", between the filing of the preliminary prospectus and the effective date of the prospectus.[129] This period must be a minimum of ten days in order to provide some opportunity for potential purchasers to consider the preliminary prospectus, digest the information it contains and come to some conclusion regarding whether they wish to purchase once the prospectus is finally qualified. Underwriters also benefit from the existence of this interval which permits them to "test the market" for a security before being firmly committed.

---

[122]Section 54. Bill 20, s. 64(2) tightens the requirement by removing the words "in his opinion" and substituting "forthwith". See Quebec Policy 6, CCH vol. 3, para. 66-017.

[123]Section 55. Bill 20, s. 58(1) provides for an amendment to the prospectus both while the preliminary prospectus is still outstanding and while the final prospectus is accepted but distribution is still continuing. It thus combines ss. 55 and 40(2) of the Act.

[124]Section 56 (Bill 20, s. 63). See Uniform Policy 2-02 "Prospectuses—Annual Re-Filings", CCH vol. 2, para. 54-872; Ontario Policy 3-01 "Fee Calculation for Annual Re-filing of Prospectuses", CCH vol. 2, para. 54-895; Manitoba Policy 3-07 "Primary Distribution Statistics", CCH vol. 2, para. 34-997.

[125]Section 62(1) (Bill 20, s. 71(1)), discussed, *supra*, part 4.05(1) through (6).

[126]Section 62(2) (Bill 20, s. 71(2)).

[127]Section 62(3) (Bill 20, s. 71(3)).

[128]Section 144.

[129]Section 36 (Bill 20, s. 66). See the Kimber Report regarding this waiting period and the use of the "red herring" or preliminary offering circular (paras. 5.24 to 5.28). See also National Policy 21 "National Advertising—Warnings", CCH vol. 2, para. 54-858.

During this period the prohibition on "trading" is relaxed to permit certain activities of a limited nature. The tombstone advertisement only may be used,[130] and even this is permitted only if the source from which a preliminary prospectus may be obtained is indicated.[131] The cryptic brevity of this notice may be summarized thus:

"a notice, circular, advertisement or letter to or [other communication] with any person or company identifying the security proposed to be issued, stating the price thereof, if then determined, the name and address of a person or company from whom purchases of the security may be made..."

The key word in this provision is "identifying". Interpreted at its narrowest it would permit only the name of the company and the most essential features of the class of shares or debt obligations to be stated. The Ontario Commission tends to adopt a narrow interpretation, although in the first public issue of Canada Development Corporation the objects of the corporation appeared in the tombstone advertisement.[132] In addition a preliminary prospectus may be circulated to potential investors and expressions of interest solicited, provided that the preliminary prospectus is forwarded no later than the point at which those approached indicate an interest in purchasing.[133] A record must be kept for the inspection of the Commission of those to whom a preliminary prospectus has been distributed.[134] It is this latter requirement which ensures that the use of the preliminary prospectus is confined to a fairly small circle of potential purchasers.

The director is empowered to order trading to cease without giving notice and the opportunity for a hearing, whenever it appears to him that the preliminary prospectus is substantially defective as to form *and* content.[135] This cessation remains until a satisfactory preliminary prospectus is filed and forwarded to each recipient of a defective one.

4.10 Civil Liability on Distribution

There are three statutory civil liability remedies applicable to distributions: the right of withdrawal, the right of rescission and the right to recover damages from directors and others connected with the issuer.[136] These rights are considered in turn.

(1) THE DUTY TO DELIVER AND RIGHT TO WITHDRAW

One of the basic objects of the statutory scheme is to attempt to ensure that a prospective purchaser considers the information which the statute requires be disclosed to him. Taking this object one step further, provision is made for the purchaser to reconsider on reading

---

[130]For a sample, see, *supra*, part 4.01(3) and footnote 5.
[131]Section 36(2) (Bill 20, s. 66(2)). This notice may contain such further information as the regulations may permit; none have been promulgated.
[132]The Financial Post, Aug. 23, 1975, p. 15.
[133]Section 36(2)(c) (Bill 20, s. 66(2)(c)).
[134]Section 37 (Bill 20, s. 68).
[135]Section 40(1) (Bill 20, s. 69).
[136]Consideration should also be given to the common law, a detailed consideration of which is beyond the scope of this book but which has undergone fundamental changes since the landmark decision of *Hedley Byrne & Co. Ltd. v. Heller & Partners Ltd.*, [1964] A.C. 465, [1963] 2 All E.R. 575 (H.L.).

the information and, if desired, to withdraw from the agreement of purchase and sale. To these ends an obligation is imposed on the vendor to deliver a prospectus to the purchaser or his agent coupled with a right to withdraw from the transaction within a specified period.[137]

Anyone receiving a purchase order or subscription for a security being distributed to the public is required to deliver or mail the prospectus or amended prospectus to the purchaser not later than midnight of the second day after entering into the agreement of purchase and sale.[138] The duty to deliver is not imposed, however, upon a vendor, acting as agent of the purchaser, who has received an order or subscription to purchase, provided that the agent is acting "solely as the agent of the purchaser with respect to the purchase and sale in question", and is not receiving compensation from the vendor of the securities. Consequently delivery of a prospectus to a purchaser does not occur where the normal agency relationship prevails between a purchaser and his broker. However, where a dealer is a member of the banking or selling group in an underwriting and purchases as principal for resale to his customer, the obligation to deliver a prospectus arises.

The purchaser is given a two-day cooling off period or automatic right of withdrawal that does not depend on misrepresentation or other deficiency.[139] This right only applies, however, where there is a duty to deliver a prospectus to the purchaser. The latter is given until midnight on the second day after receipt of the prospectus to notify the vendor that he intends not to be bound by the agreement.[140] This right would appear to be independent of the time limit on the duty to deliver set out above; thus if a prospectus was delivered outside the two-day period measured from the agreement date, the purchaser would still have an additional two days from actual delivery of the prospectus to withdraw, should he so desire. This distinction creates a formidable potential civil liability in instances where an issuer was unknowingly involved in a distribution to the public to which the prospectus requirements applied because, for example, it was mistaken in its belief that an exemption was available, or chose to ignore the law. Not having delivered a prospectus, the issuer may be subject to his purchaser's withdrawal rights in perpetuity, absent defences such as laches or waiver. This argument, however, has been rebutted in a recent adjudication *Ames et al. v. Investo-Plan Ltd.*[141] where the

---

[137]Cynics have been heard to quote "an old Wall Street saying" in reply to this obligation: "You can drag a purchaser to a prospectus but you can't make him read it".

[138]Section 64(1) (Bill 20, s. 72(1)).

[139]Section 64(2) (Bill 20, s. 72(2)).

[140]*Ibid.*

[141][1973] 5 W.W.R. 451, 35 D.L.R. (3d) 613 (B.C.C.A.). The Court rejected in a cursory fashion the view that the rescission right lasts indefinitely until a prospectus is delivered, holding instead that s. 62, the British Columbia counterpart to s. 65 of the Ontario Act, which confers a right of rescission on the purchaser, presupposes compliance with the filing provision (s. 37 in the British Columbia Act; s. 35 in the Ontario Act) and is otherwise ineffective. See

British Columbia Court of Appeal held that non-compliance with the provision requiring the filing and clearance of the prospectus before securities may be sold to the public did not render a contract for the sale of shares void or voidable so that the purchaser could rescind, except in the circumstances explicitly set down in the counterpart to s. 65 of the Act. Instead, the effect of failure to comply with the filing provision was simply to subject the issuer to the statutory penalty, a fine of $2,000.

The right is not available if the purchaser is a registrant, or if he sells or otherwise transfers beneficial ownership of the security within the two-day period otherwise than to secure indebtedness. The purchaser does not need to rely on any material misrepresentation or other ground, and may withdraw entirely at his discretion.[142]

---

the criticism of this case by S. M. Beck in 52 *Can. Bar. Rev.* 589 (1974), especially at pp. 594-5.

For early cases involving the effect of failure to qualify a prospectus or obtain a licence to sell see *Re Carpenter Ltd.; Hamilton's Case* (1916), 35 O.L.R. 626, 29 D.L.R. 683 (H.C.); *McAskill v. Northwestern Trust Co.*, [1926] S.C.R. 412, [1926] 3 D.L.R. 612, 7 C.B.R. 440; *Re Great North Ins. Co.; Painter's Case*, [1925] 1 W.W.R. 1149, [1925] 2 D.L.R. 778, 21 A.L.R. 326 (C.A.); *Re Bluebird Corporation* (1926), 58 O.L.R. 486, [1926] 2 D.L.R. 484, 7 C.B.R. 522 (C.A.); *Martin v. Clarkson* (1926), 58 O.L.R. 618, [1926] 3 D.L.R. 29, 7 C.B.R. 619 (C.A.).

[142]Apart from the right of withdrawal separately conferred in the Act, there is the question of the effect of a failure to deliver on the validity of the transaction. In *Dorsch v. Freeholders Oil Co. Ltd. et al.*, [1965] S.C.R. 670, 52 D.L.R. (2d) 658, 52 W.W.R. 304, the Supreme Court showed its reluctance to interpret prospectus delivery provisions as entailing consequent relief for the purchaser in the event of failure to follow them. The plaintiff had assigned a royalty interest and a lease-hold interest in his land to the defendant, in return for its shares and a portion of any benefits resulting. Although the defendant had prospectuses available, its agent had not supplied one to the plaintiff. The Saskatchewan Companies Act, R.S.S. 1940, c. 113 stipulated by s. 116(1) that the company furnish every person invited to subscribe for shares offered by the prospectus with a copy at the time the invitation was made and also provided by s. 129(1) that it was not lawful to issue any form of application or subscription for shares unless the form was issued with a prospectus. The Act stipulated that an allotment upon an application in contravention of s. 129 was void, but prescribed no relief for a contravention of s. 116(1).

Martland J. noted that s. 116 and s. 129 were introduced into the Act at the same time in 1933, but were not intended to cover identical ground. He construed "issue" in s. 129(1) to mean "the publication and putting into circulation" by the company of share application forms and prospectuses but not the furnishing of a prospectus to a purchaser or subscriber. He held that the company complied with s. 129 in supplying copies of the prospectus to its agent. While the latter's failure to furnish one to the plaintiff purchaser might have breached s. 116, it could not involve a breach of s. 129, since the requirements of the latter section had already been fully satisfied.

In the absence of express relief for a violation of s. 116 in the Act, Martland J. decided that at most it might render the purchase voidable; but since six years had elapsed since the purchase, and the plaintiff had attended and voted at two annual meetings, he was deemed to have waived any rescission rights. (*Ibid.*, pp. 679-80.)

A prospectus sent by prepaid mail is conclusively deemed to have been received by the addressee in the ordinary counsel of the mail.[143] The onus of proving that the time for delivery of such notice has expired is upon the vendor.[144] Finally the prospectus is required to contain a statement of this right of withdrawal.[145]

In reality the protection afforded by the two-day cooling off period is more illusory than real. In the great majority of small purchases the individual will be buying through an agent, and will not enjoy the right. In the case of larger institutions purchasing directly from a principal, they will not ordinarily exercise their right for fear of being left off the list of selected purchasers for "hot issues" on subsequent occasions.

(2) MISLEADING STATEMENTS OR OMISSIONS—RIGHT OF RESCISSION

The Act provides a right of rescission where the prospectus received by a purchaser or his agent contains an untrue statement of a material fact, or a failure to state a material fact necessary to make a statement not misleading in the circumstances.[146]

At common law, reliance on a misrepresentation would ordinarily be necessary to give rise to a right to rescind. It seems that reliance on the misrepresentation need not be proved by a plaintiff in the s. 65 action. It would be helpful if the statute expressed the concept of deemed reliance as it does in the parallel provision, s. 142. However, s. 65(7) expresses that the statutory right is in addition to and without derogation from any other right the purchaser may have at law. Moreover the right seems to be automatic on the condition of misrepresentation being satisfied: "a...purchaser...has a right to rescind...if the prospectus...contains an untrue statement...or omits to state a material fact...". Finally, the polar extreme of deemed

---

This judgment can be criticized for placing an unduly narrow construction on the term "issue"; and one might infer that the reason for attaching no consequential relief to s. 116 was that the Legislature intended the issue of a prospectus to be co-extensive in meaning with furnishing the same to a purchaser in which case the relief provided for a breach of s. 129 would apply. The lower court (the Saskatchewan Court of Appeal (1964), 48 W.W.R. 257, 45 D.L.R. (2d) 44, Hall J.A. for a unanimous court) found that "issue" did have this larger meaning and that the contract was void, applying *McAskill v. Northwestern Trust Co.*, [1926] S.C.R. 412, [1926] 3 D.L.R. 612, 7 C.B.R. 440. But, like the legendary phoenix renewing itself from the ashes of its own destruction, the contract so held void was resurrected on another principle contained in the *McAskill* case: that a new contract could be formed by conduct following a void transaction. The plaintiff's activities as a shareholder were held to be sufficient to produce this result, and so the Court of Appeal reached the same result as later did the Supreme Court but travelled a different route. *Cf. Ames v. Investo-Plan Ltd., supra*, footnote 141.

[143]Section 64(4) (Bill 20, s. 72(4)).

[144]Section 64(8) (Bill 20, s. 72(8)).

[145]Section 64(9). Bill 20, s. 61 indicates that every prospectus must contain a statement of the rights given a purchaser by ss. 72 and 129, *i.e.*, the right of withdrawal and the right of action for rescission or damages for misrepresentation in the prospectus.

[146]Section 65(1).

reliance—actual knowledge of the misrepresentation by the purchaser—is stated as a defence to rescission.

The provision sets out three circumstances negativing the right to rescind.[147] The first is where both the issuer and the underwriter who executed the certificate in the prospectus were unaware of the misstatement or omission, and could not in the exercise of reasonable diligence have discovered it. In cases where the underwriter but not the issuer can bring himself within this defence, the underwriter would ordinarily be liable to the purchaser but would have a right over against the issuer in damages. Secondly, the right of rescission is not available if the purchaser knows of the misstatement or omission at the time of purchase. Finally, the right may not be exercised if the misstatement or omission is disclosed and corrected by an amendment received by the purchaser.

As in the case of the withdrawal right the purchaser, in order to rescind, must still be the owner of the security.[148] Moreover, like s. 64 there is a further limitation as to time. The action to rescind must be commenced within 90 days from receipt of the prospectus.[149]

(3) FALSE STATEMENTS—ACTIONS AGAINST DIRECTORS ET AL.

It is curious that the statute imposes no direct civil liability on the issuer for misrepresentation. However, common law contractual principles will apply. Under the standard firm underwriting agreement the purchaser will seek his remedy in contract against the selling dealer for misrepresentation in the prospectus; where that selling dealer is not the underwriter the selling dealer will seek recourse against the underwriter. It then remains for the underwriter to sue the issuer on the underwriting agreement where the misrepresentation or other fault lay with the issuer. Most underwriting agreements contain covenants and warranties which give the underwriter the maximum amount of protection in this regard. Where they do not exist one could anticipate that a court would conclude an implied warranty exists as to truthfulness on the issuer's part.

The statutory civil liability provision which has the sharpest teeth attaches personal liability to directors and other persons associated with a prospectus. This provision has an interesting history; its roots go back to the English Directors' Liability Act of 1890, which reversed the House of Lords decision in *Derry v. Peek.*[150] In that case it was held that intention to deceive had to be shown before recovery could be had by a purchaser for a false statement in a prospectus. Negligence or recklessness in preparing the document was not sufficient. The

---

[147]Section 65(3).

[148]For other cases involving misrepresentations in prospectuses and a shareholder's right of rescission see *R. v. Garvin* (1909), 18 O.L.R. 49, 14 C.C.C. 283 (S.C.); *Fort William Commercial Chambers Ltd. v. Braden* (1914), 6 O.W.N. 24, 16 D.L.R. 864 (S.C.); affirmed 7 O.W.N. 679 (C.A.); *Johnson v. Johnson* (1913), 18 B.C.R. 563, 5 W.W.R. 525, 14 D.L.R. 756 (C.A.).

[149]Section 65(2). In Bill 20 essentially the same relief as granted by s. 65 is conferred by s. 129. The latter is a compilation of s. 65 and s. 142 of the Act. Accordingly it will be discussed after s. 142 has first been considered.

[150](1889), 14 App. Cas. 337; [1886-90] All E.R. Rep. 1 (H.L.).

Directors' Liability Act expunged the *scienter* requirement from the misrepresentation and the current statutory provision,[151] which is not altogether free from ambiguity, continues this position. Not only this, but in a strenuous attempt to turn *caveat emptor* on its head, it dispenses with proof of reliance as well. The remedy gives to every purchaser of securities to which a prospectus relates a right to recover any loss or damage he has sustained as a result of the purchase.[152]

An initial problem is raised by the term "purchaser" which is not further described. There are in fact as many as five levels of purchasers on a normal public distribution: the managing or lead underwriter, the members of the banking group, the members of the selling group, the first "public" purchaser, and subsequent "secondary" purchasers in the marketplace. The first three of these are contractually linked with the issuer directly or indirectly and are not in need of protection; it is unlikely that the remedies provided by the legislation were intended to extend to them. Similarly, in view of the fact that the requirement of a prospectus is exclusively designed to provide disclosure in a distribution to the public, the first sale by the initial "public" purchaser to other members of the public, as well as any subsequent sales, would not fall within the regulatory scheme. Thus it is the first "public" purchaser who enjoys the remedy.[153]

It is however at least arguable that a "purchaser" in the after-market buying from the initial public purchaser might enjoy the remedy, since the right is granted to "every" purchaser. The only qualification is that he be a purchaser "of the securities to which the prospectus relates". Such an interpretation is rendered improbable however by the deemed reliance provision of s. 142. The purchaser who enjoys the remedy "is deemed to have relied upon the statements made"[154] in the disclosure document whether or not a prospectus was actually received. Applying the canon of construction known as the "presumption against fundamental change", we may suppose that this deeming provision covers those at whom the prospectus is directed and not the other group constituted by purchasers in the secondary market.

We turn now from the problem of the class of persons eligible for the remedy to examine the question of what state of facts will make the remedy available. The wrong in question is in the nature of a

---

[151]Section 142.

[152]See also *Farrel v. Manchester et al.* (1908), 40 S.C.R. 339, 5 E.L.R. 293, and *Chapman v. Warren et al.*, [1936] O.R. 145, [1936] 2 D.L.R. 157 (S.C.). The CCA prospectus liability provision does not deem reliance. The plaintiff must establish that he subscribed "on the faith of the prospectus", s. 80. The CBCA deletes the substantive prospectus provisions, s. 186, relying instead on provincial securities legislation.

[153]This construction is substantiated somewhat by the language of s. 65 in granting the 90-day right of rescission. The person enjoying this right is the "party to a contract as purchaser resulting from the offer of a security in the course of distribution to the public". Once *he* purchases the security, the course of distribution to the public of that specific security is terminated or exhausted.

[154]Section 142.

misrepresentation, but the test for determining its presence is unsatisfactory.

Liability is triggered "if a material false statement is contained" in the disclosure document. There is neither a definition of this phrase in s. 142, nor is it linked by reference to the disclosure formula set out earlier in the Act[155] which requires first, full, true and plain disclosure[156] and secondly, additional information to ensure that any statement in the disclosure document (whether or not expressly required to be contained therein) is augmented to the degree necessary to make the required statement not misleading in the light of the circumstances in which it was made.[157] It would be more satisfactory if the provision under discussion were either couched in the same terms as these earlier sections or failing this followed the language used by s. 65 in providing for the right of rescission. The problem in brief is whether an absence of disclosure or an omission to state a fact can be construed as a "material false statement"; the contrary view would be that there must be some patent falsity in a statement actually made.[158]

The liability attaches to every director of the issuer, and to its chief executive officer and chief financial officer, as well as any promoter of the issuer who signed a certificate contained in the prospectus pursuant to s. 52. There are five express defences alternatively available. In each case the defendant has the burden of proof. These are:

(1) The prospectus was filed without his knowledge or consent and on becoming aware he forthwith gave reasonable public notice to that effect.

(2) Before the purchase of the securities, on becoming aware of a false statement, he withdrew his consent with reasonable public notice and with reasons.

(3) He had reasonable grounds for, and did in fact, believe the statement to be true.

(4) He had no reasonable grounds to believe an expert was not competent to make an expert report.

(5) A false statement by an official person was a correct and fair representation of that statement.[159]

It is the third of these defences that presents the most difficult interpretive problems.[160]

---

[155]Sections 41 to 46.

[156]Section 41.

[157]Section 42.

[158]See for example *R. v. Lord Kylsant*, [1932] 1 K.B. 442, 101 L.J.K.B. 97 (C.C.A.) for material half-truths, cited and discussed, *supra*, footnote 65.

[159]Section 142.

[160]The leading Canadian authority on a misleading prospectus and civil liability is *Nesbitt, Thomson & Co. Ltd. v. Pigott and J.M. Pigott Construction Co. Ltd.*, [1941] S.C.R. 520, [1941] 4 D.L.R. 353. For an analysis of the impact of statutory civil liability under the U.S. Securities Act, 1933 and a consideration of this third "due diligence" test and the English precedent, *Adams v. Thrift*, [1915] 2 Ch. 21, 84 L.J. Ch. 729, there relied on, see *Escott v. BarChris Construction Corp.* (1968), 283 F. Supp. 643 (S.D.N.Y.). One must be aware that the network of liability is much more extensive in the United

"Compensation for any loss or damage" in the section is measured according to the amount of the actual loss suffered. There can be no allowance for a prospective loss of profits because this would result in giving the plaintiff the difference between the price paid and the value of his bargain.[161]

There is no statutory limitation period expressed within which this right must be exercised. Presumably the ordinary statute of limitations for actions in contract will apply.

(4) REFORM PROPOSALS AND PROSPECTUS MISREPRESENTATION

Bill 20 clears up some of the difficulties discussed above. Section 129 contains elements of both the right of rescission and the damage action against directors *et al.* for material false statements.[162] By means of this single broad provision not only does liability initially attach in a greater variety of situations but greater flexibility is provided for in enforcing the rights conferred. Section 129(1) states in part that:

"Where a prospectus together with any amendment to the prospectus contains a misrepresentation, a purchaser who purchases a security offered thereby shall be deemed to have relied on such misrepresentation and has a right of action for rescission or damages..."

We shall examine this provision with reference to the two predecessor sections to see how they have been altered and their application expanded.

First, with respect to rescission, s. 129 imports a deemed reliance provision into the situation where the purchaser is seeking rescission; it would seem therefore to eliminate the problem discussed above where deemed reliance was not expressed in s. 65. Secondly, the new provision contains no restriction that the person seeking rescission must still be the owner. Presumably the purchaser will be governed by common law bars to rescission, and if they apply, he will be able to switch over to the alternative remedy of damages. It should also be noted that there is no 90-day time limit within which an action must be brought. Both for the action to rescind and the one for damages the general limitation periods of the Bill the lesser of three years from the date of the transaction or 180 days from first knowledge of the error will apply.[163] These are more generous time periods than the 90 days in the present Act at least for the right of rescission. However, some will argue that the predecessor open-ended provision in Bill 75[164] which gave a right to sue for one year after knowledge of the misrepresenta-

---

States than under the Canadian Acts. In particular, underwriters and experts such as auditors are expressly burdened with statutory civil liability in the U.S. but not yet in Canada.

[161]*Uncle Ben's Tartan Holdings Ltd. v. Northwest Sports Enterprises Ltd.*, [1974] 4 W.W.R. 69, 46 D.L.R. (3d) 280 (B.C.S.C.).

[162]Sections 65 and 142 of the Act.

[163]Section 137. The latter provision was included in Bill 20 in response to a number of submissions suggesting that the "aroused" plaintiff should get on with his action.

[164]Section 130.

tion first came or ought reasonably to have come to the purchasers' attention would have been more appropriate.

So far as the conditions giving rise to the right are concerned, there must be a "misrepresentation". This is defined in s. 1(1)24 in a way that reflects almost exactly the language of the former s. 65: an untrue statement of a material fact or an omission to state a material fact.

There are also important changes in the defences available to a rescission action. They are basically a modification of those existing in s. 142 of the Act. Thus the requirement that both issuer and underwriter be unaware of the falsity of the misrepresentation disappears, broadening the defences available. Basically what is needed for an effective defence under the new provision is timely withdrawal of approval of the misrepresentation with notice or a reasonable belief in the truth of the misrepresentation.

Turning to the situation where the plaintiff seeks damages, the term purchaser has been clarified by the addition of the phrase "who purchases a security offered thereby". This strongly implies that only the initial public sale after issuance is covered. Turning to the facts which give rise to liability we have already noted the definition of misrepresentation, which settles the problem discussed earlier regarding the scope of the phrase "material false statement" in the present s. 142; it is clear that an omission may qualify if it is material.[165] Another aspect in which the new section may be broader concerns the scope of the term prospectus itself. Section 142 requires the issuing of a receipt by the director in order to bring the liability provisions into operation; the broader language of s. 129 may well cover a preliminary prospectus or a document which contains the kind of information found in a prospectus but which has not been qualified in any way.

The most important way in which the scope of the section has been broadened, however, is in respect to the persons who may be made liable. These now include underwriters and every person or company required by the Regulation to file a consent or who has signed the prospectus. This represents a highly visible shift to the U.S. practice of attaching liability to experts engaged in the preparation of the prospectus.[166] Moreover, the issuer itself is now subject to statutory liability; so is the "selling security holder". This latter provision will catch control persons making a secondary primary distribution.

Bill 20[167] contains the same defences available to a defendant in an action for damages for material false statement in the Act but with several significant additions. First, the purchaser's actual knowledge of the truth vitiates his action. Secondly, the other defences are not available to the issuer or the selling security holder (underwriter or control person). Thirdly, a defendant claiming he had reasonable grounds for believing a misrepresentation to be true will have to establish that he made reasonable investigation. So too will the expert asserting reasonable grounds for belief in a misrepresentation in the

---

[165]See Bill 20, s. 1(1)22 for the definition of "material".
[166]*Escott v. BarChris, supra,* footnote 160, makes it clear that their liability is limited to the parts of the prospectus they "expertised".
[167]Section 129.

expertised portion of the statement.[168] Moreover that expert will be obliged to notify the Commission and give reasonable public notice of a misuse of his report or a misrepresentation in it.

(5) SPECIAL RESCISSION PROPOSALS FOR MUTUAL FUNDS
Bill 20 contains a special consumer protection provision applicable to mutual fund sales only.

There is a cooling-off period of two days for outright purchases of mutual fund securities and 60 days in the case of contractual plan purchases.[169] These rights are limited to purchases of $50,000 or less; the remedial provision is thus directed towards the smaller investor most apt to be imposed upon by the persuasive presence of the salesman. The extra time is designed to give him an opportunity to analyze and digest the disclosure information provided and reconsider his purchase.[170] The two-day cooling off period for lump sum sales of mutual funds differs from the two-day withdrawal right for sales of other securities in that the latter is limited to situations where a prospectus must be delivered to the purchaser. The rescission notice must be given to the seller within 48 hours after receipt of the confirmation for a lump sum purchase of mutual funds or within 60 days after receipt of the confirmation for the initial payment under a contractual plan purchase of mutual funds. It is not possible to link up two separate transactions over a period of time so as to avail oneself of the longer cooling off period where both purchases have been made outright without the use of a contractual plan. Furthermore the contractual plan rescission right applies only to payments scheduled to be made within the 60 days for rescinding contractual plan purchases.[171] The notice to the seller must be in writing and "may be given by prepaid mail, telegram or other means".[172] The language of the subsection would suggest that notice has already been "given" when a letter has been posted. In this case rescission would be effective even in cases where actual receipt occurs outside the 48-hour period. The seller is obliged to refund not simply the amount of money applicable for investment in the mutual fund but also "the amount of sales charges and fees relevant to the investment of the purchaser".[173]

4.11 Distribution Out of the Jurisdiction
A peculiar problem arises when a corporation whose securities presently trade in Ontario chooses to effect a new distribution entirely outside

---

[168]In s. 131 of Bill 20 the standard of reasonableness for the investigation or belief is expressed to be that "of a prudent man in the circumstances of the particular case".
[169]Section 136(1).
[170]The equation—size equals sophistication—obviating the need for the Act's protections, is a frequent theme in the Act. Examples are s. 19(1)9b the exemption for the sale of assets worth $100,000 or more, s. 19(2)3 the exemption for promissory notes of $50,000 or more, and s. 19(3) the exemption for security purchases of $97,000 or more.
[171]Section 136(2).
[172]Section 136(3).
[173]Section 136(5).

t ...... the OSC took the position that this was a distribution to the public requiring an Ontario prospectus. This position required that "public" be interpreted to mean "the public anywhere" and not, more restrictively, "the public in Ontario". Sometime later the OSC altered its view. For a while it held that a distribution to members of the public outside Ontario did not require an Ontario prospectus if done by a company incorporated outside Ontario, but that an Ontario prospectus would be required for such a distribution by a company incorporated within the province. Presumably the rationale for this "split approach" was that in the second case some aspects of a trade in the course of a distribution would occur in Ontario, since the Ontario incorporated company would have an Ontario head office. The questionable feature of this approach was that it too presumed that "public" in the phrase distribution to the public was not confined to the Ontario public.

Currently the OSC holds that the provincial securities legislation may embrace and protect only that province's public; it is only when the Ontario public will be the target of the distribution that a prospectus will be required. A distribution to a "public" other than the Ontario public will not require a prospectus approved by the OSC. A problem will arise, however, when (or if) those securities, after initial distribution out of the jurisdiction, ultimately find their way into the hands of an Ontario public to which they have not previously been distributed. It may be argued that according to branch one of the definition of distribution, a distribution to the public will be taking place on their resale into Ontario, requiring the seller then to qualify a prospectus.[174] If so the Commission is entitled to suspend trading in Ontario in those securities at that time. It may, however, act at a stage before the resale of unqualified securities can actually be proved, since such securities may easily become mixed with securities which are already qualified. The Commission assumes that it is expected to act in anticipation of illegal distribution in Ontario and not merely after the fact.

To summarize, the Commission will ordinarily consider suspending trading of those securities of a company already trading in Ontario when it makes a distribution outside of Ontario on two grounds: (1) on the basis of an apprehended breach of the prospectus requirements on their resale into Ontario, and (2) on the basis that a material event has occurred in the company's affairs without adequate disclosure in Ontario. Technically, of course, the issuer could satisfy the Commission's concern under ground two by filing a timely disclosure statement about the distribution.

In view of this attitude it becomes important to determine what will satisfy the OSC so as to preclude a cease-trading order. Ordinarily if the distribution is done in a jurisdiction whose prospectus standards

---

[174]See *Hretchka et al. v. A.-G. B.C., B.C. Securities Commission and Superintendent of Brokers*, [1972] S.C.R. 119, 19 D.L.R. (3d) 1; quashing appeal [1971] 1 W.W.R. 163 *sub nom. Re Hretchka et al. and Chromex Investments Ltd.*, 16 D.L.R. (3d) 273 *sub nom. Re Chromex Nickel Mines Ltd.* (B.C.C.A.), discussed, *ante*, part 2.10, and, *infra*, footnote 177, which casts doubts on this position.

are similar to those of Ontario, the qualification of the prospectus or equivalent documents in that jurisdiction may be sufficient. If, however, the distribution standards of the other jurisdictions do not satisfy the OSC, it may insist on an Ontario prospectus being qualified here.

One further problem that remains, however, when securities are distributed outside Ontario and then resold into Ontario is this: what civil liability remedies which are related to the prospectus would be available to the Ontario public purchasing the securities for the first time in Ontario? It seems probable that buyers could not use the right of rescission against the sellers (if they can be traced) or the action in damages against directors *et al.* for misrepresentation, since these seem to turn on an Ontario qualified prospectus (with a misrepresentation) being present. Possibly, the right of withdrawal extant for two days after the delivery of a prospectus may be available.[175]

All of the securities administrations in Canada have partially addressed the mirror image of this problem of out of province distributions in a national policy statement.[176] Unfortunately the thrust of the statement is simply to warn trading registrants to ensure securities in distribution elsewhere are qualified for trading in their jurisdiction. The statement does address one jurisdictional point: a trade in a registrant's jurisdiction takes place when he accepts an order in that jurisdiction even though the trade will be executed out of the jurisdiction.[177]

---

[175]See, *supra*, part 4.10(1).

[176]National Policy 20 "Trading in Unqualified Securities—Securities in Primary Distribution in Other Jurisdictions", CCH vol. 2, para. 54-857 and Saskatchewan Policy 1, CCH vol. 3, para. 69-302.

[177]The expanded definition of trade as interpreted by *Gregory and Co. Inc. v. The Quebec Securities Commission*, [1961] S.C.R. 584, 28 D.L.R. (2d) 721 and *R. v. W. McKenzie Securities Ltd. et al.* (1966), 55 W.W.R. 157, 56 D.L.R. (2d) 56 (Man. C.A.) (see, *ante*, part 1.12(2)) leaves little doubt as to the legality of this position. The difficulty of enforcing a policy prohibiting secondary trading in the province of shares which have never been qualified for distribution in the province is well illustrated in *Hretchka, supra*, footnote 174, see, also *ante*, part 2.10. In that case a federally incorporated company with its head office in British Columbia had its prospectus refused for failure of its promoters to accord with British Columbia policy in escrowing shares received by vendors for their mining claims. The company, however, successfully qualified its prospectus in Newfoundland, and the shares traded for a year in British Columbia on the over-the-counter market. The British Columbia Commission eventually agreed to let the shares be traded, but attempted to escrow 95 per cent of the shares held by the controllers of the company, including those acquired in the secondary market. On appeal to the Court of Appeal, the Court concluded the prohibition on trading by all the control persons in all of the company's shares was too general and limited it to only those shares issued to them from the company treasury, thus permitting them to sell any shares which they had purchased in the market. Leave to appeal to the Supreme Court of Canada was refused: [1972] S.C.R. 119, 19 D.L.R. (3d) 1. This is unfortunate. First it left undisturbed a Court of Appeal judgment which failed to recognize that "control persons" require a prospectus to trade whether the shares have come to them directly from treasury or through market purchases. Secondly, it left as law a decision which fetters the power of a commission to

4.12 Exemptions from Distribution Requirements

There are two methods of avoiding the elaborate disclosure requirements which attach in the case of distribution to the public.[178] The first is to use one of the specific exemptions in the Act discussed immediately below. The second is to obtain discretionary relief on application to the Commission under s. 20 or s. 59,[179] a method which will be discussed at the end of this chapter.

The express exemptions from the distribution requirements are quite extensive and will receive individual discussion. As was noted in chapter 3,[180] some of the exemptions are "dual", in that they give relief from both the registration and distribution requirements; these will now be discussed in their distribution aspect. In addition, those exemptions which relate solely to the distribution requirements will thereafter be analyzed.

(1) PROSPECTING SYNDICATES

As a preliminary we may take a category of security which avoids the usual disclosure requirements but is not the subject of an exemption *per se*. There is a separate registration regime for prospecting syndicates.[181] It occupies a separate part in the Act. This is further recognition of the peculiar significance of grass roots mining exploration activity in Ontario and other provinces in Canada.[182] Although "prospecting syndicate" is not specifically defined in the Act, the terms and conditions upon which this "exemption" is granted are set out in sufficient detail to make its intended application clear. The Act provides that once a prospecting syndicate has been filed and the director has issued a receipt for it, the "liability of the members of the syndicate or parties to the agreement is limited to the extent provided by the terms of the agreement". This removal of liability ensures that the Act's *troika* of statutory civil liability provisions—withdrawal, rescission, and claim for damages on material false statement—would not be available to a purchaser. It is probable also that common law civil liability remedies would not be available. It is improbable, however, that the "liability" thus avoided includes *quasi*-criminal prosecution under the offence provisions of the Act or a criminal prosecution under the Criminal Code.[183]

---

regulate secondary trading in the province of shares which have not been qualified for distribution in the province. See also *Re Bank of Western Canada*, [1970] 1 O.R. 427, 8 D.L.R. (3d) 593 (C.A.), leave to appeal refused, [1969] S.C.R. xii; *Ames et al. v. Investo-Plan Ltd.*, [1973] 5 W.W.R. 451, 35 D.L.R. (3d) 613 (B.C.C.A.).

[178]Hereinafter "distribution requirements".

[179]Bill 20 has one discretionary exempting section, s. 75.

[180]See, *ante*, part 3.15.

[181]These are classified as partnerships but once a receipt is issued by the director for a prospecting syndicate agreement, the filing requirements of s. 34(3) of the Partnerships Registration Act, R.S.O. 1970, c. 340, do not apply. See *Pepper Prospecting Syndicate v. Matthews*, [1950] O.W.N. 156 (H.C.).

[182]Part VI, s. 34 (in Bill 20 prospecting syndicates are dealt with in Part XIII, s. 53). British Columbia (s. 36(1)); Alberta (s. 34(1)); Saskatchewan (s. 41(1)) and Manitoba (s. 34(1)) have similar provisions; Quebec and the Atlantic Provinces do not.

[183]See *R. v. Prosser*, [1950] 1 W.W.R. 145, 9 C.R. 120 (Alta. Dist. Ct.).

The conditions upon which the exemption is enjoyed[184] make it clear that the syndicate is a device which is not intended for development going beyond the preliminary prospecting stage.[185]

The director has a wide discretion to issue a receipt for a prospecting syndicate agreement. However, in contrast to his power to accept or reject a prospectus, he is not charged with responsibility for ensuring that the syndicate agreement contains all the conditions required by the Act, presumably to ensure speedy approval and on the premise that for sums of $50,000 or less it is simply not practicable to undertake a detailed scrutiny.[186] To ensure that this relief is available only to those not actively engaged in the securities business, there is a prohibition on any registrant trading in a security issued by a prospecting syndicate either as agent for the syndicate or as principal.[187]

An exemption from the registration and distribution requirements is specified either (a) where a prospector who staked the claims sells a unit providing he delivers a copy of the qualified agreement to the purchaser who apparently can be a member of the public, or (b) where the syndicate issues units after the agreement has been filed if they are not offered for sale to the public and are sold to not more than 50 purchasers.[188] The distinction between (a) and (b), public and non-public, is curious. The prohibition contained in the limiting conditions of (b) may be avoided simply by using (a) in two steps: first arranging an issue by the syndicate to the prospector for cash and having him resell the securities (with delivery of a copy of the agreement to the purchaser) to a member of the public. Possibly such a member of the public is free to resell without delivery of a copy of the agreement.[189] Note, too, that (b) would seem to provide a ringing affirmation of the need to know and friends or business associates test of the non-public with a generous boundary of 50.[190]

---

[184]For the various items that must be set out in the syndicate agreement see the clearly articulated list in s. 34. Note that the $50,000 limit on its capital is raised to $100,000 in Bill 20, s. 53.

[185]The $100,000 short-form mining exploration company prospectus would apply at the next logical step. See Reg. 794, s. 17 and Form 17.

[186]Section 34(2), (Bill 20 s. 53(2)).

[187]Section 34(4) (Bill 20, s. 53(4)).

[188]Sections 19(2)11 and 12 and 58(2)(a) (Bill 20, ss. 35(2)14 and 15 and 74(1)(a)).

[189]This requires that the phrase in s. 19(2)11 "where such securities are sold by the prospector" be read as qualifying the noun "securities" within the text of the para. 11 exemption and not the noun "securities" in the preamble to all of the exemptions in s. 19(2). For a similar interpretive problem see the discussion of the s. 19(2)9 exemption, *infra*, part 4.12(4)(c).

[190]See discussions of the concept, *supra*, part 4.02(2). Bill 20 uses the numbers test of 25 purchasers and 50 offerees in replacing the concept public by certain limits (ss. 35(1)17 and 73(1)(m)). Note also that the old term "Registrar", now replaced by "Director" elsewhere throughout the Act, has escaped the draftsman's eye and still appears in the exemption, though corrected in Bill 20. A literal interpretation would render the exemption impossible to achieve since the office of Registrar has disappeared from the Commission.

(2) EXPRESS EXEMPTIONS—DOUBLE EXEMPTIONS FOR A TRADE

As is the case with the exemptions from registration,[191] the express exemptions from the distribution requirements focus either on the nature of the parties to a trade or the nature of the securities in a trade. All the exemptions from registration directed to the nature of the securities involved are dual exemptions in that they are exactly duplicated as exemptions from the distribution requirements. There are some additional "nature of securities" exemptions which are exemptions from the distribution requirements only; the traders involved must be registered persons or obtain some other exemption from registration.[192] Only some of the "nature of trade" exemptions from registration requirements are also exemptions from the distribution requirements, and of these some which appear to be dual exemptions are narrower in their ambit as exemptions from distribution than as exemptions from registration. We shall discuss here all three types: those exemptions which are dual exemptions, those which are parallel to registration exemptions but narrower in scope as distribution exemptions, and those which are distribution exemptions only.[193]

(a) Institutional Purchasers—Private Placements

The first group of exemptions to be considered under this heading is available for a trade in the course of distribution where the purchaser or proposed purchaser falls within a general category composed of otherwise regulated institutions and government agencies ("regulated and government purchasers"). In addition the heading includes institutions which have been expressly granted specific "exempt purchaser" status on application to the Commission. Finally it embraces those whose purchase exceeds $97,000 ("$97,000 purchasers"). All of these exempted transactions are normally referred to as "private placements" since the number of offerees is limited and the details of the issue are determined by active negotiation between the issuer and the "private placee" (usually an institution), resulting in a specifically tailored agreement.[194]

---

[191]See, *ante*, part 3.15.

[192]*E.g.*, s. 58(2)(b) and (c). Section 74 is roughly the equivalent section in Bill 20.

[193]Appendix V compares in summary form the exemptions from the registration and distribution requirements in the other Canadian jurisdictions. There is a peculiar problem which distinguishes the distribution exemptions from the registration exemptions. It may be conveniently raised here. A number of the exemptions speak of securities of a company (*e.g.*, s. 19(1) paras. 8, 9, 9a, 9b, 9c, 10 and s. 58(1)(c)) and would on their face not apply where the issuer was an unincorporated person such as a trust. Probably s. 66 which extends the application of Part VII of the Act to a "person, trust or other entity proposing to issue securities" serves to make the exemption from distribution requirements which are imposed by Part VII available to them, but not the exemption from registration requirements which are imposed by Part II of the Act. Bill 20 cures this problem by using, where appropriate, the broader term "issuer" in the text of the exemption instead of "company".

[194]Section 58(1)(a) (Bill 20, s. 73(1)(a)).

(i) Regulated and Government Purchasers

The otherwise regulated institutions are banks chartered under the federal Bank Act,[195] the Federal Government's Industrial Development Bank,[196] loan or trust corporations registered under the Ontario Loan and Trust Corporations Act[197] and insurance companies licensed under the Ontario Insurance Act.[198]

There are several reasons for exempting these agencies and institutions from both the registration and distribution requirements, and to some extent these reasons vary in accordance with the capacity in which the agencies act (either as traders in securities or purchasers of securities). The registration requirements attempt to ensure that the public, when dealing with members of the securities industry, will find at least a minimum standard of honesty, good reputation, ability, knowledge and sophistication among those professionally transacting business in the financial markets. The exempted institutions are all financial intermediaries which, as a result of the concentration prevalent in the financial markets of Canada, display, or should display, these attributes. An additional factor is the existence of instrumentalities such as the Canada Deposit Insurance Corporation, which safeguard the funds invested in some of these institutions, furthermore, they are subject to close and continuing scrutiny by various governmental bodies. Possibly also the constitutional difficulties which arise when a provincial agency attempts to regulate the activities of federally governed institutions such as the banks have contributed to the exempting of these businesses from the legislative scheme.

The exemptions relating to disclosure on distribution are of two types and again the reasons for their existence differ. The first, with which we are concerned here, is a general exemption when the purchaser is an otherwise regulated institution, provided there is a public report of the transaction identifying issuer and purchaser. The paramount reason for the exemption is that the legislation chartering these institutions imposes regulation by governmental agencies with respect to investments made by them. Also important is the fact that their position in the financial community, together with the importance of access to the financing offered by them, permits such institutions to exact disclosure at least equal to and in most cases far surpassing what is available to a normal investor under the Act. In addition, these purchasers are considered to have a degree of expertise and sophistication matched only by the most knowledgeable investors. By an application of the "need to know" test, the statutory disclosure regime appears unnecessary in the case of these institutions.

The second exemption from distribution requirements arises when certain of these institutions are offering certain of their own securities for sale to the public; this exemption and its underlying rationale will be discussed later in this chapter.[199]

---

[195]R.S.C. 1970, c. B-1.
[196]The Industrial Development Bank Act, R.S.C. 1970, c. I-9.
[197]R.S.O. 1970, c. 254.
[198]R.S.O. 1970, c. 224.
[199]*Infra*, part 4.12(4)(b).

The exemption for a government agency as purchaser is drafted in a peculiar manner. The exemption is available to "an officer or employee, in the performance of his duties as such, of Her Majesty in right of Canada, or of any province or territory of Canada, or of any municipal corporation or public board or commission in Canada". One questions why the focus should be on the human agent rather than the government organ in the framing of this exemption.[200] Once again the rationale for this exemption is the presumed sophistication of the government agency and the fact that it is otherwise regulated; one may question whether this is altogether well founded in the case of smaller municipalities or their administrative boards who frequently do not receive the advice of someone with substantial experience in the securities industry.

It is important to emphasize that the exemption from registration for these institutions is broader than its counterpart in the area of distribution. The latter exemption is available only where the exempted institution is the purchaser or proposed purchaser, whereas the exemption from registration requires only that the exempted institution be one of the parties to the trade. Accordingly an exempted institution selling securities which are qualified for distribution need not be registered, and because the trade as a whole is exempt, the purchaser is also not required to be registered.

(ii) Exempt Purchasers

Exempt purchaser status, in the strict sense now under consideration, requires for its creation specific recognition by the Commission upon application.[201] Before this will be granted it must be shown that the applicant is a sophisticated entity able to fend for itself, and can be expected to honour the investment intention caveat which is attached to this exemption in its distribution aspect.[202] The policy of the Commission is to view this exemption as essentially directed towards the recognized institutional investor, which in turn normally requires that three tests be satisfied: a substantial amount of assets under administration, investment expertise and the pooling of contributions from a great number of individuals. Mutual funds or pension funds will normally qualify. By contrast an application from an individual who incorporates a personal holding company to invest his personal fortune or from an industrial company which intends to use the exemption for investment of sporadic liquid assets will normally be

---

[200]The reason may be historical. The provincial Sale of Shares Act was redrafted in terms of persons after the Privy Council decision in *A.-G. Man. v. A.-G. Can.*, [1929] A.C. 260, [1929] 1 D.L.R. 369, [1929] 1 W.W.R. 369 (on this case and its successor, *Lymburn v. Mayland*, [1932] A.C. 318, [1932] All E.R. Rep. 291 (P. C.), see,*ante,* part 3.05(1) footnotes 50 and 54) struck down the prohibition against the sale of a federal corporation's securities without registration. Since it was only "persons", a term which did not include corporations, who were prohibited from trading without registration, so only persons were exempted. Subsequently, however, the prohibition has been extended to persons and companies.

[201]Section 19(1)3 (Bill 20, s. 35(1)4).

[202]Section 58(1)(a).

refused. Somewhat more obscure is the position of the industrial or mining company with a substantial amount of cash or a large portfolio of investment securities. In such a case the OSC will want to be satisfied that the amount of cash and nature of the portfolio are sufficient to ensure the company will be the significant participant in the institutional investor community and will respect the investment intent proviso.

The rationale for this restricted view is that the exemption permits securities to be issued and, following the exhaustion of an investment intent, to be resold into the public market without the normal prospectus disclosure. There is a disinclination to expand the number of securities which reach public hands in this manner.

It should perhaps be noted that exempt purchaser status is not of great significance. For purchases of a value of $97,000 or more the potential applicant will proceed instead under s. 19(3), the private placement provision. Mutual funds and pension funds are the most frequent users of the former exemption, since they are not generically exempted and may often wish to make purchases of less than $97,000. Recognition of exempt purchaser status is not available to individuals.

Application for exempt purchaser status is made by completing Form 9 and must be renewed annually.[203] The facts required by the Commission in order to exercise its discretion in this matter include among other things the nature of the applicant's business, the powers of investment and the restrictions stipulated by its constating instrument, and the approximate value of its investment portfolio; a statement is also requested of any other relevant reasons why the exemption is justified.[204]

(iii) $97,000 Purchasers

The final category of exempted institutions constituted by the size of the purchase involved calls for an extended discussion. The security must have an aggregate acquisition cost of $97,000.[205] The choice of such an unusual number was intended to permit the purchase of a block of securities having a face value of $100,000 (a common minimum denomination) after deduction of a discount or commission of three per cent.

Like exempt purchaser status, this exemption is not available to individuals, the apparent rationale being the sophistication of the investor. The theory is that in order to carry on business in some form

---

[203]Reg. 794, s. 7.

[204]Whereas the previously discussed classes of institutions such as banks, trust companies and government agencies were exempted in Ontario's first "securities act", the Security Frauds Prevention Act, 1928 (Ont.), c. 34, s. 3(3)(c), the provision for the *ad hoc* recognition of exempt purchasers was only added in 1963 (1962-63 (Ont.), c. 131, s. 10(1)). At the time of the publication of the OSC's Merger Report (February, 1970), there were approximately 100 exempt purchasers; the members of this group, apart from managed pension funds and mutual funds, were described in the Report as "largely substantial financial institutions which, while not licensed to do business in Ontario, represent substantial pools of capital with sophisticated investment advisers" (para. 5.09).

[205]Sections 19(3) and 58(1)(b) (Bill 20, ss. 35(1)5 and 73(1)(d)).

other than a sole proprietorship an individual will normally have obtained some professional assistance (usually legal) ensuring a minimum if not an adequate level of competent advice. It is easy to refute this premise in particular cases or where the business organization is of a rather rudimentary type. A partnership between two individuals, for example, may not require a lawyer for its formation—indeed it need not even be expressed in a written agreement. However, as a general rule there will be more opportunity for professional advice and sophistication where a business form has been adopted.[206]

The use of the $97,000 category exempts from both registration and disclosure on distribution except for the public report of the transaction. The terminology used is almost exactly the same in both cases, except that s. 58 (the exemption from prospectus disclosure) refers to the "purchaser or proposed purchaser", whereas s. 19 (the exemption for trading) refers only to the "purchaser".[207] However, there is a remedial provision which has the effect of relieving from the registration requirements those elements of trade which are antecedent to the actual purchase, so as to permit direct solicitations or negotiations with potential private placees when it is not certain that they will purchase.[208] This relieving provision does not provide a similar remedy for the exemption from the distribution requirements but the additional words "or proposed purchaser" in s. 58(1)(a) perform a similar function.[209]

One interpretive problem which the $97,000 exemption presents is whether or not the business organization must be in existence before the first aspects of a trade occur. For example may an individual be solicited[210] on the condition that he later forms a trust or a partnership with another individual to consummate the purchase? In such a case, although the offeree might have been an individual the ultimate purchaser will be the partnership, "a person other than an individual". One interpretation posits that the exemption is not available because the exemption "cuts in" where the proposed purchaser *is* a person other than an individual. It affords no protection when the proposed purchaser *will be* or *might be* a person other than an individual. The other view concedes that the exemption only comes into being when a final condition is satisfied—the purchaser *is* a person other than an individual. But it requires that s. 19(4), which deems solicitation of persons or companies for a private placement not to be a trade, operates retrospectively to wipe clean the slate of earlier "illegal"

---

[206]Merger Report (para. 5.13).
[207]Sections 58(1)(b) and 19(3) (Bill 20, ss. 73(1)(d) and 35(1)5; Bill 20 just uses "purchaser" in both cases).
[208]Section 19(4). The use of the qualifying word "direct" in s. 19(4) would seem to preclude widespread antecedent mailings or advertisements.
[209]The registration exemption for named institutions in s. 19(1)3 is not accompanied by a similar relieving provision. However it is probably not necessary, because the exemption from registration is broader where one of the parties is a named institution.
[210]Note that s. 19(4) negates the normal rule of s. 1(1)24 that the solicitation is a trade.

trading with an individual. It is submitted that the latter interpretation is too tortured a reading of the literal wording of the exemption. It would seem to misinterpret s. 19(4), which operates to exempt the solicitation stage of a trade which is never consummated, and does nothing to relax the requirement that the person or company solicited must not be an individual. One might ask how such a soliciting trader would defend against a prosecution begun after solicitation if the purchase was never completed because the individual never formed a trust. In any event it is clear that the example frustrates the spirit of the exemption, since the investor sophistication on which it is predicated is most needed precisely in the early stages of trade prior to the actual purchase.[211]

There is no particular magic in the figure of $97,000, which was taken as a rough measure of probable investor sophistication. Elsewhere in the Act[212] a figure of $50,000 is used in exempting short-term notes. The explanation given for the creation of the private placement exemption in the 1967 amendments was that it was designed "to overcome a reluctance on the part of large sources of capital within Canada and elsewhere which apparently could not be persuaded to apply for the 'exempt purchaser' status".[213] The intention was to permit the placing of debt securities of large denomination with the expectation they would be held by the purchaser to maturity. Hence the restrictive stipulation that the purchaser "purchases or proposes to purchase as principal for investment only and not with a view to resale or distribution"[214] was attached to this exemption (and subsequently to the exempt purchaser exemption as well). As it turned out both these exemptions have been heavily used for the placement of equity shares, or debt securities which are convertible into equity or have share warrants attached. This trend became particularly notice-

---

[211]The Merger Report gave a different reason for denying the exemption to the partnership formed subsequent to the start of trading. Its concern was chiefly with the possibility that several individuals each with less than $97,000 might combine in a partnership solely to make up the requisite amount. In rejecting this as unlawful (para. 5.13) the Report appears to place excessive reliance on a literalistic argument, *viz.*, that the word "security" appears in the singular in the exemption ("trade in a security which has an aggregate acquisition cost to such purchaser of not less than $97,000"). Carried to its logical limits this interpretation might prevent for example the private placement of 100,000 common shares of no par value sold at $1 each to an otherwise qualified private placee unless there was attached to the issue a condition that it be sold in a unit of no less than 100,000 shares or be evidenced by one share certificate for 100,000 shares. It might also prevent the placement of a "hybrid" security such as a $100,000 bond with warrants attached. It is doubtful that this type of technical subtlety was intended by the legislation.

[212]Section 19(2)3; s. 19(1)9b (as added by 1971, Vol. 2, c. 31, s. 3(2)) employs the $100,000 figure.

[213]Merger Report, para. 5.12. The reason for this reluctance is unclear. Perhaps some of these sources of capital were large foreign-based financial institutions which at that time did not wish to submit to Ontario's jurisdiction. Query whether that reluctance is an appropriate reason for exemption or does it suggest that market realities are paramount in drafting securities laws?

[214]Sections 19(3), 58(1)(a) and Reg. 794, s. 10.

able in the late 1960's, when great emphasis was placed on "performance" by institutions requiring them to select investments with fast growth potential. Issuers as well as investors were attracted by these exemptions because they permitted the raising of significant amounts of cash more quickly and at less expense than in the case of a prospectus distribution. These advantages were often sufficient to outweigh negative features such as the fact that the total amount that could be raised by this method was less and a lower offering price was frequently necessary to compensate for a lack of liquidity. As the conglomerate movement gained momentum through 1967 and 1968, acquisition-minded companies used these exemptions to raise cash when cash consideration was necessary for an acquisition.[215]

(iv) Private Placements—General Requirements

The requirement that a purchaser buy as principal and not as agent, which now applies when the private placement exemptions are used in the case of a distribution,[216] is designed to prevent an exempt institution from lending its status to and acting as agent for a purchaser who does not enjoy the exemption and over whom there is less control on resale.[217]

---

[215]The trend to increased equity issues through private placements in a short period of years is quite startling. The following data and analysis are taken from the Merger Report (Appendix V, p. 180); the analysis is unfortunately based on incomplete information, since only trades to $97,000 purchasers and not to exempt purchasers were reported under the regulation then in effect.

"*Review of Private Placements*

Section 7 (now s. 11) of the Regulations of the Securities Act, requires both the vendor and his agent, if any, in a private placement under section 19(3) of the Act to file with the Commission within 30 days of the placement a form reporting the placement, Form 8 (now Form 11). This is a review of such forms from May, 1967 to July, 1969. From May 1st, 1967 to December 31st, 1967, 20 forms were filed; in 1968, 78 forms were filed; and from January 1st, 1969, to July 14th, 1969, 70 forms were filed, a total of 168. The private placement as a means of raising funds is thus apparently becoming more popular. The dollar amount of such placements follows a similar trend: approximately $47 million in 1967, $133 million in 1968 and $298 million to July in 1969. The total value of securities placed pursuant to section 19(3) of the Act in the period reviewed was $478 million. The breakdown between debt and equity shares by year is as follows:

	Debt	Equity
1967	$ 47 million	$ 0.3 million
1968	83 million	50 million
	(12.5 convertible)	
1969	48 million	250 million
	(4.3 convertible)	
	$178 million	$300.3 million

In the period reviewed, 1,374 prospective purchasers were approached, 537 of whom invested under section 19(3)."

See, *ante*, chapter 2, footnote 127, for 1972 and 1973 figures for total private placements.

[216]Section 58(1)(a).

[217]The Merger Report examined this problem and found that the potential for abuse existed in the belief of some firms that they were entitled by the

The Merger Report recommended some relaxation of this requirement in the case of trust companies registered under the Loan and
Trust Corporations Act. This was effected in a 1971 amendment,[218]
which deems them to act as principal when they trade as trustees for
accounts they fully manage. One may fairly ask whether this relaxation
should not be extended to other classes of exempted institutions
performing a similar function with fiduciary powers, such as a chartered bank administering its employees' pension fund with full investment discretion.[219]

The extension of the investment intent requirement, which formerly
applied only to $97,000 purchasers, to regulated and government
purchasers and, exempt purchasers under s. 19(1)3, was another
Merger Report recommendation which found its way into the 1971
amendments. As in the case of the $97,000 exemption, a form must be
filed with the Commission by the vendor or his agent for the private
placement (Form 11), and subsequently by the purchaser in the event
of resale (Form 12).[220] The requirements of Form 11 are quite detailed.

---

exemption to purchase as agents for an undisclosed principal (para. 5.15). An
interesting example of such a misuse, which involved the s. 19(1)3 exemption,
is detailed in the Atlantic Report (pp. 1312-5). In the fall of 1962 Atlantic had
contracted to sell $5,000,000 of senior notes; this required a borrowing base or
cushion of junior debt or equity of considerable proportions in order to avoid
violation of the provision of the trust indenture pursuant to which other senior
notes had previously been issued. Accordingly Atlantic covenanted to sell
95,000 second preference shares at $25 each before October 4. Fifty thousand
of these were sold to two large exempt institutions. British Mortgage & Trust
Company agreed to take the remaining 45,000 shares on October 4 and an
additional 30,000 shares by November 15, for a total of 75,000. However the
trust company bought less than a third of these for its own account. Of the rest,
25,000 were passed on to the chairman of the Atlantic board, some were sold
by British Mortgage itself to the public and some were transferred to dealers
who had close connections with the Atlantic network of enterprises, to be sold
subsequently to the public in blocks of varying sizes. In stating that the
distribution by the trust company was permissible because of the exemption,
the Commissioner seems to have overlooked the definition of underwriter in
the Act.

For a classic instance of a similar unlawful distribution see *Crowell-Collier
Publishing Co.*, U.S. Securities Act, 1933, Release No. 3825, (1957) CCH Fed.
Securities Law Reporter, vol. 4, para. 76,539, and the discussion of the case in
D.R. Herwitz, *Business Planning*, Brooklyn, Foundation Press, 1966, at p. 213
and following.

[218]Section 58(1a) of the Act as added by 1971, Vol. 2, c. 31, s. 13(1). Bill 20, s.
73(2).

[219]The British Columbia Securities Act does not contain the Ontario amendment requiring specifically that the placee purchase as principal for its own
account. However in a "Notice Respecting Sections 21(1)(c) and 55(1) of the
Securities Act, 1967" (April 13, 1973 BCSCWS) the British Columbia Commission cautioned brokers that this was the interpretation it placed on s. 55(1)
and (2) exemptions where the purchaser or proposed purchaser was one of the
persons or institutions referred to in s. 21(1)(c) since the rationale for the
exemption was the sophistication and knowledgeability of the exempted
persons or institutions as investors.

[220]Reg. 794, ss. 10 and 11; Forms 11, 12. For an example of the type of conduct
this amendment would clearly proscribe, see, *supra*, footnote 217.

Among other things there must be a certificate of the purchaser that the purchase was made as principal for investment only and not with a view to resale or distribution; he must undertake to file Form 12 within ten days of any resale. Synoptic details from Forms 11 and 12 reports are published in the OSC's Weekly Summary. The administrative staff of the OSC contrasts the resale Form 12 with its predecessor Form 11 with a view to determining whether a purchaser's investment intent has changed rather quickly; if so it will make inquiries into the circumstances of the change.

The investment intent condition requires that the purchase is for investment only and not with a view to resale. If this restriction were interpreted literally there could never be any such purchases. All purchasers have some "view to resell" if only in contemplation of the death of a person or liquidation of a corporation. Understandably a literal interpretation is not given to this restriction but unhappily the range of interpretations varies widely.[221] A "change of circumstance" is normally regarded as sufficient for the expiration of investment intent but what degree of change and whether it must be in the issuer's or the investor's circumstances are open questions. United States lawyers have used a "rule of thumb" of two to three years for such changes in interpreting a similar provision. The TSE contemplates such a change occuring within six months and twelve months for two different types of investors in a policy statement which relates to this problem.[222]

---

[221]See the Merger Report, paras. 5.14 to 5.21, and the Wheat Report, Disclosure to Investors—A Reappraisal of Federal Administrative Policies under the '33 and '34 Acts, Washington, 1969, p. 160 for an extended discussion. Bill 20 eliminates this subjective restriction replacing it with objective criteria, to avoid the problem of subjective interpretation.

[222]"The Private Placement of Treasury Shares of Listed Companies", CCH vol. 3, para. 92-010. The "change of circumstance" doctrine has put a gloss on the requirement of investment intent which has bedevilled U.S. securities lawyers for many years. Perhaps a measure of their frustration (and proof that even securities lawyers have poetry in their souls) is this little bit of doggerel by a New York practitioner (C. Leonard Gorden) preserved for posterity in the Wheat Report, *ibid.*, at p. 169:

"If you buy stock privately,
Enlightened counsel will implore:
Heed the Act of Thirty-Three,
Subsection One of Section Four.

"Make your purchase for investment.
Have a clear and pure intent.
Do not think about divestment
Till some unforeseen event.

"Avoid the Crowell-Collier snare
Be one of few and not of many.
You need not be a millionaire
But don't go in with your last penny...

"Thereafter, changing factors which
Might make a sale by you exempt

(v) $100,000 Sale of Assets

As a postcript to the subject of private placements, we may note the recently introduced (1971) exemption for an asset sale where the vendor of assets worth more than $100,000 receives securities as consideration.[223] It is modelled on the $97,000 exemption and carries with it the same requirement of reports to the Commission. The main difference is that the "purchaser" is providing assets rather than cash (strictly speaking the issuer of the security is the purchaser, the owner of the assets is the seller).[224] Logically this exemption might also have been grouped with the "Issuer-Combination" exemptions, since it is frequently used in a business combination where the acquiror uses its shares to obtain assets rather than shares of the target company.[225] As in the two previously discussed exemptions the recipient of the securities must not be an individual and it must have the requisite investment intent. It should be noted finally that the issuer must be a company.

(vi) Private Placement Reforms

It seems appropriate at this point to consider the changes introduced by Bill 20 with respect to the private placement exemptions. First s. 35, the registration exemption, now requires that the institution both be the purchaser and be acting as a principal. This represents a considerable tightening up of this provision to deal with the situation discussed

---

Must be a bad and sudden switch
Which justifies a changed intent.

"When you have held two years or more
That sad and unforseen event
Need not be tragic as before
To justify a new intent!

"So put your stock upon the shelf;
Don't question when it will be free.
The very thought defeats itself
With legal logic's subtlety.

"With time and troubles, you may get
Advice of counsel or, much better,
Advice to sell that's safer yet—
An SEC 'no action' letter."

[223]Sections 19(1)9b and 58(1)(c) (Bill 20, ss. 35(1)15 and 73(1)(j)).

[224]It seems that the $97,000 private placement exemption requires a cash consideration, including a cheque but probably not a promissory note or other "paper," to flow from purchaser to issuer: the acquisition cost is expressly stated as "$97,000". An ingenious issuer might have availed itself of the $97,000 purchase exemption (obeying the words of the section in letter but not in spirit) by interposing a third party to whom the intended purchaser would sell his assets for cash. The purchaser would then use the cash to buy securities from the issuer under the exemption and the issuer in turn would use the money to purchase the assets from the third party (who would probably receive a fee for his temporary banking and "bailment" services).

[225]In addition such a trade might be disclosed by means of a timely disclosure statement, since for smaller companies at least an assets purchase of $100,000 or more would be a material event in the purchaser's affairs.

above of exempted institutions acting as agents. In effect the restrictions of the Act on institutions acting as agents are now extended to secondary trading as well as distributions. The same change has been effected in those parts of s. 35 dealing with exempt and $97,000 purchasers. It should be noted, however, that the $97,000 private placee may now be an individual, while in respect to exempt purchasers the proscription of individuals still obtains. In addition the requirement of investment intent has been removed entirely. Finally s. 19(4) appears to have disappeared in the Bill.

With respect to distributions, s. 73(1) of Bill 20 removes the requirement of investment intent from all the exemptions we have been considering. This is done because the exempted securities will be subject to statutory escrow provisions and certain objective rules for resale.[226]

(b) Trades to Underwriters and Registrants

Two of the dual exemptions recognize the sophistication of underwriters and registrants and the fact that they often have other sources of information available to them which obviate the need for normal disclosure. So far as the registration requirements are concerned these exemptions are based on the assumption that if at least one of the parties to the transaction holds registration the non-registered party will receive the protection that dealing with a registrant provides. The "underwriter" exemption is for a trade "between a person or company and an underwriter acting as purchaser, and...between or among underwriters".[227] Applying the provision to a typical public issue, the trade between an issuer and the purchasing underwriter is exempt under the first clause: the trade between the purchasing underwriter and the remaining members of the banking group (who buy as principals) is exempt under the second. As stated this is a dual exemption, so that not only is the issuer relieved of any requirement to obtain registration to make the initial trade to the purchasing underwriter, but the same issuer and the others along the chain are exempt from the distribution requirements at this stage.

The registrant exemption applies to "a trade in a security by a person or company acting solely through an agent who is a person or company registered for trading".[228] This exemption permits members of the public to trade without registration through their brokers. This is not a dual exemption *per se*, but s. 58(1)(d) contains an exemption from the distribution requirements which is related. It is effective only where the trade is between registrants and where the registrant purchasing is performing a true dealer function in buying for his own account. If that same dealer purchases as principal with a view to reselling the security immediately or shortly thereafter, and there is no distribution disclosure, he runs the risk of being prosecuted for engaging in a distribution to the public without notifying the Commission or qualifying a prospectus.[229]

---

[226]Section 73(4).
[227]Sections 19(1)6 and 58(1)(c) (Bill 20, ss. 35(1)9 and 73(1)(o)).
[228]Section 19(1)7.
[229]It is the concluding "catch-all" words of the definition of distribution coupled with the broad definition of underwriter which makes this so (s.

Bill 20 makes scarcely any changes in the area of registrant and underwriter exemptions. Section 35(1)10 adds a separate subparagraph exempting from registration an unsolicited order to purchase placed with a bank or trust company which is later to be executed through a registered dealer. In the Act this is covered by the regulated purchaser exemption,[230] which simply requires that either party to a trade be one of a number of named institutions.

(c) Issuer Internal Trades

Next there is a group of dual exemptions which reflect the assumption that persons intimately involved in or connected with the affairs of an issuer do not need the protection of the distribution and registration requirements. Concern for business efficacy is also a factor in some of these situations contributing to the decision to exempt. There are broadly speaking three types of transactions here: trades with promoters, employees, and existing securities holders. These will be considered in turn.

(i) Trades with Promoters

Curiously, the "promoters" exemption (applying to a "trade by an issuer in the securities of its own issue to its promoters") did not appear in the Act until the 1971 amendments.[231] It will disappear when Bill 20 is enacted since the new limited offering exemption will satisfy its purpose. "Promoter" is defined in two ways.[232] The first which focuses on entrepreneurial activity, covers persons who "take the initiative in founding or reorganizing an enterprise". The second uses a straightforward percentage test to include persons who receive ten per cent or more of a class of securities, or the proceeds therefrom, in return for the provision of services or property in connection with the founding or reorganization of the business. Perhaps the definition is too guarded in requiring that all persons who take shares in a new or recently founded venture must "take the initiative" in "promoting" the venture. This wording would exclude someone who had a more passive involvement but because he was a friend of the initiator or was a business acquaintance who trusted him, wished to provide funds. Such a person might have as much knowledge of the venture as a prospectus would provide.[233] On the other hand the exemption may be unduly permissive in not providing some circumscribing guidelines for the interpretation of the term "initiative".

1(1)25). This is a notoriously difficult concept to satisfy by proof, but the courts are prepared to accept circumstantial evidence in keeping with the maxim that one is deemed to intend the natural consequences of his actions (see *e.g.*, *R. v. MacMillan*, [1968] 1 O.R. 475, 66 D.L.R. (2d) 680, [1969] 2 C.C.C. 289 (C.A.); *R. v. Lampard*, [1969] S.C.R. 373, [1969] 3 C.C.C. 249, 4 D.L.R. (3d) 98, 6 C.R.N.S. 157; reversing [1968] 2 O.R. 470, [1968] 4 C.C.C. 201 (C.A.). These cases are discussed in chapter 9, *post*, part 9.12. See also the discussion of possible civil liability implications, *supra*, part 4.10.
[230]Section 19(1)3.
[231]Sections 19(1)9c and 58(1)(c) added by 1971, Vol. 2, c. 31, ss. 3(2) and 13(1).
[232]Section 1(1)15 (Bill 20, s. 1(1)31).
[233]As the Act presently stands a careful solicitor incorporating such a venture could resort to the incorporation of a private company and rely on the position that such a passive investor was not a member of the public, to ensure exemption from the registration as well as the distribution requirements.

(ii) Trades with Employees
The second of the "issuer-internal" exemptions has the practical aim of encouraging employees to obtain an ownership stake in their employer's business. It is based not on the "need to know" test which reflects the goal of investor protection, but on considerations which are external to securities law, at least in a narrow sense. In the U.S. the courts have been unwilling to find a specific "employee" exemption in their interpretation of the broad exemption for "non-public" offerings in the 1933 Securities Act. The key case is *SEC v. Ralston Purina Co.*[234] where the U.S. Supreme Court upheld the SEC's attack on the defendant company's employee-share purchase plan. Some senior employees were found to be exempt, but only on account of the greater amount of information available to them.[235]

In Ontario so long as the employee is not "induced to trade by expectation of employment or continued employment", the transaction is free from both the registration and the distribution requirements. It is arguable that this proviso would be violated where an employee received a substantial part of his salary in shares of his employer rather than cash, a practice which is none too rare in the case of some junior mining exploration companies. A clear violation occurs where the employer requires an employee to take his wages in shares or face dismissal.

(iii) Existing Securities Holders
The third of the "issuer-internal" exemptions is applicable to trades involving existing securities holders. It is further divided into three subsections dealing with stock dividends, reorganizations and windings-up, and rights issues.

1. Stock Dividends
The first category comprehends a trade "in a security of its own issue that is distributed or issued by a company to holders of its securities as a stock dividend or other distribution out of earnings or surplus".[236] Since the securities must be of the issuer's own issue a parent may not use this exemption to distribute to its shareholders securities of a subsidiary which it holds. The wording of the exemption does not limit its applicability to shares and shareholders so it may well be available in the case of a distribution to creditors, depending on the nature of the debt instrument held by them and the type of issue which is proposed. Broadly speaking "trade" creditors would not be included unless they held a "security" as defined in the Act.[237] With respect to creditors that do qualify, the distribution need not be made on a *pro rata* basis provided it comes out of earnings or surplus.[238]

This exemption is founded on the "need to know" test. Shareholders are thought to be already aware of their company's affairs, although

---

[234](1953), 346 U.S. 119, 73 S.Ct. 981, discussed, *supra*, footnote 30.
[235]See also *Lumley v. Broadway Coffee Co. Ltd.*, [1935] O.R. 278, [1935] 2 D.L.R. 417 (C.A.).
[236]Sections 19(1)8(i) and 58(1)(c) (Bill 20, ss. 35(1)11(i) and 73(1)(f)(i)).
[237]Section 1(1)22.
[238]Why the dual phrase "distribution or issue" is used can only be a matter of conjecture. Perhaps "distribution" connotes previously issued securities which have to be passed around. See, *supra*, footnote 13.

the ongoing information they receive is not as complete as that contained in a prospectus. However, there are also reasons of business efficacy for the exemption. A stock dividend may broaden the market for an issuer's securities if the recipient trades the share to an outsider. Furthermore, this form of dividend to shareholders permits shareholders to be rewarded without encroaching on the issuer's cash reserves, and thus encourages capital formation. The conclusion of this section prohibits promotional schemes. No commissions or other remuneration may be given in respect of the distribution except for ministerial or professional services or services performed by a registrant.

2. Reorganization or Winding-up

The second division involves a reorganization or winding-up. Here there is a dual exemption for a trade "in a security whether of its own issue or not that is distributed or issued by a company to holders of its securities as incidental to a *bona fide* reorganization or winding-up of such company or distribution of its assets for the purpose of winding-up its affairs".[239] The two categories of organic change contemplated by the section, "reorganization" and "winding-up", are nowhere defined in the Act. Although the BCA attempts to define both terms, the task of extracting a clear meaning is one to discourage even the most intrepid of interpreters.[240] Strictly speaking the BCA does not offer a separate definition of "reorganization", but that word is the general rubric under which are grouped ss. 189 through 200. These in turn contain four subheadings, "Amendment of Articles", "Restatement of Articles", "Arrangements", and "Amalgamations and Continuations".[241]

The distinguishing feature with which we are concerned is the issuance of the issuer's own securities as incidental to reorganization; accordingly not all the forms of amendment to the articles which are set out in s. 189 require this exemption. Those that do are as follows: (a) decreasing the issued capital if the corporation has shares without par value as, for example, where it cancelled one half its outstanding common shares and issued a new share certificate on a one for two basis to each shareholder representing half the number of shares that he formerly held;
(b) consolidating or subdividing any of its shares without par value;
(c) changing any of its shares with par value into shares without par value or *vice versa*;
(d) redesignating any class of shares;

---

[239]Sections 19(1)8(ii) and 58(1)(c) (Bill 20, s. 35(1)11(ii) and s. 73(1)(f)(ii)).
[240]The task is still more difficult in other jurisdictions where corporations legislation does not use the same formulation. For general guidance see J.T. English, "Corporate Acquisitions—General Factors"; D. Huberman, "Winding-up of Business Corporations"; the 1973 Select Committee Report on Mergers and Amalgamations (Hodgson Report); Commentary on Proposals for a new Business Corporations Law for Canada, part 14.00, "Corporate Re-organizations and Amalgamations"; D. G. C. Menzel, "Corporate Re-organizations and Amalgamations"; R. W. Bird, "Corporate Mergers and Acquisitions in Canada"; Morin and Chippindale, *Acquisitions and Mergers in Canada*, especially the chapter by H.L. Beck, "The Legal Aspect", p. 186.
[241]BCA, ss. 189 to 191, 192, 193 to 195 and 196 to 200, respectively.

(e) reclassifying any shares into shares of a different class;

(f) providing for restrictions on transfer of shares which would require new certificates to be issued to comply with the notice of restriction provisions;

(g) any other variation of or amendment to the articles which would change a right or condition affecting a share so as to require a new certificate or some other evidence of the change to be issued to the holder.

The restatement of articles[242] would not require the issuance of a security unless it included one of the amendments discussed above.

The third sub-species of "reorganization"—"arrangement" is quite confusing. To begin with it is defined to include the following:

(1) "a reorganization of the authorized capital of a corporation"[243] and,

(2) three of the changes in the internal capital structure which may also be effected by amendment to the articles: consolidation of shares of different classes, reclassification of shares of one class into shares of another class and variation of some feature of a share, such as a right or condition,[244] and,

(3) a reconstruction involving a sale or transfer of all or part of the undertaking, a concept which presupposes the intervention of an outside body corporate.

All these types of arrangements ordinarily require new certificates to be issued, which involves using the reorganization exemption. The first two situations logically belong under the general heading of issuer-internal trades because the issuer is distributing its own securities to its existing securities holders. In a reconstruction on the other hand, there is a transaction with an external corporation in which the issuer acquires securities of that external corporation which it then distributes to its own shareholders. To illustrate, suppose that issuer A sells its undertaking to issuer B in exchange for B's securities. A then distributes B's securities to its own (A's) security holders. It is not a case of issuer A distributing *its* securities to holders of issuer B's securities.[245]

At this point the classification concepts of the two Acts appear to be in serious conflict. The Securities Act focuses in s. 19(1)8 on trades by an issuer to its own security holders; the situation where an issuer trades its securities to others with the purpose of combining with or taking them over is reserved for s. 19(1)9. This neat division seems to

---

[242]BCA, s. 192.

[243]Presumably "reorganization of authorized capital" must be only one type of arrangement and thus only a minor subheading within the more comprehensive category reorganization; otherwise the attempt at classification is completely circular.

[244]The advantage of an arrangement is the lower majority required to effect it—the approval of three-quarters of each class of shares represented (s. 194(4)). A less attractive feature is the need for court approval (s. 194(5)). By contrast amendments to articles require unanimous approval in writing of an affected class or of at least 95 per cent if not all can be reached unless the articles stipulate a lower majority (s. 189(4)). However court approval is not required.

[245]This latter situation will be discussed under take-over bids, *post*, chapter 7.

be violated by the inclusion of "reconstruction", as defined above, in "reorganization". Moreover, "reorganization" under the BCA includes not only "arrangements" (of which the odious "reconstruction" is as we saw a sub-species) but also "amalgamations and continuations". Clearly both a reconstruction and an amalgamation require some form of combination with an external corporation. But the element which permits a reconstruction to be exempted under s. 19(1)8 as an issuer-internal trade is this: in a reconstruction the issuer receives the securities from an outside company but distributes them to its own security holders itself. It is only this latter part of the transaction with which the reorganization exemption is concerned. But this leaves uncovered the trade from the outside company. Similarly, an issuer effecting a statutory amalgamation with another company would use the issuer combination exemption (s. 19(1)9) to exchange its securities for those of the company, but would again use the reorganization exemption if it desired to distribute those newly-acquired securities to its own security holders. The distinction is not valid if, instead of looking to the recipients of the securities only, the source is also examined. In this case the rationale for the exemption begins to break down.[246]

Debate as to the meaning of reorganization cannot be resolved, but it is arguable that any meaning ascribed to the term by the Ontario Legislature in the BCA is also a valid interpretation of the concept in the Act, offspring of the same legislative will. However, the many corporations incorporated outside Ontario which are regulated by the Act may also wish to seek exemptions from the Act under a "reorganization". The concept may appear in their incorporating statute stated in different terms and perhaps with more precise definition than in the BCA.[247] The precise extent to which the interpretation of "reorganization" in the Act can be adapted to reflect the varying treatment of the term in other incorporating legislation is a matter of conjecture; it would seem reasonable, however, when examining the corporate conduct of an issuer seeking an exemption under this head, to consider the definition in the legislation under which the issuer is incorporated.

The concept of "winding-up" presents problems somewhat similar to those encountered with "reorganization". Once again there is no definition in the Act so that interpretation is dependent on the varying

---

[246]For a judicial interpretation of reorganization see *R. v. Santiago Mines Ltd.*, [1946] 3 W.W.R. 129, [1947] 1 D.L.R. 642, 2 C.R. 279, 86 C.C.C. 357 (B.C.C.A.). See also the Merger Report, paras. 6.10 to 6.17.

[247]*E.g.* see the CBCA (s. 185) where "reorganization" is defined to mean a court order made under
(a) s. 234, where "oppression" is shown,
(b) the Bankruptcy Act approving a proposal, or
(c) any other federal legislation affecting rights among the corporation, its shareholders and creditors.

The Commentary on the Draft Proposals for the CBCA in regard to this reorganization section (para. 374) makes it evident that the central idea behind this comprehensive provision is to facilitate drastic changes by court order in the capital structure of an insolvent company which is being refloated. The concept is not only very different from that of the BCA but is also clearer.

treatment accorded the term in bankruptcy legislation and the laws of the incorporating jurisdiction. Here, however, there is at least one common feature: at some point in the process the formal life of the corporation is extinguished. For Ontario corporations the natural recourse is to those sections of the BCA[248] which deal at length with both a voluntary and a court-ordered winding-up. Any organic change in a corporation which is carried out in conformity with the rules expressed in that legislation (and probably in parallel legislation of any other Canadian jurisdiction) will qualify for the exemption. A winding-up will often result in an issuer distributing to its securities holders the securities of another corporation, and the exemption is designed to cover such trades. It does not, however, cover a distribution of its own or another issuer's securities to someone who is not an existing securities holder, such as a trade creditor.

The exemption is specifically limited to *bona fide* reorganizations and windings-up; this is to prevent corporations from being manipulated in an improper fashion to avoid registration and obtain disclosure-free distribution.[249] It is also subject to the prohibition on payment of any commission or remuneration except for professional or ministerial services or the services of a registrant.

3. Rights Issue

A third dual exemption exists for "the rights issue". This is defined as "the sale by a company of its securities pursuant to the exercise of a right, transferable or otherwise, granted by the company to holders of its securities to purchase additional securities of its own issue...".[250] The typical rights issue has two distinct stages. The first is the granting or issuing of the right or option itself, normally at no charge to existing securities holders and on a *pro rata* basis. The recipients are normally given a limited period in which to exercise the right. For example rights might be issued to all common shareholders on the basis of one right for each ten common shares held by them, the shares to expire 90 days from the date of issue.

The second stage is the exercise of the right and the issue of the underlying security. This normally requires the payment of a price which is slightly discounted from the market price of the same class of shares at the time of the issuance of the rights.

A literal reading of the provision suggests that it only exempts stage two—the issue of the underlying security ("pursuant to the exercise of the right")—and not stage one—the earlier issue of the right itself. There are at least two answers to such an inconvenient interpretation. The first rejoinder, of a rather technical kind, is derived from the definition of trade. It is a trade that requires registration and it is a trade in the course of distribution that requires the disclosure documents. Trade is defined inclusively to mean a disposition of a security for valuable consideration.[251] In the normal situation the right is issued

---

[248]Sections 201 to 246.
[249]For an interpretation of *bona fide*, see *Panacea Marketing and Exploration Ltd.*, Oct. 1971 OSCB 163.
[250]Section 19(1)8(iii).
[251]Section 1(1)24(i) (Bill 20, s. 1(1)40(i)).

gratis, without consideration, to the shareholder. Therefore an exemption for the issue of the right is unnecessary. Unhappily, this is not a totally satisfactory response. It would not meet those situations where the receipt of the right actually required a cash payment or where, for example, it was issued to debt obligation holders in consideration of their forbearance from insisting on payment of interest or principal on their securities. Furthermore the fourth part of the trade definition, "any act...[or] conduct...directly or indirectly in furtherance of any of the foregoing",[252] might be linked up with the subsequent issue of the common share so as to permit the contention that the issuance of the right, albeit at no charge, was an act in furtherance of the subsequent issue of the common share for valuable consideration.

A second and more pragmatic answer to the literal interpretation is this: the subsequent sale "pursuant" to the exercise of the right is exempted, therefore the prior issue of a necessary ingredient of that sale, the right itself, is also exempt. This is the view that most practitioners using the exemption take and it makes sense, given the apparent purpose of the exemption.[253]

Rather surprisingly, the exemption permits the right to be transferred by the recipient shareholder to someone else who may not be a shareholder. Thus its rationale cannot be sought entirely in the greater amount of information about and familiarity with the affairs of the corporation possessed by the shareholders. It must also have an economic purpose—to expedite and encourage the raising of additional capital by issuers from their existing shareholder base. Thus to ensure a maximum return, the opportunity to invest may be passed along to someone else more willing to use it.[254]

This transferability of the right permits a subsidiary market to develop within the protection of the rights offering exemption. Payment is made to the shareholder who chooses not to exercise the right, thus allowing it to be exercised by someone else. Issuers making a rights offering are normally anxious that virtually all of the rights are taken up and exercised. It is thus common procedure for the issuer to pay an additional commission to brokers who will solicit and encourage shareholders to take up and exercise their rights or, if they are unwilling to do so, will prevail upon them to sell their rights to others who will. A technique which makes it more certain that there will be a full return from the rights issue is for the issuer to arrange for a "standby underwriting". An underwriter will agree for a fee, usually a discount from the price payable on exercise of the rights, to "pick up" those rights not taken up and exercise them. He in turn will distribute

---

[252]Section 1(1)24.
[253]See, *infra*, part 4.12(4)(e), for a related problem with warrants or convertible securities.
[254]The opportunity to make a rights issue under favourable conditions constitutes a disincentive to make a full public issue. The latter would ensure that a greater proportion of the purchasers of the issue were outsiders, thus broadening the shareholder base. The result would be the development of a more liquid market, which would be beneficial in the case of a number of public issuers in Canada. See, for example, the anxiety of the Merger Report in this connection paras. 1.28 and 1.29.

the newly issued underlying securities to the public relying on the phrase "transferable or otherwise" in the wording of the exemption to do so.

It is not clear what the phrase "or otherwise" adds to the word "transferable". A simple explanation would be that it is a synonym for "or not": the whole phrase would accordingly read "whether or not transferable". Another possibility is that it is intended to exempt the type of arrangement where the right itself is not transferred but underlying securities in respect of which the rights have not been taken up are sold either *pro rata* or on a "first come, first served" basis to those shareholders who have already exercised the rights issued directly to them. It is questionable whether the phrase would permit a member of the public not already a shareholder to purchase those "neglected" underlying securities; such a practice would be almost indistinguishable from a standard public distribution, notwithstanding that it forms the tag-end of an exempted rights offering. However, the idea is by no means far-fetched, since to allow such a step would be only a small advance from the wide latitude already present in the right to transfer. The fact that the Commission is entitled to insist upon disclosure approximating that of a prospectus (though without the same liabilities and obligations) points in the same direction.

A condition, requiring prior knowledge and approval of the offering by the Commission is attached to the use of this exemption. The supervisory technique being applied by the Commission here appears at first sight to be one of mere notification rather than positive qualification, but the manner in which it is exercised does not always bear this out. The statute requires written notice to be given to the Commission of the date, amount, nature and conditions of the issue, and the net proceeds assuming it is fully subscribed. The Commission is given ten days to object to the sale or to require additional information relating to the securities. The authority conferred under this provision gives the Commission a discretion (in fact exercised by the director) almost as complete as that enjoyed by the director in vetting the prospectus. The ability to insist on additional information is subject to the limitation that it must relate "to the securities" and not directly to the affairs of the issuer, but the power of the Commission to "object" within ten days is not circumscribed in any way. In theory this "negative vetting" procedure—*viz.*, "you may proceed unless we say no within ten days"—is intended as a convenient half-way house between notification, as exemplified by the take-over bid circular which merely must be deposited with the Commission, and qualification as exemplified by the prospectus, which must be carefully analyzed and fully approved by the regulator before becoming effective.

The five uniform act provinces have issued a uniform policy statement[255] detailing the requirements to be satisfied before the

---

[255]No. 2-05, "Applications under Section 19(1)(8)(iii)...", CCH vol. 2, para. 54-875. See also Ontario Policy 3-22 "'Non-Reporting' Companies: Applications for Exemption—under S. 19(1)8(iii) or S. 59", CCH vol. 2, para. 54-916 and British Columbia Policy 3.05 "Rights Offerings to Shareholders under S. 21(1)(h)(iii)", CCH vol. 2, para. 29-955.

exemption may be enjoyed. According to this statement it is not intended that the filed material will be reviewed in the same stringent fashion as prospectus filings. The requirements as set forth fall into two parts. The first stipulates that certain current information must be supplied to shareholders with or in advance of the notice of the offer. The items listed include such matters as recent reports and financial statements, details regarding the particular offer such as how long it is to remain open and how much money must be raised, and the name and financial capabilities of the underwriter (in the case of a stand-by underwriting). The Commission insists that where a minimum amount is necessary to carry out the purpose and the offering is made on a "best efforts" basis (rather than with a stand-by underwriting), the subscriptions are to be held in trust by an independent trustee until the minimum is reached, and returned in the event of a failure to reach that amount. The same trust arrangement must be made where a stand-by underwriting contains a market-out clause or similar provision.

Secondly, the Commission as opposed to the shareholders must receive a copy of the minutes of the last annual meeting together with a senior officer's statement that there have been no material changes since the date of the last audited financial statement.

The Commission has specified some of the criteria it uses in exercising its discretion. If the information specified above is supplied, the company has been holding regular annual meetings and distributing information to shareholders as required by its incorporating act, and there has been no change in management or effective control since the last annual meeting, the Commission will not normally object. Where the purpose of the offer requires that a minimum amount be raised, an acceptance period of up to 30 days will not be considered unreasonable; and for other offers a 90-day maximum is permissible.

The rights offering presents a problem for dealings with shareholders outside Canada. The problem is particularly acute in the case of shareholders who are U.S. residents, in view of the fact that U.S. registration of the securities is required before a U.S. trade with such U.S. residents can take place. The principles of corporate law in the U.S. are different as well. Frequently the decision is made to bar U.S. shareholders from the offering rather than go to the expense of qualifying the offering so that they may share in the distribution.[256]

---

[256]Professor Loss comments on this problem in his *Securities Regulation*, vol. 1, pp. 363-5. As he notes, the reluctance of Canadian corporations to make rights offers to their American shareholders is understandable from the point of view of the corporations themselves but may involve unfairness if the offer is at a price substantially below the market. This has been mitigated somewhat by the practice of the SEC in permitting the offering documents to be sent to the shareholders with a legend attached which warns them that the underlying securities are not qualified for sale in the U.S. but which also informs them that they may dispose of their rights in Canada. This procedure involves no offer or sale of any security in the U.S., and is the method most frequently used by Canadian corporations. For a tender offer where American stockholders were not so accommodated and subsequently brought legal action unsuccessfully, see *Travis v. Anthes Imperial Ltd.* (1971), 331 F. Supp. 797 (D. C. Mo.).

Bill 20 introduces few innovations in the area of "issuer-internal" exemptions. Perhaps the most important is the deletion of the exemption for promoters.[257] However a great many promoters, especially those most "in the know", will be able to take advantage of the new limited offering exemption which permits trades to 25 purchasers if certain conditions are met.[258] In addition Bill 20 adds a new subparagraph to the exemption for rights offerings[259] which makes it clear that it covers both the issuing of and trading in the right and the subsequent trade in the underlying securities.

As might be expected "issuer" replaces "company" as the source of the exempted securities, thus reflecting the general scheme of the Bill.

(d) Issuer Combinations

There are two categories of exemption whose distinguishing characteristic is the combining of the issuer with another business enterprise (or its owners or creditors) in some way. These exemptions are justified primarily on the basis of the "need to know" test, although the parties for whom the protection of the Act is thought to be unnecessary possess not so much knowledge as an ability to become knowledgeable through negotiations; it is assumed that an exempt issue of securities will only result after a carefully negotiated agreement in which those who are to receive shares as consideration (or their representatives) will have had ample opportunity to learn about the affairs of the issuer. Corporate law reporting obligations should ensure adequate dissemination of the information so acquired.

Both these categories derive from a single exempting provision (containing a staccato list of technical words, each with a particular but as yet undetermined significance) in the 1971 amendments following the recommendations of the Merger Report. The first exempts trades where securities of the issuer are exchanged in connection with:
(a) a statutory amalgamation,
(b) a (statutory) arrangement,
(c) a take-over bid as defined in s. 105, and
(d) "other mergers".
The two exempt trades in the second category are:
(e) an offer to purchase shares by way of private agreement with less than fifteen shareholders, and
(f) an offer to purchase all the shares of a private company.
We shall deal with all six of these sub-categories in turn except that (c), the take-over bid, will be left to the end.

(i) Statutory Amalgamation

As in the case of "reorganization" there is no definition of statutory amalgamation in the Act. However, there are detailed provisions[260] in most corporations legislation and in the Income Tax Act[261] which assist in the interpretation of the concept. In the BCA "Amalgamations and Continuations" is one of the four sub-headings under the broad

---

[257]Presently s. 19(1)9c.
[258]Section 35(1)17.
[259]Section 35(1)11(iii).
[260]See the BCA, s. 196; the CCA, s. 137; the CBCA, s. 185 and the 1973 Select Committee Report on Mergers and Amalgamations, chapters 4 to 7.
[261]1970-71-72 (Can.), c. 63, s. 87, as amended.

heading "Reorganization."[262] The relevant sections begin with the permission that "any two or more corporations, including holding or subsidiary corporations, may amalgamate and continue as one corporation."[263] What follows is not so much a definition of amalgamation itself as a statement of its results. As set out in the BCA[264] the effect of amalgamation is analogous to the coming together of several streams to form a river: the rights and liabilities, both criminal and civil, of the constituent elements are preserved in the successor entity, and the amalgamating corporations continue as one corporation which possesses all the property previously held by them individually.[265]

The unanswered question is the scope of the term "statutory". Is any statute of any jurisdiction eligible or is the term restricted to the BCA, the Income Tax Act, and other incorporating or taxing statutes (or some still narrower group within this list)?[266]

(ii) Arrangement

The exemption for an "arrangement" appears in the phrase "a statutory amalgamation or arrangement".[267] It is unclear whether or not the word "statutory" modifies "arrangement" as well as "amalgamation". If not, absolute drafting precision would require the presence of a comma before "arrangement". The point is of some importance if the word statutory requires as its reference only the BCA,[268] where arrangement forms one of four divisions under the broad heading "Reorganization". In view of the fact that the exemption was drafted with the intent that the other uniform act provinces would similarly amend their securities legislation, it seems improbable that any of its terms should be so limited; we may suppose that "statutory" includes at least the incorporating legislation of the uniform securities act jurisdictions, a number of which treat "arrangement" somewhat differently from Ontario.[269]

---

[262]Sections 196 and 197. For the circularity this treatment creates compare the discussion, *supra*, in the text at and after footnote 243

[263]Section 196(1). Note that "corporation" is defined in the BCA to include Ontario incorporated business corporations but not those incorporated in a jurisdiction other than Ontario (ss. 1(1)9 and 2).

[264]Section 197.

[265]Two recent Supreme Court of Canada cases emphasize the extent to which the predecessor corporations literally continue for the purpose of enforcing rights and imposing liabilities (including criminal sanctions): *R. v. Black & Decker Mfg. Co. Ltd.* (1974), 43 D.L.R. (3d) 393, 15 C.C.C. (2d) 193, 13 C.P.R. (2d) 97 (S.C.C.) and *Witco Chemical Co. Canada Ltd. v. Town of Oakville* (1974), 43 D.L.R. (3d) 413 (S.C.C.).

[266]The problem is raised in a pointed form by the treatment of amalgamation in the CBCA (s. 176(1)) where there is no definition.

[267]Section 19(1)9(a) as added by 1971, Vol. 2, c. 31, s. 3(2) (Bill 20, s. 35(1)12(a)).

[268]The discussion of this exemption in the Merger Report (paras. 6.16 and 6.17) which recommended the current phraseology refers only to the BCA, a fact which might suggest that the subsequent legislation is likewise concerned with that Act alone. It is by no means certain that this is the correct interpretation.

[269]This footnote examines how the term "arrangement" is treated in the various Canadian companies acts. The companies acts of British Columbia, Nova Scotia, Prince Edward Island, Quebec and Saskatchewan do not define

Moreover there is a good argument for the view that this exemption was intended for arrangements under any Canadian incorporating statute and not just those of the uniform act provinces. This view is suggested by the subsequent creation of a related exemption for "other mergers" (discussed below), a kind of catch all for corporate organic changes occurring under corporations legislation outside Canada. It would appear that all Canadian jurisdictions were already covered by the exemption presently under consideration.

As we saw earlier, most of the items included under the heading "arrangement" in the BCA[270] are "issuer-internal" matters, the exception being "reconstruction", which contemplates a transaction between two corporations and is defined as follows:

"a reconstruction under which a corporation transfers or sells, or proposes to transer or to sell, to another body corporate the whole or a substantial part of its undertaking for a consideration consisting in whole or in part of securities of the other body corporate and under which it proposes to distribute a part of that consideration among its shareholders of any class, or to cease carrying on its undertaking or that part of its undertaking so transferred or sold or so proposed to be transfered or sold."[271]

This definition requires two things (a) a sale of assets to a corporation for securities and (b) one of: (i) distribution of those securities to its shareholders, (ii) ceasing to carry on its undertaking, or (iii) ceasing to carry on that part of its undertaking that is sold. Part (a) alone and part (a) plus part (b) with alternative (i) are probably already exempted by the previously discussed reorganization or winding-up

---

"arrangement", yet all of them except the Prince Edward Island Act use the term. Manitoba (s. 124(1)) and Newfoundland (s. 131(4)) have definitions that are similar to the s. 193(1) definition in the BCA.

The CCA (s. 134(4)) and New Brunswick (s. 47(4)) have similar definitions of "arrangement". The CCA definition is somewhat like that in the BCA in that "arrangement" extends to any reorganization of share capital; however in the CCA definition "arrangement" includes an "amalgamation or reconstruction" whereas the BCA definition includes only a reconstruction. But the CCA definition of "amalgamation or reconstruction" is similar to the BCA definition of "reconstruction" in s. 193(1)(d). This illustrates that terms have not been well defined in this area.

The Alberta definition (s. 154(1)) is the simplest one: "arrangement... [extends] to the reorganization of the share capital of the company...".

All of the definitions take the form "arrangement includes" or "arrangement extends to". This language may be construed to give the term a wide and inclusive as opposed to a restricted ambit—perhaps it was used because the draftsmen did not have a clear idea of what an "arrangement" is.

The CBCA does not use the term arrangement, but rather speaks of "reorganization", which is defined by s. 185(1) as a court order made under (a) s. 234, (b) the Bankruptcy Act approving a proposal and (c) any other Act of Parliament that affects the rights among the corporation, its shareholders and creditors. Only one company is involved in the first two types of order, but the third potentially goes further since a second company might be involved in an order made under "any other Act of the parliament of Canada".

[270]Section 193(1).
[271]Section 193(1)(d).

exemption which is not subject to a dollar amount floor.[272] Alternatives (ii) and (iii) seem not to be covered by the reorganization exemption, since they involve no distribution to security holders. As a result the "arrangement" exemption appears to have a necessary function in the limited circumstance of an assets transfer below $100,000 in which the securities received are not distributed: transactions involving assets worth more than $100,000 appear to be exempt already by the special assets sale exemption.[273]

(iii) "Other Merger"

The "other merger" exemption is intended as a kind of omnibus clause to cover certain corporate combinations which are not explicitly covered under sub-categories (a) or (b). The specific exemption reads:

"any statutory procedure under which one company takes title to the assets of the other company which in turn loses its existence by operation of law, or under which the existing companies merge in a new company".[274]

This exemption derives from the recommendations of the Merger Report. It was intended to replace the rather cryptic exemption for a "merger or consolidation" in the predecessor Act, which was designed to accommodate business combinations occurring under the incorporating statutes of some of the U.S. states. Indeed the language of the new exemption is taken from one of the leading U.S. textbooks describing the terms "merger" and "consolidation."[275]

(iv) An Offer to Purchase Shares By Way of Private Agreement with Less than Fifteen Shareholders

One paragraph contains both the private agreement exemption and its

---

[272]Sections 19(1)8(ii) and 58(1)(c). Using s. 19(1)8(ii) in this way requires that one read the word "reorganization" in that paragraph to comprehend the issuer part of the transaction.

[273]Sections 19(1)9b and 58(1)(c). See, *supra*, part 4.12(2)(a)(v). Note however that s. 19(1)9b, the exemption for securities exchanged for assets of $100,000 or more, requires investment intent on the part of the recipient of the securities. This is not the case in s. 19(1)9.

[274]Sections 19(1)9(b) and 58(1)(c) (Bill 20, s. 35(1)12(b) and s. 73(1)(g)(ii)).

[275]Merger Report, paras. 6.13 and 6.14:

"Merger and consolidation have not been the subject of judicial interpretation in the context of securities regulation. The words appear to have been adopted from company law in the United States, and have been explained as follows:

'Technically, merger, is limited to a statutory procedure whereby one of the constituent companies takes title to the assets of the other one, which in turn loses its existence by operation of law. If none of the constituent companies remains, but instead a new entity is created into which they are merged, the process is called consolidation.' *Cases and Materials on Corporations,* Baker and Cary, 3rd edition, (Brooklyn, 1959) at p. 1435.

"These forms of statutory merger and consolidation are unknown to Ontario law. The words are used by the legal profession in a non-technical manner to describe the actual result of the business combination, e.g. where one group of shareholders is left rather than two...or to describe acquisitions other than statutory amalgamations.... Assuming adequate investor disclosure, and subject to the rules regarding resale, our recommendations are intended to bring order and clarity to this exemption...".

companion the "private company" exemption;[276] both of these, like the preceding exemption, are products of the 1971 amendments which followed the recommendations of the Merger Report.

The exempted transactions are among the "exempt offers" in that part of the Act dealing with take-over bids. Three limitations apply: (1) the issuer must be a company; (2) offering securities, and (3) acquiring shares.

Prior to the 1971 amendments these two types of now exempt transactions were a frequent source of s. 59 applications to the Commission for discretionary relief.[277] It has been suggested that the draftsman's intention would be more clearly implemented if it were expressly stated that it is exempt offers in connection with take-over bids which are the subject-matter of the exemption. Otherwise the language of the section might be open to the unintended interpretation that the offer to purchase shares could be made *by* rather than *to* less than fifteen shareholders. An ingenious issuer of shares might secure an offer to purchase from less than fifteen persons who only become shareholders after the sale.

A nice question is whether the exemption applies to up to fourteen separate agreements with shareholders connected only by the fact that the offeror is the same in each case and the shareholders all hold shares in the same company. This hypothetical situation may be taken a stage further: must all the elements in the fourteen separate agreements (excepting the number of securities acquired) be the same, or may, to take one example, different consideration be offered? The opposite extreme would be to suppose that the fourteen must all be parties to one single agreement arrived at by a common negotiating process, whether as a result of the largest shareholder acting on behalf of the rest or otherwise. The use of the adjective "private", and the fact that the words "offer" and "agreement" are used in the singular, might suggest such a restricted view. On the other hand the language from which this exemption was modelled, *viz.*, the take-over bid exempt offer prior to its 1971 amendment, reads "an offer to purchase shares by way of private agreement with individual shareholders and not

---

[276]Sections 19(1)9a and 58(1)(c) added by 1971, Vol. 2, c. 31, ss. 3(2) and 13(1).
[277]See the Merger Report, pp. 181-6; the rationale for creating the statutory exemptions is discussed in paras. 6.04 to 6.09 and 7.07 of the Report. The evolving treatment of these transactions is an interesting example of how experience with a discretionary power may demonstrate the need for an automatic or certain statutory exemption. In analyzing these s. 59 applications the Report (by three of the then six commissioners of the OSC) states (para. 6.05): "The Commission examined the needs of the selling shareholders (vendors) in the course of the section 59 applications. In the majority of cases the bargaining process leading up to the agreement satisfied the Commission that the vendors did not need prospectus protection. They were content to sell their business in exchange for shares. As to the question of whether the trade constituted primary distribution to the public,the Commission, applying the need to know philosophy, found the vendors were not the 'public'..." and (para. 6.09) "So far as the 'exempt offer' share exchange acquisitions are concerned the Commission through its treatment of the section 59 applications had created another class of exemption. We have concluded that this should be included in the statutory exemptions".

made to shareholders generally". It can be seen that the qualifying proviso in that exempt offer, excluding "shareholders generally", has been dropped from the current exemption. It can be argued that the omission of the proviso and the insertion in its place of the numbers test "less than fifteen" which came from another of the predecessor take-over bid exempt offers,[278] meant that the Legislature intended to negate entirely the qualifying force of the proviso and leave a naked numbers test instead. Probably the latter view is the preferable one; once the legislation has laid down an objective test regarding the number of shareholders that may be reached by the exempt offer, it is reasonable to suppose that the manner in which they participate in the offer, whether singly or collectively, is immaterial.[279]

A further area of obsurity in regard to this exemption concerns the time aspect. Can it be used frequently, provided that there is a distinct intervening period each time? Consider one private agreement today with fourteen shareholders, another six months later with another fourteen, a third six months later with fourteen and so on. Probably this question can best be answered equivocally the more persons for whom an exemption is sought and the more often it is used, the longer space of time should be between each use.

---

[278]Section 81(b)(i).

[279]If the intention of the reform committee whose recommendations led to the legislative change has any persuasive force, the Merger Report might provide evidence that the possibility of more than one agreement was contemplated. In recommending an exemption to parallel the "exempt offer" provisions it states "...since we have recommended limiting clause (i) to fifteen offers the second part of this exemption [exempting offers to public companies having fifteen shareholders] appears redundant." The possible relevance of the Report here raises the whole question of the admissibility and probative value of ancillary interpretive sources such as reform commission recommendations, legislative debates, and legislation committee reports in seeking to determine the legislative intent. Traditionally, Canadian (unlike U.S.) courts have been indisposed to use such interpretive tools. Recently, however, there have been some indications of a change in attitude. See for example *Re Lambert Island Ltd. and A.-G. Ont.,* [1972] 2 O.R. 659 at p. 669, 26 D.L.R. (3d) 391 at p. 401 (H.C); *Gaysek v. The Queen,* [1971] S.C.R. 888 at p. 902, 18 D.L.R. (3d) 306 at p. 317, 2 C.C.C. (2d) 545, 15 C.R.N.S. 345; *Re Ombudsman Act* (1970), 72 W.W.R. 176 at p. 180, 10 D.L.R. (3d) 47 at p. 51 (Alta. S.C.). In a case dealing with an exemption from financial reporting obligations, *Re Maher Shoes Ltd.,* [1967] 2 O.R. 684, 65 D.L.R. (2d) 105 (H.C.), the Kimber Report was quoted by the Ontario High Court without comment. An issue of construction arose in the insider-trading case, *Green v. The Charterhouse Group Canada Ltd. et al.,* [1973] 2 O.R. 677, 35 D.L.R. (3d) 161 (H.C.) and the Kimber Report was referred to. Grant J. quoted one paragraph from the chapter on insider trading in the Kimber Report, styling it as relevant "for the limited purpose of determining what was the defect or evil which the legislation intended to remedy"; he stated clearly however "the recommendations of such report cannot be referred to directly to determine the intention of the legislature in enacting the insider trading provisions." This approach was approved on the appeal in this case (1975), 12 O.R. (2d) 280 (C.A.). In *Farnham v. Fingold,* [1973] 2 O.R. 132, 33 D.L.R. (3d) 156 (C.A.) improper use of this exemption was alleged in a civil liability claim but, due to settlement, the substantive issue never came to trial.

The intent of this exemption is to provide an exemption from registration and distribution requirements which parallels the exemption from take-over bid provisions in the case of an offer to fourteen shareholders or fewer. But the exemption may, unwittingly, do more than that. It clearly exempts the trade when fourteen or less shareholders of an offeree company are *selling* their shares to an acquiror issuer. But can it also be read to exempt fourteen or fewer persons or companies *purchasing* shares, or at any rate fourteen or fewer existing shareholders *purchasing* more shares. This second interpretation would require that the "offer to purchase" shares originate with the fourteen shareholders and not with the issuer, and that the "shares" so purchased, which would have to be identified with the word security in the opening phrase "a trade in a security of a company", be those of the issuer and not those of the fourteen shareholders. If valid, such a construction would establish by the back door, as it were, a numbers test by which a distribution of the standard type could classify itself "non-public".[280] It is submitted that a court would readily reject this

---

[280]This would be an indirect anticipation of the new s. 35(1)17—limited offering exemption of Bill 20, but with much less stringent requirements (*infra*, part 4.12(3)(b)). The number fifteen as a test for non-public has a respectable antiquity. In s. 103(2)(a) of the Act certain proxy provisions do not apply where the number of shareholders is "*not more than* fifteen"; in s. 1(9) of the BCA the existence of *fewer than* fifteen shareholders permits a discretionary declaration that a company is no longer offering its shares to the public. There is no magic in numbers however until they appear in statute. For a delightfully candid account of why the number 35 was proposed for the new U.S. Uniform Federal Securities Code in an attempt to "objectify" the non-public offering exemption, see L. Loss and G. A. Blackstone, "Codification of the Federal Securities Laws" (1973), 28 *The Business Lawyer* 381 at p. 385.

In an earlier draft of this manuscript this footnote ended here. But one of my colleagues pointed out that while the footnote perhaps raised a presumption of candour and delight, in the absence of evidence it failed to satisfy the onus of proof. So—for the reader to judge—here is the passage from Professor Loss' lips (*ibid.*, at p. 385):

"Section 227(b) defines a limited offering as an offering that results in not more than 35 buyers, plus a number of institutional investors. It is of no consequence how many offerees there are. First of all, why no limit on the number of offerees? There are two reasons. First, it occurred to us half way through our deliberations that the tremendous emphasis on offerees was illogical. It goes back to a case in the House of Lords that was based on the Directors' Liability Act of 1890, on which our Securities Act was in part modelled. That statute talked about public offerings, and the House of Lords read 'offering' literally. But who is hurt if you have a lot of offerees and nobody buys, or only two people buy? Secondly, as 'offer' is defined, and will continue to be defined, it will be impossible to get a degree of definiteness unless we get away from counting offerees. So we shall count buyers.

"Now, why 35? Well, why not? Twenty-five was a good old number years ago. That was the rule of thumb that was used when I was a youngster with the Commission, and so, naturally, I brought in a draft that said 25. Then one of the Advisers at the meeting said that seemed a little low, so somebody else said 35 and Commissioner Loomis, who is one of the Advisers, said, 'We might live with 35', and I said, 'Sold'."

second interpretation. First, to identify the word "securities" with the narrower word "shares" would be a tortured use of language. Secondly, the entire legislative history of this provision which makes clear that its function is to complement the exemptions from the take-over bid requirements, precludes such a view.

(v) An Offer to Purchase Shares in a Private Company

The origins of this "private company" exemption have been discussed in the preceding section. Although "private company" has been dropped from the lexicon of the BCA in favour of the more indistinct "non-public offering company" it still remains in the Act and in many of the Canadian corporations acts,[281] albeit with some minor definitional variations. In the Act[282] the private company uses the traditional trinity of charter restrictions to define the concept. These are in summary form:

(i) the right to transfer the company's shares is restricted in the instrument of incorporation,

(ii) the number of its shareholders, exclusive of employees and former employees who remain as shareholders, is limited to 50,

(iii) any invitation to the public to subscribe for its securities is prohibited.

The exemption requires the offer to be for all the shares of the private company and not just for all of the shares held by some of the shareholders or some of the shares held by all of the shareholders. It need not, however be accepted by all.[283]

Both this exemption and the closely related one for private agreements are designed to permit an acquiring company to use securities rather than cash consideration to purchase already issued shares free of the registration and distribution requirements. If the acquiror were offering cash consideration it would of course be unnecessary to create an exemption from the distribution requirements, since the shares purchased would probably already have been distributed to the public; if not it could be argued plausibly that the acquiror in the present purchase was not the "public" either. An exemption from the registration requirement would not be necessary if the acquiror were paying cash, since the Act is normally interpreted as a "soliciting" Act designed to protect potential purchasers who are being solicited to

---

[281]See F. Iacobucci and D. L. Johnston, "The Private or Closely-held Corporation", at p. 77.

[282]Section 1(1)14.

[283]Section 19(1)9a simply says that the offer (and not the trade) must be for all the shares of the company. Whether this requirement of a complete and comprehensive offer was deliberate—to ensure that no shareholder is unwillingly left holding a minority interest beside a new controller—or was the result of a drafting oversight is an interesting puzzle. An analysis of the Merger Report gives some support to the latter possibility. The Report appears to make a slip in summarizing the exemptions from the take-over bid requirements as they appeared in the pre-1971 Act. The exemption in question was simply for "an offer to purchase shares in a private company". This slip turns up in the final recommendations of the Report (see paras. 7.06, 7.16, 7.36(2), 6.23). Bill 20 now reverts to the pre-1971 formulation (see s. 35(1)14 and s. 90(c)(ii) and, *infra*, part 4.12(2)(d)(vii)).

purchase securities. It is not a "dealing" act seeking to protect persons who are selling securities, even though the definition of trade[284] with its catch-all phrase "or other dealing in" might suggest the latter interpretation. In any case the vendors in most circumstances would fall within the isolated trade exemption.[285] On either of these grounds, then, the exemption would be unnecessary for cash offers.

(vi) Take-Over Bids

The final exemption in this group is for a trade in securities issued by a corporate offeror in a take-over bid.[286] This transaction is entirely exempted from the registration and distribution requirements; it is regulated separately, albeit less stringently, under a special section of the Act which imposes certain disclosure obligations;[287] there is no regulation at all from a registration point of view. The term "take-over bid" is defined[288] to mean:

> "an offer, other than an exempt offer, made to shareholders the latest address of any of whom as shown on the books of the offeree company is in Ontario to purchase such number of equity shares of a company that, together with the offeror's presently-owned shares, will in the aggregate exceed 20 per cent of the outstanding equity shares of the company."

In recommending that take-over bids not be subject to the kind of administrative vetting carried out with respect to a prospectus, the Kimber Report cited as a reason

> "the importance of speed and secrecy to the success of a take-over bid or a counter bid and because the procedural and substantive recommendations which comprise the suggested statutory code for take-over bids should, on a logical basis, be applicable to both cash bids and share exchange bids".

The same Report did acknowledge however

> "that the issuance by a company of its own securities as a part of a share exchange take-over bid does not differ in any essential constituent from the issuance of its securities in the course of primary distribution to the public".[289]

The reasons for providing an exemption from registration were not considered in the Report though it was clearly intended that the exemption should be dual. Certainly reasons of speed would not be a factor since a broker could be engaged quickly to handle the transactions in the same way as a trust company is now usually employed as a depository for offerees' acceptances. Similarly the registrant could be enjoined to maintain the same secrecy as the trust company. Moreover a registered broker will often be involved prior to the offer to advise on market conditions and price. Presumably the essential reason why exemption from registration is given is because a take-over bid will take place in the glare of publicity, accompanied by full disclosure and

---

[284]Section 1(1)24 (Bill 20, s. 1(1)40(i) has been amended to make this clear).
[285]Section 19(1)2.
[286]Sections 19(1)9(c) and 58(1)(c) (Bill 20, ss. 35(1)13 and 73(1)(h)).
[287]Part IX (Bill 20, Part XIX).
[288]Section 81(g) (Bill 20, s. 90(1)(h) changes "shareholders" to "security holders" and "equity shares" to "voting securities").
[289]Para. 3.24.

subject to the close and attentive scrutiny of the financial newspapers, the brokerage community and the regulatory authorities, and normally a registrant will, in fact, be involved.

The exemption is phrased so that the transaction to be exempted must first meet the definition of take-over bid. Since that definition is limited to an offer for equity shares, trades in non-voting shares or other forms of securities which might be the subject of a bid are not within the exemption. This, of course, is a problem inherent in the limited definition of take-over bid and not in the exemption itself.[290]

(vii) Reforms to Issuer Combination Exemptions

We shall summarize at this point the changes effected by Bill 20 in the area of "issuer combination" trades. These are relatively minor in all. Once again these are dual exemptions, so an examination of s. 35 will suffice for s. 73 as well. The provision dealing with amalgamations, arrangements and "other mergers"[291] remains the same. The most significant alteration occurs in connection with the "private agreements" and "private company" exemptions. These disappear from the body of s. 35, which simply provides for the exemption of trades in connection with exempt offers as defined in Part XIX regulating take-over bids.[292] One important change is that issuer has replaced company; thus the securities of unincorporated organizations may be issued as consideration under this exemption.[293] In Part XIX the definition of exempt offer[294] has two parts: the second of these reproduces the old private company exemption, except that its terms are first, relaxed to include an offer for some rather than just all the

---

[290]The problem may be illustrated in the following example. G Ltd. had purchased privately all of the class A preferred shares of M Ltd., a federally incorporated company, and had acquired by take-over bid 94 per cent of its class B preferred shares. G proceeded under the compulsory expropriation section of the CCA (s. 136) to acquire the balance of the class B shares. However there remained outstanding: (a) M bearer warrants entitling the holders to purchase a total of 30,000 class B shares if exercised within the next 15 months, and (b) M debentures in the principal amount of $250,000 convertible into class A shares over a four-year period. G applied under s. 59 for an exemption from the registration and distribution requirements to issue shares to the M warrant and debenture holders on terms analogous to those accorded the offerees in a take-over bid, assuming the conversion privileges were, in fact, exercised. Its offer was not a take-over bid as defined, and thus did not fall within the registration and distribution exemptions. Although the rather extended time period over which the shares might issue involved a departure from the Commission's customary practice, a favourable s. 59 order was granted. One might question what would have been the result if the class A preferred shares had been acquired by a take-over bid. Would shares issued to the debenture holders be trades "in connection with" a take-over bid and thus exempt?

Bill 20, s. 90(1)(h) remedies this problem by defining take-over bid to mean "an offer...to security holders", although the calculation of the definitional base is still in terms of "voting securities".

[291]Section 35(1)12.

[292]Section 35(1)14. But Bill 20, s. 90(2) makes significant changes in these exempt offers.

[293]See, *supra*, footnote 193.

[294]Section 90(2).

shares in such a company but secondly restricted to exclude private companies which are insiders of reporting issuers. The first type of exempt offer is one made and regulated through the stock exchange. It will be seen that the old exemption for the private agreement with fewer than fifteen shareholders has disappeared entirely. Presumably this exemption was felt to be too open to abuse[295] and in any case it covered some of the same ground as the new limited offering exemption.[296] The take-over bid exemption remains much the same. (The issuer must still be a company.[297]) However, the defintion of take-over bid[298] has been changed to make the object of the bid "voting securities", a category that will in certain circumstances be broader than "equity shares".[299]

(3) REFORM PROPOSALS—DOUBLE EXEMPTIONS FOR A TRADE

Bill 20 contains two new important double exemptions for a trade. Each is a *quid pro quo* for the removal of the public-private distinction from the concept of distribution.[300]

(a) Isolated Issue

The first of these exempts:

"an isolated trade in a specific security by or on behalf of an issuer, for the issuer's account, where such trade is not made in the course of continued and successive transactions of a like nature, and is not made by a person or company whose usual business is trading in securities".[301]

The language of this distribution exemption is identical to that of the exemption from registration for an isolated trade in the Act, except that the phrase "for the issuer's account" is substituted in Bill 20 in the exemption from distribution for the phrase "for the owner's account" in the Act.[302] The double phrase "for the owner's or issuer's account" appears in Bill 20 in the exemption from registration.[303] This ensures that the present single exemption from registration for an isolated secondary trade by an owner is preserved and that a new double exemption for an isolated primary trade by an issuer is created.

This exemption will be particularly useful for the issuance of smaller amounts of securities, for example to a trade creditor, not already exempted by the large dollar amount or institutional purchaser private placement exemptions.[304]

---

[295]See *Farnham v. Fingold*, [1973] 2 O.R. 132, 33 D.L.R. (3d) 156 (C.A.).
[296]Section 35(1)17. See, *infra*, part 4.12(3)(b).
[297]Section 35(1)13. See, *supra*, footnote 193.
[298]Section 90(1)(h).
[299]Note that by the definition in s. 1(1)42 debt securities are excluded from "voting security".
[300]*Supra*, part 4.02(2), esp. footnote 28.
[301]Section 73(1)(b).
[302]Section 19(1)2.
[303]Section 35(1)2.
[304]For a detailed discussion of the language of this exemption, see the isolated trade exemption, *ante*, part 3.18(2).

(b) Limited Offering

This important innovation provides a double exemption for trades by an issuer to 25 purchasers or less.[305] It is modelled in part on the similarly named exemption proposed for the American Law Institute's Federal Securities Code[306] and borrows from U.S. experience with the "non-public" offering under the 1933 Federal Securities Act.[307] It is designed to replace the subjective tests for the concept public with objective criteria that limit the range of interpretive variance. Its requirements are specified in the form of a number of conditions. The first of these is that the purchaser must be a principal. Secondly, the purchaser must either be a senior officer, director or close relative of the issuer, or be of such sophistication and experience (or have access to such sophisticated advice) that he has no need of a prospectus. This, of course, is a cryptic statutory crystallization of the current jurisprudence on the concept of public. Thirdly, there must be no special promotional campaign accompanying the sale. Fourthly, no more than 50 prospective purchasers may be solicited. This condition is expressed in the past tense "solicitations have not been made" requiring an historical count to be kept. Thus when, counting from day one, 50 persons have been solicited, the exemption is exhausted.[308] The final condition is that the number of beneficial owners as a result of trades pursuant to the exemption must not exceed 25. This last condition will not require that a count be kept throughout the issuer's lifetime to ensure the maximum is not exceeded. It is expressed in the present tense: "there are not more than twenty-five beneficial owners of securities as a result of trades pursuant to this exemption". This is a continuing condition. Thus one beneficial owner may sell to another within the group (or to the issuer for cancellation) and "his chance" may be used again. More difficult is the question whether one beneficial owner may sell to some other purchaser who enjoys an exemption so that "his chance" may be used again. It would seem so. The beneficial owner as a result of the trade pursuant to *this* exemption has disappeared. Moreover the new purchaser will still be subject to restrictions on resale.

It should be noted that the concept "beneficial ownership" rather than holder or registered owner is used. This is designed to prevent one

---

[305]Sections 73(1)(m) and 35(1)17.

[306]Tentative Draft No. 1, April 25, 1972, s. 227(b), that exemption reads:
"A limited offering is one which in the following conditions are satisfied: (A) the initial buyers of the securities are institutional investors and not more than thirty-five other persons; (B) resales of any of those securities before a date of three years after the last sale to any of the initial buyers do not result in more than thirty-five owners of those securities (apart from institutional investors and persons who become owners otherwise than the purchase) at any one time; and (C) the original offeror and all sellers in such resales comply with any rules [established by the SEC]."
See, *supra*, footnote 280, for its history.

[307]See discussion of "public", *supra*, part 4.02(2).

[308]This interpretation is confirmed by a change to the past tense in Bill 20 from the present tense in Bill 98, the change indicated by the emphasis: "solicitations in respect of the securities *have* not been made to more than 50 prospective purchasers."

exempted person holding on behalf of a number of beneficiaries and thus expanding the true owners beyond the ceiling of 25.

(4) EXPRESS EXEMPTION—DOUBLE EXEMPTION FOR SECURITIES

The exemptions under this heading are all fully dual, in contrast to those based on the nature of the trade involved. The basis for the exemptions is that (1) the securities are extremely stable, in some cases being government guaranteed; (2) they are regulated under other specific legislation; (3) the particular buyers can be expected to fend for themselves; (4) it is expedient for business or social reasons to exempt them, or (5) it is impracticable for them to be regulated by the Act.

These exemptions are reasonably straightforward. The discussion here will be limited to grouping them under the most appropriate of the five categories just mentioned (though it is apparent that some of them could easily fit under two or more headings); specific problems in their use will occasionally be subjected to more detailed treatment.

(a) Stable Securities—Government Guaranteed

The securities under this heading are solely debt obligations—"bonds, debentures or other evidences of indebtedness" and are issued or guaranteed by a recognized government.[309] The governments are those of the United Kingdom, Canada, or any of its provinces, or municipal corporations in Canada (including school debentures) "or any foreign country or any political division thereof". In addition, debt obligations of or guaranteed by the International Bank for Reconstruction and Development are exempt provided they are payable in Canadian or U.S. currency.[310]

(b) Otherwise Regulated Securities

A variety of types of securities are grouped under this heading. The volume in dollars traded in some of these is immense. The exemption reflects the self-imposed limits of "pure" securities regulation based on the premise that duplication of regulation should be avoided where possible. The first of these types, where the "other regulation" is most complete, comprehends[311] debt obligations of or guaranteed by:
(a) chartered banks,[312]
(b) loan or trust corporations registered under the Ontario Loan and Trust Corporations Act,[313]
(c) insurance companies licensed under the Ontario Insurance Act,[314]

---

[309]Sections 58(2)(a) and 19(2)1(a) (Bill 20, ss. 74(1)(a) and 35(2)1(a)).

[310]Sections 19(2)1(d) and 58(2)(a) (Bill 20, ss. 35(2)1(d) and 74(1)(a)). The I.B.R.D. is known informally as the World Bank (14 Yearbook of International Organizations 1391 (1972-73 ed.)).

[311]Sections 58(2)(a), 19(2), paras. 1(c) and 2 (Bill 20, s. 35(2), paras. 1(c) and 3 and s. 74(1)(a)).

[312]Chartered under the Bank Act, R.S.C. 1970, c. B-1.

[313]R.S.O. 1970, c. 254. Extra-provincial loan or trust corporations are required to obtain registration (s. 146) to carry on a loan or trust company business in Ontario and, once they do, their securities enjoy this exemption.

[314]R.S.O. 1970, c. 224. Extra-provincial insurers are required to obtain a licence (s. 21) if they are carrying on business in Ontario and, once they do, their securities enjoy this exemption.

(d) guaranteed investment certificates or receipts of a trust company registered under the Loan and Trust Corporations Act.[315]

Bill 20 adds an exemption for securities of registered trust companies issued in respect of accounts whose sole function is to service a retirement savings plan registered under the Income Tax Act[316] or certain types of pooled or common trust funds.[317]

The second category under the otherwise regulated exemption is that of securities issued by corporations which are operated as co-operatives under Part V of the Ontario Corporations Act.[318] The "other regulation" rationale is not so far-reaching here as for the institutions in the preceding group.[319] Until recently the term co-operative was not expressly defined in the governing legislation; rather a co-operative was simply a company or corporation (with or without share capital) to which Part V was made applicable on the issuance of letters patent or supplementary letters patent. The result[320] was that the term "co-operative" was a source of confusion, despite the fact that one could identify a common element of mutual self-help, with aims and methods varying according to context. The passing of the Co-operative Corporations Act, 1973[321] has altered the situation considerably. The Act applies to "every corporation incorporated as a co-operative by or under a general or special Act of the [legislature.]".[322] A co-operative is defined as a corporation carrying on an enterprise on a "co-operative basis".[323]

There are four requirements for an enterprise to operate on a "co-operative basis": each member or delegate must have one vote, there must be no voting by proxy, the interest on loan capital and dividends on share capital must be limited to a percentage fixed either by the statute or the articles of the particular corporation, and the corporation must be operated as nearly as possible at cost.[324] Part V of the Ontario Corporations Act is thus superseded to the extent that the new Act applies. The exemption for co-operatives in Bill 20 is limited in its scope by reference to this new statute.[325]

Possibly the co-operative exemption, like the final exemption in this

---

[315]R.S.O. 1970, c. 254. Although the reason is unclear, these certificates are apparently not viewed by their issuers as guaranteed debt obligations, and thus not already exempted under para. (b) above.

[316]1970-71-72 (Can.), c. 63.

[317]Sections 74(1)(a) and 35(2)4. It has been suggested that such plans and accounts should not be exempt but rather equated with ordinary mutual funds. For a lucid discussion of the various arguments and counter-arguments see the Canadian Mutual Funds Report (at pp. 120-7). It recommended that the exemption continue.

[318]R.S.O. 1970, c. 89, Part V; for the exemption see ss. 19(2)7 and 58(2)(a).

[319]This and other matters are considered in the Report by the Ontario Select Committee on Company Law on Co-operatives.

[320]As the Select Committee notes, *ibid* , at pp. 1-4.

[321]1973 (Ont.), c. 101.

[322]*Ibid.*, s. 3.

[323]*Ibid.*, s. 1(1)5.

[324]*Ibid.*, s. 1(1)6.

[325]Sections 35(2)10 and 74(1)(a).

group—shares of a credit union[326] could be more easily justified on grounds of business efficacy or social convenience. The credit union must be one within the meaning of the Credit Unions Act.[327]

Are the categories of "otherwise regulated" closed? One can think of numerous other industries and forms of business organization which are regulated to a sufficient degree that they might plausibly claim that the further imposition of obligations under the Act is unnecessary. An example which came before the Commission was the case of *Avoca Apartments*,[328] involving a condominium venture. An exemption was claimed both under s. 20, the Commission's "legislative" exemption and s. 59; in both instances it was refused. One may legitimately enquire why co-operative apartments are exempt and condominium apartments not. It may be because co-operatives have been in existence for some time and have become recognized by statute, while condominiums are quite recent. Furthermore, the legislative intent may have been that these two types of exemptions should be interpreted restrictively. Finally, one should not exclude the possibility that there are intrinsic differences between co-operative and condominium apartments.

(c) Adequate Knowledge on the Part of Purchasers
There is a series of securities grouped under this heading. The rationale for exempting them is that the nature of the assets covered by the security or the methods of sale are such that: (a) the purchaser will be expected to understand his investment from his present knowledge of the issuer's affairs, or (b) he is in a position to obtain satisfactory disclosure, or (c) his intimate or personal association with the venture or its promoter will give him adequate knowledge. To the extent that these assumptions are unwarranted the exemption can be justified on the grounds of the impracticability or the undue cost of any benefits to be gained from regulating the trades in question. The first three of these exemptions are subject to the caveat "if not offered to the public".[329]

---

[326]Sections 19(2)8 and 58(2)(a) (Bill 20, ss. 35(2)11 and 74(1)(a)).

[327]R.S.O. 1970, c. 96, this Act does not explicitly define the term. It simply provides that a credit union comes into being when an application by way of memorandum of association is approved by the Minister and a certificate of incorporation issued (ss. 2 and 3). The definition contained in the 1969 Select Committee Report on Credit Unions stressed certain salient features of these organizations, such as the fact that they deal exclusively in money in the form of credit, are restricted to a neighbourhood or to persons with some common bond of interest, and are open-ended in the sense that the money put in can be taken out. It is in the latter feature that they most strongly resemble co-operatives. This report and its sister Report on Co-operatives (*supra*, footnote 319) are valuable sources of information on the two types of organizations in question. It should be noted that it is only the shares, and not the other securities of a credit union, that are exempted.

For a different approach in Quebec see Policy 15 "Registration conditions and standards for the 'Caisses d'entraide economique'", CCH vol. 3, para. 66-026.

[328]July 1968 OSCB 154.

[329]On this difficult concept, see, *supra*, part 4.02(2).

The first exemption is for mortgages or other encumbrances upon real or personal property, apart from those contained in or secured by a bond, debenture or similar obligation or in a trust deed or other instrument to secure bonds or debentures or similar obligations.[330] The proviso that the securities shall not be made the subject of a public offering is waived where the offeror is registered under the Real Estate and Business Brokers Act.[331]

It can be a difficult question to determine whether the sale of an interest in real property involves an exempt mortgage transaction or the issuance of an investment contract which is subject to regulation by the Act.[332]

The second exemption is for securities evidencing indebtedness due under any conditional sales contract or other contract for the acquisition of personal property involving the retention of title.[333]

The third is for securities issued by a private company.[334] As indicated earlier, the term "private company" is defined in the Act. The most difficult issue in many instances where this exemption is used is whether a member of the public is a party to the trade.[335] With a maximum number of 50 shareholders (exclusive of employees) frequently the public is brought in.

Section 15 of the Execution Act[336] permits a sheriff who has seized the private company shares of an execution debtor to sell them to the public generally, provided that he has first determined that none of the existing shareholders of the company are prepared to buy them for a reasonable price. Such a sale would be in breach of the distribution requirement of the Act. The exemption from registration[337] for liquida-

---

[330]Section 58(2)(a) by reference to s. 19(2)4. The equivalent sections in Bill 20 are ss. 35(2)7 and 74(1)(a).

[331]R.S.O. 1970, c. 401, logically this exemption for mortgages offered to the public should also be available in the case of registration under the Mortgage Brokers Act, R.S.O. 1970, c. 278. The OSC has indicated that it was a legislative oversight which accounts for this omission in *WOCCO Investments Ltd.*, Feb. 1973 OSCB 15 at p. 20 and May 1974 OSCB 87. The latter decision was confirmed by the Ontario Divisional Court and the oversight recognized: see *Re Western Ontario Credit Corp. Ltd. and Ontario Securities Commission* (1975), 9 O.R. (2d) 93, 59 D.L.R. (3d) 501 (Div. Ct.). Bill 20 corrects this deficiency, and in fact omits reference to the Real Estate and Business Brokers Act, since registration under the Mortgage Brokers Act is deemed to be registration under the former Act. Section 35(2)7 of Bill 20 reads "registered or exempted from registration under the *Mortgage Brokers Act*", the theory being that anyone who is exempt from that Act is entitled to any privileges granted under it. This exemption within the exemption might appropriately be classed under the "otherwise regulated" heading as well. Absent registration under one of these two Acts, persons are permitted to purchase, sell or trade in mortgages without registration or disclosure requirements so long as they are not offered to the public.

[332]See *e.g., ante*, chapter 1, footnote 79.

[333]Section 19(2)5 (Bill 20, s. 35(2)8). See the new Personal Property Security Act, R.S.O. 1970, c. 344, for various categories.

[334]Section 19(2)9 (Bill 20, s. 35(2)12).

[335]See the discussion of the concept "public", *supra*, part 4.02(2).

[336]R.S.O. 1970, c. 152.

[337]Section 19(1)4.

tion of *bona fide* debts would probably exempt this trade from the registration requirements, but that exemption is not repeated as a double exemption in s. 58.[338] A court would probably resolve this conflict in favour of allowing the sale to take place unhindered on the ground that the specific permission contained in the one act ousts the general prohibition of the other.

The final exemption in this group has an enormous effect in the securities market, a fact not conveyed by the simple way it is stated in the Act. It applies to "negotiable promissory notes or commercial paper maturing not more than one year from the date of issue".[339] There is a limiting proviso which makes the exemption inapplicable when the security traded to an individual has a denomination or principal amount of less than $50,000. Because of this the stipulation that the offering be non-public is omitted in this exemption. When the purchaser is a corporation or other "person", a trade in short-term paper is exempt whatever the principal amount.

A promissory note in simplest terms is an unsecured promise to pay a certain principal amount. In practice it usually contains a covenant for interest payment and a specified term. In the exemption the note must be negotiable, *i.e.*, it must be capable of being assigned from its first holder to a subsequent holder. It is not clear why. Nor is it clear from the wording of the section whether the commercial paper must be negotiable as well. Inasmuch as the term seems to have only the vaguest of definitions anyway, an attempt to delimit it in such a restrictive fashion would seem to be contrary to the spirit of the exemption.[340]

It is only the "paper" of large commercial corporations that is "commercial paper". It has also been called "corporate paper", to distinguish it from government securities, bankers' acceptances and the notes of sales finance companies.[341]

(d) Business or Social Efficacy Factors

Several exemptions are largely based on reasons of business or social utility and to some extent the impracticability of regulation. The first of these takes its justification from the non-profit character of the enterprise.[342] It covers

"securities issued by a person or company organized exclusively for educational, benevolent, fraternal, charitable, religious or recreational purposes and not for profit, where no part of the net earnings of such person or company enure to the benefit of any security holder".

The requirements are onerous. Not only must the issuer refrain from paying dividends or interest, but on winding-up or dissolution of the

---

[338]Section 73(1)(e) of Bill 20 exempts the giving of security, as opposed to its liquidation, from the distribution requirements.

[339]Section 19(2)3.

[340]For some remarks on this type of short-term security, see C.C. Potter, *Finance and Business Administration in Canada*, 2nd ed. (Toronto, Prentice-Hall, 1970), p. 283.

[341]*Ibid.*, p. 113.

[342]Sections 58(2)(a) and 19(2)6 (Bill 20, ss. 74(1)(a) and 35(2)9).

non-profit organization holders are not to receive back anything in excess of their initial investment.

Bill 20 introduces a new but related exemption originating in the Canadian Mutual Funds Report. It exempts securities issued by an "investment club."[343] The meaning of this term is made tolerably clear by the three conditions which circumscribe the exemption's use:

"1. [the club's] shares or units are held by not more than fifty persons,

"2. it does not pay or give any remuneration under a management contract or in respect of a trade in securities except normal brokerage fees, and

"3. all of its members are required to make contributions in proportion to the shares or units each holds for the purpose of investment."

The restriction on numbers reflects the figure commonly used in the definition of a private company. An earlier exemption in Bill 20[344] exempts such an investment club from the requirement of registration as a mutual fund.

The exemption has the effect of removing the distribution requirements from the issue of units or shares in a club to members and the trading of those units or shares among members and removing the requirement that the trading members be registered. Under the Act an investment club is free from the distribution requirements only if its members are not the public, thus removing them from the reach of s. 35. It would seem that even such non-public trades are caught by the registration requirements, since s. 19 is not limited by the "public" concept.[345]

A related group of four exemptions reflects the special concern which some provincial Legislatures have shown for keeping grass roots mining exploration less encumbered by regulation that other business enterprises. These exemptions apply to securities issued and sold by a prospector for the purpose of financing a prospecting expedition (the "grubstake")[346] and those issued by a prospecting syndicate which has met the required conditions for qualifying an agreement under Part VI of the Act.[347] The final exemption in this group relates to securities issued by a mining company or a mining exploration company as consideration for mining claims where the vendor enters into such escrow or pooling agreement as the director considers necessary.[348] The

---

[343]Sections 74(1)(a) and 35(2)5.

[344]Section 34(a).

[345]For a decision determining that an investment club had grown into a public distributor see *Hawkesbury Curling and Golf Club*, July 1968 OSCB 161.

[346]Sections 58(2)(a) and 19(2)10 (Bill 20, ss. 74(1)(a) and 35(2)13).

[347]Sections 58(2)(a) and 19(2), paras. 11 and 12 (Bill 20, ss. 74(1)(a) and 35(2), paras. 14 and 15). See the discussion of prospecting syndicates, *supra*, part 4.12(1).

[348]Sections 58(2)(a) and 19(2)12a (Bill 20, s. 35(2)16). Section 74(1)(a) of Bill 20 specifically does *not* grant an exemption from the distribution requirements in this case. The situation with respect to the Ontario s. 19(2), paras. 11, 12 and 12a exemptions (made double by s. 58(2)(a)) in other provinces is

"other regulation" on which this exemption depends is the escrow or pooling requirements imposed by the director.

(e) Trades in Securities as Exempted by the Regulations

There is a final exemption as provided for by regulation.[349] One has been promulgated to date in Ontario. It is of special significance because it foreshadows the use of the reporting issuer concept for liberal exemptions in Bill 20.

"Reporting issuer" is defined to mean an issuer which is either required or voluntarily agrees to comply with the regular financial disclosure requirements.[350] The Regulation exempts both from registration and distribution requirements trades in the underlying securities of a reporting issuer which are issued on the exercise of a right or conversion privilege previously granted in a public distribution. Perhaps more important than the exemption itself is what it implies for non-reporting issuers. Their issue of underlying securities pursuant to the exercise of a right or conversion privilege will be subject to the registration and distribution requirements. This means that a non-reporting issuer effecting a distribution of a unit which has warrants or convertible securities with the warrant or conversion privilege to be exercised more than one year after the prospectus is qualified will have to continually renew the prospectus each year until the warrants or conversion privileges are used up or time-barred.

(5) STOCK EXCHANGE

(a) Stock Exchange Treasury Issue—Statement of Material Facts

The first exempt category under the stock exchange heading is a treasury issue through the stock exchange accompanied by a statement of material facts acceptable both to the Exchange[351] and to the Commission. This statement contains information substantially similar to that found in a prospectus and it is treated in the same way for

---

as follows: All of the Western Provinces have provisions similar to paras. 11 and 12: British Columbia, s. 21(2)(o),(p); Manitoba, s. 19(2), cls. 11, 12; Saskatchewan, s. 20(2)(k) and Alberta, s. 19(2)11, 12. The following are significant differences: British Columbia, s. 21(2)(o) there is no requirement of delivery of a copy by the prospector. Manitoba, s. 19(2), cl. 12 adds the words "and if the copy of the prospecting agreement is delivered to the person or company…before payment…". None of the Western Provinces have a provision like Ontario s. 19(2), para. 12a; however, Alberta added s. 19(2)12.1 "securities of a commercial syndicate within the meaning of Part 6, issued by a commercial syndicate where a commercial syndicate agreement…".

Nova Scotia, s. 19 begins "Sections 12 to 17…shall not apply to the following classes of trades or securities:" cl. (g) reads "a trade in good faith by an actual prospector of a security issued by him for the purpose of financing a prospecting expedition." Newfoundland, s. 5(h) is similar to the Nova Scotia provision. The New Brunswick Act, s. 7(i) and the Prince Edward Island Act, s. 2(3)(g) are similar to the New Brunswick provision except s. 7(i) adds the words " or for the purpose of disposing of any of his interest under a mining licence or lease wholly or partly owned by him", and Prince Edward Island, s. 2(3)(g) adds the words "any of his interests in a mining claim or property staked by or wholly or partly owned by him." Quebec has no similar provisions.

[349]Sections 19(2)13 and 58(2)(d).

[350]Reg. 794, s. 85.

[351]The only recognized exchanges are the TSE and the Alberta Stock Exchange. See, *post*, part 10.03(4).

purposes of civil liability.[352]

(b) Stock Exchange—Control Person Isolated Trade

The second of these exemptions permits isolated trades by control persons through the exchange.[353] The limiting language which it contains, "isolated trades not made in the course of continued and successive transactions of a like nature" is taken directly from the isolated trade exemption from registration,[354] but there are several significant differences between the two provisions. The word "trades" (as opposed to "trade" in the analogous exemption) permits the inference that at least two transactions are contemplated. Secondly, the exemption from registration may be enjoyed by any owner of securities, whereas the distribution exemption is only available to the owner who also happens to be a control person. The exemption is designed to give such persons a limited form of relief: they may sell off either a small part of their holdings or a large block, provided the trades are infrequent and not part of a pattern. It does not permit trading by a control person which bears the marks of a normal public distribution.

(6) SECURITIES EXEMPTED BY THE REGULATIONS

There is a final exemption for securities which have been exempted from the distribution requirements by the Regulation.[355] One has been promulgated to date.[356] It exempts certain options to sell or purchase securities (puts and calls). The option permits the holder to sell to or purchase from the option writer a specified amount of securities at a specified time provided that three conditions are satisfied:

(a) the option is written, issued or guaranteed by a member of a recognized stock exchange,

(b) the underlying securities are listed and posted for trading on a recognized exchange, and

(c) the option contracts conform to specified forms.[357]

4.13 Resale by Exempted Purchasers

Resale by purchasers of securities where the securities themselves have been exempted from the distribution requirements presents no prob-

---

[352]Section 58(2)(b) and Reg. 794, ss. 51 to 63. Ontario Policy 3.05, " Requirements with Respect to Financial Disclosure in Statement of Material Facts", CCH vol. 2, para. 54-899; Alberta Policies 3-04, "Filing a Statement of Material Facts", and 3-05, "Requirements with respect to Financial Disclosure in Statement of Material Facts", 3-13,"Recognition of Calgary Stock Exchange", CCH vol. 1, paras. 24-504, 24-505, 24-513; Quebec Policy 1, "Permission to distribute filing statements submitted to the Montreal Stock Exchange in lieu of prospectuses", CCH vol. 3, para. 66-012.

[353]Section 58(2)(c). See, *supra*, part 4.02(1) for a discussion of the definition of control person.

[354]Section 19(1)2. See, *ante*, part 3.18(2) for discussion of this concept.

[355]Section 58(2)(d).

[356]Reg. 794, s. 86.

[357]Forms 30 and 31. This Regulation results from the decision of the OSC to permit TSE members to trade in options of the Chicago Board Options Exchange. For TSE and MSE rules, see CCH vol. 3, paras. 89-496, 87-575 and following.

lems of consequence. These securities are exempt with respect to all subsequent trades, subject to any express caveats in the particular exemption such as a prohibition on offers to the public. However, where the securities have been purchased through an exempt trade, it is only *that* trade which is free, and subsequent sales may pose some difficult problems. Such exempt trades are of two kinds.

First, if the exempted purchaser in the initial sale has not received the securities as a member of the public, when he attempts to resell them (assuming the absence of another distribution exemption) he will be trading in securities not previously distributed to the public; the second sale, if to a member of the public, will be a distribution to the public subject to the prospectus requirements. From a practical standpoint it is often very difficult to determine whether the exempted purchaser was a member of the public on the initial sale. It may well depend on the entire circumstances of the issue and not just the relationship of the particular purchaser to the issuer.

Secondly, if one is certain that it was necessary to use an exemption for the first trade because that first trade was to a member of the public, then resale may occur free of the distribution requirements. The basic prohibition of s. 35 was exhausted in the first trade. There are several catches to this reasoning, however: first, there are several exemptions which contain express caveats such as those which preclude an offer to the public or impose an investment intent. Secondly, the exemption for promoters involves a trade which on its face is to a non-public person. Thus it is not necessary to have an exemption to issue securities to a promoter free of the distribution requirements, but he will hold securities which have not been previously distributed to the public. Thirdly, there may be other restrictions such as control person status.

While this may be an accurate statement of the law, it is by no means satisfactory in policy. It means that substantial amounts of securities will find their way into public hands on resales from exempted trades without prospectus disclosure, and frequently without continuous disclosure by the issuer. This unfortunate state of affairs results from the confusion over the concept of public in s. 35. What was probably intended, but not articulated in the provision, was that the prohibition would not apply on the first exempted trade but would apply on the first subsequent resale where the purchaser was a member of the public. Bill 20 seeks to rectify this serious anomaly.

To these important reforms we now turn.

4.14 Reform Proposals—Resale by Exempted Purchasers
A major objective of Bill 20 is to remove the complexity of the exemptions and reduce the restrictions on resale, thereby improving market liquidity. It attempts to achieve this objective by several important mechanical changes in the distribution process. First it deletes the reference to public in the distribution definition.[358] Whenever securities have been distributed to an exempted purchaser they have been "previously issued" and the effect of the first branch of the

---

[358]Section 1(1)12.

distribution definition is exhausted. Any restrictions on resale must be imposed as conditions of the initial exemption.

Section 73 of Bill 20 does precisely this. It states that the first trade in securities acquired pursuant to an exemption, other than a further exempt trade, is a distribution, unless certain stated conditions permitting resale are met.[359] These conditions are of three main types, tailored to reflect the kind of trade which was exempted at the time of the initial purchase. We shall examine each of them in turn. The common feature of the two most important is that the issuer of the securities must perform certain reporting obligations.

Section 73(4) deals with securities acquired pursuant to the institutional investor exemption, the assets purchaser (not less than $100,000) exemption, the exemption for escrowed shares issued as consideration for mining claims, the isolated issue and limited offering exemptions, and the exemption for trades by a registered dealer to another registered dealer buying as principal.[360] Resale is dependent on the issuer being a reporting issuer in good standing and the buyer having held the securities for a certain minimum period varying according to circumstances from six to eighteen months. Hence s. 73(4) may be called a statutory escrow provision. It also requires that no special selling efforts accompany the trade. The time does not begin to run until the issuer has become a reporting issuer.

Section 73(5) deals with securities purchased pursuant to the "issuer-internal" and "issuer-combination" exemptions and the first trade in previously issued securities of a company that has ceased to be a private company. Before resale can take place it requires that the issuer has been a reporting issuer for twelve months, that the exempt trade has been disclosed, and that no special selling effort accompany the subsequent trade. It does *not* impose a statutory escrow period.

Section 73(6) deals with securities purchased by an underwriter and simply states that the first trade by the underwriter is a distribution.

The rationale for the escrow and difference between s-ss.(4) and (5) of s.73 is that in s-s. (5) the securities being issued are for the most part those of stable well-established companies. Moreover the new issue will often be rather small in relation to the total issued capital. Furthermore the trades involved will frequently be of the sort where the recipient of the shares would not have entered the deal unless he expected to hold the shares for an extended period. As a result it was concluded that reliance on full disclosure would be sufficient. With the trades in s. 73(4), on the other hand, the securities will often be more speculative, and in some cases very large blocks of securities will be involved which could have a disruptive effect if suddenly dumped on the market. Accordingly, it was felt that the public should have the additional protection of the filing of a report by the vendor within ten days of the initial trade[361] and the intervention of a minimum hold period before resale. This hold period should permit thorough dissemination and digestion of information about the exempted trade.

---

[359]Section 73(4) to (6).
[360]Section 73(1)(a) to (d), (j), (k), (m), or (n).
[361]Section 73(3) except for s. 73(1)(k).

This scheme places considerable reliance on the continuous disclosure system. It assumes that the information provided by this system, together with any timely disclosures in the relevant period, will be absorbed and digested by research analysts, brokers and the financial news media, thus ensuring on an overall view adequate protection for resale purchasers.

The holding period before a s. 73(4) trade may be made runs from the later of the date of the exempted trade or the date the issuer became a reporting issuer. Three different periods of six, twelve and eighteen months apply depending on the investment quality of the securities concerned as determined by certain objective criteria.

(1) SIX-MONTH HOLD PERIOD

The six-month hold period applies to securities which meet the conditions of either cl. (a) and (b) together or cl. (c) alone:

(a) listed and posted on a stock exchange recognized by the Commission and

(b) comply with s. 383(1)(m) or (n) of the Insurance Act,[362] or

(c) debt obligations which comply with s. 383(1)(k) of the Insurance Act.

In all probability both the TSE and the Alberta Stock Exchange will be recognized stock exchanges for purposes of (a) above, since those two are now recognized for distributions by way of statement of material fact rather than by prospectus.[363] The conditions referred to in the Insurance Act are those which make these securities permissible for purchase by insurance companies without resort to their residual or basket clause investment powers.

(2) TWELVE-MONTH HOLD PERIOD

The twelve-month hold period applies to securities listed and posted on a recognized stock exchange or debt obligations issued or guaranteed by an issuer which has securities listed and posted on a recognized exchange.

(3) EIGHTEEN-MONTH HOLD PERIOD

The eighteen-month hold period applies to all other securities of a reporting issuer.

Obviously these provisions are designed to encourage the pursuit of reporting issuer status and the listing of securities on a recognized exchange. The eighteen-month hold period in the case of securities of a reporting issuer which has not obtained listing is intended to ensure that at least one set of annual audited financial statements is extant before resale. This requirement will force some issuers to become reporting issuers as a result of pressure from their exempted purchasers who wish to enjoy the freedom to dispose of their newly acquired property. If such purchasers wish to resell and the issuer is not a reporting issuer, they will have to find another exemption or apply for relief to the Commission.

Some questions of interpretation may arise in regard to the prohibition on a special selling effort by the issuer. The freedom to resell is premised on a theoretically perfect operation of continous disclosure—

---

[362]R.S.O. 1970, c. 224 as amended.
[363]See discussion, *supra*, part 4.12(5)(a).

234 *Distribution*

that a secondary purchaser will be induced to seek out and buy from the secondary vendor on the basis of the former's "complete and current" knowledge of the security and its price without his buying motivation arising from artificial factors such as "unusual efforts...made to groom the market or to create a demand for the securities".[364] Reliance on the underwriter definition to prosecute such a purchaser is beset with the difficult problem of proving intent. Special selling effort is given some clarification by the addition of the explanatory words "provided that...no extraordinary commission or consideration is paid in respect of such trade."[365]

It should be borne in mind that these secondary resale trades are not exempt from the registration requirements. Thus an exemption from registration will have to be used to effect the sale. The two most common will be sales through a broker[366] and isolated trades.[367]

It should also be noted that the resale provisions of Bill 20 represent a drastic modification of an earlier scheme contained in Bill 154. The latter Bill placed an even heavier emphasis on continuous disclosure, introducing the concept of a cornerstone prospectus, which would be subject to timely amendment. This idea, abandoned in Bill 20, permitted the draftsmen of Bill 154 to propose a much shorter "hold" period before resale—a mere 28 days—barely long enough for the details of any timely amendment to be absorbed and disseminated.[368]

As well as evincing an intention to promote efficiency and cost-effectiveness in distributions the system of exemptions in s. 73 is designed to increase liquidity in Canadian securities markets. The change regarding control persons is a part of this design. Lack of liquidity and thinness in the Canadian markets have often been cited as major shortcomings leading to locked-in investments and rapid and dramatic price movements when a block comes on the market. As a result institutional investors have been led to place their funds in significant volume in foreign securities markets.[369]

One of the potential dangers of the exempted distribution system is that it will leave the small investor in a decidedly second best position. The large institution will have first opportunity to purchase initial distributions with no opportunity for the small investor to participate. In many instances he will only be able to buy when the large institution decides the securities are no longer attractive to hold at the prevailing price. This is one of the more troublesome features of an increasing trend to institutionalization of the market place. Furthermore, even when the distribution employs an offering circular, the small investor is shut out from the initial opportunity to purchase through the

---

[364]Merger Report para. 4.11; see also paras. 4.12 and 4.13.
[365]Section 73(4).
[366]Section 35(1)10.
[367]Section 35(1)2.
[368]For a detailed discussion of the system proposed in Bill 154, see the Merger Report, which recommended it (chapter III); an important intellectual source was Milton Cohen, "Truth in Securities Revisited", 79 Harvard L.R. 1340, (1965-66).
[369]These problems are discussed in the Canadian Mutual Funds Report (paras. 12.62 and 12.63).

predistribution placing and can only buy in the after-market, in many cases at a premium.

4.15 Reform Proposals—Trades by Control Persons

Bill 20 will provide some welcome relief for control persons wishing to sell. The need to regulate control persons was historically based on four factors: possible inside information; a special interest in controlling the market price and possibly managing the issuer's news; a disorderly market resulting from precipitate sales of control; and the fact that the reduction of a control person's control position was significant investor information. The Merger Report concluded that insider-trading regulations mitigated the force of the first factor and an accelerated insider report could satisfy the concerns of the fourth. It concluded that a proper continuous disclosure system neutralized the force of the second factor and that restrictions on special selling efforts could alleviate the concerns of the third.[370] Section 73(7) legislates these conclusions as an exemption from the distribution requirements for sales by control persons either if another s. 73(1) exemption is available (in which case the next subsequent trade would be a distribution) or all of the following conditions are met:

(1) the issuer has been a reporting issuer for eighteen months and is not in default,

(2) the seller files with the Commission and any recognized exchange on which the securities are listed between seven and fourteen days prior to the trade

(a) a notice of intention to sell with particulars of the control position, number of securities to be sold and the distribution method and

(b) a current certificate that he has no knowledge of any unreported material change or material adverse information regarding the issuer,

(3) the seller files an accelerated insider report within three days of any trade,

(4) the notice in (2)(a) and certificate in (2)(b) are renewed at the end of 60 days and thereafter each 28 days so long as the securities concerned have not been sold or notice is filed that they are no longer for sale, and

(5) no special selling effort is made or extraordinary commission is paid.

Bill 20 also singles out for special treatment pledges of their securities by control persons and any subsequent liquidation by the pledgee. The pledge itself is defined as a trade[371] but it is exempted from registration and distribution requirements.[372] Any sale by the pledgee is exempt if the terms of s. 73(7), described above, are met. This will have the effect of precluding sales by pledgees based on inside knowledge and will serve to inform the market place of the pledgor's indebtedness and the resultant effect on control.

---

[370]See, *supra*, part 4.02(1).
[371]Section 1(1)40(iv).
[372]Sections 35(1)6 and 73(1)(e).

4.16 Discretionary Exemptions

There are two discretionary exemptions in the statute, articulated in ss. 20 and 59. They are alike in several basic aspects, but the differences between them are far more numerous. Both empower the Commission to exempt an applicant from the registration and distribution requirements and in both cases the test for permitting an exemption is that to do so would, in the Commission's opinion, not be prejudicial to the public interest. As well, both sections permit the Commission to make the order subject to such terms and conditions as it deems fit.[373]

At this point, however, the similarities end. Notice of a s. 20 order together with a summary of facts must be published as soon as practicable, and the order laid before the Legislative Assembly if it is in session.[374] The rationale for this requirement is that the protections which the Legislature has built into the legislation have been waived, and therefore the creator of those protections should be alerted. The same tabling requirement does not operate in the case of s. 59 orders even though the requirements of the Act may have been dispensed

---

[373]The Western Provinces all have provisions similar to s. 20 of the Ontario Act (Alberta, s. 20; British Columbia, s. 22; Manitoba, s. 20; Saskatchewan, s. 21), with the following differences: Alberta and Manitoba require publication in the Provincial Gazette, but not laying the order before the Assembly; the British Columbia provision reads "may be published" rather than "shall be published" and Saskatchewan has no provision requiring publication.

Manitoba and Alberta have sections similar to s. 59 of the Ontario Act (Manitoba, s. 59(1.1); Alberta, s. 59). British Columbia has no section like s. 59 but uses its s. 22 for the same purpose. Section 66(1A) of the Saskatchewan Act as added by 1970 (Sask.), c. 65, s. 5(a), is substantially different. It reads:

"(1A) Where...the Commission:
    (a)   is satisfied that the number of securities is not substantial in amount in relation to the holdings of the offeror or proposed offeror, or that the proposed purchaser is acquiring the security or securities for investment purposes with reasonable knowledge of the affairs of the issuer; and
    (b)   is of the opinion that it would not be prejudicial to the public interest;
the Commission may rule that...the trade...shall be deemed not to be a primary distribution to the public...".

The Quebec provisions are much different s. 20 "Exemption from registration":
"The commission may...at its discretion, grant an exemption from registration in the case of an issue of securities sold *en bloc* to one or more registered brokers, provided that the permission contemplated by section 50 has been given...".
"Exemption for certain companies":
"The commission may...grant to a company...an exemption...for the issuance, distribution and sale of any of its capital to its officers, directors and employees...".
Section 50 gives to the Commission power to grant exemption from registration for sale of securities "where it deems it expedient to do so". None of the Maritime Provinces has any provisions similar to Ontario s. 20 or s. 59.

[374]Section 20(2).

with to just as great an extent. Another difference is that a s. 20 order is subject to appeal but a s. 59 order is final and, apart from any effect on the Commission's decisions resulting from the implementation of the Statutory Powers Procedures Act, 1971,[375] is not subject to appeal.[376] The reason for such an order being final is to ensure speed and informality in its processing and determination; another consideration is the fact that the Commission relies in these cases on its knowledge of and feeling for the investment community and the current state of the market rather than on any clear principles of law such as would permit the application of *stare decisis*. Both of these reasons perhaps account for the fact that s. 20 is rarely used, whereas the exact opposite obtains in respect to s. 59.[377]

Section 20 is the broader of the two so far as the basis for an application is concerned. It applies to any trade, security, person or company named in the order. Section 59 on the other hand relates only to a trade or an intended trade. The Commission interprets this language to require there to be a specific trade in contemplation. Therefore it will not make the exemption available if the party applying has no specific intent to trade but merely wishes to dispose of securities in the future contingent upon a particular event taking place such as the crystallizing of a market opportunity. In the case of sales by control persons the Commission will normally attach to a favourable order a condition that the trade contemplated be executed within three months of the granting of the order with the opportunity to renew the exemption for one additional three-month period.[378] In the event of failure to sell within the time period the order is null and void. This time limitation results from the fact that there is adequate current information available and the applicant has no inside information.

The s. 20 exemption is also clearer and more straightforward. It permits the Commission to grant relief from the s. 6 registration requirement or the s. 35 prospectus requirement or both; this relief may extend to one transaction only or to all trades in a particular

---

[375] 1971, Vol. 2, c. 47

[376] Bill 20, s. 75(3) proposes in spite of the SPPA that its orders should not be subject to appeal.

[377] In the *Avoca* case, July 1968 OSCB 154, at pp. 159-60, the Commission stated "as to the [s. 20] power...[we] have only exercised it once since...1967, and then in what was the clearest possible case of legislative oversight. In the absence of like extraordinary circumstances...we do not propose to exercise it." For an idea of the frequency of s. 59 applications see the statistical summary in the Merger Report (pp. 181-6) and the Annual Reports of the Department. To date there have only been several s. 20 orders. See *Finance Corp.*, Apr. 1967 OSCB 12, and *Canada Development Corp.*, Apr. 1974 OSCB 71.

[378] See OSC Policy 3.18A "Section 59 Orders: Applications for Extensions of Time", CCH vol. 3, para. 54-912(a). See also, British Columbia Policies 3-04 "Application under s. 56(1) Primary Distribution", 3-04A, "Distribution of Securities", 3-06, "Retirement of Company Debt by Issue of Treasury Shares", and 3-24, "Application under s. 56(1)—Shareholder Approval", CCH vol. 2, paras. 29-954, 29-954a, 29-956, 29-978; Alberta Policy 3-14, "S. 59 Applications", CCH vol. 1, para. 24-514.

sequence, or a particular security, or to trading by a specific person or company. Section 59 on the other hand is far more difficult. It empowers the Commission to deem a particular trade not to be a distribution to the public and in addition, rule that registration is not required. The latter indulgence is not normally required for listed stocks; they will be traded through a registered representative using a different exemption. The flaw lies in the fact that a favourable ruling by the Commission, taking the language of the statute literally, results in the securities not having been previously distributed to the public. The effect of branch one of the distribtuion definition will not have been exhausted, and a subsequent trade in the securities, if to a member of the public, will attract the prospectus requirements of s. 35. In fact, the practice of the Commission and of securities lawyers is to interpret a favourable order to mean that the intended trade is deemed not to be a distribution to the public for the purposes of the s. 35 prospectus requirements only, and for all other purposes to be a distribution to the public. Thus when the securities are resold in a subsequent transaction the only restraints are those imposed in the order itself.

Section 59 relief is also available when doubt exists as to whether a distribution to the public has been concluded or is still in progress.[379] A favourable ruling will assure any party to the trade that if the facts in the application are correctly stated no prosecution for a violation of the Act will be launched. It is a moot question however whether a disposition by the Commission under one of these discretionary exemptions has any effect on the private civil liability remedies contained in the Act or on the common law remedies that might otherwise be available to the parties.

The Ontario Commission has set out the procedure that is to be followed in s. 59 applications in one policy statement[380] and the substantive considerations which it employs in two other policies.[381]

Bill 20 has one discretionary exemption provision.[382] An order made under this section is final and there is no appeal therefrom. It provides that the Commission may, upon the application of an interested person or company, rule that an intended trade is not subject to the registration or distribution requirements where it is satisfied that to so rule would not be prejudicial to the public interest. The Commission may in addition impose such terms and conditions as it deems are necessary. This provision is clearly similar to s. 59 in the Act in that it exempts a trade rather than a security or a person or a company. The position on resale would seem to be that each transaction must be looked at individually to see if an exemption is necessary. If so, and no

---

[379]Section 59(3).
[380]Policy 3-19 "Applications to the Commission Re Rulings—Procedure", CCH vol. 2, para. 54-913.
[381]Policies 3-18 and 3-18A "Section 59 Applications", CCH vol. 2, para. 54-912; "Section 59 Orders: Applications for Extensions of Time", CCH vol. 2, para. 54-912a respectively. See also Ontario Policy 3 "'Non-Reporting' Companies: Applications for Exemption—under S. 19(1)8(iii) or S. 59", CCH vol. 2, para. 54-916. For other jurisdictions see, *supra*, footnote 378.
[382]Section 75(1).

specific statutory exemption is available, another application under this discretionary section will be necessary, unless (as is probable) the question of resale has been dealt with in terms and conditions accompanying the first exempting order.

Chapter 5
Continuous Disclosure

5.01 Introduction
Continuous disclosure is that disclosure required of an issuer after distribution has ceased. It provides the information upon which investment decisions will be made: in the case of present security holders whether or not to sell the securities or make additional purchases; in the case of potential new investors whether or not to buy the securities. Continuous disclosure also assists in determining the price of the issuer's presently outstanding securities and the price at which a new distribution of securities might be made. Finally, it is viewed positively as an accountability technique to encourage more efficient management and negatively as a deterrent to fraud.

Continuous disclosure falls into two categories. The first is regular disclosure, which must be made at predictable fixed intervals. It includes the annual financial statements which are filed once each year within a specified time from the end of the issuer's fiscal year end, the interim financial report which must be published within a specified number of days from the ending of the first six months of the fiscal year, and the proxy information circular which must accompany the solicitation of proxies within prescribed times prior to the issuer's annual general meeting of shareholders which must itself be held within a specified number of months from the issuer's commencement of operations or the last annual general meeting.

The second category of continuous disclosure is irregular and somewhat unpredictable, because it is triggered by a material event or change in the issuer's affairs. Such a change, while it may have been the subject of careful and exhaustive planning and is thus under the issuer's control, does not occur on a cycle and never recurs in exactly the same form. Equally it may happen at a time and in a manner which is totally beyond the issuer's control. Examples of controlled change are the incorporation of a new manufacturing subsidiary, the declaration of a dividend increase, or some types of take-over bids. Examples of uncontrolled change are an explosion destroying an issuer's plant or some types of labour disputes and lawsuits.

Considered from the standpoint of Canadian legislative development, continuous disclosure is the "Cinderella" of securities regulation techniques. Long confined to an obscure role it has recently not only received recognition but been embraced with enthusiasm and elevated to a position of paramount importance among devices for the protection of the investor. This shift of emphasis is presently being reflected in legislative reform, but the change had been foreshadowed in the more informed policy requirements of government and self-regulatory agencies.[1]

---

[1]See, for example remarks by R. W. Haack, President, New York Stock Exchange, at a panel session "Some Viewpoints in Corporate Disclosure" Financial Executive Institute, October 26, 1968, where he said:

Various reasons account for the one-time neglect of continuing disclosure as well as for its present prominence. The Kimber Committee has pointed out that one reason for the heavy emphasis up until now on disclosure attending distribution is that when disclosure was first introduced, the needs of short-term creditors were of highest importance; only in recent years have the information needs of long-term creditors and "permanent" equity owners become recognized. Furthermore, the post World War II era has seen a startling increase in both the breadth and depth of equity investments in North America. The increased participation in the market of persons who lack private methods of obtaining information underlined the need for enforcing public disclosure not just at the time of an initial purchase but continuously thereafter. Another reason for the emphasis on continuous disclosure is the responsibility now assumed by government to regulate the economy by intervening with measures designed to temper cyclical fluctuations. To perform such a function effectively, current published information is necessary. Perhaps the most compelling reason for greater continuous disclosure, however, has been the growing sophistication of investment research analysts and the financial press; the continuous barrage of announcements, releases, bulletins and other analyzes which issues from these two quarters is dependent on the availability of reliable information.

5.02 Evolution of Continuous Disclosure

Even as early as the U.K. Companies Act of 1844[2] which required initial disclosure in the prospectus, an annual report had to be placed on public file with the Registrar in the ensuing years.[3] A similar requirement for annual information was, generally speaking, a part of corporations legislation in Canada. However, there was little attempt to analyze the information provided and to check for accuracy.

The 1933 U.S. Securities Act focused on initial distribution and disclosure through the prospectus. It was the 1934 U.S. Securities Exchange Act which formed the basis for a modern continuous disclosure system with its requirements of annual and interim reports as well as proxies and their accompanying information circulars; even so, it was not until 1964 that the 1934 Act was extended to securities trading off the exchanges "over the counter". About 1964, serious concern for continuous disclosure manifested itself in Canada. While the prospectus reforms of the 1933 U.S. Act and those of the 1929 English Companies Act on which they were based had influenced initial distribution requirements in Canada to some extent, the models

---

"The concept of corporate disclosure grew out of industrialization in the last century. One of the classic stories concerns the request the Exchange made in 1866 to the Delaware, Lackawanna & Western Railroad for facts and figures regarding its capitalization. The president of the railroad responded that his firm 'made no reports, and publishes no statements and has not done anything of the kind for the last five years'. But the Exchange did not permit such tight-lipped attitudes to continue for long."

[2]1844 (U.K.), chapters 110 and 111.

[3]*Ibid.*, c. 110, ss. 4 and 43.

for change in the area of secondary trading provided by the 1934 Act were largely ignored until the Kimber Report was published in 1965.

Continuous disclosure was the single most important reform technique recommended in the Kimber Report, which was of the opinion that public confidence in the securities industry would increase measurably with enhanced disclosure. This is the central theme which underlies the Report's substantive recommendations for insider-trading reporting and liability, take-over bid regulation, annual and interim financial statements, and proxy regulation.[4] The 1966 Act adopted these varied but commonly linked recommendations almost without change. They were also made part of Ontario corporations legislation so that they would also apply to Ontario incorporated companies. By 1968, British Columbia, Alberta, and Manitoba had made roughly similar changes to their companies and securities legislation. In Saskatchewan the alterations extended only to securities legislation. Two years later the CCA was amended in substantially the same way. And two years after that, roughly similar changes were made to Quebec securities legislation. Finally, in 1975 the CBCA preserved and carried slightly further the continuous disclosure philosophy.

The 1966 Act came into effect in May, 1967. Three subsequent developments in Ontario sought to supply those elements of complete continuous disclosure which were still wanting. First the TSE began by stages to require quarterly financial reports, with the result that most of its listed companies are now covered. The Exchange also amended its 1965 timely disclosure policy, and issued a new timely disclosure policy in parallel with the OSC in October, 1968. The TSE's policy applied to listed companies only. That of the OSC covered unlisted companies as well. Thirdly, the Merger Report in February, 1970 recommended a new continuous disclosure system which was articulated in Bill 154 and reproduced with important modifications in Bills 75, 98 and 20. The principal features proposed in the system were the enactment in legislation rather than policy statement of timely disclosure provisions, the requirement of quarterly reports and the application of the scheme to debt securities and non-voting shares and units as well as voting shares. Bill 154 also proposed the introduction of a cornerstone statement with annual updating and timely amendment with a view to integrating initial and continuous disclosure; it was intended that the continuous disclosure standard to be reached should be that of a prospectus.[5]

Bill 20 retreats from the objectives of Bill 154 so far as the cornerstone prospectus is concerned, on the basis that the burden involved in preparing and keeping up to date such a document would be excessive in the case of many smaller Canadian companies. The new Bill does incorporate the provisions for more frequent financial reporting and for timely disclosure. It also reflects in its provisions the recommendations of the Canadian Mutual Funds Report, many of

---

[4]Paras. 1.16 and 1.17.
[5]See chapter 2 of the Merger Report and Part XIII of Bill 154, "The Securities Act, 1972" (2nd Sess.), 29th Legislature, Ontario.

which will have a material impact on continuous disclosure standards in relation to mutual funds and investment contracts.

In the sections that follow, the three major segments of the present continuous disclosure system are discussed in turn, beginning with the requirement of annual and semi-annual financial reporting, continuing with the subject of proxy regulation, and ending with timely disclosure. Insider trading and take-over bid regulation are considered in subsequent separate chapters.

A. Regular Financial Disclosure

5.03 Application of Regular Financial Disclosure

Continuous regular financial disclosure is required from issuers in Part XII of the Act.[6] Audited financial statements must be filed with the Commission yearly[7] and unaudited statements semi-annually.[8] All information filed under this part is placed on public file at the Commission.[9] These requirements apply to issuers whose shares are posted for trading on the TSE or which have qualified a prospectus in Ontario since May, 1967 for equity shares and continue to have owners whose last address is in Ontario.[10] Chartered banks and loan, trust, and insurance companies are expressly exempted through deference to federal jurisdiction for constitutional reasons in the case of banks and, in general, because they are already uniquely regulated in regard to financial statements.[11] Companies incorporated in Ontario are also expressly exempted,[12] because their incorporating legislation applies similar requirements, but they are required to file that information with the Commission as soon as it is mailed to shareholders or when required to be mailed to shareholders, if that date is earlier.[13]

The application of Part XVII in Bill 20 differs in several important respects from that of Part XII of the Act. The concept of "reporting issuer" which Bill 20 introduces is nowhere more important than in the area of continuous disclosure. It defines the class of persons and companies who are to be subject to the reporting requirements.[14]

---

[6]Part XVII in Bill 20.

[7]Section 120 (Bill 20, s. 79).

[8]Section 130 (Bill 20, s. 78, requires these every three months).

[9]Section 135 (Bill 20, s. 139).

[10]Section 118(1)(b)(i) and (ii), (2) and s. 132(2). The plural expression "owners" is used in s. 132(2), the subsection which governs the cessation of jurisdiction, raising the presumption that there must be at least two shareholders for jurisdiction to attach.

[11]Section 118(1)(b)(iv) and (v).

[12]Section 118(1)(b)(iii).

[13]Section 134.

[14]Section 1(1)36. British Columbia led the way in August, 1973 with a "reporting company" concept in its securities (s. 2(1) and companies (s.1(1)) legislation, borrowing it from the Merger Report (para. 2.26). The British Columbia concept, however, has a longer historical reach than Bill 20's reporting issuer and, in addition, the British Columbia Superintendent of Brokers is given a discretion to apply or remove the status from a company.

Relief from the consequences of reporting issuer status is available to issuers who have less than fifteen security holders in Ontario if the Commission is satisfied the public interest would not be prejudiced. This provision is modelled on a sister provision in the BCA[15] which permits a public offering company to revert to non-public offering status.

The new Bill removes the exemption for Ontario incorporated companies and for banks, trust companies and insurance companies.[16] Moreover, "reporting issuer" includes those who have filed a take-over bid circular under the Act or its predecessor.[17] There is a further slight broadening of the impact of financial disclosure to cover issuers with any outstanding voting securities (as opposed to companies with outstanding equity shares) which have been qualified by an Ontario prospectus.[18] However, May 1, 1967 is retained as the cut-off date after which the securities must have been issued if Part XVII is to apply.

The desire to place all matters of investor protection in securities legislation is evident in the move to bring Ontario companies, banks, trust companies and insurance companies directly under the reach of the reporting requirements of the Bill.[19] In addition this change reflects the belief that the growth and diversity of operations of such issuers within the framework of an increasingly complex Canadian financial structure has made inadequate, at least so far as the provision of financial information is concerned, the protection afforded by the other forms of regulation which apply to such institutions. The constitutional validity of this change so far as the banks are concerned remains to be seen.

5.04 Content of Financial Statements

The annual financial statement must be filed with the Commission within 170 days from the end of the issuer's last completed financial year.[20] It must include a profit and loss statement, statement of surplus, a balance sheet and a source and application of funds statement. A statement of changes in net assets replaces the last-mentioned statement in the case of mutual funds. Where the corporation has completed more than one financial year the financial state-

---

[15]Section 1(9).

[16]Section 1(1)36. Bill 21, ss. 4 and 5, "An Act to amend The Business Corporations Act" (4th Sess.), 30th Legislature Ontario deletes from the BCA the provisions respecting annual and interim financial statements and insider trading and reporting since the parallel provisions in Bill 20 will now govern Ontario incorporated companies.

[17]*Ibid.*

[18]Thus unincorporated issuers such as trust based mutual funds and real estate investment trusts will be included. The Merger Report (para. 2.36) challenges this distinction between voting and non-voting securities, suggesting reporting issuer status should follow on the public issue of either. It is apparent from the context in which this questioning takes place that the authors of the Report had in mind the collapses of Atlantic Acceptance and Prudential Finance, the vast majority of where securities outstanding in public hands were debt securities.

[19]Merger Report, paras. 2.15 and 2.16.

[20]Section 120(1) (Bill 20, s. 79(1) shortens this period to 140 days).

ments are to be comparative and thus cover separately the latest completed financial year and the period covered by the immediately prior financial year.[21] Unlike the Act,[22] Bill 20 leaves the detailed requirements of the annual and the interim financial statements to the regulations.[23]

The semi-annual statement must also include the comparative statement from the previous year's corresponding six months; it is to be filed within 60 days of the date to which it is made up.[24] It is to contain a source and application of funds statements and summary financial results of operations including sales, extraordinary items of income or expense, net income before taxes, taxes and net profit or loss.[25] Here also mutual funds and investment companies must file a statement of changes in net assets instead of a source and application of funds statement.[26]

5.05 Audited Statements

An important distinction between the annual and interim financial statements is that only the former must be audited.[27] Nowhere, perhaps, is the dependence of the legislative framework on self-regulation and its attendant professionalism more manifest than in the audit requirements. The Act states that an auditor's report shall accompany the annual financial statements and that he shall make such examination as will enable him to make the report.[28] But as to the professional qualifications necessary to become an auditor, the techniques used to perform the audit, and the accounting principles employed in the preparation of the financial statement, both the legislator and the investor rely to a very large extent on the internal procedures and standards of the appropriate professional associations of accountants. The difficulty involved in maintaining an appropriate balance between such reliance on *quasi*-private bodies on the one hand and intervention by government regulatory bodies like the Commission on the other, is, as noted in chapter 10,[29] one of the continuing unresolved tensions in securities law. In the U.S. the SEC has been noticeably less hesitant to involve itself in this area than the Canadian commissions.

---

[21]Section 120(1).
[22]Sections 121 to 128.
[23]Sections 78(1) and 79(1). Note that this approach of relegating to the regulations important substantive requirements of regular financial statements has already begun. See Reg. 794, ss. 77 to 84 for provisions on reporting earnings per share and acquisitions, implementing recommendations of the Merger Report, chapter 9.
[24]Section 130(1).
[25]Section 130(1). Bill 20, s. 78, as in the case of the annual statement, banishes the detailed statement of the requirements to the Regulations.
[26]Section 120(5). Bill 20, s. 78(2) refers simply to an interim statement of the mutual fund, leaving the peculiar characteristics of that statement to be set out in the Regulations.
[27]Section 119(2) (Bill 20, s. 79(3)).
[28]Section 119.
[29]*Post*, part 10.02.

The qualification of an auditor is only vaguely expressed in the Act. The term is defined to "include" the auditor of the corporation and any other independent public accountant.[30] This void has been filled by a national policy which declares that certain auditor's reports will be unacceptable where a conflict exists by virtue of some relationship, direct or indirect, between the auditor, his partners, and associates and the issuer being reported upon, its subsidiaries or its holding company if any. This conflict relationship may arise either through the ownership of securities or the holding of positions such as director, officer or employee.[31]

The central question with respect to which the auditor must state his opinion is cast in the stylized language generally seen at the conclusion of audited financial statements, *viz.*, "whether in his opinion the financial statements...present fairly the financial position of the corporation and the results of its operations for the period under review in accordance with generally accepted accounting principles applied on a basis consistent with that of the preceding period."[32] The Act also contains several other items of cryptic guidance for the auditor. Stated in the form of positive injunctions, they provide by negative inference an indication of how much discretion is left to the individual auditor and to the professional association which issues guidelines to assist him. He is required to make "such statements as he considers necessary" in several specific situations:

(1) if the financial statements are not in accordance with the accounting records, the requirements of the Act or regulations,

(2) if the auditor has not received all the information and explanations he has required or

(3) if proper accounting records have not been kept.

The way in which the auditor's opinion is phrased has given rise to some difficulties. Obviously, if he cannot give a "clear" opinion he must state his reason for qualification even though it is not exactly covered by the four specific grounds. But a problem arises with respect to the terms "generally accepted accounting principles" and "fairly presented". In 1972 the national securities administrators issued a policy statement indicating that "generally accepted accounting principles" for securities legislation must conform to releases and guide-

---

[30]Section 118(1)(a) (Bill 20, s. 79(4)). In the Bill "reporting issuer" of course replaces "corporation" as specially defined in the Act.

[31]National Policy 3 "Unacceptable Auditors", CCH vol. 2, para. 54-840. The guidelines contained in this statement are modelled on those legislated in the BCA. The introduction of substantially more rigorous standards to ensure the independence of auditors for Ontario corporations was one of the consequences of the coming into force of that Act in 1971. The original impulse for reform came from the 1967 Interim Report of the Ontario Select Committee on Company Law, pp. 87-98, which in turn was heavily influenced by the deficiencies exposed in the Atlantic and Prudential investigations (discussed in Appendices VI and VII). See also the Securities Acts of Quebec, s. 66; Manitoba, s. 32(2); Newfoundland, s. 31(3); Nova Scotia, s. 29(3); Alberta, s. 30(a); New Brunswick, s. 29; British Columbia, s. 116 and British Columbia Commission, "Instructions to Brokers Auditors", CCH vol. 2, para. 25-576.

[32]Section 119(2). This requirement or its equivalent is reserved for the regulations in s. 79, Bill 20.

lines issued by the Research Committee of the Canadian Institute of Chartered Accountants.[33] The sanction to enforce compliance with this standard is a cease-trading order against the issuer's securities, whether or not the non-conforming financial statements are accepted for filing. Shortly thereafter the OSC threatened to issue a cease-trade order against an issuer whose audited financial statements failed to show deferred income taxes as a current liability and this departed from CICA guidelines.[34] It was not sufficient that the auditor's opinion made it clear that the statements deviated from generally accepted accounting principles. In so acting, the OSC rejected the view that by clearly noting such a deviation, a report could still be "fairly presented".[35] The Commission justified its position on the basis that for an investor to compare different issuers in the same industry there must be no departure from the CICA model.

5.06 Financial Statements—Corporations and Securities Legislation

As we have seen, Part XII is drawn so as to apply to certain corporations incorporated outside Ontario who have a sufficient connection with the province through a TSE listing or a prospectus distribution of equity shares that the continuous disclosure obligation is imposed on them. The Act contains a provision designed to adjust securities legislation requirements to accommodate the financial disclosure provisions of the issuer's incorporating legislation. Thus, it is sufficient if annual and interim financial statements made available to shareholders under incorporating legislation are filed with the Commission together with a supplement of whatever additional information is necessary to comply substantially with the Ontario requirements provided that the filing with the Commission includes an auditor's report stating that substantial compliance has been

---

[33]National Policy 27 "Generally Accepted Accounting Principles", CCH vol. 2, para. 54-864. See also, National Policy 5 "Recognition of Profits in Real Estate Transactions", CCH vol. 2, para. 54-842; National Policy 14 "Acceptability of Other Currencies in Material Filed with the Provincial Securities Administrators", CCH vol. 2, para. 54-851.

[34]These are taxes which are not payable immediately because depreciation allowances for income tax purposes are greater than the actual rate of depreciation. At about the same time, the Quebec Institute of Chartered Accountants had disciplined two chartered accountants for failure to show deferred income taxes in financial statements they prepared (Globe and Mail Report on Business, March 22, 1973).

[35]The issuer in this case submitted the opinions of four leading accountants, three of which stated that it was possible for financial statements to deviate from generally accepted accounting principles and still be presented fairly. The question is whether the adverb "fairly" modifying the verb "present" applies only to the first object, "the financial position of the corporation", or whether it also applies to the second object, "the results of its operations...in accordance with generally accepted accounting principles...". A literal reading of the subsection suggests the former view. This view is supported by the next subsection where the auditor need only give his opinion whether the statement of source and application of funds presents the information in the statement fairly, with no reference to generally accepted accounting principles.

effected.[36] No relaxation of time limits is permitted however. An issuer whose home jurisdiction does not require substantially the same reports must either put together a consolidated statement especially designed for and acceptable to the Ontario authorities or else seek an exemption either because of inability to comply or on the vague ground that it is justified in the particular circumstances.[37]

Another problem that arises with respect to continuous disclosure by non-Ontario corporations is one of enforcement. The directors and senior officers of the issuer will usually not be within Ontario's jurisdiction. The solution which has been found is not altogether satisfactory but represents the best available alternative short of devising a far more elaborate scheme. The issuer must give undertakings at the time of the distribution to comply with Part XII or face refusal of a receipt for a prospectus.[38] This technique finds its root in the Kimber Report concern over the jurisdictional and constitutional limitations of provincial legislation.[39] Another weapon in the Commis-

---

[36]Section 131. See also, British Columbia Policy 3-18 "Filing of Quarterly Reports", CCH vol. 2, para. 29-968.

[37]Section 132(1)(b) and (c)(iii) (Bill 20, s. 81(b) and (c)(ii)). It is unlikely that a complete exemption would be forthcoming. Section 83 of Bill 20 expressly permits the filing of signed copies of the documents filed in a corporation's home jurisdiction where the requirements of the home jurisdiction are substantially similar to those of Ontario.

[38]Section 133. Note that the Act states it is in the Commission's discretion to direct the director to refuse. The uniform act provinces have given a blanket direction to their directors to refuse to issue a receipt for prospectuses for equity shares until undertakings satisfying the proxy, insider trading and financial disclosure parts of the Act have been supplied (Uniform Policy 2-01 "Undertakings—Extra-Provincial Companies", CCH vol. 2, para. 54-871). See also, *ante*, part 4.06.

[39]In its chapter on Constitutional Considerations, the Kimber Committee justified both its use of undertakings and its provision for exempting federally incorporated companies in cases of conflict (Part IX). With regard to companies incorporated in other provinces, the problem is jurisdictional only, arising from the company's not being physically present in Ontario and its need to conform with its own incorporating act in internal matters. The Committee felt that the sanction of a forced exclusion from the Ontario capital market would be sufficient to make such extra-provincial issuers conform to Ontario-style reporting requirements. It favoured the use of the kind of undertakings which are provided for in s. 133. Federally incorporated companies pose a similar problem regarding enforcement, capable of being overcome by the same means. But there is one added factor: the need to avoid a conflict with any paramount federal legislation dealing with the same matters. The careful way in which s. 133 is drafted, giving the Commission a discretionary authority to exempt in such circumstances, reflects the Kimber Committee's concern to avoid a head-on collision with the federal jurisdiction.

But very recent authority suggests the Kimber Committee may have been overly sensitive. The question of whether the provisions of the CCA (or CBCA) applying to federally incorporated companies and similar provisions of the provincial securities acts applying to federally incorporated companies can stand together in the face of the doctrine of paramountcy (or the doctrine of the occupied field as it is sometimes called) has now been answered directly. In *Multiple Access Ltd. v. McCutcheon* (1975), 11 O.R. (2d) 249 (H.C.) a motion to strike out an action by a federally incorporated company (through

sion's arsenal, one particularly useful for delinquencies occurring after distribution, is the cease-trading order. Failure to file regular financial statements as required is in fact the most frequent occasion for the issuing of such orders by an overwhelming margin. This is a discretion which the Commission has delegated to the director.[40]

5.07 Exemption From Financial Statements

An elaborate exemption scheme based on the Kimber Report's recommendation is enshrined in s. 132. In the relatively short space of time since it became law this scheme has been subjected to considerable

---

the agency of the OSC under s. 114 of the Act) to recover damages from its insiders for alleged insider trading was denied. The ground for the motion was that the provisions of the CCA and the Act were duplicative (s. 100.4 and s. 113 respectively); based on federal occupation of the field, the provincial provisions should be held inoperative. Relying on a series of Supreme Court of Canada cases on duplication of provincial statutes and provisions of the Criminal Code the Court decided that mere duplication was insufficient to strike down the provincial provision. Rather, incompatability or repugnancy must be established. The Court at pp. 259-60, applied *Smith v. The Queen*, [1960] S.C.R. 776, 25 D.L.R. (2d) 225, 128 C.C.C. 145, 33 C.R. 318 (see, *post*, part 9.01) and quoted from the judgment, the following test for incompatability, at p. 800: "…there is no conflict in the sense that compliance with one law involves breach of the other. It would appear, therefore, that they can operate concurrently."

One of the few instances where there probably is incompatability between the federal and provincial provisions is in the take-over bid regulations. There the provincial acts stipulate a seven-day right of withdrawal period for tendered stock; the federal provision gives a more generous period of ten days (s. 82, para. 3 of the Act and s. 135.2(c) of the CCA). An offeror faced with a request for withdrawal on the eighth day would be required to comply under the federal provisions but under the provincial statute it is not so obligated and could properly refuse to return the stock. In recognition of this potential constitutional shoal, Bill 20 has amended the seven-day provision to ten days (s. 91(1)3).

Multiple Access also suggests that if concurrent actions could be brought under both the provincial and federal statutes, the courts are capable of harmonizing the proceedings (pp. 263-265, O.R.). Moreover, it also establishes that if two actions, one under the federal and the other under the provincial statute, establish an award of damages arising from the one transaction the courts are capable of regulating proceedings to ensure that the insider is not subjected twice to damages (p. 264, relying on *Co-operators Insurance Associations v. Kearney*, [1965] S.C.R. 106, 48 D.L.R. (2d) 1).

[40]The order for compliance power was used in these instances shortly after its introduction into the Act. However, the displeasure of the courts at being burdened by these orders led to the use of the present method. Delinquency in filing regular financial statements has resulted in the Ontario Commission issuing a policy statement warning of vigorous surveillance and enforcement (No. 3-14 "Delinquency in Filing Under Part XII, Securities Act, 1966", CCH vol. 2, para. 54-908). Normally the director's order suspending trading in securities of a delinquent issuer will be lifted as soon as it makes up-to-date filings. The general discretion to refuse a prospectus can also be used to secure compliance from current defaulters in continuous disclosure requirements (Ontario Policy 3-04 "Preliminary Prospectuses and Prospectuses", CCH vol. 2, para. 54-898).

definition in detail by an interesting series of court decisions. First, the Commission has a discretion to permit an applicant issuer to dispense with certain parts of the required financial statements. The sort of information that may be omitted includes sales volume data, earnings per share, and the comparative statement for the financial period immediately preceding the current one in both the annual and interim filings. Secondly, in the event of an issuer's inability to comply with all the details required in its statement of source and application of funds, permission to file an appropriate substitute document may be granted. Thirdly, the Commission has a discretion to exempt an applicant issuer in whole or in part where there is either a conflict or substantial similarity with the requirements of the laws of the issuer's incorporating jurisdiction or where it is otherwise satisfied in the particular case that there is adequate justification.[41] It may also attach terms and conditions. The exempting provision for conflict was primarily designed to avoid a constitutional confrontation with federally incorporated entities.[42]

The possibility of such a conflict is not solely confined to the financial disclosure provisions of Part XII of the Act. The same question arises with respect to all areas of securities law which require regular reports or filings of one kind or another. In 1971, amendments to the CCA became effective which imposed varying types of disclosure requirements with respect to take-over bids, proxies, insider trading, and annual financial statements, the model being the uniform act.[43] Shortly before this occurred British Columbia, Alberta, Saskatchewan and Ontario (but not Manitoba) issued a statement of guidelines for exemptions.[44] It declared that with the coming into force of proxy provisions in the CCA, the provisions of Part X dealing with proxy regulation no longer applied to federal corporations. However, it reminded issuers of the Part XII requirement[45] that companies subject to this part, a category which includes federal companies, were required to file with the Commission all information furnished to shareholders. This would include the proxy information circular and other proxy solicitation material needed to comply with the federal Act.

The treatment of insider-trading reports was somewhat different. The statement noted the practice of the four provincial jurisdictions to accept upon application the form of insider-trading report required in the home jurisdiction and acknowledged that they were substantially the same. It declared that a similar acceptance, upon application,

---

[41]Section 132(1). Bill 20, s. 81(c) drops the "substantial similarity" subsection because s. 83 permits substantially similar forms to be filed without the need for an application for exemption. See, *supra*, footnote 37.
[42]See, *supra*, footnote 39.
[43]The CCA went further and applied continuous disclosure requirements to private companies with assets exceeding $5 million or gross revenue exceeding $10 million yearly (CCA, s. 128(3); CBCA, s. 154(1)(b)).
[44]"Guidelines for Federal Companies: Applications For Exemptions— Amendments To The Canada Corporations Act Alberta, British Columbia and Saskatchewan", CCH vol. 2, para. 54-950.
[45]Reg. 794, s. 57(1) as am. by O.Reg. 385/70, s. 7.

would be accorded the forms filed under the new federal provisions "so long as the information required is the same".

Finally, with respect to financial statements under Part XII, the guidelines took the view that the requirements of the federal and uniform legislation were substantially the same. Exemption applications would not be necessary unless the federal company believed its statement would not meet the uniform act's requirements, in which case an application for exemption to the extent necessary would be appropriate.

In the case of applications by issuers whose home jurisdiction is in the U.S. and who are subject to SEC regulation, the practice of the uniform commissions is to exempt on condition that the SEC proxy, insider and financial disclosure forms are filed. Ontario has now made this practice more general in a policy which applies to all companies incorporated outside Ontario, the laws of whose incorporating jurisdiction require information identical to that demanded within the province; the only caveat is that the Ontario time limits must be met.[46] While issuers subject to SEC jurisdiction do not conform to requirements which are precisely "identical", it is the custom of the OSC to exempt them under the terms of this policy statement.

Bill 20 introduces certain minor changes in the area of exemptions from the financial reporting requirements.[47] The discretion given to the Commission by s. 81 to exempt a reporting issuer is of the same sort as is granted by s. 132 of the Act. However, the power to permit the omission of financial statements[48] is stated in somewhat broader terms: the exemption may relate to "comparative financial statements for particular periods of time".[49]

---

[46]Policy 3.16 "Grounds For Exemptions, Non-Ontario Companies—Parts X, XI and XII", CCH vol. 2, para. 54-910. The situation in Manitoba is different. In June, 1972 (Manitoba Policy 3.08 "Insider Reporting Exemptions", CCH vol. 2, para. 34-998) the Manitoba Commission announced that it would grant exemptions, upon application, from the insider reporting obligations only, if the incorporating jurisdiction required similar reports. These exemptions are to be available only for companies incorporated in Canada but with no local connection with Manitoba. A "local connection" is established by any one of the following:
(1) Manitoba head office,
(2) listing of shares on the Winnipeg Stock Exchange,
(3) securities in continuous primary distribution in Manitoba (other than mututal fund shares),
(4) some other connection which would make the ownership of its shares a matter of interest to Manitoba residents (*e.g.*, a Manitoba executive office with nominal head office elsewhere).
The Manitoba Commission also indicated that it would entertain applications in respect of companies whose home jurisdiction did not require insider reports but whose continued listing on a stock exchange required them. In such instances satisfactory evidence would be required as to the reasonable certainty of continued listing. See also, Alberta Policy 3.12, CCH vol. 1, para. 24-512.
[47]Sections 81 and 83.
[48]Section 81(a).
[49]From the way in which "comparative" is used in the section it would seem

We may conclude this consideration of exemptions by making the perhaps obvious point that this is a clear case for all the Canadian jurisdictions to co-ordinate their regulations so that one form would satisfy them all and avoid the need for exempting orders.

(1) TIMING OF APPLICATION FOR EXEMPTIONS

As a matter of practice the OSC insists that applications for exemptions for a stay of time, and for a variation or omission of a financial statement, be filed so that the application may be considered and granted before the operative date for filing of the required statement. Where applications are filed late, the Commission will ordinarily not grant a favourable ruling on the basis that it will not normally issue *ex post facto* rulings. However, if there are reasonable circumstances to explain the late filing and if there are no good reasons to require the issuer to file the specified statement, the Commission will give assurance that no prosecution will ensue. Consequently some issuers use the application for exemption as a method of making disclosure to the Commission of their inability to meet filing deadlines.

(2) COMPARATIVE FINANCIAL STATEMENTS AND THE BUSINESS CORPORATIONS ACT EXEMPTION

There is an inconsistent pattern between the BCA and the Act on the requirement of comparative financial statements. As we have seen, s. 132 of the Act provides for a discretionary exempting order of the Commission relieving against certain reporting requirements applying to non-Ontario incorporated companies. The BCA, applying to Ontario incorporated companies, should provide for a parallel exempting discretion in the Commission. Unfortunately, this is not entirely the case. It does provide for an exempting discretion for interim comparative statements,[50] but not for the annual comparative statements. By a generous (and probably improper) reading of s. 134 of the Act (which requires Ontario companies to file their annual financial statements with the Commission) together with s. 132 (the exempting power for non-Ontario companies) the Commission takes jurisdiction over applications and will grant an exemption from the BCA in otherwise appropriate circumstances.

Some Ontario companies, faced with the need for an exemption where the nature of their undertaking has changed substantially from the previous year to the current one have taken the view that the statements would not be truly "comparative". By reading this sense into the word "comparative" they have been able simply to dispense with the previous year's statement as not meaningful. The best that can be said for this argument is that the statute might have made the

---

that the entire statement for the current year may be omitted under Bill 20 as well as that for the preceding year though one may assume that such an exemption would be infrequently granted.

Note that s. 83 of Bill 20 amounts to a statutory enactment of Ontario Policy 3-16, *supra*, footnote 46, since the requirement of "identical information" in that policy statement has been liberally interpreted.

[50]Section 185(2). Even in this subsection the heading suggests the Commission's discretion is limited to varying the comparative period. However, the text of the subsection (and the Commission's practice) makes it clear that a larger discretion is contemplated.

requirement of two statements less open to ambiguity if the word "comparative" had simply been left out. It seems, however, that the adjective "comparative" is intended as an indication of the duration of the period to be covered by the second of two mandatory statements, and it is not as a qualitative word permitting a discretionary interpretation that one statement may be left out where truly comparative conditions do not apply. Thus the more appropriate method for dealing with a situation where the directors or auditors conclude that comparative statements would not be meaningful is as follows. They should comply with the requirement of two years' statements and explain the anomaly by way of notes to those statements or apply to the Commission for an exemption in connection with the previous year's statement. This problem disappears with Bill 20 since Ontario companies will also be subject to its requirements and entitled to avail themselves of its exemptions in this connection.[51]

(3) SALES DISCLOSURE EXEMPTIONS

The exemption from the financial disclosure requirements which has been the centre of most controversy and more jurisprudence than any other provision concerns the obligation to disclose figures for sales or gross operating revenue.[52] Thus it may be instructive to single out this exemption for more thorough consideration.

Section 132(1)(a)(ii) provides that this obligation may be dispensed with where the Commission is satisfied that it would be "unduly detrimental to the interests of the corporation" to force disclosure. The Commission must also be of the opinion that it would not be prejudicial to the public interest to grant an exemption. As we have seen, all orders issued under s. 132 may be made subject to terms and conditions.

This provision like so many others in the Act, reflects the recommendations of the Kimber Report, which considered the arguments for and against allowing an exemption of this sort and concluded that in two situations it would often be desirable: first, where a competitor (or competitors) of an applicant firm was a private company under no disclosure obligations and secondly, where the competition was provided by a large firm with several operating divisions and no division or product line reporting obligations.[53]

The present exemption in the Act is exactly the same as the corresponding exemption for Ontario companies in the BCA except that the latter does not contain the requirement of no prejudice to the public interest.[54] Applications under both Acts are now heard by the OSC.[55] The other statutes in Canada which impose the sales reporting requirement also contain an exempting procedure, with some interesting deviations from the Ontario model.[56]

---

[51]See *e.g.*, ss. 1(1)36, 76, 78 and 79. And Bill 21 "An Act to amend The Business Corporations Act" (4th Sess.), 30th Legislature Ontario removes the exempting provisions from the BCA.

[52]Section 121(1)(a).

[53]Kimber Report, para. 4.17.

[54]Section 173.

[55]As a result of 1968-9 (Ont.), c. 16, s. 6.

[56]The Alberta Securities Act uses precisely the same formula as the Ontario

There is some uncertainty regarding the permissible duration of an order for exemption. The Kimber Report intended that a fresh application should be made each year,[57] but there are a number of cases which have granted disclosure exemption for several successive years with respect to both the annual and the interim statements.[58] The language of the section as it stands is vague enough to support either interpretation.

It will be apparent from the foregoing that the OSC must consider two types of applications in the area of sales disclosure exemption: from Ontario companies under the BCA and from non-Ontario companies under the Act (*i.e.*, companies to whom Part XII is applicable). Are there any important differences in the considerations that should influence a decision under one Act or the other? At first sight the answer would seem to be no. These disclosure requirements were enacted in both the corporate and securities areas at the same time in almost identical language and with the same general goal of investor protection in mind: the conditions for exemption, it might be argued, should be the same in each case. The foregoing view was exploded in *Re Niagara Wire Weaving Co. Ltd.*[59] This was a successful

---

BCA and gives its discretion to the Alberta Securities Commission (s. 131(1)(a)(ii)). The Alberta Companies Act uses the same exempting language but gives the decision-making power to a judge of the Trial Division specially designated (s. 121(3)). The British Columbia Companies Act, s. 158(3)(4) and the British Columbia Securities Act, s. 119(3) are similar to the Alberta statutes. The Manitoba Companies Act, s. 111(3) and the Manitoba Securities Act, s. 131(1)(a)(ii) use the same language as the British Columbia and Alberta Acts but, as in Ontario, discretion to grant an exemption is exercised by the Securities Commission under both Acts. The Saskatchewan Securities Act uses the same formula as the BCA and gives the discretion to the Saskatchewan Securities Commission (s. 128(3)). The formulation of the exempting provision in the CCA, s. 129.3(1)(a) is slightly different. A company may apply for an exempting order to the Chief Justice of the Supreme Court (or a judge designated by him) in the province in which the head office of the company is located. He may grant the exemption in whole or in part when he is satisfied that disclosure "would be seriously and unfairly detrimental" to the company's interests. He is specifically required to "have regard to the interest of the public in having disclosure of the information" in so deciding. The most interesting treatment of the exemption is in the CBCA, s. 154(3). The director has the discretion to grant an order under the circumstances spelled out in the Regulation, s. 50. See also, Uniform Policy 2-11 "Policy Statement in Connection with Applications to the Commission for an Order under...s. 173(3) of the Business Corporations Act, 1970 (Ontario)", CCH vol. 2, para. 54-881.

[57]Para. 4.18.

[58]See D.L. Johnston, "Exemptions From Sales Disclosure In Regular Financial Statements: Courts, Tribunals, And Business Judgments" (1973), U. Toronto L.J. 215, on which the discussion in this part is largely based. For cases dealing with the duration of the exempting order see footnote 35 of that article.

[59][1971] 3 O.R. 633, 21 D.L.R. (3d) 305 (C.A.). This case will be referred to as "*Niagara Wire*", to distinguish it from a subsequent appeal in respect to the same company, *Re Niagara Wire Weaving Co. Ltd. (No. 2)*, [1972] 3 O.R. 129, 27 D.L.R. (3d) 548 (C.A.).

appeal by an Ontario company from a denial of an exemption by the OSC. It was held that the Commission had failed to appreciate the distinction between the purpose of the Act, which aims to enlighten investors generally, and that of the BCA, under which disclosure has the narrower aim of enabling shareholders to be better informed in appraising the management of the corporation. The case was remitted to the OSC for fresh consideration.

Another problem regarding these exemptions, one not unrelated to the foregoing, is that of the delay and duplicated effort involved in securing approval from several courts and regulatory agencies in various provinces. This is a significant problem in the case of a large company with nationwide operations. Added to this is the uncertainty involved—only one unsuccessful application frustrates the goal of obtaining permission for non-disclosure in a given year, and success in one year is by no means a guarantee of a like result in subsequent ones.[60] Little attempt, however, has been made at co-ordination, even within the five uniform act provinces. The British Columbia, Alberta, Saskatchewan and Ontario commissions have gone so far as to issue guidelines stating that financial statements produced in compliance with the CCA would satisfy the provincial Acts;[61] in policy statements, however, they have stopped short of dispensing with a separate hearing before each commission in the case of an application for exemption.[62] However, in the wake of *Niagara Wire*, and *Niagara Wire (No. 2)*, which indicated that the purposes of corporations and securities legislation were different and that the Commission could not delegate its discretion, the OSC rescinded this policy statement.[63]

Another area in which interpretive difficulties arise is that concerning the nature and scope of the detriment which must be shown by an applicant for exemption. The Act speaks of "undue" detriment, while the CCA uses the phrase "serious and unfairly" to qualify detriment.[64] Thus something more than the mere presence of detriment is required in both instances. The courts and tribunals applying the test have not failed to take note of this fact;[65] the OSC and the Court of Appeal have

---

[60]See Johnston, *supra*, footnote 58, p. 225.

[61]"Guidelines for Federal Companies: Applications for Exemptions-Amendments to the Canada Corporations Act", Mar. 1971 OSCB 24, CCH vol. 2, para. 54-950.

[62]Ontario and Alberta did so with regard to federal companies listed on the TSE or Alberta Stock Exchange applying to a Supreme Court Judge for exemption from sales disclosure (Ontario Policy 3-15 "Applications for Order for Omission of Sales or Gross Operating Revenue—Canada Corporations", CCH vol. 2, para. 54-909 and Alberta Policy 3-11, CCH vol. 1, para. 24-511) indicating that provided notice was given to the Commission on such applications, if the court granted the exemption the Commission would do so as well without a hearing.

[63]As of December 31, 1973.

[64]The CBCA deletes the qualifying words altogether (s. 150) but in the Regulation (s. 49) sets out certain circumstances which the director might conclude establishes detriment.

[65]*Re Maher Shoes Ltd.*, Oct. 1970 OSCB 141, upheld on appeal *Re Maher Shoes Ltd. and Ontario Securities Commission*, [1971] 2 O.R. 267, 17 D.L.R. (3d) 519 (C.A.). "Undue" was glossed by McRuer C.J.H.C. in the field of

rejected an application where some detriment existed but it could not be characterized as undue.

The cases also make it clear that actual as opposed to possible or hypothetical detriment from disclosure must be shown. Since the whole purpose of the application is to prevent damage from actually occurring, this requirement must be interpreted to mean that the expectation of detriment must be plausibly based and not the result of mere supposition or conjecture.[66]

A variety of terms and conditions may be attached to these exempting orders. For example, the company may be exempted but required to show the *percentage* change in its sales figures over a period of five years. Less commonly it may be simply asked to introduce a note into its statement indicating whether sales have risen or declined in the previous year. *Niagara Wire (No. 2)*[67] introduces some fine distinctions regarding the kind of conditions involving shareholder approval that can be attached. In that case the company was granted an exemption conditional on the matter being subjected to a vote at the next shareholders' meeting; if less than 90 per cent of the votes favoured omitting the figures the company was to make immediate disclosure of them. This was held to be improper as a case of unlawful delegation. Rather suprisingly the same case suggests that an order granting an exemption is valid if by a fixed date prior to its operative effect a two-thirds majority of shareholders consent to the omission. It may be questioned whether this rather more narrowly framed condition is in substance much different from the proviso which was held invalid.

The future of the exemption from sales disclosure is uncertain. U.S. experience (and precedent) suggests that it may be on the way out, but it is too early to conclude that there may not be a continuing place in the unique context of the Canadian economy for exemptions in the case of particular detriment. And in any case Canada lacks sufficient experience with continuous disclosure as a technique of corporate-securities law to be able to say that safeguards such as exemptions of this sort should be removed. However, recent trends in OSC decisions do suggest that the number of exemptions will decrease and that only situations where peculiar hardship would result—such as the one product company with a few important customers (or suppliers), *none* of whose competitors make effective disclosure—will enjoy immunity. This will be all the more probable if Canadian jurisdictions continue

---

combines law as "inordinate, excessive or oppressive": *R. v. Northern Electric Co. Ltd. et al.*, [1955] O.R. 431, [1955] 3 D.L.R. 449, 111 C.C.C. 241, 24 C.P.R. 1, 21 C.R. 45 (H.C.). Detriment has been further defined as "economic detriment" in *Niagara Wire (No. 2), supra*, footnote 59. "Seriously and unfairly" has been interpreted in a similar fashion: *Re A.E. Ames & Co. Ltd.*, [1972] 3 O.R. 405, 28 D.L.R. (3d) 435 (C.A.).

[66]See in this connection *Re Maher Shoes Ltd.*, [1967] 2 O.R. 684, 65 D.L.R. (2d) 105 (H.C.); *Re Maher Shoes Ltd. and Ontario Securities Commission*, [1971] 2 O.R. 267, 17 D.L.R. (3d) 519 (C.A.); *Re Niagara Wire Weaving Co. Ltd.*, [1971] 3 O.R. 633, 21 D.L.R. (3d) 305 (C.A.).

[67]*Re Niagara Wire Weaving Co. Ltd. (No. 2)*, [1972] 3 O.R. 129, 27 D.L.R. (3d) 548 (C.A.).

to adopt some of the more sophisticated and detailed reporting techniques presently used in the U.S. (such as cost of sales and product line reporting). Already the policy evident in new legislation of broadening disclosure requirements has narrowed the base for exemptions considerably. For example, the two categories of situations which the Kimber Committee foresaw in 1965 as creating the possibility of an exemption—where competitors were not public companies or were multi-product companies—were largely eliminated for dominion companies as of 1971.

In concluding this section on sales disclosure exemptions one may remark that there is a need for standardization in the granting of exemptions and in the legislation which authorizes them. Saskatchewan and the easternmost provinces have lagged somewhat in development of their disclosure standards, and anomalies persist in the requirements of the remaining jurisdictions. In the area of administering the exemptions, an attractive solution to the present confusion and duplication would be the pooling of existing commissions into a national securities commission with the responsibility for deciding upon exemptions on a nation-wide basis. Besides eliminating a certain amount of inefficiency and waste, such a move would provide a forum for the resolution of some of the jurisprudential problems which have been alluded to in the course of this discussion. The present situation suggests that some reweaving of loose threads in order to achieve consistency would be highly desirable.[68]

As indicated above, Bill 20 seems to leave the situation very much as it stands so far as sales disclosure exemptions are concerned.[69]

B. Proxies

5.08 The Need for Proxy Regulation
At common law each shareholder was expected to exercise his own franchise in person at shareholders' meetings.[70] As shareholders increasingly took on the status of investors and not owner-managers it became common for corporation charters to authorize voting by proxy. More recently corporation statutes have commonly made it a right of any shareholder to designate someone else (whether connected in some way with the company or not) to exercise the former's votes at shareholders' meetings. Technically speaking it is that other person who is the shareholder's "proxy". However, common usage today ascribes the name "proxy" to the written document, technically the instrument of proxy, by which the shareholder appoints another to exercise a vote on his behalf.[71] The person who holds the "proxy" is

---

[68]We may take as an example the practice of the Ontario Commission, referred to earlier, of simply issuing exempting orders under securities legislation on the strength of a court-granted exemption under the Canada Corporations Act which unfortunately was withdrawn as invalid in the light of *Re Niagara Wire Weaving Co. Ltd.*, [1971] 3 O.R. 633, 21 D.L.R. (3d) 305 (C.A.) and *Re Niagara Wire Weaving Co. Ltd. (No. 2)*, [1972] 3 O.R. 129, 27 D.L.R. (3d) 548 (C.A.).

[69]Section 81(a)(ii).

[70]*Harben v. Phillips* (1883), 23 Ch. D. 14, 48 L.T. 334 (C.A.).

[71]Kimber Report, para. 6.01.

commonly referred to as the "nominee".[72]

In the period before the Kimber Report (1965), there was no comprehensive proxy regulation framework in Canadian corporate or securities legislation. Most of the general incorporating acts did contain provisions expressly permitting the use of the proxy and dealing with various procedural matters, but these were largely restrictive in nature and confined to such matters as the provision of adequate notice of meetings and the fixing of the time for closing the list of proxies deposited. It was against this background that the Kimber Committee proposed that substantive proxy regulation be included in Ontario corporate and securities legislation as a part of a composite package of reforms emphasizing continuous disclosure.

The specific shortcomings which the Kimber Committee isolated were these. While Ontario corporations legislation gave a proxy right and laid down some rules as to the form of the proxy, they were largely inhibiting in nature and failed to give positive guidance. The law was silent regarding even such a basic question as whether proxy solicitation should be required at all, as well as when and how it should be carried out. As a result, the proxy commonly used was deficient as a form of ballot and provided an alarmingly slim base of information upon which the absentee voter was to form his judgment. In view of the importance of the proxy system in a period when large widely-held companies are dominant, this was a highly unsatisfactory state of affairs.[73]

---

[72]*Ibid.*For a thoughtful discussion of proxy rules see L. Getz, "Alberta Proxy Legislation" and L. Getz, "The Structure of Shareholder Democracy".

[73]Paras. 6.02 and 6.03.

U.S. Federal practice with regard to proxies significantly influenced the Kimber Committee in its analysis of the Ontario scene. It cited approvingly the terse conclusion (para. 6.04 from Loss, vol. 2, pp. 857-8) of Professor Loss on this topic:

"Corporate practice has come a long way from the common law's non-recognition of the proxy device. The widespread distribution of corporate securities with the concomitant separation of ownership and management, puts the entire concept of the stockholders' meeting at the mercy of the proxy instrument. This makes the corporate proxy a tremendous force for good or evil in our economic scheme. Unregulated, it is an open invitation to self-perpetuation and irresponsibility of management. Properly circumscribed, it may well turn out to be the salvation of the modern corporate system."

The Committee was probably influenced by one or two other value judgments that Professor Loss had made on the U.S. proxy regime. He said: (*ibid.*, at p. 1027):

"The proxy rules are very likely the most effective disclosure device in the SEC scheme of things. The proxy literature, unlike the application for registration and the statutory reports, gets into the hands of investors. Unlike the Securities Act prospectus, it gets there in time. It is more readable than any of these other documents. And it gets to a great many people who *never* see a prospectus. Moreover, there are indications in both management and judicial attitudes that the indirect influence of the proxy rules, through their infiltration of the general law of notice to security holders, may in the long run be more significant than their direct impact."

The Committee's recommendations, which were followed both in the 1966 Act, and in parallel amendments to Ontario corporations legislation, dealt with three main areas: the question of whether proxy solicitation should be made mandatory on the part of management and dissident shareholder groups, the nature and detail of the proxy form itself and the disclosure of information which should accompany the solicitation. These will be considered in turn following a brief section devoted to the subject of when these rules apply. This part concludes with a consideration of costs of solicitation and consequences of irregularity.

5.09 Application of Proxy Rules

The proxy rules apply to the same categories of companies as the regular financial disclosure rules except that loan and trust corporations and insurance companies are included.[74] The exemptions from the rules are basically similar to those for regular financial disclosure.[75] Since the proxy rules are new there has been little jurisprudential guidance to date regarding the finer points of their interpretation. Several cases, however, have dealt with their application. A liberal and functional approach rather than a formalistic or literal interpretation emerges from these cases. In *Re Frontier Acceptance Corp. Ltd.*,[76] Osler J. considered the Ontario corporations legislation exemption from the proxy rules for "a public company that has fewer than fifteen shareholders...".[77] He read that phrase as referring to shareholders entitled to vote only and not to all shareholders, reasoning from a functional premise that "the relatively new [proxy] provisions...are concerned with information to be given to shareholders who are entitled to vote at meetings."[78]

(*Ibid.*, at p. 866):
  "...Congressional action [enacting proxy rules]...has probably had a more beneficial effect on 'corporate democracy' in America than any other of the numerous weapons in the SEC arsenal."
[74]Section 101(a). Bill 20 applies the proxy rules and continuous disclosure requirements to reporting issuers (ss. 86 and 76 respectively). For discussion of the application of both sets of rules see, *supra*, part 5.03.
[75]*Supra*, part 5.07.
[76][1969] 2 O.R. 302 (H.C.).
[77]The Corporations Act, R.S.O. 1960, c. 71, s. 75d(2). See s. 118(2) of the current BCA.
[78]The corporation had non-voting preferred shares held by fifteen shareholders, one of which was a dominion corporation holding 14,085 shares with the other fourteen holding 1,285 shares. The parent dominion corporation also held all but a few of the common shares, the balance being held by ten shareholders of whom five were not beneficially owners thereof. The matter came before Osler J. as an application for an exempting order. He dismissed the application concluding that the sanction of the court was not required since the test of 15 *voting* shareholders was not met. He also noted that the corporation was "an interested person" entitled to bring the application.
  Another case dealing with applicability arose in connection with one of the minor chapters in the tumultuous saga of the Investors Overseas empire: *Schiowitz et al. v. I.O.S. Ltd. et al.*, [1972] 3 O.R. 262, 28 D.L.R. (3d) 40 (C.A.). IOS, a company incorporated in Canada, had a subsidiary which had been

5.10 Mandatory Solicitation of Proxies

The major policy question before the Kimber Committee was whether to make proxy solicitation mandatory or optional, *viz.*, simply to define the procedures which must be followed and the information which must be supplied in the event that either management or an insurgent group chooses to solicit proxies. Had the optional route been taken, it would have enabled management or an insurgent group to avoid the application of the new rules by simply refraining from soliciting proxies. This was the path followed in the U.S. at the time of the introduction of proxy rules in the 1934 Securities and Exchange Act. Voices were heard at a later date suggesting that the rules be made mandatory, but it was not until 1964 in the context of an extension of the proxy requirements to the over-the-counter market issuers that a shift to a mandatory policy occurred.[79]

In deciding in favour of mandatory solicitation the Kimber Committee noted that larger Canadian public companies already followed the practice of soliciting proxies for annual or special meetings. The cost of requiring other public companies to do the same would be justified, so the Committee reasoned, by the wider dissemination of corporate information thus made possible. Although it might appear that the votes so solicited would be seldom if ever needed in the making of corporate decisions, the Committee clearly felt that there was a benefit to be had by drawing the absentee shareholder into some form of participation in the affairs of the corporation, however indirect and remote.[80]

The method chosen to implement mandatory solicitation in Canada was to require that a prescribed proxy form and information circular accompany (or precede) management's notice to shareholders of meetings. Since incorporating legislation invariably requires shareholders to be notified of meetings, the effect was to make the solicitation of proxies (by management) a necessary concomitant of all general meetings, whether annual or special. The group to whom the proxy form and circular is to be sent is composed of all shareholders

---

incorporated in the Bahamas. This subsidiary was restrained from voting the parent's shares at an annual and special general meeting of the parent's shareholders as being a prohibited shareholder. The prohibition contained in s. 16A(2) and (4) of the CCA which forbids a subsidiary company to hold shares in a parent holding company and excludes any share so held from a vote, was held to be applicable even though the subsidiary was incorporated outside of Canada. This involved interpreting the prohibited "company" broadly as not limited to companies incorporated under the CCA. The court held that a non-federally incorporated company was capable of being a subsidiary in the sense intended by the prohibition, reasoning that s. 16A was a narrower enactment of the common law rule in *Trevor v. Whitworth* (1887), 12 App. Cas. 409, [1886-90] All E.R. Rep. 46 (H.L.) that a company should not directly or indirectly purchase its own shares and that the ordinary meaning of "company" includes a foreign incorporated company.

[79]The technique used to implement this change was this: when management did not solicit proxies it was required to file with the Commission and transmit to security holders information equivalent to that which would accompany a proxy solicitation. See Loss, vol. 5, pp. 2874-7.

[80]Para. 6.24.

whose latest address as shown in the books of the corporation is in Ontario and who are entitled to vote on the matters to be decided at the meeting.[81]

In the case of solicitations by persons or companies other than management it is only the information circular that is mandatory.[82] This must be in prescribed form. In the case of a management solicitation the information circular must be either an appendix or a separate document accompanying the notice of the meeting. In the case of any other solicitation it must be sent concurrently with or prior to the solicitation.[83]

The requirement of an information circular is subject to certain exceptions. First of all the solicitation of a small number of proxies (fifteen has been chosen as an arbitrary maximum) is exempt provided that the soliciting is not "by or on behalf of the management".[84] A special arrangement is made in respect of brokers holding street name certificates (registered in the name of the broker or his nominee rather than the beneficial owner).[85] Finally anyone soliciting in connection with shares he beneficially owns is exempted.[86]

The terms "solicit" and "solicitation", which are crucial in triggering the obligation to send the information circular, are defined broadly to include several types of requests which could be oral or written communications and several types of requests which must be in writing.[87]

Bill 20 contains no significant changes so far as the basic requirement of mandatory proxy forms and circulars is concerned.[88]

5.11 Form of Proxy
Where the mandatory solicitation provisions apply, the Act sets out guidelines which must be followed regarding the form of proxies. Each of these guidelines is considered in turn.

First, the form must indicate in bold-face type whether or not it is being solicited by or on behalf of management[89] and provide space for

---

[81]Section 102(1) (Bill 20, s. 86). A class of preferred shareholders which ordinarily did not vote, except for example, on the occasion of an organic change in the corporation such as a merger, would be included among the mandatory recipients of the proxy and circular should such a change be contemplated.

[82]Section 103(1)(a) (Bill 20, s. 87(1)).

[83]Section 103(1). (Bill 20, s. 87(1)(b)).

[84]Section 103(2)(a) (Bill 20, s. 87(2)(a)). Joint registered shareholders count as one.

[85]Sections 103(2)(b) and 80 (Bill 20, ss. 87(2)(b) and 49). See, *post*, part 8.06.

[86]Section 103(2)(c) (Bill 20, s. 87(2)(c)).

[87]Section 101(c) (Bill 20, s. 85(b)).

[88]Sections 85 to 87 supplemented by the regulations form a parallel with ss. 101 to 105 of the Act at almost every point. "Reporting issuer" of course replaces "corporation", and the recipients of the forms are designated "holders of...voting securities". This group will normally be co-extensive with those shareholders entitled to vote at a given meeting, although it could include holders of debt obligations given a vote under special circumstances.

[89]Section 105(a)(i). Bill 20, s. 86 leaves the requirements for the form of proxy to the regulations.

dating it.[90] Secondly, it must serve as an issue-oriented ballot. In respect to *each* matter intended to be subject to a vote the shareholder must be afforded the privilege of voting for or against the course advocated by the sender of the proxy; the analogy with a ballot is a close one here. The proxy may confer a discretionary authority with respect to matters for which a choice is not specified on the form of proxy if the form itself or the information circular clearly indicates how the proxy holder intends to vote in each case.[91] Finally, the proxy may confer discretionary authority on its holder with respect to two residual matters:

(1) Amendments or variations to matters identified in the notice of meeting; or

(2) Other matters which may properly come before the meeting.[92]

The Kimber Committee justified this ballot-box form of proxy primarily in terms of obtaining more "input" from the shareholders by providing a more efficient means for the communication of their views to management. The "for or against" proxy has the advantage that the shareholder can indicate dissent on a particular issue without going to the length of rejecting the nominee proposed by management. As elsewhere the U.S. example seems to have been foremost in the minds of the Committee members when making their recommendations on this point.[93]

There are several prohibitions affecting the proxy form. A proxy may not confer authority to vote for the election of any person as a director unless a *bona fide* proposed nominee is named in the information circular.[94] Nor may it confer authority to vote at any meeting other than the meeting specified in the notice of meeting or any adjournment thereof.[95]

The Act goes on to provide that the information circular or the form of proxy must indicate clearly that the shareholder has the right to appoint a person to represent him other than the person named in the form sent to him.[96] In order that as few proxies as possible should be invalidated by the exercise of this right "in an erroneous manner"[97]

---

[90]Section 105(a)(ii) (Bill 20, regulations).

[91]Section 105(b) (Bill 20, regulations).

[92]This permission, however, is circumscribed by a double proviso. The proxy holder must not be aware a reasonable time prior to the time the solicitation is made that any such amendments, variations or other matters are to be presented for action at the meeting and a specific statement must be made in the information circular or in the form of proxy that the proxy is in fact conferring such discretionary authority. Section 105(c) (Bill 20, regulations).

[93]Paras. 6.12 and 6.13.

[94]If the form of proxy does contain a designation of a named person as nominee, it must also provide means whereby the shareholder may designate someone else (s. 105(g) (Bill 20, regulations)). The Kimber Committee noted that it had been judicially observed that to do otherwise was not good corporate practice; it felt however that the matter should not be left to the some time vagaries of current opinion regarding good corporate practice but should be regularized as a requirement of law (para. 6.10).

[95]Section 105(d) (Bill 20, regulations).

[96]Section 105(f) (Bill 20, regulations).

[97]Kimber Report, para. 6.11.

instructions must be given in the proxy form as to the manner in which a substitute appointment may be made. Finally, the information circular or form of proxy must state both that the shares represented by the proxy will be voted and that they will be voted in accordance with the choice specified by the shareholder.[98] There is one qualification; this gives the chairman of the meeting the right to waive a ballot where he knows the outcome is not in any doubt.[99]

5.12 Information Circular

The form and content of the information circular are to be determined

---

[98]Section 105(e).

[99]Section 106. This provision grew out of the Kimber Committee's concern regarding the practical impact which the new form of proxy would have on the actual conduct of shareholders' meetings (paras. 6.15 and 6.16). Proxies require a recorded ballot rather than a show of hands. The Committee felt that some inconvenience in the conduct of meetings as a result of the introduction of the new rules was acceptable; it could not, however, justify the prospect of an elaborate ballot being required whenever a miniscule number of shareholders preferred to vote for a course opposed to that of management; hence the recommendation that the chairman of the meeting be given a discretionary power to dispense with a ballot when less than five per cent of the shares are required to be voted against a given proposal.

The articulation of this recommendation in the subsequent legislation has been unfortunate. Several drafting committees in the various jurisdictions have experimented with different formulations without achieving complete success. The provision in the Act now reads (s. 106):

"106. If the aggregate number of shares represented at a meeting by proxies required to be voted *for or against* a particular matter or group of matters carries, to the knowledge of the chairman of the meeting, less than 5 per cent of the voting rights attached to the shares entitled to vote and represented at the meeting, the chairman of the meeting has the right not to conduct a vote by way of ballot on any such matter or group of matters unless a poll is demanded at the meeting or required by the laws of the jurisdiction of incorporation of the corporation."

(Emphasis added.) The inclusion of the alternative phrase "for or" in this provision constitutes the flaw. Since it was essentially the negative nuisance or protest vote that the Kimber Committee intended to neutralize in this exemption, its recommendation that these "against" votes by themselves must reach five per cent of the total to force a formal vote should have been left untouched in the translation into law. Followed literally the legislative formula requires that all the "fors" and all the "againsts" in all the proxies be added together in calculating whether the allowable percentage has been exceeded. Thus the exemption is only available where at least 95 per cent of the voting rights are represented at the meeting by shareholders voting personally and not by proxy. Perhaps the best solution would have been to provide separately that all proxies cast in favour of a given proposal will be voted if a vote by ballot is otherwise required. As it stands all proxies are required to be voted *tout court*, which is presumably what inspired the rather clumsy insertion by the draftsman.

Bill 20 (s. 88) puts the matter right. It gives the meeting chairman a right to avoid a ballot vote unless one is demanded or there are proxies totalling more than five per cent which are to be voted against what would otherwise be the decision.

by regulation.[100] This is one area where the Act adopts the procedure which is followed generally in Bill 20 of relegating to the regulations detailed requirements which are apt to be subject to frequent changes. The form to be followed[101] specifies ten different items with instructions for the treatment of each. The information in the circular cannot be more than 30 days stale,[102] and must be presented in narrative form rather than a mechanical item by item response to the specifying requirements.[103] Where information is not known to the person soliciting the proxy and is not reasonably within his power to ascertain or procure, it may be omitted if a brief statement of the circumstances rendering it unavailable is made.[104] Furthermore an item may be dispensed with if the information is already contained in another information circular, notice of meeting or form of proxy sent to the same persons in connection with the same meeting, provided reference is made to the particular document containing that information.[105] These two provisions may be particularly useful to non-management proxy soliciting groups. The information circular and any other material distributed by the soliciting party in connection with a meeting must be placed on public file with the Commission when it is first mailed.[106] So also must proxy material governed by Ontario corporations legislation.[107]

Form 20 states[108] that the substance of any matter to be acted upon (apart from the passing of financial statements) is to be described in sufficient, though brief, detail to permit a shareholder to form a reasoned judgment concerning the matter in question. Following this, certain examples are provided of the kind of major transactions or alterations in the corporate structure that will call for such description. Not much help is given, however, in determining what degree of detail will be sufficient.[109]

---

[100]Section 108 (Bill 20, s. 85(a) (by implication)).

[101]Form 20, Reg. 794, s. 44(1).

[102]Reg. 794, s. 44(2).

[103]As we have seen the prospectus was similarly transformed following the Kimber Report emphasis on readability. See, *ante*, part 4.03, text at footnote 45. The Regulation stipulates that the information must be clearly presented with appropriate subdivisions and headings. Flexibility in the mode and sequence of presentation is permitted as is the omission of negative responses or inapplicable items (Reg. 794, s. 45).

[104]Reg. 794, s. 46.

[105]*Ibid.*, s. 47.

[106]*Ibid.*, s. 48.

[107]*Ibid.*

[108]Item 10.

[109]Some guidance is provided by the case of *Re N. Slater Co. Ltd.*, [1947] O.W.N. 226, [1947] 2 D.L.R. 311, 28 C.B.R. 31 (H.C.) which involved an internal corporate reorganization in the form of a conversion of preferred shares to common. The question in issue was the adequacy of the information circular recommending the change sent to shareholders by the directors. The purpose of the proposed exchange was left stated in very general terms, confined to such explanations as the need of the company to maintain its liquidity. There was an absence of supporting material concerning the financial position of the company which would enable a shareholder to

It would seem that a "brief description" in Form 20 includes a brief summary of the basic data from which inferences regarding the proper course of action to be followed are drawn; the data must not be summarized in so brief a fashion as to point to only one possible conclusion without an opportunity being given to examine the reasoning which led to this conclusion. Put another way it seems that value judgments must be supported by factual information.[110]

5.13 Costs of Proxy Solicitation

The problem of when the costs of proxy solicitation may properly be charged to the corporation is one which has received more attention in the U.S. than in Canada.[111] However, it would probably be correct to say that the general law of the two countries (and in England) on this topic is not dissimilar. The broad principle which governs[112] is that reasonable expenditures to allow shareholders to decide intelligently in respect to corporate policies are allowable, but not if the purpose of the solicitation is purely to maintain the directors in office. Does it follow, then, that reasonable proxy expenditures in connection with annual meetings will always be acceptable? This would be the case, one would suppose, even where the only substantial item of business on the agenda was the election of new directors, since annual meetings are required by law. Certainly any reasonable expenses would be protected under a system of mandatory proxies such as we have now in the uniform provinces, provided they meet the test of *bona fide* concern for the best interests of the company as a whole. Much the same principle would apply in the case of special meetings designed to deal with particular topics. Provided the meeting was called to deal with some matter involving a genuine issue of company policy, expenses incurred in the mandatory solicitation of proxies would be immune from attack.[113]

---

determine whether the stated conclusion regarding the company's liquidity needs was justified on the evidence at hand. Without such additional material it would be difficult to judge whether the proposed course of action would in fact be successful or whether some alternative scheme might be equally effective or even more so. It was held that more specific information should have been provided before a shareholder could make an intelligent decision on the question.

[110]The provincial commissions have not been noticeably active in applying sanctions against persons soliciting proxies where the information is inadequate or misleading. In contrast the SEC has been particularly vigorous in this regard in part perhaps because that agency is required to vet proxies and their accompanying information before they are sent. See L. Getz, "The Structure of Shareholder Democracy".

[111]There is, however, guidance in some corporations legislation. See ss. 101(7), 102(8) and 109(6) of the BCA and s. 103(5) of the CCA and s. 137(6) of the CBCA. These provisions generally reflect the principles of the discussion of common law which follows.

[112]As stated in Loss, vol. 2, pp. 859-65.

[113]*Peel v. London and N.W. Ry. Co.*, [1907] 1 Ch. 5, 23 T.L.R. 85 (C.A.) is a suitable illustration. There an attempt by dissident shareholders to enjoin the payment of proxy expenses from corporate funds was unsuccessful. The directors had called a meeting to explain their reasons for recommending a

So far we have considered only what sort of purposes are legitimate in proxy solicitation. There remains the question of what *methods* are appropriate, or perhaps better stated, what types of expenditure are permissible, assuming always that the requirement that any type of expenditure allowed must be reasonable in the circumstances. The case law gives little guidance on how far the law should go in circumscribing the methods to be employed in proxy solicitation in addition to traditional solicitation by mail.[114]

An additional problem concerns the propriety of reimbursing successful insurgents in a proxy fight from corporate funds. This question usually arises in connection with the effect of shareholder ratification, since a proposal to make reimbursement of this kind will almost always be accompanied by formal approval of a majority of shareholders. On principle one might suppose that the same principle of *bona fide* concern for corporate policy should apply as in the case of solicitation by management, and that reimbursement could be justified quite apart from ratification. Since, however, management is charged with the primary responsibility for policy, it might seem appropriate that the onus should rest on the insurgent shareholders to show that they had acted *bona fide* in the best interests of the company; at all events a higher standard of proof should perhaps be

---

certain course of action and to garner support for their view. They did this in the genuine belief that their policy was in the best interests of the company. The court held that they had a duty to provide information about the course they were advocating and were perfectly justified in attempting to secure support for it. It would seem that as long as a proxy fight involves some legitimate corporate ruling issue, this will avoid the taint of impropriety, even though the directors stand to lose their positions if unsuccessful in their solicitation of support.

The case of *Campbell v. Australian Mutual Provident Society et al.* (1908), 77 L.J.P.C. 117, 99 L.T. 3, 24 T.L.R. 623 (P.C.) adds a gloss to the principle of the *Peel* case to the effect that where directors are making a legitimate appeal for support, they are under no obligation to disseminate the proposals of those shareholders who oppose them.

[114]A case which might have clarified this matter was *Rosenfeld v. Fairchild Engine and Airplane Corp.* (1955), 128 N.E. 2d 291 (N.Y. C.A.). Unfortunately, the members of the court split three ways, with no clear ratio emerging. The plaintiff in the case sought to establish various types of expenditure as *per se* improper, while admitting that the quantum of expenditure under each head was not unreasonable. The challenged items included professional solicitation costs, public relations counsel, entertainment and chartered airplanes and limousines. None of the seven judges in the case supported the plaintiffs' contention, although three (in dissent) found that proof of such unusual expenditures going beyond the bare minimum raised an inference of possible impropriety, calling for a specific determination on the evidence in each case. One decided against the plaintiff on grounds of lack of evidence, while three others held that in general, judicial enquiry should proceed no further than the requirement of reasonableness. They did however concede that the costs of professional proxy solicitation firms should only be charged to the corporation in cases where they are used to secure a quorum. Even this has been disputed see *Levin v. Metro Goldwyn Mayer Inc.* (1967), 264 F. Supp. 797 (S.D.N.Y.).

demanded of insurgents than management in establishing proper motive.

So far as ratification is concerned, there seems no reason why it should not be generally effective: the corporate body should be able to determine how its own moneys are spent.[115] This principle, however, is still subject to qualification by that elusive concept "fraud on the minority".[116] What sort of reimbursement would constitute such a fraud is difficult to determine. Presumably, however, expenditures unreasonable as to quantum would not be shielded by ratification, nor improper heads of expenditure[117] although this is perhaps less certain. In many cases, however, ratification will be employed even when it perhaps could be dispensed with, just to make sure that no question of impropriety remains. Shareholder ratification of proxy expenditures made by management would presumably operate in the same way.

5.14 Irregularity in Proxy Solicitation—Consequence for Transactions

Perhaps the most difficult problem in the law relating to proxies is the question of when procedural irregularities will invalidate actions taken in consequence thereof. As it is primarily a matter of corporate law, the topic will not be treated in detail here.[118] The problem in this area is not what constitutes an adequate proxy or circular but rather what is the effect of an inadequate one.

Fogler v. Norcan Oils Ltd. and Gridoil Freehold Leases Ltd.[119] is a leading authority. In that case an amalgamation of two companies was approved by a majority of shareholders, approved on application to the court and a certificate of amalgamation was issued by the Registrar of Companies. The amalgamation was later attacked and the trial judge found that the proxy statement did not disclose sufficient information to enable shareholders "to judge of the fairness and propriety of the scheme". However, a majority in the Supreme Court of Canada held that there was no power in the court to set aside an amalgamation thus consummated. Apparently the attack must be launched before the certificate of amalgamation is issued. However the case suggests that if the transactions impugned in time the court will not limit itself to a consideration of formal defects but will also consider what substantial effect the irregularity had (or might have had) on the outcome.

---

[115]The problem with this approach however as a policy matter is that it turns proxy struggles into escalating "all or nothing" contests. The insurgents must spend enough to win and reclaim their expenses on ratification; otherwise the vengeful incumbent majority will deny them any reimbursement. See the powerful dissent of Van Voorhis J. in *Rosenfeld, supra*, footnote 114, on this issue.

[116]See S. M. Beck "Analysis of Foss v. Harbottle" and Gower, *Modern Company Law*, 3rd ed. (1969), pp. 562-80.

[117]If one adopted the view of the dissent in *Rosenfeld, supra*, footnote 114.

[118]On the effects of breach of statutory duty see Gower, *Modern Company Law*, 3rd ed. (1969), p. 334ff; Wegenast, *Law of Canadian Companies*, 1931, p. 709ff (on breach of prospectus provisions.)

[119][1965] S.C.R. 36, 49 W.W.R. 321, 46 D.L.R. (2d) 630.

In *Garvie v. Axmith et al.* [120] the issue was faced squarely. There proxies solicited in connection with a shareholders meeting to approve a refinancing scheme were accompanied by financial information but omitted any explanation as to how the valuation was arrived at. The court held that the circular was deficient and struck down the resolutions passed at the meeting. In so doing the court established the principle that it is the right of each shareholder to receive sufficient information to enable him to come to an intelligent conclusion whether he should vote in favour of a proposal or against it.

Murphy v. Lindzon et al.[121] involves securities legislation more directly but leaves several important questions unresolved. It was concerned with the consequences which flow from non-compliance with s. 80 of the Act relating to brokers holding street name certificates. Was compliance with that section which requires brokers to forward proxy material to beneficial owners requesting voting instructions a necessary condition to the validity of the broker's exercise of the proxy or to the validity of the shareholders' meeting? At the meeting the chairman had disallowed votes of the plaintiff which in fact would have altered the election of directors; he based his action on the ground that the plaintiff had not given evidence of compliance with s. 80. The trial judge answered the first question negatively and refused to answer the second more general question regarding the effect of non-compliance as being hypothetical and too wide. However he did state that the chairman had no right to institute of his own motion an investigation as to whether the section had been complied with. On appeal the Ontario Court of Appeal held that there were insufficient facts to decide either question, thus leaving the construction of s. 80 to another day. The case does, however, suggest the court will look to all the facts in determining what would have been the practical results of conformity with statutory provisions. One may infer from the *Murphy* case that the purpose of a particular provision is all-important. Thus one may conservatively presume that if the provision not complied with was not designed for the protection of the party seeking to invalidate the transaction, no declaration of nullity of or even voidability will follow.

C. Timely Disclosure

5.15 Present Situation—Policy Statement Only
Two of the remarkable features about timely disclosure as a current technique of securities regulation are first, that it has been introduced

---

[120][1962] 2 O.R. 65, 31 D.L.R. (2d) 65 (H.C.). For other cases involving defective proxies and shareholder action see *Pender v. Lushington* (1877), 6 Ch. D. 70 at p. 78; *Baillie v. Oriental Telephone and Electric Co. Ltd.*, [1915] 1 Ch. 503, 31 T.L.R. 643 (C.A.); *Montreal Trust Co. v. The Oxford Pipe Line Co. Ltd.*, [1942] O.R. 490, [1942] 3 D.L.R. 619 (C.A.); *Charlebois v. Bienvenue*, [1968] 2 O.R. 217, 68 D.L.R. (2d) 578 (C.A.); *Goldex Mines Ltd. v. Revill* (1974), 7 O.R. (2d) 216, 54 D.L.R. (3d) 672 (C.A.).
[121][1969] 2 O.R. 704, 6 D.L.R. (3d) 492 (C.A.); reversing [1969] 1 O.R. 631, 3 D.L.R. (3d) 423 (H.C.).

so recently and secondly, that it has been enunciated in policy statement only and not in legislation.

A timely disclosure policy statement was first issued by the OSC in September, 1968[122] simultaneously with a similar policy of the TSE which amended the latter's 1965 policy.[123] It became a uniform act policy in April, 1971[124] and was revised in December, 1971. Its enforcement depends on the use of the cease-trading power.

The phrase which best sums up the over-all aim of this policy is equality of access to information; it attempts as far as possible to see that all investors have available to them the most current information regarding an issuer, whether it be favourable or unfavourable.[125] The achievement of equality is intended to serve both a broad and a narrow purpose: first, to ensure that securities markets perform their pricing and evaluation function in the most prompt and efficient manner, and secondly, and more specifically, to prevent "insiders" (not limited to statutorily defined persons) from taking advantage of their special position.[126] These purposes are criticized as not realistic because much

---

[122]Sept. 1968 OSCB 192.

[123]The Merger Report (para. 2.10) gives this explanation: "The changes in financing patterns which led to [the Merger] study had earlier caused the Commission and the Exchange to examine their positions regarding timely disclosure. Investors were frequently acting on inadequate or misleading information. The Exchange had the power to halt or suspend trading until such time as adequate information was made available and circulated. Through an amendment to the Act [currently s. 144] the Commission was given the power to suspend trading. A coordinated study was embarked upon by the Exchange and the Commission and, as a result, in October 1968 both the Exchange and the Commission published 'timely disclosure' policies which, if not adhered to, might result in the suspension of trading until proper information was made available to the investor. Both were aimed at requiring the timely disclosure by an issuer of information relating to changes or events of a material nature concerning the affairs of the issuer which would significantly affect investor decisions".

[124]Uniform Policy 2-12 "Timely Disclosure", CCH vol. 2, para. 54-882; Quebec Policy 24, CCH vol. 3, para. 66-079.

[125]The policy statement reasons this way: "It is essential that all investors be placed on an equal footing insofar as knowledge of the material facts regarding the company which has securities in the hands of the public [*sic*]...Unfavourable facts must be disclosed as promptly, fully and plainly as favourable facts."

[126]This latter purpose has been artfully articulated by Chairman Cary of the SEC in *In the Matter of Cady, Roberts and Co.* (1961), 40 S.E.C. 907 (reproduced in Jennings and Marsh, *Securities Regulation*, 3rd ed. (1972) at pp. 1126-7 who set forth the foundation for insiders' obligation to disclose (or refrain from trading) as follows:
"...the obligation rests on two principal elements; first, the existence of a relationship giving access, directly or indirectly, to information intended to be available only for a corporate purpose and not for the personal benefit of anyone, and second, the inherent unfairness involved where a party takes advantage of such information knowing it is unavailable to those with whom he is dealing."

of professional investment involves getting accurate information first. However this should not prevent the regulatory regime from attempting to make the getting or at least the giving out as fair as possible, and to force professional investment advisors to concentrate on intelligent appraisal of information that is made available to all.

Timely disclosure may be analyzed as involving three major problem areas: what is the material information to which the policy applies, when should it be disclosed and how? To some extent the answers to these questions overlap.

The policy statement provides a comprehensive but not exhaustive listing of material information as follows:[127]

"Material changes or developments include:

"1. Actual or proposed changes in the control of the company,

"2. Actual or proposed acquisition or disposition of material assets,

"3. Proposed take-overs, mergers, consolidations, amalgamations or re-organizations,

"4. Any material discoveries, changes or developments in the company's resources, technology, products or contracts, which would materially affect the earnings of the company upwards or downwards,

"5. Proposed changes in capital structure, including stock splits or stock dividends,

"6. Indicated changes in earnings upwards or downwards of more than recent average size and changes in dividends,

"7. Any other material change in the affairs of the company which could reasonably be expected to affect materially the value of the security."[128]

The omnibus clause listed as item 7 is really a test that runs through the other six items and provides the yardstick against which materiality is measured.[129]

In a note on *SEC v. Texas Gulf Sulphur*, 82 Harv. L. Rev. 938 (1968-69), the commentator for the Harvard Law Review suggests at p. 940: "In the Texas Gulf Sulphur litigation, the SEC appears to be seeking to bring the existing securities market into the closest possible conformity with a perfectly competitive model in which all investors have equal access to relevant information". Subscription to such an ideal is implicit in much U.S. federal securities legislation.

[127]Sept. 1968 OSCB pp. 192-193 and Uniform Policy 2-12, *supra*, footnote 126.

[128]A preliminary technical point is that several of the examples refer to "a company" rather than the broader term "issuer". It is clear that the broader term should be implied. One would find it difficult for example to imagine the withdrawal by a bank sponsoring in partnership a real estate investment trust as not being subject to the timely disclosure policy simply because the trust was not a company.

[129]Clause 7 contains a fairly common test of materiality. Bill 20, s. 1(1)22 statutizes an essentially similar test. In commenting on stop-orders under the 1933 U.S. Securities Act Professor Loss (vol. 1, p. 305) identifies the other test, which is largely similar, frequently seen in the case law:

"In every stop-order proceeding the Commission does have to consider materiality, which it has defined in the common law tradition as limiting the information required 'to those matters as to which an average prudent investor ought reasonably to be informed before purchasing the security registered.' (Rule 405; see also *Charles A. Howard*, 1 SEC 6, 8, 18 FTC 626

The question of timing—when to disclose the statement—is more difficult. This topic may be better subdivided into two distinct issues: when does an item become material information and secondly, assuming an event is material information, when must it be disclosed? It is not possible to answer the first question by making a simple distinction between fact and opinion and designating information as material at the point at which it changes from being opinion to fact. This distinction breaks down if one considers an example such as a new technology or product; if sufficiently weighty, an authoritative expert opinion regarding the proposed innovation would surely be material. Furthermore the statement deals in several instances with "proposed" as well as "actual" changes, acquisitions and other reorganization; an estimate of the effect of such development inevitably takes one into the realm of conjecture. Ultimately the only way of resolving this question is to apply the materiality test sometimes supplemented with the concern as to whether disclosure of this item at this preliminary stage would be more misleading than informative. But it is generally true to say that when something can be reported as fact rather than opinion it would probably come within the statement. Moreover, and here we begin to encroach upon the "how" as opposed to the "when" of timely disclosure, the report should disclose the fact rather than the opinion.[130]

The uniform act policy statement goes into somewhat more detail regarding when one must disclose. It states that "immediate disclosure of all material and significant information...is encouraged" and that "Disclosure should be made, of a proposal or proposed change when a decision accepting or recommending acceptance of such proposal or proposed change has been made, in other cases of material change when such change has occurred or when such change has been agreed upon by the relevant parties, notwithstanding that all the details may not have been documented."
In an acquisition situation, for example, it would be appropriate to disclose when a letter of intent has been signed rather than waiting for a formal contract or for the later closing of the transaction.
The direction to disclose is not without qualification. An issuer is permitted to keep back information where a premature announcement would result in more injury than benefit. This is an area which involves

---

(1934)). The Lord Davey report of 1895, one of the periodic reports on English company law reform, used much the same language: '...every contract or fact is material which would influence the judgment of a prudent investor in determining whether he would subscribe for the shares or debentures offered by the prospectus.' Cmd. 7779 (1895) s. 14(5); see *Macleay* v. *Tait*, [1906] A.C. 24 (H.L.)."
[130]Texas Gulf Sulphur Co. learned this lesson the hard way, through extensive litigation in the U.S. In its first press release about its significant mineral find it gave opinions (about the discovery)—later judged to be misleading—rather than hard facts such as drill core results, from which investors and their specialist advisers could form *their* opinions: *SEC v. Texas Gulf Sulphur* (1968), 401 F. 2d 833 (2nd Cir.).

exceedingly difficult judgments and the qualifying provision should be quoted in full:

"The Commission recognizes that there may be cases where disclosure might occasion harm to the company which might outweigh any possible damage to the shareholder by withholding the information. Where this arises management should take every possible precaution to ensure that no trading whatsoever takes place by any insiders or individuals who are associated with the company and who may be in possession of the confidential information."

To assist in the decision the Commission invites issuers to discuss the problem with it "if management has an unusual or difficult situation confronting it"; in the case of listed securities the Exchange also should be consulted.[131]

In the December, 1971 revision[132] a paragraph was added to the policy statement stating that items 1, 2, 3 and 5 in the list of material changes quoted above "must be discussed with the Commission prior to disclosure to the investing public."[133]

Turning finally to the manner in which the information is to be divulged, timely disclosure will normally be made by a press release which goes to the Dow Jones wire service and for listed stocks to the TSE and to the appropriate members of the news media. This is a difficult area of timely disclosure policy to apply, and is perhaps best understood on a case-by-case basis. With enactment of the former policy statement into legislation in Bill 20 one may expect that Canadian jurisprudential guidance will eventually be forthcoming: until then it will be necessary to resort to the plentiful American examples which provide a veritable thicket of suggestions for interpretation.[134]

[131]The management of Texas Gulf Sulphur (see, *ibid.*) in November, 1963 chose not to disclose information from its first drill hole results (later judged to be material) from what provided to be a remarkable ore body. The justification for the decision was that the company would be seriously prejudiced by its inability to purchase surrounding mining properties at constant prices if disclosure were made. That decision itself was not impugned in the subsequent litigation.

[132]Dec. 1971 OSCB 198.

[133]In an explanatory note (Ontario Policy 3-23 "Administration: Timely Disclosure Policy: Uniform Act Policy 2-12", Dec. 1971 OSCB 201, CCH vol. 2, paras. 54-917 and 54-882) the Ontario Commission indicated that only the briefest of discussions was envisaged; for the most part it wished simply to be advised of the proposals in question. The note states that in situations where timing is critical it will be appropriate to communicate with the Commission by means of a telephone call to the chairman or vice-chairman, or in their absence to the director or chief legal investigation officer. The Commission indicated a twofold reason for requiring prior discussion:

(a) to enable it to stop trading where necessary to permit the information to be disseminated, and

(b) by being aware of developments before publication to enable it to stop trading where the market was responding to rumours and not fact.

[134]See also the illuminating pamphlet "Corporate Disclosure and Insider Information", A Panel Interview with Philip A. Loomis, Jr., then SEC General Counsel (now a Commissioner for the SEC) presented at the Fall Conference of the Financial Analysts Federation, Atlanta, Georgia, October 7, 1968.

5.16 Legislative Reform

Bill 20 introduces major changes in the area of timely disclosure. In brief the present scheme is elevated from the somewhat nebulous status of a policy statement and placed in the body of the Bill with appropriate modifications to bring it into line with the rest of the new statute. This change is coupled with a new liability provision which makes trading and "tipping" while material changes are undisclosed an offence.

The requirement that material changes be disclosed is in s. 76. It contains two distinct commands: first, the change be published forthwith by means of a press release, and secondly, that a report of the change be filed with the Commission within ten days of its occurrence.[135] There is also an escape clause[136] regarding information the publication of which would be "unduly detrimental" to the issuer.[137] The report to the Commission must still be made but may be marked "confidential" and accompanied by written reasons for non-disclosure.[138]

It is instructive to compare this provision with its predecessor, uniform act Policy 2-12. First of all the obligations imposed by the section apply to reporting issuers. This change is in keeping with the rest of Part XVII dealing with regular financial disclosure.[139] Secondly, the subject-matter which must be disclosed is a "material fact or change". This differs somewhat from the present provisions, since the definition of "material" in Bill 20[140] uses the definite word "would" in place of the vaguer "could" or "might" as used presently in the most comprehensive of the instances of material change listed in the policy statement ("change in the affairs of the company which *could* reasonably be expected to affect materially the value of the security").

There is also little change regarding the question of timing. The adjective "forthwith" in the new provisions is roughly equivalent in its general import to the language in the policy statement favouring immediate disclosure. The exemption for disclosure causing detriment is also the same. Furthermore the new section offers no guidance on the question of determining the point at which an evolving development or project becomes a material change. The major alteration is the imposition of formal reporting obligations (to the Commission) with respect to the material changes with a specific time limit of ten days.

With regard to the manner of disclosure, the obligation to issue a press release means roughly the same as the exhortation to make disclosure "through news media" contained in the present policy statement.

Bill 20 contains no specific requirement that the material change be

---

[135]The report must be filed in accordance with the Regulation.
[136]Section 76(2).
[137]For some jurisprudence interpreting this phrase in a different context see, *supra*, part 5.07(3), text at footnote 64 and following.
[138]Section 76(4) provides for this confidential status to be maintained indefinitely provided this is confirmed with the Commission every ten days.
[139]*Supra*, text at footnote 14.
[140]Section 1(1)22. See, *supra*, footnote 135 and, *post*, chapter 6, footnote 79.

discussed with the Commission prior to disclosure, but this particular feature of the present guidelines may be placed in the regulation or retained in a revamped version of Policy 2-12.

So much for the obligation to disclose. What is new is a prohibition on tipping or trading on inside information. Section 77 prohibits a person or company from (a) purchasing or selling the securities of a reporting issuer with knowledge of a material change in the affairs of the issuer which he or it knew or ought to have known had not been generally disclosed, or (b) informing another person or company about this material change before it is disclosed, other than in the necessary course of business. This provision naturally invites comparison with s. 133, the civil liability provision of the Bill, which grants an enlarged remedy to those purchasing from or selling to insiders against insiders, tippers and tippees.

As initially drafted in Bill 98, s. 77 prohibited trading by a person in possession of inside information even though he had not made use of the information as in the case of automatic dividend reinvestment or employee purchase plans. To accomodate this situation Bill 20 introduces a reverse onus defence which avoids the offence where the defendant proves he did not make use of the information.[141] Another such amendment[142] prohibits a tipper from advising another to trade where the tipper is in possession of inside information. This is intended to prevent a tipper from escaping culpability by simply advising the trade without passing on the information.

---

[141]Section 77(2) of Bill 20.
[142]Section 77(3) of Bill 20.

Chapter 6
Insider Trading

6.01 Background
Insider trading first became subject to statutory regulation in a substantial fashion with the introduction of the uniform act in Ontario in 1966. The provisions which then became a part of securities law represented an implementation of the recommendations of the Kimber Report, which had defined insider trading in a general way as denoting "purchases or sales of securities of a company effected by or on behalf of a person whose relationship to the company is such that he is likely to have access to relevant material information concerning the company not known to the general public."[1] Statutory controls were needed essentially because the development of the common law in broadening the fiduciary responsibility of corporate insiders had been stunted, in particular by an English decision at the turn of the century.[2]

---

[1]There were several statutory antecedents. An amendment in 1935 (1935 (Can.), c. 55, s. 15) added s. 96A to the Companies Act requiring directors to report their transactions in the company's shares to the annual general meeting and prohibited speculation (a purchase and sale or sale and purchase within six months) by directors in such shares. The Ontario Corporations Act commencing in 1953 (1953 (Ont.), c. 19, s. 71) required directors to report their transactions to the annual general meeting upon request by a shareholder. But these provisions, at best, served only to adumbrate a solution. And the Kimber Committee concluded: "These provisions have proved ineffectual".

[2]*Percival v. Wright*, [1902] 2 Ch. 421 (C.A.). But let the Kimber Report speak for itself (paras. 2.01 to 2.03):

"Although there is no statistical information available showing the volume of such trading, there is no doubt that it takes place. The question which the Committee considered was whether this trading is a matter of such concern to the investing public that rules to control it should be established. The Committee's conclusion...is that statutory rules are required in the public interest.

"In our opinion, it is not improper for an insider to buy or sell securities in his own company. Indeed, it is generally accepted that it is beneficial to a company to have officers and directors purchase securities in the company as they thereby acquire a direct financial interest in the welfare of the company. It is impossible to justify the proposition that an investment so made can never be realized or liquidated merely because the investor is an insider. However, in our view, it is improper for an insider to use confidential information acquired by him by virtue of his position as an insider to make profits by trading in the securities of his company. The ideal securities market should be a free and open market with the prices thereon based upon the fullest possible knowledge of all relevant facts among traders. Any factor which tends to destroy or put in question this concept lessens the confidence of the investing public in the market place, and is, therefore, a matter of public concern.

"While the existing law recognizes that in certain circumstances a director is not entitled to profit personally as the result of the use of inside information, such law is not, in our opinion, adequate to prevent or

In view of the importance the Kimber Committee attached to the "free and open [securities] market with the prices thereon based upon the fullest knowledge of all relevant facts among traders", it is somewhat surprising that it did not also recommend legislative provisions for timely disclosure of material changes. Indeed, the imposition of sanctions on trading by insiders using confidential information addresses just one end of the problem. The other is the public release of the information so it is no longer confidential. The aim is that, with the elimination of the temptation which might entice insiders to take improper advantage, the securities markets may operate in as close conformity as possible with the theoretically perfect model which the Kimber Report set forth as the ideal. In sum, the overriding objective is equality of investment opportunity.[3]

It is surprising that regulation of insider trading has come so late to the securities markets. One reason may be that business ethics operated as a partial sanction to limit some of the most flagrant kinds of insider trading. Perhaps a more practical reason is that a complete cure was hard to devise. Even the present Regulation can be easily avoided by the unscrupulous through the use of nominees and hidden brokerage accounts. And even this partial cure is expensive. The reporting scheme now operating imposes a substantial paperwork burden on the vast majority of ethical corporate insiders in an attempt to reveal or deter the unethical few.[4] But when all is said and done, the most significant reason for the absence of insider trading regulation was simply neglect, for the basic unfairness of insider trading on the basis of confidential knowledge cannot be denied. And it is indicative of the "coming of age" of present securities legislation that it has focused directly on the problem.

In this chapter we first briefly explore the common law background to insider trading and then turn to the twin statutory techniques of regulation: the obligation to report and liability for misuse of information. Changes in other Canadian securities and corporate legislation since the 1966 Ontario Act have somewhat extended the statutory controls. These extensions will be commented on in context throughout this chapter. Since the Canadian legislative framework is derived from the U.S. federal rules, these are briefly considered. Then the chapter discusses such matters as who is an insider, when he must report, when does liability arise, how liability may be enforced and the

---

discourage all the potential abuses inherent to the position of special advantage enjoyed by the insider. We believe that the law should clearly provide that the use by insiders, for their own profit or advantage, of particular information known to them but not available to the general public is wrong and that the law should give appropriate remedies to those aggrieved by such misuse."

[3]See the discussion of this objective in connection with timely disclosure, *ante*, part 5.15, especially footnotes 125 and 126.

[4]What is unfortunately lacking as a basis for the recent and future reform of the insider regulations is economic analysis of the evidence and consequences of insider trading (see the Kimber Report, para. 2.01, quoted, *supra*, footnote 2). One of the leading spokesmen for this need is Professor H.G. Manne, *Insider Trading and The Stock Market*, New York, Free Press, 1966, especially pp. 1-15.

relevant limitation periods. Bill 20 introduces significant extensions to the existing insider liability and controls as well as important reforms resulting from the Canadian Mutual Funds Report which replace in part self-regulation and policy statement controls to guard against self-dealing by those closely associated with mutual funds. These latest reform initiatives will be considered separately at the end of this chapter.

6.02 Common Law Foundation

In considering the common law background to insider trading, a distinction should be drawn for analytical purposes between any duty owed by an insider to a corporation and any duty he might owe to other securities holders of the corporation. In the first category—duty to the corporation—the common law had established a fiduciary responsibility broadly comparable to that presently established by legislation. Indeed there are several areas of insider trading where this limb of the common law may reach beyond the statutory regime.

It has long been accepted that directors and officers of a corporation have a fiduciary responsibility to it. In the hallmark case of *Regal (Hastings) Ltd. v. Gulliver*,[5] Lord Porter stated that a director must not make a profit out of property acquired by reason of his relationship to the company of which he is a director. Viscount Sankey's statement of fiduciary obligation in the same case is that the director must not realize a profit arising in the course of his position as director of the corporation. And Lord McMillan enunciated a proposition which perhaps is slightly broader in ambit.[6] The director must not realize a profit arising by use of knowledge or information acquired during his course of duty.[7]

---

[5][1942] 1 All E.R. 378, [1967] 2 A.C. 134n (H.L.) expressly adopted by the Supreme Court of Canada in *Zwicker v. Stanbury*, [1953] 2 S.C.R. 438, [1954] 1 D.L.R. 257 and in *Peso. Silver Mines Ltd. v. Cropper*, [1966] S.C.R. 673, 58 D.L.R. (2d) 1, 56 W.W.R. 641 and applied to senior officers in *Canadian Aero Service Ltd. v. O'Malley*, [1974] S.C.R. 592, 40 D.L.R. (3d) 371, 11 C.P.R. (2d) 206.

[6][1942] 1 All E.R. 378 at pp. 381-2 and pp. 391-2, respectively, [1967] 2 A.C. 134n (H.L.).

[7]The Kimber Report (para. 2.25) also referred to Professor Gower's summary of this fiduciary principle in *Modern Company Law*, 3rd ed. (1969) at pp. 546-7:

"Directors are not permitted, either during or after their service with the company, to use for their own purposes anything entrusted to them for use on behalf of the company. This principle is not restricted to property in the strict sense; it also includes trade secrets and confidential information. This principle, it is submitted, should be wide enough to cover cases, such as *Percival* v. *Wright*, in which directors have used confidential information (for example, knowledge of an impending dividend declaration or take-over bid) to speculate successfully in their company's shares. The fact that the company itself suffers no damage ought, on general principles, to be irrelevant."

But the Committee preferred not to rely on the common law, concluding thus:

A more recent House of Lords' decision, *Boardman v. Phipps,*[8] weaves together various strands of judicial thinking and is authority for the proposition that knowledge obtained in the course of a trust relationship is property subject to a trust obligation. From this, one could conclude that knowledge acquired by the director or officer in the course of his service, is clothed with the trust obligation and must not be used by him when his service ends.[9] But the most interesting feature of *Boardman v. Phipps* is that it is not limited to a fiduciary duty of directors or officers. The individual who was required to disgorge profits was the solicitor to a trust who had failed to secure approval from all of the trustees or all of the beneficiaries to use knowledge acquired during his employment by the trust for personal profit. The solicitor too wore the mantle of fiduciary responsibility. Similarly, persons employed or retained by a corporation such as lawyers, accountants or other advisers may find they are held to a strict account by the fiduciary principle.[10] Furthermore, in recent corporate reform legislation in Canada the difficulty of causing the corporation to sue offending directors when they control the company has been partly removed by the creation of the representative or derivative suit.[11] This gives a minority shareholder a statutory right to bring an action on behalf of the company subject to certain conditions.[12]

However, there are residual difficulties. For example, in the absence of a reporting obligation, it may be extremely difficult to determine when a director has abused his position. More significantly the common law has not developed a similar fiduciary responsibility owed by a substantial shareholder to the corporation when he is not also a director or officer.[13] This deficiency provided a clear invitation for

---

"However, the Committee is of the view that there is sufficient uncertainty in the present state of the law to justify a recommendation that legislation should provide a specific cause of action in favour of the company against an insider who profits from improper trading in the securities of the company." See also the Proposals for a New Business Corporations Law (Commentary, vol. 1, paras. 263 and 264) where the draftsmen concluded that the common law was adequate to establish recovery by a corporation against its insiders and for that reason recommended the excision of this limb of statutory liability from federal corporations legislation. However, they subsequently resiled from that position and the new Act leaves the former twin-limbed statutory principle intact (CBCA, s. 125(5)(b)).

[8][1967] 2 A.C. 46, [1966] 3 All E.R. 721 (H.L.).
[9]Confirmed to a point in *Canadian Aero Services Ltd. v. O'Malley, supra,* footnote 5, and *Industrial Development Consultants Ltd. v. Cooley,* [1972] 2 All E.R. 162, [1972] 1 W.L.R. 443 (H. Ct.).
[10]*Ibid.*
[11]The difficulty is enshrined in the rule in *Foss v. Harbottle* (1843), 2 Hare 461, 67 E.R. 189 (H. Ct. of Ch.). For examples of reforms see the BCA, s. 99 and the CBCA, s. 232.
[12]For the first important tests of this action see *Farnham v. Fingold,* [1973] 2 O.R. 132, 33 D.L.R. (3d) 156 (C.A.) and *Goldex Mines Ltd. v. Revill* (1974), 7 O.R. (2d) 216, 54 D.L.R. (3d) 672 (C.A.)
[13]*Farnham v. Fingold, op. cit.,* and for U.S. authority see *Perlman v. Feldmann* (1955), 219 F. 2d 173 (C.A. 2nd Cir.); *Jones v. Ahmanson,* 460 P. 2d

statutory reform.[14]

6.03 Statutory Framework in General and Its Application

The two reform techniques proposed by the Kimber Committee were the institution of compulsory reporting by insiders of every trade made by them in the securities of the corporation of which they are insiders, and the imposition of liability on insiders and certain persons or companies connected with them who use specific confidential information in their trading.[15]

The insider trading reporting and liability provisions of the Act apply only to trading by insiders in capital securities of a corporation as defined and not securities of a trust, unincorporated association or other person that would be subject to the distribution provisions. Capital securities are defined to include both shares and debt obligations whether secured or unsecured.[16] The corporation to which the reporting scheme applies is defined in the same limited way as "corporation" in Part XII, which deals with financial disclosure

---

464 (Cal. S. Ct.) and *Rosenfeld v. Black* (1971), 445 F. 2d 1337 (C.A. 2nd Cir.).
[14]The Kimber Report (para. 2.22) summarized the deficiency as follows:
"In the English case of *Percival v. Wright*, it was held that no fiduciary relationship exists between a director of a company and its shareholders. The wide scope of this decision was qualified to a certain extent by the Privy Council in *Allen v. Hyatt* where it was held that in certain special circumstances there is a fiduciary relationship. The extent to which *Allen v. Hyatt* qualifies *Percival v. Wright* is uncertain. It is probably limited to a very narrow class of case in which the shareholder and the director meet virtually face-to-face and the director is put in a fiduciary relationship by the conduct of the parties. Even if *Percival v. Wright* were judicially overruled with the result that directors would then owe a fiduciary duty to the shareholders of the company of which they are directors, the courts would be unlikely to impose such duty on insiders other than directors, such as officers or principal shareholders; nor is it likely that a fiduciary relationship would be established by jurisprudence to assist a purchaser of securities from an insider if such purchaser was not at that time a shareholder of the company. The Committee accordingly recommends that the so-called doctrine of *Percival v. Wright* be abolished by statutory enactment, to be replaced by legislative rules...governing the legal relationship between insiders of a company and persons with whom they trade in the company's securities."

It should be noted, however, that in a particularly flagrant case of "unfair dealing" between a director and the shareholders of a company, wilful concealment of material information may lead to a finding of fraud. Thus in the recent Quebec case of *R. v. Littler* (1972), 41 D.L.R. (3d) 523, 13 C.C.C. (2d) 530 (Que. Ct. Sess.); conviction upheld 65 D.L.R. (3d) 443, sentence reduced 467 (C.A.) the accused, an insider of a company, bought shares from a shareholder, without disclosing a secret arrangement to dispose of his shares to another company at a vastly increased price. The court distinguished *Percival v. Wright*, [1902] 2 Ch. 421 (C.A.) and convicted the accused of fraud. See also, *post*, part 9.10.
[15]Kimber Report, para. 2.04*ff*.
[16]Section 109(1)(a). Bill 20 changes all this so that all trading by insiders in "securities" of a "reporting issuer" will be caught. (Section 1(1)36 defines "reporting issuer".) The new provisions will apply, for example, to a debenture issued by a trust which is a reporting issuer.

requirements,[17] since parallel requirements exist in the BCA for Ontario incorporated companies.[18]

It is important to recognize that the reporting obligation is automatic and comprehensive. It applies to every trade by an insider in his corporation's capital securities whether or not he has used inside information. The liability technique is more limited. It only becomes operative when it can be shown that the insider has made use of specific confidential information with all the difficult problems of proof attendant thereto.[19] The two techniques are connected. The reporting of the trade is intended to permit the potential plaintiff corporation or shareholder to determine whether in any given trade it is likely or unlikely that the insider has used specific confidential information.[20] But here of course lies the problem. The sophisticated unscrupulous insider will either fail to report or trade through nominees to avoid discovery.

6.04 United States Rules

The Kimber Committee was primarily influenced by s. 16 of the 1934 U.S. Securities Exchange Act which requires defined insiders to report their trades. The reports are published in a monthly bulletin of the SEC. The reporting provisions of s. 16 are coupled with a "short swing" liability provision designed to prevent speculation by insiders. It makes the insider liable to disgorge any profit to the corporation when he buys and sells or sells and buys within a six-month period with certain limited exceptions. The liability is automatic. Any profit accruing from the impugned transaction must be handed over to the insider's corporation whether or not he used inside information.

---

[17]Section 109(1)(b). See, *ante*, part 5.03. The equivalent in Bill 20 is Part XVII, now retitled "Continuous Disclosure".

[18]With Bill 20 (Parts XVII and XX and s. 1(1)36) extends the application of insider trading reporting and liability provisions and continuous disclosure provisions to Ontario incorporated companies which meet the public issuance tests and consequently these provisions have been deleted from Bill 21, "An Act to amend The Business Corporations Act" (4th Sess.), 30th Legislature Ontario, ss. 4 and 5.

[19]*Green et al. v. Charterhouse Group Canada Ltd. et. al.* (1976), 12 O.R. (2d) 280 (C.A.); affirming [1973] 2 O.R. 677, 35 D.L.R. (3d) 161 (H.C.) the first case to interpret the insider liability provisions, eases the plaintiff's task by shifting the burden of proof to the defendant once the plaintiff establishes certain preliminaries.

[20]For these two techniques see ss. 110 and 113 of the Act (Bill 20, ss. 104 and 133). Similar provisions were inserted in Ontario corporations legislation, currently ss. 148 and 150 of the BCA. (Repealed by Bill 21, s. 4. See, *supra*, footnote 18.) Parallel provisions were subsequently introduced in securities and corporations legislation in Alberta and Manitoba, securities legislation in Saskatchewan and the CCA and CBCA. Quebec has recently amended its Securities Act to bring it into substantial conformity with the securities legislation of the five provinces to the west. Its insider liability section follows the somewhat broader provision contained in the federal legislation. The three Atlantic Provinces, Nova Scotia, New Brunswick and Prince Edward Island have recently considered amending their securities legislation and it seems probable that the introduction of insider reporting and liability provisions will be a high priority if such a project is carried out.

Equally, if he completes the two steps of a purchase and sale (or the reverse) but takes pains to ensure that more than six months elapse between the two, he is immune from liability under s. 16 even if he did use inside information.[21] This rather harsh short-swing automatic liability provision was enacted primarily because of the belief that substantial short-swing speculation brought enormous profits to insiders in years prior to the 1929 stock market crash and to some large extent helped to bring it about.[22]

The second U.S. provision with which more than a nodding familiarity is required in the Canadian context is Rule 10b-5, promulgated under s. 10(b) of the 1934 Securities Exchange Act. The rule, *inter alia*, brands as unlawful misstatements or omissions of material fact in connection with a securities transactions.[23] While the rule does not explicitly provide for civil liability, the courts have held that its violation constitutes a civil wrong, giving rise to a remedy in damages.[24]

6.05 Who is an Insider

The first question to be answered in the Act is: who is an insider? Here the Kimber Committee borrowed from s. 16 of the 1934 U.S. Act and opted for a statutory definition which would produce certainty and precision rather than comprehensiveness.[25] The definition of "insider"

---

[21]A remedy for this latter transgression may be found in s. 10 of the same Act.
[22]See *e.g.*, Manne, *Insider Trading and The Stock Market*, New York, Free Press, 1966.
[23]Rule 10b-5 reads as follows:
  "It shall be unlawful for any person, directly or indirectly, by the use of any means or instrumentality of interstate commerce, or of the mails, or of any facility of any national securities exchange,
  (1) to employ any device, scheme or artifice to defraud,
  (2) to make any untrue statement of a material fact or to omit to state a material fact necessary in order to make the statements made, in the light of the circumstances under which they were made, not misleading, or
  (3) to engage in any act, practice, or course of business which operates or would operate as a fraud or deceit upon any person,
  in connection with the purchase or sale of any security."
[24]*Fischmann v. Raytheon Mfg. Co.* (1951), 188 F. 2d 783 (C.A. 2nd. Cir.). The U.S. Supreme Court settled the question in a footnote in *Superintendent of Insurance of New York v. Bankers Life and Casualty Co.* (1971), 404 U.S. 6, 92 S. Ct. 165.
[25]Kimber Report (para. 2.05):
  "The Committee gave extensive consideration to the categories of persons to be included in the definition of insider. The definition must be sufficiently precise to give clear guidance to the business community, yet sufficiently flexible to prevent an insider from avoiding the intent of the legislation by artifice. While the scope of the definition should not be unnecessarily inclusive, we feel that a wide definition is preferable to a narrow one. This conclusion is based on the premise that the benefits which will be derived from reporting will be of prime importance. The fact that a person is an insider and therefore required to report does not *ipso facto* make his trading improper. In the view of the Committee, trading is improper and should be declared unlawful only if the insider does in fact abuse his position."

was structured so as to embrace three categories: directors, senior officers and shareholders "owning" more than ten per cent of the outstanding voting shares.[26]

(1) DIRECTORS

The first category—directors—involves a simple determination of fact. It is possible, however, that someone who has never formally been elected a director of a corporation but *de facto* acts as such will not be an insider within the meaning of the legislation.[27]

(2) SENIOR OFFICERS

The second class of insider is the senior officer. Here a somewhat more embroidered definition was used.[28]

The result is a category determined according to two tests: the first names positions within the corporate administrative structure (including functional substitutes, which the definition of director eschewed), and the second uses levels of compensation, *viz.*:

"i   the chairman or any vice-chairman of the board of directors, the

---

And see H.P. Crawford, "Insider Trading" and D.L. Johnston "Insider Trading Liability—A Comparison of U.S. and Ontario Legislation".

[26]Section 109(1)(c). Bill 20 contains essentially the same definition, except that the categories are grouped somewhat differently and the associate of an insider becomes an insider also (s. 1(1)18). "Corporation" has of course been replaced by "reporting issuer", in view of the fact that the Bill will apply to unincorporated associations (s. 1(1), paras. 19 and 36). Note also that "equity shares" has been replaced by "voting securities" (s. 1(1)42).

[27]One arrives at this position by inference. Section 3(a)(7) of the 1934 U.S. Act, from which the insider definitions are taken, defines "director" to mean "any director of a corporation or any person performing similar functions with respect to any organization, whether incorporated or unincorporated." Section 6(a) of the 1934 U.S. Act uses a similarly expansive formulation of the term director in requiring a majority of the board to sign the registration statement while s. 52(1) of the Ontario Act requiring the board to certify that a prospectus makes full, true and plain disclosure and s. 109(1)(c)(i) making a director an insider simply uses the term "director" without further definition. The inference is that by not including the wider wording available to it in the statutory analogies the Legislature intended to restrict the term to those who were directors formally elected.

See also the definition of officer and the "functional substitute" meaning of senior officer (*infra*, next footnote and text) where additional guidance is provided.

[28]The Kimber Committee's intent was this (para. 2.06):

"The definition should be broad enough to encompass those members of management who have access to confidential information and take part in the formulation of corporate decisions, but narrow enough to exclude junior officers, whether or not they have access to such information. Trading by such junior officers entails different considerations. Senior management itself would have an interest in ensuring that these persons do not trade on the basis of confidential information. The policing of such activity may well be left to management."

The conclusion in these last two sentences is the crucial one. The extension of liability to all employees in the 1971 amendments to the CCA (s. 100.4) and continued in the CBCA (s. 125(1)(d)), and in the 1973 Quebec Securities Act (s. 151) reflects a different conclusion. The CBCA, effective December, 1975, makes an even greater leap by extending liability to knowledgeable "tippees" (s. 125(1)(f)).

president, any vice-president, the secretary, the treasurer or the general manager of a company or any individual who performs functions for the company similar to those normally performed by an individual occupying any such office, and

"ii each of the five highest paid employees of a company, including any individual referred to in subparagraph i."[29]

As a result of this more comprehensive definition a company which designated its senior financial officer, manager of finance or comptroller instead of treasurer or vice-president—finance would find him included within the senior officer category. Also a mining development company might find its chief geologist in the insider category because he is highly rewarded for specialized skills on which the company is peculiarly dependent even though he is not a member of the formal executive hierarchy.[30]

The question of what forms of remuneration should be included may sometimes present problems in determining whether an individual is an insider on the basis of how much he is paid. For example, if cash bonuses are included, a company which provides significant incentives may find its leading salesman in a given year within the five highest paid employees, even though he is not an officer and will probably drop out of the group in a leaner year. If other forms of fringe benefits are included, a company heavily dependent on sophisticated technology might find the benefit package provided to its most

---

[29]Section 1(1)23 (s. 1(1)39 of Bill 20 substitutes "issuer" for company: otherwise the definition is the same).

[30]One corporation whose senior management apparently placed great emphasis on the safe and expert transportation of its executives from place to place discovered shortly after the insider reporting requirements were introduced that its chief pilot was among its five highest paid employees and was therefore a statutory insider.

"Officer" is defined in the Act to mean (s. 1(1)11):

"the chairman or any vice-chairman of the board of directors, the president, vice-president, secretary, assistant secretary, treasurer, assistant treasurer or general manager of a company, or any other person designated an officer of a company by by-law or similar authority."

Due either to the "functional substitute" extension or the remuneration test a company can have a senior officer who is not an officer.

The "functional substitute" language is derived from U.S. precedent. The instructions to the SEC insider reporting forms define officer to mean "a president, vice-president, treasurer, secretary, comptroller, and any other person who performs for an issuer, whether incorporated or unincorporated, functions corresponding to those performed by the foregoing officers". In a published opinion of the SEC's General Counsel further guidance is given. An assistant would be an officer if his chief was so inactive that the assistant was really performing his chief's function. However, an assistant, although performing some functions which might be those of his chief, would not be an "officer" so long as his duties were under the supervision of his chief (U.S. Fed. Sec. Law Rep., CCH vol. 3, para. 26-058). The CCA broadly follows the U.S. approach, categorizing "officers" as insiders and defining officer to mean "the chairman or vice-chairman of the board of directors, the president, vice-president, secretary, treasurer, comptroller, general manager, managing director or other individual who performs" similar functions (ss. 100(1) and 3(1)).

brilliant research scientist, composed perhaps, of pension contributions, stock options and a share in the royalties or patents originated by him, would bring him into the insider group. Since the premise of this second branch of the definition is that the best rewarded individuals in a company might be most privy to confidential information regardless of the function they perform, it seems a broad test of "pay" is appropriate. A reasonable guide in cases of choice might be the "aggregate remuneration paid"[31] to senior officers, which is a disclosure item in the prospectus and proxy information circular, coupled with some detailed instructions on what is included and what is excluded.[32]

It is a difficult policy question to determine how far down the chain of employment and how far outside the nexus of permanent employment the Legislature should go in designating insiders. The Kimber Committee chose a limited and more certain ambit and the Act reflects this conservative choice.[33]

(3) TEN PER CENT VOTING SHAREHOLDERS

When one turns to the third category of the insider definition based on share ownership, the interpretive difficulties are considerable. This

---

[31]The Kimber Committee recommended the test of "direct remuneration paid by the company or its subsidiaries" (para. 2.07) although, as we have seen, the actual legislation is more cryptic.

[32]See *e.g.*, Form 13, item 16 and Form 20, item 6 which exclude pension and insurance benefits and stock options from the terms. The Kimber Committee recommended a floor of $20,000 per annum (para. 2.07) for the "highest paid" test which the Legislature eschewed; one might infer from this that at least for smaller companies all forms of remuneration should be included. The Employment Standards Act, R.S.O. 1970, c. 147 as am., s. 1(i) defines the term "wages", which is presumably narrower than "pay", in a comprehensive way to include "any form of remuneration for work or services performed", but not tips and other gratuities. Another interpretive tool consistent with the broad test might be the amounts which may be deducted by a company as current employment expenses for income tax purposes.

[33]The Kimber Committee's reasons were these (paras. 2.08 and 2.09):

"The Committee considered the position of other employees who receive confidential information in the course of their employment, and who might use the information to their private advantage by trading in the securities of the company which employs them. While the use of such confidential information is improper, we do not recommend any legislative rules with respect to this trading. As with junior officers, the policing of any such abuse can be left to management.

"A similar conclusion was reached in regard to professional persons, such as lawyers, accountants and financial agents. The improper use of confidential information by professional advisers cannot be condoned, but the disciplining of such persons, who abuse the confidence placed in them, must be left to the companies who retain them and the professional bodies to which they belong. The Committee is prepared to assume the principles of the proposed legislation are at present or will be incorporated in the ethical codes of the bodies governing such professional advisers."

As we shall see when we turn to the second statutory technique for regulating insider trading liability, Canadian legislation subsequent to the 1966 Act has to some extent departed from this policy choice of the Kimber Committee, although as a delimitation of reporting responsibility, it remains intact.

category classifies as an insider "any person or company who *beneficially owns, directly or indirectly,* equity shares of a corporation carrying more than 10 per cent of the voting rights attached to all equity shares of the corporation for the time being outstanding".[34] And to make things more complex the 1968 amendments to the Act grafted an additional branch onto this category: "any person or company who *exercises control or direction over*" ten per cent of the voting equity shares.[35]

In choosing the ten per cent test, the Kimber Committee was guided by a concept broader than control of a corporation; rather the rationale was to include those who have opportunity of access to confidential information or influence over management.[36] At the same time, it concluded that non-voting shares or debt securities did not generally provide such opportunity, although there are certainly particular situations where this assumption may be challenged.[37]

In enacting the ten per cent test into law a minor change was made from the U.S. model. All the outstanding equity shares of the corporation were taken as the base against which the calculation is made rather than using as a separate base for separate calculation each class of equity shares presently outstanding. This simplifies matters

---

[34]Section 109(1)(c)(ii). Bill 20, s. 1(1)18(iii), leaves this unchanged, except that "voting securities of a reporting issuer" replaces "equity shares of a corporation". This change makes it clear that non-voting preferred shares are excluded (just as voting preferred will be included) and as noted above reflects the necessary alterations consequent on making the continuous disclosure system applicable to unincorporated entities.

[35]Section 109(1)(c)(iii). Alberta (s. 108(1)(c)(iii)); Manitoba (s. 108(1)(c)(iii)); Quebec (s. 139(c)(iii)); the CCA (s. 100(1)(c)) and the CBCA (s. 121(1)(c)), all have similar provisions. British Columbia does not but includes an associate of an insider as an insider (s. 106(1)(c)(iii)). Saskatchewan does not have this branch and the Atlantic Provinces have no insider legislation. Bill 20 includes "control or direction" together with "direct or indirect beneficial ownership" in the same paragraph (s. 1(1)18(iii)).

[36]Para. 2.10.

[37]*Ibid.* In its recommendations for take-over bid regulations it chose the arbitrary figure of 20 per cent as roughly equivalent to control, although in later amendments to the CCA the federal draftsmen chose ten per cent. The Kimber Committee justified the choice of ten per cent in the insider area rather pragmatically (para. 2.10):

"The substantial shareholder may technically be an 'outsider' rather than an 'insider' but by virtue of his relationship with the company he should be treated for these purposes as if he was in fact a member of management. In determining what percentage of the outstanding shares of a company held by a person would place such person in the position of being an insider, the Committee has concluded that it is necessary to take a figure which to some extent is arbitrary. In view of the lengthy, and apparently satisfactory, experience in the United States, the Committee recommends that the legislation in Ontario adopt the S.E.C. rule that any person who is, directly or indirectly, the beneficial owner of more than ten percent of the outstanding securities of any class of equity securities of a company be deemed to be an insider of that company. [Securities Exchange Act of 1934, s. 16] It may be noted that the Jenkins Report also selected ten per cent as the appropriate figure for this purpose [paras. 141 *et seq.*]."

somewhat because shareholders are customarily in the habit of totalling up all the votes outstanding in determining their voting position rather than looking at a particular class of shares.[38]

The ten per cent test contains an exclusionary proviso to accommodate underwriters during a distribution. This proviso excludes equity shares acquired by the underwriter in the course of distribution of the shares when such shares were acquired by the underwriter in his capacity as such. The exemption disappears as soon as distribution to the public by him ceases.[39] It is to be noted that it only applies in the calculation of the underwriter's percentage position. For purposes of calculating the ten per cent position of others his shares are part of the base.

The consuming difficulty in the ten per cent test, however, is the meaning of "beneficially owns, directly or indirectly". The intent of this extending provision is clear. It is to prevent a person with a ten per cent or greater voting stake in a corporation from using some artifice or improper device to shield himself from involvement with insider obligations. But how far courts will go in interpreting the word "indirectly" can only be a matter of conjecture at this point.[40]

---

[38]The definition of equity share (and in Bill 20, voting security) is designed to make this calculation as simple as possible. However there are still hazards. Equity share means "any share of any class of shares of a company carrying voting rights under all circumstances and any share of any class of shares carrying voting rights by reason of the occurrence of any contingency that has occurred and is continuing" (s. 1(1)7). Full voting rights are not necessary to make the latter class equity shares provided the contingency is satisfied. Thus a class of preferred shares carrying rights to elect two directors when two consecutive annual dividends are missed become equity shares when the non-payment contingency occurs. Thus, too, a class of preferred shares which carries no voting rights at any time except on a resolution to wind up or effect some other organic change apparently become equity shares the moment notice of a meeting to consider such a change is sent (or is it only when the resolution is laid before the meeting?).

These same hazards will continue under Bill 20, where the definition of voting securities contains unaltered the same proviso regarding contingent voting rights (s. 1(1)42). For a different approach to the calculation of voting rights for the take-over bid definition, see, *post*, part 7.03, especially footnote 17.

[39]There may be some difficulty in determining when that underwriter's distribution does in fact cease (see, *ante*, part 4.08, footnote 122). In *Consolidated Montclerg Mines Ltd.*, June 1967 OSCB 12 the OSC concluded that the sale of securities which had been purchased by an underwriter for the purpose of market maintenance was part of a primary distribution to the public. Logically it seems an underwriter engaging in market maintenance operations need not count shares so purchased for insider purposes; although the case is strictly speaking authority only on the point of whether a prospectus is required for their sale. It should be noted that the provision terminating the underwriter's exemption on the close of distribution does *not* contain the subjective test of the underwriter's opinion as called for by the requirement that he notify the Commission when distribution ceases. Thus an objective test might be inferred.

[40]The *Ames-Kaiser* case, June 1972 OSCB 98 illustrates the difficult fact situations that may arise. In this case a holding company was incorporated in

We may turn now to the second branch of the influential shareholder category, persons who "exercise control or direction over" more
than ten per cent of the equity shares. This provision attempts to cover
another legal form through which a shareholder might be in a position
to exercise substantial influence over a corporation and thus have
access to specific confidential information. However, this branch also
presents some substantial interpretative problems. First, it is clear
that the exercise of "control or direction" is not limited to a neat
concept of legal ownership to be contrasted with the more abstruse
concept of beneficial ownership in the first sub-category. If legal title
to ten per cent of the voting rights had been intended that could have
been stated. The "exercise of control or direction" test comprehends
something more. But how far does it go? For example, is control
transferred when shares are pledged with another person? Must the
voting rights be vested in the pledgee?[41] Is the test satisfied when
shares are subjected to a voting trust or shareholders' agreement?
What is the effect of a restriction on transfer as regards the exercise of
"control or direction"? The provision also creates problems for a trust
company which may not be in a position to know when various

Canada by U.S. residents who were insiders of Kaiser Resources Canada Ltd.
by virtue of their position as directors or senior officers with that company or
its U.S. parent. Kaiser Resources Canada was distributing its shares in
Canada only. The insiders wished to participate but the shares were not
qualified for distribution under U.S. law. Moreover, the Canadian prospectus
stated that the shares would not be distributed to U.S. residents. The insiders,
as U.S. residents, sought to insulate themselves from direct or indirect
beneficial ownership of the shares by a two-step procedure. They formed a
company which purchased some of the shares being distributed and created a
trust to hold their shares in the holding company. The OSC concluded that the
prospectus qualifying the shares failed to make full, true and plain disclosure
when it said the shares would not be offered to U.S. residents. Thus, it
implicitly found that the U.S. resident Kaiser insiders acquired indirect
ownership of the shares.

Consider the following example: three shareholders of a public company
each own 20 per cent of its equity shares; they form a private company and all
transfer their shares to it. No one of them controls it, but through it they
together effectively own 60 per cent of the public company. It is submitted
that this would constitute indirect beneficial ownership by them of the public
company. For interpretive purposes it is important to note that the phrase
"beneficially owns, directly or indirectly" has been directly copied from s.
16(b) of the U.S. 1934 Act. Therefore, some of the U.S. court decisions and
interpretive policies of the SEC may have an influential role to play in the
elucidation of its meaning, and are of more than passing interest. We may note
here some U.S. cases where indirect beneficial ownership was found: *Newmark
v. RKO General Inc.* (1970), 425 F. 2d 348 (2nd Cir. C.A.) and *American
Standard Inc. v. Crane Co.*, 1973 Decisions, CCH Fed. Sec. Law Rep. para.
94-061 (N.Y. Dist. Ct.). See also Op. Gen. Counsel, Sec. Ex. Act Rel. 1965
(1938) as quoted in Loss, vol. 2., pp. 1104-5.

[41] In this connection see Bill 20, s. 1(1)40(iv) which defines a pledge by a control
person as a trade. And see the new s. 107 in Bill 20, which requires a registered
shareholder who is not the beneficial owner, but who knows or should know
the beneficial owner is an insider, to report, except where the transfer is a
pledge and the insider has reported.

holdings of one issuer held in different departments and in different portfolios or trusts in the trust company taken cumulatively exceed a ten per cent interest in the voting rights of the issuer's equity shares.[42]

(4) INTER-CORPORATE HOLDINGS

The categories of insiders are considerably expanded and complicated by three basic provisions which deal with inter-corporate holdings. First, every director or senior officer of a company that is itself an insider of an issuer corporation is deemed to be an insider of the issuer.[43] Secondly, a company is deemed to own beneficially securities beneficially owned by its affiliates.[44] Thirdly, a person (which does not include a company) is deemed to own beneficially securities beneficially owned by a company controlled by him or by an affiliate of such company.[45] Three definitions dealing with the concepts of "affiliate", "control" and "subsidiary" in the context of companies spin out the web. One company is deemed to be an "affiliate" of another if:

(a) one is the subsidiary of the other, or
(b) both are subsidiaries of the same company, or
(c) each is controlled by the same person or company.[46]

One company is deemed to be "controlled" by another person or company or by two or more companies where more than 50 per cent of the votes for electing directors of the former are held by or for the latter and are potentially sufficient to elect a majority. This deeming provision does not apply if the shares are held only as security.[47]

One company is deemed the "subsidiary" of another if

"(a) it is controlled by,
   (i)   that other, or
   (ii) that other and one or more companies each of which is controlled by that other, or
   (iii) two or more companies each of which is controlled by that other; or
"(b) it is a subsidiary of a company that is that other's subsidiary."[48]

---

[42]And probably a broker whose possession of various clients' street name certificates representing shares in one issuer exceeding ten per cent of the voting rights is an insider because the broker is empowered to vote them once he has sent the proxy forms on to his clients and received no direction (s. 80). But must he wait until the eve of the annual meeting before making the calculation? If so, is he only an insider from that point to the close of the meeting at which point the proxy's life terminates?

[43]Section 109(2)(a) (Bill 20, s. 1(1)18(ii)). But directors and senior officers of the issuer are not insiders of the parent company. The CBCA (s. 125(2)(a) and (b)) corrects this anomaly.

[44]Section 1(7) (Bill 20, s. 1(6)).

[45]Section 1(6) (Bill 20, s. 1(5). The "exercise of control" test added in 1968 would include some of the situations covered by these provisions.

[46]Section 1(2) (Bill 20, s. 1(2)).

[47]Section 1(3). Bill 20, s. 1(3) is the same, except that "voting securities" replaces "equity shares".

[48]Section 1(4) (Bill 20, s. 1(4)). Bill 20 effects no significant changes in the inter-corporate holdings area. Note, however, that "reporting issuer" replaces "corporation" as specially defined in Part XII of the Act.

One writer has charted out some relationships that can arise by virtue of these provisions in the following illustration:[49]

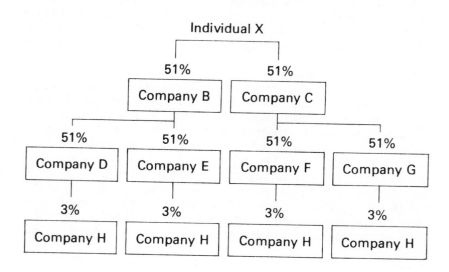

Applying the deeming provisions, X owns twelve per cent of company H's shares and is therefore its insider. Companies B, C, D, E, F, and G each own the shares owned by each other and are insiders of H. Each of their directors and senior officers are insiders of each other company including H. H is not an insider of each of the other companies and the directors or senior officers of H are not insiders of each of the other companies.

The reporting requirements in a large inter-corporate holding empire could become impossibly complicated in the absence of qualification. Some simplification has been introduced by regulation[50] and by the Commission's exempting power.[51]

(5) CORPORATION INSIDER OF ITSELF

Finally, some of the Canadian legislation makes the corporation an insider of itself. The first to do so was the BCA in 1971[52] but only in respect of purchases and sales of common shares and not other capital securities such as preferred shares. More recently the CBCA[53] did so

---

[49]Morley Carscallen, *Ontario Securities and Companies Legislation*, p. 21.
[50]Reg. 794, s. 66.
[51]Section 116. The CBCA (s. 2(1), (2) to (5), and s. 125(2)) does a more thorough job of establishing this inter-corporate framework.
[52]Section 41. See D.L. Johnston, "Public Offering Companies and Non-public Offering Companies under the Ontario Business Corporations Act", at p. 6.
[53]Section 121(1) "insider".

for purchases or other acquisitions by a corporation of its own shares or those issued by an affiliate.

6.06 Timing of Reports

An insider must file a report on the prescribed form with the Commission within ten days after the end of the month in which he became an insider.[54] For any change in direct or indirect beneficial ownership of or control or direction over securities a report must be filed within ten days following the end of the month in which the change takes place.[55]

For reporting purposes ownership is deemed to pass at the time an offer is accepted by the purchaser or vendor or his agent thus ignoring the normal five-day settlement period and other delays which might arise in the settlement process.[56] The report form requires that the capacity in which the reporting person qualifies as an insider be indicated. He is also required to designate the class of security, the amount or number he holds and the nature of his ownership.[57] The form for reporting a change requires the transaction date and the price per share or unit along with the balance position at the end of the month for which the report is given. Every transaction involving a change must be reported and not simply the cumulative effect of a series of transactions. Furthermore the nature of the transaction must be shown.[58]

---

[54]Section 110(1); Reg. 794, Form 21 (Bill 20, s. 104(1)).

[55]Section 110(3); Reg. 794, s. 50, Form 22 (Bill 20, s. 104(2)). This time frame would permit up to 41 days to elapse between a transaction and its publication. The Kimber Committee (para. 2.15) adopted it from the SEC rules because it appeared "...to be a practical and fair provision" in preference to the Jenkins Committee's recommendation of a report within seven days, which placed "too heavy a burden on the insider and is not necessary". As a result of the Merger Report recommendations (paras. 7.13 and 7.36(3)), this time period was reduced to three days in the case of take-over bids effected as exempt offers through market purchases (s. 110(a), both for the acquisition of the initial 20 per cent of voting securities and for the five per cent accretions thereafter). Bill 20 will impose the accelerated three-day report on some other trades, such as certain transactions by control persons, as a condition of removing other restrictions on the trades (s. 73(7)).

[56]Section 109(2)(c) (Bill 20, s. 103(2)(c)).

[57]The initial report does not require a statement of acquisition price. This omission was presumably designed to accommodate those insiders who had held their securities for a considerable period of time at the time the legislation first came into effect and would not have records showing initial acquisition price or average prices. But now ten years after its enactment this state of affairs no longer exists, and it would seem that the initial report form requirement should be amended to include specification of price.

[58]The examples designated are purchase, sale, exercise of an option, transaction not on the open market (with particulars) gift, and stock dividend. A transaction which is the disposition or acquisition of a "put" (option to sell), call ("option to buy") or other transferable option with respect to a capital security is deemed to be a change of beneficial ownership in that underlying capital security (s. 109(2)(b)).

The entire report of each insider is available for public inspection at the Commission.[59] In addition, summaries are produced in each monthly bulletin of the Commission, although details such as price and date of transactions are not reproduced therein.[60] Several other provincial jurisdictions use the Ontario bulletin as their publication vehicle.[61] It has become the practice of a number of the financial newspapers in Canada to produce a brief summary of the most significant insider transactions each month.

There is a host of mechanical provisions in the form of regulations and policy statements which attempts to clarify and simplify the reporting provisions.[62]

6.07 Exempting Provisions

Satisfaction of any one of three conditions permits the Commission to exempt an insider, on application, from the reporting obligation:[63] (i) a conflict with requirements of the incorporating jurisdiction, (ii) a substantial similarity to these requirements, or (iii) the broader ground of adequate justification for exemption in the circumstances of

---

By policy statement in 1970 "Initial Insider Trading Reports—The Filing of 'Nil' Reports," Ontario Policy 3-13, Aug. 1970 OSCB 114, CCH vol. 2, para. 54-907, the OSC began to require an initial "nil" report from a senior officer or director on his becoming such even though he neither owned nor exercised control or direction over any securities. The intent of that policy was to identify as a matter of public record all the senior officers and directors of the corporation concerned and to remind them of their insider position. The validity of that policy in terms of the existing legislation is open to some question. Section 110(1) is ambiguous. Section 110(2) would seem to have no purpose unless a nil report is not required. But the new provisions of Bill 20 (s. 104(1)) left no doubt that the newly-fledged insider must file a nil report, if that is the applicable state of affairs. However, in a recent about-face the OSC rescinded the nil report policy (Nov. 6, 1975 OSCWS 1). It is anticipated that the regulations providing details of the reporting requirement of Bill 20, s. 104(1) will eliminate reports. The CCA (s. 100.1) and the CBCA (s. 122) require nil reports. See also, British Columbia Policy 3-23 "Initial Insider Trading Reports—Filing of 'Nil' Reports, s. 107, The Securities Act 1967", CCH vol. 2, para. 29-973; Alberta Policy 3-10 "Initial Insider Trading Reports", CCH vol. 1, para. 24-510; Quebec Policy 22 "Insider Trading", especially s. 4, CCH vol. 3, para. 66-076.
[59]Section 111(1). Although Bill 20 does not continue this provision, it will presumably be taken care of by regulation.
[60]Section 111(2) (Bill 20, s. 119). A similar monthly bulletin is published by the federal Department of Consumer and Corporate Affairs for CCA and CBCA reports.
[61]See Nov. 1967 OSCB 78.
[62]See Reg. 794, s. 66 and Uniform Policy 2-09 "Insider Trading Reports—Loan and Trust Companies", CCH vol. 2, para. 54-879; Uniform Policy 2-10 "Insider Trading—Persons Required to Report In More Than One Capacity", CCH vol. 2, para. 54-880; Ontario Policy 3-12 "Preparation of Insider Trading Reports", CCH vol. 2, para. 54-906; Ontario Policy 3-24 "Insider Trading Reporting: Failure to File—Late Filing", CCH vol. 2, para. 54-918.
[63]Section 116(1). See the fuller discussion of similar exemptions from financial disclosure requirements, *ante*, part 5.07.

the particular case. The major change initiated by Bill 20 in this area[64] is to dispense with the need for an application where the ground for the exemption sought falls into the substantial similarity category. Instead the reports required by the incorporating jurisdiction may simply be filed. The problem of determining what is "substantial" remains.

While the conflict provisions would extend to a substantive clash between the Ontario requirements and those of any other jurisdiction, the immediate intent of this exempting condition was to prevent Ontario rules applicable to federally incorporated companies being completely nullified by the presence of conflicting federal corporations legislation pursuant to the paramountcy doctrine.[65]

⟋ The exempting category based on the Commission's just and equitable discretion presents the most interesting problems.[66] Because the insider net becomes so wide through the provisions dealing with inter-corporate holdings the exempting provision is frequently used. The test of access to specific confidential information is the guiding principle in such exemptions.[67] In addition to the access test the

---

[64]Section 120.

[65]See the Kimber Report, paras. 9.04, 9.05 and 9.07 and the discussion of this portion of the report, *ante*, part 5.06, footnote 39.

[66]Cost of compliance is not a satisfactory ground. In *Reeves Macdonald Mines Ltd.*, June 1967 OSCB 11, the OSC refused to exempt a federal company with executive offices in Vancouver whose shares were listed both on the Toronto and Vancouver Stock Exchanges from the insider reporting requirements and the proxy and financial disclosure requirements. The basis of the application was that there were only 50 Ontario shareholders with relatively little trading in Ontario and the costs outweighed the benefits. The Commission explained that:

"The theory of disclosure...is not related to the original distribution of shares but rather is concerned with the public who have bought and still hold securities and who should receive continuing and timely information regarding the company. The size of the company or the number of its shareholders or the possible inconvenience of its staff do not in themselves constitute a basis upon which to grant an exemption..."

[67]The pattern for a great many of these exemptions was cut in one of the first decisions under the new Act, *British American Oil Co. Ltd.*, June 1967 OSCB 9. There, an application was made on behalf of the insiders of the British American Oil Company Limited ("B.A.") pursuant to s. 116 of the Securities Act, 1966, for an order exempting all of the insiders of B.A. excepting the directors and senior officers of the company itself from the insider reporting requirements. B.A. was 68 per cent owned by Gulf Oil (U.S.). Gulf also controlled some 140 subsidiaries throughout the world and directly and indirectly was involved in numerous joint ventures and partnerships. B.A. itself had 75 subsidiaries, including Royalite Oil Company Limited and Shawinigan Chemicals Limited. Gulf and its directors and senior officers were insiders of B.A. Also the 140 subsidiaries of Gulf, as well as their directors and senior officers were insiders of B.A.; and so were the 75 subsidiaries of B.A., as well as their directors and senior officers. The OSC said:

"...the only purpose of the legislation is to bring to the attention of the public the view that those in a position to know most about a company's affairs take of the company's shares at the particular prices at which they are then trading. This being so, common sense dictates that in the complex of

Commission has recently imposed a further requirement. It may request affidavits from certain non-exempted insiders that they will not disclose specific confidential information to exempted insiders where the two groups are linked by interlocking directorates.[68]

---

companies there are only certain groups of individuals who are privy to what might be viewed as executive or policy knowledge which would affect their market decisions. On [the applicant's] evidence this interchange between B.A. and its affiliates would be confined to Gulf, Royalite and Shawinigan...Accordingly, we have granted an exemption from the reporting requirements of Part XI to all of the insiders of B.A. excepting the directors and senior officers of B.A. itself, Gulf and its directors and senior officers, Royalite and its directors and senior officers and Shawinigan and its directors and senior officers".

[68]The first case of this kind involved an application by company B. Several of its affiliates were related not simply by a common parent but by interlocking directors as demonstrated in the following diagram. X and Y were individuals and directors:

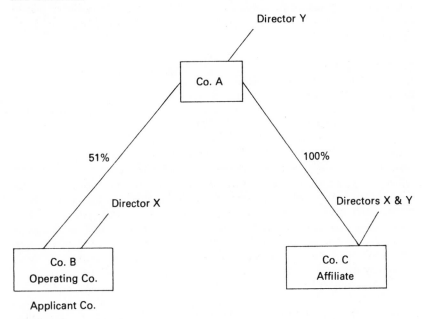

X and Y could be carriers of confidential information about company B, the applicant company, to the board of company C. This possibility was scotched by X and Y filing affidavits that they would not disclose any confidential information about company B to the insiders of company C. On this basis the insiders of company C were exempted from reporting requirements.

The clearest guide to insider reporting exemptions is found in Information Statement No. 9, December 1974, CCA Bulletin, vol. 4, No. 12. See also Saskatchewan Policy 6 "Elimination of Certain Insider Trading Reports", CCH vol. 3, para. 69-307; Alberta Policy 3-12 "Grounds for Exemptions", CCH vol. 1, para. 24-512; Ontario Policy 3-16, CCH vol. 2, para. 54-910; Manitoba Policy 3.08, CCH vol. 2, para. 34-998.

The Ontario Commission's practice on exemption applications is to require the applicant to state which of the insiders have access to specific confidential information and to exempt all other insiders permanently on the condition that if the situation changes with regard to access the order will terminate and a new application must be brought. This practice relies heavily on the care and sense of responsibility of the applicant in determining which of the insiders have access. Furthermore, the general principle of a perpetual exemption whose termination is brought about by a change which the applicant to some extent controls is questionable.

Exemptions are frequently sought on behalf of insiders who are participants in a payroll deduction stock option plan. If the amount of regular deduction from pay required to exercise the option is relatively small an exemption will be granted from monthly reports with a year-end report sufficing.[69] Normally the exemption will be subject to the condition that a report be filed when an option is exercised after the instructions have been changed. In addition the exemption will not normally apply either to resale by the insider of the optioned securities or to transactions in securities other than those taken down under the option.

6.08 Insider Liability
(1) LIABILITY IN GENERAL
In dealing with insider liability we seek to answer three main questions: first, in what circumstances will liability arise, secondly, what range of persons are to be made subject to liability and thirdly, to whom is there liability? It is the answers to the first and second of these questions which reveal the chief differences between insider reporting obligations, already discussed, and the liability provisions. Broadly speaking, liability arises only where use is made of specific confidential information by an insider to the detriment of an opposite party in a securities transaction. Reporting on the other hand is required whenever an insider trades. The second important distinction is that for purposes of liability the insider category has been broadened to include "associates" and "affiliates" of insiders as more narrowly defined.

We may begin by quoting the pertinent provision of the Act:

"Every insider of a corporation or associate or affiliate of such insider, who, in connection with a transaction relating to the capital securities of the corporation, makes use of any specific confidential information for his own benefit or advantage that, if generally known, might reasonably be expected to affect materially the value of such securities, is liable to compensate any person or company for any direct loss suffered by such person or company as a result of such transaction, unless such information was known or ought reasonably to have been known to such person or company at the time of such transaction, and is also accountable to the corporation for any direct benefit or advantage received or receivable by such

---

[69]A test of no more than $200 a month has been used in some exemptions. *British American Oil Co. Ltd.*, June 1967 OSCB 9 was the first such decision.

insider, associate or affiliate, as the case may be, as a result of such transaction."[70]

The succeeding paragraphs will discuss and analyze particular aspects of s. 113 in greater detail. The various concepts which the section contains, form in effect a series of tests, each of which must be met for liability to arise. The provisions of Bill 20 will be considered as occasion requires.

(2) "CONFIDENTIAL"

The requirement of confidentiality will rarely be an issue, since information that is capable of affecting market price and is not generally known will in almost all circumstances be confidential. *Green et al. v. Charterhouse Group Canada Limited et al.*,[71] Canada's only completed insider trading case to date, revolved around knowledge among directors of an impending take-over bid at a premium price, a situation which is normally clothed in confidentiality until the bid is formally made. One problem which may arise in such situations is this: must the information be imparted in confidence, or is confidentiality an inherent quality which is unaffected by the manner in which the user of the information acquires it? The second alternative would seem to be the preferable interpretation, since otherwise affiliates and associates of insiders who receive information casually or accidentally would escape liability. This would scarcely seem to be the intent of the section.[72]

(3) "SPECIFIC" INFORMATION

Section 113 requires that the information used in cases of insider liability be specific. The Court of Appeal for Ontario considered this requirement briefly in *Green v. Charterhouse*.[73] The Court chose as an example the evolution of the proposed take-over bid in that case from a statement of general aims and intentions on the part of the offeror to a precisely articulated scheme of acquisition involving a definite price per share. The principal personal defendant, who was involved in the negotiations at all stages, was a certain Godbout. The lower court held that at all times up to about two weeks before the time of the insiders' trades, Godbout's knowledge was only general, presumably because there was no firm proposal for a take-over bid. In reversing the lower court on this point (although affirming the trial court's dismissal of the suit), the Court of Appeal held that the negotiations had ripened to specificity prior to the impugned trades because the bidder had indicated a specific price he was prepared to offer if certain other contingencies such as a satisfactory examination of the offeree's financial records by the offeror's accountant were met. It is not altogether clear what general guidance may be extracted from this

---

[70]Section 113(1) (BCA, s. 150(1) (repealed by Bill 21, s. 4. See, *supra*, footnote 18.)

[71](1976), 12 O.R. (2d) 280 (C.A.); affirming [1973] 2 O.R. 677, 35 D.L.R. (3d) 161 (H.C.). See the comment regarding the High Court decision in 51 *Can. Bar Rev.* 676 (1973).

[72]Directors and officers of a corporation do not present the same problem, since when they receive information about a corporation in the course of duty, they do so at least impliedly in confidence.

[73]*Supra*, footnote 71.

finding apart from the somewhat unenlightening statement that the specific is the opposite of the general. It seems clear, however, that specific here means more than "precisely detailed" or "narrowly defined". The contrast is not so much between broad and narrow concepts, as between those entities which are uncertain and contingent and those which have evolved into immediate and palpable realities. The latter will almost inevitably have had to be made more precise and detailed, and thus specificity in the conceptual sense is an inevitable accompaniment of their approach to actuality. But the dominant and most important feature would appear to be the extent to which the information involves something which has happened or is about to happen.

The adjective "specific" is not found in s. 133 of Bill 20. It has been replaced, as has "confidential", by the concept of "material change not generally known" which covers much the same ground.[74]

(4) A MARKET IMPACT TEST

Not all specific confidential information meets the test envisaged by s. 113. There is the additional qualifying phrase "that, if generally known, [it] might reasonably be expected to affect materially the value of such securities". This is sometimes called the market impact test. The standard is objective—what the reasonable investor would take into account in buying or selling. Furthermore, the requirement that the value be affected materially provides in effect a *de minimis* rule, ensuring that information which might create extremely minor price fluctuations will not create problems. The objective standard and the inclusion of the word "material" tend to make the threshold at which liability arises a high one. On the other hand, the phrase "*might* reasonably affect materially the value" (as opposed to "*would*") should logically have the opposite effect, since it suggests that *possible* and not just probable changes in value (provided that reasonableness is present) will meet the requirements of the section. These suggestions must of course remain tentative in the absence of judicial interpretation.[75] For comparison, we may consider the two tests for market impact which have developed under Rule 10b-5, one of two U.S. federal securities statutory liability provisions impinging on insider trading.[76] These tests are discussed in the *Texas Gulf Sulphur* case.[77] The first holds that the insider's duty to disclose information arises only in those situations which are reasonably certain to have a substantial effect on the market price of the security, the second that it must only be information to which the reasonable man would attach significance. The first and more stringent standard might be termed one of objectivity and omniscience and clearly comes closer than the second to adopting the standpoint of specialized knowledge and expert

---

[74]Sections 1(1)22 and 133.

[75]*Green v. Charterhouse, supra,* footnote 71, did not deal with this point.

[76]Rule 10b-5 has proved to be a very flexible instrument and has provided great impetus to the development of the law in the area by judicial interpretation. See, *supra,* footnote 23.

[77]*SEC v. Texas Gulf Sulphur* (1968), 401 F. 2d 833 (2nd Circ.). See, *ante,* part 5.15, especially footnotes 136 and 137

judgment. It would appear from the language of s. 113 that Ontario has chosen to enact in law the second and more relaxed of these tests.

Bill 20 incorporates the market impact test in the definition of "material".[78] In Bill 20, facts or changes which are material are those which would reasonably be expected to have a significant effect on the market price of a security of an issuer.[79]

(5) CORPORATE PURPOSE

In the *Green* trial judgment, Grant J. suggested that the information in question must have been acquired for "corporate purposes" before liability will attach.[80] On appeal, however, Arnup J.A. indicated that he would not so confine confidential information. Thus, although it is likely that an insider would acquire his information through his position, his access to and participation in the corporate business, this is not a necessary condition for the operation of the section.[81] For example, it is apparently the case that an insider who hears first of an important external event which will affect the stock market, such as the assassination of a president, may trade to his advantage in securities of another company with impunity, but if he happens to trade in his own company's shares, he will be liable. This result follows even though his insider connection with his company had nothing to do with his acquiring the information first.

(6) "MAKE USE OF"

Perhaps one of the most important ways in which the imposition of liability is restricted under current legislation is by the requirement that the insider "make use" of the specific confidential information at his disposal. Both the trial and appeal court decisions in *Green v. Charterhouse* dismissed the plaintiff's case on this point.[82] The defendant insider had indeed purchased Green's shares at a time when possessed of knowledge of an impending take-over, but there was evidence that the initiative came from Green himself and that the essential concern of the insiders was to prevent his shares from swamping the market rather than turning a profit for themselves. The test as to whether use has been made of the information looks then to the dominant motive of the insider or the effective cause of his trading activity. He will not be liable if it can be established that he would have bought or sold in any event.

In *Green v. Charterhouse,* the evidence permitted a clear-cut finding that insider information was not involved in the decision to purchase. What of the situation where motives are mixed, and there is more than one contributing cause? The statutory language does not provide explicit guidance, but the Court of Appeal in *Green* suggested

---

[78]Section 1(1)22.
[79]Therefore the test of liability has changed in that the Bill uses "material changes", *i.e.,* changes that *would* reasonably be expected to have a significant effect on the market price, instead of specific confidential information that *might* reasonably be expected to affect materially the value of securities.
[80][1973] 2 O.R. 677 at pp. 740-1, 35 D.L.R. (3d) 161 (H.C.); affd 12 O.R. (2d) 280 (C.A.).
[81]Pages 309-10.
[82]*Supra*, footnote 80, at pp. 737-40, pp. 306-9 respectively.

that liability will attach in cases where the confidential information is "a factor" in an insider's decision to trade.[83]

The "make use of" requirement disappears from the initial fact situation giving rise to liability in Bill 20, only to reappear as a defence.[84] In its place, s. 133(1) of the Bill simply states that all insiders who trade with the knowledge of an undisclosed material change are liable. However, s. 133(1)(c) specifically provides for the exculpation of the insider who can prove that though he traded he did not make use of knowledge of a material change.[85]

(7) "IN CONNECTION WITH A TRANSACTION RELATING TO THE SECURITIES"

Conceivably an insider could make use of confidential information in some way that was to the advantage of himself or his friends without actually engaging in a trade. Under present legislation he would not be liable. The Act may be contrasted in this respect with the American Rule 10b-5, the most commonly invoked U.S. insider provision. Rule 10b-5 can occasion liability in cases where an insider or issuer has done no more than issue misleading information which has caused loss in a securities trade to those who (reasonably) relied upon it.[86]

Not only must the insider trade, he must also, under s. 113 of the Act, trade *with* the person for whose loss he is to be made liable. In more technical language, there must be privity between the insider and the plaintiff who seeks compensation. This is so whether a purchase or a sale is involved. This requirement places a considerable obstacle in the way of a would-be plaintiff, who must be able to identify the particular insider with whom he dealt. Where the parties are dealing through the mechanism of a stock exchange in a period of high investor excitement and feverish trading activity, the principals to a given trade will often be hard to track down.

Although it is not stated in so many words, it would appear that privity will still be required under s. 133 of Bill 20. That section speaks of a need to compensate "the" purchaser or vendor of "such securities", clearly implying a direct nexus between the parties.[87]

---

[83]The Court of Appeal decision in *Green* (p. 307) used just that language, *viz.* "a factor" as opposed to "*the* factor". Thus, the intent to take advantage of the insider position need not be the *causa causans* or even the "primary intent" to use the language of tax cases: *Regal Heights Ltd. v. M.N.R.*, [1960] S.C.R. 902, 26 D.L.R. (2d) 51, [1960] C.T.C. 384, 60 D.T.C. 1270 for liability to attach. A "secondary intention" to profit from the insider position will suffice. But it seems there must be some intent. Mere happenstance resulting in insider profit will not give rise to liability.

[84]Section 133.

[85]Examples might be automatic employee stock purchase or dividend reinvestment plans where a trade on behalf of an insider is triggered by some neutral event (*e.g.* a dividend payment even though it occurs at a time when the insider is aware of a material undisclosed change).

[86]The *Texas Gulf Sulphur, supra,* footnote 77, case is enlightening in this regard. Note the comments of the Court of Appeal in *Green v. Charterhouse, supra,* footnote, 80.

[87]This is one area in which the draftsmen of the Bill have not perhaps been sufficiently adventurous. Although the requirements of privity (or its equivalent in tort) makes excellent sense and responds to our deepest sentiments

(8) CROSS-OVER PROFIT-TAKING IN TAKE-OVER BIDS

The restriction of insider liability to losses occasioned by a trade in the capital securities of the insider's company directs attention to one of the major gaps in present Ontario legislation. Where a take-over bid is in preparation, insiders of the offeror company (and occasionally insiders of the offeree) will often be aware of the projected scheme months in advance. Since the offeror ordinarily pays a premium price for the shares of the offeree company, the latter are an attractive investment in the period prior to the take-over bid becoming generally known. The possibilities for abuse are obvious. But as the Ontario statute law stands, the insider is not accountable for profits made or losses occasioned by this trading in the shares of another company. Suspicion that insider profits have been made in take-over situations has been one reason for the drive in recent years to subject such acquisitions and the transactions surrounding them to closer scrutiny. It is doubtful if the present restrictive approach can be justified. It is true that an insider owes a peculiar obligation to the shareholders of his own corporation not to take advantage of them; but the rationale behind the imposition of insider liability is somewhat broader than this. The fundamental idea is that persons with special knowledge derived from a privileged position should not be able to use that knowledge to the direct detriment of members of the general public.[88]

Once a decision to acquire has been made, the offeree company's shares are immediately affected in value. An insider of another company who intervenes to prevent an offeree shareholder from

---

regarding what is just in instances where damages suffered are unique, such as particular contracts or torts, there is less need for it where we are dealing with homogeneous items such as shares. Each victim has suffered the same type of loss as the rest, whereas each insider, trading improperly has caused damage to *someone*, even if that someone cannot easily be singled out. Given these facts and the formidable evidentiary problems involved in matching the parties to a transaction, some relaxation of the privity requirement might seem desirable. The liability imposed by s. 133 is neither tortious nor contractual, but rather a special creation of a statute dealing with the peculiar problems of modern business transactions, and it would not perhaps be incongruous to adjust the requirements of traditional theory to fit the unusual problems raised by this rather specialized branch of human activity.

The major opposing consideration is the fact that the various persons trading with insiders may have suffered varying amounts of damage, depending on when they sold or bought, and at what price. In view of the tendency of the market to fluctuate in periods where vital information is being withheld, the discrepancies involved could be quite considerable. The injustice of making an insider liable for a particular quantum of damage which he may not in fact have caused must be weighed against the desirability of giving maximum efficacy to the rules which seek to eliminate an abusive practice.

[88]See *Cady Roberts and Company* (1961), 40 S.E.C. 907, quoted *infra*, footnote 105. It should be noted that at common law a director stood in a fiduciary relationship to his company, not to the shareholders: *Percival v. Wright*, [1902] 2 Ch. 421 (C.A.). Once the decision has been made to use a statutory enactment to break the impasse created by the latter case, there seems no reason to draw the line at shareholders (current, past or future) of the insider's own company if the abuse in question in fact extends to a wider group than those shareholders.

reaping the benefits of this increase in value has surely caused "direct" loss to that shareholder in the spirit if not the letter of s. 113. Furthermore, the two parties are very unequal—the insider knows what the shares are really worth while the shareholder does not. The combination of inequality of position and the capacity to cause direct detriment justifies the imposition of a *quasi*-fiduciary duty on the insider.[89]

(9) MEASURE OF DAMAGES

Once the requirements for liability have been met, the amount involved must be determined. Securities transactions present special difficulties in this area. The critical aspect is the choice of an appropriate time frame within which to measure a rise or fall in share prices. For example, we may suppose that a shareholder purchases from an insider in a falling market. If he held the shares long enough it is conceivable that they might eventually rise in value to the point at which he acquired them, in which case his loss would be nil. Clearly, there is a problem in determining at what point the shareholder who has held the shares so acquired has suffered a loss. If the same shareholder has in fact sold the shares, is he to be entitled in every instance to the full difference between purchase and selling price, regardless of how long he held them? Similar difficulties exist in the converse situation where it is the insider who purchases. American jurisprudence has evolved a test to deal with this problem that has had

---

[89]The Kimber Report dealt with the "cross-over" situation only by disclosure and not liability. It stated (para. 3.08):

"Perhaps the most controversial feature of take-over bid transactions in recent years has been centred on the allegations made in the press and elsewhere that such transactions have led to 'insider trading' profits, benefitting directors and other insiders. Certain aspects of insider trading dealt with in Part II of this report applied to take-over bid transactions. The insider trading rules will require the disclosure of the trading by insiders of the offeror and the offeree company in the shares with their respective companies. Other aspects are dealt with by the Committee's recommendations as to the contents of take-over bid circulars...which will require, in certain circumstances, the disclosure of holdings of the insiders of one company in the securities of the other company."

Disclosure in such a situation involves the directors of the offeror company disclosing in a take-over bid circular any trading in the shares of the offeree company within the preceeding six-month period, together with a statement of the number of shares held at that date. Trading by directors of the offeree company in securities of the offeror are required to be disclosed in the director's circular. But that document need only be issued if the directors of the offeree company choose to take a public position either for or against the take-over bid. The CCA in 1971 was the first legislation in Canada to create insider reporting and liability provisions for this cross-over situation. It does so by deeming directors and officers of the offeror company to be insiders of the offeree company and *vice versa*, for six months prior to the take-over bid (ss. 100.1(5) and 100.4(3)). Since 1973 the Quebec Act has contained a similar provision (ss. 151 and 153). The CBCA goes one step further and includes as well business combinations through acquisitions of assets or an amalgamation (s. 125(3)(a), (b) and (5)). Bill 20 deals with the problem differently, but effectively, by rendering the insider liable for trading with knowledge in any securities.

considerable success and currently enjoys widespread acceptance. This is the so-called "New York rule". The way in which it works is as follows: the shareholder-victim is held to be under a duty to mitigate his losses. Accordingly he is notionally supposed to have sold or repurchased his shares, as the case may be, within a reasonable time after disclosure of the confidential information which he lacked at the time of the transaction.[90] The measure of damages is the loss he suffers in thus seeking to regain his original position. In the case of a purchaser, the sale is supposed to take place at the lowest price which obtained during the period in which divestment could reasonably have been carried out. Conversely, a seller is deemed to have re-purchased at the highest price which obtained during the equivalent period. The shareholder is thus given the benefit of the doubt, as is only proper, but at the same time, a mechanism is provided whereby damages can be fixed by reference to prices obtaining in the immediate aftermath of the episode which gave rise to liability and the enquiry need not be carried forward indefinitely into the future.

(10) DEFENCES TO LIABILITY AND THE PROBLEM OF PARTIAL DISCLOSURE

Liability under s. 113 presupposes an inequality between the insider and the other party in terms of the information at their disposal. The best defence available to the insider is to show that this inequality did not in fact exist—that the plaintiff either knew of the facts in question or ought reasonably to have known of them. Section 113 of the Act expressly recognizes both these defences. They appear in even more explicit terms in Bill 20.[91]

One important observation should be made at this point: for disclosure to be a defence it must be full and not partial disclosure. Another way of stating this requirement is that it is the information itself and not merely the fact that it exists which must be revealed. The question of what constitutes adequate disclosure arose in *Green v. Charterhouse*.[92] One Sinclair, a director of Imbrex Ltd. whose shares

---

[90]A fairly recent American authority in this area, *Reynolds v. Texas Gulf Sulphur Co.* (1970), 309 F. Supp. 548 at p. 563, adopted a period of 20 trading days. Grant J. and the Court of Appeal followed the lead of this case in *Green et al. v. Charterhouse Group Canada Ltd. et al.*, [1973] 2 O.R. 677 at p. 755, 35 D.L.R. (3d) 161 (H.C.); affd 12 O.R. (2d) 180 (C.A.). Bill 20, s. 133(5) statutizes this solution by stipulating a period of 60 days and using an *average* market price test.

[91]Section 133(1). A third has now been added, *i.e.*, that the insider did not make use of the information. See, *supra*, part 6.08(6). Whether or not a person had actual knowledge of certain information, is of course, a pure question of fact. While in individual cases there may be problems with regard to credibility or with respect to the proper inferences to be drawn, questions of actual knowledge should for the most part be readily capable of resolution. Much greater difficulty is apt to ensue in those instances where it is contended for the defendant that knowledge should be *imputed* to the plaintiff on the basis of one or more types of public disclosure. The decision as to what a plaintiff should have been aware of in given circumstances involves an element of legal judgment. This will be discussed more fully in connection with the topic of dissemination and digestion periods.

[92]*Supra*, footnote 90.

were involved, wrote to Green a few days before the transactions which formed the subject of the case, and informed him that negotiations in progress could result in an offer at a premium price being made for Imbrex's shares. This letter came at a time when the offeror company had virtually committed itself to making a bid at a stipulated price in the next two weeks. The Court of Appeal was quite explicit in holding that Sinclair's letter did not fulfil the requirements of a defence under s. 113. In the words of Arnup J.A.: "the resulting obligation is discharged by disclosure of 'such information'. It is not discharged by disclosing that it exists, without saying what it is."[93] In view of the fact that Sinclair's letter in fact told Green a fair bit of what was going on and was more than a bare statement that "there is confidential information which might affect your decision to sell your shares", the ruling of the court on this point must be taken as demanding a fairly high standard of completeness and detail of disclosure before an insider can feel free to trade. He must, it would seem, tell all that he knows without the omission of material particulars. The actual facts in *Green v. Charterhouse*, so far as the issue of partial or complete disclosure is concerned, involved the defence of actual knowledge in the plaintiff, inasmuch as Green did receive the information in the letter such as it was. The problem will not arise in the same form in cases where the defence is one of imputed knowledge, but the holding here suggests that defendants who have not been entirely candid when they could have told all will not receive a sympathetic hearing when pressing for a generous interpretation of what the plaintiff should have inferred from the limited facts at his disposal.

(11) DISSEMINATION AND DIGESTION

Even the most complete disclosure will not be effective unless the information is distributed broadly enough to reach all those affected by it in a form which they can understand. American jurisdictions have realized for some time that to assume that satisfactory disclosure has taken place the moment an initial press release or the equivalent thereof has been issued is to adopt a mechanical test which ignores the realities of the situation and provides too easy an out for the possessors of confidential information. The transactions which gave rise to the extensive *Texas Gulf Sulphur* litigation[94] afford a classic illustration of this point. An insider who traded several hours after information regarding an important find had been placed on the Dow Jones news service was nevertheless held liable, since the information was not yet widely enough known and investors had insufficient time to assess and react to it. The question as to what constitutes an adequate dissemination and digestion period will depend on a number of factors which vary from case to case, making it impossible to lay down rigid rules. The nature and complexity of the information in question, the class of security and type of corporation involved, the medium adopted in communicating with the public, the availability of alternate and

---

[93](1976), 12 O.R. (2d) 280 at pp. 308-9 (C.A.).
[94]*SEC v. Texas Gulf Sulphur* (1968), 401 F. 2d 833 (2nd Cir.).

perhaps more effective modes of disclosure, all these matters should be taken into consideration.[95]

---

[95]Helpful guidance as to the kind of judgment that is required is provided by a more recent American decision, *In the matter of Certain Trading in the Common Stock of Faberge, Inc.*, Securities Exchange Act of 1934 Rel. No. 10174, May 25, 1973, CCH Fed. Sec. Law Rep., para. 79-378. See also comments on *Green et al. Charterhouse Group Canada Ltd.*, 51 *Can. Bar Rev.* 676 (1973), at footnote 27.

A useful comment on waiting periods for insiders is contained in the American Bar Association's comment letter on material, non-public information sent to the SEC in October, 1973:

"Dissemination of previously undisclosed material information concerning an issuer, through press releases, news wire releases, articles and the like, constitutes only the threshold of disclosure. While certain previously undisclosed information (e.g., dividend notices, or loss or receipt of major contracts) may be susceptible to immediate and reliable interpretation, the initial disclosure of most material corporate information can hardly be deemed to effect comprehensive dissemination of the information in question and its varying implications for the ongoing operations of the issuer, particularly if such information is complex or technical in any significant respect. By establishing waiting period guidelines, reasonable opportunity is furnished for the information to percolate through, and be analyzed by, the financial community and financial press.

"While selection of any waiting period must in part be arbitrary, the periods reflected in this suggestion are meant to be responsive to the needs and realities of the disclosure process, as we understand them. For those larger issuers whose releases are summarized for transmission by wire services promptly after receipt and are then republished in financial journals the following morning, the intervention of a single full trading day after the wire service publication should suffice to take into account the realities of the reactions of securities professionals and their clients as well as the demands of broader investor dissemination. For less significant issuers who may have to accomplish dissemination by mailings to their security-holders or publication in local or trade journals, the intervention of a calendar week after commencement of mailing or release for publication should likewise suffice to take into account the vagaries of the mails and the infrequency of local and trade journal publication schedules. In neither event do we feel it inequitable to require insiders to refrain from trading during these relatively short periods in order to reach the 'safe harbour' afforded by compliance with this suggestion."

The trial court judgment in *Green et al. v. Charterhouse Group Canada Ltd. et al.*, [1973] 2 O.R. 677 at pp. 743-4, 35 D.L.R. (3d) 161, gave some basis for believing that no dissemination or digestion period existed under the Ontario statute and that the insider was free to trade once news appeared on the Dow Jones tape. However, the Court of Appeal (p. 301) expressly disassociated itself from the trial judgment on this point and impliedly adopted the concept of dissemination and digestion with specific reference to its treatment in *Texas Gulf Sulphur, supra*, footnote 94, at p. 854.

Bill 20 is no more explicit regarding the need for dissemination and digestion than its predecessor. In one important respect, however, it may result in a more stringent standard for adequate disclosure. Section 133(1) exculpates from liability if the insider has "reasonable grounds to believe that such material fact or change has been generally disclosed", in addition to duplicating the defence in s. 113 of the Act where the information "ought reasonably to have been known to" the plaintiff.

(12) PROCEDURE AND THE BURDEN OF PROOF

In general terms the plaintiff in an insider trading case has the burden of establishing his case on a balance of probabilities. This is in accordance with the normal rules which operate in any civil action. The question arises, however, whether the plaintiff, having proved his case to some extent, may call in aid any presumptions which would shift the onus to the insider. And if it should be held that such a presumption exists, there is the further question of whether it merely operates to cast the burden of adducing evidence on the defendant or instead actually shifts the burden of proof, creating a separate legal issue where the insider must establish his case on a balance of probabilities.

Both at the trial and at the appellate level it was held in *Green v. Charterhouse*[96] that such a shifting of burdens does occur. In both cases there was agreement that the critical stage at which this occurs is when the plaintiff has shown that the insider possessed confidential information and nevertheless proceeded to trade. The question then becomes: did he "make use" of the information in the sense which we have already discussed? Grant J. held that the insider is under an "onus of explanation" to show that he did not. This expression is ambiguous, and it remains uncertain as to precisely what type of onus the learned trial judge had in mind. In any case the Court of Appeal disregarded his formulation in favour of a clear holding that the presumption is one which shifts the burden of proof; from this point to the end of the case the legal burden is on the defence so far as the issue of "making use" of the information is concerned. This ruling of the Court, while it does not smooth out all the difficulties facing a plaintiff in an action of this sort, does provide him with important assistance on a critical point once certain basic preliminary facts are in evidence.[97]

6.09 Categories of Persons Subject to Liability

The discussion of what constitutes an "insider" for reporting purposes need not be repeated here. Such persons are of course subject to civil liability as well. It was noted in the previous section that the Act makes liable "affiliates" and "associates" of insiders. The definitions of both these terms involve some ⌐omplexity. "Affiliate" applies to companies only. It centres on the concept of "control" of a corporation by means of the ability to elect its directors. Companies are affiliates of each other if one is the subsidiary of the other, if both are subsidiaries of a third company or both are controlled by the same person or company.[98]

"Associates" on the other hand are a more mixed group, and include

---

[96][1973] 2 O.R. 677 at p. 736, 35 D.L.R. (3d) 161 (H.C.); affd 12 O.R. (2d) 280 (C.A.).

[97](1976), 12 O.R. (2d) 280 at p. 307. As regards the separate defence that the plaintiff knew or ought to have known of the information in question the persuasive burden is of course on the defendant from the beginning.

[98]Section 1(2). The concept of subsidiary is defined in terms of control. See s. 1(4) of the Act.

individuals, corporations and in some instances even trusts.[99] The definition has five distinct subgroupings. The leading idea would appear to be that all those should be included with whom the insider has such close contacts either in business or private life as to render it highly probable that confidential information will not be withheld from them. The persons covered by the definition are the immediate family of the insider, relatives living in the same house and partners acting in a partnership capacity. Corporations included are those in which the insider owns ten per cent or more of the voting stock. Once a person's holdings in an organization approach this level it becomes probable that a sizeable part of his personal fortune is invested in the enterprise, in which case the temptation may be there to assist it to gain an improper advantage, or at any rate as the owner of such a sizeable block of stock, it is more than likely that the insider is either involved in the running of the company or has close contacts at the personal level with the management. The ten per cent test is of course arbitrary, but not wholly unreasonable. With trusts or estates it suffices if the insider has a substantial interest in them.[100]

It will be immediately obvious that liability under s. 113 of the Act is vastly extended by the inclusion of the two categories just described.[101] Those who remain unaffected are the large class of "tippees" who are neither associates, affiliates or insiders as defined for reporting purposes. "Tippees", an American expression, may be roughly defined as all those who are "tipped off" with respect to confidential information and proceed to make use of it to their advantage. In the broadest sense, it may be thought of as including persons such as employees who may pick up information on the job without its being made the subject of special communication. There is much to be said, in logic at least, for restraining all those who *in fact* profit from a privileged position, not just those who in addition meet certain minimum *indicia* of a privileged position as objectively specified.

The solution of the "tippee" problem has been attempted, at least, in Bill 20. Section 133 speaks of any person or company "who [trades] with knowledge of a material change", a formulation broad enough to include all those who acquire confidential information, whether through an explicit "tip" from an insider, through access to files or memoranda while working for the company[102] or through any other

---

[99]Section 1(1)2.

[100]Or manages them, whether he is formally called a trustee or not.

[101]The need to include affiliates as well as associates, despite the breadth of the latter concept, is clear if one considers the case of the subsidiary company which owns no stock of its parent. The parent is not an associate, but it is an affiliate.

British Columbia goes even one step further and imposes reporting obligations on associates (s. 106(1)(c)(iii)). The Quebec Act substitutes the term "related person" for "associate" (ss. 139(a) and 113(b)). The CBCA removes the distinction between distributing and non-distributing companies for liability purposes (s. 125(1) and (5)) though retaining it for reporting (s. 121(1)).

[102]In the CCA (s. 100.4(1)); CBCA (s. 125(1)(d)) and the Quebec Act (s. 151),

means whatsoever. This is essentially the "full access" test of liability as it is known and applied in the U.S. It is important to note however that the same defences available to insiders proper will be available to tippees. And it is conceivable that in some circumstances a tippee will have reasonable grounds to suppose that information has become public when an insider would not. Some such interpretation of the standard of what is reasonable seems necessary to protect tippees who may be unsophisticated and whose access to the information is of a relatively innocent kind.[103]

Some idea of the probable scope of the new section in this area may be gained from an examination of U.S. cases. In *Cady Roberts and Company*[104] liability was imposed on a partner of a brokerage firm who sold stock on a tip from another partner who was an insider. Although on the facts the partner would have been held liable as an associate under present Ontario law, the case is of importance for its classic statement of the full access test in terms of underlying principle:

"Analytically, the obligation [not to trade] rests on two principle elements; first, the existence of a relationship giving access, directly or indirectly, to information intended to be available only for a corporate purpose and not for the personal benefit of anyone, and second, the inherent unfairness involved where a party takes advantage of such information knowing it is unavailable to those with whom he is dealing."[105]

Some years later in *SEC v. Texas Gulf Sulphur Co.*,[106] the point was made that the existence of a legitimate corporate reason for not disclosing the information does not affect the obligation on the insider to refrain from trading in the relevant period. In that case the chief geologist and two of his subordinates, a geophysicist, another geologist, and an attorney on the company staff were all held liable. None of these persons would have been senior officers or associates under the present Ontario legislation, although they would have been liable as employees under the CCA, CBCA or the Quebec Act. More recently in *SEC v. Merrill Lynch*,[107] the access test was extended still further when fifteen institutional investors, who were clients of the well-known brokerage firm, disposed of stock on a tip and were subsequently found liable. The information originated in the underwriting division of the firm and was passed on to the general brokerage division from where it was transmitted to this privileged class of

---

liability has already been extended to employees and those retained by the company and in the CBCA effective December, 1975 (s. 125(1)(f)) to knowledgeable tippees.

[103]This question should not be confused with the subject of what the *plaintiff* ought reasonably to have known (see, *supra*, part 6.08(10) on defences). Here we are concerned with what was reasonable conduct on the part of the defendant.

[104](1961), 40 S.E.C. 907, CCH Fed. Sec. Law Rep. paras. 4845.39; 22781.764; 26,265.16.

[105]40 S.E.C. 907 at p. 912.

[106](1968), 401 F. 2d 833 at p. 848 (2nd Cir.).

[107](1968), 43 S.E.C. 933, CCH Fed. Sec. Law Rep. vol. 2, para. 22781.135.

customer. Although the precise limits of s. 133 of Bill 20 remain to be
determined, a general thrust towards a broadening of liability is clear.

6.10 To Whom is There Liability
(1) PROBLEM OF DOUBLE RECOVERY

The discussion so far has focused primarily on the plaintiff-security
holder who has had dealings with an insider to his detriment. Section
113 of the Act also, however, makes the insider accountable to his
corporation for any benefit derived from the transaction. In effect the
insider is made by statute a fiduciary agent of the corporation in
respect to his gains through insider trading, just as he would be at
common law with respect to bribes or secret profits. The purpose of
this enactment is clearly not to enrich the corporation but to place an
additional deterrent in the path of the insider. The problems of proof
facing the individual shareholder who has been taken advantage of
have already been alluded to, and cost considerations are of course
another factor which tend to discourage the instigation of actions
against insiders. The creation of an enforceable right in the corporation, which will normally have such greater resources at its disposal,
should at least in theory help to inhibit those tempted to engage in an
improper trade.[108]

The language of the section makes it clear that there is double
liability. Unfortunately, however, it does not explicitly state whether
there can also be double *recovery, i.e.*, whether the insider can be
compelled to pay out twice in cases where he is sued by both the
shareholder *and* the corporation. The Kimber Committee,[109] was
opposed to double recovery, but its recommendation that this bar be
explicitly established in the statute was ignored. When two distinct
rights of action are created in two separate parties, the inference to be
drawn, in the absence of evidence or authority to the contrary, is that
the same parties are entitled to enforce their rights without regard to
each other's actions.[110]

---

[108]Besides having the financial resources to bring an action and secure
evidence the corporation should on occasion be able to recover where the
insider has clearly traded and made a profit but the parties to the individual
trade cannot be identified or are unwilling to take action on their own behalf.

[109]Para. 2.30.

[110]Such an interpretation would appear to receive at least some support in an
obiter dictum of Grant J. in *Green et al. v. Charterhouse Group Canada Ltd.
et al.*, [1973] 2 O.R. 677 at p. 740, 35 D.L.R. (3d) 161 (H.C.); affd 12 O.R. (2d)
280 (C.A.). He observes that the rights of the corporation appear to be much
broader than those of the person who sues in respect of a direct loss. The drift
of his remarks is admittedly somewhat ambiguous. The language of s. 113,
joining the two differently articulated remedies with the conjunctive word
"and" supports Grant J.'s suggestion. But double recovery may turn entirely
on who sues first. An outsider is entitled to recover *any loss* he has suffered
from the insider. The corporation may force the insider to disgorge to it *any
profit* he has received. If the outsider recovers first, may the insider not defend
against his corporation's suit by responding that his profit has now been
extinguished? Bill 20, s. 133(3) resolves the ambiguity by providing for double
recovery against insiders, associates and affiliates, though not, it seems against
tippees.

Provisionally then it may be stated that double recovery is the law in Ontario. This result appears, and is, harsh, but may receive some justification in an increased deterrent effect.[111]

(2) WHO MAY INSTIGATE THE ACTION

Once a corporation has been given a right of recovery as described in the previous section, the problem remains of ensuring that the right is exercised. This area is not without difficulty; it is not hard to imagine instances where the directors of a corporation will be reluctant to proceed against an insider who is either one of themselves or a close associate. Recognizing this, the Act provides a means by which individual shareholders may compel the company to act by seeking an order before a High Court Judge.[112] This procedure is available to any person or company that is currently the owner of capital securities of the corporation in question or was so at the time of the insider transaction complained of. Conditions precedent to jurisdiction under the section are: first, that reasonable grounds exist for supposing that the company has an action under s. 113 and second, that it has upon request failed to commence an action or diligently prosecuted the same.[113] If these conditions are met the judge is empowered to make an order requiring the Commission to commence or continue an action in the company's name. The order may make such provision regarding security for costs and other matters as is needful in the circumstances.[114]

---

[111]*Cf.*, the use of treble damage suits in the U.S. which have proved effective in the regulatory area generally, not just in securities law.

[112]Section 114.

[113]The request must be written and the corporation has 60 days in which to act in response to it.

[114]The involvement of the Commission in assisting in the furtherance of a civil action by a company is a noteworthy innovation. It was recommended by the Kimber Committee (paras. 2.27 to 2.29).

The discretion given the judge regarding costs is particularly important. Section 114 was designed to allow an applicant to be relieved of cost worries in appropriate circumstances. One worrisome approach to the exercise of this discretion was displayed by Addy J. in granting an application for an order that an action be commenced against *Multiple Access Ltd.* (unreported Feb. 6, 1973). He ordered that the complainant shareholder indemnify the OSC and the company if the action were unsuccessful. It remains to be seen whether subsequent applicants will be treated with equal rigour.

The summary procedure under s. 114 provides a mechanism by which the resources and expertise of the Commission may be invoked by shareholders who may often lack both. The major limitation on the effectiveness of this mechanism is the fact that the shareholder must still assume the initiative to the extent of bringing application under the section. For various reasons, whether ignorance, fear, or inertia, shareholders will often be unwilling to take this step. And if the trend indicated by the *Multiple Access* case continues their reluctance will be understandable. A logical solution to the difficulty might appear to be to permit the Commission to initiate an application on its own when it determines through investigation or information reaching it that such a step would be appropriate. This in fact is the course which reform has taken in Bill 20. Section 134(1) states that the Commission as well as security holders of the corporation may make application before a judge in the same manner and under the same conditions as presently stipulated in s. 114 of the

6.11 Limitation Periods

Section 113(2) limits the period in which an action may be commenced to "two years after the date of completion of the transaction that gave rise to the cause of action". The time therefore begins to run at the date of completion of the transaction rather than the potentially later date when a victim discovers that specific confidential information has been used to his disadvantage. A person who discovered for the first time two years after the transaction that he had dealt with an insider who was acting on confidential information would be without redress. The U.S. approach, as embodied in Rule 10b-5 is that the limitation period begins to run at the time the injured person makes actual or constructive discovery of what has taken place.[115] Despite a number of submissions that the U.S. model should be followed, Bill 20 repeats the limitation concept of the Act, though it extends the time for suit to three years from the date of the transaction.[116]

6.12 Mutual Funds and Conflicts of Interest—Mutual Funds Report

The topic of conflicts of interest as it applies to mutual funds may be appropriately considered at this point, since Bill 20 has attempted for the first time in Canadian securities legislation to control the problems created by such conflicts through a regulatory scheme involving restrictions on self-dealing and insider trading.[117] The new rules are included in Part XX of Bill 20 along with the generally applicable insider trading provisions. They have their origin in the Canadian Mutual Funds Report,[118] which examined conflicts of interest in a broad context. The Report recommended specific legislative controls for self-dealing and insider trading because it had come to the

---

Act. This provision is analogous to one introduced in the 1971 amendments to the CCA (s. 100.5(1)) which gave the responsible Minister a unilateral right to initiate a civil suit on the corporation's behalf. Curiously enough this ministerial prerogative was dropped from the new CBCA enacted in 1975, although the corporation's right of action itself is preserved. With this enactment the enforcement of the insider trading liability laws would seem adequately provided for, to the extent that this is possible by means of mechanisms created by the law itself.

[115]The length of the limitation period itself varies from state to state, but three years is common. British Columbia has recently adopted the U.S. model for the commencement of the period and has extended its length to six years (s. 111(1)). The Limitations Act, 1975 (B.C.), c. 37, s. 16(1), repealed s. 111(2) of the British Columbia Securities Act which had followed the uniform act pattern in providing a limitation of two years.

[116]Section 137. The CCA and CBCA (ss. 100.4(2) and 125(6) respectively) have adopted a preferable course in providing for alternative limitation periods: two years from the date of the completion of transaction or, if it was a transaction that should have been subject to an insider report, within two years from the time of reporting. The CBCA takes one additional step by prohibiting short sales and trading in puts and calls by insiders (s. 124).

[117]For a generalized description of the mutual fund industry, and of the requirements of registration in Bill 20 for mutual funds and their management and distribution companies see, *ante*, part 3.19.

[118]For the remainder of this chapter styled "the Report".

conclusion that there was no feasible technique available whereby those responsible for the operation of the mutual fund could be subjected to continuing scrutiny by unit holders or by a "surrogate" on their behalf. Before examining those specific controls in Bill 20, it is first necessary to consider the broader control techniques.

The typical mutual fund operation involves a mutual fund contracting with a management company for management services and with a distribution company for distribution services. The financial rewards accorded to the three different parties involved are thus distinct and flow from different sources: consequently there may be temptations on the part of those who provide services to make investment decisions for purposes other than the good of the mutual fund unit holders. A choice must be made between two basic philosophies regarding the nature of mutual funds before these temptations can be controlled.

The first point of view holds that the mutual fund is simply the method by which the management company provides the service of investment management to an investor. The second proposes that the mutual fund is an enterprise, separate from the management company and consisting of an investment portfolio operated for the benefit of its participants. The enterprise then contracts with the management company for investment advice and administrative services which it may reject at any time. In the second situation the investor would be much more influenced by a belief that he had a stake in the enterprise.

Assisted by a consumer survey of mutual fund products and its own analysis of the industry in Canada, the Report concluded that the first philosophy rather than the second accorded with the realities of investor expectation and the manner in which such funds are actually managed in Canada. This choice had an important bearing on the acceptance or rejection of various techniques by the Committee in its recommendations aimed at controlling conflicts of interest.

Before coming to grips with the question of the prohibition against self-dealing and insider trading, the Report considered a number of other methods, some of which it chose to adopt; these will primarily be found as conditions of registration for the mutual fund, the management company or the distribution company in the regulation and policy statement changes which will be necessary with the adoption of Bill 20.[119] Six important techniques were considered, under the heads of disclosure, independent directors, voting rights, an independent trustee with supervisory powers, auditors, and internalization of the sales and management function.[120]

Although the Report placed heavy emphasis on disclosure, it concluded that it was not practical to require release of the details of all the transactions which might or might not show conflicts of interest. Furthermore, consistent with its over-all view of the nature of mutual funds, the Report noted that it would be wrong to assume that share or unit holders would be fully able to understand such an ultimate degree of disclosure or act effectively on it.

---

[119]See, *ante*, part 3.19.
[120]Report, pp. 148-91.

The use of independent directors as a controlling technique had some important antecedents. The U.S. Investment Company Act of 1940[121] required that 40 per cent of the board of directors, governors or trustees of the mutual fund be outsiders, that is, independent from its staff and from the management or distribution companies associated with it. Understandably the concept of outsider required detailed definition. The Canadian Mutual Fund Association ("the CMFA") had adopted the same requirement as a self-regulatory technique, but with no attempt to define independence. In rejecting proposals for a statutory requirement that the board of directors or equivalent body of each mutual fund contain a specified percentage of members who would be independent of management the Report was guided by three principal considerations.[122] First, it concluded on the basis of a U.S. SEC report[123] that the use of independent directors had not effectively solved the problems that arise from the separation of mutual fund management from ownership. Secondly, and more specifically, this technique of independence, so the SEC study concluded, did not resolve what the study considered to be major problem areas, *i.e.*, management compensation, allocation of brokerage and the setting of sales load levels. Thirdly, the Report concluded from experience in both Canada and the U.S. that an extremely broad and rigorous test would be necessary to attempt to ensure independence in this area and that it was not worth the effort.

By contrast, the Report chose to follow the 1940 U.S. Act in the area of shareholders' voting rights, even though the SEC appraising report drew attention to some very substantial shortcomings in this accountability technique. As a condition of registration for a fund the Report recommended that a majority vote by unit holders should be required at intervals no greater than every two years for approval of management contracts and that prior approval of unit holders be required for material amendments to the management or distribution contract, to agreements for the custody of assets and to the statement of investment objectives and practices.

In the United Kingdom, mutual funds take the form of unit trusts; before the Board of Trade gives them permission to distribute units they must have an independent trustee with supervisory powers.[124]

---

[121]Hereinafter referred to as the "1940 U.S. Act".

[122]At pp. 164-5.

[123]Report of the Securities and Exchange Commission on the Public Policy Implications of Investment Company Growth, Washington, 1966.

[124]The Report quoted at p. 173 from D.C. Corner and H. Burton, *Investment and Unit Trusts in Britain and America*, Elek Books, 1968, p. 12:

"'The Investment Company Act, 1940, required investment companies to provide security arrangements for the underlying securities of their portfolios satisfactory to the SEC, or to deposit such securities with a trustee approved by the SEC. The sole function of such trustees is that of custodian. Trustees of British unit trusts have many other duties to perform; in general, they are watchdogs of the interests of the unit holders, and make sure that the provisions of the trust deed and the provisions of the Prevention of Frauds (Investment) Act, 1958, as implemented by the Board of Trade regulations, are not violated. Depending upon the provisions of the trust deed, the main duties of trustees are: to buy and to sell underlying

The Report concluded it would be inappropriate to import this British precedent to Canada, which has a substantially different tradition and where methods of organization in the mutual fund industry have developed along different lines. The reasons are various—considerations of cost, the difficulty in determining which organizations would be appropriate to serve as trustees, the problem of competition involved in one trust company serving as independent trustee of another trust company's mutual fund, and finally a "reason of principle" also used to reject a proposal for independent directors; that independent trustees would lack a direct stake in the success of the enterprise and yet would be expected to pass judgment on the business decisions of the management company.

The Report placed very heavy emphasis on the role of the auditor.[125] In keeping with a legislative trend in Canada,[126] it recommended a number of provisions dealing with auditors of mutual funds to be enacted as conditions of registration. These include the following: power in the regulatory authority (the "administrator") to appoint an auditor when the office is vacant; independence of the auditor from the mutual fund; disqualification of a person or firm from acting as auditor if mandated by the administrator; specified standards with respect to the auditor's report and the degree of examination necessary before expressing his opinion; requirements with respect to his dismissal by management accompanied by a vote of the shareholders thereon under conditions of full disclosure; permission for the auditor to include in his report reference to any matters which, in his opinion, constitute evidence of violations of law or impropriety even though they do not materially affect the financial statements; and a requirement that he report to the administrator any matters which might constitute evidence of violations of law.

Finally, the Report considered imposing a requirement that the managementand sales functions be internalized rather than permitting them to be conducted by separate organizations under contract.[127] It concluded that such a requirement would be inappropriate first, because it is too great a change for the benefits to be obtained,

---

securities on instruction from the management, but to veto investments if not permitted by the deed, or if they consider them not to be in the best interests of the unit holders; to see that distributions are not inflated by underlying securities always being bought cum dividend and sold ex dividend; to receive the income of the fund and distribute it to the unit holders; to maintain and keep up to date a register of unit holders; to see that no certificate of units is issued before they are possessed of equivalent asset value; to take steps to remove management from office on good cause; and to be satisfied with sales promotion literature before it is used. All these duties are not necessarily assumed by all trustees, and trustees probably try to keep their responsibilities down to a minimum. The trustees in Britain are mostly high quality banks, especially the Big Five, and high class insurance companies. They receive fees for their services which are normally paid out of the gross remuneration of managements."'

[125]At pp. 177-8.
[126]See for example the 1967 Report of the Select Committee on Company Law, chapter 10, and the Ontario BCA, ss. 167 to 171.
[127]At pp. 188-91.

secondly, there is considerable doubt as to whether it would make any difference and thirdly, it would serve to discourage a variety of financial complexes from developing within and beyond the Canadian mutual fund industry.

Against this background the Report recommended specific rules with respect to self-dealing, insider trading and related areas. Most of these appear in the provisions of Bill 20.

6.13 New Statutory Regime for Mutual Funds

The legislative scheme envisaged by the Report had a threefold aspect: provisions to define transactions which are abusive, remedies to be applied when abuses have been detected, and procedures to facilitate the disclosure of abusive transactions.

(1) ABUSIVE TRANSACTIONS

The closest analogue was the 1940 U.S. Act, which established rather rigorous controls, a primary influence being the evidence of "very serious abuses" uncovered in the study leading to the legislation.[128] That Act prohibits transactions with affiliated persons as defined in the Act and in some instances transactions involving the affiliate of an affiliate.[129]

The Report rejected this U.S. approach because of the very heavy administrative burden imposed on the agencies involved in granting exemptions, the sophistication of staff required and the difficulty of achieving consistency and uniformity in exemptions. In addition it concluded that the ability of such an exemption apparatus to function in Canada was doubtful in the absence of a single national authority. As a result the Report looked to other models. Its choice fell closer to home upon the newly enacted fiduciary duty of directors and officers in the BCA[130] and the self-dealing provisions enacted in certain areas of recent federal legislation.[131]

The BCA furnishes a general standard for measuring fiduciary obligations, while the analogous federal legislation provides a model

---

[128]Report, p. 278. The legislative aim is stated at the outset of the Act as follows:
"The national public interest and the interest of investors are adversely affected—...
(2) when investment companies are organized, operated, managed, or their portfolio securities are selected, in the interest of directors, officers, investment advisers, depositors, or other affiliated persons thereof, in the interest of underwriters, brokers, or dealers, in the interest of special classes of their securities holders or in the interest of other investment companies or persons engaged in other lines of business, rather than in the interest of all classes of such companies' securities holders;...[Investment Company Act of 1940, s. 1(b)(2)]."
[129]The definition of affiliate itself is exceedingly complex (Report, pp. 279-80). Such transactions may only be entered into with an exemption from the SEC.
[130]Section 144.
[131]Investment Companies Act, 1970-71-72 (Can.), c. 33, s. 9; Canadian and British Insurance Companies Act, R.S.C. 1970, c. I-15, s. 33 as am. R.S.C. 1970, c. 19 (1st Supp.), s. 8; Trust Companies Act, R.S.C. 1970 c. T-16, s. 68.4 new by R.S.C. 1970, c. 47 (1st Supp.), s. 25(11); Loan Companies Act, R.S.C. 1970, c. L-12, s. 60.3 new by R.S.C. 1970, c. 24 (1st Supp.), s. 25.

for specific prohibitions of certain types of transactions, but in a fashion which avoids the complexity of the U.S. requirements with the already noted heavy administrative burden with regard to the granting of exemptions. Bill 20 sets out the general standard in s. 115(1):

"Every person or company responsible for the management of a mutual fund shall exercise the powers and discharge the duties of its office honestly, in good faith and in the best interests of the mutual fund, and in connection therewith shall exercise the degree of care, diligence and skill that a reasonably prudent person would exercise in the circumstances."[132]

Although the Report recommended that it be omitted an unnecessary, the draftsmen of Bill 20 also added the duty of care, diligence and skill (*i.e.*, the director's duty in its non-fiduciary aspects) from the BCA—the latter half of the provision quoted above. This duty is placed on the management of the mutual fund whether the management remains within the fund in the hands of the board of directors or is provided externally by contract.[133]

The specific self-dealing prohibitions encompass a narrower class of persons or companies than the U.S. legislation on which they are modelled; they prohibit direct investments only as opposed to the wider range of transactions prohibited by the U.S. Act. Thus Bill 20[134] prohibits the mutual fund, its management company or distribution company[135] from knowingly making an investment by way of loan to certain functionaries of these companies or a spouse or child of any such functionary or any person (plus defined relatives and related groups) who is a substantial unit holder or shareholder of the mutual fund, the management company or the distribution company. Similarly, investments are prohibited in any issuer that is a substantial unit holder of any of the three above-mentioned entities, in any issuer in which the mutual fund alone or with a related mutual fund or funds is a substantial shareholder, or in an issuer in which any functionary or spouse or child has a significant interest or in which a substantial unit holder of the fund, management company or distribution company has a significant interest.[136] Pursuant to the recommendations of the

---

[132]See E.E. Palmer, "Directors Powers and Duties"; F. Iacobucci, "The Business Corporations Act, 1970: Management and Control", 21 U. of T. L.J. 543, at p. 550; S. Lavine, *The Business Corporations Act* (Toronto, Carswell, 1971), pp. 227-232; L. Hebb, The Law Society of Upper Canada, "BCA 1970 Rights and Obligations of Directors"; Special One-Day Programme, Nov. 1970.

[133]Section 115(2) of Bill 20 provides as an interpretive addition to the statement of the duty of managers that "a person or company is responsible for the management of a mutual fund if he has a legal power or right to control the mutual fund or if in fact he is able to do so." The reasons for adopting the federal and Ontario precedents are set out in paras. 922 and 923 of the Report.

[134]Section 109(1).

[135]Section 109(2).

[136]Section 109(3). These provisions are made applicable to investments held at the time Bill 20 comes into force (s. 109(4)). In a corollary provision the mutual fund, management company and distribution company are prohibited from knowingly entering into a contract or other arrangements which would result in them being directly or indirectly contingently liable in respect of any of the

Report, the Commission is given both a broadening and a narrowing discretion. In s. 112 it is empowered to exclude an investment or class of investments from the operation of ss. 109 to 111 once satisfied that an abusive transaction would not occur.

A final prohibition denies a mutual fund the right to make any investment in consequence of which a person or company related to the mutual fund would receive any fee or other compensation except fees paid pursuant to a contract which is mentioned in the prospectus.[137] The Commission has a discretion to exempt.

(2) REMEDIES FOR ABUSIVE TRANSACTIONS

The second element of the regime deals with remedies and procedural problems including costs. Here the Report considered existing precedents in the Act and the recent federal self-dealing provisions[138] and concluded they were inadequate. In their place it recommended a broad discretion in a court to choose a remedy appropriate for a particular case from a range including rescission, damages and injunctions. The choice of procedures would permit a unit holder or the administrator to initiate and continue an action in the name of the mutual fund with provisions for making interim costs available to the initiator. In order not to discourage such actions, costs would not be available against the initiating party.[139] Unfortunately, Bill 20 for the most part ignores these recommendations and relies on the enforcement scheme available for other offences under the Act.[140]

Dealing with insider trading *per se*, however, Bill 20 adopts the novel recommendations of the Report. One of the latter's major concerns was the use by an insider of the confidential information that the mutual fund is about to trade in a particular security, thus possibly

---

prohibited investments referred to above (s. 111). Investment is defined (s. 108(a)) broadly to mean the purchase of shares or debt obligations or other evidence of indebtedness and loans to individuals but not to include an advance or loan that is merely ancillary to the main business of the mutual fund, management company or distribution company. Significant interest is interpreted in a rather elaborate definition that turns on the beneficial ownership either directly or indirectly of more than ten per cent of the outstanding shares or units of an issuer by a person or company, or more than 50 per cent of such units in the case of a group of persons or companies (group is not defined). Appropriate deeming provisions (s. 108(d)) extend beneficial ownership through a whole pyramid of interlocked companies or other issuing institutions. Voting securities owned by an underwriter during the course of distribution are excluded in determining the percentage of voting rights attached to voting securities owned by an underwriter.

Section 117 of Bill 20, provides for similar self-dealing prohibitions in the case of a new class of registrant, the portfolio manager, who is retained by a client to manage an investment portfolio.

[137]Bill 20, s. 114. "Related person or company" is defined in s. 103(1)(c) as any person or company whose securities are a prohibited investment for the mutual fund, its management company or its distributing company by the terms of Part XX of the Bill.

[138]*Supra*, footnotes 130 and 131.

[139]At pp. 296-9. Compare the experience with insider trading liability, *supra*, footnote 114.

[140]*Post*, chapter 9.

affecting the market-price. Section 118 specifies that this is an offence. It states:

"No person or company who has access to information concerning the investment program of a mutual fund or the investment portfolio managed for a client by a portfolio manager shall purchase or sell securities of an issuer for his or its account where the portfolio securities of the mutual fund or the investment portfolio managed for a client by a portfolio manager include securities of that issuer and where the information is used by the person or company for his or its direct benefit or advantage."[141]

The access test is used to cast a net spreading far beyond the carefully defined class of insiders employed for other purposes in the Act. An equally broad provision has been added to the liability section for insider trading in tandem with the more general provision examined earlier.[142] It attaches liability to "any person or company who has access to information concerning the investment program of a mutual fund that is a reporting issuer or the investment portfolio manager for a client by a portfolio manager and uses that information for...direct benefit or advantage to purchase or sell securities of an issuer...where the portfolio securities of the mutual fund or the investment portfolio managed for the client by a portfolio manager include securities of that issuer is accountable to the mutual fund or the client of the portfolio manager, as the case may be, for any benefit or advantage received or receivable as a result of such purchase or sale."

The confidential information involved is information in regard to the investment program of the mutual fund. The provision is of a somewhat hybrid character. It uses the all-inclusive access test as a basis for liability, but at the same time requires that information be used for the advantage of the person or company trading—language not unlike that of s. 113 of the Act. The section is restitutionary in nature, involving a handing-over of benefits received to the mutual fund whereas in s. 133(1) of Bill 20, the remedy may also be used to compensate an outsider for loss he has suffered.[143]

The provisions for enforcing liability and disposing of the costs attendant thereto follow the provisions of the Report and represent a substantial departure from the procedures of the Act. As in the case of a reporting issuer, the Commission itself, and not just a security holder of the mutual fund, may apply to begin an action on behalf of a mutual fund where the fund has failed to commence or prosecute diligently an action available to it.[144] The order consequent on the application may either require the Commission to start the action or authorize the person or company making the application to start it. In the area of

---

[141]It parallels the more general insider trading prohibition (s. 77) new in Bill 20. As one can see the section expands this prohibition to include information concerning the investment program of an investment portfolio manager for a client by a portfolio manager.

[142]Section 133(2). This subsection parallels the more general insider trading liability provision (s. 133(1)) new in Bill 20.

[143]Section 133(3) which creates the latter remedy is confined to s. 133(1) liability.

[144]Section 134(2).

costs, the BCA derivative suit is used as a model to give considerable discretion to the court.[145]

(3) DISCLOSURE OF POTENTIALLY ABUSIVE TRANSACTIONS

Bill 20 imposes a duty on the management company to report within 30 days after the end of the month any transaction involving a related person or company of the mutual fund.[146]

Turning to insider trading *per se*, Bill 20 accepts the Report's recommendation that somewhat lighter treatment than that accorded other mutual fund conflicts of interest is appropriate. Because the adoption of forward pricing would render unnecessary insider trading reporting and liability provisions with respect to dealings by insiders in the capital securities of the fund itself, Bill 20 specifically exempts mutual fund insiders from the standard reporting requirements.[147]

---

[145]Section 134(2) of Bill 20; BCA, s. 99.
[146]Section 116. The Commission has an exempting discretion. The reports are summarized in the Commission's monthly publication s. 119.
[147]Section 104(1).

Chapter 7
Take-Over Bids

7.01 Introduction

Take-over bids first became the subject of substantial regulation in Canada with the introduction of the Act in 1966. Rules governing take-over bids together with those parts of the Act relating to proxy solicitation, insider trading and regular financial disclosure were major innovations of the Kimber Committee. That Committee defined the take-over bid as a commercial transaction "whereby a company or a bidding group has sought to acquire legal or effective control of another company by a procedure which has become known as a 'take-over bid'".[1] Deliberately excluded from this definition were "other types of transactions whereby two or more companies combine their business operations by way of, say, a statutory amalgamation or by way of asset acquisition".[2] The Committee concluded that statutory amalgamations and assets acquisitions did not require legislative reform. These latter forms of business combination did receive subsequent consideration in the OSC's Merger Report which looked at them along with take-over bids and made reform proposals.

The take-over bid is perhaps the most dramatic occurrence in corporate life. Its success or failure often has incalculable consequences for affected parties. Because of this dramatic quality, abuses or inequities that occur in connection with such bids often achieve great notoriety.

Since the Kimber study there has been a significant increase in business combinations in general and take-over bids in particular, although the pace has moderated in the past few years. Indeed this trend had begun several years before the Committee was appointed.[3]

---

[1]Kimber Report, chapter 3, particularly para. 3.01. See also the Hodgson Report, chapters 10 to 17. In discussing the need for legislation the Kimber Committee stated (para. 3.01): "There has been, in the past several years, criticism by the general public, the financial community and the press concerning both the form and effect of [these] commercial transactions...". One of the principal events which led to the creation of the Kimber Committee was the take-over bid by Shell Oil Ltd. for Canadian Oil Ltd. Numerous allegations of trading by persons with confidential knowledge of the bid were made, although a subsequent investigation disclosed no impropriety by any of the principals of either company. However, it is important to note that the Kimber Committee was not moved to recommend legislation by the occurrence of a rash of celebrated scandals or volumes of evidence of abusive practices. The Report states (para. 3.07):

"The Committee was not appointed to perform a fact-finding function in the sense of seeking evidence as to the wrongs or harms which the shareholding public may have suffered as a result of the absence of statutory regulation of the take-over bid transaction."

[2]Kimber Report, para. 3.02.

[3]The Merger Report (pp. 187-92) states that from:

"May 1st, 1967 when Part IX came into force, to December 31st, 1969, 87 take-over bid circulars have been filed...Of the [offerors] analysed...17 were

318

Since the take-over bid regulatory framework is relatively new there is a scarcity of case-law and administrative guidelines to assist in its interpretation.[4] An understanding of the scheme and its operation must rest primarily on a consideration of the legislation itself and an analysis of the various policy reports and other regulatory models which influenced its creation or amendment.

In this chapter we look first at the broad purpose of the legislation as well as the definition of a take-over bid and the exemptions therefrom. This is followed by a consideration of the substantive rules which impose certain time limits on the various stages of the take-over bid process. Finally we look briefly at several special problems and the civil liability provisions.

7.02 Purpose of Legislation

In examining the regulatory structure a fundamental question concerns the intent underlying the legislation. Its primary purpose is to provide protection to the offeree. This aim is accomplished in three principal ways: by giving the offeree information relevant to his decision whether to accept or reject the offer; by ensuring that he has time to assess the information and make a reasoned decision; and by requiring that he be treated equally with other offerees both in terms of price and in respect to the portion of his securities which will be taken up in an oversubscribed partial bid.[5]

Offeree protection must, however, be weighed against other competing interests; it must not be emphasized to the point where it is extremely difficult or expensive to effect a take-over bid. For example,

---

federally incorporated, 17 were incorporated in the U.S. and 46 were provincially incorporated of which 28 were incorporated in Ontario...

"Six unconditional bids were made for all of the class of equity shares of the offeree outstanding....

"The offers made for only common shares of the offeree company were by far the most prevalent, almost 84% of the total offers....Nine more offers were made for both common shares and either preferred shares or warrants of the offeree."

[4]For detailed consideration of Canadian take-over bid legislation see: P. Anisman, "Takeover Bid Legislation in Canada: The Definitions, Exemptions and Substantive Requirements"; P. Anisman, *Takeover Bid Legislation in Canada: A Comparative Analysis*; D. B. Morin and W. Chippindale, *Acquisitions and Mergers in Canada*; Merger Report; Proposals for a New Business Corporations Law for Canada, vol. I, part 16.00; R.W. Bird, "Corporate Mergers and Acquisitions in Canada"; J.P. Williamson, *Securities Regulation in Canada*, and Supplement; W.P. Rosenfeld, "Corporate Acquisitions"; G.E. Creber, "Take-over Bids, Insider Trading and Proxy Requirements"; Hodgson Report.

[5]A bid made for only part of the total securities outstanding, such as one for 50 per cent of the outstanding common shares, is a partial bid. If 75 per cent of the outstanding common shares are tendered in response it is oversubscribed, and only two out of every three shares tendered will be taken up, unless the partial condition is waived. A bid subject to a condition of a minimum level of tendering response, *e.g.*, that at least 50 per cent of the outstanding shares be deposited before the shares deposited will be taken up, is a conditional bid.

the offeror should not be unduly exposed to competition from rival bidders, nor should the management of the offeree company be permitted simply to entrench itself.[6]

Particular take-over bids may, for example, lead to monopolies or oligopolies in restraint of trade, or to increased foreign ownership in a given industry. Measures designed to regulate or combat such developments are appropriately left to statutes which embody distinct policy choices in these areas.

The current legislation in Canada is found in the five uniform acts, in the CCA (since the 1971 amendments) and the CBCA where substantially similar take-over bid regulations apply if the offeree company is federally incorporated, and in the recently amended Quebec Securities Act.[7]

In examining the roots of the Canadian legislation it is of interest to consider the situation as it existed in the comparable jurisdictions of Great Britain and the United States at the time when the Kimber Committee made its report. Both then and now the United Kingdom had a code of conduct to protect offerees which was largely a matter of self-regulation.[8] In the U.S. there was then no specific and comprehensive take-over bid regulation, although other provisions of federal securities legislation had a significant impact in the area.[9]

The Kimber Committee considered the approaches of these other two jurisdictions, but designed a regulatory framework which was unique. In so doing it concluded that an attempt to effect self-

---

[6]While it was inevitable that any form of regulation would place some obstacles in the way of using the take-over bid technique, the Kimber Committee's basic attitude regarding the merits of such bids was clearly one of neutrality (para. 3.07):

"The Committee's recommendations concerning the adoption of the mandatory statutory code pertaining to take-over bids are made on an analytical basis designed to protect the general public by averting potential abuses while impeding as little as possible the use of the take-over bid technique." And para. 3.03:

"...it has not been suggested to the Committee, nor is the Committee of the view, that the take-over bid is apparently harmful either to the general public, to the shareholders of the companies involved, or to the economy of the province or the country as a whole. On the contrary, the Committee recognizes that take-over bids can, in many cases, have positive advantages to the companies involved, to their shareholders and to the economy generally."

[7]The presence of a take-over bid section in the federal companies legislation raises again the difficult question (discussed, *ante*, parts 1.06, 1.07) whether the regulation of take-over bids is most appropriately placed in corporate or securities legislation or both.

[8]The U.K. rules are contained in the City Code on Take-overs and Mergers (Revised in 1969 and in February, 1972) which is administered by the Panel on Take-overs and Mergers. For a comparative discussion, see Anisman, *Takeover Bid Legislation in Canada*, especially p. 3, footnote 13.

[9]The U.S. situation is vastly different today with the introduction of amendments to the U.S. federal legislation in 1970 (Public Law 91-567, 84 Stat. 1497 (1970), amending 15 U.S.C. ss. 78n (1970) (Williams Act)). The result is that now the U.S. regulation of take-over bids is more rigorous than in Canada.

regulation which had been successful in the U.K. would not be adequate in Canada.[10]

7.03 Bid Defined

The take-over bid is an attempt to acquire control of another company through acquisition of its voting shares. It is defined as:[11]

"...an offer, other than an exempt offer, made to shareholders the latest address of any of whom as shown on the books of the offeree company is in Ontario to purchase such number of equity shares of a company that, together with the offeror's presently-owned shares, will in the aggregate exceed 20 per cent of the outstanding equity shares of the company".

In using an arbitrary test, 20 per cent of the outstanding equity shares, the Kimber Committee opted for certainty rather than attempting to measure actual control. Other models, which the Committee rejected, preferred the varying functional concept of control.[12]

The choice of a fixed percentage indicates a concern to have a clear and objective standard; the fact that the figure chosen was 20 per cent and not 51 per cent is an explicit indication that the Committee and

---

[10]Kimber Report (paraphrasing paras. 3.03 to 3.06): The Committee was at all times mindful that its recommendations would have to be implemented in a Canadian context. British experience was less relevant than it might otherwise have been because of a differing financial structure and other special factors operating in the post-war period. In the U.S., on the other hand, take-over bids were less common than in Canada, making their regulation a less urgent concern. In addition, the comprehensive disclosure requirements under the various existing U.S. laws made it somewhat more difficult either for insider trading to take place unchecked or for unprincipled offerors to take advantage of ill-informed shareholders.

In Britain the principal move toward self-regulation was taken in 1959, when various associations (including the London Stock Exchange) combined to produce a document entitled "Notes on Amalgamations of British Businesses" (revised in 1963). Canada followed this lead in 1963, when a responsible and influential group of associations prepared and issued "A Recommended Code of Procedure to be Applied in Connection with Take-Over Bids". The Kimber Committee made extensive use of this document when dealing with the take-over bid area. It noted however, that the voluntary code of conduct contained therein had been far from universally followed; only the sanction of law, so the Report concluded, could secure adequate enforcement on an overall basis.

[11]Section 81(g).

[12]Kimber Report, para. 3.09. To take one example, the U.K. Licenced Dealers' Rules (confirmed by the Jenkins Report) defined a take-over bid as "an offer to acquire securities of a corporation made to more than one holder of those securities calculated to result in any person acquiring, or becoming entitled to acquire, control of that corporation...". The concept of control was defined by the same rules functionally to mean "control direct or indirect, or by means of any right, over the exercise of a majority of the voting power at meetings of the corporation excluding the voting power of holders of classes of securities...having only limited voting rights."

the legislation intended to regulate effective rather than legal control.[13] There are companies with widespread shareholdings where less than 20 per cent of the voting shares might be sufficient for effective control; leaving such cases outside the definition is one of the compromises involved in the adoption of an arbitrary but certain formula.[14] Equally, there are situations where substantially more than 20 per cent would be necessary to acquire effective control.[15] The specific percentage test eliminates the vagueness and unpredictability that would arise in leaving it to a potential offeror to determine whether its bid was in fact an attempt to acquire control.

Defining a take-over bid in terms of equity shares involves a focus on voting shareholdings only, a limitation which fails to take account of the possibility that the acquisition by an offeror of securities other than equity shares might through the occurrence of some contingency result in a later change of control in the offeree company. For example, a successful bid for warrants or convertible debentures, once the conversion privilege was exercised after the successful bid, might result in an offeror holding in excess of 20 per cent of the voting rights.[16]

---

[13]Kimber Report, para. 3.11. *Cf.*, the definition of controlled company (s.1(3)).
[14]When take-over bid regulation was introduced to the CCA in 1971 a lower percentage, ten per cent, was chosen (s.135.1; CBCA, s.187). A further distinction should be made between effective control during a take-over bid and in its absence. For example, for some years prior to the contest between Rothmans and Philip Morris for Canadian Breweries Ltd. in 1969, it was thought that the eleven per cent interest sold by Argus Corporation Ltd. to Philip Morris at a premium over market price constituted effective control of Canadian Breweries. The emergence of a rival, Rothmans, which ultimately was successful in acquiring over 50 per cent of the outstanding equity through the open market in the face of Philip Morris' formal bid for 50 per cent, demonstrated how illusory the previous notion of effective control was when battle was joined. See "Rothmans, Canadian Breweries: Happily Ever After?" Financial Post, June 14, 1969, p. 17.
[15]Once again the Canadian Breweries take-over furnishes an appropriate example. At the close of the contest Rothmans held slightly more than 50 per cent. Philip Morris had more than 20 per cent tendered in response to the bid but not its desired 50 per cent. Philip Morris quite clearly did not have effective control.

This drive for certainty in the Act creates certain anomalies. Thus one who presently holds fifteen per cent of the outstanding equity shares in a company and wishes to obtain only an additional six per cent will be subject to the take-over bid regulations should he choose to acquire the additional six per cent by a general offer to shareholders. This result obtains even when there is another shareholder clearly in control, such as a 51 per cent shareholder who will continue to hold legal and effective control of the offeree company and is not inclined to respond to the offeror's bid. At the other end of the scale we may take the case of a shareholder who already holds 51 per cent of the outstanding equity shares of a company wishing to increase his holdings by a small percentage. If he chooses to do so through an offer to shareholders generally and not by private agreement, the requirements of the take-over bid section of the Act must be complied with.

[16]Or, in a situation where voting rights attached to the preferred shares when dividends were missed, a bid might be made for the non-voting preferred shares of an offeree company with a declining earnings trend in the expecta-

The legislation now ignores the distinction between classes of equity shares although originally this was not the case. It was the 1971 amendments which introduced the simpler concept of taking all outstanding equity shares as a base from which the 20 per cent is calculated regardless of the existence of classes.[17]

It is the total effect of a bid that is looked at in determining whether the 20 per cent test has been met. Thus the 20 per cent is an aggregate composed of the offeror's presently owned shares coupled with the shares he will acquire if the bid is successful.[18]

Any arrangement ("acting jointly or in concert") between two or more offerors results in their being treated as one.[19] The jurisdictional

---

tion that it would soon have to suspend dividend payments; such an event commonly involves voting rights attaching to the preferred shares in question. See the CBCA definition of share for take-over bid purposes (s. 187) which corrects some of these anomalies as does s. 91(1) of Bill 20.

[17]This is the case for calculating ten per cent shareholder insiders but the test is ten per cent of the *votes* attached to all equity shares outstanding rather than ten per cent *in number* of all outstanding equity shares (*ante*, part 6.05(3)). The Kimber Committee had recommended that a take-over bid be defined in terms of a class of equity shares (para. 3.11). The failure to persist in following this more discriminating recommendation evidences a desire for simplicity. The CBCA (s. 187) returns to the class concept. It also includes any offer by an issuer to repurchase its own shares as a take-over bid (s. 187).

To calculate percentage holdings on the basis of the number of voting shares outstanding rather than the total votes attached to shares outstanding is clearly to apply an imperfect test of control. To take an extreme example, acquisition of legal control might occur without the necessity to comply with the take-over bid regulations. Suppose that a company has 1,000 class A shares outstanding with ten votes attached to each, and 5,000 class B shares outstanding with one vote each. An offeror holding one class A share makes an offer for three-quarters of the remaining 999 class A shares. If successful, he would have 51 per cent of the total voting rights of the company but still escape the take-over bid regulations because he would hold only thirteen per cent of the outstanding shares. It is submitted that the take-over bid might be better defined in terms of 20 per cent of the outstanding votes.

[18]Section 81(g) uses the conjunctive phrase "together with" to combine the offeror's present holdings with those to be purchased under the offer. The number of "presently-owned shares" is determined as at the time the take-over bid is made (s. 81(f)). Thus any shares purchased through an exempt offer, *e.g.* through the market, after the bid is made would seem to be excluded from the aggregate used in applying the test.

[19]Offeror is defined broadly in s. 81(e) to mean

"a person or company, other than an agent, who makes a take-over bid, and includes two or more persons or companies,

(i) whose take-over bids are made jointly or in concert, or

(ii) who intend to exercise jointly or in concert any voting rights attaching to the shares for which a take-over bid is made".

The CCA (s. 135.1) gains added flexibility in this area by broadening the definition of take-over bid; after the word "offer" it inserts "or offers, (other than an exempt offer) directly or indirectly made at approximately the same time...". The CBCA (s. 187) uses a slightly different formulation for added flexibility and prudently includes as a take-over bid an offer by a company to repurchase its own shares, specifying particular rules applicable to such bids.

nexus for the Act is offeree shareholders with Ontario addresses on the books of the target company. This is one of the few instances in the Act where provincial geographical boundaries are explicitly recognized as setting a limit to the scope of a provision. The federal legislation on take-over bids uses as its jurisdictional nexus federal incorporation of the offeree company.[20] Thus, for example, where a bid is made for a federally incorporated company with its head office and most of its shareholders in New Brunswick and a much smaller number in Ontario, the offeror will have to comply with the federal Act for any bid, and additionally with the Ontario Act if it extends its offer to Ontario shareholders. If the same company were incorporated in New Brunswick, compliance with the Ontario Act only, would be necessary.

Bill 20 introduces no radical change in the definition of take-over bid.[21] Clarity has been added by the substitution of "voting securities" for equity shares.

7.04 Exempt Offers

The legislation defines four types of offers which are expressly designated as exempt and therefore not subject to the take-over bid rules. These are considered in turn.[22]

(1) PRIVATE AGREEMENT EXEMPTION

The first exempt offer is "an offer to purchase shares by way of private agreement with fewer than fifteen shareholders and not made to shareholders generally".[23]

---

[20]Sections 135.1 and 3(1). On securities regulation and geographical boundaries, see also, *ante*, part 1.12(2).

[21]Section 90(1)(h). Bill 20 (ss. 90(1)(c) and 91) does, however, introduce the concept of an "issuer bid" which is "an offer made by an issuer to purchase, redeem or otherwise acquire any or all of a class of *its* securities" and applies the take-over bid rules to such bids. Bill 20 (s. 91(1)) also requires a take-over bid to be made to holders of warrants or securities convertible into the voting securities sought.

[22]The Kimber Committee would have given only the private company and "market purchasers" a clear exemption in the legislation, leaving other particular cases, such as "an offer made to a limited number of shareholders of a public company" to the discretion of a Supreme Court Judge (para. 3.11). Bill 20 as we shall see marks a partial reversion to the view of the Committee. Note also that while the take-over bid as defined is exempted from the registration and prospectus requirements explicitly (s. 19(1)9(c) and s. 58(1)(c)), not all of the exempt offers as defined (which *ex hypothesi* are not take-over bids) are exempted from the registration and prospectus requirements in precisely the same terms. Compare ss. 19(1)9a, 58(1)(c), 81(b)(i) and (iii).

[23]Section 81(b)(i). The CCA (s. 135.1) parallel exemption uses the pre-1971 Ontario Act language. The CBCA (s. 187) is worded to resolve some of the problems discussed above. It reads: "to fewer than fifteen shareholders to purchase shares by way of separate agreements."

For a consideration of some of the interpretive difficulties in this provision see, *ante*, part 4.12(2)(d)(iv). In *Farnham v. Fingold*, [1973] 2 O.R. 132, 33 D.L.R. (3d) 156 (C.A.), allowing an appeal from [1972] 3 O.R. 688, 29 D.L.R. (3d) 279 (H.C.), it was alleged that a control group of offeree shareholders had breached the Act by artificially lowering their number below fifteen, thereby giving rise to a civil cause of action in the remaining shareholders. The case was settled before this issue could be tried.

Originally it was private agreements in general that were exempt; the provision limiting the number of offerees came as a result of the 1971 amendments following the Merger Report.[24] The exemption would be considerably broadened if one could assume that the fourteen offerees must be all from one province. Probably such a geographic limitation may be inferred. Take as an example a Quebec company with most of its shareholders in Quebec and only ten shareholders in Ontario. If private agreements are made with the ten Ontario shareholders and an additional ten shareholders in Quebec, have the terms of the exemption been exceeded? So long as Ontario alone is considered, fewer than fifteen shareholders are involved, but in fact the offer is directed to 20 shareholders in all. Two arguments from the language of the statute suggest that such an offer was not intended to be exempt. First, the exemption speaks of "shareholders" rather than "offerees". The latter term is defined with a geographic limitation to mean "a person or company to whom a take-over bid is made and whose latest address as shown on the books of the offeree company is in Ontario".[25] "Shareholders" is not thus restricted in scope. Secondly, the definition of take-over bid attaches an Ontario address requirement to shareholders as offerees but does not establish equity shares held in Ontario as the base for the 20 per cent test. The inference is that although the persons to be protected are limited to Ontario, the criteria for deciding what size and type of transactions fall within or without the regulatory requirements are not so circumscribed. There are some grounds, therefore, for supposing that the omission of any express reference to a geographical unit in defining this exempt offer was deliberate. On the other hand there is reasonably clear authority[26] that provincial securities legislation should not attempt to protect extra-provincial investors, unless some aspect of the transaction occurs within its borders.[27] On the basis of this authority it is submitted that a provincial act should have no regard for events outside its borders in determining whether one of its exemptions is met (or exhausted).

(2) PRIVATE COMPANY EXEMPTION

The second exempt offer is "an offer to purchase shares in a private company".[28] The Act defines a private company as one having three

---

[24]*Ante*, part 4.12(2)(d)(iv).

[25]Section 81(c).

[26]*Hretchka et al. v. A.-G. B.C., Securities Commission and Superintendent of Brokers*, [1972] S.C.R.119, 19 D.L.R. (3d) 1, [1972] 1 W.W.R. 561. See also, *ante*, part 1.12(2).

[27]*Gregory and Co. Inc. v. The Quebec Securities Commission*, [1961] S.C.R. 584, 28 D.L.R. (2d) 721 and *R. v. W. McKenzie Securities Ltd. et al.* (1966), 55 W.W.R. 157, 56 D.L.R. (2d) 56 (Man.C.A.). See also, *ante*, part 1.12(2).

[28]Section 81(b)(iii). Logically it is the second. As set out in the Act it is the third exempt offer. The parallel federal exemptions read: CCA (the definition of "exempt offer" in s. 135.1) "an offer to purchase shares in a private company or in a public company that has fewer than fifteen shareholders..."; CBCA (s.187(c)) "an offer to purchase shares of a corporation that has fewer than fifteen shareholders...".

prescribed charter restrictions: a maximum number of shareholders, limited transfer rights and a prohibition on a public offering of its securities.[29] It would seem that to enjoy this exemption a company must reflect these restrictions in its constitution precisely and without variation. This may create difficulties where a company's incorporating legislation permits or requires a private company to have slightly different limiting provisions.[30]

The rationale for this exemption has the same basis in practicality as the exemption for private agreements. In addition, shareholders in a private company will normally be closely associated one with another and with the company's management. Close ties of this sort should mean that all the shareholders and not just a favoured few will be able to respond in an informed way to a take-over bid as well as to present a common bargaining front.

There is no numerical limitation on the number of shareholders to whom this exempt offer may be made. Also there is no prohibition against dealing with all of the shareholders at once "shareholders generally". This would permit, for example, solicitations by mail. The exemption simply recognizes that private companies should be treated differently for purposes of securities regulation.[31]

(3) MARKET PURCHASE EXEMPTION

The third exemption is for "market purchases". It exempts "an offer to purchase shares to be effected through the facilities of the stock exchange or in the over-the-counter market, where such purchases are reported in accordance with section 110a".[32] This exemption is based on the theory that free market forces operating in the recognized markets either of a stock exchange or the over-the-counter market with cash consideration will provide the necessary protection to offerees.[33] Put another way, in a take-over bid the bidder seeks out the

---

[29]Section 1(1)14. See the discussion, *ante*, part 4.12(2)(d)(v).

[30]For example, the third restriction in the private company definition under the CCA (s. 3(1)) prohibits any invitation to the public to subscribe for shares or debentures. "Debenture" is defined in that Act to include debt obligations which carry a charge on any assets (s. 3(1)), thus excluding, to take one example, an unsecured promissory note. The corresponding provision in the Securities Act contains a blanket prohibition on any invitation to the public to subscribe for its securities, secured or unsecured. It is possible therefore, to have a company incorporated as a private company under the CCA in such a way as to permit the issuance of its promissory notes to the public. On a strict interpretation a bid for the shares of that company would not be an exempt offer under Ontario legislation.

[31]The exemption was specifically recommended by the Kimber Report, para. 3.11.

[32]Section 81(b)(ii).

[33]The phrase "a stock exchange" does not contain the usual phrase "recognized by the Commission". Therefore it would not seem to be limited in its application under the Ontario Act to the Toronto Stock Exchange. Thus the purchases could be through the Montreal Stock Exchange even though Ontario shareholders were selling. Notwithstanding the occurrence of a "trade" in Ontario, the exemption would still apply. In the absence of further guidelines in the Act, it is arguable that purchases on any stock exchange so-called, anywhere, would qualify. The CCA (s. 135.1) and the CBCA (s. 187)

offeree in the privacy of his home or office with a persuasive argument; on the other hand, in the case of market purchases, the bidder is simply accepting shares which have already been anonymously offered; a shareholder chooses whether to enter that market or not without being subjected to solicitation.[34]

The term "over-the-counter market" may present some interpretative difficulty.[35] As generally understood, however, the over-the-counter market denotes the trading which takes place between dealers (either as principals or on behalf of clients) in securities which are not listed on the stock exchange. The "counter" in question is that of the dealer. Since securities of this sort cannot mechanically be traded through the facilities of a stock exchange, their only ready market is with a dealer who is prepared to transact business in that security.[36]

---

use the phrase "a recognized stock exchange". This raises the question of what constitutes recognition. In the absence of a policy statement similar to Ontario's Policy 3-17 "Recognition of Toronto Stock Exchange", CCH vol. 2, para. 54-911 in which only the TSE is recognized (*post*, part 10.03(4)) perhaps one must employ a pragmatic test, *viz.*, would the public generally or at any rate those members of it who ordinarily participate in trading, view this institution as a stock exchange? See also, Alberta Policy 3-13 "Recognition of Calgary Stock Exchange", CCH vol. 1, para. 24-513.

[34]The Merger Report, para. 7.11, explains the exemption as follows: "No special effort is made to force the offeree shareholder to sell. He bases his decision on the market price of the securities and, when a formal take-over bid is outstanding for part of the shares, may be influenced into taking the lower market price by the fact that he can dispose of all and not merely part of his holdings."

Recently the OSC has used its general cease trading power to suspend the operation of this exemption due to certain difficulties with partial or conditional bids effected through the exchange. The suspension will be lifted for particular bids whose terms are satisfactory to the Commission.

[35]For discussion of this term, see, *ante*, part 3.04(2). Lack of understanding as to its meaning caused this part of the "market purchase" exemption to be omitted from the first draft of the federal legislation modelled on the original Ontario legislation, though it was subsequently restored: see "An Act to Amend the Canada Corporations Act", R.S.C. 1970 (1st Supp.), c. 10, s. 24, which added s. 135.1, and the CBCA s. 187.

[36]Since the creation of this exemption in the 1966 Act, Ontario has passed regulations to require reporting by registrants of all trades in the over-the-counter market (Reg. 794, ss. 73 to 76 and Policy 3-21 "Publication of Unlisted or Over-the-Counter Quotations", CCH vol. 2, para. 54-915 and Policy 3-25 "Ontario Over-the-Counter Market Manual for Registrants", CCH vol. 2, para. 54-935). Unfortunately the definition provided there of over-the-counter market, which is intended to sweep in all trades by registrants in unlisted securities, is too wide as it stands to be used for the purpose of the take-over bid exemption. Intended for reporting purposes, that definition is inclusive and not exhaustive. Section 73(b) reads:

"'over-the-counter market' includes all trading in securities other than trades in securities that are listed and posted for trading on any stock exchange recognized by the Commission for the purpose of this Part where the securities are traded through the facilities of such stock exchange pursuant to the rules of such stock exchange."

The exemption is contingent on the fulfilment of a timely reporting requirement imposed on offerors by the insider trading provisions of the Act.[37] The aim of this requirement is to let offeree shareholders know in reasonably good time that a "take-over bid" through the market exemption is under way so that they may make an informed decision whether to sell or to hold on the chance of a higher price.[38]

The reporting technique employed is for insider trading reports to be filed by the acquiror within three days after his holdings reach 20 per cent of the outstanding equity shares and within the same period in the case of each additional five per cent thereafter.[39] The three days begin to run as of the day the ownership level is attained.[40] Some have argued that the reports should be immediate on the day of the trade since time is a crucial factor. The Merger Report concluded as much as three days could be necessary to ensure that the required information could be accurately assembled, but this is now open to question. A way of signalling control, approaching more closely to the ideal at least in theory, would be a requirement that a market bidder announce his intention to acquire 20 per cent and report all trades daily from the date of the announcement. This, however, raises the problem of deciding when an intent to acquire control has been formed as well as imposing an administrative burden in the producing of daily reports.

The Merger Report opted for an intermediate course which would touch the most significant shifts in control without treading on points of particular difficulty. Such information as is obtained by this compromise approach is not made available in the most useful form. Rather than appearing as press releases the reports are placed on public file with the Commission, appearing in the next issue of the OSC Weekly Summary.[41] Their utility will depend on perceptive brokers or journalists reacting to market change by investigating the insider trading report public files at the Commission and then disseminating the information to their clients or readers. The present situation seems unfortunate in view of the fact that an acquisition of 20 per cent is normally a material change falling under the timely

---

This provision is so broadly stated that if it were used as a guide to "over-the-counter" in the take-over area it would make redundant the exempt offers for private agreements and private company exempt offers; such a result suggests that it is inapplicable. See also British Columbia, "Over-The-Counter Manual for Registrants", CCH vol. 2, para. 29-975; Quebec Policy 5 "Shares Traded Over-The-Counter in Quebec", CCH vol. 3, para. 66-106.

[37]Section 110a.

[38]In justifying this reporting requirement the Merger Report (para. 7.12) noted that the fact of an impending change in control or an actual change is an important item of investor information and should therefore be subject to timely disclosure policy. Both the U.S. and Britain had already adopted differing approaches to deal with this problem while maintaining the principle that such purchases should be immune from take-over bid rules *per se*.

[39]Section 110a(1) and (2).

[40]Ownership is deemed to pass at the time an offer to sell is accepted or an offer to buy is accepted by the principal or his agent, and not on the closing of the transaction (s. 109(2)(c)).

[41]The CCA Bulletin does not publish these reports.

disclosure policy to which the market must be alerted in a more vigorous fashion, albeit one in the control of the bidder and not the offeree company. It would be of assistance if the Commission made a declaration to this effect and placed the reporting obligation on the offeror.[42]

(4) COMMISSION ORDERED EXEMPTIONS

The last of the four exemptions is one established by order of the Commission.[43] The Commission's power in this area is a discretionary one similar to the exempting authority which it exercises with respect to proxies, insider trading, financial disclosure and the prospectus and registration requirements in connection with a distribution.[44] The wide discretion with which the Commission is endowed is conveyed by the usual sweeping phrase "where in its opinion such an order would not be prejudicial to the public interest" and as in other cases it is empowered to impose such terms and conditions as it considers appropriate. Any person or company may apply for the order, although in the normal situation it will be the offeror.

An application for a Commission order under s. 90 should also be accompanied, where the consideration offered involves securities, by an application under s. 59 for an exemption of the trade in those securities from the distribution and registration requirements. This is necessary because there is no automatic statutory exemption under ss. 19 and 58 for a take-over bid that is exempted by Commission order from the take-over bid requirements, as there is for actual take-over bids. The definition of take-over bid[45] specifically excludes exempt offers.

(5) BILL 20—EXEMPT OFFERS

Bill 20 introduces some important changes. Only the exemption for offers to purchase shares in a private company remains substantially as is.[46] The exemption by Commission order is retained, but it is given a broader formulation designed to make clear that an exemption may be granted from any requirement in the part of the Act dealing with take-over bids.[47] The exemption for "market purchases" is also retained, but with a severe limitation placed upon its use.[48] First the over-the-counter market portion of the exemption disappears altogether. The stock exchange market exemption is subject to rules promulgated by a recognized exchange and accepted by the Commis-

---

[42]Under Bill 20, such an acquisition would be a material change subject to s. 76. See text, *ante*, part 5.16.

[43]Sections 81(b)(iv) and 90.

[44]See, *ante*, part 4.16, part 5.07, part 5.09, footnote 75, and part 6.07. This responsibility was originally vested by the 1966 Act in a designated Judge of the High Court and then subsequently transferred to the Commission on the recommendation of the Merger Report (para. 7.17). In the similar provisions of the CCA (s. 135.91) and CBCA (s.197(1)) the power resides with a High Court Judge.

[45]Section 81(g).

[46]Section 90(2)(b). But even it has experienced change. It is qualified thus "provided that the private company is not an insider of a reporting issuer".

[47]Section 101. This power was only implicit in s. 90 of the 1966 Act which allowed terms and conditions to be imposed in exempting an offer.

[48]Section 90(2)(a).

sion. These rules will permit small amounts of securities to be purchased or small premiums to be paid by a take-over bidder through the exchange but subject bids with a substantial premium attached to be rigorously regulated by the exchange. The exempt offers will also be subjected to the accelerated insider trading reporting rules requiring reports within three days of acquiring 20 per cent and each additional five per cent.[49]

Most severely affected is the exemption for private agreements. This is entirely eliminated. Possibly as a result of recent evidence of abuse, the framers of the Bill have concluded that the maintenance of the exemption is no longer justified, despite the inconvenience entailed by subjecting many small size transactions to legislative requirements and the undoubted sophistication of many of the offerees in such "private" transactions. The elimination of this exemption needs to be considered in the light of the parallel provision,[50] which requires take-over bids to be made to all shareholders whose address is in Ontario. The combined effect of these changes is to prohibit take-overs where only a proportion of the offeree company shareholders are able to participate. This prohibition, together with the scaling-down of the market purchase exemption, should result in all shareholders receiving timely notice of attempts to take over control and allow them to share equally in any enhanced value which the desire of a particular offeror to acquire control lends to their holdings. These changes were chiefly aimed at preventing the sale of control at a premium by a portion of the shareholders.[51]

7.05 Time Limits and Other General Provisions

Time limits are imposed on take-over bids to give the management of the offeree company an opportunity to analyze the bid and report to its shareholders if it so wishes, and to give the shareholders a reasonable opportunity to assess the bid in the light of the information required to be disclosed and other factors before coming to a conclusion to accept or reject. In addition there is a maximum time limit imposed within which the transaction must be consummated in order to ensure that the consideration for tendered shares passes within a reasonable period of time; otherwise the offeree shareholder will be left in a position of suspense, having tendered his shares but not having realized upon them. The major rule of the first type requires that the bid must remain open for the deposit of shares for at least 21 days from the date it is made.[52]

The offeror is also prohibited from taking up and paying for any shares deposited within the first seven days.[53] This restriction is

---

[49]Section 105.
[50]Section 91(1)1.
[51]See, *infra*, part 7.14.
[52]Section 82, para. 1. The Act gives some guidance on the mechanics of delivering take-over bids. They are to be sent by prepaid mail to offerees and are deemed conclusively to have been dated as of the date on which they were sent (s. 83; Bill 20, s. 94). Does this preclude delivery by hand?
[53]Section 82, para. 2.

designed to operate in conjunction with a provision which allows anyone who deposits within the first seven days to withdraw at any time before the expiry of the same seven-day period.[54] This withdrawal right is particularly designed for the small and unsophisticated shareholder who without seeking a broker's advice deposits his securities in immediate reaction to the take-over bid. The sophisticated offeree shareholder will normally wait until the last several days of the 21-day period of the bid to assess the response of the offeree company's management and the market, and in particular to await the possible emergence of a rival bidder. A rival bidder may either operate through the market, in which case the price of the stock is apt to rise higher than the take-over bid offer, or may make a formal take-over bid with better terms. Where a partial bid has been made, a shareholder may prefer to sell to a rival bidder in the market and have all his shares taken up at a lower price than have only a part taken up at the higher take-over bid price. An additional seven days withdrawal right is given whenever the terms of the take-over bid are varied.[55] The draftsmen of the CCA concluded that seven days was an insufficient period for the bid to reach the offeree through the mails, to give the offeree directors time to prepare and send a directors' circular and get it into the hands of offerees, and give them a chance to reflect on the proposal. Hence they extended the withdrawal period to ten days.[56]

There are particular considerations applicable to a partial bid (for less than all the outstanding shares) which are not present with a total bid. To enable the provisions for *pro rata* acceptance to take effect and eliminate any resort to a "first come—first served" procedure, the offeror is prohibited from taking up and paying for deposited shares until 21 days have expired.[57] To prevent an unreasonably long one-sided commitment on the part of the depositing shareholders, the period of time during which shares may be deposited in response to a partial bid or any extension of it is limited to a total of 35 days.[58] An additional provision to satisfy the same objective requires that in a partial bid, if all the terms and conditions not waived by the offeror have been met, shares deposited must be taken up and paid for within fourteen days after the last day for deposit.[59] Where the number of shares deposited exceeds the number for which the offer was made, acceptance must be made *pro rata* unless the offeror changes his mind and decides to take all.[60]

Some partial bids pose particular difficulties. For example, a bid may be made for Ontario held shares of a federally incorporated company. If an offeror who obtains over 90 per cent of the shares wishes to take advantage of the compulsory acquisition powers

---

[54]Section 82, para. 3.

[55]Section 82, para. 3, responding to a Merger Report recommendation (para. 7.24).

[56]Section 135.2. Bill 20, s. 91(1)4 follows this lead. One may question whether even this period is sufficient.

[57]Section 82, para. 4 (Bill 20, s. 91(1)6).

[58]Section 82, para. 5 (Bill 20, s. 91(1)7).

[59]Section 82, para. 6 (Bill 20, s. 91(1)8).

[60]Section 82, para. 7 (Bill 20, s. 91(1)9).

provided by the CCA in order to buy up the rump minority of less than ten per cent, the two time limits of 35 days for deposit and an additional fourteen days for payment create an impossible obstacle since one of the qualifying conditions for compulsory acquisition is that the bid be outstanding for at least four months.[61] Relief must be obtained through an application for an exemption which will extend the time limit to the period stipulated by the provisions of the federal Acts.[62]

The Merger Report[63] brought about a number of changes in the mandatory provisions applicable to take-over bids. Where a right of appraisal is available to an offeree shareholder, normally as a result of provisions contained in corporations legislation, he must be so advised by the offeror.[64] Similarly, where a right of compulsory acquisition or appraisal exists,[65] the offeror must indicate if it intends to avail

---

[61]CCA, s. 136; CBCA, s. 199(2).

[62]These exemptions are customarily granted as requested. The CCA gives the offeror four months in which to solicit tenders from 90 per cent of a class of shares (or 90 per cent of each class where more than one class are bid for). If the goal of 90 per cent is reached in the four months, the offeror has another two months in which to give notice of his desire to acquire any "dissenting" shareholder's shares. The dissenting shareholder is given a month from the date of the notice to seek court adjudication, failing which the offeree company is obliged to register the offeror as the new shareholder and to accept the consideration from the offeror to be held in trust. Accordingly, a period of seven months in all may be involved—four months for deposits and three months after that for compulsory acquisition and the payment of consideration. In the corresponding section of the CBCA, the offeror may acquire dissenting shareholder's shares within 60 days after termination of the take-over bid or within 180 days after the date of the bid, requiring the dissenting shareholder to elect either to accept the terms of the take-over bid, or to demand payment of the fair value of his shares as determined under s. 199(9) to (17), *i.e.*, upon application to a court by the offeror or offeree within 20 days after it has paid the money or consideration to the offeree corporation as required under s. 199(6).

For cases involving the application of this provision, see *Rathie v. Montreal Trust Co. and B.C. Pulp and Paper Co. Ltd.*, [1953]2 S.C.R. 204, [1953] 4 D.L.R. 289; *Esso Standard (Inter-Amer.) Inc. v. J.W. Enterprises Inc. and Morrisroe*, [1963] S.C.R. 144, 37 D.L.R. (2d) 598; *Re Waterous and Koehring-Waterous Ltd.*, [1954] O.W.N. 580, [1954] 4 D.L.R. 839 (C.A.); *Re John Labatt Ltd. and Lucky Lager Breweries Ltd.* (1959), 29 W.W.R. 323, 20 D.L.R. (2d) 159 (B.C.S.C.); and *Re Shoppers City Ltd. and M. Loeb Ltd.*, [1969] 1 O.R. 449, 3 D.L.R. (3d) 35 (H.C.). For a discussion of this and related corporate organic changes affecting dissenting shareholders, see J.T. English, "Corporate Acquisitions—General Considerations", at pp 624-29 and P. Anisman, *Takeover Bid Legislation in Canada.*

[63]Chapter 7.

[64]Section 82, para. 8.

[65]Such as the situation we have already examined, where the offeree company is federally incorporated and the bidder has acquired 90 per cent of the outstanding shares within four months. The Hodgson Report, chapter 17, also recommended a right of compulsory acquisition for Ontario companies legislation. The Report however also recommended that the minority should have the right to *require* an offeror corporation to purchase their shares when the offeror corporation "becomes the beneficial owner of 90% of the shares of

itself of this privilege.[66] Where a take-over bidder intends to make exempt purchases in the market during the course of the bid, this intention must be set out in the take-over bid circular.[67] And if it does so when its bid is a partial bid, it is precluded from reducing the number of shares it is willing to take up by the number of shares purchased in the market.[68] Another provision is designed to ensure that depositing shareholders do receive the consideration offered if their shares are left on deposit more than a certain period of time. Where a total bid is made, even though it continues to be outstanding beyond 35 days (as in the case of compulsory acquisitions) the offeror is obliged to take up and pay for shares tendered at the expiration of that 35-day period or abandon it.[69] This provision will have particular application in cases where the offeror has made the tendering of a minimum percentage a condition of the offer. The offeror will have to choose between waiving the condition or abandoning the offer.[70]

A rather controversial condition resulting from the Merger Report prohibits the offeror from attaching conditions to the take-over bid. There are two exceptions to this restriction: it may withdraw if in a partial bid it has established a minimum number of shares which must be deposited and that minimum number is not met or if the action of the offeree's board subsequent to the offer materially changes the undertakings, assets or capital of the offeree.[71] At the very least withdrawal should also have been permitted in the case of any action of any government body independent of the offeror, to accommodate situations such as a veto by the provincial energy board of the take-over bid by one gas company for another. This prohibition is intended to negative "market out clauses" in take-over bids. Because it is so narrowly drawn there have been an increased number of applications for exemptions by offerors seeking to incorporate a wider variety of conditions in their bids.[72]

---

a corporation *including* in such 90% any shares beneficially owned by an affiliate of the offeror." These recommendations have yet to be implemented.

[66]Section 82, para. 8 (Bill 20, s. 91(1)10).

[67]Section 82, para. 9 (deleted from Bill 20).

[68]*Ibid.*

[69]Section 82, para. 11 (Bill 20, s. 91(1)13).

[70]Query what will happen in the case of further shares deposited *after* the expiry of 35 days. If these additional shares still do not bring the total up to the figure stated in the original condition it would appear that the offeror could refuse to take them up.

[71]Section 82, para. 10.

[72]The Merger Report justified its recommendation regarding conditions this way (para. 7.25):

"On occasion an offeror includes in its tender offer what are known as 'market out' clauses. These escape clauses give the offeror a very substantial discretion to withdraw its offer during or even at the end of the offering period regardless of whether or not it has received the minimum number of shares tendered for. These clauses are not responsive to defensive tactics of the offeree's board of directors. They are appropriate to an underwriting in which the dealer assesses the market before going firm on his commitment. We recommend that such escape clauses be prohibited in take-over bids. The offeree is committed to sell his shares once they are tendered and the

In a further attempt to achieve equity the Act stipulates that where the offeror increases the consideration offered while the bid is outstanding he is obliged to pay the additional premium to those shareholders whose deposited shares he has already taken up and paid for.[73] This increase also constitutes a variation in the terms of the bid, giving shareholders who have already deposited their shares a new seven-day right of withdrawal.[74] This right may be exercised by a shareholder who responded to a partial bid believing at the outset that there would not be a large oversubscription and that most or all of his shares would be taken up. The shareholder may anticipate that the increased consideration offered by the bidder will produce an overwhelming response so as to leave him with a very large proportion of his shares not taken up and paid for. As a result he may now wish to withdraw and retain them all (or perhaps to liquidate his entire holdings in the market during the currency of the bid).

In the case of a cash bid the offeror is obliged to make "adequate arrangements to ensure that the required funds are available to effect payment in full" for deposited shares.[75] This is usually done by appointing a trust company as depository and providing it with funds to effect payment or by arranging a line of credit with a bank evidenced by a letter of commitment.

7.06 Reforms in the General Provisions

Bill 20 effects a number of modifications to the mandatory provisions just discussed. The shareholders' right of withdrawal is now extended to ten days from the date of the take-over bid,[76] and this enlarged time

---

period of withdrawal has run. The offeror ought to be similarly committed subject to his share objective being achieved."

While the prohibition on escape clauses may have been drafted too broadly, there is a very real possibility of unfairness if there is no check on an offeror's withdrawal rights. The parallel with "market out" clauses in an underwriting agreement is an illuminating one. The latter provide an escape not only for extraneous or neutral causes but also for reasons which relate to the business judgment of the underwriter and are thus to some extent within his control. The following is an example of a rather typical market out clause in an underwriting agreement:

"If prior to 8:00 p.m. Eastern Standard Time on the day on which qualification for sale to the public of the Debentures in all the Provinces of Canada has been completed-

(a) There should develop, occur or come into effect any catastrophe of national or international effect or any accident, government regulation or other occurrence of any nature whatsoever which, in our opinion, seriously affects or will seriously affect the financial markets or your business, or

(b) The state of the financial markets becomes such that debentures cannot, in our opinion, be profitably marketed,

we shall be entitled to terminate our obligations hereunder by written notice...not later than 10:00 am. Eastern Standard Time on the second business day following the Qualification Date."

[73]Section 84 (Bill 20, s. 92(3)).

[74]Section 82, para. 3 (Bill 20, s. 92(2)). And Bill 20, s. 92(1) requires that offerees be recirculated.

[75]Section 85 (Bill 20, s. 95).

[76]Section 91(1)3 and 4. Bill 20, s. 91 also applies the general rules to issuer bids. See, *supra*, footnote 21.

period also applies in the case of a fresh right of withdrawal caused by a variation in the terms of the bid.[77] A new provision prescribes how notice of withdrawal is to be communicated.[78] Some of the most important changes occur in the prohibition against attaching conditions to take-over bids.[79] The exception for material changes introduced by the board of directors in the assets or undertaking of the company has been expanded to include actions taken after the bid: (a) by senior officers of the offeree in recognition of the fact that persons in such positions can have just as important an effect on a company as the directors, and (b) by a person or company other than the offeror. Secondly, in order that there should be no rewards for concealment on the part of the directors of the offeree company, offers may be conditioned on there being no *undisclosed* changes *before* the date of the take-over bid. In addition the description of what actions of the directors and senior officers will be proper subjects for a condition of withdrawal has been simplified as well as clarified by the substitution of the phrase "effects a material change in the affairs of such company" for "materially changes the undertakings, assets, or capital of the offeree company". Conditions of withdrawal may now include failure to obtain the approval of a governmental or regulatory authority prior to the expiration of the offer. In cases where such approval is required, another new provision permits the period after which an offeror is bound to take up and pay for securities deposited to be enlarged from 35 to a maximum of 95 days.[80]

7.07 Disclosure Requirements

All take-over bids must be accompanied by a take-over bid circular containing prescribed information in prescribed form. In the case of a bid where a part or all of the consideration consists of securities of the offeror additional information modelled on the prospectus disclosure requirements must also be contained in the take-over bid circular.

Directors of an offeree company are not obliged to make any public response to a bid. However, if they choose to recommend acceptance or rejection of a bid they must send to each offeree a directors' circular with prescribed information.[81] An individual director or officer may recommend acceptance or rejection of an offer but in such a case he must send with his communication a directors' circular in the prescribed form.[82] What the phrase "recommend acceptance or rejection" fails to answer, however, is whether expressions of opinion or statements of fact short of an overt or firm recommendation are permissible without following the prescribed formalities. In recognition of the fact that it may require a number of days to make a full appraisal after a

---

[77]Section 92(1).
[78]Section 91(1)5.
[79]Section 91(1)11.
[80]Section 91(1)13.
[81]Section 87. Bill 20, s. 98(1) requires a directors' circular in any event, which may or may not contain a recommendation from the directors.
[82]Section 87(4) (Bill 20, s. 98(3)). Section 98(6) of Bill 20 requires that all communications sent under s. 98 be by prepaid mail to each offeree at his latest address.

surprise bid, offeree directors are permitted to advise shareholders that they should not tender their shares until further communication is received from the directors. They must then send a directors' circular at least seven days prior to the offer's expiry.[83]

A take-over bid circular must be approved and delivery authorized by the offeror's directors.[84] Similar authority must be obtained for a directors' circular.[85] Both circulars must contain a "full, true and plain disclosure" certificate similar to that required from an issuer in a prospectus.[86] Experts such as auditors or engineers must consent to the use of their reports in either circular and the consent itself must be reproduced in the appropriate circular.[87]

7.08 Contents of Take-Over Bid Circular

There are two types of take-over bid circulars: those where the consideration is cash only and those where the consideration is partially or totally securities. In the former, the contents of the circular include the bare bones of the transaction. In the latter, the contents include in addition information about the offeror's securities[88] equivalent to that found in a prospectus.

Thus in the cash take-over bid the circular must describe the number of any securities of the offeree company beneficially owned directly or indirectly by the offeror and other listed parties; the particulars of any conditions in a conditional take-over bid, the particulars of the method and time of payment of the consideration to be paid, a statement that any deposited shares may be withdrawn by the offeree within seven days; a summary showing the volume of trading and price range of the shares of the offeree in the six-month period preceding the date of the take-over bid and the particulars of any arrangement between the offeror and any of the directors or senior officers of the offeree and of any information known to the offeror that indicates a material change in the financial position or prospects of the offeree since its last published financial statement.[89]

Where a take-over bid is made on behalf of an undisclosed principal the offeror is deemed to be the principal.[90] A 1971 amendment requires

---

[83]Section 87(2) (Bill 20, s. 98(4) and (5)). The Bill *requires* that the directors advise the offerees not to tender their securities while they are considering recommending acceptance or rejection of the bid.
[84]Section 89(1).
[85]Section 89(2).
[86]Sections 89a and 99. This requirement resulted from the recommendation of the Merger Report which considered that take-over bid circulars should be equated with prospectuses for disclosure and liability purposes. However the Report stopped short of recommending vetting by a regulatory agency (paras. 7.18 and 7.19).
[87]Sections 88 and 94. Section 96(2) of Bill 20 leaves this matter to the regulations.
[88]Section 95.
[89]Section 91. Bill 20 (s. 96(2) and (3)) reduces the bulk of the section devoted to take-over bids considerably by leaving the contents of an offeror's circular to be prescribed (and more easily changed) by regulation. Bill 20, ss. 97 and 100 apply the circular rules to issuer bids.
[90]Section 92(1).

the identity of the offeror to be disclosed where the take-over bid is made for less than all of the outstanding equity shares owned by the offerees.[91]

7.09 Contents of Directors' Circular

The purpose of the directors' circular is two fold: first, to communicate the disposition of the offeree's board about the bid to offeree shareholders with some brief supporting detail, and secondly, to ensure that when such communication is effected all possible conflicts of interest are disclosed. Thus the circular must set out debt and equity holdings in the offeree by its insiders and associates accompanied by a statement as to which of those persons intend to accept the offer.[92] The same group must also disclose their holdings of the offeror's securities. If the directors or senior officers have entered into some arrangement with the offeror providing for the retention or retirement of such securities or have any interest in material contracts to which the offeror is a party, this too must be revealed. If the offeror's circular has not, in the directors' opinion, adequately set out the volume of trading and the price range of the shares sought to be acquired in the six months prior to the offer, the directors' circular must remedy the deficiency. Finally two "catch-all" provisions designed to ensure completeness require disclosure of facts known to the directors or senior officers that indicate a material change in the position or prospects of the offeree since the last financial statement, and other material facts not disclosed under the preceding headings.[93]

7.10 Administrative Review of Circulars

Neither a take-over bid nor a directors' circular is required to be qualified with the Commission prior to its being sent to offerees. The regulatory technique followed is one of notification only—the material must simply be filed with the Commission on the date on which it is first sent to offerees.[94]

The Kimber Committee gave careful consideration to the question of whether circulars should be subject to a more thorough screening, before opting for the simpler procedure.[95] While it conceded that a bid which involved. the exchange of securities as consideration did not "differ in any essential constituent from the issuance of securities" in a distribution, it recommended against requiring pre-delivery vetting on the rather pragmatic ground of "the importance of speed and secrecy to the success of a take-over bid or a counter bid". Another important factor was the desire to achieve uniformity in the rules governing take-over bids and to avoid the complexity which a distinction based on the type of consideration offered would entail. Compli-

---

[91]Section 92(2). See, *infra*, part 7.13.
[92]Section 96. Bill 20 (s. 98(1)) leaves details to the regulations.
[93]*Ibid.*
[94]The circular and all supporting or supplementary material must be filed. The Commission has the power to order a cessation of trading in the event that it discovers deficiencies or misrepresentations in the filed material.
[95]Para. 3.24.

ance with the statutory regime, it was thought, could be ensured through the enforcement provisions of the Act.[96]

The Merger Report considered the question of prior review and recommended no change.[97] It did note that the considerations which had weighed so heavily with the Kimber Committee—speed and secrecy—were no longer applicable in quite the same way as a result of developments in the intervening years. In particular, timely disclosure policy requires that plans for a take-over bid be announced prior to the formal offer at least in the event of unusual movements in the stock of either offeror or offeree. However, the Report concluded that the flexibility permitted by present arrangements was worth preserving. It was also of the opinion that "take-over bid circulars for the most part had been responsibly and accurately prepared", a view which helps to explain the Committee's sanguine attitude towards the *status quo* in this area but one which is not universally shared. Equating the take-over bid circular with the prospectus for civil liability purposes apparently seemed to be adequate reinforcement of an already satisfactory state of affairs. In general it is clear that the Merger Report was heavily influenced by the notification philosophy. That Report primarily emphasizes disclosure accompanied by tougher civil liability and enforcement sanctions. It resiles, however, from demanding pre-effective bureaucratic review to ensure that the disclosure standards are met, and in its place gives increased prominence to after-the-fact surveillance and private civil remedies.

7.11 Necessity to Submit Bid to Offeree Company

The Kimber Committee decided that it was not appropriate to require the offeror to submit its bid to the directors of the offeree company prior to sending it to the offerees. In doing so it rejected the model of the U.K. Licenced Dealers' rules, which required this to be done at least three clear business days prior to the mailing to offerees. The Committee was largely influenced by the consideration that shares are the personal property of the person who holds them; in strict legal theory an offer to buy them does not concern the company in which the shares are held.[98] One might argue that offeree directors are in the best position to evaluate the take-over bid and constitute the most knowledgeable, if not the most objective, source of advice for offerees.[99] On the other hand there may often be a conflict between the

---

[96]The Kimber Committee did not extend civil liability for misrepresentations (already applicable to prospectuses by s. 142) to the material contained in offerors' and directors' circulars. This had to wait for the Merger Report which recommended the requirement of certificates warranting full, true and plain disclosure and the imposition of statutory civil liability on directors and officials who signed the certificate (*infra*, part 7.15).

[97]Para. 7.18.

[98]Para. 3.13.

[99]More recently, amendments to the 1934 U.S. Act have required that offeree directors be notified prior to a bid. The 1934 Securities Exchange Act (s. 13(d)(1)) provides that any person who acquires more than five per cent of a class of shares send a notification statement to the issuer.

interests of the directors and those of offeree shareholders, as for example, in a badly managed company. In such cases lack of objectivity is a factor which must weigh heavily but will not always be perceived.

7.12 Mandatory Directors' Circular

Bill 20 fundamentally alters the significance of the directors' circular by making it mandatory. Shareholders are presumed to benefit from having the information specified in these circulars even when the directors have no opinion one way or other regarding the proposed take-over. This represents an important reversal of the stand taken by the Merger Report which recommended against mandatory circulars for fear of forcing offeree directors "into the role of investment advisers".[100]

The Bill simply states that the board of directors of the offeree company *shall* send a directors' circular to each offeree.[101] It then additionally provides that the board *may* include in the circular a recommendation to accept or reject the bid.[102] The board *must*, if it is considering recommending acceptance or rejection, advise the offerees of this fact[103] and advise them not to tender until further communication is received from the directors. Unchanged is the requirement that where a notice is sent that a recommendation will be forthcoming, the decision must follow at least seven days prior to the expiry of the offer.[104]

7.13 Identity of Bidder

The 1966 Act permitted the cash bidder to remain anonymous.[105] The Kimber Committee concluded that it was not necessary for such a bidder to identify himself since offerees are primarily influenced by price.[106] The Committee recognized that the identity of the bidder in a cash take-over bid could conceivably influence offerees, *e.g.* a bidder who would derive a special benefit from a take-over bid by the reduction of competition. Such a person might be expected to pay a higher price than another bidder who did not have such an interest. It was thought, however, that the positive consequences of identification were outweighed by the danger of discouraging take-over bids through compulsory disclosure. The Merger Report considered the same question[107] and its compromise recommendations were adopted in the

---

[100]This recommendation was made even though the writers of the Report were "disappointed to note that the 87 take-over bid circulars filed with the Commission from May, 1967 to December, 1969 elicited a response of only 46 directors' circulars." The provisions of Bill 20 accord with the position taken by the 1973 Select Committee on Company Law (pp. 36-7).
[101]Section 98(1).
[102]Section 98(2).
[103]Section 98(4). This is a significant change. The 1966 Act says "*may* advise".
[104]Section 98(5).
[105]Section 92.
[106]Para. 3.18.
[107]Para. 7.31, where it is noted that the recently amended U.S. federal regulations under the 1934 Securities Act required the cash bidder to be identified.

1971 amendments.[108] Thus a cash bidder is now permitted to retain his anonymity where a total bid is made, but his identity must be revealed in a partial bid. The rationale is that in the case of partial bids which are overtendered, the offeree shareholders will continue to be associated with the enterprise as fellow shareholders of the take-over bidder. The entry on the scene of a new controlling interest or group can have an important impact on the fortunes of a company. In order to assess this impact properly, the Report concluded that the offeree shareholders should know the identity of the partial bidder before deciding whether to accept or reject, given that they would continue to have a shareholding association with it. On the other hand a total bid would "take them out" entirely.

Bill 20 goes one step further and requires the offeror's identity to be disclosed in all take-over bid circulars.[109] The drafters of the Bill decided that the interest of offeree shareholders in knowing with whom they are dealing should override the desire of some offerors to remain anonymous even in the total bid situation.

7.14 Sale of Control at a Premium

When control of a company is sold *via* private agreement under the present legislation, the transaction may be classified as an exempt offer provided that the number of vendors is less than fifteen.[110] And if securities of the acquiring company form part of the consideration, an exemption is provided from the registration and prospectus requirements of the Act.[111] Often the sale of control involves the payment of a premium to the controlling shareholder(s) with no similar offer to other shareholders who in consequence are left with two choices: to sell their shares on the market at a price lower than that received by the controlling shareholder(s) or to remain as shareholders and accept the change. Two policy questions arise which have been the subject of widespread and, at times, emotional debate: first, should the private agreement exemption for sale of control with or without a premium be permitted at all, and secondly, if it is retained, should the law require a subsequent general offer to all shareholders on the same terms or some other "sharing" with them of the premium. It was this latter issue which most seriously divided the Select Committee on Company Law.[112] The majority favouring the *status quo* concluded:[113]

> "that shares of a corporation are a form of personal property and that the owner should be entitled to dispose of them by private agreement on whatever terms he may consider advisable without interference on the part of the legislature....To impose the obligation of a general offer to shareholders would reduce the incentive for

---

[108]Section 92.
[109]Section 102.
[110]Section 81(b)(1).
[111]Sections 19(1)9a and 58(1)(c).
[112]See Hodgson Report, pp. 30 *et seq.*
[113]*Ibid.*, at p. 30.

a person to develop and manage a business by denying such person
a well merited premium for his shares."
The minority concluded that the exemption in the Act should be
conditional on the party acquiring control making an offer within 60
days after the acquisition of control to the remaining shareholders on
the premise that:[114]

"...each share in the capital of a company is the same as every other
share of the same class and entitles the holder to an aliquot interest
in the company. When a controlling shareholder sells control, the
thing he is really selling is corporate assets and the right to control
the use of those assets and those assets belong to all of the
shareholders, not merely the controller."

The minority recommended that the acquisition of 20 per cent of the
voting shares of a company *via* private agreement should be deemed
to be acquisition of control for the purpose of determining if a general
offer should be made. They also recommended that the Commission
should have discretion to exempt acquirors from making a general
offer.

Bill 20 now proposes a change even more fundamental than that
envisaged by the dissenting view in the Committee Report. Not only
do the mandatory general rules applicable to all take-over bids require
that a bid must be made to all shareholders[115] but the exempt offer for
private agreements has been removed entirely from the Act. As a
result there can be no private take-overs not subject to regulation, and
the regulations require that all shareholders must participate equally.

7.15 Civil Liability in Take-Over Bids

We have already noted the assimilation of take-over bid and directors'
circulars to prospectuses for purposes of civil liability.[116] Section 100a
provides for a right of rescission in an offeree in similar terms and with
similar defences as the right of rescission given in s. 65 to purchasers
of securities in the course of distribution to the public. Section 144a
provides for an action in damages for material false statements in the
take-over bid or directors' circular in similar terms and with similar
defences as the analogous action for material false statement in the
prospectus.[117]

Bill 20 consolidates ss. 100a and 144a; s. 130 provides that where a
take-over bid circular contains a misrepresentation every offeree is
deemed to have relied on the misrepresentation and has a right of
action for rescission[118] or damages against three possible categories of

---

[114]*Ibid.*, at p. 31.

[115]Section 91(1)1.

[116]*Supra*, part 7.10

[117]Alberta and Manitoba alone of the other jurisdictions have provisions
similar to s. 100a and s. 144a: R.S.A. 1970, c. 333, as am., ss. 99.1, 140.1; R.S.M.
1970, c. S-50, ss. 99.1, 141.1. For a discussion of take-over bids and insider
trading see, *ante*, part 6.08(8).

[118]The deemed reliance is arguably novel in Bill 20 for the rescission action
though not for the action in damages. In the Act s. 144a expressly deemed
reliance. Section 100a was silent, simply giving a rescission right where the
misrepresentation occurred. See, *ante*, part 4.10(2) and (3).

parties: the offeror, the directors of the offeror at the time the circular was signed, and all other persons who signed a certificate in the offending circular. This cause of action and its defences are parallel with the provisions in s. 129 of the Bill for liability in connection with a defective prospectus.[119]

Bill 20 also introduces a new liability provision with respect to directors' circulars.[120] The remedy is confined to damages, and the range of potential defendants is restricted to directors and officers of the offeree company. The offeree company itself is not liable. Apart from this, there is no difference in the rules applicable to the two types of circular.

---

[119]The defence that the offeree knew of the misrepresentation will mitigate the harshest aspects of the deemed reliance provision.
[120]Section 130(2).

Chapter 8
Regulation of Trade
Generally

8.01 Introduction

We have discussed earlier the requirement that anyone trading in securities must first possess a licence to trade unless an exemption is available.[1] Most of the rules affecting the conduct of traders are appended to the licence requirement as conditions of registration or are found in the internal codes of the self-regulatory organizations.[2] There are, however, rules of general application expressed in the Act which regulate trading conduct, yet fall into neither of these two categories; if one classifies them according to purpose they may be ranged under the general heading of anti-fraud techniques. The breach of any one of these general trading rules will be an offence under the Act. Several of them apply indiscriminately to registrants and non-registrants alike; others only apply to registrants.

All of the rules discussed in this chapter appear in Part VIII of the Act.[3] They may be conveniently divided in two for analytical purposes: disclosure requirements and prohibited acts. In the event the rules are breached there are in some instances civil remedies (*e.g.* rescission) contained in the legislation. This raises the question whether the expressed sanction or remedy is exhaustive. Where no civil remedies are explicitly provided, one faces a difficult task in deciding whether civil remedies may be inferred on a statutory tort or related theory.[4] This is essentially a problem of statutory interpretation: was it the legislative intent to permit the wronged party to be restored to his pre-contract position (or obtain damages in respect of his loss) on the theory that such a wrongfully obtained contract is voidable or void?[5]

A. Disclosure Requirements

8.02 Confirmation of Trade

Registered traders are required in the case of each trade to send a confirmation notice to the customer containing prescribed particulars.[6] This requirement applies whether the trader has acted as

---

[1] *Ante*, chapter 3.
[2] *Post*, chapter 10.
[3] Sections 67 to 80, entitled "Trading in Securities Generally". Bill 20, Part XII, ss. 36 to 52.
[4] Bill 20 has a special section creating statutory torts when certain specified sections are breached (s. 132). In the case of sections not referred to in s. 132, the problem arises in deciding whether this means that no civil remedy is available.
[5] For a discussion of some of the jurisprudence see, *ante*, part 4.10.
[6] Section 67 (Bill 20, s. 36).

principal or agent. The notice must be sent or delivered "promptly", although no further assistance is given in the Act as to the meaning of that term.[7] The following information must be provided:

(1) quantity and description,

(2) consideration,

(3) whether or not the registrant acted as a principal or agent,

(4) if the registrant acted as agent in a stock exchange trade, the name of the other registrant who was party to the trade,

(5) the date and name of the stock exchange, if any, upon which the transaction took place,

(6) the commission, if any, charged in respect of the trade,

(7) the name of the salesman, if any, in the transaction.

As well as providing the customer with a written record, this information can be used by him to compare his trade with other activity in that particular stock at a similar time in order to ascertain whether his broker took appropriate steps to obtain the best deal or "fill" possible. This is particularly important in the case of trading in unlisted stocks, which lack one central auction market place. The publication in the newspapers of daily volume and price information with respect to such stocks is an almost essential adjunct in enabling the information provided to serve its purpose. If the customer notes that details of the confirmation are widely at variance with the quotations published in a newspaper, he can begin an inquiry with his broker or if necessary can take the matter up with the appropriate regulatory officials.[8]

Bill 20 introduces few alterations in the confirmation slip requirement.[9] The only major change is in the fourth of the required items: a dealer acting as agent must report the name of the other party to the trade in all cases, and not just when the trade is on a recognized exchange. In view of the fact that the information is perhaps most useful in connection with over-the-counter trades, the extension of this obligation appears desirable. Bill 20 also contains a number of completely new confirmation rules applicable to mutual funds.[10] The requirements which they impose are in addition to the normal confirmation information previously discussed. The extra items which must be included are:

(1) The price per share or unit at which the trade was effected.

---

[7]For some guidance see *Laskin v. Bache & Co.*, [1972] 1 O.R. 465, 23 D.L.R. (3d) 385 (C.A.).

[8]A fairly elaborate mechanism has been established as a condition of registration in Ontario in the last few years to deal with the public reporting of over-the-counter market trades. See Reg. 794, ss. 73 to 76, Ontario Policy 3-21 "Publication of Unlisted or Over-The-Counter Quotations", CCH vol. 2, para. 54-915, and "Condition of Registration Over-The-Counter Trading Reports, OTC Manual for Registrants", CCH vol. 2, para. 54-935. See also, British Columbia "Over-The-Counter Market Manual for Registrants", CCH vol. 2, para. 29-975; Quebec Policy 5 "Shares Traded Over-The-Counter in the Province of Quebec", CCH vol. 3, para. 66-016.

[9]Section 36(1).

[10]These derive from the recommendations of the Canadian Mutual Funds Report, chapter 14.

(2) The amount deducted by way of sales charges or service fees, and any other deductions.[11]

Where the mutual fund trade is effected pursuant to a contractual plan[12] yet another series of statements must be included which will enable an investor to determine what portion of his consideration is allotted to investment, as opposed to sales and other charges, and the timing and manner of such allocation.[13] Most licensed traders subject to these rules, whether regular brokers or mutual fund distributors, now use modern data processing service bureaus to process the information and forward it to the customer on their behalf.[14]

Several short forms are permitted to reduce the bulk of confirmation information. For example, it is sufficient to identify the salesman acting for the customer and the trader on the other side of the transaction by means of a code or symbols. The slip must state, however, that the real name will be furnished on request.[15] The licensed trader who employs this exception is required to file the code or symbols and their meaning with the Commission and give notice within five days of any change in or addition to them.[16] Upon the Commission's request the licensed trader who acted as agent in a trade is required to disclose to the Commission the broker or other person on the other side of the trade.[17] This information could also be obtained under an investigation order, but since its disclosure is specifically provided for here, the Commission is relieved of the necessity of bringing more onerous sanctions into play. Ascertaining the identities of traders and of the principals for whom the traders are acting is particularly important in an attempt to trace an insider trade or a market manipulation scheme. However, the use of this power is not restricted to such portentous occasions and events. A quiz circular to brokers to elicit the names of persons beneficially buying and selling is a common first step in an informal investigation following unusual fluctuations in a stock; in many cases a perfectly satisfactory explanation is at hand.

8.03 Principal's Notification

When a licensed trader acts as principal in the sale of his own securities or the purchase of securities for his own account, and in the same transaction acts as agent on someone else's behalf, he has acted with a conflict of interest. The resolution of this conflict raises questions of some perplexity. The problem is and will continue to be endemic in the securities industry so long as the functions of broker and dealer are not divorced.[18] One of the general trading rules

---

[11]Section 36(2).

[12]Defined in s. 1(1)6.

[13]Section 36(3).

[14]For a case holding that this processing service in itself is not trading in securities requiring a licence see *Re Ontario Securities Commission and C.A.P. Ltd.*, [1972] 1 O.R. 205, 22 D.L.R. (3d) 529 (H.C.).

[15]Section 67(2) (Bill 20, s. 36(4)).

[16]Section 67(3) (Bill 20, s. 36(5)).

[17]Section 67(4) (Bill 20, s. 36(6)).

[18]The two roles are separate in the U.K. but not in the U.S. For an example of

attempts to mitigate the effects of conflict by requiring its disclosure. A registrant (except where he is trading with another registrant or where one of the exemptions from registration in s. 19(1) or (2) is available) is required to state that he proposes to act as principal in all written communications before a contract is entered into or any consideration is received. Where the preliminaries of the trade are oral, the written confirmation of the contract must state that the trader has acted as principal.[19] However, the prophylactic purpose of this disclosure is largely frustrated by a qualifying provision which stipulates that a statement made in compliance with the principal's notification requirement does not prevent the licensed trader from acting as agent.[20] It is this provision which has permitted the present standard practice of stating on *all* confirmation slips that the broker may have been acting as principal, a form of notification which fails to flag those trades where he was in fact so acting.

So far as the consequences of failure to make the required statement are concerned, a licensed trader who errs in this fashion will be subject to the offence provisions of the Act;[21] and if the omission is deliberate or reflects ineffective internal firm rules or has occurred before, it will jeopardize the trader's continued registration. However, the Act goes further and positively states civil liability consequences flowing from the delinquency. The party to the contract who should have received notification is entitled to rescission by giving written notice of the same to the trader within 60 days of the delivery of the security.[22] The 60-day rescission period only applies in the case where the licensed trader executed some of the preliminaries to the trade in writing without the required disclosure. Where all the preliminaries were oral with the exception of the required final written confirmation, the registrant's client has only seven days from delivery of the written confirmation to serve written notice of rescission.[23] The difference between the seven-day and 60-day limitation periods may be explained by the fact that written contracts usually involve larger amounts, requiring greater opportunity for assessment of one's rights. It is not altogether clear, however, that this should result in such a marked difference between the two provisions. The major defect in this remedy, however, is that there is no mechanism which will enable a client to know that his broker was buying or selling as principal at the relevant times; and even if the client does find out, there may be

---

the conflict see *SEC v. Merrill Lynch* (1968), 43 S.E.C. 933, CCH Fed. Sec. Law Rep. vol. 2, para. 22781.135, discussed, *ante*, chapter 6 at footnote 107. See also, *infra*, footnote 28.

[19]Section 70(1), (2) and (4).

[20]Section 70(3).

[21]Section 137.

[22]Section 71(1) (Bill 20, s. 135(1)). An additional provision in the same section appears redundant. It states that in the case of a purchase *from* the registrant, the purchaser must still be the owner of the security purchased. At common law (or rather in equity) "rescission of contract" would not be available in the case of a transaction where the purchasing party was not in a position to effect "restitutio in integrum"; other purchased securities of the same class would not suffice.

[23]Section 71(2) (Bill 20, s. 135(2)).

insurmountable difficulties in the way of proving that the securities bought or sold by the customer were the identical ones sold or bought by the broker.[24]

The Act reverses in this area the usual rule that proof lies with the plaintiff. It establishes that the registrant has the onus of proving compliance with the notification provision in the event of an action for rescission.[25] The advantage thus given the plaintiff is counterbalanced somewhat by a provision which requires an action of this sort to be commenced within three months from the date of service of notice of rescission, a considerable modification of the usual moratorium.[26]

Bill 20 contains the requirement of notification when acting as principal in terms almost identical to those of the Act.[27] However, the requirement of notification in the case of a contract entered into orally has been removed, as has the corresponding restricted right of rescission. Instead, the Bill relies on an obligation imposed on the registrant to disclose as part of the confirmation of trade slip the capacity in which he acted. Failure to provide this information results in a right of rescission under the general rescission remedy in s. 130(2).

8.04 Particulars Identifying Traders and Conflicts of Interest

There are several requirements designed to make customers aware of the extent of registrant holdings the potential conflicts of interest arising therefrom.[28] First, advisers must print on any of their written communications a statement of any financial or other direct or indirect interest they may have in any of the securities referred to.[29]

Bill 20 broadens the scope of the disclosure required of registered advisers considerably. The financial or other interests not just of the adviser himself but of any "partner, director, officer or a person or company that would be an insider of the adviser if the adviser was a reporting issuer" must be prominently indicated on all literature sent out.[30]

Entirely new in Bill 20 is a provision extending certain disclosure of interest requirements to registered dealers who issue written recommendations that securities be bought, sold or held.[31] The dealer must prominently indicate whether in the immediate past year it has acted as an underwriter or financial adviser to the issuer of the securities in question or is currently such an adviser or whether it will receive any fee for its recommendation.

---

[24]On similar difficulties involved in tracing insider trading, see *ante*, part 6.08(7).

[25]Section 71(3) (Bill 20, s. 135(4)).

[26]Section 71(4) (Bill 20, s. 137).

[27]Section 39.

[28]For examples of principal-agent conflicts of interest see *Elliott v. Dobson*, [1954] O.R. 185, [1954] 2 D.L.R. 510 (H.C.) and *Brown v. Premier Trust Co. and Holmes*, [1947] O.R. 50, [1947] 1 D.L.R. 593 (H.C.).

[29]Section 72. Some further guidance to the ambit of this requirement is given by the inclusion in the legislation of five specific cases where disclosure is required.

[30]Section 40.

[31]Section 41.

The Act requires every registered partnership or company to publish on all letterheads, circulars or other stationery, or in a prospectus where its name appears as underwriter, the name of each person who has a direct or indirect interest of five per cent or more of the capital of the partnership or company.[32]

Another series of provisions circumscribe advertising of the fact of registration. This topic perhaps belongs more under prohibited acts, but a brief summary may be given here. A registrant may not use the name of another registrant in its communications unless it is the partner, officer or agent of the other or has its written authorization.[33] The fact of registration may not be advertised,[34] nor may representations be made whether written or oral that the Commission has passed upon the financial standing, fitness or conduct of any registrant or upon the merits of any security.[35] Finally, unregistered persons or companies are prohibited from holding themselves out as being registrants, either directly or indirectly.[36]

8.05 Short Position

The sale of a security not owned by the seller at the time it is sold is called a short sale.[37] The successful completion of such a transaction requires that the seller purchase or borrow by the delivery date a security matching the one which he has contracted to sell. For sales through the stock exchange delivery must occur within five days after the contract of sale is written.[38] Short sales are common in the securities industry and in themselves constitute a type of speculation.[39] The short seller believes that the price of the security will decline between the time he enters into a contract and the time of delivery. He realizes his profit on the difference between the contract price and the lower amount he has to pay in later purchasing or borrowing the security to satisfy his obligation as seller. If the price does not change or increase in the intervening period then the short seller incurs a loss.

---

[32]Section 73. Bill 20 retains this requirement unchanged except for the substitution of the more concise term "registered dealer" and the specific inclusion for greater clarity of the preliminary prospectus in the documents which must display the required names (s. 42).

[33]Section 74 (Bill 20, s. 43).

[34]Section 75 (Bill 20, s. 44).

[35]Section 77 (Bill 20, s. 46).

[36]Section 76 (Bill 20, s. 45).

[37]Section 11.27 of the TSE by-laws defines short sales and provides for their regulation, CCH vol. 3, para. 89-426.

[38]*Ibid.*, s. 13.02

[39]The percentages of short sales to total trading on the TSE for a five-year period on a volume basis were as follows:

1969	2.20 per cent
1970	1.40 per cent
1971	1.35 per cent
1972	1.07 per cent
1973	1.32 per cent

(Source: TSE Annual Reports).

As a technique in the securities industry, short selling remains the centre of controversy. The main argument on its behalf is that it serves as a moderating force when the price of a security (or the market generally) experiences an undue price rise not based on concrete economic evidence such as increased profitability of the issuer or easier credit in the economy. On the other hand, it is argued that short selling tends to emphasize and accelerate a decline either in a single stock or the market generally to a level below that at which it would stabilize if governed by its own supply and demand forces without the additional impetus provided by speculation.

The rules relating to trades generally accept the fact of short sales and provide for their recognition through a special disclosure provision.[40] This requirement is not limited in its application to registered traders, but applies to anyone selling securities, although reliance is placed on registered traders to collect the information. Anyone placing an order for the sale of a security through a registrant must indicate to the registrant at the time of placing the order that he does not own the security; if acting as an agent with the knowledge that his principal does not own the security he must make a similar declaration to the registrant on the principal's behalf.[41]

8.06 Registrant's Treatment of Proxies

Both as a matter of convenience to the customer and to oblige their broker, customers will often leave their securities in a registrant's custody. Often too the securities will be registered in "street form" or "street name", that is, in the broker's name or in the name of the broker's nominee. Those securities registered in the customer's name but held by the broker will often bear an endorsement in blank.[42] These practices make the execution of a subsequent sale far simpler than if the securities were kept by the customer or placed by him in a safety deposit box.[43] However, the practice of using street names does interpose a third party between an issuer and the beneficial security holder, since the share register will show only the street name.

A curious compromise rule provides a communication bridge between the issuer and the party with the ultimate beneficial interest where a broker holds the shares. It also gives the benefical owner some

---

[40]Figures for outstanding short sales are regularly published in the financial newspapers, though not by force of law; they serve as a barometer reflecting the current conditions and expectations in the securities industry.

[41]Section 79. See also, Uniform Policy 2-08 "Declaration as to Short Position-Listed and Unlisted Securities", CCH vol. 2, para. 54-878.

[42]The customer signs the reverse side of the certificate to effect a transfer but with the name of the transferee left blank. It will be filled in later—after a sale takes place.

[43]Canada has not yet developed a central securities depository designed to immobilize certificates in a particular location. The Canadian Depository for Securities Ltd. was incorporated under the Canada Corporations Act in 1970 (Canada, House of Commons Debates, 28th Parliament, 2nd Sess., 1970, vol. 8, at p. 8486) but has not yet begun to operate. For a review of this and related developments see I.F.G. Baxter and D.L. Johnston, "Transfer of Investment Securities—Some Current Proposals" and Baxter and Johnston, "New Mechanics for Securities Transactions".

control over how the shares are voted.[44] Where shares of a company[45] are registered in the name of a registrant or his nominee and are not beneficially owned by him, he is prohibited from voting these shares at any meeting of shareholders unless he

(a) forwards a copy of the notice of the meeting, the financial statements, the information circular and any other material other than the form of proxy at no expense to the beneficial owner,[46] and

(b) requests voting instructions stating that if they are not received at least 24 hours prior to the proxy deposit expiry time[47] a proxy may be given or the shares otherwise voted at the registrant's discretion.[48] Companies are obliged to furnish the registrant with the appropriate number of copies of material to be forwarded.[49] A positive obligation is placed on registrants to vote or give proxies according to written voting instructions received from the beneficial owner,[50] and if requested by the beneficial owner, the registrant shall give the proxy to the owner or his nominee.[51] None of these provisions gives the registrant the right to vote shares that he is otherwise prohibited from voting.[52] There is also an important declaratory provision which stipulates that the failure of a registrant to comply with these provisions does not affect the validity of a shareholders' meeting or proceedings taken at it.[53]

Bill 20 qualifies the freedom of action available to the registrant or nominee.[54] Instead of allowing the registrant to vote the shares after he has forwarded the proper information and advised the beneficial owner that they will be voted if instructions are not received by a certain time, there is a prohibition (followed by a qualification) on the voting of such shares by registrants. To enable the registrant to vote them, the beneficial owner must take the initiative and so instruct

---

[44]Note that the rule does not apply in the case of holdings of securities other than shares. Bill 20, s. 49 introduces the term voting securities in place of shares.

[45]Again the provision lacks breadth in not including shares of a person. Bill 20, s. 49 refers to voting securities of an issuer.

[46]Section 80(1).

[47]If an expiry time is not specified in the notice then the time is 24 hours prior to the time fixed for the meeting.

[48]Section 80. The registrant is precluded from voting shares registered in his name or his nominee if he does not know who is the beneficial owner of the shares, by s. 80(2).

[49]Section 80(3) (Bill 20, s. 49(3)).

[50]Section 80(4) (Bill 20, s. 49(4)).

[51]Section 80(5) (Bill 20, s. 49(5)).

[52]Section 80(7). For example, a clause in a street name agreement reserving the voting rights to the beneficial owner would probably suffice as an "other prohibition" which would prevent the registrant from voting the shares even if he had complied with the provisions permitting the forwarding of proxy material with a request for instructions.

[53]Section 80(6). See *Murphy v. Lindzon et al.*, [1969] 2 O.R. 704, 6 D.L.R. (3d) 492 (C.A.).

[54]Section 49. It also replaces "shares of a company" with "voting securities of an issuer".

him. Bill 20 also makes the provisions outlined above applicable to "custodians" of mutual fund shares or units.[55]

There is one more innovation of Bill 20 approximately subsumed under the heading of disclosure. This is a provision which permits the Commission to order that any sales material intended to be used in a distribution must be filed with it first.[56] The Commission's authority to make an order may on analysis be broken down into two distinct phases: it must first be "satisfied" that the registrants' past conduct in regard to sales literature engenders a reasonable belief that protective measures are necessary; if so, the Commission *may* then decide to require prior submission of the material. In theory the Commission could be convinced that present circumstances outweigh past conduct so as to prevent an order issuing in a particular case. The Bill goes on to offer comprehensive definitions of "advertising" and "sales literature".[57] The latter is covered by the section, whether it is given to the prospective customer or merely shown to him. When an order is made, it may be either a blanket prohibition or a qualified one requiring deletions in the material.[58] In addition the Bill expressly provides for rescission or variation of the order on application by the registered dealer affected.[59]

B. Prohibited Acts

8.07 Residential Sales

The Act prohibits "door-to-door" peddling of securities. Presumably this prohibition recognizes the sophisticated nature of securities and the potential dangers inherent in permitting a skilled salesman to use his persuasive tactics on the average householder. The prohibition is expressed in this way:[60]

"No person or company shall,
  (a) call at any residence; or
  (b) telephone from within Ontario to any residence within or outside Ontario,
 for the purpose of trading in any security with any member of the public."

A call probably means a personal visit, although the word is not defined in the Act. It seems that this provision is intended to preclude any opportunity for two-way dialogue, but one-way communication such as by letter or telegram is permissible.[61]

---

[55]Section 49(1) through (6). "Custodian" is defined (s. 49(6)) to mean a "custodian of securities issued by a mutual fund held for the benefit of plan holders under a custodial agreement or other arrangement with a person or company engaged in, or administering a contractual plan in relation to, the distribution of securities of the mutual fund."
[56]Section 51.
[57]Section 51(2).
[58]Section 51(3).
[59]Section 51(4).
[60]Section 68(1).
[61]These one-way communications would, however, be trading activities within s. 1(1)24 requiring registration. It is also to be noted that the prohibition does

Unlike the registration for trading requirement where trading with *any* persons is comprehended, calls at or to the residence of "non-public" persons are permissible.[62] Residence is defined inclusively as[63] "any building or part of a building in which the occupant resides either permanently or temporarily and any premises appurtenant thereto". While some scope may be given to the residual meaning of residence not expressed in the words of the definition, it does not cover the potential customer's business office or place of employment, or a public meeting place.[64] An exemption[65] from this prohibition is provided which is based in part on the distinction between public and private but extends beyond it to cover the situation where the customer himself takes the initiative in requesting information. Thus calls are exempt to or at the residence of:

(i) a close personal friend, a business associate or a customer with whom a habit of trading has developed, or

(ii) a person who has made a written request for information provided that the call relates only to the specific security for which information was requested.

In addition this prohibition is not applicable in the case of "a trade in any security in respect of which registration is not required". There is some ambiguity to this qualification.[66]

This prohibition does not affect salesmen of some other financial instruments which do not fall within the Act. Life insurance salesmen, for example, whose governing legislation does not preclude calls at residences, have a considerable competitive advantage, which is increased by the fact that they may also hold a licence to sell mutual funds. In recognition of this the Canadian Mutual Funds Report

---

not prevent a person outside the jurisdiction from telephoning into it. However, telephoning from outside the jurisdiction to initiate sales was held sufficient to establish trading within the receiving jurisdiction on a charge of failing to register; see *R. v. W. MacKenzie Securities Ltd. et al.* (1966), 55 W.W.R. 157, 56 D.L.R. (2d) 56 (Man. C.A.). See also B.C. Policy 3-12 "Calling at or Telephoning Residences", CCH vol. 2, para. 29-962.

[62]See, *ante*, part 4.02(2).

[63]Section 68(3) (Bill 20, s. 37(3)).

[64]Thus to use a simple illustration, a securities salesman would violate the prohibition if he called at a farmer's home or met him in the adjacent barn, but might escape the ambit of the prohibition if he intercepted him on his tractor in the field.

[65]Section 68(2).

[66]Presumably the antecedent to which "in respect of which" refers is "trade" and not "security". Thus, the exemption almost certainly does not apply to the activities of advisers which are exempted from registration by s. 18; that section is concerned with persons and institutions rather than trades and securities. It probably applies to situations covered by the s. 19(3) exemption "in respect of a trade where the purchaser is a person...or company...*if* the trade is in a security...not less than $97,000." Similarly there is a probable exemption for calls in connection with the eleven types of trades exempted from registration by s. 19(1). It certainly applies to the s. 19(2) registration exemption for trades in certain types of securities since this is the narrowest possible construction of the exemption.

recommended that the prohibition be lifted.[67] That recommendation is followed in Bill 20, which lifts the general ban and in its place gives a discretion to the director to prohibit calls or telephoning by a named person or company.[68] The director is required to first give the affected trader an opportunity to be heard.[69]

8.08 Future Representations

The Act prohibits any one, whether registrant or not, who is intending to effect a trade from making any written or oral representation that he or anyone else will resell or repurchase or will refund all or any of the purchase price of the security traded.[70] There is an understandable exception for securities that carry a right of redemption or repurchase by the issuer.[71] There is also an exception where the representation is made to a purchaser other than an individual if it is contained in a signed agreement for the purchase of a security costing more than $50,000.[72]

The second type of prohibited representation is an undertaking regarding future price or value.[73] Although usually observed in form, this provision is frequently contravened in spirit by persuasive estimates which fall short of an outright violation. The key word is "undertaking", which strictly construed implies a guarantee.[74] Such a restricted interpretation permits suggestions, inferences and educated guesses indicating that, healthy price increases are to be expected in the case of a particular security.[75]

Finally, representations that a security will be listed on the stock exchange or that application for listing has or will be made are forbidden without the written permission of the director.[76] It seems that a restrictive view is taken of this prohibition as well. This can be illustrated by the case of *R. v. Coles*[77] where the Ontario Court of Appeal upheld an appeal from a conviction based on the statement that the stock "would be or would likely be listed". The Court of Appeal concluded that there could be no breach of the section without a representation that the stock "will be listed".

Where the director's relieving permission is granted it is usually in distributions where an exchange listing in the near future is contemplated. He will then normally require that the prospectus contain a statement of the application for listing.

---

[67]The Mutual Funds Report, pp. 552-6, contains a discussion of this broadening provision; it reflects a new philosophy which assumes greater sophistication on the part of the consumer than earlier regulators conceded.
[68]Section 37(1). The order may be on terms and conditions.
[69]Section 37(2).
[70]Section 69(1) (Bill 20, s. 38(1)).
[71]Section 69(1) (Bill 20, s. 38(1)).
[72]Section 69(4) (Bill 20, s. 38(4)).
[73]Section 69(2) (Bill 20, s. 38(2)).
[74]The heading for the subsection reads "promises".
[75]*E.g.*, "We are *very* confident that it will double in price in two months".
[76]Section 69(3).
[77][1970] 1 O.R. 570, 9 D.L.R. (3d) 65, [1970] 2 C.C.C. 340 (C.A.), *per* Laskin J.A. (as he then was).

The prohibition against future representations is continued almost unaltered in Bill 20.[78] One small but important clarification is made regarding repurchases and refunds. An additional exemption is provided where there is a right of the owner to require redemption or purchase of his securities.[79]

8.09 Margin Purchases

Purchases on margin are a common practice in the securities industry, particularly in the more speculative types of shares. In transactions of this sort the purchaser only pays to the trader purchasing on his behalf a certain percentage, say 30 per cent, of the purchase price, and leaves the security purchased with the trader as collateral for the amount outstanding.[80] Generally the trader will take that security and pledge it with a bank in return for a loan permitting him to finance the credit he has granted to his margin customer. When the market price of the securities held on margin falls below the earlier purchase price, the customer is required to pay an additional sum necessary to bring his account back up to the required percentage of the total market price of the security. Alternatively, the trader may sell a portion of the margin securities to maintain the appropriate margin percentage after first giving notice to the customer.[81]

Several of the conditions of registration[82] govern the maintenance by a broker of securities equivalent to the number held on margin. One of the general trading rules attempts to attain a similar objective. It gives the margin customer an "option" to treat his contract with a registrant as "void" and obtain rescission where the registrant or any member or employee of the firm sells securities for an account in which he or the firm or member has a direct or indirect interest if the effect would be to reduce the amount of securities below the amount the firm should be carrying for all customers.[83]

The value of this provision is somewhat questionable. The customer will normally not discover that a broker has violated the rule, in

---

[78]Section 38.

[79]Section 38(1).

[80]The purchaser achieves a leverage effect which is in inverse proportion to the percentage paid on the total sum. Commodity futures provide the best opportunity in this respect, with minimum percentages as low as ten per cent.

[81]In connection with margin requirements, see *Burke v. Cory*, [1959] O.W.N. 129, 19 D.L.R. (2d) 252 (C.A.); *Laskin v. Bache & Co.*, [1972] 1 O.R. 465, 23 D.L.R. (3d) 385 (C.A.); *R. H. Deacon & Co. Ltd. v. Varga; DuDomaine Third Party*, [1973] 1 O.R. 233, 30 D.L.R. (3d) 653 (C.A.); appeal dismissed by the Supreme Court of Canada (1974), 41 D.L.R. (3d) 767*n*. The exchange rules governing such purchases are contained in the TSE by-laws, ss. 16.15 to 16.19, CCH vol. 3, paras. 89-635 to 89-649.

[82]See chapter 3, *ante*, part 3.11(4).

[83]Section 78(1) (Bill 20, s. 47(1)). The customer is entitled to exercise this option to treat the contract as void by notice sent by prepaid mail to the registrant. The language of the statute, in giving the customer an option to treat a contract as void (rather than simply stating that the contract is voidable at the option of the customer), is rather curious if not contradictory. The "option" is not available where the reduction was unintentional. Bill 20, s. 47(1) replaces the term "void" with "voidable".

circumstances short of the broker's bankruptcy, and in this latter contingency it is probably not desirable that the margin customer should have such an advantage in proving his claim over other clients of the firm.

8.10 Special Rules Applicable to Mutual Funds

Several of the recommendations of the Mutual Funds Report have been adopted in the general trading rules in Bill 20. First, to prevent a secondary trading market in mutual funds from developing, registrants are prohibited from purchasing or selling mutual fund units except in accordance with the terms of an agreement between the registrant and a distribution company selling the units under a distribution contract.[84] There are two important exceptions to this prohibition. First, the Commission has a discretion to waive the prohibition where adequate arrangements exist:

(1) to permit the distribution company or mutual fund to carry out adequately its responsibilities relating to the distribution of such shares or units;

(2) for the distribution company to prevent dealers in the shares or units of the mutual fund from taking undue advantage of the availability of the right to redeem the shares or units of the mutual fund; and,

(3) to facilitate enforcement of the penalty prescribed by the regulations for the early redemption of shares or units of the mutual fund in a transaction in which the total consideration paid or to be paid by the purchaser for the shares or units is more than $50,000.

Secondly, the prohibition is not applicable to units which have not been qualified with the Commission by a prospectus in the last fifteen months.[85] This latter exception reflects the view that the transferability of mutual funds should not be restricted when the fund is no longer issuing to the public.

Bill 20 contains a provision designed to stimulate price competition.[86] It prohibits mutual funds and distribution companies from using any device or arrangement to prevent registrants, other than their own employees, from reducing sales charges, provided that the sole purpose of the proposed reduction is to enable the ultimate purchaser to purchase the units at a proportionately lower price.[87] An exception to this provision entitles the distribution company to refuse to sell the units to or through another trader if the distributor has "reasonable cause to believe and does believe", that the other trader:

(1) is operating a secondary market in the units,

(2) is using them as "loss leaders", *i.e.*, selling them not at a profit but for advertising or to attract customers for profitable securities,

(3) is engaging in misleading advertising in those securities, or

---

[84]Section 50(1).
[85]Section 50(3).
[86]Section 52(1). The Mutual Funds Report (334-47) contains an extended discussion of resale price maintenance and other competition inhibiting techniques used by mutual funds which have distribution companies.
[87]Section 52(1).

(4) is not providing the level of servicing that purchasers might reasonably expect.[88]

---

[88]Section 52(2).

Chapter 9
Enforcement

9.01 Introduction

There are a variety of sanctions, all falling under the general head of enforcement, which are employed to make securities regulation work. Only if the standards of conduct laid down by the Act are obeyed will the goal of investor protection and other related objectives be attained. Some of these enforcement techniques have been discussed in a specific context, but the present chapter attempts a comprehensive though superficial survey. One reason for considering all the provisions of this sort in one place is that any one fact situation can often be dealt with in several different enforcement ways; another is simply that enforcement is a distinct topic in securities regulation under the anti-fraud head.

A particularly noticeable aspect of this topic is the simultaneous involvement of both federal and provincial jurisdictions. Constitutional difficulties are an ever-present danger. However, Canadian courts have adopted a permissive attitude to the use by the provinces of criminal type sanctions in the area of securities legislation, even when the offending conduct is clearly covered by the express provisions of the federal Criminal Code; the theory is that if the provinces are to be permitted to pursue in their legislation the goal of investor protection, this necessarily entails giving them some latitude in taking measures to secure compliance with that legislation.[1]

The range of enforcement techniques may be visualized as a broad spectrum; at one end of the scale the sanctions employed are purely civil and regulatory, while at the other extreme of criminal acts the penalty may be a substantial jail sentence. The discussion in the present chapter will proceed through this spectrum, beginning with sanctions attaching to the licence, namely, reprimand, suspension or cancellation. Next come cease-trading orders of which there are three types in the legislation, followed by orders for compliance. The next topic is offences against the Act or Regulation punishable by fine. Here there are two broad types: the first applies particular sanctions for breaches of the take-over bid, proxy, insider trading and financial disclosure provisions of the Act, whereas the second, which adds the

---

[1]Nowhere is this relaxed attitude to possible constitutional conflict seen more clearly than in the Supreme Court of Canada's judgment in *Smith v. The Queen*, [1960] S.C.R. 776, 25 D.L.R. (2d) 225, 128 C.C.C. 145, 33 C.R. 318. The case involved the central anti-fraud provision of the Act, which almost exactly duplicated in its language the fraud offence in the Criminal Code. However, the provincial enactment was permitted to stand on the basis that its purpose was to ensure the effective operation of securities regulation, whether in its disclosure, licensing or investigative aspects, and not to punish criminal conduct as an end in itself. For a parallel case dealing with civil liability provisions in the Act and the CCA which relies on *Smith*, see *Multiple Access Ltd. v. McCutcheon* (1975), 11 O.R. (2d) 249 (H.C.) discussed, *ante*, part 5.06 at footnote 39.

sanction of a jail sentence, deals with all other offences against the Act and Regulation. Lastly we consider violations of the Criminal Code.

A. Securities Legislation Contraventions

9.02 Sanctions Against the Licence

As we saw in chapter 3, those participants in the securities industry who earn their living from the industry must for the most part be registered in one capacity or another.[2] The exception is partners and officers of dealers, and they must belong to a registered firm before they can act.[3] One of the most powerful incentives to encourage registrants to maintain proper standards of professional conduct is the threat of having their licence taken away by the regulatory authorities. The power to do this is given to the Commission by s. 8(1), which permits that body, after giving the registrant a hearing, to suspend or cancel any registration where it appears to be in the public interest to do so. An interim fifteen-day suspension may be made without a hearing where appropriate.[4]

The drafting of this provision is not artful; consequently, there is some uncertainty as to the type of orders that may issue under it. This uncertainty has two aspects: as to the range of sanctions which may be used, and as to the range of persons (or companies) against whom they may be employed. Read literally, s. 8 permits the Commission to cancel a registration altogether or suspend it for a period of time (*e.g.,* one week, six months, etc.) but does not permit a reprimand for misconduct to be issued with no accompanying suspension. In fact the Commission interprets its power as including an authority to issue reprimands, and has acted on this interpretation.[5]

---

[2]Section 6.

[3]Section 6(1)(b).

[4]Section 8(2).

[5]See, for example, the reprimand of a senior officer in *In the Matter of A.E. Ames & Co.,* June 1972 OSCB 98. This practice can be justified by a kind of a reasoning the Commission has been expressly given the power to impose the more severe sanctions, a cancellation and suspension and therefore by implication has the power to impose the lesser sanction of a reprimand. This type of argument is not altogether convincing, however. One might equally well apply, particularly to punitive provisions, the maxim which states that that which is expressed renders inactive that which is left unspoken (*expressum facit cessare tacitum*). Moreover the Commission is exercising a delegated power. If a power is not expressly granted, particularly in the area of "criminal sanctions", it should not be implied. Not only this, but the sequence of the words in s. 8 does not particularly favour the theory of implied authority: "suspend" comes before "cancel", the less severe before the more severe of the two powers. The reverse order, had it been followed, might have suggested a power in the Commission to moderate the penalty imposed by introducing fine distinctions and gradations.

The question of word order is a relatively minor matter. A more substantial flaw in the theory of implied authority is that other statutes granting disciplinary powers to adjudicative tribunals expressly include reprimand as part of a standard trinity of sanctions including also cancellation and suspension. See *e.g.* the Law Society Act, R.S.O. 1970, c. 238, s. 34 which reads:

The other problem as far as the scope of s. 8 is concerned stems from the fact that it applies literally to registrants only. Can the sanction be employed against a trading officer or partner? This problem is tied in with the previous one, as the issue will only arise where the Commission wishes to administer some relatively light sanction such as a reprimand to a non-registrant. For more serious matters it will generally be desirable and appropriate to strike at the offender's firm instead.[6]

Bill 20 makes explicit the present practice of the Commission, at least so far as the application of a less severe form of sanction is concerned.[7] It provides for an order to "suspend, cancel, restrict or impose terms and conditions upon the registration or reprimand the registrant". As a result the sanction can be modified in any fashion desired to suit the demands of the circumstances. The section still speaks, however, in terms of registrants and registration and does not contain any modifications designed to deal with the aforementioned problem of non-registered partners and trading officers. Perhaps the appropriate solution in a particular case is to make the registrant firm's continued registration contingent on *it* taking certain action to suspend or dismiss certain of its non-registrant employees.[8]

"If a member is found guilty of professional misconduct or of conduct unbecoming a barrister and solicitor after due investigation by a committee of Convocation, Convocation may by order cancel his membership in the Society by disbarring him as a barrister...or...suspend his rights and privileges as a member for a period to be named or may by order *reprimand* him or may by order make *such other disposition* as it considers proper in the circumstances."

(Emphasis added.) Section 37 of the same statute provides for a reprimand by a committee of Convocation where the committee concludes that the graver sanctions of disbarment, suspension or reprimand in Convocation are not warranted. While it is a truism that each statute is unique and not subject to binding precedent so far as its interpretation is concerned, the phrasing employed in similar statutes dealing with related matters is most persuasive.

[6]The *Ames* decision, *supra*, footnote 5, shows the Commission acting on the assumption that it may reprimand such persons. This attitude involves a rather liberal construction of its powers, but does not seem too unrealistic once one concedes a power to reprimand at all, since s. 6 requires such persons to be "approved" by the director. A reprimand could be seen as a form of "disapproval". The difficulty is the fact that the persons affected are not registrants. Their activities are regulated in lock step with other persons and institutions that are registered, but this is not the same thing as actual registration. It may be questioned therefore if the Commission's viewpoint in this area is tenable on a strict view of the law. One can understand a power to cancel implying a power to reprimand, but it is more difficult to see how a power to affect registrants can imply a power to affect non-registrants even if they may be closely connected with registrants. A related jurisdictional problem stems from the fact that current registration (*e.g.* of a salesman), is the basis for discipline and once registration is voluntarily surrendered, jurisdiction ends (see, *ante*, part 3.13, especially footnote 134).

[7]Section 26.

[8]Bill 20 also contains a new provision (s. 26(3)) regarding surrender of registration. The Commission in its discretion may accept such a surrender in lieu of making a disciplining order, if the registrant has discharged its financial

The uses of the sanction against the licence are many and varied, but they have one common thread—the power to suspend can only be directly used to control the activities of registrants. But indirectly of course, the activities of others will be controlled, since so much of the business of the securities industry is done through registrants.[9]

9.03 Cease Trading

It is noteworthy that the Commission was without the direct power to issue a cease-trading order of general application until the 1968 amendments to the Act. Long before that, however, there were less comprehensive powers of the same type which could be used in a variety of situations. These earlier powers—exemption denial and cease distribution orders—are discussed after the newer cease-trading order.

(1) SECTION 144 CEASE-TRADING ORDERS

The general power[10] gives the Commission a broad discretion to order trading to cease in respect of particular securities. The Commission need only be convinced that such action is in the public interest. It may impose terms and conditions as it deems appropriate and designate whatever duration it chooses for the halt.

Certain safeguards circumscribe the use of this power. The Commission is prohibited from ordering trading to cease without first arranging for a hearing, unless in its opinion the length of time required for a hearing could be prejudicial to the public interest.[11] In that event the Commission is empowered to make a temporary order which must expire fifteen days from its making.[12] The Commission is

---

obligations to clients and the public interest will not be harmed. The acceptance of the surrender may be made subject to terms and conditions. This provision reflects and carries further guidelines already expressed in a policy statement (Uniform Act Policy 2-07 "Surrender of Registration-Other Than Salesmen", CCH vol. 2, para. 54-877) which states that when a registrant indicates a desire to withdraw, a suspension will normally follow until evidence of the discharge of client obligations has been presented. When this has been done the suspension *may* be lifted, and once lifted it is mandatory that the registration be regarded as having been voluntarily terminated. The new subsection in the Bill operates in virtually the same way, except that it is phrased more sensitively and is slightly broader. It will permit a voluntary surrender to override a suspending order at any time, whereas the current policy statement requires that notification of a desire to surrender be given before the initial suspension.

Until mid-1975 the OSC would publish a notice that a firm's "registration had been suspended (pending audit clearance)" on its application to leave the industry. Since then the more felicitous phrasing "placed in suspension at the firm's request" has been used to avoid the impression of regulatory disapprobation.

[9]The reported decisions on the registration sanction are legion. See the index to reported decisions of the Ontario, Quebec and British Columbia Commissions in Appendix III.

[10]Section 144(1) (Bill 20, s. 126(1)).

[11]Section 144(2) (Bill 20, s. 126(3)).

[12]The wording of this provision for a temporary order in the absence of a hearing, literally applied, could produce a somewhat inconvenient result. It suggests that the Commission has a discretion to impose a temporary order

also expressly empowered to extend the temporary order for such additional period as it considers necessary if it is not provided with satisfactory information within the fifteen-day period.

In exercising this power the Commission is faced with some of its most difficult problems of judgment. The cease-trade order is a blunt rather than a discriminating instrument. When applied to restrain the trading activities of a few, it also affects many other persons who hold the issuer's securities and who cannot sell them. More serious still is the fact that a cease-trading order with respect to a particular security may damage the reputation of the issuer and depress the price of its securities even though the reason for the cessation of trading has no connection with any event which, objectively considered, would reduce the price of the particular stock.

The range of situations in which the cease-trading power can and has been used is quite wide. On occasion it has been employed in cases of flagrant abuse such as a clearly established fraud involving a particular promoter and a particular security. On the other hand it may be the appropriate instrument in situations where there is no question of delinquent behaviour, such as a valuable mineral discovery which calls for a freeze period to permit knowledge of that discovery to be disseminated generally through the market place. Far more frequent are the intermediate cases where the power is used to discipline an issuer who has failed to satisfy his annual or interim financial reporting requirements.[13] The Commission has delegated to

---

only for fifteen days and not for a lesser period of time. But, under Bill 20, the Commission could order trading to be suspended on day one until the expiry of day four with the foreknowledge that arrangements had been made for a hearing in the matter to be held on day four; at the actual hearing a decision could be made to extend the order or not. Another situation calling for the same kind of flexibility arises where the Commission wishes a 24-hour halt to permit dissemination of some important news. As things stand now it must impose a halt of fifteen days duration and then lift it 24 hours later, rather than restricting its original order to the shorter period. Bill 20 rephrases the section to read: "...the Commission may make a temporary order, which shall not be for longer than fifteen days from the date of the making thereof...".

[13]The following statistics regarding the different uses of the cease-trading power in s. 144 represent an analysis of the instances in which the power was used over a two and one-half month period in 1974 (April 1 to June 13):
Temporary orders for failure to make statutory filings: 24
Permanent orders for failure to comply with Part XII: 21
Temporary orders pending announcement of financial status of the company or statement by the company or announcement of offer to purchase: 3
Temporary orders for trading without prospectus: 1
Permanent orders for trading without complying with registration and prospectus provisions: 1
Permanent orders due to receiver's inability to make available to the public information about a proposal in bankruptcy because of a mail strike: 1
For a categorization of the instances of s. 144 orders in reported decisions of the Ontario, British Columbia and Quebec Commissions, see Appendix III. For an example of flexibility in lifting cease-trade orders see Ontario Policy 3-31 "Cease Trading Orders: Applications for Partial Revocation to Establish a Tax Loss", CCH vol. 2, para. 54-956.

the director its responsibility for cease-trade orders in the latter cases.[14] However, it has retained the power to vary the director's order in specific instances when an application comes before it. For example, it may vary the order to permit a new promoter to receive shares with a view to reviving the company so that it will be able to prepare proper financial statements. In the great majority of instances, however, it will be the director who exercises the power of revocation when the issuer begins to comply with Part XII.

The most notable change in the general cease-trading power in Bill 20 is a new provision which expressly permits an order halting trading to be made in situations where an issuer has not disclosed a material change but has reported in confidentially to the Commission.[15] In view of the fact that such action on the Commission's part may well force the hand of an issuer which has attempted to keep private certain data, the release of which will be detrimental to itself, one may anticipate that orders will be made sparingly in such a situation, and only where clearly demanded by the pace of developments.

(2) SECTION 19(5) EXEMPTION DENIAL ORDERS

The Commission has a second and less sweeping cease-trading power which is of greater antiquity.[16] It enables the Commission to stop trading by way of a denial of the exemptions from the registration requirement with respect to specified trades[17] or specified securities.[18] Since the use of an exemption is necessary for any trade in securities except one that is entirely between two registered persons, this power has a wide ambit. As with the general cease-trading power, the grounds which permit the Commission to act are very broadly expressed— where in its opinion such action is in the public interest. While the scope of the order is defined with respect to trades or securities, the sanction applies to a named person or company.[19] The courts take a strict view of the formal requirement that the person or company with respect to whom exemptions are denied must be named.[20]

---

[14]OSC Order, October 27, 1971.

[15]Section 126(2). The specific provision permitting s. 126(2) to override s. 76(3) which permits a confidential report to the OSC rather than public disclosure of a material event is perhaps an example of the draftsman acting *ex abundanti cautela*, but in view of the fact that s. 76(3) is the newer of the two sections and of narrower scope, it was perhaps wise to nip in the bud any argument that here is an example of the specific ousting the general. This is particularly the case when one reflects that it may be the information provided by the confidential report under s. 76(3) which permits the Commission to assess current market developments with respect to the security in question from a position of full knowledge and conclude that a cease-trading order is necessary.

[16]Section 19(5) (Bill 20, s. 127(1)).

[17]Section 19(1) and (3).

[18]Section 19(2).

[19]Section 19(5) (Bill 20, s. 127(3)).

[20]In *Re Clark and Ontario Securities Commission*, [1966] 2 O.R. 277, 56 D.L.R. (2d) 585 (C.A.), the OSC found that without the shareholders' knowledge, Clark, after having "resigned" as auditor of a company to become its signing officer, had participated in raising additional funds from share-

The procedural safeguards are similar to those which exist in the case of the general cease-trading power.[21]

Potentially the denial of exemption power has a wide range of uses; not all of them have been employed with any frequency. For example, an insider who made a practice of using specific confidential information might be denied trading exemptions even though no civil action had been brought against him. The same approach could be taken against a person who was not an insider or associate according to the statutory definition but who held a position giving him access to specific confidential information and abused the confidence of that position by trading on the basis of the information. Recently the Commission has begun to use this power against those who are chronically deficient in their insider reporting obligations. And more generally it has used this power to punish where for various reasons it is either undesirable or impracticable to prosecute for contravention of the Act.[22] But as with other enforcement devices, punishment is seldom if ever an end in itself, the desire to induce positive compliance, whether with the Act generally or some specific directive made under it, is seldom absent.[23]

---

holders of which less than 30 per cent went into its treasury. Trading exemptions were denied to Clark and to any company of which he was a director or officer so long as he continued in that capacity. Only Clark had been named in the notice of hearing. On appeal to the Supreme Court of Ontario under s. 29 of the Act, it was held that the extension of the order to any company of which Clark was an officer or director "was beyond or outside the powers" of the Commission. The Court remarked that if broader authority were necessary it should be obtained by statutory amendment. It seems that the denial could have been extended to the company(ies) of which Clark was currently a director or officer if it (or they) had been named in the notice of the hearing as well as the order. It is by no means clear, however, whether those companies and their other shareholders deserved to be drawn in unless it could have been shown that the whole of their trading operations was influenced and dominated by the activities of the offending Clark.

[21]Briefly, the Commission cannot make an order without a hearing unless in its opinion the length of time required for a hearing could be prejudicial to the public interest (s. 19(6)). In such an instance the Commission is empowered to make a temporary order "which *expires* fifteen days from the date of the making thereof" (s. 19(6)) (emphasis added). The use of the word "shall" to mark the expiry date of the order is not found in s. 19 (as it is in s. 144). It is at least plausible to argue that the force of the word "shall" in s. 144 is to establish an outer boundary or absolute limit for expiration but that the Commission may in its discretion fix upon a date prior to the lapse of a full fifteen days. The unqualified word "expires" in the temporary denial of exemption power may suggest that fifteen days' duration is an invariable property of orders made under the section, precluding a discretion to make a more temporary order. Bill 20 (s. 127(2)) gives the Commission power to make a temporary order "which shall not be for longer than fifteen days from the date of the making...".

[22]See *A Company*, June 1968 OSCB 129; *Midgaul Investments Ltd. and Stanley Hawkins*, June 1970 OSCB 91; *Pyrotex Mining and Exploration Co. Ltd.*, June 1968 OSCB 143. In the latter case an order was made in conjunction with suspension proceedings under.s. 8.

[23]An unusual case in the area of compliance which makes this point is *Buschell*

An order may be aimed at paralyzing a company's activities in general until compliance is effected, or it may be used to forestall a specific transaction either because it will be a breach of the Act or because it is undesirable to let it go forward in view of the inadequate disclosure being provided to some of the participants.[24]

Bill 20 grants the Commission the power to deny exemptions in terms similar to those in the Act. As with general cease-trading orders, the Bill provides for temporary orders lasting for less than fifteen days.[25] The Bill will not permit unrestricted renewal of the denial order, in keeping with the view that this is a less drastic remedy than the general cease-trading order; however, it does go so far as to permit a denial of exemptions to be extended in cases where a hearing has actually been commenced, in which case the Commission may extend the order until the hearing is concluded.[26]

(3) SECTION 62 CEASE DISTRIBUTION ORDERS

The third specific cease-trading power relates to distributions only. It is difficult to see why it must continue as a separate power in the Act in the light of the broad and sweeping authority given by general cease-trade power.[27] Section 62(1)[28] gives the Commission a discretion to order that all distribution of securities shall cease where after the issuance of a final receipt for prospectus any of the six specific conditions for prospectus refusal set out in s. 61 exist.[29] There are procedural requirements for temporary orders without a hearing similar to those for general cessation orders and exemption denials. The effect of a cease distribution order is precisely spelled out. No further trade is to be made in the course of distribution (as opposed to a secondary trade) of the securities named in the order by any person or company and the prospectus receipt is revoked.[30] If the Commission

---

Lake Mines et al., June 1958 OSCB 1, where a s. 19(5) order was made in the face of the refusal of a company and its officers and directors to comply with the requirements of the Companies Act. See also *International Negotiators Ltd. and Albert Gould*, Oct. 1965 OSCB 2; *New Hosco Mines et al.*, Nov. 1968 OSCB 259. *New Hosco* involved a flouting of the TSE disclosure requirements. In the same general connection see *Mercantile Bank and Trust Co. Ltd.*, Oct. 1973 OSCB 173.

[24]An example of the latter situation is *Panacea Mining and Exploration Ltd.*, Oct. 1971 OSCB 163. In that case the Commission denied the exemptions in s. 19(1)(8)(ii) and (9) where on a winding-up it was proposed to distribute to the shareholders of an Ontario corporation shares of a corporation in another jurisdiction as consideration for the assets of the Ontario corporation. In the Commission's view, the proposed arrangement would have had the effect of depriving the Ontario shareholders of the information the company had undertaken to provide in filing and distributing its shares under an Ontario prospectus.

[25]Section 127. See, *supra*, footnote 21.

[26]Section 127(2).

[27]Section 144.

[28]Bill 20, s. 71(1).

[29]See, *ante*, part 4.05. As noted there, Bill 20 adds three extra grounds for refusal.

[30]Section 62(3).

finds it necessary to suspend trading in the securities of an issuer in the course of distribution for reasons other than the six specified circumstances in s. 61 then the general cease trade or exemption denial powers can be used.

A similar cease distribution power exists in connection with the distribution of securities of a finance company.[31] Under this power where the director reports to the Commission that the finance company has not supplied the additional information which the director may require, the Commission is empowered to order trading to cease in those securities of the finance company then being distributed.

(4) NOTICE PROVISIONS FOR CEASE-TRADING ORDERS

The notice provisions for the three cease-trading orders differ somewhat, reflecting their different purposes.[32] For example the s. 144 cease-trading provisions expressly permit the Commission to publish the required notice in a newspaper. The notice provisions for the other two orders do not, although the Commission is not precluded from doing so.

In fact, it is the practice of the Ontario Commission to publish in its weekly summary, notices of trading suspension, denials of exemptions and cessation of distribution hearings or any other hearing prescribed by the Act wherever there is substantial probability that persons other than those directly and immediately affected may have an important interest. But this is done only in a relatively small number of cases.[33]

9.04 Order for Compliance

A novel enforcement technique which appeared in the Act for the first time in 1968[34] is the order for compliance.[35] It is a civil remedy and does not carry any criminal or *quasi*-criminal consequences other than potential contempt of court proceedings if it is violated. Compliance order applications are tried as civil matters before a Judge of the High Court rather than as *quasi*-criminal or criminal matters before a provincial court judge. This procedure is available to the Commission where it appears that any person or company has failed to comply with or is violating any provision of the Act or the regulations; the order is distinct from and can be used in addition to any other penalty for

---

[31]Section 63(2).

[32]See ss. 5, para. 1, 144(3), 19(7) and 62(3).

[33]An obvious case calling for more ample provision for notice arises where the Commission must review a proposal of the TSE to change its commission rate structure (for citations see, *post*, part 10.03(4) at footnote 37). In a recent case where an application to remove a freeze order was made by new management of a company whose assets had been frozen pending an investigation of alleged fraud by the former management, the OSC insisted that the applicant notify all shareholders of the hearing to give minority shareholders a chance to make submissions although it is questionable whether they were primarily affected. In cases of doubt the tendency is to give notice.

[34]1968 (Ont.), c. 123, s. 40.

[35]Section 143(1) (Bill 20, s. 125(1)). This technique was recommended by the Kimber Committee (para. 2.20).

non-compliance or violation which may have already been imposed. The judge has wide powers to make such order as he thinks fit.

The advantages of this power are several. First, the civil evidentiary and legal burdens of proof apply instead of the standards applicable in criminal matters, permitting the Commission to establish its case more easily. Secondly, a proceeding of this kind does not damage reputations in the same way as a prosecution under one of the offence provisions. A third and perhaps less concrete consideration is this: in a case before a High Court Judge as opposed to one brought in provincial court, the relevant law will be applied in a less simplistic and more interpretative fashion; Canadian jurisprudence in the area should benefit as a result. Bill 20 retains the order for compliance but with an important addition. Where it is a company or some other person not an individual which has failed to comply with the Act or Regulation, an order may issue against the directors or senior officers of the organization or entity involved.[36]

The experience of Ontario and the other Canadian provinces with compliance orders is relatively limited. As a result there is little jurisprudence to provide detailed guidance as to how this particular enforcement technique is to be used in the various situations which may arise.

The Ontario Commission at one point began to use the order for compliance to require issuers deficient in filing their regular financial statements to bring them up-to-date. Given the large number of delinquent issuers, the choice of this enforcement technique soon resulted in the court becoming impatient. Furthermore it seemed unnecessarily harsh to subject officers of a dormant company to a choice between maintaining current disclosure on pain of contempt proceedings or winding-up the company. Consequently the Ontario Commission soon switched to using the cease-trading power to deal with this problem.[37]

---

[36]Section 121(1)(b). This is to overcome the problem exposed in *Re Saskatchewan Securities Commission v. Premier Products Ltd. and Gray* (1973), 36 D.L.R. (3d) 476 (Sask. Q.B.) where a company was delinquent in its financial reporting requirements and the court held that an order for compliance might be made against the company itself but not its officers. They could only be disciplined by a prosecution for authorizing or acquiescing in a breach of the Act.

[37]As we have seen, this power is in fact exercised by the director on a delegated basis, OSC Order, October 27, 1971.

Apart from the financial reporting cases, the first instance in which the compliance section was used was in *OSC v. Canadian Magnesite Mines Ltd.*, Sept. 1969 OSCB 174, where an order was made restraining any disposition of certain shares in the company. The securities in question had originally been the subject of a non-public distribution and were thus caught by s. 35 so far as resale was concerned; some of them had in fact already been improperly resold. The order was threefold, freezing for two years those shares not yet resold, requiring those already resold to be the subject of an OSC ruling before a further resale, and ordering the company to comply with the distribution requirements in all future public issues.

9.05 Offences Against the Act or Regulations

There are four separate offence provisions confined to specific parts of the Act and a general offence provision for any other contravention of the Act or Regulation. All are summary conviction proceedings. All carry a reasonable diligence defence with respect to the offences involving false statement of material fact or failure to state material facts.[38] The four specific provisions dealing respectively with take-over bids, proxies, insider reporting and financial disclosure are considered first.

(1) TAKE-OVER BID VIOLATIONS

An offeror who fails to send a take-over bid circular or sends one that contains false statements or is misleading, or who fails to comply with

---

In *OSC v. Robert Sajo*, Aug. 1970 OSCB 120, the court restrained the respondent from trading without registration and distributing shares without a prospectus.

In a more recent adjudication, *OSC v. Roy A. Burton*, June 1974 OSCWS 3A, the court restrained an insider from further failure to comply with insider trading reporting provisions.

These three instances give some idea of the varied situations where an order will be sought. They all involved a judgment of the Commission, based on the particular circumstances, that the extra authority of a judicial rather than a merely administrative order was desirable to secure compliance and prevent future violations. Various factors could contribute to a decision to proceed this way. Past conduct of a reprehensible nature is one possibility, or the display of a particularly contumacious attitude in continuing the violation which is the subject of the order; or there could be reasons peculiar to an individual case making it desirable to achieve greater certainty of effect and give a broader warning to others by going before a court.

Does the basis for the order dissolve when the defendent complies during the course of the trial? It would seem that once the matter has reached the trial stage an order could issue requiring a person to comply promptly in the future.

What *kind* of order may issue, assuming that its basis has not been dissolved by prior voluntary compliance and that there are proper persons available against whom it may be made? The material facts which form the basis for the order are present breaches of the Act; does this affect the scope of the order that may be made once the law has been applied to the facts, confining it to restraining present violations, or may it provide a sanction against future breaches as well? The latter, it is submitted, is the correct position; the jurisdictional base and the resultant order are two different things, not necessarily on all fours with one another. And logically even a restraint of a present breach has a future effect; it would not be a convenient result to suppose that an offender could momentarily discontinue violating the Act and then start in again with impunity on the ground that he was committing a fresh breach not covered by the order. These considerations would of course not apply in the case of a breach different in *kind*. The view here expressed is supported by the wide language of s. 143, which empowers the judge to make the order recommended by the Commission or "such other order" as he thinks fit.

[38]Sections 100(4), 103(5), 112(3) and 137(2). Curiously there is no separate offence for such positive misstatements in Part XII continuous disclosure offences and hence no due diligence defence. That suggests that the liability for failure to comply with Part XII (s. 136) is strict. For a discussion of reasonable diligence see, *ante*, part 4.10(3) and *R. v. Revenue Properties Ltd.* (1971), CCH vol. 3, para. 70-028, and, *infra*, part 9.05(5).

requirements regarding equal consideration to all or the securing of funds to make payment, is guilty of an offence. The penalty is a fine of up to $25,000 or imprisonment for a term not to exceed one year, or both. Furthermore every person or company who authorizes, permits or acquiesces in the violation is guilty of an offence and liable to a maximum fine of $2,000 and/or imprisonment of up to one year.[39]

A similar sanction attaches to the directors of an offeree company who err in connection with the directors' circular. Every director of the offeree company who authorizes, permits or acquiesces in a recommendation to offeree shareholders "by means of a directors' circular...without complying with" the statutory requirements or so acts where the directors' circular contains a material omission or misleading information is guilty of an offence and liable to a fine of not more than $2,000.[40]

(2) PROXY VIOLATIONS

The second type of specific offence has to do with the proxy requirements of Part X. Where management of a company omits to send out mandatory proxies, the company will be guilty of an offence carrying a penalty of no more than $1,000, and directors or officers who authorize, permit, or acquiesce in the failure to comply will be subject to the same penalty.[41] An offence is provided for in almost identical terms when a person or company fails to send out an information circular of required type[42] to accompany the sending of proxies.[43] Both the failure to send out a circular altogether and non-trivial mistakes and omissions in the actual circular sent will be offences.

(3) INSIDER REPORT VIOLATIONS

The third substantive offence provision provides sanctions designed to enforce the insider trading reporting requirements of Part XI. As with proxy sanctions, failure to comply may result in a fine of up to $1,000, and where a company commits the offence, directors and officers who authorize, permit or acquiesce are subject to the same penalty.[44] A similar offence occurs where a report is filed that is false or misleading by reason of misstatement or omission of material fact. The reasonable diligence defence available in the take-over bid sanctions and the proxy offence is also provided here.[45]

(4) FINANCIAL DISCLOSURE VIOLATIONS

The last provision in the quartet, punishes failure to comply with the financial disclosure requirements of Part XII; non-disclosing compa-

---

[39]Section 100(1). Contrast these penalties with the lighter ones for the remaining three specific offences in this quartet.
[40]Section 100(2) and (3). *Quaere* whether an oral recommendation or a written communication such as an advertisement aimed at the public generally, or a letter to shareholders which does not recommend but sets out "facts" which establish a one-sided case, are forms of communication sufficiently distinct from a directors' circular that an offence does not lie.
[41]Section 102(2).
[42]Reg. 794, s. 44(1) and Form 20.
[43]Section 103(3).
[44]Section 112(1). For the cynical insider this sanction is scarcely more than a licence to evade the law. U.S. federal legislation is substantially more severe.
[45]Section 112(3).

nies attract a fine of up to $1,000[46] and acquiescing directors or officers of a delinquent company are once again liable to a fine up to the same amount.[47]

(5) GENERAL OFFENCE PROVISION

The general offence provision operates as a basket to catch all other failures to comply with the provisions of the Act or the Regulation.[48] It is divided into four parts dealt with in separate paragraphs. The first of these covers misleading statements or omissions made by a person or company in any material, evidence or information given under the Act or the Regulation to the Commission, its representative, the director or any person appointed to make an investigation or audit. Such statements will be an offence when they are false or misleading at the time of making in the light of the surrounding circumstances or omit to state any material fact so as to make the statement false or misleading. The next part deals with misleading statements or omissions in any of the documents required to be furnished under the Act or Regulation. The test of falsity is the same as in the case of the previous offence, and is expressed in identical terms. The third paragraph is more concise and simply provides that it is an offence to contravene the Act or the Regulation. A similar offence for any failure to observe or comply with any order, direction or other requirement made under the Act or Regulation rounds out the package. Provision is made for an exception in the case of actions or omissions that constitute an offence under the four specific provisions discussed above.[49] Summary conviction under the general offence provision carries with it a fine not to exceed $2,000 and/or imprisonment not to exceed one year.[50] Every director or officer who permitted, authorized or acquiesced in such offence is also guilty of an offence and is liable to a fine of up to $2,000 and/or imprisonment.[51] The standard reasonable diligence defence is available for the first and second general offence provisions but not for the third and fourth.[52] In effect statements as to the existence of facts are protected but acts of contravention are not.[53]

---

[46]Section 136.
[47]*Ibid.*
[48]Section 137(1).
[49]*Ibid.*
[50]*Ibid.*
[51]Section 137(3).
[52]Section 137(2).
[53]This distinction may have important consequences. For example, someone charged with failing to file a prospectus while being a control person and selling his shares cannot, it seems, rely on his lawyer's opinion that he was not a control person even though he may have shown more than reasonable diligence in securing the opinion and has no knowledge of the control person tests. However the same person who files a prospectus disclosing his holdings but mistaken advice from his lawyer fails to state that he is a promoter may be able to use the defence.

But see *R. v. Dalley*, [1957] O.W.N. 123, 8 D.L.R. (2d) 179, 118 C.C.C. 116, 25 C.R. 269, *sub nom. R. ex rel. Irwin v. Dalley* (C.A.) where the defence of reliance on counsel's opinion was rejected. The defendant must satisfy two conditions, *viz.*, that he did not know *and* in the exercise of reasonable

Bill 20 displays much tidier drafting of the offence provisions. All offence provisions including the four specific ones presently in the Act are consolidated in s. 121. It provides that every person or company that:

(1) makes a statement in any material submitted under the Act or regulations that is a misrepresentation,

(2) makes a statement in any report, release, application, preliminary prospectus and prospectus, information circular, take-over bid circular, financial statement, return or other document required to be filed, that is a misrepresentation,

(3) contravenes the Act or regulations,

(4) fails to observe any direction, decision, ruling, order or other requirement made under the Act or regulations

is guilty of a summary offence and liable in the case of a person or company to a fine of $25,000, and in the case of an individual to a fine of $2,000 and/or to a one-year jail sentence. This standardization of penalties brings the insider, proxy and financial disclosure sanctions up to the level of severity of the take-over bid and general offence provisions of the Act.

The reasonable diligence defence is retained for the first two "statement" parts of the offence.[54] The provision dealing with directors or officers who authorize, permit, or acquiesce in offences is unchanged, except that the offenders may be directors and officers of a person other than an individual.[55] Such unincorporated entities, it will be noted, are now to be subject to the higher maximum fine of $25,000; it is thought that there is no good reason for distinguishing them from companies in this respect. Another change worth remarking upon is the replacement of misleading statements and commissions by the single term "misrepresentation" as now defined in the Bill.[56] A final addition not to be disregarded is the inclusion of the word "release" in s. 121(1)(b): "makes a statement in any application, *release*, report", etc. The release which is meant is a press release required by the new timely disclosure provisions.[57]

Bill 20 breaks new ground in s. 132, which creates a statutory tort. The section provides that a person or company

(1) that trades without qualifying a prospectus,

(2) fails to comply with the requirements of distribution during the waiting period,

---

diligence could not have known that the statement was false or misleading. The U.S. federal statutes provide a parallel defence by building a *mens rea* element into the offence itself. See Loss, vol. 3, pp. 1984 and 1987 and Supplement, pp. 416-27.

See also *R. v. Campbell and Mlynarchuk* (1972), 10 C.C.C. (2d) 26, [1973] 2 W.W.R. 246 (Alta. Dist. Ct.); *R. v. Maclean* (1974), 17 C.C.C. (2d) 84, 46 D.L.R. (3d) 564, 27 C.R.N.S. 31 (N.S. Co. Ct.); *R.v. MacPhee* (1975), 24 C.C.C. (2d) 229 (N.S. Prov. Mag. Ct.); *R. v. Seemar Mines Ltd.* (1974), 23 C.C.C. (2d) 54 (Ont. Prov. Ct.).

[54]Section 121(2).
[55]Section 121(3).
[56]Section 1(1)24.
[57]Section 76.

(3) fails to deliver a prospectus to each purchaser; or
(4) contravenes subsection (4), (5) or (7) of s. 73, the resale distribution provision, or
(5) contravenes the take-over bid circular provision
is liable to the purchaser or offeree for rescission or damages. This statutory tort was created to provide an additional avenue of relief to purchasers and offerees. The section also performs the signal service of helping to resolve in this area the persistent problem of deciding when a statutory directive is meant to have civil consequences and if so, what. Unfortunately, it provides no express guidance on a further problem which immediately arises, whether the expressed remedy is intended to be exhaustive. This question has two aspects: one is whether the situations listed in s. 132 are the only ones to which the remedy applies; the second is whether remedies other than those in s. 132 are available in the situations listed there. It has been argued elsewhere[58] that s. 132 should be limited to those offences expressly mentioned, but on the second issue the better view would seem to be that s. 132 is intended not to derogate from other modes of recovery which may be available. However, the matter, is far from certain.

9.06 Procedural Requirements

The consent of the Minister is necessary to launch proceedings under the general offence and the take-over bid offence provisions.[59] By contrast, the Commission must give its consent to prosecute for insider reporting deficiencies, presumably to serve as a filter to screen out minimal departures from the norm.[60] No such Commission or ministerial leave is necessary to prosecute irregularities in proxy solicitation and the filing of regular financial statements. This requirement of consents to prosecute together with the scale of fine or imprisonment attached to each of the offences provides a rough guide as to the degree of gravity with which different types of offending conduct are viewed, though one can point to plenty of exceptions which will not fit easily into this pattern.

Provisions exist to co-ordinate the enforcement provisions between provinces. Where a provincial judge, magistrate or justice of one province or territory of Canada issues a warrant for the arrest of a person on a securities charge, a provincial judge or justice in the jurisdiction in which the accused is thought to be located may endorse the warrant on satisfactory proof of the handwriting of the first judicial officer.[61] The endorsement is sufficient authority for all constables within the territorial jurisdiction of the endorsing judge to execute it.[62]

---

[58]*Ante*, chapter 4, at footnote 142.
[59]Section 138(1).
[60]Section 112(4). In Bill 20 offences relating to insider reporting obligations are standardized within s. 121, which means that ministerial consent will be required under s. 122 of Bill 20 before proceedings are instituted.
[61]Section 149(1) (Bill 20, s. 124(1)).
[62]*Ibid.*

The time limitations expressed in the Act are quite important, since the investigation of any substantial securities fraud may be complex and lengthy. No proceedings for the enforcement of the Act may be commenced in a court more than one year after the facts upon which the proceedings are based first came to the knowledge of the Commission.[63] In the case of proceedings other than in a court, such as those before the Commission or the director, a two-year limitation period applies.[64] The difficult question is what constitutes knowledge on the part of the Commission. For example, when an issuer discloses all directors' holdings in a proxy information circular, does this circular when filed impart constructive knowledge to the Commission which will prevent it in the future from taking action against those directors who have failed to file insider trading reports in previous years? The Commission has taken the position that it does.

B. Criminal Code Offences

In this section we deal with the most severe type of sanction, prosecution under the Criminal Code.[65] Of those offences which are particularly relevant to securities regulation, some are quite general in scope, such as fraud and conspiracy, while others are directed more specifically at activities unique to the securities industry, *e.g.* wash trading and publishing falsehoods in prospectuses. Furthermore, there are general provisions in the Code such as those dealing with perjury (s. 120), false statements in extra-judicial proceedings (s. 122), use of mails (s. 339), and forgery (s. 324) which may be of tangential significance to our topic. Criminal Code prosecution will be undertaken where the conduct of the accused has been flagrant or persistent, or is clearly indicative of malice. Furthermore, severe loss or damage arising from the accused's activities may also be a factor in a decision to prosecute, provided the requisite intent is present.

The following discussion will focus on conspiracy, spreading false news, false pretences or statements, fraud, false prospectus, wash trading, gaming, short sales against margin accounts, and breach of trust by public officials.

9.07 Conspiracy

Section 423 deals with, *inter alia*, the indictable offences of conspiracy to commit an indictable offence carrying with it the same penalty as the latter offence and conspiring to effect an unlawful purpose or to effect a lawful purpose by unlawful means punishable by a maximum penalty of two years' imprisonment. The gist of the offence lies in the

---

[63]Section 138(2) (Bill 20, s. 128(1)).

[64]Section 138(3). Bill 20, s. 128(2) changes the wording of this latter provision somewhat to read "No proceedings under this Act shall be commenced before the Commission more than two years...". The change is primarily for purposes of clarification, to make it express that administrative hearings before the Commission are not "in a court" and cannot benefit from the shorter limitation period.

[65]R.S.C. 1970, C-34 as am. The section numbers which follow refer to "the Code".

unlawful agreement; no overt act in performance of the agreement need be established—the offence is complete when the agreement is made.[66] The section results in a significant interlocking of federal and provincial jurisdictions, as is illustrated by the decision of the Supreme Court of Canada that "unlawful purpose" is not restricted to Code offences, but includes offences under provincial statutes.[67] It would thus appear that "unlawful means" includes non-compliance with provincial securities regulatory requirements.

9.08 Spreading False News
Section 177 deals with the offence of wilful publication of a statement, tale or news known to be false and which causes or is likely to cause injury or mischief to a public interest.[68] It carries a penalty of up to two years' imprisonment.

Matters which are the subject of regulatory legislation such as investor protection concern the "public interest"[69]; if so, the section could be directed to promotional abuses or could serve as a sanction to curb flagrant abuses involving the spread of misinformation which threaten to frustrate the aims of the timely disclosure requirements.

9.09 False Pretences or Statements
Sections 319 and 320, dealing with false pretences and false statements, fall in that category of offence whose central characteristic is the deception of another person in a manner which leads to his disadvantage. The penalties vary, according to the consequences of deception, with the *maxima* ranging from two to ten years in prison. By s. 319 a false pretence is defined as a representation of fact,[70] present or past, known by its maker to be false and made with a fraudulent intent to induce the person to whom it is made to act upon it. The offence includes obtaining by a false pretence of anything "in respect of which the offence of theft may be committed", or causing it to be delivered to another person. The representation may be "by words or otherwise": for example, assent to the false representation of another may amount to a false representation by conduct by the one who assents.[71]

---

[66]*R. v. Deal* (1956), 18 W.W.R. 119, 114 C.C.C. 325, 23 C.R. 354 (Sask. C.A.).
[67]*Wright, McDermott and Feeley v. The Queen*, [1964] S.C.R. 192, 43 D.L.R. (2d) 597, [1969] 2 C.C.C. 201; *R. v. Thodas et al.* (1970), 73 W.W.R. 710, 10 C.R.N.S. 290, [1970] 5 C.C.C. 260 *sub nom. R. v. Layton, ex p. Thodas* (B.C.C.A.).
[68]*R. v. Hoaglin* (1907), 12 C.C.C. 226 (N.W.T.S.C.). The first and one of the rare prosecutions under this section was that of an expatriate American merchant who advertised a close-out sale at the turn of the century as follows: "Americans not wanted in Canada. Investigate before buying lands and taking homesteads in this country." The accused was found guilty, the injured public interest being the national desire to attract settlers to Canada. While the case is somewhat of an historical curiosity, it is not difficult to imagine a similar incident occurring today.
[69]See *R. v. Kirby* (1970), 1 C.C.C. (2d) 286, 13 *Crim L.Q.* 128 (Que C.A.).
[70]See *Gagnon v. The Queen* (1953), 110 C.C.C. 350, 19 C.R. 127 (Que C.A.) on the distinction between obtaining by false pretences and obtaining by fraud.
[71]See *R. v. Grosvenor* (1914), 10 Cr. App. R. 235 (C.C.A.).

Section 319(2) is a saving provision for "puffing" or disparaging: "Exaggerated commendation or depreciation of the quality of anything is not a false pretence unless it is carried to such an extent that it amounts to a fraudulent misrepresentation of fact." Since one can scarcely conceive of a statement, known to be false, made without fraudulent intent, the distinction between mere exaggeration and a false pretence must depend on the "knowledge" of the maker of the statement; in other words much of what is stated as a matter of fact represents not knowledge, but opinion, particularly in a commercial context. Section 319(2) presumably recognizes this fact. Fraud is an offence which carries with it a significant element of moral censure, and so the courts are understandably reluctant to infer its existence; they will tend rather to make allowances for the moral atmosphere of a given milieu.[72]

Turning to false statements as opposed to false pretences, everyone is guilty of an offence who knowingly makes or causes to be made with intent that it should be relied on, any false statement in writing respecting the financial condition or means or ability to pay of himself or any other person, firm, or corporation in whom he is interested or for whom he acts, for the purpose of procuring financial benefits for himself or such other person, firm, or corporation.[73] The obtaining of such benefit when a false statement is known to have been made and has been relied on is an offence even though another may have made the statement.[74]

The element of reliance is essential to securing a conviction both in the case of a false pretence and a false statement.[75] Even in the absence of reliance, however, it would appear that in appropriate circumstances there might be a conviction for an attempt.

---

[72]*R. v. Bryan* (1875), Dears. and Bell 265, 169 E.R. 1002 at p. 1004 (C.C.A.) is one such example albeit from the ancient past. There, Lord Campbell C.J. stated (in a passage which displays a questionable assumption of the equality of buyer and seller in the market place):
"...it could never have been the intention of the Legislature to make it an indictable offence for a seller to exaggerate the quality of that which he was selling anymore than it would be an indictable offence for the purchaser, during the bargain, to depreciate the quality of the goods and to say that they were not equal to that which they really were."
[73]Section 320(1)(c). See *R. v. Campbell* (1912), 23 Que. K.B. 400, 5 D.L.R. 370, 19 C.C.C. 407 (C.A.); *R. v. Lyons*, [1939] 3 D.L.R. 625, 72 C.C.C. 65, [1939] 2 W.W.R. 255 (Sask. C.A.).
[74]Section 320(1)(d).
[75]See *R. v. Thornton* (1926), 37 B.C.R. 344, 46 C.C.C. 249 (C.A.); *R. v. Castle*, [1937] O.W.N. 245, 68 C.C.C. 78 (C.A.); *R. v. Jones and Manlove* (1935), 49 B.C.R. 422, [1935] 2 D.L.R. 718, 63 C.C.C. 145 (C.A.). In *Jones,* the representations in issue concerned guarantees, money in the company treasury and the nature of the offering as being from treasury stock. In *Castle*, the representations concerned book value of assets, encumbrances and cash on hand. The purchaser had discovered the falsity of the representations after an initial purchase, yet additional purchases were made. With respect to the initial purchase and sale, a conviction for obtaining was secured, notwithstanding the fact that the evidence might lead one to infer that the representations had not been material to the decision as to whether to purchase the securities.

It is essential that the false pretence relates to a matter of fact either present or past, as opposed to future events or promises. Whether or not a statement of intention about future conduct is a statement of existing fact, such a statement does not amount to a false pretence.[76]

Because s. 319 deals with positive representations of fact, the offence does not appear to extend to representations of a misleading nature, *i.e.*, those involving partial truth or giving rise to ambiguity. On the other hand it is arguable that any representation made with an intent to induce reliance consists of more than an objective matter of fact; that which is a matter of fact must have contextual significance.[77]

9.10 Fraud

Among offences which involve the victim being placed under a prior apprehension of some kind, fraud occupies a central place. Section 338 reads:

"(1) Every one who, by deceit, falsehood or other fraudulent means, whether or not it is a false pretence within the meaning of this Act, defrauds the public or any person, whether ascertained or not, of any property, money or valuable security, is guilty of an indictable offence and is liable to imprisonment for ten years.

"(2) Every one who, by deceit, falsehood or other fraudulent means, whether or not it is a false pretence within the meaning of this Act, with intent to defraud, affects the public market price of stocks, shares, merchandise or anything that is offered for sale to the public, is guilty of an indictable offence and is liable to imprisonment for ten years."

The key distinction to be kept in mind is the difference between convincing a person of the existence of a certain state of affairs which does not exist (false pretences) and persuading him to do something by a falsehood (fraud). The former is not an offence *per se*, but the latter is. "To deceive is by falsehood to induce a state of mind"; "to defraud is by deceit to induce a course of action".[78]

The element of falsity is not confined by the restricted definition of false pretences; the deception need not relate to a matter of fact. It is thus an offence to obtain property on the promise of future payment without the intention of paying.[79]

It is the second of the two offences that relates most closely to securities regulation. However, the first count is also relevant to the topic, and since the case law dealing with it is more extensive, it will receive most attention.

Section 338(1) makes it an offence to induce an individual to part with property of some kind. Assuming that the elements of fraud are

---

[76]*R. v. Dent* (1955), 39 Cr. App. R. 131 (C.C.A.); *R. v. Thimsen* (1940), 55 B.C.R. 103, [1940] 2 W.W.R. 165, [1940] 3 D.L.R. 158, 73 C.C.C. 315 (C.A.).
[77]See *Farris v. The Queen*, [1965] 2 O.R. 396, 50 D.L.R. (2d) 689, [1965] 3 C.C.C. 245 (C.A.).
[78]Buckley J. in *Re London and Globe Finance Corp. Ltd.*, [1903] 1 Ch. 728 at p. 733, [1900-3] All E.R. Rep. 891 at p. 893.
[79]*R. v. Stanley* (1957), 119 C.C.C. 220, 26 C.R. 180, 22 W.W.R. 71 (B.C.C.A.); *R. v. Gregg*, [1965] 3 C.C.C. 203, 44 C.R. 341, 49 W.W.R. 732 (Sask. C.A.).

otherwise present, the question arises whether it will be a defence that the complainant as it turned out made a good bargain. In *R. v. Phillips*,[80] it was implicit in the court's reasoning that it was no defence that the defrauded person received value for the consideration given.[81]

Unless the contrary is expressly provided for by statute,[82] an actionable wrong must usually involve a positive act. The type of representation involved in s. 338 is no exception. In *R. v. Charters*,[83] the charge arose in a private sale transaction where the accused had failed to disclose that customs duty was payable in respect of the subject-matter. An acquittal was entered, because:

"...there was no misrepresentation or fraud. There was not even innocent misrepresentation. There was non-disclosure of what was, perhaps, a material fact, but that is not sufficient to justify a conviction for an offence under this section. It cannot be held that the appellant deceived the complainant, *viz.*, that he by falsehood induced a state of mind in him, or that he defrauded him *viz.*, that he by deceit influenced the complainant's conduct. Nor does the evidence establish that the appellant employed other fraudulent means against the complainant."[84]

Although the *Charters* decision is still a correct statement of the law, it is important to note that in a case where the accused has made a number of misleading statements accompanied by positive steps made possible by these statements, a conviction may still occur even though the central deception involved is the withholding of information for which (considered in isolation) there is no legal obligation to disclose. In *R. v. Littler*,[85] the president and chief shareholder of a company confidentially received a firm take-over bid at a price approximately three times the current value of the shares. Before closing the transaction he proceeded to purchase substantial minority holdings in the company at a price less than half that fixed for the take-over bid. In negotiations with him the representatives of the minority group were led to believe that rumours of an impending purchase of the shares were false, and this, together with his action in carrying out the transactions in question was sufficient to convict the accused of fraud. The defence relied in it submissions on the principle that a director is under no duty to disclose material facts to shareholders. The court qualified this principle in deciding that directors cannot

---

[80](1928), 35 O.W.N. 119 (C.A.).

[81]The same approach was followed in *R. v. Knelson and Baran* (1962), 39 W.W.R. 264, 133 C.C.C. 210, 38 C.R. 181 (B.C.C.A.), where the court held, without reference to *Phillips*, that the offence was sufficiently made out where it was proven that the purchase was induced by falsehood, *i.e.*, that the shares did not have the attributes, excepting value, ascribed to them.

[82]As in the definition of misrepresentation in Bill 20, s. 1(1)24.

[83](1957), 119 C.C.C. 223 (Ont. C.A.).

[84]*Ibid.*, at p. 225. The approach taken in *Charters* was followed in *MacKrow v. The Queen*, [1967] S.C.R. 22, [1967] 1 C.C.C. 289.

[85](1972), 41 D.L.R. (3d) 523, 13 C.C.C. (2d) 530 (Que. Ct. Sess.); 65 D.L.R. (3d) 443, 467 (C.A.).

mislead as to the true purpose of transfers of shares from the shareholders to themselves.[86]

Another potential issue concerns jurisdiction. What degree of connection with Canada must the fraudulent activity have? *Re Chapman*,[87] involving a conspiracy is a decision of some significance for fraud in securities transactions. It was common ground that there had been a solicitation of U.S. residents only, in furtherance of a fraudulent scheme. With respect to the words "public or any person" in the section, the court held that they were not limited to the Canadian public or persons in Canada. It was sufficient therefore that something necessary to the realization of the scheme, *viz.*, receipt of money from U.S. subscribers, took place in Canada.[88]

In today's world many fraudulent schemes inevitably involve corporations. It is important therefore to consider the application of the section to business organizations of this type and their officers and servants. Not surprisingly the defrauding of a company by its own officers and directors comes within the purview of the offence. In *Cox v. The Queen; Paton v. The Queen*, the Supreme Court of Canada held that a corporation could be so defrauded, stating:[89]

"If all the directors of a company should join in using its funds to purchase an asset which they knew to be worthless as part of a scheme to divert those funds to their own use they would, in my opinion, be guilty...of defrauding the company of those funds. Even supposing it could be said that, the directors being 'the mind of the company' and well knowing the true facts, the company was not deceived (a proposition which I should find it difficult to accept), I think it clear that in the supposed case the directors would have defrauded the company, if not by deceit or falsehood, by 'other fraudulent means'."

This principle has been carried to its logical extreme by holding that even a "one-man" company can be so defrauded by the individual who is its directing mind: *R. v. Marquardt*.[90] This is one instance in which "conceptual thinking" and policy objectives mesh together neatly. As the court in *Marquardt* observed:

---

[86]In the same way that *Allen v. Hyatt* (1914), 26 O.W.R. 215, 17 D.L.R. 7 (P.C.) qualified this broad principle of *Percival v. Wright*, [1902] 2 Ch. 421 (C.A.). *Littler* is pertinent to civil insider trading liability, *ante*, part 6.02, especially footnote 14

[87][1970] 3 O.R. 344, [1970] 5 C.C.C. 46, 11 C.R.N.S. 1 *sub nom. R. v. Chapman* (C.A.); leave to appeal refused [1970] 3 O.R. 353n, [1970] 5 C.C.C. 55n (S.C.C.).

[88]An important extension of this principle is contained in the form of new amendments to the Criminal Code, 1974-75-76 (Can.), c. 93, s. 36, proclaimed in force April 26, 1976. These changes envisage the enlarging of the offence of criminal conspiracy to cover corporate and stock market frauds which are planned in Canada and executed elsewhere as well as the converse situation where the conspiracy takes place outside Canada but the deception is perpetuated in this country. The new provisions are in response to a resolution passed by the Canadian Bar Association at its 1974 annual meeting.

[89][1963] S.C.R. 500 at pp. 512-3, [1963] 2 C.C.C. 148, 40 C.R. 52.

[90](1972), 6 C.C.C. (2d) 372, 18 C.R.N.S. 162, [1972] 3 W.W.R. 256 (B.C.C.A.).

"Even if this company was a 'one man company' owned and controlled by the appellant, he had no right to deplete the assets of the company and thus prejudice the rights of creditors. Nor is it any answer to say that the creditors were ultimately paid off once it is established that assets of the company were depleted by the fraudulent action of the appellant."[91]

Section 338(2) has attracted little litigation. Despite its apparent limitation to fraudulent stock exchange and public market transactions, the subsection is not so circumscribed in its application.[92]

9.11 False Prospectus

Section 358 is of chief interest in connection with false prospectuses; however, it also imposes liability in the case of false statements or accounts, whether written or oral. Subsection (1) provides:

"(1) Everyone who makes, circulates or publishes a prospectus, statement or account, whether written or oral, that he knows is false in a material particular, with intent

(a) to induce persons, whether ascertained or not, to become shareholders or partners in a company,

(b) to deceive or defraud the members, shareholders or creditors, whether ascertained or not, of a company,

(c) to induce any person to entrust or advance anything to a company, or

(d) to enter into any security for the benefit of a company,

is guilty of an indictable offence and is liable to imprisonment for ten years."

With respect to the requisite intent, it is, of course, a well-established principle of the criminal law that intention may be arrived at by inference. Assuming the existence of material falsity and knowledge thereof, all that is required to complete the elements of the offence in the case of a prospectus is for the document to be filed with a provincial securities commission; the very making of such a filing should suffice to show the intent to induce persons to become shareholders of the company.[93] In the case of statements or accounts in satisfaction of the continuous disclosure requirements these obligations have been established with the underlying objective of investor protection; a failure to observe them and the deliberate provision instead of information false in a material particular gives rise to the inference of an intent to deceive or defraud the members, shareholders or creditors of a company.[94]

It is sufficient for the offence if it is a probable consequence that the recipient of such information will be deceived; there is no requirement of actual detriment. The "actus" of the offence is complete with the "circulation" or "publication" of the required information either through filing with the Commission or mailing it to interested parties (*e.g.*, shareholders).

---

[91]*Ibid.*, at p. 374, C.C.C.
[92]*R. v. Bolcev* (1951), 102 C.C.C. 239 (Ont. C.A.).
[93]*R. v. Liversidge* (1970), 73 W.W.R. 29 (B.C. Co. Ct.).
[94]Section 358(1)(b).

The section creates only one offence: the three terms "making, circulating or publishing" a false prospectus are merely alternative descriptions of the means of committing the offence.[95] The falsity contemplated by the section is not confined to that which would constitute a "false pretence".[96] The expression "any person" includes all persons of the class to whom the prospectus was intended to be given.[97]

If filing constitutes publication, the interesting problem arises of what happens when the material falsity supervenes or only comes to light sometime later than the date of first filing. In *R. v. Liversidge*[98] it was held that the "publication" continued as long as the filing in question remained the current one. Thus the offence may occur when no amendment to the public file is made after a material change occurs.[99]

It is no defence that the representation was objectively somewhat ambiguous if subjectively speaking there was knowledge of this ambiguity and an intent to deceive or induce reliance by means of it.[100]

Another important question concerns the extent to which misleading omissions will be treated as false statements within the meaning of the section. In *R. v. McLeod*[101] the Supreme Court of Canada, reversing the British Columbia Court of Appeal, upheld the conviction of a company director which arose out of the publication of a balance sheet which omitted to show the amount of a loan as a corresponding liability. The Supreme Court held that the positive statement complained of was false by reason of omission, *i.e.*, the shareholders were deceived by it.[102]

---

[95]*Cox v. The Queen; Paton v. The Queen, supra*, footnote 89.
[96]*Ibid.*
[97]*Ibid.*
[98]*Supra*, footnote 93.
[99]*Davidson v. The Queen*, [1971] 4 W.W.R. 731, 3 C.C.C. (2d) 509 *sub nom. R. v. Davidson* (B.C.C.A.).
[100]See *R. v. Johnston*, [1932] O.R. 79, [1932] 1 D.L.R. 655, 57 C.C.C. 132 (C.A.), where the accused was convicted. The prospectus contained after the name of the company the words: "No Bonds. No Mortgages". The prospectus also contained an engraving of a building with the same words on the sides of the building. This elicited the following rejoinder from the court at p. 83, O.R.:
"While a close scrutiny, such as would be given to the prospectus by a financial company or one accustomed to examine documents with great care and minuteness, would have disclosed that the company, the stock of which was being offered and promoted by the prospectus, was ultimately to acquire the property free from bond or mortgage, it is, I think, clear that the ordinary reader with the attention usually paid to such documents, would believe that the representation was that the property spoken of as what the company had been 'incorporated...to own and operate...free and clear of bonds and mortgages', was then, 'free and clear of bonds and mortgages'."
[101][1941] S.C.R. 228, 75 C.C.C. 305, [1941] 1 D.L.R. 773; reversing [1940] 3 W.W.R. 625, [1941] 1 D.L.R. 578, 75 C.C.C. 78, 55 B.C.R. 439 (C.A.).
[102]The majority of the Court of Appeal had considered that the Crown's case depended on proving the making of a statement false in a material particular and not "a statement rendered false by the omission of material particulars". To this extent, it may be that the majority in the Court of Appeal decided the case on technical grounds, although it is equally clear that the dissenting

The *McLeod* decision was followed in *R. v. Colucci.*[103] The accused, a broker-dealer, was convicted for distributing a circular to shareholders which extracted a favourable passage from the report of an engineer in respect to sampling conducted on property belonging to a company in which those circularized were shareholders. A most unfavourable part of the report, which recommended in effect that no further investigation was justified and that all option arrangements should be cancelled, was neither set out nor referred to. McLennan J.A. delivering the judgment of the court, stated:

"...common sense and reason would indicate that the section of the *Code* which makes it an offence to deceive, must of necessity include deceiving by an omission of a material particular."[104]

Hitherto in considering the type of falsehood envisaged by the section we have assumed the element of materiality. However, this too requires some attempt at definition if clarity is to be achieved in all cases. The decision in *R. v. Lord Kylsant*,[105] held that materiality is to be determined with reference to a particular document in its entirety as interpreted by the average reasonable man. There is furthermore in the *Colucci* case an incipient definition of materiality as being that which the average reasonable man would consider as material to his decision whether or not to make an investment. In the words of McLennan J.A:

"There can be no question in this case that the matter omitted was material. No shareholder...would consider even holding his shares let alone buying further had the report...including the recommendations been summarized in the circular letter."[106]

In *R. v. Bishirgian et al.*[107] the English Criminal Court of Appeal came to a similar conclusion in a case in which a prospectus stated that the proceeds of the offering were to be used to buy a controlling interest in another company, omitting to disclose that the acquiree company was engaged in a highly speculative venture. Lord Hewart L.C.J. stated:

"In order to ascertain the question whether this document was false in a material particular or in all material particulars, one may ask oneselves [*sic*] this question: 'If the facts had been revealed or even clearly indicated, would any man of sense have put his money into it?'".[108]

As with all criminal offences, the instances in which a conviction is appropriate are substantially circumscribed by the defence of mistake of fact.[109]

---

judgment, the reasons of which the Supreme Court adopted, gives effect to substantive considerations which were not fully dealt with by the majority.
[103][1965] 2 O.R. 665, [1965] 4 C.C.C. 56, 46 C.R. 256 (C.A.).
[104]*Ibid.*, at p. 668, O.R.
[105][1932] 1 K.B. 442, 101 L.J.K.B. 97 (C.C.A.).
[106]*Supra*, footnote 103 at p. 688, O.R.
[107](1936), 25 Cr. App. R. 176, [1936] 1 All E.R. 586.
[108][1936] 1 All E.R. 586 at p. 594.
[109]*R. v. Harcourt* (1929), 64 O.L.R. 566 (C.A.) is an illustration of this cardinal principle. The accused, whose responsibility for making a false statement was not seriously in dispute, escaped criminal liability on the basis that he had

9.12 Fraudulent Manipulation of Stock Exchange Transactions

Section 340 makes an offence of the practice colloquially known as "wash trading". It reads:

"Every one who, through the facility of a stock exchange, curb market or other market, with intent to create a false or misleading appearance of active public trading in a security or with intent to create a false or misleading appearance with respect to the market price of a security,

(a) effects a transaction in the security that involves no change in the beneficial ownership thereof,

(b) enters an order for the purchase of the security, knowing an order of substantially the same size at substantially the same time and at substantially the same price for the sale of the security has been or will be entered by or for the same or different persons, or

(c) enters an order for the sale of the security, knowing that an order of substantially the same size at substantially the same time and at substantially the same price for the purchase of the security has been or will be entered by or for the same or different persons,

is guilty of an indictable offence and is liable to imprisonment for five years."

In *R. v. Jay*[110] the accused had engaged in a considerable number of transactions in which the purchases and sales were substantial by equivalent. His ultimate objective was apparently to acquire a substantial holding and secure election to the company's board. With respect to the correspondence of purchases and sales it was successfully argued that the accused was engaged in price stabilization and not market manipulation. With respect to the elements of the offence and requisites of proof, the court stated:

"In order to succeed the Crown would have to prove, with respect to each of those purchase orders, that a substantially corresponding sale order had been entered by the accused at substantially the same time so that when the purchase and sale of the quantity specified would be completed they would offset one another with no profit to the accused. The Crown would have to go further and prove beyond a reasonable doubt that those corresponding purchase and sale orders were entered with intent to create a false or misleading appearance of active public trading.

---

relied in good faith on statements made to him by a mining engineer. *Davidson v. The Queen*, [1971] 4 W.W.R. 731, 3 C.C.C. (2d) 509 *sub. nom. R. v. Davidson* (B.C.C.A.), is illustrative of the same limitation; the accused was a director of a company which had issued a prospectus stating that it was the holder of certain mineral claims. During the currency of the prospectus the claims expired; the accused arranged to have the claims registered in his name to hold the beneficial interest in trust for the company. Contrary to the accused's alleged belief that the arrangement had been effectuated, the claims were not recorded in his name. On appeal from a conviction, the British Columbia Court of Appeal held that in law the accused was entitled to have had the trial jury instructed as to a defence of mistake of fact.

[110][1965] 2 O.R. 471, [1966] 1 C.C.C. 70 (C.A.).

"...Parliament must have recognized that such corresponding purchase and sale orders could be entered without the specified intent.[111]

A broader approach was subsequently taken in *R. v. MacMillan*.[112] The accused was charged with an offence under para. (b) of the section. The charges arose out of certain cross trades involving two companies controlled by the accused and friends and family for whose accounts the accused had a blanket authority to deal. While the rules of the stock exchange required that the floor trader announce that the trade was a cross and that any intervenor bids at the price announced be met before the execution of the trade, the trade was recorded to the public on the ticker tape without particulars, thereby creating the false or misleading appearance of active public trading. With respect to the elements of the offence the court rejected a defence argument that the cross-trading was not prohibited unless it involved fictitious persons or persons involved with the accused in a fraudulent conspiracy. As to intent, McLennan J.A. speaking for the court, observed:

"As already stated, it is beyond dispute that the cross-trade created a false or misleading appearance of active public trading. The appellant was a knowledgeable person with respect to trading in securities; she was interested financially in different ways in the shares...and she must be taken, in the absence of evidence from which some other reasonable explanation might be inferred, not only to have foreseen the probable result of the large cross-trade but to have as her real and dominant intention in carrying out the transactions the probable result so foreseen."[113]

With respect to a suggestion that the only intent was to benefit friends, the court observed that as a result of the accused's trading on their behalf, the actual benefit enjoyed was as a direct consequence of the public demand in response to the appearance of active public trading.

In *R. v. Lampard*[114] the broadening trend continued,[115] although the conviction was reversed on jurisdiction grounds by the Supreme Court of Canada. There the accused, a broker, was charged with 29 counts alleging trading which involved no change in beneficial ownership. The accused was acquitted at trial on the basis that the Crown had failed to establish beyond a reasonable doubt that the accused had intended to create a false and misleading appearance of active public trading. An appeal to the Court of Appeal was allowed. The Court held that in the first instance the evidence on each count should be considered separately in determining whether there was the requisite

---

[111]*Ibid.*, at p. 473, O.R.
[112][1968] 1 O.R. 475, 66 D.L.R. (2d) 680, [1969] 2 C.C.C. 289 (C.A.) This was the prosecution of the central character in the Windfall Royal Commission inquiry (see Appendix VIII).
[113]*Ibid.*, at pp. 481-2, O.R.
[114][1969] S.C.R. 373, [1969] 3 C.C.C. 249, 4 D.L.R. (3d) 98, 6 C.R.N.S. 157; reversing [1968] 2 O.R. 470, [1968] 4 C.C.C. 201 (C.A.).
[115]And thus deflecting a movement within the federal Department of Justice and the provincial securities commissions to amend the offence by reversing the onus of proof.

intent. Since, however, all of the transactions were similar, the Court held it would be proper in such circumstances to consider the accused's conduct with respect to the other counts cumulatively in order to determine whether there was intent. It was also noted that the absence of proved motive was to be distinguished from the proved absence of any motive the final conclusion was that the only reasonable inference to be drawn from the facts was "that the respondent was engaged in a scheme or plan to create a false and misleading appearance of active public trading...". McLennan J.A. reiterating a theme from the judgment in *MacMillan*, stated:

> "He [the accused] had been in the brokerage business for many years and must be taken in the absence of evidence from which some other reasonable explanation may be inferred, not only to have foreseen that each wash trade would create a false appearance of active public trading, but to have intended that result."[116]

9.13 Gaming

Section 341 prohibits gaming in stocks or merchandise and establishes a penalty of five years' imprisonment. The essence of the offence consists in speculating on the rise or fall of prices. The section provides that once an agreement is established to sell or acquire stocks or merchandise, the burden of proving a *bona fide* intention to make or to accept delivery rests on the accused.

From a practical standpoint the most important problem that arises in connection with this section is whether it renders illegal the commodity futures market. This is a market in which the participants contract to buy or sell a quantity of a given commodity several months ahead at a price fixed at the time of the contract. This is a great convenience for those suppliers or users of the commodity who must plan ahead on the basis of costs or revenues that are largely known in advance. The element of speculation lies in the fact that the contract price and the market price at the time of performance may vary greatly. If the contract price is higher than the market price, the seller has made a profit; if it is lower, it is the buyer who stands to gain from the arrangement.

Early cases in Ontario and the Supreme Court of Canada took a rather literal view of the section, holding that the test of legitimacy with regard to such contracts was whether there was a *bona fide* intention that actual delivery should take place as between buyer and seller. The leading case enunciating this principle was *Beamish v. Richardson*[117] where 24 futures contracts, some of which *had* resulted in delivery, were held to be illegal. Rather than the goods actually changing hands, accounts were debited and credited between the parties.[118] The same principle was applied but with an opposite result

---

[116][1968] 2 O.R. 470 at p. 476.

[117](1914), 49 S.C.R. 595, 16 D.L.R. 855, [1914] 6 W.W.R. 1258 .

[118]See also *R. v. Harkness* (1905), 10 O.L.R. 555, 10 C.C.C. 199 (C.A.) and *Pearson v. Carpenter & Son* (1904), 35 S.C.R. 380, 25 C.L.T. 26 for the same approach. Other cases in the same line are: *Beyea v. Johnston & Ward*, [1930] 4 D.L.R. 421, 2 M.P.R. 287 (N.B.C.A.); *Betcherman v. E.A. Pierce & Co.*, [1933] O.R. 505, [1933] 3 D.L.R. 99 (C.A.) reversed on appeal, [1934] 2 D.L.R. 449 (S.C.C.); *Bank of Toronto v. Sweeney et al.*, [1927] 2 W.W.R. 597, 21 Sask.

in *Turner v. Alberta Pacific Grain Co.*[119] where the contract was upheld. In determining intention, relevant factors were the percentage of the price paid by the purchaser at the time of the contract and whether or not the parties were engaged in a business which used the particular commodity or were in the business of actually trading in it, and whether the quantity ordered was such that actual delivery could reasonably be contemplated. The line of authority culminating in *Beamish* was overruled in *Prudential Exchange Co. Ltd. v. Edwards*,[120] which held that the previous case had been misunderstood, and all that was required was a binding legal obligation on both sides, even though the buyer may have intended immediately to resell his purchase or the seller intended to perform by purchasing from someone else at the last minute. Despite its seeming inconsistency with the language of the section, as things stand the *Prudential* case is the governing authority in this area at the present time. And consequently, trading in naked commodity futures contracts thrives.

9.14 Short Sales Against Margin Accounts

Section 342 in effect deals with selling short against margin accounts of customers. The section creates an indictable offence with liability to imprisonment for five years for a broker who is employed by a customer to buy and carry on margin shares and thereafter sells shares of the issuer for any account in which he, the firm, or one of its principals, has a direct or indirect interest, if the effect is intentionally to reduce the amount of such shares he would normally carry for all customers. The manifest intention of this provision is to protect purchasers of stock on margin. There do not appear to be any reported cases under the section. It may be conjectured that its objectives are being fulfilled in large part by means of self-regulation and administrative practice.[121]

9.15 Breach of Trust by Public Officials

Section 111 makes it an offence for a public officer[122] to commit fraud

---

L.R. 670 (K.B.); *Topper Grain Co. Ltd. v. Mantz*, [1926] 2 W.W.R. 140, [1926] 2 D.L.R. 712 (Alta. S.C.); *Hansen v. Lechtzier*, [1925] 4 D.L.R. 1008 (Man. K.B.); *Medicine Hat Wheat Co. v. Norris Commission Co.*, [1919] 1 W.W.R. 161, 45 D.L.R. 114, 14 A.L.R. 235 (C.A.); *James Richardson & Sons v. Gilbertson* (1917), 39 O.L.R. 423, 39 D.L.R. 56, 28 C.C.C. 431 (H.C.); *Smith Grain Co. v. Pound*, [1917] 3 W.W.R. 516, 36 D.L.R. 615 (Sask. S.C.).
[119][1938] 1 W.W.R. 97, [1938] 1 D.L.R. 277, 69 C.C.C. 258 (Alta. C.A.).
[120][1939] S.C.R. 135, [1939] 1 D.L.R. 465, 71 C.C.C. 145.
[121]See the Act, s. 78 and discussion, *ante*, parts 8.05 and 8.09. Section 78 establishes a civil liability penalty for the same misconduct by a broker by giving the customer the right to have the contract treated as void. The drafting of s. 78 is preferable, particularly in its treatment of the broker and the affected shares. Section 79 of the Act requires a declaration by any person or company of a short position.
[122]In *Martineau v. The Queen*, [1966] S.C.R. 103, [1966] 4 C.C.C. 327, 48 C.R. 209 the Supreme Court of Canada held that the "official" described in s. 110, which creates another offence against the administration of law and justice, refers to elected or appointed officers discharging a "public duty". Note the definitions of "official and office" in s. 107. In *R. v. Pruss*, [1966] 3 C.C.C. 315,

or a breach of trust in connection with the duties of his official office. The section is found in the part of the Code dealing with "Offences against the Administration of Law and Justice". It expressly states that the official's duty is not to be defined by analogy with the duty of a trustee to a private person. There may still be an offence even where there would be no actionable wrong in private law.

Not only is the private law analogy not available regarding the person to whom the duty is owed; the subject-matter of the trust is also not to be understood in terms of civil law trust relationships. In *R. v. Campbell*[123] it was alleged that the accused, the OSC director, had actively sought to prevent the cessation of trading or de-listing of a certain mining stock on the TSE. The Court of Appeal with whose reasons the Supreme Court of Canada concurred concluded that the offence under s. 111 was the breach of trust by an official in connection with the duties of his office; the section did not require the existence of any trust property. Wells J.A. (as he then was) stated:

"In our opinion s. 103 [now s. 111] is wide enough to cover any breach of the appropriate standard of responsibility and conduct demanded of the accused by the nature of his office as a senior civil servant of the Crown, acting as he was, as Director of the Ontario Securities Commission."[124]

Of the traditional prerequisites for a valid trust it seems that one only is necessary: the trust must have been constituted, in other words, the official must have been duly and properly appointed.

The second branch of the offence, "fraud" by a public official, does not seem to have been subjected to extensive judicial interpretation. But here as well, civil law concepts would not seem entirely appropriate. The kind of activity covered by the ban would seem to be wilful exploitation of a public position for economic gain whether or not the exploitation involves appropriating funds or property belonging to the public. The element of "inducement by deceit", so prominent in civil fraud, appear here to be unnecessary.

---

47 C.R. 358, 55 W.W.R. 83 (Y.T. Mag. Ct.) it was held that an employee of a company under contract to the Federal Government did not fall within the section. Presumably the company that employed him would not either, unless the arrangement with the government was so permanent that a status rather than a contractual relationship resulted.

[123][1967] 2 O.R. 1, [1967] 3 C.C.C. 250, 50 C.R. 270 (C.A.); affd 2 C.R.N.S. 403 (S.C.C.). The accused's acquittal on a charge of breach of trust was set aside and apparently the charge was not re-laid. This case arose from the events investigated in the Windfall Royal Commission (see Appendix VIII).

[124]*Ibid.*, at p. 6, O.R.

Chapter 10
Self-Regulation

10.01 General Framework

Self-regulation in a particular segment of the securities industry may be described in a minimal fashion as the establishment and enforcement of rules governing the activities of that particular segment by its members.[1] A self-regulatory framework may develop for a variety of reasons. It may be to permit persons or companies with some common features to conduct their businesses more efficiently and profitably, either through an exchange of information or through the improved public relations which a formal association with perhaps a permanent staff may make possible. Another aim may be to ensure a higher standard of ethical conduct in the business in question. Moreover, the desire to "pre-empt" impending regulation by governmental authority with rigid standards is undoubtedly a motive in some cases. Finally, "voluntary" self-regulation may be the direct result of pressure by government authorities on a certain segment of the industry.[2] The government authority may have concluded that regulation is necessary but at the same time may be disinclined to impose direct controls either because of a lack of funds or in the belief that the necessary restraints can be most effectively provided by the industry itself.[3]

10.02 How is the Effectiveness of Self-Regulation to be Measured

The Canadian Mutual Funds Report stated the potential advantages of effective self-regulation as follows:[4]

"If the members of a particular industry can effectively supervise themselves and discipline members whose behaviour is detrimental

---

[1]The Canadian Mutual Funds Report went further than this in its definition of the term and included an explicit reference to government bodies as authorizing self-regulation and to the public interest as the norm or standard by which it is to be judged (p. 723): "any arrangement under which an industry association is looked to by a government agency to apply controls over its members in the public interest, in circumstances where the agency might otherwise apply such controls directly." See the valuable discussion of self-regulation generally in that Report at pp. 722-32.

[2]As in the case of the formation of the Ontario Broker-Dealers' Association in 1947. See, *infra*, part 10.05.

[3]There are varying degrees of government involvement in the design of a self-regulatory framework with defined goals and responsibilities. The comments of the Canadian Mutual Funds Report are apposite in this connection (p. 723):

"At the one extreme, it [self-regulation] could refer to an association of industry participants, operating independently of government, which voluntarily established a code of conduct and censured or expelled members who failed to adhere to it. At the other extreme it could refer to the complete delegation by government of regulatory powers to an industry association."

[4]Page 724.

386

to the public interest, considerable benefits will result. The governmental agencies concerned will be able to devote their resources to other activities. The industry concerned will keep its own house in order, thereby maintaining a favourable reputation with the public and with the government. In addition, an industry association may well be able to apply disciplinary techniques more effectively than could a governmental agency. Considerations of moral standards and good business practice can often be more readily appreciated by persons who are actively engaged in a particular business than by an administrator who is less familiar with day-to-day practice and with the possible implications of various types of improper behaviour. Another advantage, particularly relevant during the period of separate administration, is that an industry association can be organized on a national basis without constitutional difficulties."

In its balanced approach the same Report outlined several negative features of leaving control in the hands of non-public bodies:[5]

"Those who criticize reliance on self-regulation do not ordinarily question the value of the advantages described in the preceding paragraph. They simply regard such advantages as unattainable. To permit the assumption of responsibilities by a self-regulatory association which does not properly exercise those responsibilities results in a mere facade of public protection that may well be more dangerous than would be no protection at all. This would be particularly true if governmental agencies relied on proper performance by the self-regulatory association, and therefore failed to exercise similar responsibilities. These are the most important criticisms, but others are also advanced. It is said that a trade association with official powers tends to become monopolistic and anti-competitive. This, also, results in a decrease rather than an increase in the quality of public protection. Finally, if membership in the self-regulatory association is not either held by or available to all participants in the industry concerned, those who are members may receive the competitive advantage over those who are not."

The Report then suggested five basic conditions which must be met before a successful self-regulatory system could operate:[6]

(1) an association genuinely representative of the industry in question;

(2) active supervision of the association by an administrator;

(3) ready availability of information as to policies, rules and their enforcement;

(4) a permanent staff to deal with routine matters; and

(5) a willingness on the part of the association to impose necessary discipline on its members.

We shall concentrate on the self-regulatory organizations in the securities industry which operate in Ontario. Those which receive some tangible recognition in the Act and Regulation are the Toronto Stock Exchange (TSE), the Ontario District of the Investment Dealers' Association of Canada (IDA), the Ontario Broker-Dealers' Associ-

---

[5] Pages 724-5.
[6] Pages 725-6.

ation (BDA), and the Canadian Mutual Funds Association (CMFA).[7]

10.03 Toronto Stock Exchange
(1) FUNCTION AND STRUCTURE OF THE TSE
The function of the TSE is to provide facilities and rules for the buying and selling of securities of listed issuers.[8] The Toronto Exchange first commenced operations in 1852 and was incorporated by statute in 1878.[9] The Act of 1878 continued with amendments until its replacement by the Toronto Stock Exchange Act in 1969.[10] The Exchange is a non-profit corporation formed with the object of operating a stock exchange in Ontario for trading by the members and other authorized persons in a manner that does not contravene the Act and Regulations or rulings made thereunder.[11] The management is to be by a board of governors consisting of the president, who is the chief executive and administrative officer, two public directors and ten

---

[7]There are other professional associations which operate in fulfilment of one or more of the purposes of a self-regulatory body (*supra*, part 10.01) but do not receive express acknowledgement in the Act or in the subordinate legislation made under it. Examples of these are an independent mutual funds association, the Toronto Bond Traders Association and the Toronto Financial Analysts Society.

[8]The Kelly Report approved the statement of function provided by the TSE to the Porter Commission (p. 104):

> "The chief function of stock exchanges is to facilitate the purchase and sale of shares as between investors by bringing together in one place orders from those who wish to buy and those who wish to sell. The price at which a share transaction is carried out on the exchange is determined by these forces of demand and supply in such shares at that time, as represented by the best price which one or more investor(s) is willing to pay (the bid) and the best price which one or more investor(s) is willing to accept (the offering)."

The Canadian Securities Course, 1971, p. 229, defines an "organized stock exchange" as "a market place where buyers and sellers of securities meet under competitive conditions to trade with each other and where prices are established according to the laws of supply and demand." It points out that on Canadian exchanges trading is carried on in common and preferred shares, rights and warrants, while in some European and United States exchanges, bonds are traded along with stocks.

[9]See J. R. Kimber and L. Lowe, "The Toronto Stock Exchange", at p. 193.

[10]1968-69 (Ont.), c. 132, now R.S.O. 1970, c. 465. The Toronto Stock Exchange Act is summary in its contents, being only twelve sections long. It is supplemented by the provisions of the Ontario Corporations Act, R.S.O. 1970, c. 89 which apply to the Exchange with only minor exceptions (s. 11).

[11]Toronto Stock Exchange Act, ss. 5, 4(1) and (3). And to dispel any doubt s. 12 of the Toronto Stock Exchange Act states that nothing in it is to derogate from the powers of the Commission; it explicitly provides, however, that the Exchange may "impose any additional or higher requirement within its jurisdiction" (s. 4(3)). This explicit right to raise standards above those which the OSC might impose as conditions of registration could have significance on appeals from a TSE disciplinary decision where the expected standard of conduct or the penalty imposed are more onerous than that which the Commission would have applied had it heard the case as a tribunal of first instance. See, *ante*, chapter 2, especially footnote 54.

persons elected each year by the members.[12] The president is appointed by the board and may be removed only by a two-thirds vote.[13] The two public directors, who cannot be members, are elected by the board yearly on the president's recommendation and with the approval of the Lieutenant Governor in Council. No officers of the Exchange other than the chairman and vice-chairman of the board and the secretary and the treasurer can be appointed without the president's approval.[14] No officers other than these four may be members of the Exchange.[15] In fact the secretary and the treasurer are part of the permanent staff and are not board members.[16]

The board is explicitly given power to govern and regulate the Exchange, the partnership and corporate arrangements of members and other persons authorized to trade on the Exchange including requirements as to financial condition, and the business conduct of members and other persons authorized to trade and of their employees, agents and other persons associated with them.[17]

(2) INTERNAL RULES OF THE TSE

The general by-law of the Exchange is a long and rather complicated document broken into some 21 separate parts, with a number of ancillary instructions on various topics as well as twelve policy statements.[18] Only the merest outline of these provisions can be given here.

From a regulatory standpoint the by-law broadly speaking covers three areas: the qualifications for becoming (and remaining) a member of the Exchange qualified to trade, the requirements for listing on the Exchange enabling an issuer's securities to be traded, and the manner in which trading is conducted in listed securities by members.

(a) Rules as to Membership

Part III of the by-law deals with membership. It deals with the different classes of members and the formalities of application to the Exchange and sets out qualifications such as citizenship, active involvement in the securities business and an absence of excessively close or otherwise inappropriate links with other members. Part V contains certain additional provisions which apply in the case of members which are corporations, notably the requirement that directors and shareholders of members be approved by the Exchange. Part VI contains similar stipulations with respect to the partners of members who are unincorporated firms. Part VII requires Exchange approval before a member or a director, shareholder or partner of a member becomes involved with an affiliated company as defined in the by-law. Part VIII regulates members' employees.

Part XVIII has certain requirements regarding the financial position of members. Among other things it authorizes the imposition of minimum net free capital requirements by the Exchange, and provides

---

[12]Toronto Stock Exchange Act, ss. 9 and 6.
[13]Section 7(1).
[14]Section 8.
[15]Section 8(2).
[16]Kimber and Lowe, *op. cit.*, footnote 9, p. 196.
[17]Section 10.
[18]For the full text see CCH vol. 3, para. 89-102.

for the manner in which members' accounts shall be audited. Members are also required to disclose details of their financial condition to customers on request. Detailed instructions for the auditing of member firms have been prepared in the form of regulations pursuant to Part XVIII. These are an appendage to the general by-law itself.[19]

Part XVII provides for disciplining of members and attendant procedures. Discipline may be imposed either for a failure to meet basic qualification requirements or (far more frequently) for infractions of the rules governing broker conduct.

(b) Rules as to Listed Issuers

The rules relating to the listing of issuers' securities on the Exchange are contained in Part XIX of the by-law.[20] The Exchange has a general power to list such issuers as it may determine. It may also de-list if they fail to comply with the terms of original listing or contravene the general requirements or if the Exchange concludes it is in the public interest so to act.[21]

The policy on minimum listing standards require satisfaction of two basic tests: financial soundness, whether looked at from the standpoint of minimum assets, adequate working capital or proven earnings, and "market depth", measured by the total value and spread of shares in the hands of the public.[22] The requirements, particularly so far as working capital, earnings and assets are concerned, vary considerably according to the industry—industrial, investment and real estate issues standing in one category, computer companies in another, mining companies in a third and oil and gas companies (split into producing and exploration companies) in a fourth. The converse topic of suspension and de-listing is dealt with by way of a separate policy statement.[23]

Quite apart from the policy statements discussed above, the reporting requirements imposed on listed issuers in Part XIX of the general by-law provide guidance as to the sort of company that is considered desirable for listing.

It is clear that those companies providing the fullest disclosure are the most acceptable. But in any case, whatever their previous practice the issuers accepted for listing must file a variety of information with the Exchange and in some respects the requirements are more stringent than those imposed under the Act. Changes in outstanding capital, whether debt or equity, and other "material changes"[24] must

---

[19]CCH vol. 3, para. 90-951. The Toronto Stock Exchange Act, s. 10(c) specifically authorizes the making of regulations under the by-law.

[20]The term "issuer" is used here because there are a few securities of unincorporated issuers listed, for example, units of real estate trusts. However, the by-law refers to listed companies.

[21]The precise criteria used to determine when an issuer is suitable for listing are not necessarily specified in the body of the by-law but may be contained in policies or circulars as they are sometimes called. The applicable provisions here are in Part VII, "Minimum Requirements for Listing Securities on the Toronto Stock Exchange", CCH vol. 3, paras. 92-038 to 92-061.

[22]*Ibid.* See also, Kimber and Lowe, "The Toronto Stock Exchange", at p. 198.

[23]CCH vol. 3, paras. 92-062 to 92-064.

[24]The definition of this term is less comprehensive but similar to that contained in Uniform Act Policy 2-12, CCH vol. 2, para. 54-882.

be reported, and annual, semi-annual and quarterly financial statements are required. The listed issuer must hold annual meetings accompanied by the sending of proxies to all shareholders; it must also inform the Exchange and its shareholders promptly of any action regarding dividends or the allotment of share rights. Finally listed issuers must conform to the Exchange's timely disclosure policy to ensure the market is a fully informed one.[25]

(c) Rules as to Trading

Most of the TSE rules regarding the conduct of trading and matters associated therewith are contained in Parts XI and XVI. Trading on the floor of the Exchange is regulated in Part XI. The rules in this section are lengthy and detailed, and from the standpoint of securities regulation this is the most important part of the whole by-law. Part XII contains special rules applicable to off-the-floor trades. Part XIII on the "clearing house", deals with details of the execution of trades once contracted, in particular the delivery of securities or the handing over of cheques in settlement. Part XIV deals with situations where trades are not carried out according to plan, whether through neglect or default or the insolvency of one of the parties. Commission charges are dealt with in Part XV, whereas Part XVI contains a number of miscellaneous rules concerned for the most part with the manner in which customers' accounts are to be handled. Part XXI regulates trading in "O.C.C. Options"—call options issued by the Options Clearing Corporation.

As the existence of these various by-laws and the numerous rulings and decisions made under them would indicate, the Exchange exists not only to provide a forum in which purchases and sales of securities can be conveniently transacted; it also attempts to provide a market of a certain quality. The adjective that is perhaps most expressive of the quality aimed at is "orderly". This means not only that the members of the Exchange should be honest in their dealings but that the market mechanism should function fairly and efficiently without wild swings in the price of securities owing to shortages (whether accidental or contrived) in the supply of a certain stock or the unchecked proliferation of misleading and unsurely based rumours. A phrase which is sometimes used, "continuous auction market", conveys something of the ideal towards which the Exchange, certainly in recent years, has striven.

A standard technique used to curb excessive speculative fever on the stock exchange is to raise the margin requirements, *i.e.*, the percentage of the total purchase price which must be paid, the balance being a debt owed by the margin customer to his broker. Occasionally the margin requirement in a particular stock will be raised when it experiences heavy speculative trading activity.[26]

---

[25]CCH vol. 3, para. 92-004. The policy is similar to that of the OSC discussed, *ante*, part 5.15, especially footnote 124.

[26]In March, 1973, for example (Globe & Mail, Wednesday, March 14, 1973, p. B8) the TSE raised margin to 100 per cent on United Siscoe Mines Ltd. Its price had risen from $3.05 in January, opening at $10.25 on March 13 and rising to a record $12.25 on the same day before margin trading was

Another method of moderating undue trading activity in a stock is the prohibition of short selling. This is often coupled with an increase in the margin requirements.[27]

The most important technique for maintaining an "orderly" and fair market is the trading halt. This is frequently used when material information about an issuer is to be released to permit the information to be disseminated and digested. Normally a realignment of price takes place before trading resumes. The imposition and duration of a halt may vary but in general:

(1) If an announcement appears in the morning newspapers there is no halt.

(2) If an announcement appears on the Dow Jones service before the opening or during the morning the halt is for two hours.

(3) If an announcement is made during the afternoon the halt is for the remainder of the day's session.

Longer halts are normally avoided because they violate the principle of liquidity and depress members' commission income. Also U.S. markets (which influence duration of halts as to interlisted issuers) tend to halt for even shorter periods. In any case the Exchange depends on its members to ensure that any client trading is fully aware of the information which occasioned the halt.

(3) PRIVATE CLUB OR PUBLIC SERVICE INSTITUTION: THE EXCHANGE'S STAFF AND MEMBERS

The Exchange is under the direction of its governing authority, the board. However of necessity much of the routine business must be done by a permanent staff. In recent years, the TSE has felt considerable pressure to move toward greater public accountability. One response has been to distinguish the staff more clearly from the elected board and give it broader authority over the day-to-day control of trading activities on the Exchange, although subject to board approval. Much of the impetus for structural reforms of this kind came from the recommendations of the Kelly Report in 1965.[28]

That Report laid down a number of basic principles. First, the Exchange must be regarded by its members and by the public as an entity which exists apart from its members to serve the public generally. Secondly, the function of the board of governors and of the administrative staff must be considered and their duties redistributed. Thirdly, regarding discipline the board should lay down policy and the sanctions available for infractions, and would review specific decisions of the administrative staff when a request was made for a review on the grounds of improper application of established policy. However, the

---

eliminated. It then fell to $9.35, but nevertheless accounted for more than ten per cent of the day's trading. In a notice announcing the margin increase, the Exchange stated that action was not a reflection on the merits of the stock. This was the first occasion when margin trading was eliminated since April, 1970 when securities of Seaway Multi-Corp. Ltd. "were put on 100 percent margin because of delivery problems" (TSE Notice No. 684, April 9, 1970).

[27]On March 30, 1973, the TSE followed the Montreal based Canadian Stock Exchange in imposing both these restrictions on no less than six different securities (TSE Notice No. 1006, March 30, 1973).

[28]See Appendix VIII which describes this Report in detail.

day-to-day administration and application of the rules and initial investigations were to be conducted by the permanent staff free from the influence of the governors and other members.

The strengthening of the staff's role which has decidedly occurred may perhaps be epitomized by a change in 1973[29] which gave the staff the power to make immediately effective decisions regarding such matters as increasing margin requirements or prohibiting short selling. Such decisions are still subject to approval by the board (and thus lapse or become ineffective in the case of rejection), but in view of the delicate judgment called for in complicated fact situations, decisions of professional administrators are not apt to be overturned.

The Kelly Report also envisaged that public governors would "engender a greater measure of confidence in the public mind" by keeping "the public better informed of what goes on within the Exchange". A public governor "would have an independence such as a President or Chief Executive Officer, who holds employment under the Board of Governors, could never have. More important, his presence would stand as an assurance by the Governors to the public that their functions were being performed in the interest of maintaining the Exchange as a public institution."[30] As we have seen, this recommendation too has been put into effect.

(4) THE EXCHANGE IN RELATION TO THE COMMISSION

The Act recognizes self-regulation by the Stock Exchange in several instances. It has long required the Commission's consent before the business of a stock exchange in Ontario could be carried on.[31] The Ontario Commission has extended that recognition only to the TSE.[32] It will, however, on occasion extend recognition to other exchanges such as the Vancouver, Montreal or Alberta exchanges in regard to certain aspects of their activities deemed to be carried on in Ontario.[33] There may be some question as to what constitutes a stock exchange when a particular institution carries on some of the activities traditionally part of the exchange function.[34]

---

[29]Proposed by-law No. 106, June, 1973, now enacted as by-law 11.69, CCH vol. 3, para. 89-489.

[30]Page 116.

[31]Section 140(1) (Bill 20, s. 22(1)).

[32]Ontario Policy 3-17 "Recognition of Toronto Stock Exchange", CCH vol. 2, para. 54-911. See also, Alberta Policy 3-13 "Recognition of Calgary Stock Exchange", CCH vol. 1, para. 24-513.

[33]The chief example to date has been the granting of permission for securities which have qualified a statement of material facts for distribution through the Calgary (now the Alberta) Exchange to be traded into Ontario.

[34]For example, what is the status of an institution set up to carry on a fourth market (trading in listed stock by direct buyer-seller contact without using a broker). The appearance of Instinet (Institutional Networks Corporation) in the U.S. and the decision of the OSC to exclude it from Ontario have been noted, *ante,* part 3.04(2), footnote 43. That decision was based on the fact that Instinet lacked registration to trade in Ontario and so its activities would be in breach of the Act. The Commission did not go on to consider whether Instinet was a stock exchange requiring recognition as such.

The Commission may in time extend the scope of "outsider" recognition. For example the Act requires that the confirmation notice sent by a registrant to his client state the name of the trader from or to or through whom the security was traded if the registrant was acting as an "agent in a trade upon a stock exchange recognized by the Commission". The reason for this requirement is to permit a customer to trace his trade at least to the agent on the other side. It might be advisable to recognize exchanges outside of Ontario in this limited area of confirmation slip disclosure.[35]

The substantive powers of the Commission over the Exchange owe much to the recommendations of the Kimber and Kelly Reports. The OSC now has a discretion to make any direction or determination or ruling with respect to the following matters:

(1) The manner in which any stock exchange in Ontario carries on business;

(2) Any by-law, ruling, instruction or regulation of it;

(3) Trading on or through the facilities of it or with respect to any security listed and posted for trading on it;

(4) To ensure that companies whose securities are listed and posted for trading on it comply with the Act and Regulation.[36]

These provisions give the Commission a very broad authority to supervise the affairs of the Exchange. Consequently the Exchange will normally consult with the OSC as a matter of course before embarking on a change which will have lasting effects such as a new by-law, although the more routine by-law changes will be first enacted by the Exchange and then forwarded to the Commission for review.

In matters which attract widespread public interest where it is desirable to hear from a number of viewpoints, such as the question of

---

Another corporation whose proposed activities bear some resemblance to those of a stock exchange is the Canadian Securities Depository incorporated under the CCA in 1970 (described, *infra*, part 10.07). Since it has not yet begun to function the issue of whether it is carrying on the business of a stock exchange in Ontario has yet to be faced.

The objects of the Toronto Stock Exchange as set out in the Act of 1878 (c. 65, s. 2) provide limited guidance as to what a stock exchange is. These objects are basically modelled on those set out in the Montreal Stock Exchange Act passed four years earlier (Act of Incorporation, 1873-74 (Que.), c. 54, s. 2 as am.). The objects of the Winnipeg Stock Exchange (Act of Incorporation, 1903 (Man.), c. 72, s. 2) follow the same model. The TSE objects are:

"to compile records and publish statistics, to acquire and distribute information respecting stock, shares, bonds and debentures; to provide and regulate a suitable building or room or rooms for a stock exchange and offices in the City of Toronto, to promote the observance of such regulations and requirements as may be by by-law established not contrary to law, to which ends the Corporation is hereby empowered by vote of the majority at annual, quarterly or special meetings of the said Corporation, to make and establish such proper and needful rules, regulations and by-laws for its government as they may deem expedient and necessary for the interest and administration of the property and affairs of the said corporation."

[35]Section 67(1)(e) requires disclosure of "the day and the name of the stock exchange, if any, upon which the transaction took place". This requirement also raises the issue of what is a stock exchange.

[36]Section 140(2). Bill 20, s. 22(2), cl. (d) changes "companies" to "issuers".

commission rate structure, the Commission will convene a more formal public hearing and invite submissions from all interested parties.[37]

A specific right of hearing and review by the Commission is granted to anyone who "feels aggrieved" by any disposition of the Exchange.[38] The procedures are similar to those which accompany the hearing and review of a disposition of the director.[39]

The best examples of a more active use of the OSC's supervisory powers have been the commission rate increase decisions.[40] In the first of these in June, 1967, a proposal for an eleven per cent over-all increase in brokerage commissions charged by members of the TSE was considered. The increase was approved by the OSC as not contrary to the public interest. The proceedings were short and the written decision summary in nature but several principles of fundamental public importance were established. The first is that the OSC has the jurisdiction to undertake a full measure of responsibility for rate regulation in the securities industry. A more timid interpretation of the Commission's powers might have concluded that commission rates were part of the internal business of the Exchange and not part of the regulatory framework. An intermediate position might have moved the OSC to intervene only when the increase showed a *prima facie* case of disregard of the public interest but in normal circumstances not to review a change in the by-law with respect to brokerage rates. The test the TSE was required to meet was that the new rates not be prejudicial to the public interest; approval was not to be granted simply on the basis that no one was able to establish that the rates would be unconscionable or excessive or would impair the efficiency of capital markets.

Secondly, the Commission chose to consider the Exchange decision after it had taken the form of a firm proposal rather than to enter into informal consultation and negotiation with the Exchange at the first manifestation of a desire for a change. Thus the Exchange had first to formulate what it considered to be an appropriate rate structure and then defend it rather than to develop a consensus with the OSC through mutual discussion. Thirdly, the Exchange proposal was tested in a public hearing with an opportunity for interested third parties to make representations regarding the merits or demerits of the proposal though not to cross-examine witnesses.

In the second decision on rates the procedural edifice already established was significantly reinforced. Considerable uncertainty still obtained regarding the most appropriate type of rate reviewing mechanism.[41] The Exchange proposed a substantial restructuring of commission rate schedules producing an increase in the total commis-

---

[37]For TSE commission rate hearings see June 1967 OSCB 16-17; Aug. 1973 OSCB 107; Nov. 1974 OSCB 199; Aug. 1975 OSCB 193.

[38]Section 140(3) (Bill 20, s. 22(3)). The phrase "feels aggrieved" could be more precisely defined. Bill 20 rephrases the section to say: "any person or company directly affected", which presumably provides an objective standard.

[39]*Ibid.* See, *ante*, part 2.10.

[40]Section 140(2), *supra*, footnote 36.

[41]Aug. 1973 OSCB 107.

sion return to brokers. The OSC reviewed the proposals in detail approving the idea of an increase but not in the amount suggested; it also gave its blessing in part to the restructuring of the rate schedule but indicated a need to go further in this respect. The manner in which the Commission made its decision reflected the greater complexity of the securities industry in 1973 (as opposed to 1967) and a desire by the OSC to delve more deeply into that industry's financial condition.[42] The formal hearings in this case extended over five days, with a substantial number of briefs and interventions from third parties. The Commission stressed that inasmuch as the brokerage industry operated as a cartel with fixed commission rates, close scrutiny of those rates was necessary to ensure that they were fair to the public, given the absence of the kind of price competition which might be depended upon to establish a "fair" level. The decision went further and requested that the Exchange give careful attention to the possibility of eliminating a fixed commission rate structure within the near future.[43]

---

[42]Such an approach raises fundamental questions. In the absence of free competition to determine a "fair rate" how far short of public utility rate regulation does the Commission's power of review fall? The OSC specifically said it did not intend to assume powers of review as deep and broad as utility rate regulation tribunals. But is there any half-way house? The decision hints at some answers.

[43]The OSC had recently completed its Industry Ownership Study giving it the opportunity to develop a deeper understanding of the industry, its structure and practices, and in particular its financial condition. The OSC indicated that while a detailed analysis of the brokerage industry's financial condition comparable to that done by government agencies regulating rates in public utilities such as communications, gas or electricity was not appropriate due to the lesser frequency of rate changes in the brokerage industry, the evidence before it was insufficient. In particular the Commission was critical of cost accounting methods in the securities industry which were incapable of isolating the cost of share brokerage in an integrated firm which carried on a number of other functions such as bond trading, underwriting, money market dealings, investment counselling, and acting as a fiscal agent. In an effort to remedy these deficiencies it was proposed that the two bodies—the Exchange and the Commission—should work jointly on a study over a two-year period to develop a greater understanding of the matter.

The Commission also assessed the impact of rates on different kinds of customers. It was particularly concerned to keep smaller individual investors in the market, though it approved a tapering schedule of progressively increasing volume discounts in favour of the larger institutional investor. As evidence of this concern for the small investor the Commission rejected the Exchange's proposal to increase the minimum commission rate from $5 to $12. While approving the proposal to move towards a completely flat structure, *i.e.,* a Commission levied as a flat percentage of the dollar amount of the trade regardless of the price of the share, it requested the Exchange to consider whether a completely flat rate structure was feasible (though retaining the volume discounts) over the next several years.

In dealing with the specific question before it of appropriate adjustments to brokerage rates, the Commission rejected the proposal which would have yielded an 8.8 per cent increase in gross commissions and instead permitted an increase of 5.24 per cent. The lesser figure was that first put forward by the TSE and later amended at the urging of the membership of the Montreal Exchange who insisted on a structure which would charge more for larger

A final point on the Exchange in relation to the OSC, the Act requires the former to keep a record showing the time at which each transaction on the Exchange took place.[44] It is obliged to supply to any customer of any member, upon production of a written confirmation of any transaction with such member, particulars of the time at which the transaction took place and verification or otherwise of the matters set forth in the confirmation.[45]

The other major instance in which the Act recognizes the TSE is in connection with auditing responsibilities. In this area similar provisions apply to recognized stock exchanges, the IDA (Ontario district), and the BDA.[46] Each of these self-regulatory agencies is obliged to employ an over-all auditor (for the exchange, district association or association, as the case may be) with specified qualifications. The appointment of this person is subject to the approval of the Commission.[47] Moreover, each agency must strike a panel of members'

---

institutional trades, thus producing the greater over-all increase. The Montreal Exchange favoured the establishment of a national rate structure of which the proposed increases would form a part. Of necessity such a structure would have to take into account the needs of firms in areas less encouraging than Ontario for carrying on a securities business. The OSC was persuaded that the rate of return to members on their invested capital was insufficient to insure a financially healthy brokerage industry in which the more efficient members would be encouraged to expand; it therefore approved the 5.24 per cent increase, but concluded that events between the time of the initial and the amended proposals were not so critical as to justify the additional three and a half per cent increase. Part of the OSC's reluctance to accept the further increase came from the fact that it had no assurance that the test period on the basis of which the increase was calculated (Dec. 1972 to Apr. 1973) was sufficiently representative of a market which by its very nature is unusually cyclical. As a result the real impact of the proposed new structure could not be determined. This uncertainty was another factor leading to the aforementioned recommendation of a more detailed study covering a longer period down to March 1975.

The more detailed statistical information thus acquired may permit the OSC to make a more detailed scrutiny of future applications for rate increases. Meanwhile the Commission has already decided on a request by the brokerage industry for an interim rate increase in the difficult conditions which prevailed in the second half of 1974. A special surcharge to end by July 31, 1975 was approved to apply to orders of $5,000 or more. (Nov. 1974 OSCB 199). This was subsequently extended until November 30, 1975 (Aug. 1975 OSCB 193) but the Commission has given notice that it wishes to consider in hearings in 1976 the broad issue of fully negotiable charges *versus* minimum fixed rates. Significant in any discussion will be the fact that rates on the New York Stock Exchange have been fully negotiable since May, 1975. This makes possible considerably lower commission rates for Canadian institutional investors trading in interlisted shares (listed on both the TSE and NYSE) south of the border.

[44]Section 141 (Bill 20, s. 23).
[45]*Ibid.*
[46]Part V, "Audits", ss. 30 to 33. Each of these organizations is also recognized for purposes of separate classification in the categories of registration, *ante,* part 3.03(2).
[47]Sections 30 and 31 (Bill 20, ss. 19 and 20).

auditors with approved qualifications. Each member then appoints an auditor from the panel. That auditor makes the examination of the financial affairs of the member as required by the by-laws, rules or regulations applicable to members of the class and reports thereon through the agency auditor.[48] The governing framework established by the self-regulatory agency with respect to the practice and procedure in the examinations must be satisfactory to the Commission.[49]

The extensive supervisory powers that reside in the Commission with respect to the TSE are not present to the same degree with the other recognized self-regulatory organizations. To these we now turn.

10.04 Investment Dealers' Association of Canada

The IDA is an unincorporated non-profit entity with a constitution and by-laws which may be changed by its national executive committee subject to ratification by two-thirds of its members. The objects of the association are six in number: to encourage saving and investment; to promote as well as enforce high standards of business conduct among its members; to promote stability in the industry through establishing minimum capital, insurance and other requirements; to foster communication among members and facilitate cooperation with other bodies and institutions public and private; to provide the industry with a public voice with which to support good legislation affecting the financial system and oppose unsatisfactory proposed laws; and to upgrade the competence of persons employed in the securities industry and inform the public.[50]

The Association springs from an association of Toronto bond dealers in 1914. By merger in 1916 with a similar group in Montreal, the Bond Dealers Association of Canada was formed. The name was changed in 1925 to the Investment Bankers' Association of Canada, and as a result of amendments to the Bank Act in 1934 which restricted the use of the words "bank" and "banker" the present name was adopted in 1935. The original three districts have grown to six. They are the Pacific, Alberta, Mid-Western, Central, Quebec and Atlantic. Applications for membership are vetted by the district executive committee and the national executive committee with an opportunity for individual members to object to executive decisions. To be eligible for membership at least 60 per cent of the dealer's gross profits for the twelve-month period immediately prior to application must derive from "the underwriting, distributing or buying and selling, either as principal or agent, from or to the public in Canada, of investment securities", including bonds, debentures, notes and shares of an investment character. The distinguishing of investment and

---

[48]Section 31(1) (Bill 20, s. 20(1)).
[49]Section 31(2). Bill 20, s. 20(2) introduces a modification. The by-laws, rules and regulations of the self-regulatory organizations are to be "subject to the approval" of the Commission rather than just satisfactory. The purpose of the change is to make the relationship between the Commission and these organizations more certain. The expression "shall be satisfactory" is not absolutely explicit as to the need for approval prior to any alteration.
[50]The Canadian Securities Course 1971, p. 217, CCH vol. 1, para. 820.

speculative securities is left to the district executive committee's discretion although the Association's by-laws contain a definition.[51] There are several other requirements for members. Adequate books and records must be kept, the dealer's own securities must be clearly distinguished and kept separate from those of the customer, adequate insurance must be arranged for and maintained, prescribed financial statements must be submitted for approval, provincial licensing or registration requirements must be complied with, entrance fees and other prescribed levies must be met, and a contribution to the National Contingency Fund must be made.[52]

In its published statements the IDA ascribes to itself eight principle functions as an organization.[53] The first of these is the protection of the investing public through regulation of the type of business carried on by members and the imposition of financial requirements such as maintenance of minimum net free capital in accordance with the nature and volume of business conducted and contribution to the National Contingency Fund. The Fund was established in 1969. Its present treasury is $1,500,000. Payments may be made to clients of members who have experienced losses due to a member's failure.[54]

A second function is the mutual protection of IDA members. This is done principally through the submission of briefs and recommendations to government and other regulatory authorities. The third task of the IDA is the maintenance of high ethical standards, chiefly through the medium of business conduct committees established in each district which investigate complaints against members in that area.

A fourth activity of the Association involves the manner in which secondary trading in treasury bills, bonds, debentures and unlisted shares is conducted. In the two principal centres, Toronto and Montreal, this function is performed by the Toronto and Montreal Bond Traders Associations composed of representatives from investment dealers, chartered banks and other financial organizations. These two bond traders' associations are obliged by their by-laws to accept IDA decisions with respect to unlisted trading.

---

[51]The definition is of the non-exhaustive type which we have encountered in various places in the Act. The eligible debt securities listed are the bonds, notes and debentures of governments and corporations both private and public (including religious institutions) provided the debtor is not in arrears. So far as equities are concerned, preferred shares not in default are eligible, as are common shares of a company with proven earning power. There is a residual category composed of securities designated by the district and national committees as being of investment calibre (The Canadian Securities Course, 1971, p. 220, CCH vol. 1, para. 821, by-law No. 1, 1.1(g)).

[52]The Canadian Securities Course, p. 219. See also the by-laws of the IDA, CCH vol. 1, para. 821, in particular by-law No. 2, "Membership".

[53]The Canadian Securities Course, 1971, pp. 220-4.

[54]For the U.S. practice see the SEC's "Study of Unsafe and Unsound Practices for Brokers" which led to the Securities Industry Protection Act effective April, 1971 (CCH Federal Securities Law Reporter, Special Studies, para. 74, 801). The initial *corpus* of that fund was $75 million, with power to borrow up to an additional $1 billion from the U.S. Government.

Fifthly, the IDA oversees the education of members' employees and the public. At the present time the formal education programme is the responsibility of the Canadian Securities Institute, formed in 1971 by the IDA in conjunction with the Montreal, Toronto and Vancouver Stock Exchanges. Its function is to organize and administer two courses—an elementary outline and an advanced correspondence course—both designed to train new employees of member firms and to educate the investing public generally about the securities business and investing. The first of these courses was organized by the IDA itself in 1947; since that time the Association and its successor, the Institute, have graduated approximately 20,000 enrollees.

To round out the list the Association also provides statistical data including a compilation of bid and ask quotations and trading volume figures for unlisted industrial stocks in Ontario; it publishes a range of other materials, designed to assist its members in the performance of their tasks; and it maintains a liaison with the stock exchanges and other associations which are part of the investment community.

10.05 Broker-Dealers' Association of Ontario

The Ontario BDA was forced on the junior and more speculative segment of the securities industry by an act of the provincial legislature in 1947.[55] Its creation formed part of a programme of the OSC to give a more structured form to self-regulation in the industry. The BDA Act sketched out in general terms the objects of the Association; the making of regulations to carry out these goals was left in the hands of a board of governors, subject to the approval of the OSC. Among its various powers, the board may prescribe the qualifications for membership in the association, regulate the manner in which members carry on their businesses, prescribe a code of ethics, and provide for discipline or expulsion of those members who violate the code or any of the regulations.[56] As part of its disciplining function the board may initiate an investigation of members' affairs.

The primary purposes to which the various rules of the Association are directed may be summed up under three headings: adequate financial resources, competence, and ethical conduct. The aim is to ensure that members adhere to at least minimum standards in each area. For example, charging an unconscionable consideration or indiscriminately soliciting orders are included in the definition of "unethical conduct", and sanctions may issue against those who engage in either practice.

In addition to rules which impose certain standards on members as entities, the Association directly regulates the principal activity of members, namely, trading in unlisted securities. This function includes the setting of hours for trading, the issuing of cease-trading

---

[55]1947 (Ont.), c. 8. See also J.P. Williamson, *Securities Regulation*, pp. 275-278; J. Baillie, "Protection of the Investor in Ontario" and W.W. Cameron, "Regulation and Distribution of Securities in Ontario".

[56]See *R. v. Broker-Dealers' Association of Ontario, ex p. Saman Investment Corp. Ltd.*, [1971] 1 O.R. 355, 15 D.L.R. (3d) 385 (H.C.), and *Re Imrie and Institute of Chartered Accountants of Ontario*, [1972] 3 O.R. 275, 28 D.L.R. (3d) 53 (H.C.).

orders with respect to specific unlisted securities, and the fixing of a maximum offering price for new issues distributed through individual broker dealers who belong to the organization.

Dealers registered for trading in securities under the Act are classified as broker dealers only if they are members of the Association.[57] They may be either full members, who must carry a broker's bond, or associate members—employees of members who are registered as salesmen. Membership must be renewed yearly, so that the conduct of members is subject to periodic scrutiny by the board.[58]

The membership of the BDA has fallen off markedly in the years since the Association's inception. From a high point of close to 250 members in the late 1940's, it shrank to something less than 200 in the early 1950's; and by 1974 the number had dwindled to thirteen and in 1975 there were less than ten. There are several causes for the dramatic decline. One major one is the substantial shift in interest among Ontario investors from penny speculative securities to more expensive, better established securities of investment quality. Another is the tighter regulation of vendor consideration, the mandatory placing in escrow of promoter's stock, and the limits imposed on underwriting and distribution mark-ups in connection with flotation of natural resource issues; all these reforms have lessened the opportunity for profit. A more subtle but nevertheless important influence has been the general thrust of the various regulatory authorities to increase standards of registration and business practices among broker dealers; as a result Ontario has become a less attractive forum within which to operate.

10.06 Canadian Mutual Funds Association

The CMFA was founded in 1962 as a trade association for the sharing of ideas among its members and the carrying out of public relations activities for the industry. Its proposed activities also included compiling and distributing statistics, maintaining liaison with government agencies and administering the Canadian Mutual Fund salesman training course, which most jurisdictions require as a condition precedent to registration as a mutual fund salesman.[59] Seven years later the Mutual Funds Report appeared which examined the CMFA in terms of the five criteria for an adequately functioning self-regulatory body noted at the beginning of this chapter.[60] It found that the Association failed to satisfy them all. As of December 31, 1968 only 41 of the 136 mutual funds qualified for sale in Canada were members and only fourteen of the 92 management companies associated with mutual funds qualified for sale in Canada were members. However, in

---

[57]The Act, Reg. 794, s. 2(1)(2); see, *ante*, part 3.03(2)(b).

[58]It should be noted that until 1960, the regulations of the BDA were published in the *Ontario Gazette* as promulgated. But by an amendment to the Regulation Act in 1960 (1960 (Ont.), c. 103, s. 1(1)) the regulations under the Broker Dealer Act, 1947 were expressly excluded from the definition of "Regulations" in the Regulation Act; as a result they are no longer to be found in the *Ontario Gazette*, or in the Revised Regulations of Ontario.

[59]Canadian Mutual Funds Report, p. 727; *ante*, part 3.19.

[60]*Supra*, text at footnote 6.

terms of size and volume of business the proportion of the industry contained in the CMFA was much more substantial—some 86 per cent of the assets of all Canadian organized mutual funds then qualified for Canadian sale.[61] All of its members used a direct sales force and sold mutual funds with a basic sales charge rate in the upper part of the spectrum. No mutual fund organized outside Canada was included in its membership and until early 1969 when one independent sales force was admitted to membership the Association consisted entirely of Canadian organized mutual funds, their management and distribution companies. The Report made no finding with respect to active supervision of the Association by governmental authorities.[62] It concluded that policies and rules were publicly available from the Association with one very important exception: no information relating to enforcement was publicized. While there was a permanent staff to carry out its functions as earlier described, the Association had no substantial or significant disciplinary authority, and the Report found that it was reluctant to take disciplinary proceedings against members.[63] The Association has established a requirement that auditors of its members conduct an annual inspection and report to a central audit committee. The OSC[64] has applied a substantially similar requirement to all mutual funds.

10.07 Canadian Securities Depository

The Canadian Depository for Securities Ltd. was incorporated under the CCA in 1970 as a non-profit corporation "to provide facilities for the custody and transfer of securities owned or held by its participants and to alleviate the necessity for the physical delivery of certificates representing such securities".[65] Its sponsoring authorities were the Canadian Bankers Association, the Canadian Life Insurance Association, the CMFA, the IDA, the Trust Companies Association, and the Montreal, Toronto and Vancouver Stock Exchanges.

It is designed to hold "on deposit eligible securities" that are owned by its participants and keep track of each participant's share of the total securities on deposit as well as accrued interest, and dividends.[66] It will function by effecting delivery of eligible securities, which will include both listed and unlisted securities, resulting from purchases and sales of securities between participants *via* an accounting entry only as opposed to the physical transfer of a certificate.[67] Despite early

---

[61]Canadian Mutual Funds Report, p. 727.

[62]*Ibid.*, p. 728.

[63]*Ibid.*, p. 729.

[64]Conditions of Registration, Feb. 17, 1969, CCH vol. 2, para. 54-981 as subsequently amended, and p. 266 of the Report.

[65]Canadian Securities Course, 1971, p. 225.

[66]*Ibid.*, p. 226.

[67]See I.F.G. Baxter and D.L. Johnston, "Transfer of Investment Securities—Some Current Proposals", at pp. 194-5 describing it as follows:

"...It was recommended by an industry report in January, 1969 which identified 9 chartered banks, 16 insurance companies, 16 trust companies, 17 investment companies, 43 mutual funds, and 215 stock exchange and investment dealers' association members as potential participants. In con-

optimism, it has not yet begun to function, though counterparts in the U.S. and Vancouver are now well established.[68]

10.08 Financial Analysts Federation

The Financial Analysts Federation is a North American organization with constituent societies in local regions. It has public relations objectives as well as educational and ethical aims. It examines candidates and grants the designation "Chartered Financial Analyst" on successful completion of its training programme.

---

cept it was intended to include in its membership at the very outset a variety of financial institutions and not simply member brokers of one stock exchange. In this respect it is dissimilar to the U.S. depository which originally included only brokers, although now it includes some banks as members. Eligible securities for the Canadian depository would include securities of a number of stock exchanges, unlisted securities and also bonds and debentures. In this latter respect it would be more comprehensive than the present U.S. depository. Most of the shares of a given company are to be consolidated into a large denomination certificate, called a 'jumbo' certificate, held in the depository's name. In addition the depository would contain several smaller denomination certificates of the same company for transfers out of the system. Like the U.S. depository, transfers between members would be made entirely within the system with no need for movement of the certificates."

[68]This slowness in getting the depository into operation is a matter of concern. Plans were first formulated over 20 years ago. Such a depository has been operating in New York for over five years. Since the paper work in securities transactions is unusually cumbersome (about 75 separate steps have been identified) and rising costs have made it difficult for brokers to service small investors, the delay raises a certain uneasiness. See I.F.G. Baxter and D.L. Johnston, "Transfer of Investment Securities", and "New Mechanics for Securities Transactions". The Vancouver Stock Exchange has shown greater celerity, establishing a depository for its listed stock in 1975 and extending it to TSE listed securities in 1976 (Globe and Mail, June 9, 1976).

Appendix I
Selective Bibliography

Canadian articles, books or reports on securities regulation referred to in this book.*

Anisman, P. *Takeover Bid Legislation in Canada, A Comparative Analysis*, CCH Canada, 1974.
"Takeover Bid Legislation in Canada: The Definitions, Exemptions and Substantive Requirements" (1972), University of Western Ont. L.R.1.
Atlantic Report. See Ontario.
Baillie, J.C., and Grover, W.M.H., *Proposals for a Mutual Funds Law for Canada*, Ottawa: Information Canada, 1974.
"Securities Regulation in the Seventies", in Ziegel (ed.) *Canadian Company Law*, vol. 2, 343.
"Discovery-Type Procedures in Security Fraud Prosecutions" (1972), 50 Can. B. Rev. 496.
"The Protection of the Investor in Ontario" (1965), 8 Can. Pub. Admin. 172-268, 325-432.
Banwell, P.T. "Proposals for a National Securities Commission" (1969), 1 Queen's L.J. 3.
Baxter, I.F.G., and Johnston, D.L., "Transfer of Investment Securities—Some Current Proposals" (1972), 10 Osgoode Hall L.J. 191.
"New Mechanics for Securities Transactions" (1971), 21 U. of Toronto L.J. 336.
Beatty Report. See OSC.
Beck, H.L. "The Legal Aspect" in Morin and Chippindale (ed.) *Acquisitions & Mergers in Canada*, Toronto, 1970, p. 186.
Beck, S.M. "An Analysis of Foss vs. Harbottle", in Ziegel (ed.) *Canadian Company Law*, vol. 1, 545.
Comment on *Ames et al. v. Investo-Plan Ltd. et al.* (1974), 52 Can. B. Rev. 589.
Bird, R.W. "Corporate Mergers and Acquisitions in Canada" (1968), 18 U.N.B.L.J. 16.
Bouchard Report. See Quebec.
Bray, H.S. "Recent Developments in Securities Administration in Ontario: The Securities Act, 1966", in Ziegel (ed.) *Canadian Company Law*, vol. 1, 415.
Bray Report. See Ontario.
Cameron, W.W. "Securities Legislation Administration and Marketing in the Province of Ontario, 1956", Nov./56 OSCB 4-28.
"Regulation and Distribution of Securities in Ontario" (1954), 10 U. of Toronto L.J. 199.

---

*For a complete bibliography prior to 1966, see J.P. Williamson, Securities Regulation in Canada, 1960, and Supplement, 1966.

Canada *Proposals for a New Business Corporation's Law for Canada,* vols. I & II, Ottawa: Queen's Printer, 1971.
  Royal Commission on Banking and Finance: Report, Ottawa: Queen's Printer, 1964 ("Porter Report").
  Royal Commission on Canada's Economic Prospects: Final Report, Ottawa: Queen's Printer, 1958 ("Gordon Report").
  Proposals for a Mutual Funds Law for Canada. See Baillie.
Canada and the Provinces, *Report of the Canadian Committee on Mutual Funds and Investment Contracts,* Ottawa: Queen's Printer, 1969 ("Mutual Funds Report").
Canadian Securities Institute. *The Canadian Securities Course,* Toronto: Canadian Securities Institute, 1971.
Canadian Securities Law Reporter. 3 vols., CCH Canada Ltd., Toronto: current ("CCH").
Carscallen, M.P. Ontario Securities and Companies Legislation, Toronto: Institute of Chartered Accountants of Ontario, 1966, Supplement, 1967.
Committee to Study the Requirements and Sources of Capital and the Implications of Non-Resident Capital for the Canadian Securities Industry. *Report,* Toronto Stock Exchange, May, 1970 ("Moore Report").
Conway, G.R. *The Supply of and Demand for Canadian Equities,* Toronto: Toronto Stock Exchange, 1970.
Cranston, R.R. Comment on *Green v. Charterhouse Group* (1974), U.T. Faculty L. R. 175.
Crawford, H.P. "Insider Trading" (1965), 8 *Canadian Bar Journal* 400.
Creber, G.E. "Take-Over Bids, Insider Trading and Proxy Requirements", 1968 LSUC Lectures 235.
Dey, P.J. "Securities Reform in Ontario: The Securities Act, 1975", Canadian Business Law Journal, Sept. 1975, vol. 1, no. 1, 20-53.
  "Exemptions under the Securities Act of Ontario" (1972), LSUC Lectures 127.
Emerson, H.G. "An Integrated Disclosure System for Ontario Securities Legislation", in Ziegel (ed.) *Canadian Company Law,* vol. 2, 400.
English, J.T. "Corporate Acquisitions—General Considerations" in Ziegel (ed.) *Canadian Company Law,* vol. 1, 603.
Fullerton, D.H. *The Bond Market in Canada,* Toronto: The Carswell Co., 1962.
Getz, L. "Alberta Proxy Legislation" (1970), 8 Alberta L. Rev. 18.
  "The Structure of Shareholder Democracy" in Ziegel (ed.) *Canadian Company Law,* vol. 2, ch. 6.
Gordon Report. See Canada.
Grange Report. See Ontario.
Hodgson Report. See Ontario.
Huberman, D. "Winding-Up of Business Corporations" in Ziegel (ed.) *Canadian Company Law,* vol. 2, 273.
Hughes Report. See Ontario.
Iacobucci, F. "The Business Corporations Act, 1970: Creation and

Financing of a Corporation and Management and Control of a Corporation" (1971), 21 U. of Toronto L.J. 416-440 and 543-575.

Iacobucci, F. and Johnston, D.L. "The Private or Closely-Held Corporation" in Ziegel (ed.) *Canadian Company Law*, vol. 2, 68.

Johnston, D.L. Case Comment on *Green v. The Charterhouse Group* (1973), 51 Can. B. Rev. 676.

"Exemptions from Sales Disclosure in Regular Financial Statements: Courts, Tribunals, and Business Judgments" (1973), U. of Toronto L.J. 215.

"Public Offering Companies and Non-Public Offering Companies Under the Ontario Business Corporations Act, 1970" (1971-72), 5 Ottawa L.R. 1.

"Insider Trading Liability—A Comparison of U.S. and Ontario Legislation" Sept./68 OSCB 199.

Kelly Report. See Ontario.

Kimber, J.R. and Lowe, L. "The Toronto Stock Exchange" 1972 LSUC Lectures 193.

Kimber Report. See Ontario.

Lavine, S. *The Business Corporations Act: An Analysis*, Toronto: Carswell, 1971.

Law Society of Upper Canada. *1972 Lectures: Corporate and Securities Law*; 1968 Lectures: *Company Law*; 1950 Lectures: *Company Law*, Toronto: Richard De Boo Ltd. ("LSUC Lectures").

Langford, J.A. and Johnston, D.L. "The Case for a National Securities Commission", 1968 U. Toronto Commerce J. 21; "Cansec", Nov./67 OSCB 61.

Lennox, O.E. "Securities Legislation and Administration", 1950 LSUC Lectures 81.

Martin, S., Laiken S.N., Haslam, D.F. *Business Combinations in the '60's: A Canadian Profile*, published jointly by the Canadian Institute of Chartered Accountants and the School of Business Administration, The University of Western Ontario, London, 1970.

McRuer Report. See Ontario.

Menzel, D.G.C. "Corporate Reorganizations and Amalgamations" 1968 LSUC Lectures 273.

Merger Report. See OSC.

Moore Report. See "Committee".

Morin, D.B. and Chippendale, W. ed. *Acquisitions and Mergers in Canada*, Toronto: Methuen, 1970.

Mulvey, T. *Company Capitalization Control*: Report Upon Securities Legislation in Canada and Elsewhere by the Undersecretary of State [Canada], Ottawa: 1913.

Mutual Funds Report. See Canada and the Provinces.

Neufeld, E.P. *The Financial System of Canada; Its Growth and Development*, Toronto: MacMillan, 1972.

Ontario. Report of the Committee on Commodities Trading, Toronto, 1975 ("Bray Report").

Legislative Assembly Select Committee on Company Law: Report on Mergers, Amalgamations and Certain Related Matters, Toronto: Queen's Printer, 1973 ("Hodgson Report").

Ontario—*continued*
    Report of the Minister's Committee on Franchises dealing with referral sales, multi-legal sales and franchises, Toronto, July 1971 ("Grange Report").
    Legislative Assembly Select Committee on Company Law: Report on Co-operatives, Toronto: Queen's Printer, 1971.
    Legislative Assembly Select Committee on Company Law: Report on Credit Unions, Toronto: Queen's Printer, 1969.
    Royal Commission Appointed to Inquire into the Failure of Atlantic Acceptance Corp. Ltd.: Report, 4 vols. Toronto: Queen's Printer, 1969 ("Hughes Report").
    Royal Commission on Civil Rights: Report, 5 vols. Toronto: Queen's Printer, 1968-71 ("McRuer Report").
    Legislative Assembly Select Committee on Company Law: Interim Report. Toronto: Queen's Printer, 1967 ("Lawrence Report").
    Royal Commission to Investigate Trading in the Shares of Windfall Oils and Mines Ltd.: Report, Toronto: Queen's Printer, 1965 ("Kelly Report").
    Committee on Securities Legislation in Ontario: Report, Toronto: Queen's Printer, 1965 ("Kimber Report").
Ontario Securities Commission. *Report of the Securities Industry Ownership Committee,* Toronto: OSC, 1972 ("Industry Ownership Report").
    Report of the Committee of the OSC on the Problems of Disclosure Raised for Investors by Business Combinations and Private Placements, Toronto: OSC, 1970 ("Merger Report").
    Report of Commissioner D.S. Beatty on Matters Related to the Financing of Mining Exploration and Development Companies, Toronto: OSC, 1968 ("Beatty Report").
Palmer, E.E. "Directors Powers and Duties" in Ziegel (ed.) *Canadian Company Law,* vol. 1, 365.
Parizeau Report. See Quebec.
Peters, J.R., *Economics of the Canadian Corporate Bond Market,* Montreal: McGill - Queen's University Press, 1971.
Porter Report. See Canada.
Quebec. Department of Financial Institutions, Companies and Co-operatives, *Study on the Securities Industry in Quebec,* Interim Report, 1971; Final Report, 1972, Quebec City, Official Publisher ("Bouchard Report").
    Study Committee on Financial Institutions: Report, Quebec City: Official Publisher, 1969 ("Parizeau Report").
Rosenfeld, W.P. "Corporate Acquisitions" 1972 LSUC Lectures 367.
Shaw, D.C. and Archibald, T.R. *The Management Change in the Canadian Securities Industry,* 8 studies, Toronto: Toronto Stock Exchange, 1972-1976.
Thomson, C.R. "Concepts and Procedures in Hearings Before the Ontario Securities Commission", 1972 LSUC Lectures 95.
Ware, J.G. "The Role of the Trustee under Trust Indentures" (1968), 26 U.T. Faculty L.R. 45.

Williamson, J.P. *Securities Regulation in Canada*, Toronto: University of Toronto Press, 1960 and Supplement, Ottawa, 1966.

Windfall Report. See Ontario.

Ziegel, J.S., ed., *Studies in Canadian Company Law*, 2 vol. Toronto: Butterworth, 1967 and 1973.

"Constitutional Aspects of Canadian Companies", in Ziegel (ed.), *Canadian Company Law*, vol. 1, chapter 5, p. 149.

Appendix II
Index to Policy Statements

National Policy Statements

409

412   *Appendix II*

Alberta Securities Commission Policies

British Columbia Securities Commission Policies

Saskatchewan Securities Commission Policies

Appendix III
Index to Decisions of The Ontario, Quebec And British Columbia Securities Commissions*

1. Ontario Securities Commission Monthly Bulletin Decisions (January, 1949 to June, 1975) OSC Bulletin Reference

Section of the
Act in Issue

S. 1(1)
PARA. 6a(i)
May/59 p. 15; June/67 p. 12; June/67 p. 35; June/67 p. 36; June/67 p. 37; July/67 p. 12A; Sept./67 p. 32; Oct./67 p. 56; Dec./67 p. 97; June/68 p. 126; July/68 p. 154; July/68 p. 161; July/68 p. 179; Apr./71 p. 39
PARA. 6a(ii)
June/67 p. 34; June/67 p. 38; June/67 p. 40; July/67 p. 9A; July/67 p. 10A; July/67 p. 14A; Sept./67 p. 32; Oct./67 p. 56; Dec./67 p. 97; Jan./68 p. 12; June/68 p. 126; Apr./69 p. 52; May/69 p. 83; Mar./70 p. 52; Oct./73 p. 173
PARA. 11 (1950)
Mar./54 p. 1
PARA. 22
Mar./58 p. 1; Jan./66 p. 27; June/67 p. 21; July/68 p. 154; Aug./68 p. 187; Aug./70 p. 120; Sept./70 p. 128; Nov./70 p. 161; Apr./71 p. 39; Oct./72 p. 226; Feb./73 p. 15; Mar./74 p. 50; May/74 p. 87; Nov./74 p. 209; Mar./75 p. 93
PARA. 24
Oct./50 p. 1; Apr./51 p. 6; Apr./56 p. 3; Oct./60 p. 1; June/62 p. 1; June/65 p. 13; June/68 p. 129; Oct./72 p. 226
PARA. 25
Sept./67 p. 22

---

*See also N.M. Chorney, *Index to Canadian Securities Cases*, 1949-1976 Law Society of Upper Canada, Toronto, 1975, and Supplements, 1976

OSC Decisions—*continued*
S. 8—*continued*
  AS SALESMAN
Feb./50 p. 1; Apr./50 p. 8; Oct./50 p. 3; Feb./51 p. 3; Feb./51 p. 5;
Nov./51 p. 1; Jan./52 p. 2; Feb./52 p. 2; Feb./52 p. 3; Feb./52 p. 4;
Apr./52 p. 4; Nov./52 p. 12; June/53 p. 4; Apr./55 p. 1; Nov./55 p. 1;
June/56 p. 1; Apr./57 p. 1; July-Aug./57 p. 1; Dec./58 p. 4; Sept./59 p.
1; Oct./60 p. 1; Nov./60 p. 1; Nov./60 p. 2; Jan./61 p. 1; Apr./62 p. 1;
Apr./62 p. 2; June/62 p. 1; Dec./62 p. 2; Dec./62 p. 5; Apr./63 p. 1;
May/63 p. 1; June/63 p. 5; Nov./64 p. 3; Nov./64 p. 8; Nov./64 p. 9;
Dec./64 p. 7; Apr./65 p. 1; Apr./65 p. 2; July-Aug./65 p. 1; July-Aug./65
p. 3; Sept./65 p. 10; Oct./65 p. 9; Nov./65 p. 12; Feb./66 p. 2; Feb./66 p.
5; Mar./66 p. 17; July-Aug./66 p. 6; July-Aug./66 p. 12; July-Aug./66 p.
14; Nov./66 p. 2; Jan./67 p. 27; Jan./67 p. 28; Jan./67 p. 34; Feb./67 p.
10; Mar./67 p. 22; Apr./67 p. 14; Apr./67 p. 16; May/67 p. 25; June/67
p. 24; June/67 p. 26; June/67 p. 30; Aug./67 p. 19; Sept./67 p. 28;
Sept./67 p. 37; Oct./67 p. 58; Dec./67 p. 86; Jan./68 p. 5; Jan./68 p. 9;
Feb./68 p. 19; Feb./68 p. 24; Feb./68 p. 25; June/68 p. 135; Sept./68 p.
220; Sept./68 p. 222; Nov./68 p. 246; Nov./68 p. 263; Nov./68 p. 266-1;
Feb.-Mar./69 p. 24; Feb.-Mar./69 p. 34; Feb.-Mar./69 p. 37; July/69 p.
123; July/69 p. 136; Sept./69 p. 160; Feb./70 p. 23; July/70 p. 108;
Apr./71 p. 42; Apr./71 p. 50; July/71 p. 89; Sept./71 p. 135; Apr./72 p.
44; June/72 p. 118; June/72 p. 123; Jan./75 p. 30; Mar./75 p. 103
  AS SCHOLARSHIP DEALER
Apr./69 p. 60
  AS SECURITIES ADVISER
Sept./54 p. 1; Mar./55 p. 3; Oct./56 p. 1; Oct./56 p. 5; Apr./57 p. 14;
June/57 p. 1; Jan./59 p. 2; Jan./59 p. 5; Apr./66 p. 2; Feb./67 p. 3;
Feb./67 p. 7; June/67 p. 4; Oct./68 p. 230
  AS SECURITY ISSUER
Apr./53 p. 3; Apr./55 p. 1; July-Aug./65 p. 10; Sept./65 p. 12
  AS TRADING OFFICER
Sept./59 p. 1; Sept./59 p. 12; May/61 p. 4; Jan./66 p. 14; Jan./66 p. 21;
June/67 p. 30; Feb./68 p. 19; July/68 p. 164; Apr./71 p. 42; Apr./71 p.
50; Jan./72 p. 7; June/72 p. 98; Jan./75 p. 30; Mar./75 p. 103
  GROUNDS FOR CANCELLATION
General principles Nov./53 p. 14; June/56 p. 1; Jan./66 p. 14; Jan./66
p. 21; Nov./68 p. 266-1
Breach of duty to employer Apr./67 p. 16; Sept./69 p. 160
Breach of duty to public Feb./49 p. 20; Nov./49 p. 7; Apr./50 p. 3;
Feb./51 p. 5; Nov./52 p. 7; Nov./52 p. 9; Dec./52 p. 8; Nov./53 p. 1;
Nov./53 p. 14; May/55 p. 1; Nov./55 p. 1; May/61 p. 4; Oct./61 p. 5;
Jan./62 p. 1; Jan./63 p. 1; July-Aug./65 p. 1; May/66 p. 3; Jan./67 p. 28;
Mar./68 p. 54; Mar./68 p. 57; June/68 p. 135; July/68 p. 164; Sept./69
p. 160
Breach of TSE by-laws Nov./53 p. 1; Nov./53 p. 14
Conduct at hearing Oct./50 p. 3; Apr./52 p. 4; Sept./59 p. 8
Consent July-Aug./66 p. 9
Conversion Nov./60 p. 1; Apr./65 p. 2; July-Aug./66 p. 14; Feb./68 p. 24;
June/72 p. 123

OSC Decisions—*continued*

S. 8—*continued*

Conviction/charge Oct./50 p. 3; Dec./58 p. 4; Jan./61 p. 1; Nov./61 p. 1; Dec./62 p. 2; Dec./62 p. 5; Nov./64 p. 8; Nov./64 p. 9; Dec./64 p. 7; Apr./65 p. 2; Jan./67 p. 27; May/67 p. 25; June/72 p. 118

Dealing in stolen property Feb./68 p. 19

Delegation of responsibility Nov./49 p. 7; Apr./51 p. 2; Sept./51 p. 1; Feb./52 p. 1; Dec./52 p. 8

Failure to appear Apr./65 p. 2; Mar./67 p. 22; Aug./67 p. 19; Feb./68 p. 24; June/68 p. 135

Failure to know client Feb./50 p. 1; Apr./50 p. 8; Nov./53 p. 14; Apr./67 p. 16; Mar./68 p. 57; July/68 p. 164; June/72 p. 123

Failure to supervise Nov./51 p. 1; Oct./52 p. 1

False/incomplete application Oct./50 p. 3; Feb./51 p. 3; Feb./51 p. 5; Feb./52 p. 3; Feb./52 p. 4; Dec./58 p. 4; Jan./59 p. 5; Jan./61 p. 1; Dec./62 p. 2; Dec./62 p. 5; June/63 p. 1; Nov./64 p. 8; Nov./64 p. 9; Dec./64 p. 7; Sept./65 p. 10; Oct./65 p. 9; Jan./67 p. 27; May/67 p. 25; June/72 p. 118

Fraud Apr./62 p. 1; Apr./62 p. 2; June/63 p. 1; Mar./67 p. 22; June/72 p. 123

Fronting Feb./51 p. 5; Feb./51 p. 7; Feb./51 p. 9; June/51 p. 3; Dec./52 p. 8; Jan./67 p. 28; June/67 p. 24

High-pressure sales tactics Feb./49 p. 16; Feb./49 p. 29; Nov./49 p. 7; Apr./50 p. 8; Feb./51 p. 4; Feb./51 p. 7; Feb./51 p. 10; Feb./52 p. 2; Apr./52 p. 1; Apr./52 p. 6; July-Aug./53 p. 1; Nov./53 p. 1; Nov./53 p. 14; May/55 p. 1; June/56 p. 1; July-Aug./57 p. 1; Sept./59 p. 1; Sept./59 p. 8; Feb./60 p. 1; July-Aug./66 p. 14; Apr./67 p. 16; Mar./68 p. 57; Sept./68 p. 222; June/72 p. 123

Insolvency Apr./52 p. 2; Dec./52 p. 3; July-Aug./66 p. 14; Apr./67 p. 16; Aug./67 p. 19

Insufficient funds to achieve objects July-Aug./65 p. 10

Judgment/experience Apr./51 p. 6; June/52 p. 6; Mar./55 p. 3; Feb./66 p. 5; July/68 p. 164

Lack of independence Nov./49 p. 7; Apr./50 p. 3; Sept./50 p. 3; Oct./50 p. 2; Feb./51 p. 3; Feb./51 p. 4; Apr./51 p. 6; June/51 p. 3; July-Aug./51 p. 3; July-Aug./52 p. 1; Oct./52 p. 6; Dec./52 p. 3; Feb./53 p. 1; Mar./55 p. 3; Jan./59 p. 2; Jan./59 p. 5; Jan./67 p. 28

Lack of service Sept./50 p. 3; Oct./50 p. 2; July-Aug./51 p. 3; Mar./53 p. 1

Manipulative trading May/55 p. 1; Sept./59 p. 1; Sept./59 p. 8

Misrepresentation Feb./51 p. 5; Feb./51 p. 7; Feb./51 p. 9; Feb./51 p. 10; Jan./52 p. 2; June/52 p. 6; Nov./55 p. 1; June/56 p. 1; Apr./57 p. 1; July-Aug./57 p. 1; June/63 p. 1; Jan./67 p. 28; Mar./68 p. 57; June/72 p. 123

Overloading Feb./50 p. 1; Apr./50 p. 3; Apr./50 p. 8; Feb./51 p. 5; Apr./52 p. 1; Apr./52 p. 6; July-Aug./53 p. 1; Nov./53 p. 1; June/56 p. 1; July-Aug./57 p. 1; Feb./60 p. 1; June/72 p. 123

Policy violations

Extensive campaign/sales outside Ontario Feb./50 p. 1; Feb./51 p. 7; Feb./51 p. 10; Feb./52 p. 1; Apr./52 p. 6; June/53 p. 3; July-Aug./53

OSC Decisions—*continued*
S. 8—*continued*

p. 1; May/54 p. 1; May/54 p. 9; June/56 p. 1; Sept./59 p. 1; Sept./59 p. 8; Feb./60 p. 1; Feb./60 p. 8

Information and opinion May/54 p. 3; Oct./56 p. 1; Apr./57 p. 17; June/57 p. 1; Oct./61 p. 1; Jan./62 p. 1; May/66 p. 3

Non-residence Apr./52 p. 4; Nov./52 p. 12

Prior discipline Feb./50 p. 1; Apr./50 p. 8; June/56 p. 1; Feb./60 p. 1; Oct./61 p. 5; Mar./68 p. 54

Prior misconduct Nov./49 p. 7; Sept./59 p. 12; Oct./61 p. 5; Jan./62 p. 1; Apr./67 p. 16; Sept./68 p. 222

Promotional campaign Feb./49 p. 16; Feb./49 p. 29; Nov./49 p. 7; Apr./50 p. 3; Dec./52 p. 8; Apr./57 p. 1; May/66 p. 3; Mar./68 p. 57

Promotional literature Feb./49 p. 16; Feb./49 p. 20; Nov./49 p. 7; Feb./51 p. 10; Apr./51 p. 2; Apr./51 p. 4; Nov./53 p. 1; Nov./53 p. 14; May/54 p. 3; Nov./54 p. 12; Feb./60 p. 1; May/61 p. 4; Oct./61 p. 5; Feb./62 p. 1; Dec./65 p. 12; May/66 p. 3; Mar./68 p. 57

Unsatisfactory operation Oct./50 p. 2; Feb./51 p. 4; Apr./51 p. 6; July-Aug./51 p. 3; Nov./51 p. 1; Oct./52 p. 1; Mar./53 p. 1; Sept./54 p. 1; Oct./56 p. 1; Apr./57 p. 14; June/57 p. 1; Sept./59 p. 1; Sept./59 p. 8; Feb./67 p. 3; Feb./67 p. 7

Statutory violations

S. 6 Feb./51 p. 4; Nov./51 p. 1; Oct./52 p. 6; Nov./53 p. 1; Nov./53 p. 14; May/55 p. 1; June/57 p. 1; Oct./60 p. 1; May/61 p. 4; Feb./66 p. 2; Feb./66 p. 5

S. 15(2) Feb./51 p. 4; Feb./51 p. 9; Feb./52 p. 1; Oct./52 p. 5; Sept./54 p. 1

S. 35 Feb./49 p. 20; Apr./50 p. 3; Apr./51 p. 6; June/51 p. 3; Apr./52 p. 2; Apr./52 p. 7; Nov./52 p. 7; Nov./52 p. 9; June/53 p. 3; July-Aug./53 p. 1; July/68 p. 164

S. 52 Jan./67 p. 28; Nov./52 p. 7; Nov./52 p. 9; Feb./62 p. 1; July-Aug./65 p. 10

S. 53 Oct./51 p. 4; Apr./52 p. 2; Apr./52 p. 7; Nov./52 p. 7; Nov./52 p. 9

S. 54(1) Nov./49 p. 7

S. 56 Nov./52 p. 7; Nov./52 p. 9

S. 64 Jan./52 p. 2; Oct./52 p. 1; Dec./52 p. 8; Feb./62 p. 1

S. 67(1) Feb./50 p. 1; Apr./50 p. 3; Apr./50 p. 8; Sept./59 p. 1; Feb./60 p. 1; May/61 p. 4; July-Aug./66 p. 14

S. 68 Feb./49 p. 16; Oct./52 p. 1; July-Aug./53 p. 1; May/54 p. 1; May/54 p. 9; Apr./57 p. 1; Sept./59 p. 1; Feb./60 p. 1; Feb./60 p. 8; Mar./68 p. 57

S. 69(2) Jan./52 p. 2; June/56 p. 1; July-Aug./57 p. 1; July-Aug./65 p. 1; July-Aug./65 p. 3

S. 69(3) Jan./52 p. 2

S. 70(1) Apr./51 p. 6

S. 72 July-Aug./52 p. 1; Feb./53 p. 1; Nov./53 p. 1; Nov./53 p. 14; Mar./55 p. 3

S. 73 Apr./52 p. 1; Apr./52 p. 6

S. 137(1) (b) Apr./57 p. 1

426 *Appendix III*

OSC Decisions—*continued*
S. 8—*continued*
Policy violations
Extensive campaign/sales outside Ontario Aug./49 p. 5; June/53 p. 4
Full-time employment Nov./65 p. 12; July-Aug./66 p. 6; Feb.-Mar./
69 p. 34
Information and opinion Mar./51 p. 4; Oct./56 p. 5; Sept./61 p. 2;
July-Aug./63 p. 1; Nov./65 p. 8; Dec./65 p. 14; Mar./66 p. 9; Apr./66
p. 2; June/67 p. 26; June/67 p. 30; Sept./67 p. 37; Apr./71 p. 42;
Apr./71 p. 50
Prior discipline Sept./59 p. 1; June/67 p. 30; Aug./67 p. 5; July/69 p.
123
Promotional literature Mar./53 p. 3; Apr./53 p. 3; June/61 p. 1;
July-Aug./61 p. 8; Sept./61 p. 2; July-Aug./63 p. 1; Oct./65 p. 6; Nov./65
p. 8; Jan./66 p. 14; Mar./66 p. 6; May/66 p. 1; Sept./67 p. 37; Oct./67 p.
58; Jan./68 p. 9; July/69 p. 123
Promotional campaign Dec./52 p. 1; July-Aug./63 p. 1; Oct./65 p. 6;
Jan./66 p. 14; Jan./66 p. 21; Mar./66 p. 9; Apr./66 p. 8; Jan./67 p. 34;
Sept./67 p. 37; July/69 p. 123
Unsatisfactory operation Mar./53 p. 3; Oct./56 p. 5; Apr./66 p. 2;
Feb./68 p. 19; Feb.-Mar./69 p. 34; Dec./70 p. 170; Jan./75 p. 30
Statutory violations
S. 6 June/62 p. 1; Feb./66 p. 2; Feb./66 p. 5; June/66 p. 2; May/67 p.
9; Feb.-Mar/69 p. 37
S. 15(3) Nov./60 p. 2
S. 35 Apr./51 p. 6; June/53 p. 4; Apr./55 p. 1; June/66 p. 2; May/67
p. 9; Apr./71 p. 42; Apr./71 p. 50; Jan./75 p. 30
S. 53 Aug./67 p. 5; Aug./67 p. 13; Apr./71 p. 42; Apr./71 p. 50; June/72
p. 98
S. 55 Sept./65 p. 12
S. 56 Mar./63 p. 1
S. 64 Dec./52 p. 1
S. 67(1) Apr./51 p. 1; Apr./69 p. 60; Apr./72 p. 44
S. 68 Mar./51 p. 4; June/53 p. 4; Sept./59 p. 1; May/62 p. 4; June/62
p. 1; June/62 p. 3; June/67 p. 30; Sept./67 p. 37; July/69 p. 123
S. 69 June/66 p. 2
S. 69(2) July-Aug./66 p. 12; July/69 p. 123
S. 73 Sept./61 p. 2; Apr./69 p. 60
TSE suspension July/72 p. 158
Violation of securities laws of another jurisdiction Sept./59 p. 1;
Feb.-Mar./69, p. 37; Apr./72 p. 44; June/72 p. 98
Conditions for Reinstatement
Audit requirements Dec./70 p. 170
Capital requirements Apr./69 p. 60; Aug./70 p. 119; Dec./70 p. 170
C S C enrolment/completion Apr./67 p. 14; Sept./67 p. 28; Oct./67 p.
58; Jan./68 p. 9; Feb.-Mar./69 p. 24; Sept./71 p. 135; Apr./72 p. 44
Disclosure Apr./69 p. 60
New filing and acceptance Sept./65 p. 12
Non-participation of individual in company affairs June/67 p. 30
Recission of unlawful contracts Apr./69 p. 60
Severence of individual's connection with company June/66 p. 2

OSC Decisions—*continued*

S. 9
RE-REGISTRATION
Hearing and procedure May/64 p. 1
Suitability
General principles Jan./49 p. 10; June/49 p. 17; Mar./64 p. 1; May/64 p. 1; Nov./66 p. 5; Nov./67 p. 75
AS BROKER-DEALER
Grounds for Refusal
No change in material circumstances Nov./50 p. 2; Nov./62 p. 1; Dec./63 p. 1; Mar./64 p. 1; July-Aug./65 p. 13
AS SALESMAN
Grounds for Refusal
False/incomplete application Feb./50 p. 7
Knowledge and training Feb./50 p. 7
No change in material circumstances June/49 p. 17; May/50 p. 3; Feb./51 p. 12; June/51 p. 2; Mar./52 p. 3; Feb./53 p. 4; Apr./53 p. 6; Jan./56 p. 1; June/58 p. 5; Jan./59 p. 7; Nov./59 p. 1; Mar./64 p. 6; June/65 p. 2; June/65 p. 4; Nov./65 p. 5; Mar./66 p. 24; Nov./66 p. 5
AS TRADING OFFICER
No change in material circumstances Sept./65 p. 4
CHANGE IN MATERIAL CIRCUMSTANCES
Re Broker-Dealer
Improved business judgment June/64 p. 1
New capital Nov./50 p. 1
New evidence Jan./52 p. 3
New management Nov./50 p. 1
Re Salesman
Change in character June/64 p. 3; July-Aug./66 p. 17
Sponsorship Jan./49 p. 11

S. 12
June/53 p. 4; Feb./60 p. 8; May/60 p. 1

S. 13
June/53 p. 4

S. 18
(c) Dec./69 p. 190
(d) Oct./54 p. 1; Feb./67 p. 3

S. 19(1)
PARA. 2
Nov./64 p. 6; Jan./66 p. 27; Aug./71 p. 125
PARA. 3
General Mar./74 p. 60
Reg. s. 7 recognition June/67 p. 35; July/67 p. 12A
PARA. 5
May/67 p. 9

OSC Decisions—*continued*
S. 19(1)—*continued*
PARA. 8
Nov./51 p. 1
iii OSC Consent Objection
Orders May/69 p. 83; Sept./69 p. 166
Conditions of Consent
Undertaking as to resale May/69 p. 83

S. 19(2)
PARA. 3
Dec./60 p. 4
PARA. 4
Feb./73 p. 15; May/74 p. 87
PARA. 6
July/68 p. 16; July/68 p. 161
PARA. 9
June/49 p. 14; Nov./49 p. 12; Feb./50 p. 8; Sept./50 p. 5; Jan./58 p. 1;
July-Aug./64 p.1
PARA. 12
Jan./66 p. 35

S. 19(3)
Sept./67 p. 32; Mar./74 p. 60

S. 19(5) Denial of Exemptions
General principles Mar./55 p. 1; June/58 p. 1; Dec./58 p. 1; Nov./64 p.
6; Dec./65 p. 18; Jan./66 p. 27; Mar./68 p. 49; June/68 p. 129; Nov./68
p. 259; Mar./70 p. 52; June/70 p. 91; Oct./71 p. 163; Mar./74 p. 60
S-s. (1) Sept./57 p. 1; June/58 p. 1; Nov./58 p. 3; Dec./58 p. 1; Nov./65
p. 14; Nov./65 p. 18; June/68 p. 143; Nov./68 p. 243; Oct./73 p. 173
except (1)7 Oct./63 p. 1; Jan./64 p. 1; May/65 p. 2; May/66 p. 27
S-s. (1)2 Apr./56 p. 3; Oct./57 p. 1; Oct./65 p. 2; Mar./67 p. 19; Nov./68
p. 259; Jan./69 p. 9; Apr./69 p. 45; May/69 p. 90; Mar./70 p. 52; June/70
p. 91; July/70 p. 111
S-s. (1)6 Oct./55 p. 9; Feb./56 p. 1; Mar./56 p. 2; Apr./56 p. 3; Nov./56
p. 1; Oct./57 p. 1; Jan./58 p. 1; Mar./59 p. 1; June/59 p. 1; July-Aug./59
p. 1; May/60 p. 1; Nov./61 p. 7; Dec./60 p. 9; May/62 p. 1; Mar./70 p.
52; June/70 p. 91; July/70 p. 91; July/70 p. 111; Oct./71 p. 163
S-s. (1)7 Nov./56 p. 1; Oct./65 p. 1; Mar./67 p. 19; Dec./67 p. 91;
Nov./68 p. 259; Jan./69 p. 9; Apr./69 p. 45; May/69 p. 90; Mar./70 p. 52;
June/70 p. 91; July/70 p. 111
S-s. (1)8 June/55 p. 1; Sept./55 p. 2; Oct./55 p. 2; Oct./55 p. 5; Nov./56
p. 1; Oct./57 p. 1; Jan./65 p. 2; Jan./65 p. 4
ii Oct./71 p. 163
iii May/66 p. 26
S-s. (1)9 Jan./65 p. 2; Jan./65 p. 4; Oct./71 p. 163
S-s. (2) June/53 p. 4; Oct./55 p. 2; Oct./55 p. 5; Apr./56 p. 3; Sept./57
p. 1; Jan./58 p. 1; June/58 p. 1; Nov./58 p. 3; Dec./58 p. 1; Mar./59 p.
1; Apr./60 p. 1; May/60 p. 1; July-Aug./60 p. 3; Dec./61 p. 1; Dec./61 p.
3; May/62 p. 1; Jan./63 p. 1; Oct./63 p. 1; Jan./64 p. 1; Nov./65 p. 14;

OSC Decisions—*continued*

S. 19(5)—*continued*

Nov./65 p. 18; May/66 p. 27; June/68 p. 143; Nov./68 p. 243; Oct./73 p. 173

S-s. (2)d (1950) Nov./56 p. 1; Oct./57 p. 1

S-s. (2)1 Nov./61 p. 1; Nov./61 p. 4; (a) Nov./56 p. 1

S-s. (2)3 Oct./57 p. 1

S-s. (2)6 Oct./57 p. 1; June/67 p. 21

S-s. (2)7 Dec./60 p. 1

S-s. (2)9 Oct./57 p. 1; Apr./65 p. 4; June/65 p. 13

S-s. (2)10 Feb./49 p. 14; Jan./51 p. 1; Oct./57 p. 1; Mar./61 p. 1; Dec./61 p. 1

S-s. (2)11 Feb./49 p. 14; Jan./51 p. 1; Oct./57 p. 1; Mar./51 p. 1; Dec./61 p. 1

S-s. (2)12 Oct./57 p. 1; Mar./61 p. 1; Dec./61 p. 1

S-s. (3) Nov./68 p. 259; Jan./69 p. 9; Apr./69 p. 45; May/69 p. 90; July/70 p. 111; Mar./70 p. 52; June/70 p. 91; Oct./73 p. 173; Mar./74 p. 60

S. 19 (6)

Oct./65 p. 2; June/68 p. 143; Nov./68 p. 259; May/69 p. 90; Oct./71 p. 163; Oct./73 p. 173; Mar./74 p. 60; July/75 p. 189

S. 20

EXEMPTION FROM SS. 6 AND 35

General principles Sept./67 p. 22; Sept./67 p. 32; July/68 p. 154; July/68 p. 161; Jan./75 p. 22

Orders

General Apr./67 p. 12; June/67 p. 19; July/67 p. 9A; July/67 p. 13A; Sept./67 p. 22; Jan./75 p. 22

Policy Nov./69 p. 179; Mar./70 p. 44; May/70 p. 75; Sept./70 p. 129; Apr./74 p. 71

Conditions of Exemption

TSA safeguards undertakings as to filings and updating Apr./67 p. 12; June/67 p. 19 July/67 p. 13A; Jan./75 p. 22

S. 21

Jan./58 P. 1; Mar./68 p. 35; Dec./73 p. 203

S-S. (4)

Mar./68 p. 57

S. 23

Feb./49 p. 14; Oct./56 p. 1; Apr./57 p. 1; Nov./57 p. 1; Nov./61 p. 7

S. 24

Aug./67 p. 20A

S. 25

Nov./57 p. 1

OSC Decisions—*continued*

S. 58
(2) (b)
Apr./57 p. 1; Oct./65 p. 1; May/67 p. 5; Apr./69 p. 52

S. 59
General principles July/68 p. 176; Apr./69 p. 69
S-S. (1)
May/72 p. 81
S-S. (3)
Mar./68 p. 49; July/68 p. 179
Conditions of Determination
Shareholder/class approval May/72 p. 81
Subscription agreement May/72 p. 81
Undertaking as to resale May/72 p. 81
Voting trust agreement May/72 p. 81

S. 61
(1) PROSPECTUS APPROVAL
General principles Feb./66 p. 7; Oct./66 p. 15; May/67 p. 22; July/68 p. 154; Feb./75 p. 57; Apr./75 p. 131
Grounds for Refusal
Illegality Apr./62 p. 4; Apr./62 p. 9
Investment policy Sept./71 p. 133; Oct./72 p. 215
Irresponsible action of officers Jan./65 p. 2; Jan./65 p. 4
Name similarity Oct./70 p. 138
Potential conflict of interest Jan./66 p. 3; Jan./66 p. 5
Speculative investment intent Jan./66 p. 3; Jan./66 p. 5
S. 40(1)5(1960) Advisory Board Requirement Dec./65 p. 2; Dec./65 p. 6; Jan./66 p. 5
S. 61(1)(a)(ii) Apr./62 p. 9; Feb./66 p. 17
S. 61(1)(a)(iii) Sept./65 p. 7; Dec./65 p. 2; Dec./65 p. 6
S. 61(1)(b) Jan./66 p. 5; Feb./66 p. 7; Feb./66 p. 17; Oct./66 p. 15; Oct./66 p. 20; Oct./66 p. 23; Sept./65 p. 7; May/67 p. 21; May/67 p. 22; Feb./75 p. 57
S. 61(1)(c) Jan./65 p. 2; Jan./65 p. 4; Feb./66 p. 17; Oct./66 p. 23; May/67 p. 21; May/67 p. 22
S. 61(1)(e) Oct./72 p. 215
Conditions of Approval
Undertakings as to future conduct, Dec./65 p. 2; Oct./70 p. 138
(d) Escrow
General principles Nov./49 p. 3; Jan./66 p. 10; Sept./66 p. 1; Dec./66 p. 2; Dec./66 p. 5; Sept./68 p. 224; Mar./74 p. 65
RELEASE FROM ESCROW
Grounds for Consent
Abandonment of properties subject to escrow Apr./71 p. 38
Consent to release in another jurisdiction Sept./68 p. 224
Contribution to company position Nov./49 p. 3; Jan./66 p. 10; Sept./66 p. 1; Dec./66 p. 2

OSC Decisions—*continued*

S. 113
Apr./69 p. 69

S. 116 Exemption From Part XI
General June/67 p. 11
(1) APPLICATIONS
(b) June/67 p. 34; June/67 p. 35; June/67 p. 36; June/67 p. 37; June/67 p. 38; June/67 p. 40; July/67 p. 10A; July/67 p. 11A; Nov./67 p. 78
(c) June/67 p. 9; June/67 p. 11; June/67 p. 35; June/67 p. 37; July/67 p. 13A
Conditions of Exemption
Annual reporting June/67 p. 9; June/67 p. 35
Undertaking to file other materials June/67 p. 34; June/67 p. 35; June/67 p. 36; June/67 p. 37; June/67 p. 38; June/67 p. 40; July/67 p. 10A; July/67 p. 11A; Nov./67 p. 78

S. 132 Exemption From Part XII
General Mar./74 p. 57
(1) APPLICATIONS
(a)(ii) June/67 p. 34; June/67 p. 35; June/67 p. 36; June/67 p. 13A
(a)(iv) June/67 p. 39; July/67 p. 10A
(c)(ii) June/67 p. 34; June/67 p. 40; July/67 p. 11A
(c)(iii) June/67 p. 11; June/67 p. 34; June/67 p. 35; June/67 p. 36; June/67 p. 37; June/67 p. 38; June/67 p. 39; July/67 p. 9A; July/67 p. 10A; July/67 p. 11A; July/67 p. 12A; Feb./74 p. 23; Mar./74 p. 57
CONDITIONS OF EXEMPTION
Change in filing period July/67 p. 9A
Filing of 24 week interim statements June/67 p. 37; June/67 p. 39; July/67 p. 9A
Filing of 28 week interim statements June/67 p. 34; June/67 p. 35; June/67 p. 36; June/67 p. 37
Time extension for filing June/67 p. 39
Undertaking to file other materials June/67 p. 34; June/67 p. 40; July/67 p. 11A

S. 137
S-s. (2) Apr./68 p. 117

S. 138
S-s. (2) Apr./60 p. 1; Nov./64 p. 2; Nov./64 p. 6; June/67 p. 6; Oct./67 p. 53; Mar./68 p. 35; Mar./68 p. 57
S-s. (3) Mar./75 p. 103

S. 140
S-s. (2) June/67 p. 15; Feb./70 p. 9; Aug./73 p. 107; Nov./74 p. 199
S-s. (3) July/69 p. 110; May/72 p. 87; Feb./73 p. 26; Nov./73 p. 181; June/74 p. 125; June/74 p. 139

OSC Decisions—*continued*
Reg. s. 26—*continued*
No adverse effect on public or creditors Nov./61 p. 24; May/64 p. 5;
Oct./68 p. 230
Property with merit Mar./53 p. 3
Reliance on legal advice Jan./52 p. 3; Dec./52 p. 5; Oct./58 p. 1; June/68
p. 129
Reliance on superiors May/64 p. 5
Special service Nov./61 p. 4; Aug./67 p. 9
Sponsorship/supervision Feb./50 p. 6; July-Aug./63 p. 3

The Business Corporations Act
S. 119(2)
July/67 p. 7A; Apr./75 p. 139

**S. 173(3) Exemption From Disclosure of Sales or Gross
Operating Revenue**
APPLICATIONS
General principles Oct./70 p. 141; Nov./71 p. 178; Jan./72 p. 13
Orders June/67 p. 7; July/67 p. 5A; July/67 p. 6A; July/67 p. 7A;
July/70 p. 109; Oct./70 p. 141; Apr./71 p. 40; Nov./71 p. 178; Jan./72 p.
13
CONDITIONS OF EXEMPTION
Interim and P/L statements to show % change prior period and from
average 5 years immediately preceding June/67 p. 7; July/67 p. 5A;
July/67 p. 6A; July/67 p. 7A; Nov./71 p. 178
Shareholder approval July/69 p. 5A

S. 185
(2); S. 152 Mar./74 p. 57; Apr./75 p. 139 Apr./75 p. 139

2. Quebec Securities Commission Weekly Summary Decision Decision 1970 to June 1975
Section of Act in Issue

S. 1
PARA. (11)
(a) Vol. iii: 65 p. 1; Vol. v:6 p. 1; Vol. vi:13 p. 6
(b) Vol. iii:65 p. 1

S. 9
Vol. iv:29 p. 1; Vol. iv:39 p. 1; Vol. vi:19 p. 16

S. 13
Vol. iii:80 p. 4; Vol. iii:82 p. 3; Vol. iv:34 p. 1

S. 14
Vol. iii:65 p. 1

QSC Decisions—*continued*

S. 17 Recognition As Trading Officer
Vol. ii:27 p. 3

S. 19 Transfer Of Employment
Vol. iii:82 p. 3
CONDITIONS OF APPROVAL
Undertakings Vol. iii:82 p. 3

S. 20 Exemption From Registration
(b) Vol. v:14 p. 8
(e) Vol. ii:7 p. 1; Vol. ii:10 p. 3; Vol. ii:12 p. 4; Vol. ii:12 p. 6; Vol. ii:23 p. 4; Vol. ii:27 p. 3; Vol. ii:27 p. 4; Vol. ii:28 p. 4; Vol. ii:29 p. 1; Vol. ii:30 p. 3; Vol. ii:30 p. 4; Vol. ii:31 p. 3; Vol. ii:35 p. 4; Vol. ii:41 p. 3; Vol. ii:48 p. 3; Vol. v:2 p. 2; Vol. vi:17 p. 5
(d) Vol. i:5 p. 6; Vol. i:11 p. 2; Vol. i:21 p. 3; Vol. i:23 p. 3; Vol. i:26 p. 3; Vol. ii:7 p. 4; Vol.ii:12 p. 1; Vol. ii:16 p. 4; Vol. ii:16 p. 6; Vol.ii:17 p. 6; Vol. ii:24 p. 4; Vol. ii:25 p. 2; Vol. ii:33 p. 4; Vol. ii:34 p. 5; Vol. ii:34 p. 6; Vol. ii:38 p. 4; Vol. iv:34 p. 1
Other Vol. ii:53 p. 2; Vol. iv:42 p. 2; Vol. v:2 p. 2; Vol. v:3 p. 4; Vol. v:4 p. 3
GROUNDS FOR OBJECTION
Change in control Vol. ii:7 p. 1
Inadequate information Vol. ii:7 p. 1
Policy Listing Vol. ii:7 p. 1
Prejudice to shareholders Vol. ii:7 p. 1
CONDITIONS OF NON-OBJECTION
Approved by bondholders/shareholders Vol. i:5 p. 6; Vol. ii:16 p. 6; Vol. ii:38 p. 4; Vol. vi:23 p. 5
Conditions on re-sale Vol. ii:17 p. 6; Vol. ii:25 p. 2; Vol. ii:27 p. 27 p. 3; Vol. ii:27 p. 4; Vol. ii:28 p. 4; Vol. ii:30 p. 4; Vol. ii:35 p. 4
CSE consent Vol. i:11 p. 2
Escrow Vol. i:5 p. 6; Vol. i:21 p. 3; Vol. ii:7 p. 4; Vol. ii:10 p. 3; Vol. ii:12 p. 1; Vol. ii:16 p. 6; Vol. ii:34 p. 5; Vol. ii:34 p. 6
Filing amended listing Vol. i:23 p. 3
Limited distribution Vol. ii:12 p. 4; Vol. ii:12 p. 6; Vol. ii:30 p. 3
Listing Vol. ii:23 p. 4
Maximum subscription Vol. v:4 p. 3
Minority Protection Vol. vi:23 p. 5
Purchase for investment Vol. i:26 p. 3; Vol. ii:27 p. 3; Vol. ii:27 p. 4; Vol. ii:41 p. 3
Satisfaction of CSE conditions Vol. ii:29 p. 1
TERMS OF NON-OBJECTION
Additional shares contingent upon earnings Vol. ii:24 p. 4
(g) Vol. ii:55 p. 6; Vol. iv:7 p. 2

S. 21
Vol. i:36 p. 2

QSC Decisions—*continued*

S. 25 Continued Fitness For Registration
AS BROKER
Vol. i:1 p. 1; Vol. i:4 p. 2; Vol. ii:22 p. 2; Vol. ii:23 p. 3; Vol. iii:60 p. 1;
Vol. iii:63 p. 1; Vol. iii:83 p. 4; Vol. iii:88 p. 1; Vol. iv:2 p. 4; Vol. iv:19
p. 3; Vol. iv:22 p. 3; Vol. iv:26 p. 6; Vol. iv:48 p. 3; Vol. v:44 p. 9; Vol. v:47
p. 2; Vol. v:49 p. 7
AS INVESTMENT COUNSEL
Vol. iii:83 p. 4; Vol. iii:88 p. 1
AS SALESMAN
Vol. ii:39 p. 1; Vol. iv:22 p. 4; Vol. iv:22 p. 5; Vol. vi:24 p. 5
AS SECURITY ISSUER
Vol. ii:22 p. 3; Vol. iv:22 p. 3
GROUNDS FOR CANCELLATION
Breach of duty to public Vol. vi:15 p. 4; Vol. vi:24 p. 5
Breach of MSE by-laws Vol. vi:15 p. 4
Consent Vol. iv:48 p. 3; Vol. v:47 p. 2
Failure to know client Vol. iii:88 p. 1; Vol vi: 24 p. 5
Judgment/Experience Vol. iii:60 p. 1
Lack of independence Vol. v:49 p. 7
Policy violations
    Minimum free capital Vol. iii:60 p. 1; Vol. iii:63 p. 1
    Over-the-counter Vol. iii:60 p. 1; Vol. vi:15 p. 4
Statutory violations
    S. 16 Vol. iii:88 p. 1
    S. 23 Vol. iii:88 p. 1; Vol. vi:15 p. 4
    S. 50 Vol. vi:15 p. 4
    S. 160 Vol. vi:15 p. 4
Unsatisfactory operation Vol. iii:88 p. 1
GROUNDS FOR SUSPENSION
Breach of duty to public Vol. iv:22 p. 3
CSE suspension Vol. ii:22 p. 2; Vol. ii:23 p. 3
Inadequate information Vol. ii:22 p. 3
Lack of independence Vol. v:44 p. 9
Pending investigation Vol. iii:83 p. 4
Policy violations
    Minimum free capital Vol. iv:19 p. 3
    Over-the-counter Vol. i:1 p. 1; Vol. i:4 p. 2
Promotional campaign Vol. ii:39 p. 1
Promotional literature Vol. iv:22 p. 3
Statutory violations: S. 16 Vol. iv:22 p. 4; Vol. iv:22 p. 5; S. 55 Vol. iv:22
p. 4; Vol. iv:22 p. 5
CONDITIONS FOR REINSTATEMENT
Administration reserve Vol. iv:22 p. 3
Undertaking to comply Vol. i:4 p. 2; Vol. iv:22 p. 3

S. 26 Restricted Registration
Vol. i:20 p. 1; Vol. ii:27 p. 3; Vol. ii:28 p. 4; Vol. iii:85 p. 5

3. British Columbia Securities Commission Weekly Summary Decisions Dec. 8/72 to June 1975
Section of the Act in Issue

S. 2
(1) "Promotion" Dec. 20/1974
"Security" Sept. 13/1974; Nov. 15/1974; May 30/1975

S. 6
Mar./2 1973
(3) Mar./7 1975

S. 7
(2) RECOGNITION AS TRADING OFFICER
Grounds for Refusal
Knowledge and training Dec./8 1972
Reputation and past conduct June/15 1973
Violation of securities laws of another jurisdiction Dec./8 1972
(3) Jan./17 1975; Mar./7 1975

S. 8 Registration Renewal
General Mar./7 1975; June/20 1975
GROUNDS FOR REFUSAL
As Broker-Dealer
Principals of the firm: Knowledge and training Dec./8 1972; Violation of securities laws of another jurisdiction Dec./8 1972
As Salesman
Knowledge and training July/20 1973; July/12 1974
Prior misconduct as registrant Dec./7 1973
Reputation and past conduct Jan./5 1973
As Security Issuer
Principals of the firm: Reputation and past conduct June/15 1973; Aug./16 1974

S. 9 Continued Fitness For Registration
General Mar./7 1975; May/23 1975; June/27 1975
AS BROKER
Mar./15 1974; Nov./1 1975; Jan./17 1975; Mar./7 1975
AS BROKER-DEALER
Mar./15 1974; Apr./26 1974; Nov./1 1974; Jan./17 1975; Mar./7 1975
AS SALESMAN
Dec./22 1972; Jan./5 1973; Jan./12 1973; Jan./19 1973; Jan./26 1973; Feb./2 1973; Feb./9 1973; Feb./16 1973; Mar./9 1973; Mar./30 1973; Apr./27 1973; May/4 1973; July/13 1973; Sept./28 1973; Oct./26 1973; Nov./2 1973; Nov./9 1973; Dec./7 1973; Jan./25 1974; Feb./1 1974; Feb./8 1974; Mar./22 1974; Sept./20 1974; Oct./18 1974; Nov./29 1974;

BCSC Decisions—*continued*
S. 9—*continued*
Dec./20 1974; Feb./28 1975; Apr./4 1975; Apr./25 1975; May/9 1975;
May/23 1975; June/6 1975; June/20 1975; June/27 1975
GROUNDS FOR CANCELLATION
Breach of conditions of registration Mar./15 1974; Feb./28 1975;
Apr./4 1975; Apr./25 1975
Breach of undertaking May/23 1975
Consent Apr./26 1974
Conviction/charge Sept./20 1974; Dec./29 1974
Manipulative trading May/4 1973
Statutory violations: S. 65 (1) June/20 1975
GROUNDS FOR SUSPENSION
Breach of conditions of registration Dec./22 1972; Jan./5 1973; Jan./12
1973; Jan./19 1973; Jan./26 1973; Feb./2 1973; Feb./9 1973; Feb./16
1973; Mar./9 1973; Mar./30 1973; Apr./29 1973; Sept./28 1973; Oct./26
1973; Nov./2 1973; Nov./9 1973; Dec./7 1973; Jan./25 1973; Feb./1 1974;
Feb./8 1974; Mar./22 1974
Breach of undertaking Nov./29 1974
Failure to know client Mar./15 1974; Oct./18 1974; Mar./7 1975; May/9
1975; June/27 1975
Judgment/Experience July/13 1973
Lack of supervision Jan./17 1975; Mar./7 1975
Manipulative trading May/9 1975; June/27 1975
Statutory violations: S. 7 Mar./15 1974; Oct./18 1974; Mar./7 1975; S.
37 Mar./7 1975
VSE suspension Nov./1 1974
Conditions for Reinstatement
CSC enrolment/completion July/13 1973
Registered Representatives Exam Completion July/13 1973

S. 13
June/27 1975.

S. 21
S-S. (1)
(c) Oct./11 1973; (h) (iii) Feb./28 1975
S-S. (2)
(m) Dec./7 1973; Apr./5 1974; Apr./26 1974; Mar./7 1975
S-S. (3) DENIAL OF EXEMPTIONS
General principles Jan./11 1974; Apr./26 1974; Nov./29 1974
Hearing procedure and scope Mar./2 1973
S-s. (1)(b) Mar./2 1973
S-s. (1)(d) Mar./2 1973
S-s. (1)(f) Mar./2 1973
S-s. (1)(g) Mar./2 1973
S-s. (2)(m) Apr./26 1974; May/24 1974; Sept./20 1974; Jan./31 1975;
Feb./14 1975; Apr./25 1975.

BCSC Decisions—*continued*

S. 22 Exemption From SS. 7 and 37
ORDERS
General Dec./15 1972; Feb./16 1973; Mar./9 1973; May/11 1973; May/18 1973; May/25 1973; July/27 1973; Aug./10 1973; Nov./9 1973; May/24 1974; Aug./2 1974; Nov./15 1974; Dec./6, 1974; Feb./2 1975; Feb./7 1975; Apr./11 1975; Apr./18 1975; May/2 1975; June/6 1975
  CONDITIONS OF EXEMPTION
Dec./15 1972; Feb./16 1973; May/11 1973; Aug./10 1973; Aug./2 1974
Maximum Subscription May/2 1975
Offering material and information May/25 1973; Aug./2 1974; Feb./7 1975; May/2 1975
Protection of purchasers Feb./7 1975
Purchase for Investment Dec./6 1974
Sale through registrants Dec./15 1972; Feb./16 1973; May/11 1973; Aug./10 1973; Aug./2 1974; Apr./11 1975; May/2 1975

S. 28
May/16 1975

S. 30
Jan./11 1974; Mar./7 1975

S. 31
Jan./11 1974

S. 56
Orders Dec./8 1972; Dec./15 1972; Dec./22 1972; Jan./5 1973; Jan./12 1973; Jan./26 1973; Feb./2 1973; Feb./16 1973; Feb./23 1973; Apr./20 1973; June/8 1973; June/29 1973; Aug./24 1973; Oct./19 1973; Nov./30 1973; Feb./15 1974; Apr./26 1974; May/31 1974; Sept./13 1974; Oct./25 1974; Apr./4 1975
  CONDITIONS OF DETERMINATION
Conditions as to re-sale Dec./15 1972; Jan./26 1973; Feb./16 1973
Holding for 6 months Dec./8 1972
Holding for 6 months and conditions as to re-sale Dec./8 1972; Dec./15 1972; Dec./22 1972; Jan./12 1973; Feb./16 1973
Holding for 12 months and conditions as to re-sale Feb./23 1973
Purchase for investment June/8 1973; Feb./15 1974
Sale through registrants Feb./23 1973
Sale through VSE Jan./5 1973; Jan./12 1973
Sale through VSE within 60 days Dec./8 1972; Feb./2 1973
Satisfaction of TSE condition Nov./30 1973
Undertaking to file materials Oct./25 1974
VSE acceptance of agreement and periodic reports Dec./8 1972; Jan./12 1973

BCSC Decisions—*continued*

S. 58
(1) PROSPECTUS APPROVAL
Conditions of Approval
S-s. (1)(e) agreement Jan./26 1973; Apr./6 1973; Apr./20 1973; May/18 1973
Grounds for Refusal
General principles June/15 1973
Irresponsible action of officers June/15 1973
(d) Escrow
General principles Dec./8 1972

S. 59 Cease-Trade
Orders May/11 1973; Dec./7 1973; Dec./21 1973
Grounds for Orders
S. 52 Dec./7 1973; Dec./21 1973
Violation of Securities laws of another jurisdiction May/11 1973

S. 65
(2)(a)(i) Dec./7 1973

S. 77A Cease-Trade
General Jan./11 1974
ORDERS
(1) Dec./15 1972
(2) Dec./8 1972; Dec./15 1972; Dec./22 1972; Jan./12 1973; Jan./19 1973; Jan./26 1973; Feb./9 1973; Feb./16 1973; Mar./23 1973; May/18 1973; June/1 1973; June/8 1973; July 6 1973; July/13 1973; July/27 1973; Aug./17 1973; Aug./31 1973; Sept./7 1973; Sept./21 1973; Oct./5 1973; Dec./7 1973; Jan./11 1973; Feb./8 1974; Feb./15 1974; May/3 1974; Aug./3 1974; Sept./13 1974; Feb./28 1975; May/30 1975
GROUNDS FOR ORDERS
Breach of Companies Act Dec./15 1972; Dec./22 1972; Jan./12 1973; Aug./17 1973
Breac of VSE By-laws Aug./17 1973; Aug./9 1974
Inadequate information Jan./12 1973; June/1 1973; Feb./8 1974
Material change Feb./16 1973; June/1 1973; June/8 1973; July/13 1973; July/27 1973; Sept./7 1973; May/3 1974
Pending application to VSE Dec./22 1972
Policy violations Sept./21 1973; Aug./9 1974
Statutory violations
   S. 7 July/6 1973; Oct./5 1973
   S. 37 Oct./5 1973; Feb./15 1974; Nov./15 1974; Feb./28 1975
   S. 52 Dec./7 1973
   S. 99 Jan./12 1973; Jan./26 1973
   S. 109 Jan./12 1973; Jan./26 1973; Aug./9 1974
   S. 133 Dec./8 1972; Dec./15 1972; Jan./12 1973; Jan./26 1973; Aug./9 1974
VSE suspension/delisting Jan./19 1973; Jan./26 1973; Feb./9 1973; Feb./16 1973; Mar./23 1973; May/18 1973; June/1 1973; Aug./31 1973

BCSC Decisions—*continued*

S. 101 Exemption From Part X

(2) APPLICATIONS

(b) Dec./8 1972; Dec./15 1972; Jan./19 1973; Feb./2 1973; Mar./9 1973; Mar./23 1973; Apr./13 1973; Apr./20 1973; May/11 1973; May/18 1973; May/25 1973; June/1 1973; June/8 1973; July/6 1973; Sept./21 1973; Oct./5 1973 Oct./19 1973; Nov./2 1973; Dec./7 1973; Dec./14 1973; Feb./8 1974; Feb./15 1974; Mar./29 1974; Nov./22 1974; June/27 1975

Conditions of Exemption

Undertaking to file and mail other materials Dec./8 1972; Dec./15 1972; Jan./19 1973; Feb./2 1973; Mar./9 1973; Mar./23 1973; Apr./13 1973; Apr./20 1973; May/11 1973; May/18 1973; May/25 1973; June/1 1973; June/8 1973; July/6 1973; Sept./21 1973; Oct./5 1973; Oct./19 1973; Nov./2 1973; Dec./7 1973; Dec./14 1973; Feb./8 1974; Feb./15 1974; Mar./29 1974; Nov./22 1974; June/27 1975

(c) Aug./16 1974

S. 114 Exemption From Part XI

(1) APPLICATIONS

(b) Dec./8 1972; Dec./15 1972; Jan./12 1973; Jan./19 1973; Feb./2 1973; Feb./23 1973; Mar./2 1973; Mar./9 1973; Mar./16 1973; Mar./23 1973; Apr./13 1973; Apr./20 1973; May/11 1973; May/18 1973; May/25 1973; June/1 1973; July/6 1973; Aug./10 1973; Aug./24 1973; Sept./21 1973; Oct./5 1973; Oct./19 1973; Nov./23 1973; Nov./30 1973; Dec./7 1973; Dec./14 1973; Jan./11 1974; Jan./18 1974; Jan./25 1974; Feb./8 1974; Feb./15 1974; Mar./29 1974; Apr./5 1974; Apr./11 1974; Apr./26 1974; Nov./1 1974; Nov./22 1974; Dec./6, 1974; Jan./10 1975; Feb./7 1975; Apr./4, 1975; Apr./18 1975; June/27 1975

(c) May/11 1973; June/1 1973; June/8 1973; June/29 1973; Aug./10 1973; Sept./28 1973; Oct./5 1973; Oct./19 1973; Nov./9 1973; Nov./30 1973; Feb./8 1974; Apr./11 1974; June/7 1974; Aug./16 1974; Sept./20 1974; Oct./4 1974; Nov./15 1975; Nov./22 1974

Conditions of Exemption

Annual reporting Feb./2 1973; May/11 1973; Nov./15, 1974

Limitations on voting rights June/1 1973

Limitation on Canadian holdings Aug./16 1974

No beneficial ownership Apr./11 1974; Sept./20 1974; Nov./22 1974

Periodic reporting Oct./5 1973; June/7 1974

Semi-annual reporting Sept./28 1973

Undertaking to file other materials Dec./8 1972; Dec./15 1972; Jan./12 1973; Jan./19 1973; Feb./2 1973; Feb./23 1973; Mar./2 1973; Mar./9 1973; Mar./16 1973; Mar./23 1973; Apr./13 1973; Apr./20 1973; May/11 1973; May/18 1973; May/25 1973; June/1 1973; July/6 1973; Aug./10 1973; Aug./24 1973; Sept./21 1973; Oct./5 1973; Oct./19 1973; Nov./23 1973; Nov./30 1973; Dec./7 1973; Dec./14 1973; Jan./11 1974; Jan./18 1974; Jan./25 1974; Feb./8 1974; Feb./15 1974; Mar./29 1974; Apr./5 1974; Apr./11 1974; Apr./26 1974; Nov./1 1974; Nov./22 1974; Dec./6 1974; Jan./19 1975; Feb./7 1975; Apr./4 1975; Apr./18 1975; June/27 1975

VSE Listing Aug./16 1974

BCSC Decisions—*continued*

S. 129 Exemption From Part XII
(1) APPLICATIONS
(b) Dec./8 1972; Dec./15 1972; Jan./19 1973; Feb./2 1973; Mar./9 1973;
Mar./23 1973; Apr./13 1973; Apr./20 1973; May/11 1973; May/18 1973;
May/25 1973; June/1 1973; June/8 1973; July/6 1973; Sept./21 1973;
Oct./5 1973; Oct./19 1973; Nov./30 1973; Dec./7 1973; Dec./14 1973;
Feb./15 1974; Mar./29 1974; Aug./16 1974; Nov./22 1974; June/27 1975
(c) Nov./15 1974; June/10 1975

S. 137
(1) July/12 1974; (3) Apr./18 1975

S. 140
(1) Jan./11 1974
(a) Mar./2 1973
PROSECUTIONS
S. 7 Dec./8 1972; Feb./9 1973; Mar./2 1973; Mar./16 1973; May/4 1973;
May/18 1973; June/22 1973; Sept./28 1973; Nov./16 1973; Jan./18 1974;
Feb./22 1974; Mar./22 1974; Apr./5 1974; May/10 1974; June/7 1974;
July 15, 1974; Sept./20 1974; Oct./4 1974; Oct./11 1974
S. 37 Mar./16 1973; May/4 1973; Jan./18 1974; Feb./22 1974; Apr./5
1974; July/5 1974; Jan./17 1975
S. 55 Oct./19 1973
S. 109 Dec./8 1972
False prospectus July/13 1973
False prospectus and theft Apr./13 1973

Appendix IV
Control Person
Distribution

450

Appendix IV
Control Person Distribution

This table compares the Ontario definition with the other Canadian provincial jurisdictions. Words additional to or different from the Ontario definition are underlined. For the position under U.S. federal legislation see Loss, *Securities Regulation,* Vol. 2, ch. 5, pp. 766, 768, 772, 774, 776, 782, 770 and The American Law Institute Federal Securities Code, Tentative Draft No. 1, April 25, 1972, s. 221.

Ont. s. 1(1)6(b)(ii)	B.C. s. 2(1)	Alta. s. 2(1) (6.1)(ii)	Sask. s. 2(1) (o)(ii)	Man. s. 1(1) 16 (ii)
Distribution to the public: trades in previously issued securities to the public where the securities form all or a part of or are derived from the holdings of any person, company or any combination of persons or companies holding a sufficient number of any of the securities of a company to materially affect the control of such company, but any person, company or any combination of persons or companies holding more than 20% of the outstanding equity shares in a company shall in the absence of evidence to the contrary be deemed to materially affect the control of such company, whether such trades are made directly to the public or indirectly to the public through an underwriter or otherwise, and includes any transaction or series of transactions involving a purchase and sale or a repurchase and resale in the course of or incidental to such distribution.	similar to Ontario except: — "primary distribution to public" of a person or company "affect the control of the person or company" — no 20% provision B.C. adds (iii): Trades made by a company for the purpose of distributing to the public its previously issued securities which it has purchased.	similar to Ont. in all respects	similar to Ont. except: — "primary distribution to the public" — no 20% provision	similar to Ont. except: — "primary distribution to the public" — no 20% provision

N.S. s. 1(1) (h)(ii)	N.B. s. 1	Nfld. s. 2 (e)(ii)	P.E.I.	Quebec s. 50
— "primary distribution to the public" — applies to "trades in previously distributed securities for the purpose of redistributing" whereas Ont. definition applies to "trade in previously issued securities for the purpose of distributing" similar to Ont. except: adds words "or of the securities from which such securities have been derived — no 20% provision N.S. adds after "underwriter"; "optionee, sub-underwriter, sub-optionee or otherwise" — but does not include trades through registrants acting as agents of purchaser, or sale by a person not engaged in distribution or redistribution	similar to N.S.	similar to N.S.	No definition	In the case of an issue of corporate shares which have already been the object of an initial sale or distribution to the public, but which are held by a person or company, or by a group of persons or companies acting together, to an extent representing the control of the company or the majority of a particular class of shares of its capital stock, the permission of the Commission must also be obtained to sell, offer for sale or distribute them again to the public, en bloc or to an extent representing the control of the company or of the particular class of shares concerned whether such sale, offer or distribution be made directly as principal or indirectly through an agent, broker or salesman. Comment: This is a narrower test than "materially affecting control", but it embraces effective rather than *de jure* control of the company, which in many circumstances will arise from holdings of considerably less than a majority of the voting shares.

Appendix V
Exemptions from Registration and Distribution Requirements— Comparative Canadian Analysis

The following is a summary of the *major* differences only with respect to the exemption provisions of the provincial securities acts. It illustrates how far the Canadian provinces have yet to go to achieve the desirable goal of uniformity. The general scheme in each act is a provision requiring registration, a provision exempting certain trades and classes of securities from registration, a provision prohibiting distribution unless something is filed and finally a provision that either enumerates exemptions from filing (this is done in Nova Scotia and Newfoundland) or incorporates the registration exemptions as exemptions from filing (this is done in the other provinces) or both. The following is a list of such provisions in each act. For the sake of brevity the analysis will not refer to the full section number in each case, but rather only to the paragraph or subsection number as the case may be.

Ont.	s. 6, 19, s. 35, s. 58	N.S.	s. 3, s. 4. 12, s. 19
B.C.	s. 7, 21, s. 37, s. 55	N.B.	s. 5, s. 7, s. 13, s. 13(12)
Man.	s. 6, s. 19, s. 35, s. 58	Nfld.	s. 4, s. 5, s. 13, s. 20
Sask.	s. 6, s. 20, s. 42, s. 65	P.E.I.	s. 2, s. 2(3), s. 8, s. 13
Alta.	s. 6, s. 19, s. 35, s. 58	Que.	s. 16, ss. 20 and 21, s. 50, s. 52

1. Institutional Purchasers: Ontario 19(1)3, 19(1)9b, 19(3), 58(1)(a), (b); British Columbia (para. (c)); Manitoba (para. (3)); Saskatchewan (para. (c)) and Alberta (para. 3) all have provisions like Ontario s. 19(1)3. The Manitoba provision does not contain the words "other than an individual". Nova Scotia, New Brunswick and Newfoundland (all para. (c)) have provisions similar to the Ontario one, except all leave off the last clause "or any other trade where...". Prince Edward Island (para. (c)) is like Nova Scotia (para. (c)) except it contains the words "or is registered as a broker". Quebec s. 20(c) reads "a sale made in the performance of his duties by an officer or employer of Her Majesty...or by...". Section 20(g) reads "sale...to insurance or trust companies or to chartered banks...". Only Alberta (para. 9.2) has a provision like Ontario 19(1)9b. Manitoba (s-s. (3)), Saskatchewan (s-s. (3)) and New Brunswick (reg., s. 8(f)) have provisions like Ontario s. 19(3).

All of the jurisdictions that have the exemptions discussed above have incorporated them in their equivalent of Ontario s. 58, with one exception. There is a question as to whether the provisions of New Brunswick regulation s. 8 are true exemptions.

Also Manitoba s. 58 differs from Ontario s. 58 in that it applies the words "for investment only..." to both 19(1)3 and 19(3). The B. C. and Saskatchewan provisions do not contain the words "for investment only and not...".

2. *Trades to Underwriters or Registrants*: Ontario 19(1), paras. 6, 7, 58(1)(c) and (d). Only British Columbia (paras. (f), (g)); Manitoba (paras. 6, 7), Saskatchewan (paras. f, g) and Alberta (paras. 6, 7) have provisions like Ontario 19(1), paras. 6, 7. Nova Scotia (4(o)) and Newfoundland (5(p)) exempt "a trade where one of the parties is registered under the Act as a broker or as a salesman...".

All of the uniform act jurisdictions have incorporated these exemptions in their equivalent of Ontario 58. Nova Scotia (4(o)) and Newfoundland (5(p)) have not done so with their exemption from registration. New Brunswick (13(12)(e)) exempts from 13 trades where the purchaser is a registered broker acting as principal.

3. *Trades with Promoters*: Ontario 19(1)9c, 58(1)c. Only Alberta (para. 9.3) has a provision like 9c, and it is included within 58 as an exemption from filing.

4. *Trades with Employees*: Ontario 19(1)10, 58(1)c. British Columbia (para. j); Manitoba (para. 11), Saskatchewan (para. k) and Alberta (para. 10) all have provisions like Ontario 19(1)10. The Manitoba provision adds the words "all or any of the directors, officers" and also adds paragraphs ((ii) and (iii)) dealing with options to acquire securities and trades in mining, oil or gas claims respectively. Nova Scotia (para. 4(m)) is like the Ontario provision but it applies to "securities traded by a company..." and not to trade by a company of securities of its own issue as the Ontario definition does. The Nova Scotia definition also applies to employees of subsidiaries or affiliates. New Brunswick 7(1) and Newfoundland 4(m) are like the Nova Scotia definition except they apply to employees of the company only. Quebec and Prince Edward Island have no provisions like para. 10; however in the Quebec Act, 20, the Commission has power to grant an exemption where a company sells it shares to its officers, directors and employees or those of its affiliates.

All of the uniform act provinces, New Brunswick, Nova Scotia, Newfoundland, and Quebec have incorporated this exemption in their equivalent of Ontario 58. Prince Edward Island has no such exemption in 2(3), but in reg., s. 9(4) "securities traded by a company with its employees who are not [so] induced..." are exempt from 8.

5. *Stock Dividends and Reorganization and Winding-Up*: Ontario 19(1)8(i), (ii), (iii). All of the provinces except Quebec have provisions similar to the Ontario provisions. British Columbia (h); Manitoba (8); Saskatchewan (h); Alberta (8); Nova Scotia, New Brunswick, Newfoundland, Prince Edward Island (all (e)). The Atlantic Provinces'

provisions have minor differences. Quebec 20(e) reads in part "...the issuance, distribution or sale of shares, debentures or other securities of a person or company to the holders of securities already issued..." See 20(f) with respect to reorganization.

6. *Issuer Combinations*: Ontario 19(1)9(a), (b), (c), 9a. British Columbia (ii); Manitoba (10); Saskatchewan (j) and Alberta (9) all have provisions like Ontario 9(a), (b), (c), except that all use the words "...in connection with a consolidation, amalgamation, merger or reorganization of either company...or a take-over bid...". The Atlantic Provinces provisions (all (f)) are like the British Columbia provision except that the Nova Scotia provision does not include reorganization or the words "or the holders of securities of the other company." With respect to Quebec see 20(f), which uses the words "...for the purpose of merging and amalgamating...or of reorganizing...".

7. *Double Exemption Based on Securities*: Ontario 19(2)1, 2, 58(2)(a). British Columbia (21(2)(a), (e)); Manitoba (19(2)(1), (2)); Saskatchewan (20(2)(a), (b)) and Alberta (19(2)1, 2) all have provisions similar to the Ontario provision except that Manitoba provision 2(a) reads "...or the payment of the principal and interest of which..." and 2(b) reads "issued for school, hospital, immigration, drainage, elderly and infirm persons housing...". The Western Provinces equivalent of Ontario 58(2)(a) also includes these exemptions.

In the Atlantic Provinces' acts these provisions are not found in the respective equivalent of Ontario 19, which in Nova Scotia is 4. Section 19(h)(g) of the Nova Scotia Act exempts from 12 securities of Canada or any province and those of any known corporation. Regulation, s. 19 exempts from 3(1)(2) of the Act securities of Great Britain and of the trustees of any school section in the province. Regulation s. 26(2) exempts from 12 securities of Great Britain, and of any trustee of any school section and the bonds of the International Bank for Reconstruction and Redevelopment (IBRD).

New Brunswick regulation, s. 8 "approves" certain classes of trades including trades in securities of Great Britain, debentures and bonds of any municipality, city, town or school district in Canada, and securities of the IBRD.

Newfoundland 17(h) exempts from 11 securities of Canada, any province, city, town or municipality and (4) exempts known corporations. Regulation, s. 15 exempts from 3(1)(2) securities of Great Britain and reg., s. 22 exempts from 11 securities of Great Britain and bonds of the IRBD.

Prince Edward Island 13(2) exempts from 8 securities of Canada, or any province or territory or municipal corporation, public board or commission in Canada. Regulation, s. 9 exempts from 8 securities of Great Britain and regulation, s. 7 exempts securities of Great Britain from 2(1), (2).

Quebec 21(a) exempts from registration bonds or other evidences of indebtedness issued or guaranteed by Canada, or any Province, the U.S. or any state, the IRBD, any municipal or school corporation in Canada or certain others named in the Civil Code or the regulations. Section 52(c) includes the exemptions in 21 (NOTE: 20(h) and Reg., O.C. 731).

8. Adequate Knowledge: Ontario 19(2)3, 4, 5, and 58(2)(a). British Columbia 21(2)(g), (h), (i); Manitoba 19(2), (3), (4), (5); Saskatchewan 20(2)(c), (d), (e) and Alberta 1(2)3, 4, 5 are all similar to the Ontario provisions, except that British Columbia (h) does not have the clause "except by a person or company registered", Manitoba (4) does not have the clause "if such mortgages or other encumbrances are not offered", and Saskatchewan (c) reads "from the date of issue of the securities" and has no $50,000 stipulation. All of the equivalents in the legislation of the Western Provinces to Ontario 58(2)(a) include these exemptions.

Nova Scotia 4(i) has no $50,000 stipulation and is like the Saskatchewan provision re negotiable promissory notes. Section 4(h) reads "with respect to securities secured by mortgages" and (j) dealing with conditional sales contracts differ from the Ontario provision. Newfoundland (4(i), (h), (j)) and P.E.I. (2(3)(i), (j), (k)) provisions are similar to the N.S. provisions. New Brunswick has no provision dealing with negotiable promissory notes. The Atlantic Provinces' equivalents to Ontario 58 include these exemptions. Quebec 21(c) concerns promissory notes and negotiable instruments and is basically similar to Ontario 19(2)3.

9. Business or Social Efficacy: Ontario 19(2)6, 58(2)(a). British Columbia (2(j)); Manitoba (2(6)); Saskatchewan (2(f)); Alberta ((2)6); Nova Scotia ((k)), New Brunswick (Reg., s. 8(e)); Newfoundland ((k)), and Prince Edward Island ((3)1) all have provisions similar to the Ontario provision with the following exceptions: Manitoba adds the words "and no commission or other remuneration is paid...", New Brunswick and Prince Edward Island do not include the word "religious". Quebec 20(e) refers to companies "incorporated without pecuniary gain, provided that no commission or remuneration is paid...". All provinces except *possibly* New Brunswick (see note re reg., s. 18) include this exemption in their equivalents of Ontario 58.

10. Resale by Exempted Purchasers: Ontario 19(4). Only Manitoba (19(4)); Saskatchewan (20(4)); Alberta (19(4)) and New Brunswick (reg., s. 8(g)) have provisions similar to Ont. 19(4). The N.B. provision does not include the word "direct".

Note re New Brunswick Reg, s. 8: There is a problem of statutory interpretation with respect to this regulation. It provides that certain classes of trades and securities are approved by the Board under s. 7. It is unclear if this means s. 7 of the Act or the regulations. Regulation, s. 8(g) reads in part "section 1 of the Act and section 7 hereof" which clearly means s. 7 of the regulations. Regulation, s. 7(1) reads in part "of section 1 of this Act". These provisions indicate that it is arguable that unless there is a specific reference to the Act, then the reference is to the regulations.

Assuming that the reference is to the Act, there is yet another problem. Section 7(m) exempts from registration trades or securities of which registration is not required by the regulations. Regulation, s. 8 does not "not require" registration, it merely approves certain trades and securities. If so the list in reg., s. 8 is not incorporated into s. 7 and therefore is not a list of exemptions from s. 5.

The following arguments support the proposition that reg., s. 8 refers to s. 7 of the Act and the list in reg., s. 8 is a list of exemptions from s. 5: The language of reg., s. 8 is similar to the language of the exemptions in the Act, reg., s. 8 only makes practical sense if it refers to the Act and New Brunswick has often copied the uniform act provinces and in these provinces the reg. s. 8 provisions are exemptions from the registration provision.

It is submitted that reg., s. 8 does refer to the Act and its provisions are exemptions from s. 5.

Appendix VI
The Demise of Prudential Finance Corporation Limited

(1) Brief History

Founded in 1928, Prudential Finance conducted directly and through a wholly-owned subsidiary a consumer loan and sales finance business in London, Ontario. In 1961 the company was under pressure from its bank, its major source of funds; as a result a controlling interest was sold by its principal shareholder to Mr. J. B. Brien in return for $200,000 and the assumption of liabilities. In the same year it began to issue short-term notes to the public. The predecessor of the present exemption for negotiable promissory notes or commercial paper maturing not more than one year from the date of issue (s. 19(2)3 and s. 58(2) of the Act) permitted the issuance of such notes to the public without registration or the qualification of a prospectus; the proviso was not then in the Act which limited use of the exemption in the case of sales to individuals to notes in denominations of $50,000 or more in principal amount. The business was rapidly expanded; gross income (before provision for interest expense and bad debt) rose from approximately $100,000 in 1961 to about $1,500,000 in 1963.[1] In late 1962 Prudential proposed to refinance itself by offering debentures to holders of its short-term notes; its solicitors advised that the intended transaction would be exempt under the predecessor to the present reorganization exemption.[2]

(2) The Prospectus

Before this reorganization could be carried out, the Securities Act was amended (as of July 1, 1963) so as to eliminate the exemption for the sales of short-term notes in denominations of less than $50,000 to individuals, by the imposition of the above-mentioned proviso. This move resulted from the widespread use of this exemption by finance companies offering up to ten per cent interest on short-term notes with little information available to their investors.[3]

---

[1] Report on The Investigation Into The Affairs of Prudential Finance Corporation Limited, Clarkson Gordon & Company (hereinafter cited, Clarkson Gordon Report), at pp. 4-5, tabled in the Ontario Legislature on March 22, 1967 (Ontario Debates, 27th Legislature, 5th Sess., 1967, pp. 1634-5).

[2] Section 19(2)1 of the Securities Act, R.S.O. 1960, c. 363 was the predecessor to the current exemption for an offering to existing securities holders under s. 19(1)8(iii) and s. 58(1)(c).

[3] See the Report on Prudential Finance by Mr. B.C. Howard, Chief Legal Investigation Officer, Ontario Securities Commission (Appendix B, p. 14). Called the "Staff Report", it was tabled in the Ontario Legislature on March 22, 1967 (Debates, *op. cit.* footnote 1, pp. 1634-5).

Even though the exemption for exchange of securities with existing securities holders was still available, Prudential determined to qualify its debentures by a prospectus, as a means of offsetting "the adverse publicity affecting all finance companies because of the activities of the '10 percenters'".[4] The new offering was needed to overcome the company's precarious (and not ntirely unique) liquidity situation owing to its use of short-term borrowings as a base for long-term loans. The exchange of five-year debentures for short-term notes was intended as a first step. The second stage was to be an offer of preferred shares to the debenture holders as a means of "rolling over" their debentures when they fall due. The financial statements in the prospectus indicated liability to about 8,000 noteholders of $8 million.[5]

The Staff Report explained the Commission's decision to accept the prospectus this way:

"Though the staff of the Commission recognized that the Company's financial position was such that it would have difficulty continuing in business successfully, the staff also recognized the fact that if the Company's prospectus was not accepted the 8,000 noteholders then tied into the Company, would suffer financial loss.

"In these circumstances, the Commission staff were persuaded that the Company, if properly managed, might be able to overcome its financial difficulties and thereby avoid severe loss to its existing noteholders. Accordingly, the prospectus was accepted for filing on June 20, 1963."[6]

It is apparent from the Minister's statement in the House when tabling the final investigation report that he viewed the Commission's discretion as one involving a determination of future financial viability:

"...In June, 1963 the then Chairman of the [OSC]...concluded that he should permit [Prudential] to continue its public financing through a prospectus. This decision was made after consulting with the prospectus staff and after providing that adequate disclosure was made on the face page of the prospectus of the inherent risks involved in lending money to the Company in return for an unsecured short term note. While the risks involved appeared to be adequately disclosed in the prospectus he was mindful of the consequences of refusal. It was clear that the Company, having embarked on an acquisition program, was not generating profits. However, to refuse the prospectus would doom the Company to failure and the approximately 8,000 individuals involved to a virtually certain loss because of the lack of liquidity. There were two main considerations open to the Chairman and, in coming to his conclusions, [he] was exercising the discretion vested in him, as Chairman by the Securities Act of that date. This obviously was a judgment decision which all people in responsible positions are obliged to make from time to time.

---

[4]*Ibid.*, at p. 16.
[5]*Ibid.*, at p. 17.
[6]*Ibid.*, p. 17.

"It is apparent that the Chairman and his staff were not aware of the deceit subsequently uncovered through extensive investigation. As stated in the Clarkson, Gordon and Company report of March 1967:

"Had the true position been shown, it is reasonable to assume that Prudential would have been barred from selling its securities to the public!"[7]

The Clarkson, Gordon investigation report concluded that Prudential was in fact insolvent at the date of its audited financial statements in the June 1963 prospectus. Although the consolidated earnings statement acknowledged a loss for the most recent year, it showed substantial profits for the previous nine years with a subsisting net worth of nearly a half million dollars.[8] The two major reasons for the discrepancy between the information filed and the actual state of affairs were the recording of recently purchased assets by Prudential of an amount exceeding their fair value by almost $1 million and inadequate provision for bad debts. The inflated assets had been sold to Prudential by a company wholly owned by Brien who controlled Prudential itself. The transfer was in satisfaction of a debt owed to Prudential by the other company of almost $4 million. The assets in question were comprised largely of shares of and amounts owing by companies controlled by Brien.[9] The practice of making inadequate allowances for bad debts had existed in the period preceding 1961, but the problem had been compounded by Prudential's rapid expansion and loans to Brien-controlled companies.

(3) Last Steps and Failure

The prospectus expired in July 1964. Thereafter, at least in Ontario and some other jurisdictions, Prudential could only raise money from existing securities holders usually by "rolling over" their notes as they matured. Notwithstanding the existence of the exemption for such transactions, the OSC insisted that Prudential deliver to existing securities holders a document equivalent to a prospectus in the case of such subsequent purchases. In retrospect, it is clear that this prospectus dated December 4, 1964, was as deficient as the June 1963 prospectus.

In the fall of 1965 Prudential advised the OSC that it had ceased to sell securities to its own securities holders in Ontario. In spite of this, following a hearing in March 1966 the OSC denied Prudential the use of the exemption.[10] Sales continued in some jurisdictions outside Ontario.[11] In November 1966 the trustee for the debenture holders was unable to obtain satisfactory financial information from Prudential and insisted on an investigation. Bankruptcy ensued.[12]

In the assessment by the Clarkson, Gordon report, the failure was the direct result of:

---

[7]*Debates, op. cit.*, footnote 1, p. 6401.
[8]Prudential Finance Company prospectus dated June 14, 1963.
[9]Clarkson, Gordon Report pp. 5-7.
[10]Under s. 19(5) of the Act.
[11]Clarkson, Gordon Report, pp. 11-2.
[12]*Ibid.*, p. 7.

"1. The inability of the company to earn sufficient revenues to cover heavy administrative and overhead costs resulting from rapid expansion, to meet the high cost of borrowed funds and to absorb the losses incurred on speculative loans and investments.

"2. Losses incurred on investments in and loans and advances to:
(a) non-subsidiary and unrelated companies,
(b) subsidiary companies,
(c) companies controlled by [Brien]".[13]

(4) Consequences

The Commission ordered an investigation conducted by its staff into trading matters in connection with Prudential and related companies and persons. By a separate order, Clarkson, Gordon & Co. was appointed to examine "the documents, records, properties and matters" of Prudential, its subsidiaries, and Brien.[14] The entire Clarkson, Gordon & Co. Report was tabled in the Ontario Legislature shortly after it was completed, whereas excerpts only of the Staff Report were tabled initially. The reason for not making the whole Staff Report public emerged one and one-half years later, when the Minister tabled the final Staff Report as submitted by the OSC Chairman together with documentary exhibits and transcripts of evidence:

"The complete report was not made public·at the time since portions of the report contained evidence that was intended to be placed before the Courts in the recommended Securities Act proceedings against officials of the Company."[15]

On the instructions of the Attorney-General's staff, the first criminal charges were laid against Brien within two weeks of Prudential's bankruptcy. He was convicted under the Criminal Code on two counts of fraud and one of theft, and received four years concurrent imprisonment on each conviction.[16] Two officers and two employees of Prudential were fined for unlawful trading under the Securities Act. Prudential and a subsidiary company were also convicted for unlawful trading under the Act but, being insolvent, received suspended sentences.[17]

Following the Staff Report, four joint charges under the Securities Act were laid against Brien, two officers of Prudential, one of whom was then believed to be employed by a finance company in Venezuela, and Prudential's auditor. They were charged with making false and misleading statements in the prospectus. The auditor was expelled from the Ontario Institute of Chartered Accountants.[18]

When these charges came to trial, the technical defence was raised that the consent to prosecute had been improperly signed; it was the Attorney-General, so the argument ran, the Minister responsible for securities regulation in the period prior to the coming into force of the 1966 Act when the alleged offences had been committed, from whom

---

[13]*Ibid*, at p. 2.
[14]Staff Report, p. 6.
[15]Debates, *op. cit.*, footnote 1, p. 6402.
[16]*Ibid.*
[17]*Ibid.*
[18]*Ibid.* at pp. 6402-3.

the required authorization should have been sought, and not the Minister of Consumer and Commercial Affairs, who took over responsibility for the new 1966 Act. The Provincial Court Judge upheld the defence and ruled that he had no jurisdiction to hear the charges. An application to the Supreme Court of Ontario to reverse the ruling was refused, and on the advice of the Attorney-General's staff no further appeal was made.[19]

(5) Ministerial Responsibility

This technical defence had been anticipated and considered by the Commission staff and a legal opinion given by the Chairman to the Minister to the effect that he, and not the Attorney-General, was the appropriate Minister to sign the consent to prosecute.[20] When the converse proved true, the resulting failure of the charges initiated under this consent was one of the bases for a two-pronged attack on the Minister in the House. His reply[21] —that he was entitled to rely on the OSC and its staff—is found in the text.[22]

(6) Government Responsibility

The attack on the Minister also took the form of a claim that the Government had a responsibility to compensate the defrauded creditors of Prudential on the theory that the Commission's acceptance of the prospectus in June 1963 enabled Prudential to continue selling its securities and thereby induced the purchasers to buy. The Government resolutely opposed this demand. In tabling the final Staff Report the Minister referred to his statement at the tabling of earlier excerpts in which he had said: "In my view, it would be quite improper to provide reimbursement to Prudential creditors out of public funds...the financial critic of the official Opposition appears to have endorsed the government's sentiment. More recently, editorial comment has given further approval to the position taken by the government".[23]

The Minister had also stated that the Government "would do everything in its power to assist creditors of Prudential in pursuing other available remedies." The Commission was authorized to retain independent legal counsel in order to provide an opinion regarding possible recovery by the Prudential creditors against the trustee for the debenture holders or anyone else. The results were not encouraging.

(7) Trustee Liability

The possibility of recovery against the trustee by the creditors was rendered most improbable by the terms of the trust deed. This aspect of the Prudential debacle, together with the Atlantic disaster, was a prime factor leading to the enactment of the mandatory trust indenture provisions of the BCA in 1971.[24]

---

[19]*Ibid.*, at p. 6404.
[20]*Ibid.*, at pp. 6303-4.
[21]*Ibid.*, p. 6405.
[22]*Ante*, part 2.13 at footnote 137.
[23]Debates, *op. cit.*, footnote 1, p. 6405.
[24]They apply as of January, 1971 to all debt obligations then outstanding or

The Clarkson, Gordon Report pointed out the following anomalies in the indenture agreements (judged by contemporary standards):[25]

"1. The trust indentures contained a provision setting a maximum relationship of secured indebtedness to subordinate capital (as defined) but did not otherwise place any limits on the total amounts of securities that Prudential...could issue.

"2. Financial covenants ordinarly required by investment dealers and institutional investors were not contained in the trust indentures.

"3. There was no restriction placed on the payment of dividends.

"4. The indentures did not require Prudential...to maintain any financial ratios often found in trust deeds of finance companies.

"5. It does not appear that the indentures defined what actions constituted default.

"6. The trust indentures placed extremely limited obligations on the trustee and required the trustee to accept the instructions of the company in respect of a number of matters.

"7. By November, 1965 almost all of the collateral [for the secured notes] was represented by notes of subsidiary companies of Prudential Finance. [The definition of 'Acceptable Collateral' and 'Finance Receivables' in the trust indentures permitted this and provided that the trustee might rely on certificates of value provided by Prudential in establishing the worth of the collateral.] The trust indenture specifically freed the trustee from making an inquiry or an investigation of the qualification of Finance Receivables as acceptable collateral.

"8. From time to time in 1964 and in one instance during 1965, the trustee made advances to Prudential on secured call loans or short-term notes [they were retired by April, 1965].

"9. The trustee acted under two series of sinking fund debentures issued under a first and supplementary trust deed and under a second trust indenture covering secured notes."

(8) Commission Liability

The final chapter in the Prudential story is the suit by its creditors for damages against the OSC.[26] The plaintiff securities holders alleged the OSC failed to properly perform the duties imposed on it in respect of the 1963 prospectus and other documents filed with the Commission by Prudential until March 1966. They sought damages for breach of trust and of contract, deceit, common law negligence and negligence in performing statutory duties. As we saw in chapter 2, the Commission was successful in its application to dismiss the action on the ground that it was not an entity suable in damages.[27]

---

subsequently issued under a trust indenture by an Ontario incorporated company no matter where issued, and by non-Ontario incorporated companies where the offerees are the public in Ontario. (BCA, ss. 57 to 62). See *ante*, part 4.07.

[25]Pages 26-9.

[26]*Westlake et al. v. The Queen*, [1971] 3 O.R. 533, 21 D.L.R. (3d) 129 (H.C.); aff'd [1972] 2 O.R. 605, 26 D.L.R. (3d) 273 (C.A.); affd 33 D.L.R. (3d) 256, [1973] S.C.R. vii.

[27]Part 2.02, *ante*, at footnote 14.

Appendix VII
The Collapse of Atlantic Acceptance Corporation Limited—Some of the Causes, Some of the Cures

The collapse of Atlantic Acceptance may be traced initially to a cheque that bounced in June 1965. A bank in Toronto refused to honour the cheque drawn by Atlantic for $5,000,000 because of insufficient funds on deposit. Atlantic had written the cheque as repayment for a week-end loan from a Montreal lender. Since Atlantic's continued business operations depended on its ability to borrow, and that ability rested on its solvency, the dishonoured cheque triggered the demise of the corporation and brought down the entire financial empire which surrounded it as well.

Atlantic Acceptance was then the sixth largest sales finance company in Canada, with stated assets exceeding $150,000,000 and more than 130 acceptance and small loans offices in every province in Canada except Quebec. Its outstanding debt obligations were $130,000,000. On the face of it the assets exceeded liabilities to securities holders by a reasonable margin.

The reality was very different. Four years of extensive analysis of the assets and liabilities of Atlantic and its subsidiaries disclosed an estimated loss on Atlantic's part of $70,000,000.[1] Senior note holders holding claims amounting to $127,000,000[2] expected to receive between 75 per cent and 80 per cent on the dollar.[3] The holders of subordinated debt (more than $19,000,000 worth), of junior subordinated debt (in excess of $5,000,000)[4] and of equity shares (shown in the consolidated balance sheet at December 31, 1964 as worth more than $16,000,000)[5] were wiped out.

Atlantic Acceptance commenced operations on a modest scale in 1953 in Hamilton, Ontario. In a series of giant strides, principally from 1961 forward, it acquired or incorporated a number of subsidiaries, opened many new offices and took on substantial risks, and as an inevitable concomitant of such free-wheeling practices, kept returning to the money-market with an increasing appetite. A notable feature of this growth was "lending long and borrowing short", *i.e.*, lending out money with repayment extended over a substantial period of time

[1]Atlantic Report, pp. 1, 2, 1582.
[2]Valued at December 31, 1967, p. 104.
[3]September, 1969, p. 1582.
[4]At December 31, 1967, p. 104.
[5]Page 1586.

while raising the funds for those loans by issuing notes with relatively short maturities. This required a continual "roll-over" or refinancing of the loan. The terms of Atlantic's trust indenture were such that when default occurred in June 1965 all of these obligations became immediately payable; and as a matter of course there was no hope of raising further funds in the money-market. It was this aspect of Atlantic's difficulties which caused the Report to recommend[6] that finance companies should be required to maintain "total liquidity", defined as the maintenance of an amount of cash and unused bank credit equal to short-term debt maturing at any time.

Another characteristic of the rapidly expanding Atlantic group was the complexity of its accounts, and the unscrupulousness and duplicity with which they were manipulated. The securities industry depends on detailed accounting principles being honestly and fairly applied to the affairs of a corporation. The disclosures of the Atlantic Report pointed up the vulnerability of the industry to exploitation of this dependence. Atlantic used a number of misleading techniques to demonstrate healthy profits and induce lenders to invest in its securities. For example, current income was inflated for the year in which a given loan was made by adding in an abnormally high percentage of the pre-computed interest charge in cases where the repayment of principal and interest was spread over a number of years. With repayment proceeding in the form of a fixed sum paid each year, most of the payment in the first years represented interest, whereas the reverse obtained as the loan approached maturity. The interest of course could be shown as income, while the repayment of principal could only appear as the return of invested capital. A related technique was to acquire new business as rapidly as possible, permitting even greater amounts of income to be shown in the current year, whatever the later consequences. Unfortunately, the accounting principles applied to finance companies were imprecise, and did not establish fixed parameters of a kind which when applied across the industry would have permitted reasonable comparisons between competitors. Following the public hearings, but prior to the publication of the Atlantic Report, the Federated Council of Sales Finance Companies produced the Canadian Sales Finance Companies Long Form Report and made financial disclosure in accordance with the criteria established in this report compulsory for all its members. These criteria required that the percentage of pre-computed interest taken into income in the year in which the transaction was made be specified. Later the Atlantic Report recommended that disclosure by finance companies to their securities holders should include an explanation of the method by which unearned interest was subsequently taken into income. Furthermore, tests designed to determine whether the percentage was too high for the character of the loans outstanding were to be applied regularly, and their results disclosed in the same reports.[7]

Another example of deceptive accounting, rooted in conflict of interest and grafting fraud to slackness, involved several Atlantic

---

[6]Page 1573.
[7]Pages 1576-7.

subsidiaries. The parent's funds were lent through these subsidiaries to a number of worthless enterprises. Atlantic's chairman as well as two chartered accountants whose firm audited the subsidiaries' accounts had substantial personal interests in some of these borrowing firms. The existence of these subsidiaries permitted a massive cover-up of Atlantic's real financial weakness. The consolidated shareholders' equity, for Atlantic and its subsidiaries at December 31, 1964 was stated to be $16,000,000. In fact it should have been a negative amount. The reported profit for the year ended December 31, 1964 of $1,000,000 ought to have been recorded as a loss of $17,000,000. The corporation had a great many bad debts concentrated in its subsidiaries[8] which should have been shown as bad, resulting in a loss. However, with the accountants' complicity, Atlantic's chairman adopted the practice of transferring the debt from one company to another at full value and then capitalizing the arrears of interest in a new loan. A highly respected national accounting firm was the auditor of the consolidated accounts of the parent company (at the insistence of the company holding the controlling share interest in Atlantic), but when it came to the figures for the subsidiary companies this firm simply relied on and did not penetrate the subordinate audit. The two accountants were subsequently convicted of fraud for their activities. Atlantic's chairman died before the inquiry was completed.

The Report was critical of this accounting practice which permitted auditors of a parent company to avoid inquiries into the subsidiaries' audits; at the least (it was postulated) they should have been required to disclose in their opinion on the consolidated statement. Which subsidiaries they had not audited themselves. Mr. Justice Hughes recommended that the parent auditor should only be permitted to rely on the work of subsidiary auditors to the extent that the parent auditors accepted responsibility for that work on a principal-agent basis.

Generally the Report shows impatience at the slowness of the accounting profession to resolve the difficulty itself, particularly in view of the fact that U.S. standards had been conspicuously superior for some time. Mr. Justice Hughes said:[9]

"Since the collapse of Atlantic the views of the accounting profession, as propounded by the Canadian Institute of Chartered Accountants, in company with those of other governing bodies in the English-speaking world, have altered to reflect the opinion that the primary auditor should take more responsibility for the auditing procedures applied by the auditors of subsidiary companies, or secondary auditors as they are sometimes called. The final determination of what can be described as a polite controversy, cautiously undertaken and replete with hair-splitting refinements, has yet to be declared, even after the lapse of four years, and it is perhaps time that public regulatory authorities concerned themselves with this vital aspect of the preparation of published financial statements."

---

[8] Page 1586.
[9] Pages 1589-90.

This criticism is a reminder of one of the fundamental tensions which runs through the whole of securities regulation. To what extent should the public regulatory agencies, or alternatively the self-regulatory organizations in the industry itself, create professional accounting standards in the absence of action by the appropriate professional body? In the U.S. the enterprise of the SEC has been most noticeable in this area; on numerous occasions it has taken the lead in creating accounting principles for the SEC filings which subsequently have found general acceptance with the various American accounting bodies. In Ontario and the rest of Canada, by contrast, the tendency has been for the Commission to wait for the professional accounting associations to take the initiative; in more pressing circumstances it may take steps to nudge those bodies into action.[10] Only when there is a case urgently demanding action and a great deal of public pressure on the regulatory agency to take the initiative has it done so.[11] It may be noted that the creation of the Financial Disclosure Advisory Board suggests a more active role by the OSC in this connection.

Another major problem in the Atlantic set-up was what might be styled management by watertight compartments. Operating in virtual isolation from his fellow managers. Atlantic's chairman carefully kept information from other directors and subordinate officers of the corporation, particularly regarding loans to companies in which he had a personal interest; as a result they were excluded from participation in most of the critical decisions. In the light of this the Report recommended[12] that authorization by the board of directors of a finance company should be required where one borrower or group of associated borrowers receives a loan exceeding five per cent of the excess of the finance company's tangible assets over its liabilities. It was also suggested that there be periodic reviews of lending agreements with such borrowers, with certification to the finance company's securities holders by the directors that they have no knowledge of a breach of any such agreement. The rigour of these requirements is qualified by a stipulation that the directors be entitled to rely on unaudited statements in determining the excess of assets and liabilities, unless they have reason to doubt their accuracy.

Like the ravages of a loathsome disease, the effects of conflicts of interest manifest themselves throughout Atlantic's corporate history. As indicated, the chairman of Atlantic made a practice of concealing from his fellow directors any conflicts which affected him personally. He did not normally indicate that considerable sums were being lent by Atlantic to enterprises in which he had a substantial interest, particularly when those enterprises had gone beyond the point of financial recovery. The actions of a number of directors on the Atlantic board furnish examples of a similar kind. On some occasions there was no disclosure of the conflict of interest present, while at other times the minutes of director's meetings show that the director concerned

---

[10]See, however, the Merger Report, chapter 9, dealing with the business acquisition formula and its subsequent adoption in the Act in s. 126(3)17.
[11]See, for example, National Policy Statement No. 5 on "Recognition of Profits in Real Estate Transactions", CCH vol 2, para. 54-842.
[12]Page 1611.

declared that he had an interest and then refrained from voting. Until Ontario corporations became subject to the new BCA, a cryptic declaration of the fact of potential conflict followed by abstention from voting on the issue was sufficient under the applicable company law. The BCA now requires that the nature and extent of the interest must be declared, and the director must still refrain from voting.[13] Moreover he must be acting honestly and in good faith, and the contract or transaction must be in the best interests of the corporation—otherwise it will not be immune from voidability. As a supplement to the minimal disclosure requirement then existing the Report recommended that the directors' minutes should record the nature and extent of the interest declared and that the minutes' correctness should be acknowledged by the signature of the affected director.

As a finance company Atlantic Acceptance was not subject to the regulatory restrictions placed upon loan and trust companies. The Report recommended that similar supervision be imposed. Moreover it suggested that the failure of Atlantic and Prudential Finance in Ontario, and the similar fate which had struck several other such companies in other jurisdictions in Canada and U.S. was an indication that particular requirements for the regulation of finance companies were needed.[14] It was proposed that incorporation of finance companies should not be a matter of right as is now the case for business corporations in Ontario but would only be possible by issuance of letters patent in the discretion of the Lieutenant-Governor in Council under a separate act passed for their regulation. An inspector-general would supervise their operation and obtain a report on such information as he deemed necessary. The same official would be furnished with copies of all reports made by a finance company to any of its lenders.

An intensive scrutiny of the affairs of British Mortgage and Trust Company, whose loans to and investments in Atlantic companies caused it to disappear as an independent entity,[15] formed the basis for the Report's extensive recommendations regarding changes in the Ontario Loan and Trust Corporations Act. The lessons from British Mortgage also influenced recommendations for changes in the manner in which the Securities Act is administered and in related provincial and federal regulatory legislation. At the same time, while suggesting changes in the legislative framework, the Report opted strongly for increased disclosure and shunned any increase in direct regulation. This philosophy is contained in two revealing sentences:[16]

"I say with deliberation, after long contemplation of the sorry performance of Atlantic Acceptance Corporation and British Mortgage and Trust Company, that it is unwise and short-sighted to construct legislation based upon experience with one or two backsliders, and with a view to protecting the public from what really amounts to a breach of faith, or of the law, which prescribed sanctions, if resolutely applied, are able to deter or punish. There-

---

[13]BCA, s. 134.
[14]Page 1618.
[15]See text, chapter 2 at footnote 143.
[16]Page 1649.

fore I propose, the following recommendations, to place less emphasis on artificial limitations and restrictive ratios than is placed at present, and more upon disclosure of information, flexible regulation, and the prompt enforcement of sanctions as occasion requires."[17]

In other recommendations the Report runs against the trend of current corporation law reform. It cautions against too high a standard of conduct for directors and against making minority shareholder's suits too readily available. In this connection Mr. Justice Hughes interprets the new directors' liability provision (s. 144) of the BCA as permitting a director to be sued for mere error in judgment (not acting in the best interests of the company). He suggests that the test should be changed to occasion liability only for fraudulent or negligent decisions or those made in bad faith. The Report also recommends that the provisions in the BCA regarding the costs of a representative suit be changed and placed in the discretion of the court. It was suggested finally that the indemnification provision in the same Act be altered to permit a director or officer of a finance company to be indemnified if the shareholders so decree.[18]

---

[17]In another characteristic passage Mr. Justice Hughes demonstrates his belief in the use of *ex post facto* sanctions rather than prior "preventive interference" and insists that sanctions for white collar fraud be stern (p. 1678):

"Practitioners of commercial fraud will always have victims who are susceptible to flattery and greed, but there will be fewer victims if the laws designed to protect them are more vigorously applied, and penalties exacted on a scale of frequency comparable to those achieved in other categories in crime, more easily detected and less harmful in their effect on public confidence. Prejudice is largely responsible for the belief that there is one law for the rich and another for the poor; nevertheless, there is some substance to this easy generalization in the field of commercial fraud, because of the difficulty of detection, the unwillingness of businessmen to prosecute their own associates and accept unfavourable publicity, and the sheer load of work which falls upon law enforcement agencies in keeping abreast of more blatant offences affecting public order and decency. The answer to the problem presented by adventurers like C.P. Morgan, [Atlantic's chairman] W. L. Walton, Harry Wagman, [the two chartered accountants subsequently jailed] Elias Rabbiah, Jack Tramiel, Eugene Last and others of that ilk, [entrepreneurs associated with companies to which Atlantic lent money] is to make transgression more costly by increasing the likelihood of detection, speedy trial and suitable punishment. As to what is suitable punishment is not for me to say, but it is worthy of note that parole authorities have found swindlers and thieves more difficult to rehabilitate than offenders of a more violent and spectacular type."

[18]Page 1625.

Appendix VIII
Windfall Oils
and Mines Ltd.

The event which has had the most profound impact on self-regulation, and particularly the Toronto Stock Exchange (TSE), in recent years is the Royal Commission Report on Windfall Oils and Mines Ltd. The Windfall story begins with the announcement on April 16, 1964 by Texas Gulf Sulphur (TGS) of its spectacular base metal discovery near Timmins, Ontario. On April 18, Mrs. Viola McMillan, the promoter of Windfall and wife of its president, George McMillan, purchased four mining claims in the township adjoining the strike and sold them to Windfall.[1] Windfall was listed on the TSE and by the middle of June had arranged for a distribution of its shares through the Exchange.

A drilling programme for the claims was prepared and drilling commenced on July 1. From July 2 forward, various rumours, most of which originated with the drilling crew, suggested a significant find which in at least some of the reports that circulated merited comparison with the TGS discovery.

George McMillan had physical custody of the drill core from July 3 on and examined it on a number of separate occasions. The Royal Commission later determined that a person of average mining experience (far less than McMillan's) could easily have recognized that the core was worthless. As early as July 6 several samples were assayed in Toronto and a negative report given to Mrs. McMillan. On the same day a consulting geologist had made a visual examination of the core and gave a negative appraisal, but took a sample away for further study. A Windfall press release on July 7 stated that it was diamond drilling claims in proximity to the TGS strike and that the core was being sampled. On July 10 the TSE demanded an up-to-date statement from the company by the following Monday, July 13 and threatened to suspend trading in the event of failure to comply. Windfall did produce a statement on the date specified, but it did no more than indicate that the core sample from the completed portion of the first drill hole had yet to be sent for assay and that some difficulties were being experienced in building core storage facilities on the site. A meeting between officials of the OSC and TSE and the McMillans resulted in a public statement being issued on July 15. But far from resolving questions as to the actual value of Windfall's claims, the statement simply explained that since drilling of the first hole was incomplete the core had not yet been sent for assay and that the company would not release any information until the assay had been completed. After unwarranted delays, in part occasioned by the first hole being drilled far deeper than necessary, samples of the complete

---

[1]Report, pp. 22, 27.

core were sent for assay on July 24 without any instructions as to urgency. In the meantime the consulting geologist had reported to the McMillans on July 13 that his analysis of four core samples in his possession showed negative results. On July 29 the completed assays were mailed to Windfall and at a directors' meeting the following day the envelope was opened: the result—no significant mineralization. An announcement to this effect was made after the close of trading that evening.

Between June 26 and July 31, 13,388,000 shares of Windfall were traded with a total dollar value of $36,690,000.[2] The price moved from 60 cents on June 26 to a high of $5.50 on July 21, dropping to 40 cents after July 31. During this period the Report estimated that the two McMillans and companies controlled by them realized net profits from their own trading of $1,305,000. TSE member firms trading on their own account and partners or directors of member firms realized net profits of $514,000; other persons employed by TSE member firms (who were required to pay a commission for their trading) incurred a net loss of $286,000. A group whom the Report categorized as miscellaneous large traders sustained a net loss of $1,124,000.[3] Finally a group with accounts trading under $5,000 incurred net losses of $1,326,000. The estimated brokerage commissions realized by TSE members on Windfall trades was $1,187,000.[4] As an indicator of the relative value to exchange members from trading in Windfall this figure may be compared with total commissions of $150,000 and $160,000 from trading in Massey-Ferguson Ltd. and Steel Company of Canada Ltd. shares in the period March 8 to April 9, 1965. During that period Massey was on the ten most active traders list for eighteen of 25 trading days and Stelco was on that list for 21 of the 25 days.[5]

What were the consequences? First, the criminal sanctions were relatively minor. Charges of wash trading were brought against Viola McMillan and a conviction registered.[6] The same charge was brought against one of the brokers involved[7] and resulted in an acquittal. Criminal charges of breach of trust in public office were brought against the director of the OSC but he, too, was acquitted.[8] At the time of the events in question there was no statutory regulation of insider trading and consequently no statutory remedies were available against those who traded while possessing special knowledge. Not only this

---

[2]*Ibid.*, at p. 166.
[3]*Ibid.*
[4]*Ibid.*, at p. 168.
[5]*Ibid.*, at p. 176.
[6]*R. v. MacMillan*, [1968] 1 O.R. 475, 66 D.L.R. (2d) 680, [1969] 2 C.C.C. 289 (C.A.). She served eight weeks of the resulting nine-month jail sentence.
[7]See *R. v. Breckenridge* (1968), CCH vol. 1, para. 725.95 (Ont. Co. Ct.).
[8]*R. v. Campbell*, [1967] 1 O.R. 1, [1967] 3 C.C.C. 250, 50 C.R. 270 (C.A.); appeal to the Supreme Court of Canada dismissed without reported reasons 2 C.R.N.S. 403. The director of the Commission and his wife were trading in Windfall shares during the period of intense activity and Mrs. McMillan had lent 5,000 shares to the director's wife to cover her short sale. The director had urged the TSE not to suspend trading and was involved in the discussions resulting in the mid-July press release.

but shares listed and posted for trading on the TSE were exempt from regulation by the OSC. In the case of mining companies the authorized capital and not just the issued capital was listed with the result that the OSC had no jurisdiction whatsoever over the primary distribution.

The entire story is a graphic illustration of the need for effective timely disclosure. The Commission Report found the Exchange to be at fault in not requiring earlier public statements by Windfall to quell the rumours and in not insisting on immediate release of the assay information which the McMillans received from time to time notwithstanding the fact that the results available at a given juncture may have been partial and incomplete if judged by the most rigorous standards of accuracy. The responsibility of the Exchange was lessened somewhat by the unfortunate intervention of the OSC director. The effects of the press release of July 15, which that resultant intervention helped bring about, were particularly regrettable. It appears as if the OSC as well as the TSE had given their blessing to the delay in completing the first drill hole and assaying the drill core; the inference seemed irresistible to many that something promising existed which required more complete analysis for accurate appraisal.[9]

The lasting impact of the Windfall affair emerges from the recommendations of the Royal Commission Report, which in the years since 1965 has exerted a substantial influence on the restructuring of the stock exchange in Ontario and in refashioning the relationship between the Exchange and the OSC. Among the various suggestions arising from the Kelly Report, the one perhaps most calculated to disturb complacency relates to the conflict of interest which arises when a broker acts both as principal and agent. The Report proposed that the two functions be severed.[10]

---

[9]For some years a debate raged as to whether core information from a first drill hole or earlier core stages in a first drill hole should be released immediately or whether all comment should be postponed until at least three drill holes had been completed in a mineralized area so as to give a three-dimensional analysis which would permit a complete appraisal of the results. The Windfall fiasco, when coupled with the lessons of the first TGS press release which interposed value judgments rather than statements of fact, indicate that an early release of factual information is to be preferred.

[10]It referred to a 1936 Securities and Exchange Commission study of the same problem (p. 108, referring to the "Report on the feasibility and advisability of the complete segregation of the functions of Dealer and Broker" 1936, United States Government Printing Office) which stimulated the New York Stock Exchange to establish a rule that where a member firm traded as principal on the floor of the exchange on a particular day the firm then must forego engaging in any commission business during that day. The result of this rule was that the volume of trading by members on the floor for their own or their firm's account was reduced "to a completely insignificant amount" (Kelly Report, p. 109). The Kelly Report acknowledged that the complete severence recommended in the U.S. did not come to fruition because it was given over to the SEC for further study and presumably, with the passage of time, SEC supervision of the major U.S. exchanges provided sufficient resolution of the principal-agent wedded function conflict. The Kelly Report observed that no similar government supervisory relationship then existed in Ontario.

It recognized however that such a radical alteration of the industry structure probably would be unacceptable in the Ontario context at the time (and indeed this has proved to be the case to date); as an alternative the Report recommended that member firms of the Exchange and persons associated with them be permitted only to buy securities for investment which would be required to be held for a period of time and in circumstances which would be carefully defined. Records would be kept of all such trades in order to preclude member firms acting for public customers from taking advantage of opportunities for short swing trades. This somewhat more muted proposal has also not been implemented.[11]

The Kelly Report also recommended that primary distribution through the facilities of the TSE should cease. This recommendation was not carried out though substantial modifications in the methods of primary distribution through the Exchange have since been made. It was also of the opinion that a junior mining exchange might be set up separately from the TSE as a means of facilitating the financing of mining exploration and development. This latter suggestion was qualified by a recommendation that junior mining financing be made the subject of a further study by an expert committee. This in fact was done several years later resulting in the Beatty Report.[12]

Some of the other consequences of the Windfall Commission were these. It called for listing standards to be made more stringent in order to remove from the Exchange "shell" companies who were carrying on no business of significance and whose shares had ceased to be traded to any extent. Purchasing the charter of one of these dormant companies was an inexpensive method of securing listing on the TSE without being subjected to much scrutiny.[13] Consequently, in October 1965 the Exchange developed the following specific criteria:[14]

"[To] suspend from its Trading List the shares of companies in the mining and oil category...which...have less than $25,000 net liquid assets and have failed to carry out, directly or indirectly, exploration or development work to any appreciable extent for a period of one year. In each case shares shall remain suspended until the Exchange is satisfied as to the financial condition and programme of work of the company concerned. If by the expiration of one year the Exchange has not been so satisfied, the shares will be delisted."

The number of listed mining companies declined from 435 at year end 1965 to 384 at year end 1966 as a result of this new policy.[15]

The production of the Kelly Report required a great deal of investigative work and interpretation of the information gathered. At least one by-product of this activity should prove of considerable utility. This was the development of an electronic data processing system which successfully analyzed 26,418 separate transactions in

---

[11]*Ibid.*, at pp. 108-10.
[12]Referred to in chapter 4, *ante*, part 4.05(3) at footnote 69.
[13]Page 14. See also the Kimber Report's critical remarks on shell companies at para. 7.14.
[14]Now found in s. 8.03, item 6, of TSE Policies, Part VIII, Suspension and Delisting, June 1971, CCH vol. 3, para. 92-064.
[15]Globe and Mail Report on Business, Nov. 28, 1967, p. B5.

13,338,000 Windfall shares worth $36,690,000 traded on the TSE between June 26, and June 31, 1964, a pioneering accomplishment.[16] It should prove of value in any subsequent investigations, particularly in following the details of insider trading.

Finally, one study conducted by the Windfall Commission would fascinate behavioural psychologists. A representative sample of 727 persons trading in Windfall during the period analyzed were asked a number of questions regarding their motives and intentions for the future. Of the total, 69 per cent indicated that it was likely or very likely they would trade in speculative mining securities again, and of those who sustained a loss as a result of their Windfall transactions, 63 per cent answered affirmatively on this point.[17]

---

[16]Page 159 and following.
[17]Page 150.

Table of Cases

A

B

C

D

E

H

I

J

K

L

R

S

T

U

V

W

Z

Index

A